ENCYCLOPEDIA OF

GRAPHICS
FILE FORMATS

ENCYCLOPEDIA OF

GRAPHICS FILE FORMATS

James D. Murray and William vanRyper

O'REILLY & ASSOCIATES, INC.
103 Morris Street, Suite A
Sebastopol, CA 95472

Encyclopedia of Graphics File Formats
by James D. Murray and William vanRyper

Editor: Deborah Russell

Production Editor: Ellen Siever

Printing History:

      July 1994   First Edition

ISBN: 1-56592-058-9   [10/94]

TABLE OF CONTENTS

PART TWO
Graphics File Formats

PART THREE
Appendices

LIST OF FIGURES

LIST OF TABLES

PREFACE

Why did we write this book? The short answer is that *graphics file formats are immortal.* Like it or not, data files from the dawn of the computer age are still with us, and they're going to be around for a long time to come. Even when the way we think about data itself changes (as it inevitably will), hundreds of millions of files will still be out there in backup storage. We'll always need a way to read, understand, and display them.

Computer technology evolves rapidly. Hardware, particularly on the desktop, turns over every year or so. Software can become obsolete overnight with the release of a new version. The one thing that remains static is data, which for our purposes means information stored in data files on disk or tape. In this book we're interested in one specific type of data—that used for the interchange and reconstruction of graphics images.

Graphics data files are structured according to specific format conventions, which are (or should be) recorded in format specification documents written and maintained by the creator of the format. Not all formats are documented, however, and some documents are so sparse, poorly written, or out of date that they are essentially useless. Moreover, some format specifications are very difficult to obtain; the creator of the format might have moved; the format might have been sold to another organization; or the organization that owns the format might not actively support or distribute it. These facts make it difficult for the person who needs to find out about the specifics of a particular graphics file format to locate and understand the file format specification. We wrote this book because we saw a need for a centralized source of information, independent of the commercial marketplace, where anyone could obtain the information needed to read graphics files.

When we set out to write this book, we asked the obvious questions: How would we implement an existing format? What resources would we need? Ideally, we would like to have on hand a good book on the subject, and perhaps some working code. Barring that, we'd make do with the original format specification and some advice. Barring that, we'd scrape by with the format specification alone. This book provides as much of this as possible; the format specification is here in most cases, as is some code—even some advice, which, because it's coming from a book, you're free to take or leave as you choose.

To give you some idea about what was on our minds during the planning of this book, we'd like to mention some issues that frequently come up for programmers who need to learn about and implement file formats. In the course of writing this book, both of us (as consultants and veteran users of networked news and bulletin board systems) talked with and observed literally hundreds of other programmers. The following is a sampling of questions frequently asked on the subject of graphics file formats, and comments on how we have addressed them in this book:

"How can I get a copy of the written specification for format XYZ?"

Rarely does a day go by without a request for a written format specification—TIFF, GIF, FaceSaver, QRT, and many, many more. Unfortunately, although a few sparse collections exist online and in books, there is no single source for even the most common format specifications. One of the goals of this book is to gather as many as possible of the original specification documents in one place.

"I'm trying to implement specification XYZ. I'm having trouble with ABC."

Programmers almost always believe that only the specification document is needed in order to implement a file format. Sadly, if you read a few format specifications, you'll soon discover that there is no law requiring that documentation be written clearly. Specifications, like all technical documents, are written by people with varying degrees of literacy, knowledge, and understanding of the subject in question. Consequently, they range from clearly written and very helpful to unorganized and confusing. Some documents, in fact, are nearly useless. The programmer is eventually forced to become conversant with the oral tradition.

Even if the specification document is well done, written between the lines is a complex set of assumptions about the data. How complicated can a format be? After hours of fiddling with color triples, index map offsets, page tables, multiple header versions, byte-order problems, and just plain bad design, you may well find yourself begging for help, while the clock counting your online dollars ticks on. Another goal of this book is to provide a second opinion for use by programmers who find themselves confused by the contents of the documents.

"What does Z mean?"

In this case, Z is basic technical graphics information. Everything a programmer needs to know to read, write, encode, and decode a format is in the specification document, right? Unfortunately, writers of format specifications often use vocabulary foreign to most programmers. The format might have been created, for instance, in support of an application that used terminology from the profession of the target users. The meaning of a term might have changed since the time the format was written, years ago. You might also find that different format specifications have different names for the same thing (e.g., color table, color map, color palette, look-up table, color index table, and so on). In this book, we provide basic guidance whenever possible.

"What is an X.Y file?"

If you scan the computer graphics section of any online service, bulletin board system, or news feed, you will find numerous general questions from users about graphics files, the pros and cons of each format, and sources of image files. Surprisingly, there is no single source of information on the origin, use, and description of most of the graphics file formats available today. Some of this information, particularly on the more common formats (e.g., TIFF, GIF, PCX), is scattered through books and magazine articles published over the last ten years. Other information on the less common formats is available only from other programmers, or, in some extreme cases, from the inventor of the format. Another goal of this book is to include historical and contextual information, including discussions of the strengths and weaknesses of each format.

"Is there a newer version of the XYZ specification than version 1.0?"

Occasionally, this question comes from someone who, specification in hand, just finished writing a format reader only to have it fail when processing sample files that are known to be good. The hapless programmer no doubt found a copy of the format specification, but not, of course, the latest revision. Another of our goals is to provide access to the latest format revisions in this book and to update this information periodically.

"How can I convert an ABC file to an XYZ file?"

Programmers and graphic designers alike are often stumped by this question. They've received a file from a colleague, an author, or a client, and they need to read it, print it, or incorporate it in a document. They need to convert it to something their platform, application, or production environment knows how to deal with. If this is your problem, you'll find this book helpful in a number of ways. In the first place, it will give you the information you need to identify what this file is and what its conversion problems are. We'll give you specific suggestions on how to go about converting the file. Most importantly, on the CD-ROM that accompanies this book, we've included a number of software packages that will convert most graphics files from one format to another. Whether you are operating in an MS-DOS, Windows, OS/2, UNIX, or Macintosh environment, you should be able to find a helpful tool.

About This Book and the CD-ROM

We'd like to make it easier for you to understand and implement the graphics file formats mentioned in this book. Where does information on the hundreds of graphics file formats in use today come from? Basically, from four sources:

- Format specifications. These should be the ultimate references, shouldn't they? Unfortunately specifications aren't always available (or useful!). Nevertheless, they are the starting point for information about file formats.

- Secondary sources (magazine articles, books). These are most useful when the specification isn't handy and when the author can provide some kind of insight or relevant experience.

- Sample code. This is all we usually want, isn't it? Unfortunately the sample code may not work right, may be out of date, or may be too platform-specific for your present needs.

- Sample images. Images fully conforming to the format specification might not seem like a source of information until you actually need something on which to test your application.

What we've tried to do is to collect these four elements together in one place. Of course not all were available for every format, and sometimes we weren't allowed to include the original specification document on the CD-ROM that accompanies this book. Nevertheless, we've pulled together all the information available. Taken together, the information provided in this book and in the materials on the CD-ROM should allow you to understand and implement most of the formats.

Our primary goal in writing this book is to establish a central repository of graphics file format specifications. Because the collected specification documents (not to mention the sample images and associated code and software packages!) total in the hundreds of megabytes, the best way to put them in your hands is on a CD-ROM. What this means is that the CD-ROM is an integral part of the book, if only for the fact that all this information couldn't ever be crammed between two covers.

We've written an article describing each graphics file format; this article condenses and summarizes the information we've been able to collect. In some cases this information is extensive, but in other cases it's not much. This is the name of the game, unfortunately. When we do have adequate information, we've concentrated on conveying some understanding of the formats, which in many cases means going through them in some detail. Remember, though, that sometimes the specification document does a better job than we could ever do of explaining the nitty-gritty details of the format.

On the CD-ROM, you'll find the original format specifications (when available and when the vendors gave us permission to include them). If we know how to get the specifications, but couldn't enlist the aid of the vendors, we tell you where to go to find them yourself. Also on the CD-ROM is sample code that reads and writes a variety of file formats and a number of widely-used third-party utilities for file manipulation and conversion. Finally, we've included sample images for many formats.

Who Is the Book For?

This book is primarily for graphics programmers, but it's also for application programmers who need to become graphics programmers (if only for a little while). It's also for people who need a quick way to identify a graphics file of unknown origin. If you're not a graphics programmer, but want to get up to speed quickly, you'll find that Part I of the book requires little prior knowledge of computer graphics. It will help you become familiar with concepts associated with the storage of graphics data. In fact, a working knowledge of a programming language is useful, but not absolutely essential, if you're only looking for the big picture.

But, note that this book is also written to accommodate the specific needs of other types of readers. If you just want some background on graphics file formats, you might want to read Part I and refer, as needed, to the articles in Part II and the appendices in Part III. If you're in search of implementation guidance, you will want to refer to the articles and example code. Of course if you're a computer graphics professional, you might be interested primarily in the specification documents and tools on the CD-ROM accompanying this book.

In the unlikely event that you are creating your own new graphics file format, we fervently hope that this book provides you with some perspective on your task, if only by exhibiting the decisions, good and bad, that are frozen in the formats described in these pages.

How to Use the Book

This book is divided into three parts.

Part One, Overview, is an introduction to those computer graphics concepts that are especially helpful when you need to work with graphics file formats.

- Chapter 1, *Introduction*, introduces some basic terminology, and gives an overview of computer graphics data and the different types of graphics file formats (bitmap, vector, metafile, and the less frequently used scene description, animation, and multimedia) used in computer graphics. This chapter also lists and cross-references all of the formats described in this book.

- Chapter 2, *Computer Graphics Basics*, discusses some concepts from the broader field of computer graphics necessary for an understanding of the rest of the book.

- Chapter 3, *Bitmap Files*, describes the structure and characteristics of bitmap files.

- Chapter 4, *Vector Files*, describes the structure and characteristics of vector files.

- Chapter 5, *Metafiles*, describes the structure and characteristics of metafiles.

- Chapter 6, *Platform Dependencies*, describes the few machine and operating system dependencies you will need to understand.

- Chapter 7, *Format Conversion*, discusses issues to consider when you are converting between the different format types (e.g., bitmap to vector).

- Chapter 8, *Working with Graphics Files*, describes common ways of working with graphics files and gives some cautions and pointers for those who are designing their own graphics file formats.

- Chapter 9, *Data Compression*, describes data compression, particularly as compression techniques apply to graphics data and the graphics files described in this book.

- Chapter 10, *Multimedia*, surveys multimedia formats and issues.

Part Two, Graphics File Formats, describes the graphics file formats themselves. There is one article per format or format set, and articles are arranged alphabetically. Each article provides basic classification information, an overview, and details of the format. In many cases we've included short code examples. We've also indicated whether the specification itself (or an article that describes the details of the format) is included on the CD-ROM that accompanies this book, as well as code examples and images encoded in that format. Also provided in the articles are references for further information.

Part Three, Appendices, contains the following material:

- Appendix A, *What's On the CD-ROM?*, tells you what's on the CD-ROM accompanying the book and how to access this information.

- Appendix B, *Graphics and Imaging Resources*, suggests additional online sources of information.

We also include a Glossary, which gives definitions for terms in the text. "For Further Information" sections throughout the book list suggestions for further reading.

Conventions Used in This Book

We use the following formatting conventions in this book:

- **Bold** is used for headings in the text

- *Italics* are used for emphasis and to signify the first use of a term. Italics are also used for email addresses, FTP sites, directory and filenames, and newsgroups.

- All code and header examples are in `Constant Width`.

- All numbers in file excerpts and examples are in hexadecimal unless otherwise noted.

- All code and header examples use the following portable data types:

CHAR	8-bit signed data
BYTE	8-bit unsigned data
WORD	16-bit unsigned integer
DWORD	32-bit unsigned integer
LONG	32-bit signed integer
FLOAT	32-bit single-precision floating point number
DOUBLE	64-bit double-precision floating point number

All source code that we produced is written in ANSI C. (This is relevant only if you are still using one of the older compilers.)

Terminology of Computer Graphics

Computer graphics is in flux, and people working in the field are still busy creating vocabulary by minting new words. But they're also mutating the meanings of older words—words that once had a clear definition and context.

Computer graphics is also an emerging field, fertilized by electronics, photography, film, animation, broadcast video, sculpture, and the traditional graphic arts. Each one of these fields has its own terminology and conventions, which computer graphics has inherited to some degree.

Complicating matters, we're now in the era of electronic graphic arts. Color display adapters and frame buffers, paint and imaging programs, scanners, printers, video cameras, and video recorders are all being used in conjunction with the computer for the production of both fine and commercial art. A glance at any glossy magazine ad should give you some idea about how pervasive the mixing of digital and traditional media has become, if only because the overwhelming majority of magazines are now digitally composed. Indeed, the distinctions between traditional and computer art are becoming blurred.

Today, we can find graphic artists producing work in traditional media, which is scanned into digital form, altered, re-rendered with a computer, and then distributed as original. While this is not a problem in itself, it nonetheless accelerates the reinjection of traditional terminology into computer graphics, countering any trend toward standardization. This will inevitably cause contradictions. Some are already apparent, in fact, and you'll probably notice them when we discuss the details of the formats.

There is no one, single, consistent set of terms used across all of computer graphics. It is customary to cite standard references (like the classic *Computer Graphics: Principles and Practice* by James D. Foley, Andries vanDam, et al) when arguing about terminology, but this approach is not always appropriate. Our experience is that usage in this field both precedes and succeeds definition. It also proceeds largely apart from the dictates of academia. To make matters worse, the sub-field of graphics file formats is littered with variant jargon and obsolete usage. Many of the problems programmers have implementing formats, in fact, can be traced to terminological misunderstandings.

In light of this, we have chosen to use a self-consistent terminology that is occasionally at odds with that of other authors. Sometimes, we have picked a term because it has come into common use, displacing an older meaning. An example of this is *bitmap*, which is now often used as a synonym for *raster*, making obsolete the older distinction between *bitmap* and *pixelmap*. Occasionally, we have been forced to choose from among a number of terms for the same concept. Our decision to use the term *palette* is one example of this.

For some of the same reasons, we use the term *graphics*, and avoid *graphic* and *graphical*. We all have to face up to the fact that the field is known as *computer graphics*, establishing a persistent awkwardness. We have chosen to use graphics as a noun as well as an adjective.

We believe that the choices we made represent a simplification of the terminology, and that this shouldn't be a problem if you're already familiar with alternate usage. Should you have any questions in this area, our definitions are available in the Glossary.

About the File Format Specifications

In preparing this book, we have made a monumental effort to collect, all in one place, the myriad graphics file format specifications that have, until now, been floating on the Internet, hiding in the basements of various organizations, and gathering dust on individual application authors' bookshelves and in their private directories. We've done our best to locate the specifications and their caretakers (perhaps the original author, and perhaps the vendor that now maintains or at least owns the specification) and to obtain permission to include these documents on the CD-ROM that accompanies this book. In most cases, we have been able to obtain permission, but in some cases we have not.

There were several reasons for our failure to gain permission, some simple and some more complex. Although neither of us is a lawyer (or a bureaucrat!) or is particularly interested in legal issues, we did encounter some legalities while gathering these specifications. Given our special perspective on the world of graphics file formats, we want to share our reactions to these legalities with you—perhaps in the hope that we'll see fewer problems in the future.

Here are the reasons why we couldn't include certain format specifications on the CD-ROM; here, we use the word "caretaker" to indicate either the author or owner of the specification or the organization that now has responsibility for its maintenance or distribution.

- **We couldn't find the caretaker**. We simply couldn't find out who owned the specification of some of the formats we knew about. This may or may not have been the vendor's fault, but try as we did, we just couldn't find the information. Here's where you can help us. If you know of a format that you yourself find useful, let us know what it is and how you think we might be able to obtain permission to include it in a future edition of this book.

- **The caretaker couldn't find the specification**. Strange, but true. This happened twice. To be honest, these were both small companies. But still. . .

- **We couldn't get past caretaker bureaucracy**. In some cases, we simply couldn't get through to the correct person in the organization in 18 months of trying. We know it's hard to believe. It seems that you could walk into any installation and in a few minutes figure out who knows what and where they are. We thought so too before we started this project. In fact, executive management at several vendors professed a willingness to provide us with information, but simply couldn't figure out how to do so. Here too, maybe our readers can help. . .

- **The caretaker wouldn't allow us to include the format.** In some cases, we found this reasonable. One obvious case was the BRL-CAD specification, which is massive and readily available. The U.S. government will send it to you if you ask for it. Other companies prefer to license the information as part of a developer's kit. Still others wished to restrict the currency of older formats, presumably so they wouldn't be bothered by users calling them up about them. Although we are philosophically in disagreement with vendors in this latter group, we are willing to admit that they have a point. Some companies, however, feel that releasing information on their formats would somehow give their competitors an advantage or would otherwise be to their own disadvantage. We hope they'll change their minds when they see how many other formats are represented here and how useful this compendium is to everyone—programmers and vendors alike. Finally, several vendors have taken the most extreme position that information on their formats is proprietary and have used legal means to prevent developers from working with them. This last case is the most alarming, and we discuss it further below.

We find it hard to understand why vendors have patented their formats and/or used contract law arguments to restrict access to information on their formats. It seems obvious enough to us—and to others in the industry—that the way to get people to purchase your products is to make them easy to work with, not only for users, but for developers, too. Historically, this has been the case. Vendors who locked up their systems necessarily settled for a smaller share of the market.

Although some vendors seem nearly paranoid, we suspect that the majority that restrict their formats don't have a clear idea what they're selling. This is particularly true for vendors of large, vertically integrated systems, where the format plays a small, but key, role in the overall product strategy.

Nevertheless, whether justified in our view or not, the restriction is real and serves as an alarming and dangerous precedent. As the various parts of the computer industry converge, competition for market share is necessarily increasing. There is a tendency for entities in the business to grow larger and more corporate. What one company does, its competitors must do to stay in the market. At least they consider doing it.

Now, the reality of the situation is that no vendor can restrict information totally and indefinitely. This is particularly the case with file formats. Vendors generally seek to protect their formats through a combination of encryption and legal remedies. However, a person who buys the application which produces the restricted format as output buys a generator of an infinite number of samples. Because applications are judged, among other things, by the speed with which they produce output, and because encryption and obfuscation schemes take time to both implement and use, not much time and effort has gone into making formats unbeatable. To date, encrypted and obfuscated formats have been pretty easy to crack.

An example that comes to mind is Adobe's Type 1 font format encryption. This was used by Adobe to protect its font outlines, but knowledge of the encryption scheme was fairly widespread in certain commercial circles before Adobe publicized it. Whether this resulted in commercial losses to Adobe from piracy of their outlines is hard to say. It certainly generated a good deal of ill will in the industry and ultimately proved futile.

This being the case, some vendors have taken to the courts to protect their formats. We find this behavior futile and ill-conceived. Even if it has a short-term benefit on revenues, the long-term losses due to a restricted market and developer ill-will seem to outweigh this benefit. In a sense, it is a form of monopolistic behavior, or certainly a type of positioning designed to support future monopolistic behavior.

Now, it's a fact of life that almost every format that has made it to the market has been reverse-engineered. This has seldom been for profit—more for the challenge. If you truly have a need to track down the information, it's certain that it can be found through the Internet, provided the information exists.

Is it legal to possess this information? This isn't clear at this time. Certainly it's illegal if the information was stolen from a vendor prior to publication. We, by the way, know of no instance where a restricted format has ever been stolen from a vendor. If you use or publicize information a vendor has tried to restrict legally, however, you run the risk of becoming involved in the legal affairs of the vendor, regardless of how that information was obtained. We do wish to point out that the legal way to influence the behavior of a commercial entity is in the marketplace.

The best-known vendor in recent years that has tried to restrict developers, through legal means, from obtaining information on its format is Kodak in the case of Photo CD, as we describe in the Kodak Photo CD article in part II.

In summary, although we could not include information on several of the formats we might have wished to, that information is almost surely available somehow for you to study so you'll understand more about format construction. However, if the format is legally restricted, you probably can't use it in your application, and there's no use thinking otherwise.

About the Examples

You'll find short code examples associated with some of the articles, but in most cases the full examples are not included in the file format articles themselves. We have done this mainly because many of the code examples are quite long, and we wanted to make it easier to find information in the book. All of the code is included on the accompanying CD-ROM.

The examples are, in most cases, C functions which parse and read (or write) format files. The examples are just that—examples—and are meant to give you a jump-start reading and writing image files. These are generally not standalone applications. In most cases, we wrote this code ourselves during the writing of the book or as part of other projects we've worked on. In some cases, code was contributed by other programmers or by those who own the file format specifications described in this book. We've also referred you to the source code for certain software packages on the CD-ROM that handle specific types of file formats—for example, the libtiff software, which provides extensive code illustrating the handling of TIFF files.

The examples are usually written in a platform-independent manner. There is a bias for integer word lengths of 32 bits or less, for the simple reason that the overwhelming majority of files written to date have been on machines with a 32-bit or smaller word size. All examples and listings in this book and on the code disk are written in ANSI C.

The code is provided for illustrative purposes only. In some cases, we have spent considerable time constructing transparent examples, and it's not necessarily an easy job. So be forewarned: if you use our code, absolutely no attempt has been made to optimize it. That's your job!

Can you use our code freely? In most cases, yes. We and O'Reilly & Associates grant you a royalty-free right to reproduce and distribute any sample code in the text and companion disk written by the authors of this book, provided that you:

1. Distribute the sample code only in conjunction with and as a part of your software product

2. Do not use our names or the O'Reilly & Associates name to market your software product

3. Include a copyright notice (both in your documentation and as a part of the sign-on message for your software product) in the form:

"Portions Copyright (C) 1994 by James D. Murray and William vanRyper"

Please also note the disclaimer statements on the copyright page of this book.

Note as well that it is your responsibility to obtain permission for the use of any source code included on the CD-ROM that is not written by the authors of this book.

About the Images

Along with the specification documents and code, we have collected sample images for many of the graphics file formats. You can use these sample images to test whether you are successfully reading or converting a particular file format.

About the Software

We are not the first programmers who have discovered how cumbersome and troublesome graphics file formats can be. We have elected to organize the chaos by writing a book. Other programmers among us have responded by writing software that reads, converts, manipulates, or otherwise analyzes graphics files. Many of them have kindly agreed to let us include their software on the CD-ROM that accompanies this book. The packages we have elected to include provide an excellent sampling of what is available in the world of publicly available software. Although many of these packages are readily available on the Internet or via various PC bulletin board systems, their noncommercial nature should not in any way suggest that they lack value. These are excellent packages, and we are very grateful that we have been able to include them here. They should help you considerably in your dealings with graphics files.

We include the following software packages on the CD-ROM:

For MS-DOS:

  IMDISP (Image Display)
  ISO MPEG-2 Codec (MPEG Encoder and Decoder)
  pbmplus (Portable Bitmap Utilities)
  VPIC

For Windows:

  Conversion Assistant for Windows
  Paint Shop Pro
  PhotoLab
  PictureMan
  WinJPEG (Windows JPEG)

For OS/2:

GBM (Generalized Bitmap Module)
PMJPEG (Presentation Manager JPEG)

For UNIX:

FBM (Fuzzy Bitmap Manipulation)
ISO MPEG-2 Codec (MPEG Encoder and Decoder)
JPEG (Independent JPEG Group's JPEG Library)
libtiff (TIFF Library)
pbmplus (Portable Bitmap Utilities)
SAOimage (Smithsonian Astrophysical Observatory Image)
xli
xloadimage
xv (X Viewer)

For the Macintosh:

GIFConverter
GraphicsConverter
JPEGView
NIH Image
Sparkle

Which Platforms?

Most of the graphics file formats we describe in Part II of this book originated on a particular platform for use in a particular application—for example, Mac-Paint on the Macintosh. Despite their origins, most files can be converted readily to other platforms and can be used with other applications, as we describe later in this book. There are a few issues that you need to be aware of, though, having to do with the platform on which you are working or the platform on which a particular graphics file was developed. These issues are summarized in Chapter 6, *Platform Dependencies*.

Request for Comments

As you might imagine, locating and compiling the information that went into this book was no easy task, and in some cases our way was blocked, as we've discussed earlier. We're sure that some of the information we searched for is out there—somewhere!

We'd like to continue improving future editions, and for this we'll need all the help we can get. In addition to correcting any errors and omissions, we'd particularly like to expand our coverage of some of the more obscure graphics file formats that we might not know about or were unable to collect in time for publication. Also, if we were wrong, we want to know about it.

If you're in a position to help us out, or if you have any comments or suggestions on how we can improve things in any way, we'd love to hear from you. Please write, email, or call:

O'Reilly & Associates, Inc.
103 Morris Street, Suite A
Sebastopol CA 95472
800-998-9938 (in the U.S. or Canada)
707-829-0515 (international/local)
707-829-0104 (FAX)
Internet: *bookquestions@ora.com*
UUCP: *uunet!ora!bookquestions*

Acknowledgments

Writing this book, and collecting the voluminous material that is included on the CD-ROM that accompanies it, was a huge effort made possible only by the extraordinary generosity and common sense of a great many people. When we set out to collect the vast set of file format specifications in common use today, we frankly expected to be able to persuade only a small fraction of the specification owners and vendors that contributing them freely to this effort would be a good idea for them. We were convinced that it was a good idea, of course, but given the practicalities of bureaucracy, competition, and the many demands on people's time, we were not optimistic about conveying that conviction to others in the graphics community.

It was not an easy effort, and sometimes we nagged, wheedled, and otherwise made nuisances of ourselves, but people came through for us in the most remarkable way. To all those who contributed specifications, images, and their expertise to this effort, thank you. We hope it pays off by increasing the general awareness of people in the market and by substantially reducing the number of support calls to those who maintain the file formats. We have tried to list all those who helped us, but there were so many over such a long period of time that we are bound to leave a few names off the list. Don't be shy about reminding us, and we'll include your names next time. To all those listed and unlisted, please accept our thanks.

Individuals who helped us obtain and understand specifications include the following: Keith Alexander, Chris Allis, Jim Anderson, Tony Apodaca, Jim

Atkinson, Ron Baalke, David Baggett, Dan Baker, Cindy Batz, Gavin Bell, Steve Belsky, Celia Booher, Kim Bovic, Neil Bowers, John Bridges, Richard Brownback, Rikk Carey, Steve Carlsen, Timothy Casey, Wesley Chalfant, Buckley Collum, Freda Cooke, Catherine Copetas, António Costa, Stephen Coy, John Cristy, William Darnall, Ray Davis, Tom Davis, Bob Deen, Michael Dillon, Shannon Donovan, John Edwards, Jerry Evans, Lee Fisher, Jim Fister, Chad Fogg, Michael Folk, Roger Fujii, Jean-loup Gailly, Gary Goelhoeft, Bob Gonsales, Debby Gordon, Hank Gracin, Joy Gregory, Scott Gross, Hadmut, Paul Haeberli, Eric Haines, Eric Hamilton, Kory Hamzeh, William Hanlon, Fred Hansen, Paul Harker, Chris Hecker, Bill Hibbard, Michael Hoffman, Steve Hollasch, Terry Ilardi, Neale Johnston, Mike Kaltschnee, Lou Katz, Jim Kent, Pam Kerwin, Craig Kolb, Steve Koren, Don Lancaster, Tom Lane, Ian Lepore, Greg Leslie, Glenn Lewis, Paul Mace, Britt Mackenzie, Mike Martin, Pat McGee, Brian Moran, Mike Muuse, JoAnn Nielson, Gail Ostrow, Joan Patterson, Jeff Parker, Brian Paul, Brad Pillow, Andrew Plotkin, Jef Poskanzer, John Rasure, Dave Ratcliffe, Jim Rose, Randi Rost, Carroll Rotkel, Stacie Saccomanno, Jim Saghir, Barry Schlesinger, Louis Shay, Bill Shotts, Rik Segal, Mark Skiba, Scott St. Clair, John Stackpole, Marc Stengel, Ann Sydeman, Mark Sylvester, Spencer Thomas, Mark VandeWettering, Greg Ward, Archie Warnock, David Wecker, Joel Welling, Drew Wells, Jocelyn Willett, James Winget, and Shiming Xu.

Thanks to these organizations that shared their specifications and helped us in other ways: 3D/Eye, Adobe Systems, Aldus, Andrew Consortium, Apple Computer, Autodesk, Avatar, Carnegie Mellon University, C-Cube Microsystems, Commodore Business Machines, CompuServe, Computer Associates, Digital Equipment Corporation, Digital Research, DISCUS, DuPont, IBM, Inset Systems, Intel Corporation, ISEP.INESC, Jet Propulsion Laboratory, Khoral Research, Kofax Image Products, Kubota Pacific Computer, Lawrence Berkeley Laboratory, Massachusetts Institute of Technology, Media Cybernetics, Metron Computerware, Microsoft, National Aeronautics and Space Administration, National Center for Supercomputer Applications, National Oceanic and Atmospheric Administration, Novell, Paul Mace Software, Pittsburgh Supercomputing Center, Pixar, Princeton University Department of Computer Science, RIX SoftWorks, Silicon Graphics, Sun Microsystems, Time Arts, Truevision, University of Illinois, University of Utah Department of Computer Science, University of Wisconsin at Madison, U.S. Army Ballistic Research Lab, U.S. Army Research Laboratory, Wavefront Technologies, X Consortium, and ZSoft.

Very special thanks to those who read the manuscript of this book and made thoughtful and helpful comments on the content and organization: Dr. Peter Bono, Jim Frost, Tom Gaskins, Lofton Henderson, Dr. Tom Lane, Tim O'Reilly, Sam Leffler, Dr. Anne Mumford, and Archie Warnock. Double thanks to Lofton Henderson, who prepared CGM images for us under a tight deadline, and to Tom Lane, who reviewed the CD-ROM as well. We could not have done this without you!

Many thanks to Shari L.S. Worthington, who let us include in this book many of the Internet resources she compiled for her article, "Imaging on the Internet: Scientific/Industrial Resources" in *Advanced Imaging*, February 1994.

We are very grateful to those who contributed software that will allow you to convert, view, manipulate, and otherwise make sense of the many file formats described in this book. We could not include all of these packages on the CD-ROM (for this version, at least), but we appreciate very much your generosity. Thanks to these individuals: Dan Baker, Robert Becker, Alexey Bobkov, John Bradley, Mike Castle, John Cristy, Orlando Dare, D.J. Delorie, Guiseppe Desoli, Chris Drouin, Stefan Eckart, Mark Edmead, Chad Fogg, Oliver Fromme, Mike Fitzpatrick, Jim Frost, Aaron Giles, Graeme Gill, Maynard Handley, Jih-Shin Ho, Robert Holland, David Holliday, Allen Kempe, Andrew Key, Michail Kutzetsov, Tom Lane, Sam Leffler, Thorsten Lemke, Leonardo Loureiro, Eric Mandel, Michael Mauldin, Frank McKenney, Kevin Mitchell, Bob Montgomery, David Ottoson, Jef Poskanzer, Igor Plotnikov, Eric Praetzel, Wayne Rasband, Mohammed Ali Rezaei, Rich Siegel, Davide Rossi, Y. Shan, Doug Tody, Robert Voit, Archie Warnock, Ken Yee, Norman Yee, and Paul Yoshimune. And thanks to these organizations: Alchemy Mindworks, Bare Bones Software, Carnegie Mellon University, CenterLine Software, Express Compression Labs, DareWare, Goddard Space Center, Handmade Software, Honeywell Technology Center, Independent JPEG Group, Labtam Australia Pty Ltd, MTE Industries, National Institutes of Health, National Optical Astronomy Observatories, Peepworks, PixelVision Software, Phase II Electronics, Stoik Ltd, TBH-SoftWorx, University of Waterloo. Special thanks to Rich Siegel and Leonard Rosenthal, who offered the use of their BBEdit and Stuffit products, as well as their knowledge of the Macintosh.

Many, many thanks to all the good people at O'Reilly & Associates who made this book happen: to our editor, Debby Russell, who guided this effort from beginning to end; to Gigi Estabrook, who tirelessly collected permissions and documents from the many vendors; to Ellen Siever who as production manager got an enormous book out under incredible time pressure; to Nicole Gipson, Jessica Hekman, Mary Anne Weeks Mayo, Kismet McDonough, Clairemarie Fisher O'Leary, and Stephen Spainhour who worked on the production team; to Chris Tong, who produced the index; and to Chris Reilley, who created the figures. Special thanks to Len Muellner and Norm Walsh who spent many long hours developing tools, filters, and magical potions that tamed the SGML beast.

We are also very grateful to those who produced the CD-ROM that accompanies this book: to Debby Russell, who headed up the effort; to Terry Allen, who converted and otherwise beat the files into submission; to Norm Walsh and Jeff Robbins, who lent their expertise in PC and Macintosh environments; and to Dale Dougherty, Lar Kaufman, Linda Mui, Tim O'Reilly, Eric Pearce, and Ron Petrusha, who all contributed their knowledge of CD-ROM technology, their experiences with other projects, and their opinions about how we ought to proceed. Thanks to Jeff Moskow and Ready-to-Run Software, who did the final CD-ROM development for us.

A special thank you to P.J. Mead Books & Coffee of Orange, California, where James D. Murray sought caffeine and solace during the long days and nights of writing and revising this book.

Finally,

This book is dedicated to my son, James Alexander Ozbirn Murray, and his mother, Katherine

James D. Murray

To all sentient beings working with graphics file formats.

William vanRyper

## PART ONE

Overview

Introduction

Why Graphics File Formats?

A graphics file format is the format in which graphics data—data describing a graphics image—is stored in a file. Graphics file formats have come about from the need to store, organize, and retrieve graphics data in an efficient and logical way. Sounds like a pretty straightforward task, right? But there's a lot under the covers, and that's what we're going to talk about.

File formats can be complex. Of course they never seem complex until you're actually trying to implement one in software. They're also important, in ways that often aren't obvious. You'll find, for instance, that the way a block of data is stored is usually the single most important factor governing the speed with which it can be read, the space it takes up on disk, and the ease with which it can be accessed by an application. A program simply must save its data in a reasonable format. Otherwise, it runs the risk of being considered useless.

Practically every major application creates and stores some form of graphics data. Even the simplest character-mode text editors allow the creation of files containing line drawings made from ASCII characters or terminal escape sequences. GUI-based applications, which have proliferated in recent years, now need to support hybrid formats to allow the incorporation of bitmap data in text documents. Database programs with image extensions also let you store text and bitmap data together in a single file. In addition, graphics files are an important transport mechanism that allows the interchange of visual data between software applications and computer systems.

There is currently a great deal of work being done on object-based file systems, where a "data file" may appear as a cluster of otherwise unrelated elements and may be just as likely to incorporate graphics data as not. Clearly, traditional data classification schemes are in need of revision. Nevertheless, there will remain an enormous amount of graphics data accessible only by virtue of our ability to decode and manipulate the files we find around us today.

The Basics

Before we explore the details of any particular file formats, we first need to establish some basic background and terminology. Because we're assuming you have a general working knowledge of computers and know some programming, we'll start with some definitions. You'll find that we've simplified and condensed some of the terminology found in standard computer graphics references. The changes, however, always reflect modern usage. (You'll find a discussion of our rationale in the Preface.)

In what follows, we will be speaking of the *output* of a computer graphics process, or the production of a *graphic work* by a program. We don't mean to seem anthropomorphic here. The author of the work is usually human, of course, but his or her contribution is *input* from the point of view of this book. We're mainly concerned about the portion of the output that comes from a program and winds up in a file. Because the program is the last thing that "touches" the data before it winds up on disk or tape, we say that a graphic work is produced by a program, rather than by a human being. (In this case, we are referring to the form in which the data is stored, and not its meaning or content.)

Graphics and Computer Graphics

Traditionally, *graphics* refers to the production of a visual *representation* of a real or imaginary object created by methods known to graphic artists, such as writing, painting, imprinting, and etching. The final result of the traditional graphics production process eventually appears on a 2D surface, such as paper or canvas. *Computer graphics*, however, has expanded the meaning of *graphics* to include any data intended for display on an *output device*, such as a screen, printer, plotter, or film recorder.

Notice what's happened here. Graphics used to refer to the *actual output*, something you could see. Now it means something only *intended* for display, or something meant to be turned into output. This distinction may seem silly to experienced users, but we've watched artists new to computers struggle with this. Where is the graphic output from a paint program? Does it appear as you compose something on the screen? Where is the representation when you write your work to a file? Does it appear for the first time when another program displays it on a screen or paper?

In the practice of computer graphics, creation of a work is often separate from its representation. One way to put it is that a computer graphics process produces *virtual output* in memory, or persistent output in a file on permanent media, such as a disk or tape. In other words, even though a program has written a file full of *something*, output doesn't yet exist from a traditional point of view because nothing has been displayed anywhere. So we say that *graphics data* is the *virtual output* of a program, from which a representation of the work can be constructed, or can be reconstructed from the persistent graphics data saved to a file, possibly by the same program.

Rendering and Images

In the interest of clarity, most people make a distinction between creation and *rendering* (sometimes also called *realization*). Traditionally, an *image* is a visual representation of a real-world object, captured by an artist through the use of some sort of mechanical, electronic, or photographic process. In computer graphics, the meaning of an image has been broadened somewhat to refer to an object that appears on an output device. Graphics data is rendered when a program draws an image on an output device.

You will also occasionally hear people speak of the computer graphics *production pipeline*. This is the series of steps involved in defining and creating graphics data and rendering an image. On one end of the production pipeline is a human being; on the other end is an image on paper, screen, or another device. Figure 1-1 illustrates this process.

Graphics Files

For the purpose of this book, graphics files are files that store any type of persistent graphics data (as opposed to text, spreadsheet, or numerical data, for example), and that are intended for eventual rendering and display. The various ways in which these files are structured are called graphics file formats. We will examine several categories of graphics file formats later in this chapter.

People sometimes talk of rendering an image to a file, and this is a common and perfectly valid operation. For our purposes, when an image is rendered to a file, the contents of that file become persistent graphics data. Why? Simply because the data in the file now needs to be re-rendered as virtual graphics data before you can see what it looks like.

Although the image is once again turned into graphics data in the process of rendering it to the file, it is now once more merely data. In fact, the data can now be of a different type. This is what happens in file conversion operations, for example. An image stored in a file of format type 1 is rendered (by a conversion program) to a second file of format type 2.

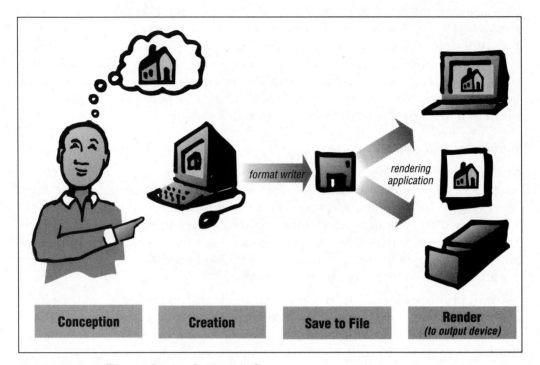

FIGURE 1-1: *The graphics production pipeline*

Which Graphics Files Are Included . . .

Although we've tried in this book to stick to formats that contain graphics data, we've also tried to make sure that they are used for data interchange between programs. Now, you'd think that it's always perfectly clear whether a file contains graphics data or not. Unfortunately, this isn't always the case. Spreadsheet formats, for instance, are sometimes used to store graphics data. And what about data interchange? A format is either used to transfer data from one program to another or it isn't, right? Again, it's not so simple.

Some formats, like TIFF, CGM, and GIF, were designed for interprogram data interchange. But what about other formats, such as PCX, which were designed in conjunction with a particular program? There is no easy answer, but these two criteria—graphics data and data interchange—will take you a long way, and we've tried as much as possible to follow them here.

The section below called "Format Summaries" contains a complete list of all of the formats described in this book.

. . . And Which Are Not

For the purposes of this book, we're excluding three types of files that contain graphics data but are outside the scope of what we are trying to accomplish here: *output device language* files, *page description language* files, and *FAX* files.

Output device language files contain hardware-dependent control codes that are designed to be interpreted by an output device and are usually used to produce hardcopy output. We exclude these, because they usually have a short lifetime as temporary files and with few exceptions are not archived or exchanged with other machines. Another reason is practical: many of the hundreds of types of printers and plotters built over the years use vendor-specific control information, which the market has traditionally ignored. By far the most common output device languages in use are Printer Control Language (PCL) and variants, used to control the Hewlett-Packard LaserJet series of laser printers and compatibles, and Hewlett-Packard Printer Graphics Language (HPGL), used to control plotters and other vector devices.

Page description languages (PDLs) are sophisticated systems for describing graphical output. We exclude page description languages from our discussion, because the market is dominated by Adobe's PostScript and because the specification is voluminous and extremely well-documented in readily available publications. We do, however, provide an article describing Encapsulated PostScript format; that article briefly discusses EPS, EPSF, and EPSI formats.

FAX-format files are usually program-specific, created by an application designed to support one or more FAX modems. There are many such formats, and we do not cover them, because they generally are not used for file exchange. We do, however, include a brief article on FAX formats that discusses some of the issues you'll face if you use these formats.

Graphics Data

Graphics data is traditionally divided into two classes: *vector* and *bitmap*. As we explain below, we use the term *bitmap* to replace the older term *raster*.

Vector Data

In computer graphics, vector data usually refers to a means of representing lines, polygons, or curves (or any object that can be easily drawn with lines) by numerically specifying *key points*. The job of a program rendering this key-point data is to regenerate the lines by somehow connecting the key points or by drawing using the key points for guidance. Always associated with vector data is attribute information (such as color and line thickness information) and a set of conventions (or rules) allowing a program to draw the desired objects.

These conventions can be either implicit or explicit, and, although designed to accomplish the same goals, are generally different from program to program.

Figure 1-2 shows several examples of vector data.

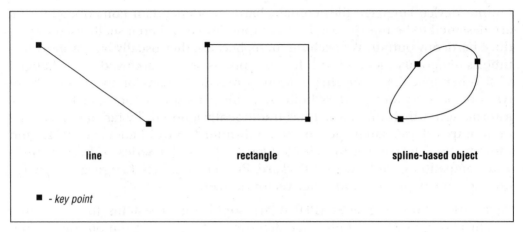

FIGURE 1-2: *Vector data*

By the way, you may be familiar with a definition of the word vector which is quite precise. In the sciences and mathematics, for instance, a vector is a straight line having both magnitude and direction. In computer graphics, "vector" is a sort of catch-all term. It can be almost any kind of line or line segment, and it is usually specified by sets of endpoints, except in the case of curved lines and more complicated geometric figures, which require other key points to be fully specified.

Bitmap Data

Bitmap data is formed from a set of numerical values specifying the colors of individual *pixels* or *picture elements* (*pels*). Pixels are dots of color arranged on a regular grid in a pattern representing the form to be displayed. We commonly say that a bitmap is an *array of pixels*, although a bitmap, technically, consists of an *array of numerical values* used to set, color, or "turn on" the corresponding pixels on an output device when the bitmap is rendered. If there is any ambiguity in the text, we will make the distinction clear by using the term *pixel value* to refer to a numerical value in the bitmap data corresponding to a pixel color in the image on the display device.

Figure 1-3 shows an example of bitmap data.

In older usage, the term *bitmap* sometimes referred to an array (or "map") of single bits, each bit corresponding to a pixel, while the terms *pixelmap*, *graymap*, and *pixmap* were reserved for arrays of multibit pixels. We always use the term

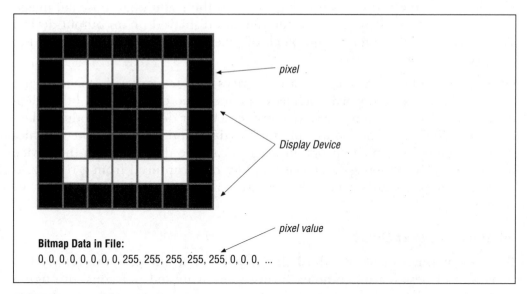

Bitmap Data in File:
0, 0, 0, 0, 0, 0, 0, 0, 255, 255, 255, 255, 255, 0, 0, 0, ...

FIGURE 1-3: *Bitmap data*

bitmap to refer to an array of pixels, whatever the type, and specify the *bit depth*, or *pixel depth*, which is the size of the pixels in bits or some other convenient unit (such as bytes). The bit depth determines the number of colors a pixel value can represent. A 1-bit pixel can be one of two colors, a 4-bit pixel one of 16 colors, and so on. The most commonly found pixel depths today are 1, 2, 4, 8, 15, 16, 24, and 32 bits. Some of the reasons for this, and other color-related topics, are discussed in Chapter 2, *Computer Graphics Basics.*

Sources of Bitmap Data: Raster Devices

Historically, the term *raster* has been associated with cathode ray tube (CRT) technology and has referred to the pattern of rows the device makes when displaying an image on a picture tube. Raster-format images are therefore a collection of pixels organized into a series of rows, which are called *scan lines.* Because raster output devices, by far the most popular kind available today, display images as patterns of pixels, pixel values in a bitmap are usually arranged so as to make them easy to display on certain common raster devices. For these reasons, bitmap data is often called raster data. In this book, we use the term *bitmap data.*

As mentioned above, bitmap data can be produced when a program renders graphics data and writes the corresponding output image to a file instead of displaying it on an output device. This is one of the reasons bitmaps and bitmap data are often referred to as *images,* and bitmap data is referred to as *image data.* Although there is nothing to see in the traditional sense, an image can be readily reconstructed from the file and displayed on an output device. We will occasionally refer to the block of pixel values in a bitmap file as the *image* or *image portion.*

Other sources of bitmap data are raster devices used to work with images in the traditional sense of the word, such as scanners, video cameras, and other digitizing devices. For our purposes, we consider a raster device that produces digital data to be just another source of graphics data, and we say that the graphics data is rendered when the program used to capture the data from the device writes it to a file. When speaking of graphics data captured from a real-world source, such as a scanner, people speak redundantly of a *bitmap image,* or an *image bitmap.*

What About Object Data?

People sometimes speak of a third class: *object data.* In the past, this referred to a method of designating complex forms, such as nested polygons, through a shorthand method of notation, and relying on a program's ability to directly render these forms with a minimal set of clues. Increasingly, however, the term is used to refer to data stored along with the program code or algorithmic information needed to render it. This distinction may become useful in the future, particularly if languages which support object-oriented programming (such as Smalltalk and C++) become more popular. However, for now we choose to ignore this third primitive data type, mainly because at the time of this writing there are no standardized object file formats of any apparent commercial importance. In any case, the data portions of all objects can be decomposed into simpler forms composed of elements from one of the two primitive classes.

Figure 1-4 shows an example of object data.

Other Data

Graphics files may also include data containing structural, color, and other descriptive information. This information is included primarily as an aid to the rendering application in reconstructing and displaying an image.

From Vector to Bitmap Data . . .

Twenty-five years ago, computer graphics was based almost entirely on vector data. Random-scan vector displays and pen plotters were the only readily obtainable output devices. The advent of cheap, high-capacity magnetic media, in the form of tapes and disks, soon allowed the storage of large files, which in turn created a need for the first standardized graphics file formats.

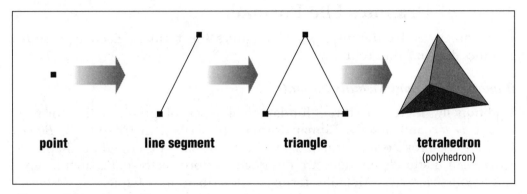

FIGURE 1-4: *Object data*

Today, most graphic storage is bitmap-based, and displays are raster-based. This is due in part to the availability of high-speed CPUs, inexpensive memory and mass storage, and high-resolution input and output hardware. Bitmap graphics is also driven by the need to manipulate images obtained from raster digitizing devices. Bitmap graphics is important in applications supporting CAD and 3D rendering, business charts, 2D and 3D modelling, computer art and animation, graphical user interfaces (GUIs), video games, electronic document image processing (EDIP), and image processing and analysis.

It is interesting to note that the increased emphasis on bitmap graphics in our time corresponds to a shift toward the output end of the graphics production pipeline. By volume, the greatest amount of data being stored and exchanged consists of finished images in bitmap format.

. . . And Back Again

But the trend toward bitmap data may not last. Although there are certain advantages to storing graphics images as bitmap data (we cover these in the section called "Pros and Cons of Bitmap Format Files" in Chapter 3, *Bitmap Files)*, bitmap images are usually pretty bulky. There is a definite trend toward networking in all the computer markets, and big bitmap files and low-cost networks don't mix. The cost of sending files around on the Internet, for example, can be measured not only in connect costs, but in lost time and decreased network performance.

Because graphics files are surely not going to go away, we expect some sort of vector-based file format to emerge somewhere along the line as an interchange standard. Unfortunately, none of the present vector formats in common use is acceptable to a broad range of users (but this may change).

Types of Graphics File Formats

There are several different types of graphics file formats. Each type stores graphics data in a different way.

Bitmap, Vector, and Metafile Formats

Traditionally, there are three fundamental types of graphics file formats: *bitmap*, *vector*, and *metafile*. Bitmap formats (described in Chapter 3, *Bitmap Files*) are used for storing bitmap data. Vector formats (described in Chapter 4, *Vector Files*), naturally enough, are designed to store vector data, such as lines and geometric data. Metafile formats (described in Chapter 5, *Metafiles*) accommodate both bitmap and vector data in the same file. So far, essentially all of our digital graphics storage needs have been satisfied by using these three format types.

Scene, Animation, and Multimedia Formats

In addition to the traditional bitmap, vector, and metafile formats, there are three other types of formats which we include in this book, all of lesser importance: *scene format*, *animation*, and *multimedia*.

Scene format files (sometimes called *scene description* files) are designed to store a condensed representation of an image or *scene*, which is used by a program to reconstruct the actual image. What's the difference between a vector-format file and a scene-format file? Just that vector files contain descriptions of portions of the image, and scene files contain instructions that the rendering program uses to construct the image. In practice it's sometimes hard to decide whether a particular format is scene or vector; it's more a matter of degree than anything absolute.

Animation formats have been around for some time. The basic idea is that of the flip-books you played with as a kid. Rapidly display one image superimposed over another to make it appear as if the objects in the image are moving. Very primitive animation formats store entire images that are displayed in sequence, usually in a loop. Slightly more advanced formats store only a single image, but multiple color maps for the image. By loading in a new color map, the colors in the image change, and the objects appear to move. Advanced animation formats store only the differences between two adjacent images (called frames) and update only the pixels that have actually changed as each frame is displayed. A display rate of 10-15 frames per second is typical for cartoon-like animations. Video animations usually require a display rate of 20 frames per second or better to produce a smoother motion.

Multimedia formats are relatively new and are designed to allow the storage of data of different types in the same file. Multimedia formats usually allow the inclusion of graphics, audio, and video information. Microsoft's RIFF and Apple's QuickTime are well-known examples, and others are likely to emerge in the near future. (Chapter 10, *Multimedia*, describes various issues for multimedia formats.)

Hybrid Formats and Hypertext

There are three other classes of formats which we should also mention. While not covered in detail in this book, these may become important in the future. These are the various *hybrid text*, *hybrid database*, and *hypertext* formats. Currently, there is a good deal of research being conducted on the integration of unstructured text and bitmap data ("hybrid text") and the integration of record-based information and bitmap data ("hybrid database"). As this work bears fruit, we expect that hybrid formats capable of efficiently storing graphics data will emerge and will become steadily more important.

Hypertext formats allow the arrangement of blocks of text so as to facilitate random access through links between the blocks. Hypertext formats that have been extended to allow the inclusion of other data (including graphics) are becoming known as *hypermedia*. Hypertext and hypermedia formats may also gain importance in the future. We don't cover them in this book chiefly because they're generally not used for data exchange between platforms.

Elements of a Graphics File

As mentioned in the Preface, different file format specifications use different terminology. In fact, it's possible that there is not a single term with a common meaning across all of the file formats mentioned in this book. This is certainly true for terms referring to the way data is stored in a file, such as field, tag, block, and packet. In fact, a specification will sometimes provide a definition for one of these terms and then abandon it in favor of a more descriptive one, such as a chunk, a sequence, or a record.

For purposes of discussion in this book, we will consider a graphics file to be composed of a sequence of data and data structures, called *file elements*, or *data elements*. These are divided into three categories: fields, tags, and streams.

Fields

A *field* is a data structure in a graphics file that is a fixed size. A fixed field has not only a fixed size but a fixed position within the file. The location of a field is communicated by specifying either an absolute offset from a landmark in a file, such as the file's beginning or end, or a relative offset from some other data. The size of a field either is stated in the format specification or can be inferred from other information.

Tags

A *tag* is a data structure which can vary in both size and position from file to file. The position of a tag, like that of a field, is specified by either an absolute offset from a known landmark in the file, or through a relative offset from another file element. Tags themselves may contain other tags or a collection of related fields.

Streams

Fields and tags are an aid to random access; they're designed to help a program quickly access a data item known in advance. Once a position in a file is known, a program can access the position directly without having to read intervening data. A file that organizes data as a *stream*, on the other hand, lacks the structure of one organized into fields and tags, and must be read sequentially. For our purposes, we will consider a stream to be made up of *packets*, which can vary in size, are sub-elements of the stream, and are meaningful to the program reading the file. Although the beginning and end of the stream may be known and specified, the location of packets other than the first usually is not, at least prior to the time of reading.

Combinations of Data Elements

You can imagine, then, pure fixed field files, pure tag files, and pure stream files, made up entirely of data organized into fixed fields, tags, and streams, respectively. Only rarely, however, does a file contain data elements of a single type; in most cases it is a combination of two or more. The TIFF and TGA formats, for example, use both tags and fixed fields. GIF format files, on the other hand, use both fixed fields and streams.

Fixed-field data is usually faster and easier to read than tag and stream data. Files composed primarily of fixed-field data, however, are less flexible in situations in which data needs to be added to or deleted from an existing file. Formats containing fixed fields are seldom easily upgraded. Stream data generally requires less memory to read and buffer than field and tag data. Files composed primarily of stream data, however, cannot be accessed randomly, and thus cannot be used to find or sub-sample data quickly. These considerations are discussed further in Chapters 3, 4, and 5.

Converting Formats

You often need to convert a graphics file from one format to another—for printing, for manipulation by a particular desktop publishing program, or for some other reason. Although conversion to and from certain file formats is straightforward, conversion of other formats may be quite hair-raising. You will find conversion particularly problematic if you need to convert between basic format types—for example, bitmap to vector.

Fortunately, there are some excellent products that handle most of the complexities of conversion for you. If you are using UNIX and are lucky enough to be converting between the formats supported by the pbmplus (Portable Bitmap Utilities) package (a freely available set of programs developed by Jef Poskanzer that we've included on the CD-ROM), your job will be an easy one. Rather than converting explicitly from one graphics file format to another (for example, from PCX to Microsoft Windows Bitmap [BMP]), pbmplus converts any source format to a common format and then converts that common format to the desired destination format.

We also provide a number of other conversion programs on the CD-ROM, including the MS-DOS pbmplus port, Conversion Assistant for Windows, GraphicsConverter for the Macintosh, and many more publicly available programs.

Try these programs out and see which best suits your formats and applications. You may also want to consider buying HiJaak, an excellent commercial product developed by Inset Systems that converts to and from most of the common file formats.

Chapter 7, *Format Conversion*, contains a discussion of converting between types of graphics file formats.

Compressing Data

Throughout the articles included in Part II of this book, you'll see references to methods of *data compression* or *data encoding*. Compression is the process used to reduce the physical size of a block of information. By compressing graphics data, we're able to fit more information in a physical storage space. Because graphics images usually require a very large amount of storage space, compression is an important consideration for graphics file formats. Almost every graphics file format uses some compression method.

There are several ways to look at compression. We can talk about differences between physical and logical compression, symmetric and asymmetric compression, and lossless and lossy compression. These terms are described in detail in Chapter 9, *Data Compression*. That chapter also describes the five most common methods of, or algorithms for, compression, which we mention here briefly:

- Pixel packing—Not a method of data compression per se, but an efficient way to store data in contiguous bytes of memory. This method is used by the Macintosh PICT format and by other formats that are capable of storing multiple 1-, 2-, or 4-bit pixels per byte of memory or disk space.

- Run length encoding (RLE)—A very common compression algorithm used by such bitmap formats as BMP, TIFF, and PCX to reduce the amount of redundant graphics data.

- Lempel-Ziv-Welch (LZW)—Used by GIF and TIFF, this algorithm is also a part of the v.42bis modem compression standard and of PostScript Level 2.

- CCITT encoding—A form of data compression used for facsimile transmission and standardized by the CCITT (International Telegraph and Telephone Consultative Committee). One particular standard is based on the keyed compression scheme introduced by David Huffman and known widely as Huffman encoding.

- Joint Photographic Experts Group (JPEG)—A toolkit of compression methods used particularly for continuous-tone image data and multimedia. The baseline JPEG implementation uses an encoding scheme based on the Discrete Cosine Transform (DCT) algorithm.

Each of the articles in Part II lists the compression algorithms used for the particular graphics file format described.

Format Summaries

Table 1-1 lists each of the graphics file formats that we describe in this book, along with an indication of what type of format it is (bitmap, vector, metafile, scene description, animation, multimedia, or other [for "other" formats, refer to the appropriate article in Part II]).

In some cases, a format may be known by a number of different names. To help you find the format you need, we've included Table 1-2, which lists the names by which graphics file formats may be known, or the file extensions they may have, with cross-references to the names under which they appear in Part II of this book.

Graphics files on most platforms use a fairly consistent file extension convention. Of the three platforms with the largest installed base (MS-DOS, Macintosh, and UNIX), all use a similar *name.extension* file-naming convention. The other platforms that are popular for computer graphics (Amiga, Atari, and

VMS) use a roughly similar naming convention. VMS, for example, uses the convention *name1.name2:version*, where *version* is an integer indicating the number of the file revision. Most of the 3-character names in Table 1-2 appear as graphics file extensions.

TABLE 1-1: *Graphics File Formats Described in This Book*

Format	Type
Adobe Photoshop	Bitmap
Atari ST Graphics Formats	Bitmap and Animation
AutoCAD DXF	Vector
BDF	Bitmap
BRL-CAD	Other
BUFR	Other
CALS Raster	Bitmap
CGM	Metafile
CMU Formats	Multimedia
DKB	Scene Description
Dore Raster File Format	Bitmap
Dr. Halo	Bitmap
Encapsulated PostScript	Metafile (Page Description Language)
FaceSaver	Bitmap
FAX Formats	Bitmap
FITS	Other
FLI	Animation
GEM Raster	Bitmap
GEM VDI	Metafile
GIF	Bitmap
GRASP	Animation
GRIB	Other
Harvard Graphics	Metafile
Hierarchical Data Format	Metafile
IGES	Other
Inset PIX	Bitmap
Intel DVI	Multimedia
Interchange File Format	Bitmap
JPEG File Interchange Format	Bitmap
Kodak Photo CD	Bitmap
Kodak YCC	Bitmap
Lotus DIF	Vector
Lotus PIC	Vector
Lumena Paint	Bitmap
Macintosh Paint	Bitmap

Format	Type
Macintosh PICT	Metafile
Microsoft Paint	Bitmap
Microsoft RIFF	Multimedia
Microsoft RTF	Metafile
Microsoft SYLK	Vector
Microsoft Windows Bitmap	Bitmap
Microsoft Windows Metafile	Metafile
MIFF	Bitmap
MPEG	Other
MTV	Scene Description
NAPLPS	Metafile
NFF	Scene Description
OFF	Scene Description
OS/2 Bitmap	Bitmap
P3D	Scene Description
PBM, PGM, PNM, and PPM	Bitmap
PCX	Bitmap
PDS	Other
Pictor PC Paint	Bitmap
Pixar RIB	Scene Description
Plot-10	Vector
POV	Vector
Presentation Manager Metafile	Metafile
PRT	Scene Description
QRT	Scene Description
QuickTime	Other
Radiance	Scene Description
Rayshade	Scene Description
RIX	Bitmap
RTrace	Scene Description
SGI Image File Format	Bitmap
SGI Inventor	Scene Description
SGI YAODL	Scene Description
SGO	Vector
Sun Icon	Bitmap
Sun Raster	Bitmap
TDDD	Vector and Animation
TGA	Bitmap
TIFF	Bitmap
TTDDD	Vector and Animation
uRay	Scene Description
Utah RLE	Bitmap
VICAR2	Bitmap

Format	Type
VIFF	Bitmap
VIS-5D	Vector
Vivid and Bob	Scene Description
Wavefront OBJ	Vector
Wavefront RLA	Bitmap
WordPerfect Graphics Metafile	Metafile
XBM	Bitmap
XPM	Bitmap
XWD	Bitmap

TABLE 1-2: *Format Names, Cross-Referenced to Articles in This Book*

Name or Extension	Format Name in Book
3D Interchange File Format	SGI Inventor
ADI	AutoCAD DXF
Amiga Paint	Interchange File Format
Andrew Formats	CMU Formats
ANI	Atari ST Graphics Formats
ANM	Atari ST Graphics Formats
AutoCAD Drawing Exchange Format	AutoCAD DXF
AVI	Microsoft RIFF
AVS	Intel DVI
AVSS	Intel DVI
Ballistic Research Laboratory CAD Package	BRL-CAD
Binary Universal Form for the Representation of Meteorological Data	BUFR
Bitmap Distribution Format	BDF
BMP	Microsoft Windows Bitmap
BMP	OS/2 Bitmap
BND	Microsoft RIFF
Bob	Vivid and Bob
BPX	Lumena Paint
BSAVE	Pictor PC Paint
BW	SGI Image File Format
C16	Intel DVI

Name or Extension	Format Name in Book
CAL	CALS Raster
CALS	CALS Raster
CE1	Atari ST Graphics Formats
CE2	Atari ST Graphics Formats
CE3	Atari ST Graphics Formats
CHT	Harvard Graphics
CLP	GRASP
CLP	Pictor PC Paint
CMI	Intel DVI
CMQ	Intel DVI
CMU Bitmap	CMU Formats
CMU Bitmap	CMU Formats
CMY	Intel DVI
ColoRIX VGA Paint	RIX
Computer Aided Acquisition and Logistics Support	CALS Raster
Computer Graphics Metafile	CGM
CUT	Dr. Halo
Data Interchange Format	Lotus DIF
DBW_uRay	uRay
DCX	PCX
DEGAS	Atari ST Graphics Formats
DIB	Microsoft Windows Bitmap
DIB	OS/2 Bitmap
DIF	Lotus DIF
Digital Video Interface	Intel DVI
Dore	Dore Raster File Format
DVI	Intel DVI
DXB	AutoCAD DXF
DXF	AutoCAD DXF
EPS	Encapsulated PostScript
EPSF	Encapsulated PostScript
EPSI	Encapsulated PostScript
Facsimile File Formats	FAX Formats
FAX	FAX Formats
FII	FLI
FLC	FLI
Flexible Image Transport System	FITS
FLI Animation	FLI
Flic	FLI
FLM	Atari ST Graphics Formats

Name or Extension	Format Name in Book
FM 92-VIII Ext. GRIB	GRIB
FM 94-IX Ext. BUFR	BUFR1
FNT	GRASP
FTI	FITS
GDI	GEM VDI
GEM Vector	GEM VDI
GEM	GEM Raster
Graphics Interchange Format	GIF
Grid File Format	VIS-5D
Gridded Binary	GRIB
GL	GRASP
Graphical System for Presentation	GRASP
Haeberli	SGI Image File Format
HDF	Hierarchical Data Format
I8	Intel DVI
I16	Intel DVI
IC1	Atari ST Graphics Formats
IC2	Atari ST Graphics Formats
IC3	Atari ST Graphics Formats
ICB	TGA
ICC	Kodak YCC
ICO	Sun Icon
IFF	Interchange File Format
ILM	Interchange File Format
ILBM	Interchange File Format
IMA	Intel DVI
IMB	Intel DVI
IMC	Intel DVI
IMG	GEM Raster
IMG	Intel DVI
IMI	Intel DVI
IMM	Intel DVI
IMQ	Intel DVI
IMR	Intel DVI
IMY	Intel DVI
Initial Graphics Exchange Specification	IGES
Intel Real-Time Video	Intel DVI
Inventor	SGI Inventor
IRIS	SGI Inventor

Name or Extension	Format Name in Book
JFI	JPEG File Interchange Format
JFIF	JPEG File Interchange Format
JPEG	JPEG File Interchange Format
JPG	JPEG File Interchange Format
Khoros Visualization/Image File Format	VIFF
Lotus Picture	Lotus PIC
MAC	Macintosh Paint
Machine Independent File Format	MIFF
Macintosh Picture	Macintosh PICT
MacPaint	Macintosh Paint
McIDAS	VIS-5D
MET	Presentation Manager Metafile
Microray	uRay
MPEG-1	MPEG
MPEG-2	MPEG
MPG	MPEG
MSP	Microsoft Paint
NEO	Atari ST Graphics Formats
Neutral File Format	NFF
North American Presentation Layer Protocol Syntax	NAPLPS
OBJ	Wavefront OBJ
Object File Format	OFF
OVR	Pictor PC Paint
P10	Plot-10
PAC	Atari ST Graphics Formats
PAL	Dr. Halo
Parallel Ray Trace	PRT
PBM	PBM, PGM, PNM, and PPM
PC Paint	Pictor PC Paint
PC Paintbush File Format	PCX
PC1	Atari ST Graphics Formats
PC2	Atari ST Graphics Formats
PC3	Atari ST Graphics Formats
PCC	PCX
PCT	Macintosh PICT
Persistance of Vision	POV
pbmplus	PBM, PGM, PNM, and PPM
PGM	PBM, PGM, PNM, and PPM
Photo CD	Kodak Photo CD

Name or Extension	Format Name in Book
Photoshop 2.5	Adobe Photoshop
PI1	Atari ST Graphics Formats
PI2	Atari ST Graphics Formats
PI3	Atari ST Graphics Formats
PIC	GRASP
PIC	Lotus PIC
PIC	Pictor PC Paint
PIC	Pictor PC Paint
PICT	Macintosh PICT
Pittsburgh Supercomputer Center 3D Metafilea	P3D
PIX	Inset PIX
PIX	Lumena Paint
Planetary Data System Format	PDS
Planetary File Format	VICAR2
PM BMP	OS/2 Bitmap
PM DIB	OS/2 Bitmap
PNM	PBM, PGM, PNM, and PPM
PNTG	Macintosh Paint
Portable Bitmap Utilities	PBM, PGM, PNM, and PPM
POV-Ray	POV
Powerflip Format	SGI YAODL
PPM	POV
Presentation Manager	OS/2 Bitmap
Quick Ray Trace	QRT
QuickDraw Picture Format	Macintosh PICT
QuickTime Movie Resource Format	QuickTime
QTM	QuickTime
RAS	CALS Raster
RAS	Sun Raster
RDI	Microsoft RIFF
RenderMan Interface Bytestream	Pixar RIB
Resource Interchange File Format	Microsoft RIFF
RFF	Dore Raster File Format
RGB	Atari ST Graphics Formats
RGB	SGI Image File Format
RGBA	SGI Image File Format
RIB	Pixar RIB

Name or Extension	Format Name in Book
Rich Text Format	Microsoft RTF
RIFF	Microsoft RIFF
RIFX	Microsoft RIFF
RIX Image File	RIX
RLA	Wavefront RLA
RLB	Wavefront RLA
RLE	SGI Image File Format
RLE	Utah RLE
RMI	Microsoft RIFF
RTF	Microsoft RTF
RTV	Intel DVI
Run-length Encoded Version A	Wavefront RLA
Run-length Encoded Version B	Wavefront RLA
SCN	RTrace
SEQ	Atari ST Graphics Formats
SET	GRASP
SFF	RTrace
SGI	SGI Image File Format
SGI	SGI Image File Format
Showcase	SGO
Silicon Graphics Object	SGO
SLD	AutoCAD DXF
SLK	Microsoft SYLK
SYLK	Microsoft SYLK
Symbolic Link Format	Microsoft SYLK
T3D	TDDD
Targa Image File	TGA
Tag Image File Format	TIFF
Tek Plot-10	Plot-10
Textual 3D Data Description	TTDDD
TN1	Atari ST Graphics Formats
TN2	Atari ST Graphics Formats
TN3	Atari ST Graphics Formats
TNY	Atari ST Graphics Formats
TPIC	TGA
Turbo Silver 3D Data Description	TDDD
TXT	GRASP
UC1	Atari ST Graphics Formats
UC2	Atari ST Graphics Formats

Name or Extension	Format Name in Book
UC3	Atari ST Graphics Formats
VDI	GEM VDI
VDA	TGA
Visualization-5D	VIS-5D
Vivid	Vivid and Bob
VMG	RIX
VST	TGA
WAV	Microsoft RIFF
Wavefront Object	Wavefront OBJ
Windows BMP	Microsoft Windows Bitmap
Windows DIB	Microsoft Windows Bitmap
Windows Metafile	Microsoft Windows Metafile
WMF	Microsoft Windows Metafile
WPG	WordPerfect Graphics Metafile
X BitMap	XBM
X PixMap	XPM
X Window Dump	XWD
YCC	Kodak YCC
Yet Another Object Description Language	SGI YAODL

## CHAPTER 2

Computer Graphics Basics

To understand graphics file formats, you need some background in computer graphics. Of course, computer graphics is an enormous subject, and we can't hope to do it justice here. In general, we assume in this book that you are not a novice in this area. However, for those who do not have an extensive background in computer graphics, this chapter should be helpful in explaining the terminology you'll need to understand the discussions of the formats found later in this book.

If you're interested in exploring any of these topics further, far and away the best overall text is *Computer Graphics: Principles and Practice* by James D. Foley, Andries van Dam, S.K. Feiner, and J.F. Hughes. This is the second edition of the book formerly known throughout the industry as "Foley and van Dam." You'll find additional references in the "For Further Information" section at the end of this chapter.

Pixels and Coordinates

Locations in computer graphics are stored as mathematical coordinates, but the display surface of an output device is an actual physical object. Thus, it's important to keep in mind the distinction between physical pixels and logical pixels.

Physical Pixels

Physical pixels are the actual dots displayed on an output device. Each one takes up a small amount of space on the surface of the device. Physical pixels are manipulated directly by the display hardware and form the smallest independently programmable physical elements on the display surface. That's the ideal, anyway. In practice, however, the display hardware may juxtapose or overlay several smaller dots to form an individual pixel. This is true in the case of most analog color CRT devices, which use several differently colored dots to display what the eye, at a normal viewing distance, perceives as a single, uniformly colored pixel.

Because physical pixels cover a fixed area on the display surface, there are practical limits to how close together two adjacent pixels can be. Asking a piece of display hardware to provide too high a resolution—too many pixels on a given display surface—will create blurring and other deterioration of image quality if adjacent pixels overlap or collide.

Logical Pixels

In contrast to physical pixels, *logical pixels* are like mathematical points: they specify a location, but are assumed to occupy no area. Thus, the mapping between logical pixel values in the bitmap data and physical pixels on the screen must take into account the actual size and arrangement of the physical pixels. A dense and brightly colored bitmap, for example, may lose its vibrancy when displayed on too large a monitor, because the pixels must be spread out to cover the surface.

Figure 2-1 illustrates the difference between physical and logical pixels.

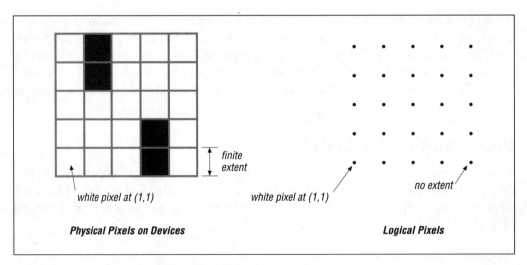

FIGURE 2-1: *Physical and logical pixels*

Pixel Depth and Displays

The number of bits in a value used to represent a pixel governs the number of colors the pixel can exhibit. The more bits per pixel, the greater the number of possible colors. More bits per pixel also means that more space is needed to store the pixel values representing a bitmap covering a given area on the surface of a display device. As technology has evolved, display devices handling more colors have become available at lower cost, which has fueled an increased demand for storage space.

Most modern output devices can display between two and more than 16 million colors simultaneously, corresponding to one and 24 bits of storage per pixel, respectively. *Bilevel,* or *1-bit,* displays use one bit of pixel-value information to represent each pixel, which then can have two color states. The most common 1-bit displays are monochrome monitors and black-and-white printers, of course. Things that reproduce well in black and white—line drawings, text, and some types of clip art—are usually stored as 1-bit data.

A Little Bit About Truecolor

People sometimes say that the human eye can discriminate between 2^{24} (16,777,216 colors), although many fewer colors can be perceived simultaneously. Naturally enough there is much disagreement about this figure, and the actual number certainly varies from person to person and under different conditions of illumination, health, genetics, and attention. In any case, we each can discriminate between a large number of colors, certainly more than a few thousand. A device capable of matching or exceeding the color-resolving power of the human eye under most conditions is said to display *truecolor.* In practice, this means 24 bits per pixel, but for historical reasons, output devices capable of displaying 2^{15} (32,768) or 2^{16} (65,536) colors have also incorrectly been called truecolor.

More recently, the term *hicolor* has come to be used for displays capable of handling up to 2^{15} or 2^{16} colors. *Fullcolor* is a term used primarily in marketing; its meaning is much less clear. (If you find out what it means, exactly, please let us know!)

Issues When Displaying Colors

It is frequently the case that the number or actual set of colors defined by the pixel values stored in a file differs from those that can be displayed on the surface of an output device. It is then up to the rendering application to translate between the colors defined in the file and those expected by the output device. There is generally no problem when the number of colors defined by the pixel values found in the file (source) is much less than the number that can be displayed on the output device (destination). The rendering application in this case is able to choose among the destination colors to provide a match for each source color. But a problem occurs when the number of colors defined by the pixel values exceeds the number that can be displayed on an output device. Consider the following examples.

In the first case, 4-bit-per-pixel data (corresponding to 16 colors) is being displayed on a device capable of supporting 24-bit data (corresponding to more than 16 million colors). The output device is capable of displaying substantially more colors than are needed to reproduce the image defined in the file. Thus, colors in the bitmap data will likely be represented by a close match on the output device, provided that the colors in the source bitmap and on the destination device are evenly distributed among all possible colors. Figure 2-2 illustrates this case.

The quantization process results in a loss of data. For source images containing many colors, quantization can cause unacceptable changes in appearance, which are said to be the result of *quantization artifacts*. Examples of common quantization artifacts are banding, Moire patterns, and the introduction of new colors into the destination image that were not present in the source data. Quantization artifacts have their uses, however; one type of quantization process, called *convolution*, can be used to remove spurious noise from an image and to actually improve its appearance. On the other hand, it can also change the color balance of a destination image from that defined by the source data.

In the next case, the output device can display fewer colors than are defined by the source data. A common example is the display of 8-bit-per-pixel data (corresponding to 256 colors) on a device capable of displaying 4-bit data (corresponding to 16 colors). In this case, there may be colors defined in the bitmap which cannot be represented on the 4-bit display. Thus, the rendering application must work to match the colors in the source and destination. At some point in the color conversion process, the number of colors defined in the source data must be reduced to match the number available on the destination device. This reduction step is called *quantization*, illustrated in Figure 2-3.

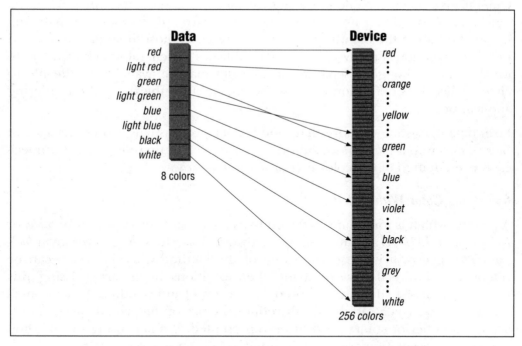

FIGURE 2-2: *Displaying data with few colors on a device with many colors*

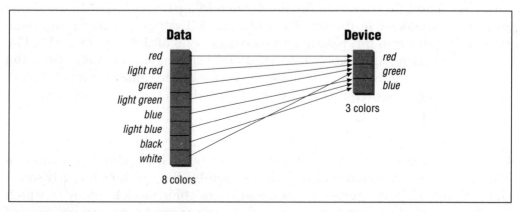

FIGURE 2-3: *Displaying data with many colors on a device with few colors*

Pixel Data and Palettes

Obviously, pixel values stored in a file correspond to colors. But how are the colors actually specified?

One-bit pixel data, capable of having the values 0 and 1, can only fully represent images containing two colors. Thus, there are only two ways of matching up pixel values in the file with colors on a screen. In most situations, you'll find that a convention already exists that establishes which value corresponds to which color, although a separate mechanism may be available in the file to change this. This definition can also be changed on the fly by the rendering application.

Pixel data consisting of more than one bit per pixel usually represents a set of *index values* into a *color palette*, although in some cases there is a direct numerical representation of the color in a *color definition scheme*.

Specifying Color With Palettes

A palette, which is sometimes referred to as a *color map, index map, color table,* or *look-up table (LUT)*, is a 1-dimensional array of color values. As the synonym *look-up table* suggests, it is the cornerstone of the method whereby colors can be referred to indirectly by specifying their positions in an array. Using this method, data in a file can be stored as a series of index values, usually small integer values, which can drastically reduce the size of the pixel data when only a small number of colors need to be represented. Bitmaps using this method of color representation are said to use *indirect*, or *pseudo-color*, storage.

Four-bit pixel data, for instance, can be used to represent images consisting of 16 colors. These 16 colors are usually defined in a palette that is almost always included somewhere in the file. Each of the pixel values making up the pixel data is an index into this palette and consists of one of the values 0 to 15. The job of a rendering application is to read and examine a pixel value from the file, use it as an index into the palette, and retrieve the value of the color from the palette, which it then uses to specify a colored pixel on an output device.

Figure 2-4 illustrates how a palette may be used to specify a color.

The palette is an array of colors defined as accurately as possible. In practice, each palette element is usually 24 bits, or three bytes, long, although to accommodate future expansion and machine dependencies, each element is sometimes stored as 32 bits, or four bytes. Curiously, color models, many of which existed prior to the computer era, are often built around the equal partition of the possible colors into three variables, thus neatly fitting into three bytes of data storage. (We include a discussion of color models in the section called "Color" later in this chapter.)

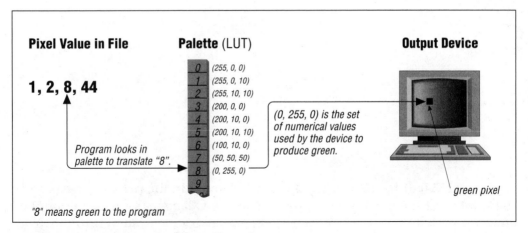

FIGURE 2-4: *Using a palette to specify a color*

What this means is that palettes are three or four times as large as the maximum number of colors defined. For instance, a 4-bit color palette is:

```
3 bytes per color X 16 colors = 48 bytes in length
```

or:

```
4 bytes per color X 16 colors = 64 bytes in length
```

depending on whether three or four bytes are used to store each color definition.

In a similar way, 8-bit pixel data may be used to represent images consisting of 256 colors. Each of the pixel values, in the range 0 to 255, is an index into a 256-color palette. In this case, the palette is:

```
3 bytes per color X 256 colors = 768 bytes in length
```

or:

```
4 bytes per color X 256 colors = 1024 bytes in length
```

Issues When Using Palettes

Let's say that the value (255,0,0) represents the color red in the color model used by our image format. We'll let our example palette define 16 colors, arranged as an array of 16 elements:

```
(  0,  0,  0)
(255,255,255)
(255,  0,  0)
(  0,255,  0)
(  0,  0,255)
```

```
(255,255,  0)
(  0,255,255)
(255,  0,255)
(128,  0,  0)
(  0,128,  0)
(  0,  0,128)
(128,128,  0)
(  0,128,128)
(128,  0,128)
(128,128,128)
(255,128,128)
```

Because (255,0,0) happens to be the third element in the palette, we can store the value 2 (if the array is zero-based, as in the C language), with the implied convention that the values are to be interpreted as index values into the array. Thus, every time a specification for the color red occurs in the pixel data, we can store 2 instead, and we can do likewise for other colors found in the image.

Color information can take up a substantial amount of space. In some cases, the use of palettes makes color storage more efficient; in other cases, storing colors directly, rather than through palettes, is more efficient.

In the larger, more complex image formats, indirect storage through the use of palettes saves space by reducing the amount of data stored in the file. If you are, for example, using a format that stores three bytes of color information per pixel (a commonly used method) and can use up to 256 colors, the pixel values making up the bitmap of a 320x200 pixel image would take up 192,000 (320 * 200 * 3) bytes of storage. If the same image instead used a palette with 256 3-byte elements, each pixel in the bitmap would only need to be one byte in size, just enough to hold a color map index value in the 0-to-255 range. This eliminates two of every three bytes in each pixel, reducing the needed storage to 64,000 (320 * 200 * 1) bytes.

Actually, we have to add in the length of the palette itself, which is 768 (256 * 3) bytes in length, so the relevant data in the file would be 64,768 bytes long, for a savings of nearly a factor of three over the former storage method. (Note, however, that if the amount of bitmap data in the file is very small, the storage overhead created by the inclusion of the palette may negate any savings gained by changing the storage method.)

Indirect color storage through the use of palettes has several advantages beyond the obvious. First, if you need to know how many actual colors are stored in an image (i.e., a 256-color image does not always contain 256 colors), it is a simple task to read through the palette and determine how many of its elements are being used or are duplicates of others. Unused elements in most formats are usually set to zero.

Palettes are also handy when you want to change the colors in an image. If you want to change all of the red pixels in the rendered image to green, for instance, all you need do is change the appropriate value defining the color red in the palette to the appropriate value for green.

As we've mentioned, the use of palettes is not appropriate in every case. A palette itself uses a substantial amount of space. For example, a palette defining 32,768 colors would take up a minimum of 98,304 bytes of storage space. For this reason, images containing more than 256 colors are generally stored in *literal, absolute,* or *truecolor* format (rather than in palettes), where each pixel value corresponds directly to a single color.

Palettes were devised to address the problem of the limited number of colors available on some display devices. However, if an output device does not provide hardware assistance to the application software, use of a palette-based format adds an extra level of complication prior to the appearance of the image on the display device. If the display device can support truecolor, it may be better to use a format supporting truecolor, even though the image may have only a few colors. As a general rule, images containing thousands or millions of colors are better stored using a format which supports truecolor, as the number and size of the elements needed in a palette-based format may cause the size of the palette needed to approach the size of the bitmapped image data itself.

Before we continue the discussion of how colors are stored in a file, we have to digress briefly to talk about how colors are defined. Discussion of palettes resumes in the section below called " . . . And Back to Palettes."

A Word About Color Spaces

Colors are defined by specifying several, usually three, values. These values specify the amount of each of a set of fundamental colors, sometimes called *color channels,* which are mixed to produce composite colors. A *composite color* is then specified as an ordered set of values. If "ordered set of values" rings a bell for you (in the same way as might "ordered pair"), rest assured that it also did for the people who create color definitions. A particular color is said to represent a point in a graphic plot of all the possible colors. Because of this, people sometimes refer to a color as a point in a *color space.*

RGB is a common color definition. In the RGB color model or system, the colors red, green, and blue are considered fundamental and undecomposable. A color can be specified by providing an RGB triplet in the form (R,G,B). People sometimes think of color triplets in terms of percentages, although percentages are not, in fact, used to express actual color definitions. You might characterize colors in the RGB color model as follows:

(0%, 0%, 0%)	Black
(100%, 100%, 100%)	White
(100%, 0%, 0%)	Red
(50%, 50%, 50%)	Light gray

and so on.

There are many refinements of this, and you can always find somebody to argue about what numbers specify which color. This is the basic idea, though. Each of these RGB triplets is said to define a point in the RGB color space.

When storing color data in a file, it's more practical to specify the value of each color component, not as a percentage, but as a value in a predefined range. If the space allotted for each color component is a byte (eight bits), the natural range is 0 to 255. Because colors are commonly defined using 24 bits, or three bytes, the natural thing to do is to assign each of the three bytes for use as the value of the color component in the color model. In RGB color, for instance, using three bytes for each color, colors are usually stored as RGB triplets in the range 0 to 255, with 0 representing zero intensity and 255 representing maximum intensity.

```
RGB = ([0-255], [0-255], [0-255])
```

Thus, the pixel values in the previous example would be:

(0,0,0)	Black
(255,255,255)	White
(255,0,0)	Red
(127,127,127)	Light gray

This example assumes, of course, that 0 stands for the least amount, and 255 for the most amount of a particular color component. Occasionally, you will find that a format creator or application architect has perversely chosen to invert the "natural" sense of the color definition, and has made RGB (0, 0, 0) white and RGB (255, 255, 255) black, but, fortunately, this is rare.

The section later in this chapter called "How Colors are Represented" describes RGB and other color systems.

Some More About Truecolor

The word *truecolor* comes up in discussions about images that contain a large number of colors. What do we mean by large in this context? Given current hard disk prices, as well as the fact that few people have personal control of more than one gigabyte of disk space, most people consider 100 to 200K to be significantly large. Recall from the discussion above that a palette containing 256 color definitions uses a maximum of 64 bytes of storage, and that a palette with 32,768 or more colors uses nearly 100K, at a minimum. In light of this, 256 is not a "large" number of colors. Most people consider 32,768, 65,536, and 16.7 million colors to be "large," however. And this is only the space a palette takes up; we're not even talking about the image data!

Instead of including in a file a huge palette in which pixel values are indices into the palette, pixel values can be treated instead as literal color values. In practice, pixel values are composed of three parts, and each part represents a component color in the *color model* (e.g., RGB) in use. Pixel values from images containing 32,768 or 65,536 colors are typically stored in two successive bytes, or 16 bits, in the file, because almost all machines handle data a minimum of one byte at a time. A rendering application must read these 16-bit pixel values and decompose them into 5-bit color component values:

```
16 bits = 2 bytes = (8 bits, 8 bits) => (1, 5, 5, 5) = (1, R, G, B)
```

Each 5-bit component can have values in the range of 0 to 32. In the case of 32,768-color RGB images, only 15 bits are significant, and one bit is wasted or used for some other purpose. 65,536-color RGB images decompose the 16-bit pixel value asymmetrically, as shown below, in order to get use out of the extra bit:

```
16 bits = 2 bytes = (8 bits, 8 bits) => (6, 5, 5) = (R, G, B)
```

Actually, a more common subdivision is:

```
16 bits = 2 bytes = (8 bits, 8 bits) => (5, 6, 5) = (R, G, B)
```

Here, the extra bit is given to the green component, because the human eye is more sensitive to green than it is to red and blue. The color component order is arbitrary, and the order and interpretation of the color components within a pixel value varies from format to format. Thus, components of a 16-bit pixel value may be interpreted as (G,B,R) just as readily as (R,G,B) and (B,R,G). Specifying RGB colors in the sequence (R,G,B) has some appeal, because the colors are arranged by electromagnetic frequency, establishing their order in the physical spectrum.

24-bit pixel values are stored in either three bytes:

```
24 bits = 3 bytes = (8 bits, 8 bits, 8 bits) = (R,G,B)
```

or four bytes:

```
24 bits = 4 bytes = (8 bits, 8 bits, 8 bits, 8 bits)
                  = (R,G,B, unused)
```

Equal division among the color components of the model, one byte to each component, is the most common scheme, although other divisions are not unheard of.

... And Back to Palettes

Earlier in this chapter we introduced the use of palettes. Here, we continue with the discussion of different types of palettes and illustrate with some actual examples.

Types of palettes

There are several different ways to talk about palettes.

A *single-channel palette* contains only one color value per element, and this color value maps directly to a single pixel color. Each element of a single-channel palette might have the following form, for example:

```
(G) = (223)
```

A *multiple-channel palette* (or *multi-channel palette*) contains two or more individual color values per color element. Each element of a 3-channel palette using red, green, and blue might have the following form, for example:

```
(R,G,B) = (255,128,78)
```

Here, R specifies the value of one channel, G specifies the value of the second channel, and B specifies the value of the third channel. If an image contains four color components, as with the CMYK color system described later in this chapter, then a 4-channel color map might be used, and so on.

Pixel-oriented palettes store all of the pixel color data as contiguous bits within each element of the array. As we noted above, in an RGB palette, each element in the palette consists of a triplet of values. This corresponds to the way pixel values are stored in the file, which is usually in RGB or BGR order:

```
(RGBRGBRGBRGBRGB . . . ) or (BGRBGRBGRBGRBGR . . . )
```

Thus the palette looks like this:

```
(RGB)(RGB)(RGB)  or  (BGR)(BGR)(BGR)
```

In a plane-oriented palette, pixel color components are segregated; corresponding color-channel values are stored together, and the palette looks like it is made up of three single-channel palettes, one for each color channel. This corresponds to the way pixel values are arranged in the file (i.e., as multiple color planes):

```
(RRRRR . . . GGGGG . . . BBBBB)  or  (BBBBB . . . GGGGG . . . RRRRR)
```

Thus, a small palette might look like this:

```
(R) (R) (R) (G) (G) (G) (B) (B) (B)
```

or:

```
(B) (B) (B) (G) (G) (G) (R) (R) (R)
```

Although this may look like a single palette containing three color planes, it is usually best to visualize it as three separate palettes, each containing a single color plane. This way you will have no trouble calling the first item in each color plane element zero.

It should be clear from the above discussion that both single- and multi-channel palettes can be pixel- or plane-oriented. For instance:

- A single-channel pixel-oriented palette contains one pixel value per element.

- A multi-channel pixel-oriented palette also contains one pixel per element, but each pixel contains two or more color channels of data.

- A single-channel plane-oriented palette contains one pixel per index and one bit per plane.

- A multi-channel plane-oriented palette contains one color channel value per element.

Figure 2-5 illustrates these different types of palettes.

As noted above, the number of elements in a palette is usually a power of two and typically corresponds to the maximum number of colors contained in the image, which is in turn reflected in the size of the pixel value in the file. For example, an 8-bit pixel value can represent 256 different colors and is accompanied by a 256-element palette. If an image has fewer colors than the maximum size of the palette, any unused elements in the palette will ideally be set to zero. Several formats, most notably CGM and TGA, have the ability to vary the number of elements in the palette as needed. If a TGA image contains only 57 colors, for instance, it may have only a 57-element palette.

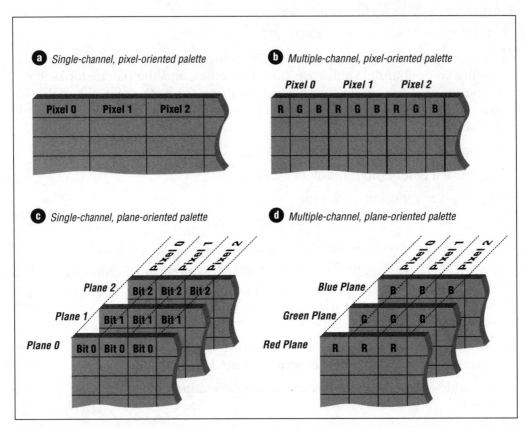

a *Single-channel, pixel-oriented palette*

Pixel 0	Pixel 1	Pixel 2	

b *Multiple-channel, pixel-oriented palette*

Pixel 0   Pixel 1   Pixel 2

R	G	B	R	G	B	R	G	B	

c *Single-channel, plane-oriented palette*

Plane 2 — Bit 2 Bit 2 Bit 2
Plane 1 — Bit 1 Bit 1 Bit 1
Plane 0 — Bit 0 Bit 0 Bit 0

d *Multiple-channel, plane-oriented palette*

Blue Plane — B B B
Green Plane — G G G
Red Plane — R R R

FIGURE 2-5: *Types of palettes*

It is also interesting to note that the usable elements in a palette are not always contiguously arranged, are not always ordered, and do not always start with the zero index value filled. A 2-color image with a 256-color palette (yes, it's been done) may have its colors indexed at locations 0 and 1, 0 and 255, 254 and 255, or even 47 and 156. The locations are determined by the software writing the image file and therefore ultimately by the programmer who created the software application. (We choose not to comment further.)

Examples of palettes

Let's look at a few examples of palettes. The simplest is the 2-color, or monochrome, palette:

```
/* A BYTE is an 8-bit character */
typedef struct _MonoPalette
{
    BYTE Color[2];
```

```
} MONO_PALETTE;
MONO_PALETTE Mono = { {0x00, 0x01} };
```

In this example, we see a 2-element array containing the color values 0x00 and 0x01 in elements 0 and 1 respectively. In the file, all pixel values are indices. A pixel with a value of 0 serves as an index to the color represented by the value 0x00. Likewise, a pixel with a value of 1 serves as an index to the color represented by the value 0x01. Because this bitmap contains only two colors, and each pixel color may be represented by a single bit, it may seem easier to store these values directly in the bitmap as bit values rather than use a palette. It is easier, of course, but some palette-only formats require that this type of palette be present even for monochrome bitmaps.

This is a more practical example, a 16-element palette used to map a gray-scale palette:

```
/* A BYTE is an 8-bit character */
typedef struct _GrayPalette
{
    BYTE Color[16];
} GRAY_PALETTE;
GRAY_PALETTE Gray =
{
    {0x00,
    0x14,
    0x20,
    0x2c,
    0x38,
    0x45,
    0x51,
    0x61,
    0x71,
    0x82,
    0x92,
    0x92,
    0xa2,
    0xb6,
    0xcb,
    0xe3,
    0xff}
};
```

Notice in these two examples that each color element is represented by a single value, so this is a single-channel palette. We could just as easily use a 3-channel palette, representing each gray color element by its RGB value.

```
typedef struct _RGB
{
    BYTE    Red;     /* Red channel value */
    BYTE    Green;   /* Green channel value */
    BYTE    Blue;    /* Blue channel value */
} RGB;

RGB Gray[16] =
{
    {0x00, 0x00, 0x00},
    {0x14, 0x14, 0x14},
    {0x20, 0x20, 0x20},
    {0x2c, 0x2c, 0x2c},
    {0x38, 0x38, 0x38},
    {0x45, 0x45, 0x45},
    {0x51, 0x51, 0x51},
    {0x61, 0x61, 0x61},
    {0x71, 0x71, 0x71},
    {0x82, 0x82, 0x82},
    {0x92, 0x92, 0x92},
    {0xa2, 0xa2, 0xa2},
    {0xb6, 0xb6, 0xb6},
    {0xcb, 0xcb, 0xcb},
    {0xe3, 0xe3, 0xe3},
    {0xff, 0xff, 0xff}
};
```

This last example is an example of a pixel-oriented multi-channel palette. We can alter it to store the color information in a plane-oriented fashion like this:

```
TYPEDEF struct _PlanePalette
{
    BYTE    Red[16];    /* Red plane values */
    BYTE    Green[16];  /* Green plane values */
    BYTE    Blue[16];   /* Blue plane values */
} PLANE_PALETTE;

PLANE_PALETTE Planes =
{
    {0x00, 0x14, 0x20, 0x2c, 0x38, 0x45, 0x51, 0x61,  /* Red plane */
    0x71, 0x82, 0x92, 0xa2, 0xb6, 0xcb, 0xe3, 0xff},
    {0x00, 0x14, 0x20, 0x2c, 0x38, 0x45, 0x51, 0x61,  /* Green plane */
    0x71, 0x82, 0x92, 0xa2, 0xb6, 0xcb, 0xe3, 0xff},
    {0x00, 0x14, 0x20, 0x2c, 0x38, 0x45, 0x51, 0x61,  /* Blue plane */
    0x71, 0x82, 0x92, 0xa2, 0xb6, 0xcb, 0xe3, 0xff}
};
```

Finally, let's look at a real-world example, the IBM VGA palette in wide use. This 256-color palette contains a 16-color sub-palette (the "EGA palette"), a 16-element gray-scale palette, and a palette of 24 colors, each with nine different variations of saturation and intensity. Notice that the last eight elements of the palette are not used and are thus set to zero:

```
struct _VgaPalette
{
    BYTE      Red;
    BYTE      Green;
    BYTE      Blue;
} VGA_PALETTE;
VGA_PALETTE VgaColors[256] =
{
/* EGA Color Table */
{0x00, 0x00, 0x00}, {0x00, 0x00, 0xaa},
{0x00, 0xaa, 0x00}, {0x00, 0xaa, 0xaa},
{0xaa, 0x00, 0x00}, {0xaa, 0x00, 0xaa},
{0xaa, 0x55, 0x00}, {0xaa, 0xaa, 0xaa},
{0x55, 0x55, 0x55}, {0x55, 0x55, 0xff},
{0x55, 0xff, 0x55}, {0x55, 0xff, 0xff},
{0xff, 0x55, 0x55}, {0xff, 0x55, 0xff},
{0xff, 0xff, 0x55}, {0xff, 0xff, 0xff},

/* Gray Scale Table */
{0x00, 0x00, 0x00}, {0x14, 0x14, 0x14},
{0x20, 0x20, 0x20}, {0x2c, 0x2c, 0x2c},
{0x38, 0x38, 0x38}, {0x45, 0x45, 0x45},
{0x51, 0x51, 0x51}, {0x61, 0x61, 0x61},
{0x71, 0x71, 0x71}, {0x82, 0x82, 0x82},
{0x92, 0x92, 0x92}, {0xa2, 0xa2, 0xa2},
{0xb6, 0xb6, 0xb6}, {0xcb, 0xcb, 0xcb},
{0xe3, 0xe3, 0xe3}, {0xff, 0xff, 0xff},

/* 24-color Table */
{0x00, 0x00, 0xff}, {0x41, 0x00, 0xff},
{0x7d, 0x00, 0xff}, {0xbe, 0x00, 0xff},
{0xff, 0x00, 0xff}, {0xff, 0x00, 0xbe},
{0xff, 0x00, 0x7d}, {0xff, 0x00, 0x41},
{0xff, 0x00, 0x00}, {0xff, 0x41, 0x00},
{0xff, 0x7d, 0x00}, {0xff, 0xbe, 0x00},
{0xff, 0xff, 0x00}, {0xbe, 0xff, 0x00},
{0x7d, 0xff, 0x00}, {0x41, 0xff, 0x00},
{0x00, 0xff, 0x00}, {0x00, 0xff, 0x41},
{0x00, 0xff, 0x7d}, {0x00, 0xff, 0xbe},
```

```
{0x00, 0xff, 0xff}, {0x00, 0xbe, 0xff},
{0x00, 0x7d, 0xff}, {0x00, 0x41, 0xff},
{0x7d, 0x7d, 0xff}, {0x9e, 0x7d, 0xff},
{0xbe, 0x7d, 0xff}, {0xdf, 0x7d, 0xff},
{0xff, 0x7d, 0xff}, {0xff, 0x7d, 0xdf},
{0xff, 0x7d, 0xbe}, {0xff, 0x7d, 0x9e},
{0xff, 0x7d, 0x7d}, {0xff, 0x9e, 0x7d},
{0xff, 0xbe, 0x7d}, {0xff, 0xdf, 0x7d},
{0xff, 0xff, 0x7d}, {0xdf, 0xff, 0x7d},
{0xbe, 0xff, 0x7d}, {0x9e, 0xff, 0x7d},
{0x7d, 0xff, 0x7d}, {0x7d, 0xff, 0x9e},
{0x7d, 0xff, 0xbe}, {0x7d, 0xff, 0xdf},
{0x7d, 0xff, 0xff}, {0x7d, 0xdf, 0xff},
{0x7d, 0xbe, 0xff}, {0x7d, 0x9e, 0xff},
{0xb6, 0xb6, 0xff}, {0xc7, 0xb6, 0xff},
{0xdb, 0xb6, 0xff}, {0xeb, 0xb6, 0xff},
{0xff, 0xb6, 0xff}, {0xff, 0xb6, 0xeb},
{0xff, 0xb6, 0xdb}, {0xff, 0xb6, 0xc7},
{0xff, 0xb6, 0xb6}, {0xff, 0xc7, 0xb6},
{0xff, 0xdb, 0xb6}, {0xff, 0xeb, 0xb6},
{0xff, 0xff, 0xb6}, {0xeb, 0xff, 0xb6},
{0xdb, 0xff, 0xb6}, {0xc7, 0xff, 0xb6},
{0xb6, 0xdf, 0xb6}, {0xb6, 0xff, 0xc7},
{0xb6, 0xff, 0xdb}, {0xb6, 0xff, 0xeb},
{0xb6, 0xff, 0xff}, {0xb6, 0xeb, 0xff},
{0xb6, 0xdb, 0xff}, {0xb6, 0xc7, 0xff},
{0x00, 0x00, 0x71}, {0x1c, 0x00, 0x71},
{0x38, 0x00, 0x71}, {0x55, 0x00, 0x71},
{0x71, 0x00, 0x71}, {0x71, 0x00, 0x55},
{0x71, 0x00, 0x38}, {0x71, 0x00, 0x1c},
{0x71, 0x00, 0x00}, {0x71, 0x1c, 0x00},
{0x71, 0x38, 0x00}, {0x71, 0x55, 0x00},
{0x71, 0x71, 0x00}, {0x55, 0x71, 0x00},
{0x38, 0x71, 0x00}, {0x1c, 0x71, 0x00},
{0x00, 0x71, 0x00}, {0x00, 0x71, 0x1c},
{0x00, 0x71, 0x38}, {0x00, 0x71, 0x55},
{0x00, 0x71, 0x71}, {0x00, 0x55, 0x71},
{0x00, 0x38, 0x71}, {0x00, 0x1c, 0x71},
{0x38, 0x38, 0x71}, {0x45, 0x38, 0x71},
{0x55, 0x38, 0x71}, {0x61, 0x38, 0x71},
{0x71, 0x38, 0x71}, {0x71, 0x38, 0x61},
{0x71, 0x38, 0x55}, {0x71, 0x38, 0x45},
{0x71, 0x38, 0x38}, {0x71, 0x45, 0x38},
{0x71, 0x55, 0x38}, {0x71, 0x61, 0x38},
{0x71, 0x71, 0x38}, {0x61, 0x71, 0x38},
```

```
{0x55, 0x71, 0x38}, {0x45, 0x71, 0x38},
{0x38, 0x71, 0x38}, {0x38, 0x71, 0x45},
{0x38, 0x71, 0x55}, {0x38, 0x71, 0x61},
{0x38, 0x71, 0x71}, {0x38, 0x61, 0x71},
{0x38, 0x55, 0x71}, {0x38, 0x45, 0x71},
{0x51, 0x51, 0x71}, {0x59, 0x51, 0x71},
{0x61, 0x51, 0x71}, {0x69, 0x51, 0x71},
{0x71, 0x51, 0x71}, {0x71, 0x51, 0x69},
{0x71, 0x51, 0x61}, {0x71, 0x51, 0x59},
{0x71, 0x51, 0x51}, {0x71, 0x59, 0x51},
{0x71, 0x61, 0x51}, {0x71, 0x69, 0x51},
{0x71, 0x71, 0x51}, {0x69, 0x71, 0x51},
{0x61, 0x71, 0x51}, {0x59, 0x71, 0x51},
{0x51, 0x71, 0x51}, {0x51, 0x71, 0x59},
{0x51, 0x71, 0x61}, {0x51, 0x71, 0x69},
{0x51, 0x71, 0x71}, {0x51, 0x69, 0x71},
{0x51, 0x61, 0x71}, {0x51, 0x59, 0x71},
{0x00, 0x00, 0x41}, {0x10, 0x00, 0x41},
{0x20, 0x00, 0x41}, {0x30, 0x00, 0x41},
{0x41, 0x00, 0x41}, {0x41, 0x00, 0x30},
{0x41, 0x00, 0x20}, {0x41, 0x00, 0x10},
{0x41, 0x00, 0x00}, {0x41, 0x10, 0x00},
{0x41, 0x20, 0x00}, {0x41, 0x30, 0x00},
{0x41, 0x41, 0x00}, {0x30, 0x41, 0x00},
{0x20, 0x41, 0x00}, {0x10, 0x41, 0x00},
{0x00, 0x41, 0x00}, {0x00, 0x41, 0x10},
{0x00, 0x41, 0x20}, {0x00, 0x41, 0x30},
{0x00, 0x41, 0x41}, {0x00, 0x30, 0x41},
{0x00, 0x20, 0x41}, {0x00, 0x10, 0x41},
{0x20, 0x20, 0x41}, {0x28, 0x20, 0x41},
{0x30, 0x20, 0x41}, {0x38, 0x20, 0x41},
{0x41, 0x20, 0x41}, {0x41, 0x20, 0x38},
{0x41, 0x20, 0x30}, {0x41, 0x20, 0x28},
{0x41, 0x20, 0x20}, {0x41, 0x28, 0x20},
{0x41, 0x30, 0x20}, {0x41, 0x38, 0x20},
{0x41, 0x41, 0x20}, {0x38, 0x41, 0x20},
{0x30, 0x41, 0x20}, {0x28, 0x41, 0x20},
{0x20, 0x41, 0x20}, {0x20, 0x41, 0x28},
{0x20, 0x41, 0x30}, {0x20, 0x41, 0x38},
{0x20, 0x41, 0x41}, {0x20, 0x38, 0x41},
{0x20, 0x30, 0x41}, {0x20, 0x28, 0x41},
{0x2c, 0x2c, 0x41}, {0x30, 0x2c, 0x41},
{0x34, 0x2c, 0x41}, {0x3c, 0x2c, 0x41},
{0x41, 0x2c, 0x41}, {0x41, 0x2c, 0x3c},
{0x41, 0x2c, 0x34}, {0x41, 0x2c, 0x30},
```

```
{0x41, 0x2c, 0x2c}, {0x41, 0x30, 0x2c},
{0x41, 0x34, 0x2c}, {0x41, 0x3c, 0x2c},
{0x41, 0x41, 0x2c}, {0x3c, 0x41, 0x2c},
{0x34, 0x41, 0x2c}, {0x30, 0x41, 0x2c},
{0x2c, 0x41, 0x2c}, {0x2c, 0x41, 0x30},
{0x2c, 0x41, 0x34}, {0x2c, 0x41, 0x3c},
{0x2c, 0x41, 0x41}, {0x2c, 0x3c, 0x41},
{0x2c, 0x34, 0x41}, {0x2c, 0x30, 0x41},
{0x00, 0x00, 0x00}, {0x00, 0x00, 0x00},
{0x00, 0x00, 0x00}, {0x00, 0x00, 0x00},
{0x00, 0x00, 0x00}, {0x00, 0x00, 0x00},
{0x00, 0x00, 0x00}, {0x00, 0x00, 0x00}
};
```

Color

Understanding how colors are defined in graphics data is important to understanding graphics file formats. In this section, we touch on some of the many factors governing how colors are perceived. This is by no means a comprehensive discussion. We just want to make sure that you to have an appreciation of some of the problems that come up when people start to deal with color.

How We See Color

The eye has a finite number of color receptors that respond to the full range of light frequencies (about 380 to 770 nanometers). As a result, the eye theoretically supports only the perception of about 10,000 different colors simultaneously (although, as we have mentioned, many more colors than this can be perceived, though not resolved simultaneously).

The eye is also biased to the kind of light it detects. It's most sensitive to green light, followed by red, and then blue. It's also the case that the visual perception system can sense contrasts between adjacent colors more easily than it can sense absolute color differences, particularly if those colors are physically separated in the object being viewed. In addition, the ability to discern colors also varies from person to person; it's been estimated that one out of every twelve people has some form of color blindness.

Furthermore, the eye is limited in its ability to resolve the color of tiny objects. The size of a pixel on a typical CRT display screen, for example, is less than a third of a millimeter in diameter. When a large number of pixels are packed together, each one a different color, the eye is unable to resolve where one pixel ends and the next one begins from a normal viewing distance. The brain, however, must do something to bridge the gap between two adjacent differently colored pixels and will integrate, average, ignore the blur, or otherwise adapt to the situation. For these reasons and others, the eye typically perceives many fewer colors than are physically displayed on the output device.

How a color is created also plays an important role in how it is perceived. Normally, we think of colors as being associated with a single wavelength of light. We know, however, that two or more colors can be mixed together to produce a new color. An example of this is mixing green and red light to produce yellow light, or mixing yellow and blue pigments to produce green pigment. This mixing of colors can also occur when an object is illuminated by light. The color of the object will always mix with the color of the light to produce a third color. A blue object illuminated by white light appears blue, while the same object illuminated by red light will appear violet in color.

One implication of this is that images rendered to different devices will look different. Two different color monitors, for example, seldom produce identically perceived images, even if the monitors are the same make and model. Another implication is that images rendered to different types of devices will look different. An example is the difference between an image rendered to a monitor and one rendered to a color hardcopy device. Although there are numerous schemes designed to minimize color-matching problems, none is wholly satisfactory.

For these and other reasons, the accurate rendition of color is full of difficulties, and much work continues to be done. Although a number of mechanical devices have recently appeared on the market, they are for the most part designed to work with one type of output device. The ultimate arbiter of color quality will always be the person who views the image on the output device.

How Colors are Represented

Several different mathematical systems exist which are used to describe colors. This section describes briefly the color systems most commonly used in the graphics file formats described in this book.

NOTE

Keep in mind that perception of color is affected by physiology, experience, and viewing conditions. For these reasons, no system of color representation has yet been defined, or indeed is likely to be, which is satisfactory under all circumstances.

For purposes of discussion here, colors are always represented by numerical values. The most appropriate color system to use depends upon the type of data contained in the file. For example, 1-bit, gray-scale, and color data might each best be stored using a different color model.

Color systems used in graphics files are typically of the *trichromatic colorimetric* variety, otherwise known as *primary 3-color systems*. With such systems, a color is defined by specifying an ordered set of three values. Composite colors are created by mixing varying amounts of three *primary colors,* which results in the creation of a new color. Primary colors are those which cannot be created by mixing other colors. The totality of colors that can be created by mixing primary colors make up the color space or *color gamut.*

Additive and subtractive color systems

Color systems can be separated into two categories: *additive* color systems and *subtractive* color systems. Colors in additive systems are created by adding colors to black to create new colors. The more color that is added, the more the resulting color tends towards white. The presence of all the primary colors in sufficient amounts creates pure white, while the absence of all the primary colors creates pure black. Additive color environments are self-luminous. Color on monitors, for instance, is additive.

Color subtraction works in the opposite way. Conceptually, primary colors are subtracted from white to create new colors. The more color that is added, the more the resulting color tends towards black. Thus, the presence of all the primary colors theoretically creates pure black, while the absence of all primary colors theoretically creates pure white. Another way of looking at this process is that black is the total absorption of all light by color pigments. Subtractive environments are reflective in nature, and color is conveyed to us by reflecting light from an external source. Any color image reproduced on paper is an example of the use of a subtractive color system.

No color system is perfect. As an example, in a subtractive color system the presence of all colors creates black, but in real-life printing the inks are not perfect. Mixing all ink colors usually produces a muddy brown rather than black. The blacks we see on paper are only approximations of the mathematical ideal, and likewise for other colors.

The next few sections describe some common color systems. Table 2-1 shows corresponding values for the primary and achromatic colors using the RGB, CMY, and HSV color systems.

TABLE 2-1: *Equivalent RGB, CMY, and HSV values*

	RGB	CMY	HSV
Red	255,0,0	0,255,255	0,240,120
Yellow	255,255,0	0,0,255	40,240,120
Green	0,255,0	255,0,255	80,240,120
Cyan	0,255,255	255,0,0	120,240,120
Blue	0,0,255	255,255,0	160,240,120
Magenta	255,0,255	0,255,0	200,240,120
Black	0,0,0	255,255,255	160,0,0
Shades of Gray	63,63,63 127,127,127 191,191,191	191,191,191 127,127,127 63,63,63	160,0,59 160,0,120 160,0,180
White	255,255,255	0,0,0	160,0,240

RGB (Red-Green-Blue)

RGB is perhaps the most widely used color system in image formats today. It is an additive system in which varying amounts of the colors red, green, and blue are added to black to produce new colors. Graphics files using the RGB color system represent each pixel as a color triplet—three numerical values in the form (R,G,B), each representing the amount of red, green, and blue in the pixel, respectively. For 24-bit color, the triplet (0,0,0) normally represents black, and the triplet (255,255,255) represents white. When the three RGB values are set to the same value—for example, (63,63,63) or (127,127,127), or (191,191,191)—the resulting color is a shade of gray.

CMY (Cyan-Magenta-Yellow)

CMY is a subtractive color system used by printers and photographers for the rendering of colors with ink or emulsion, normally on a white surface. It is used by most hard-copy devices that deposit color pigments on white paper, such as laser and ink-jet printers. When illuminated, each of the three colors absorbs its complementary light color. Cyan absorbs red; magenta absorbs green; and yellow absorbs blue. By increasing the amount of yellow ink, for instance, the amount of blue in the image is decreased.

As in all subtractive systems, we say that in the CMY system colors are subtracted from white light by pigments to create new colors. The new colors are the wavelengths of light reflected, rather than absorbed, by the CMY pigments. For example, when cyan and magenta are absorbed, the resulting color is yellow. The yellow pigment is said to "subtract" the cyan and magenta components from the reflected light. When all of the CMY components are subtracted, or absorbed, the resulting color is black. Almost. Whether it's possible to get a perfect black is debatable. Certainly, a good black color is not obtainable without expensive inks.

In light of this, the CMY system has spawned a practical variant, CMYK, with K standing for the color black. To compensate for inexpensive and off-specification inks, the color black is tacked onto the color system and treated something like an independent primary color variable. For this reason, use of the CMYK scheme is often called 4-color printing, or process color. In many systems, a dot of composite color is actually a grouping of four dots, each one of the CMYK colors. This can be readily seen with a magnifying lens by examining a color photograph reproduced in a glossy magazine.

CMYK can be represented as either a color triple, like RGB, or as four values. If expressed as a color triple, the individual color values are just the opposite of RGB. For a 24-bit pixel value, for example, the triplet (255,255,255) is black, and the triplet (0,0,0) is white. In most cases, however, CMYK is expressed as a series of four values.

In many real-world color composition systems, the four CMYK color components are specified as percentages in the range of 0 to 100.

HSV (Hue, Saturation, and Value)
HSV is one of many color systems that vary the degree of properties of colors to create new colors, rather than using a mixture of the colors themselves. Hue specifies "color" in the common use of the term, such as red, orange, blue, and so on. Saturation (also called chroma) refers to the amount of white in a hue; a fully (100 percent) saturated hue contains no white and appears pure. By extension, a partly saturated hue appears lighter in color due to the admixture of white. Red hue with 50 percent saturation appears pink, for instance. Value (also called brightness) is the degree of self-luminescence of a color—that is, how much light it emits. A hue with high intensity is very bright, while a hue with low intensity is dark.

HSV (also called HSB for Hue, Saturation, and Brightness) most closely resembles the color system used by painters and other artists, who create colors by adding white, black, and gray to pure pigments to create tints, shades, and tones. A tint is a pure, fully saturated color combined with white, and a shade is a fully saturated color combined with black. A tone is a fully saturated color with both black and white (gray) added to it. If we relate HSV to this color mixing model, saturation is the amount of white, value is the amount of black, and hue is the color that the black and white are added to.

The HLS (Hue, Lightness, and Saturation) color model is closely related to HSV and behaves in the same way.

There are several other color systems that are similar to HSV in that they create color by altering hue with two other values. These include:

- HSI (Hue, Saturation, and Intensity)
- HSL (Hue, Saturation, and Luminosity)
- HBL (Hue, Brightness, and Luminosity)

None of these is widely used in graphics files.

YUV (Y-signal, U-signal, and V-signal)

The YUV model is a bit different from the other colorimetric models. It is basically a linear transformation of RGB image data and is most widely used to encode color for use in television transmission. (Note, however, that this transformation is almost always accompanied by a separate quantization operation, which introduces nonlinearities into the conversion.) Y specifies gray scale or luminance. The U and V components correspond to the chrominance (color information). Other color models based on YUV include YCbCr and YPbPr.

Black, White, and Gray

Black, white, and gray are considered neutral (achromatic) colors that have no hue or saturation. Black and white establish the extremes of the range, with black having minimum intensity, gray having intermediate intensity, and white having maximum intensity. One can say that the gamut of gray is just a specific slice of a color space, each of whose points contains an equal amount of the three primary colors, has no saturation, and varies only in intensity.

White, for convenience, is often treated in file format specifications as a primary color. Gray is usually treated the same as other composite colors. An 8-bit pixel value can represent 256 different composite colors or 256 different shades of gray. In 24-bit RGB color, (12,12,12), (128,128,128), and (199,199,199) are all shades of gray.

Overlays and Transparency

Certain file formats are designed to support the storage of still images captured from video sources. In practice, images of this sort are often overlaid on live video sources at render time. This is a familiar feature of conventional broadcast television, where still images are routinely shown next to live readers on the evening news.

Normal images are opaque, in the sense that no provision is made to allow the manipulation and display of multiple overlaid images. To allow image overlay, some mechanism must exist for the specification of transparency on a per-image, per-strip, per-tile, or per-pixel basis. In practice, transparency is usually controlled through the addition of information to each element of the pixel data.

The simplest way to allow image overlay is the addition of an *overlay bit* to each pixel value. Setting the overlay bit in an area of an image allows the rendering application or output device to selectively ignore those pixel values with the bit set. An example is the TGA format, which supports data in the format:

```
(15 bits) = (R,G,B) = (5 bits, 5 bits, 5 bits)
```

Actually, this 15-bit pixel value is stored in 16 bits; an extra bit is left over which can be used to support the overlaying of images:

```
(R,G,B,T) = (16 bits) = (5 bits, 5 bits, 5 bits, 1 bit overlay)
```

The image creator or rendering application can toggle the overlay bit, which is interpreted by the display hardware as a command to ignore that particular pixel. In this way, two images can be overlaid, and the top one adjusted to allow holes through which portions of the bottom image are visible.

This technique is in widespread, but not obvious, use. A rendering application can selectively toggle the overlay bit in pixel values of a particular color. More to the point, the application can turn off the display of any area of an image that is not a particular color. For example, if a rendering application encounters an image of a person standing in front of a contrasting, uniformly colored and lighted screen, the application can toggle the overlay bits on all the pixel values that are the color of the screen, leaving an image of the person cut out from the background. This cut-out image can then be overlaid on any other image, effectively adding the image of the person to the bottom image.

This assumes, of course, that the color of the screen is different from any colors in the person portion of the image. This is often how broadcast television weather reporters are overlaid on background maps and displays, for instance. Certain conventions inherited from traditional analog broadcasting technology are in widespread use in the broadcasting industry, including the use of a particular blue shade for background screens. When used in this way, the process is called chromakeying.

A more elaborate mechanism for specifying image overlays allows variations in transparency between bottom and overlaid images. Instead of having a single bit of overlay information, each pixel value has more (usually eight bits). An example is the TGA format, which supports data in the format:

```
(24 bits) = (R,G,B) = (8 bits, 8 bits, 8 bits)
```

Because this 24-bit pixel value is stored in 32 bits, an extra eight bits are left over to support transparency:

```
(R,G,B,T) = (8 bits, 8 bits, 8 bits, 8 bits transparency)
```

The eight transparency bits are sometimes called the *alpha channel*. Although there are some complications in the TGA format, an ideal 8-bit alpha channel can support 256 levels of transparency, from zero (indicating that the pixel is meant to be completely transparent) to 255 (indicating that the pixel is meant to be opaque).

Transparency data is usually stored as part of the pixel data, as in the example above, but it may also appear as a fourth plane, stored the same way as palette data in planar format files. It can, however, be stored as a separate block, independent of other image and palette information, and with the same dimensions as the actual image. This allows manipulation of the transparency data independent of the image pixel data.

For Further Information

In this chapter, we have been able to touch upon only a small part of the science of computer graphics and imaging. For additional information, see the references cited below.

Books About Computer Graphics

The following books are some of the best texts available on the subject of computer graphics. Many of them contain detailed chapters on specific application areas, such as imaging, ray tracing, animation, art, computer-aided design, and 3D modelling.

Artwick, Bruce A., *Applied Concepts in Microcomputer Graphics.*, Prentice-Hall, Englewood Cliffs, NJ, 1984.

Conrac Corporation, *Raster Graphics Handbook,* second edition, Van Nostrand Reinhold Company, New York, NY, 1985.

Foley. James. D., van Dam, Andries, Feiner, S.K., and Hughes, J. F., *Computer Graphics: Principles and Practice,* second edition, Addison-Wesley, Reading, MA, 1990.

Hearn, Donald and Baker, M. Pauline, *Computer Graphics*, Prentice-Hall, Englewood Cliffs, NJ, 1986.

Netravali, Arun N. and Haskell, Barry G., *Digital Pictures: Representation and Compression*, Plenum Press, New York, NY, 1988.

Newman, William N. and Sproull, Robert F., *Principles of Interactive Computer Graphics,* second edition, McGraw Hill, New York, NY, 1973.

Rogers, David F. and Adams, J. Alan, *Mathematical Elements for Computer Graphics,* second edition, McGraw Hill, New York, NY, 1990.

Rogers, David F., *Procedural Elements for Computer Graphics.*, McGraw Hill, New York, NY, 1985.

Rosenfeld, Azriel and Kak, Avinash C., *Digital Picture Processing*, second edition, Academic Press, San Diego, CA, 1982.

Sharpe, L., "Tiling: Turning Unwieldy Drawings into Neat Little Packets," *Inform*, Association for Image and Information Management, March, 1989.

Watt, Alan, *Fundamentals of Three-Dimensional Computer Graphics*, Addison-Wesley, Reading, MA, 1989.

Books About Color and Colorimetry

The following books are excellent reference works on color, its measurement, and its effects on the human psycho-biological system.

Benson, K. Blair, *Television Engineering Handbook,* second edition, McGraw Hill, New York, NY, 1986.

Billmeyer, Fred W. and Saltzman, Max, *Principles of Color Technology*, second edition, John Wiley & Sons, New York, NY, 1981.

De Grandis, Luigina, *Theory and Use of Color*, translated by Gilbert, John, Harry N. Abrams, Inc., New York, NY, 1986.

Foley. James. D., van Dam, Andries, Feiner, S.K., and Hughes, J. F., *Computer Graphics: Principles and Practice*, second edition, Addison-Wesley, Reading, MA, 1990.

Hunt, R.W.G., *Measuring Color*, second edition, E. Horwood, New York, NY, 1991.

Hunt, R.W.G., *The Reproduction of Color,* third edition, John Wiley & Sons, New York, NY, 1975.

Hunt, R.W.G., *The Reproduction of Color in Photography, Printing and Television*, Fountain Press, Tolworth, England, 1987.

Judd, Deane B., *Color in Business, Science, and Industry,* third edition, John Wiley & Sons, New York, NY, 1975.

Kueppers, Harald, *Color; Origin, Systems, Uses,* translated by Bradley, F., Von Nostrand Reinhold Ltd., London, England, 1973.

Optical Society of America, Committee on Colorimetry, *The Science of Color,* Washington, DC, 1963.

Wyszecki, Gunter and Stiles, W. S., *Color Science: Concepts and Methods, Quantitative Data and Formulae,* second edition, John Wiley & Sons, New York, NY, 1982.

## CHAPTER 3

Bitmap Files

Bitmap files vary greatly in their details, but they all share the same general structure. This chapter looks at the components of a typical bitmap file. Later on in this chapter we'll get into explanations of the details, but for now let's just get a feel for the overall structure. We'll explain as necessary as we go along.

Bitmap files consist of a header, bitmap data, and other information, which may include a color palette and other data.

A warning: inexplicably, people continue to design applications which use what are sometimes called raw formats. Raw format files consist solely of image data and omit any clues as to their structure. Both the creator of such files and the rendering applications must somehow know, ahead of time, how the files are structured. Because you usually can't tell one raw format file from another (except perhaps, by examining their relative sizes), we'll confine our discussion in this chapter to bitmap files, which at least contain headers.

How Bitmap Files Are Organized

The basic components of a simple bitmap file are the following:

Header
Bitmap Data

If a file contains no image data, only a header will be present. If additional information is required that does not fit in the header, a footer will usually be present as well:

Header
Bitmap Data
Footer

An image with a palette may store the palette in the header, but it will more likely appear immediately after the header:

Header
Palette
Bitmap Data
Footer

A palette can also appear immediately appear after the image data, like a footer, or be stored in the footer itself:

Header
Bitmap Data
Palette

Scan-line tables and *color correction tables* may also appear after the header and before or after the image data:

Header
Palette
Scan Line Table
Color Correction Table (here)
Bitmap Data
Color Correction Table (or here)
Footer

If an image file format is capable of holding multiple images, then an image file index may appear after the header, holding the offset values of the starting positions of the images in the file:

Header
Palette
Bitmap Index
Bitmap 2 Data
. . .
Bitmap *n* Data
Footer

If the format definition allows each image to have its own palette, the palette will most likely appear before the image data with which it is associated:

Header
Palette
Bitmap Index
Palette 1
Bitmap Data
Palette 2
Bitmap 2 Data
. . .
Palette *n*
Bitmap *n* Data
Footer

We'll now look at the parts of a bitmap file piece by piece.

Header

The header is a section of binary- or ASCII-format data normally found at the beginning of the file, containing information about the bitmap data found elsewhere in the file. All bitmap files have some sort of header, although the format of the header and the information stored in it varies considerably from format to format. Typically, a bitmap header is composed of fixed fields. None of these fields is absolutely necessary, or found in all formats, but this list is typical of those formats in widespread use today. The following information is commonly found in a bitmap header:

Header
Palette
Bitmap Index
Palette 1
File Identifier
File Version
Number of Lines per Image
Number of Pixels per Line
Number of Bits per Pixel
Number of Color Planes
Compression Type
X Origin of Image
Y Origin of Image
Text Description
Unused Space

Later in this chapter we will present examples of headers from several actual formats, containing fields similar to those presented above.

File Identifier

A header usually starts with some sort of unique identification value called a *file identifier, file ID,* or *ID value.* Its purpose is to allow a software application to determine the format of the particular graphics file being accessed.

ID values are often *magic values* in the sense that they are assigned arbitrarily by the creator of the file format. They can be a series of ASCII characters, such as BM or GIF, or a 2- or 4-byte word value, such as 4242h or 596aa695h, or any other pattern that made sense to the format creator. The pattern is usually assumed to be unique, even across platforms, but this is not always the case, as we describe in the next few paragraphs. Usually, if a value in the right place in a file matches the expected identification value, the application reading the file header can assume that the format of the image file is known.

Three circumstances arise, however, which make this less than a hard and fast rule. Some formats omit the image file identifier, starting off with data that can change from file to file. In this case, there is a small probability that the data will accidentally duplicate one of the magic values of another file format known to the application. Fortunately, the chance of this occurring is remote.

The second circumstance can come about when a new format is created and the format creator inadvertently duplicates, in whole or in part, the magic values of another format. In case this seems even more unlikely than accidental duplication, rest assured that it has already happened several times. Probably the chief cause is that, historically, programmers have borrowed ideas from other platforms, secure in the belief that their efforts would be isolated behind the "Chinese Wall" of binary incompatibility. In the past, confusion of formats with similar ID fields seldom came about and was often resolved by context when it did happen. Obviously this naive approach by format creators is no longer a survival skill. In the future, we can expect more problems of this sort as users, through local area networking and through advances in regional and global interconnectivity, gain access to data created on other platforms.

This third circumstance comes about when a vendor—either the format creator or format caretaker or a third party—changes, intentionally or unintentionally, the specification of the format, while keeping the ID value specified in the format documentation. In this case, an application can recognize the format, but be unable to read some or all of the data. If the idea of a vendor creating intentional, undocumented changes seems unlikely, rest assured that this, too, has already happened many times. Examples are the GIF, TIFF, and TGA file formats. In the case of the GIF and TGA formats, vendors (not necessarily the format creators) have extended or altered the formats to include new data types. In the case of TIFF, vendors have created and promulgated what only can be described as *convenience revisions*, apparently designed to accommodate coding errors or application program quirks.

File Version

Following the identification value in the header is usually a field containing the file version. Naturally enough, successive versions of bitmap formats may differ in characteristics such as header size, bitmap data supported, and color capability. Once having verified the file format through the ID value, an application will typically examine the version value to determine if it can handle the image data contained in the file.

Image Description Information

Next comes a series of fields that describe the image itself. As we will see, bitmaps are usually organized, either physically or logically, into lines of pixels. The field designated *number of lines per image*, also called the *image length, image height*, or *number of scan lines*, holds a value corresponding to the number of lines making up the actual bitmap data. The *number of pixels per line*, also called the *image width* or *scan-line width*, indicates the number of pixels stored in each line.

The number of bits per pixel indicates the size of the data needed to describe each pixel per *color plane*. This may also be stored as the *number of bytes per pixel*, and is more properly called *pixel depth*. Forgetting the exact interpretation of this field when coding format readers is a common source of error. If the bitmap data is stored in a series of planes, the *number of color planes* indicates the number of planes used. Often the value defaults to one. There is an increasing tendency to store bitmaps in single-plane format, but multi-plane formats continue to be used in support of special hardware and alternate color models.

The number of bits in a line of the image can be calculated by multiplying the values of *number of bits per pixel, number of pixels per line*, and *number of color planes* together. We can determine the number of bytes per scan line by then dividing the resulting product by eight. Note that there is nothing requiring *number of bits per pixel* to be an integral number of 8-bit bytes.

Compression Type

If the format supports some sort of *encoding* designed to reduce the size of the bitmap data, then a *compression type* field will be found in the header. Some formats support multiple compression types, including *raw* or *uncompressed* data. Some format revisions consist mainly of additions or changes to the compression scheme used. Data compression is an active field, and new types of compression accommodating advances in technology appear with some regularity. TIFF is one of the common formats which has exhibited this pattern in the past.

For more information about compression, see Chapter 9, *Data Compression*.

x and y Origins

x origin of image and *y origin of image* specify a coordinate pair that indicates where the image starts on the output device. The most common origin pair is 0,0, which puts one corner of the image at the origin point of the device. Changing these values normally causes the image to be displayed at a different location when it is rendered.

Most bitmap formats were designed with certain assumptions about the output device in mind, and thus can be said to model either an actual or virtual device having a feature called the *drawing surface*. The drawing surface has an implied origin, which defines the starting point of the image, and an implied orientation, which defines the direction in which successive lines are drawn as the output image is rendered. Various formats and display devices vary in the positioning of the origin point and orientation direction. Many place the origin in the upper-left corner of the display surface, although it can also appear in the center, or in the lower-left corner. Others, although this is far less common, put it in the upper- or lower-right corner.

Orientation models with the origin in the upper-left corner are often said to have been created in support of hardware, and there may be some historical and real-world justification for this. People with backgrounds in mathematics and the natural sciences, however, are used to having the origin in the lower-left corner or in the center of the drawing surface. You might find yourself guessing at the background of the format creator based on the implied origin and orientation found in the format. Some formats include provisions for the specification of the origin and orientation.

An image displayed by an application incorporating an incorrect assumption about the origin point or orientation may appear upside down or backwards, or may be shifted horizontally some fraction of the width of the drawing surface on the output device.

Sometimes the header will contain a text description field, which is a comment section consisting of ASCII data describing the name of the image, the name of the image file, the name of the person who created the image, or the software application used to create it. This field may contain 7-bit ASCII data, for portability of the header information across platforms.

Unused Space

At the end of the header may be an unused field, sometimes referred to as *padding, filler, reserved space*, or *reserved fields*. Reserved fields contain no data, are undocumented and unstructured and essentially act as placeholders. All we know about them are their sizes and positions in the header. Thus, if the format is altered at some future date to incorporate new data, the reserved space can be used to describe the format or location of this data while still maintaining backward compatibility with programs supporting older versions of the format. This is a common method used to minimize version problems—creating an initial version based on a fixed header substantially larger than necessary. New fields can then be added to reserved areas of the header in subsequent revisions of the format without altering the size of the header.

Often format headers are intentionally padded using this method to 128, 256, or 512 bytes. This has some implications for performance, particularly on older systems, and is designed to accommodate common read and write buffer sizes. Padding may appear after the documented fields at the end of the header, and this is sometimes an indication that the format creator had performance and caching issues in mind when the format was created.

Reserved fields are sometimes only artifacts left over from working versions of the format, unintentionally frozen into place when the format was released. A vendor will normally change or extend a file format only under duress, or as a rational response to market pressure typically caused by an unanticipated advance in technology. In any case, the upgrade is almost always unplanned. This usually means that a minimal amount of effort goes into shoehorning new data into old formats. Often the first element sacrificed in the process is complete backward compatibility with prior format versions.

Examples of Bitmap Headers

To give you some idea about what to expect when looking at bitmap headers, we'll take a look at three typical ones. We'll start with one of the least complex (Microsoft Windows Bitmap), and proceed to two that are more complex (Sun raster and Kofax raster).

To do this, we'll provide a C data structure, which will provide an idea of the size and relative position of each field in the headers.

Example 1: Microsoft Windows Bitmap Version 1.x Format Header

```
//
// Header structure for the MS Windows 1.x Bitmap Format
//      a BYTE is an unsigned char
//      a WORD is an unsigned short int (16-bits)
//
typedef struct _WinHeader1x
{
//
//   Type     Name      Offset   Comment
//
     WORD     Type;     /* 00h   File Type Identifier (always 0)   */
     WORD     Width;    /* 02h   Width of Bitmap in Pixels          */
     WORD     Height;   /* 04h   Height of Bitmap in Scanlines      */
     WORD     Width;    /* 06h   Width of Bitmap in Bytes           */
     BYTE     Planes;   /* 08h   Number of Color Planes             */
     BYTE     BitsPixel; /* 09h  Number of Bits Per Pixel           */
} OLDWINHEAD;
```

As you can see from the comments, this particular header contains a file identification value, the width and height of the image, the width of a single line of the image (in bytes), the number of color planes, and the number of bits per pixel. This information is close to the bare minimum required to describe a bitmap image so it can be read and rendered in an arbitrary environment.

Note that the Windows 1.x header contains no information about color or image data compression. A more advanced image format will have provisions for both color information and at least a simple compression scheme. An example of a more elaborate header is that found in the Sun raster image file format shown in the next example:

Example 2: Sun Raster Format Header

```
//
// Header structure for the Sun Raster Image File Format
//   a WORD here is an unsigned long int (32 bits)
//
typedef struct _SunRasterHead
{
//
// Type    Name       Offset    Comment
//
    WORD    Magic;     /* 00h    Magic Number (59a66a95h)     */
    WORD    Width;     /* 04h    Width of Image in Pixels      */
    WORD    Height;    /* 08h    Height of Image in Pixels     */
    WORD    Depth;     /* 0Ch    Number of Bits Per Pixel      */
    WORD    Length;    /* 10h    Length of Image in Bytes      */
    WORD    Type;      /* 14h    File Format Encoding Type      */
    WORD    MapType;   /* 18h    Type of Color Map             */
    WORD    MapLength; /* 1Ch    Length of Color Map in Bytes  */
} SUNRASHEAD;
```

The Sun raster header contains information similar to the Windows 1.x bitmap header illustrated above. But note that it also contains fields for the type of data encoding method and the type and size of the color map or *palette* associated with the bitmap data.

Neither of the two headers mentioned above contains a text description field. One such header that does is that associated with the Kofax Image File Format shown in Example 3.

Example 3: Kofax Raster Format Header 0

```
//
//   Header structure for the Kofax Raster Image File Format
//     a LONG is a signed long int (32 bits)
//     a SHORT is a signed short int (16 bits)
//
typedef struct _KofaxHeader
{
//
//   Type    Name           Offset     Comment
//
     LONG    Magic;         /* 00h    Magic Number (68464B2Eh)    */
     SHORT   HeaderSize;    /* 04h    Header Size                 */
     SHORT   HeaderVersion; /* 06h    Header Version Number       */
     LONG    ImageId;       /* 0Ah    Image Identification Number */
     SHORT   Width;         /* 0Ch    Image Width in Bytes        */
     SHORT   Length;        /* 0Eh    Image Length in Scanlines   */
     SHORT   Format;        /* 10h    Image Data Code (Encoding)  */
     CHAR    Bitsex;        /* 11h    Non-zero if Bitsex Reversed */
     CHAR    Color;         /* 12h    Non-zero if Color Inverted  */
     SHORT   Xres;          /* 14h    Horizontal Dots Per Inch    */
     SHORT   Yres;          /* 16h    Vertical Dots Per Inch      */
     CHAR    Planes;        /* 18h    Number of Planes            */
     CHAR    BitsPerPixel;  /* 19h    Number of Bits Per Pixel    */
     SHORT   PaperSize;     /* 1Ah    Original Paper Size         */
     CHAR    Reserved1[20]; /* 1Ch    20-byte Reserved Field      */
     LONG    Dcreated;      /* 30h    Date Created                */
     LONG    Dmodified;     /* 34h    Date Modified               */
     LONG    Daccessed;     /* 38h    Date Accessed               */
     CHAR    Reserved2[4];  /* 3Ch    4-Byte Reserved Field       */
     LONG    Ioffset;       /* 40h    Index Text Info Offset      */
     LONG    Ilength;       /* 44h    Index Text Info Length      */
     LONG    Coffset;       /* 48h    Comment Text Offset         */
     LONG    Clength;       /* 4Ch    Comment Text Length in Bytes*/
     LONG    Uoffset;       /* 50h    User Data Offset            */
     LONG    Ulength;       /* 54h    User Data Length in Bytes   */
     LONG    Doffset;       /* 58h    Image Data Offset           */
     LONG    Dlength;       /* 5Ch    Image Data Length in Bytes  */
     CHAR    Reserved3[32]; /* 60h    32-byte Reserved Field      */
} KFXHEAD;
```

Note that the Kofax header is considerably larger than either the Windows bitmap or Sun raster headers. Included are fields which describe the horizontal and vertical resolution, paper size of the image subject, offset values of different types of data stored in the file, and the time and date that the image was created, last modified, and accessed.

Also note the appearance of several fields marked *reserved*. The Kofax format is intentionally padded to 128K bytes to accommodate common read and write buffer sizes. It uses only 72 bytes of the header in the revision presented here, but is padded to 128 bytes. The Kofax format specification promises that the first 128 bytes of every Kofax image file will be the header, regardless of future revisions. Applications are thus free to ignore the reserved data, and the format is presumably designed to allow this without dire penalty. See the general discussion of reserved fields in the section above called "Unused Space."

Optimizing Header Reading

Header reading speed can be optimized by looking at the ways in which your application uses the data, because reading the header data can usually be performed in several ways. If only selected values in the header are needed, the application can calculate the offset of the data from some key landmark such as the start of the file. The application can then seek directly to the data value required and read the data value. The offset values appearing in the comments in the header examples above can be used as offset arguments for the seek function used.

If most of the data contained in the header is needed by the application, then it may be more convenient to read the entire header into a buffer or pre-allocated data structure. This can be performed quickly, taking advantage of any efficiencies provided by an integral power of two-block reads, as mentioned above. All of the header data will be available in memory and can be cached for use when needed. One problem, however, occurs when the byte order of the file is different from the native byte order of the system on which the file is being read. Most block read functions, for example, are not designed to supply automatic conversion of data. Another problem may arise when data structures are padded by the compiler or runtime environment for purposes of data member alignment. These problems and others are discussed in more detail in Chapter 6, *Platform Dependencies*.

Bitmap Data

The actual bitmap data usually makes up the bulk of a bitmap format file. We'll assume you've read Chapter 2, *Computer Graphics Basics*, and that you understand about pixel data and related topics like color.

In many bitmap file formats the actual bitmap data is found immediately after the end of the file header. It may be found elsewhere in the file, however, to accommodate a palette or other data structure which may be present. If this is the case, an offset value will appear in the header or in the documentation indicating where to find the beginning of the image data in the file.

One thing you might notice while looking over the file format specifications described in Part II of this book is the relative absence of information explaining the arrangement of the actual bitmap data in the file. To find out how the data is arranged, you usually have to figure it out from related information pertaining to the structure of the file.

Fortunately, the structuring of bitmap data within most files is straightforward and easily deduced. As mentioned above, bitmap data is composed of pixel values. Pixels on an output device are usually drawn in scan lines corresponding to rows spanning the width of the display surface. This fact is usually reflected in the arrangement of the data in the file. This exercise, of deducing the exact arrangement of data in the file, is sometimes helped by having some idea of the display devices the format creator had in mind.

One or more scan lines combined form a two-dimensional grid of pixel data; thus we can think of each pixel in the bitmap as located at a specific logical coordinate. A bitmap can also be thought of as a sequence of values that logically maps bitmap data in a file to an image on the display surface of an output device. Actual bitmap data is usually the largest single part of any bitmap format file.

How Bitmap Data Is Written to Files

Before an application writes an image to a file, the image data is usually first assembled in one or more blocks of memory. These blocks can be located in the computer's main memory space or in part of an auxiliary data collection device. Exactly how the data is arranged then depends on a number of factors, including the amount of memory installed, the amount available to the application, and the specifics of the data acquisition or file write operation in use. When bitmap data is finally written to a file, however, only one of two methods of organization is normally used: scan-line data or planar data.

Scan-line data

The first, and simplest, method is the organization of pixel values into rows or scan lines, briefly mentioned above. If we consider every image to be made up of one or more scan lines, the pixel data in the file describing that image will be a series of sets of values, each set corresponding to a row of the image. Multiple rows are represented by multiple sets written from start to end in the file. This is the most common method for storing image data organized into rows.

If we know the size of each pixel in the image, and the number of pixels per row, we can calculate the offset of the start of each row in the file. For example, in an 8-bit image every pixel value is one byte long. If the image is 21 pixels wide, rows in the file are represented by sets of pixel values 21 bytes wide. In this case, the rows in the file start at offsets of 0, 21, 42, 63, etc. bytes from the start of the bitmap data.

On some machines and in some formats, however, rows of image data must be certain even-byte multiples in length. An example is the common rule requiring bitmap row data to end on long-word boundaries, where a long word is four bytes long. In the example mentioned in the preceding paragraph, an image 21 pixels wide would then be stored in the file as sets of pixel values 24 bytes in length, and the rows would start at file offsets 0, 24, 48, 64. The extra three bytes per row are padding. In this particular case, three bytes of storage in the file are wasted for every row, and in fact, images that are 21 pixels wide take up the same amount of space as images 24 pixels wide. In practice, this storage inefficiency is usually (but not always) compensated for by an increase of speed gained by catering to the peculiarities of the host machine in regard to its ability to quickly manipulate two or four bytes at a time. The actual width of the image is always available to the rendering application, usually from information in the file header.

In a 24-bit image, each image pixel corresponds to a 3-byte long pixel value in the file. In the example we have been discussing, an image 21 pixels wide would require a minimum of 21 x 3 = 63 bytes of storage. If the format requires that the row starts be long-word aligned, 64 bytes would be required to hold the pixel values for each row. Occasionally, as mentioned above, 24-bit image data is stored as a series of 4-byte long pixel values, and each image row would then require 21 x 4 = 84 bytes. Storing 24-bit image data as 4-byte values has the advantage of always being long-word aligned, and again may make sense on certain machines.

In a 4-bit image, each pixel corresponds to one-half byte, and the data is usually stored two pixels per byte, although storing the data as 1-byte pixel values would make the data easier to read and, in fact, is not unheard of.

Figure 3-1 illustrates the organization of pixel data into scan lines.

Planar data

The second method of pixel value organization involves the separation of image data into two or more planes. Files in which the bitmap data is organized in this way are called planar files. We will use the term *composite image* to refer to an image with many colors (i.e., not monochrome, not grayscale, and

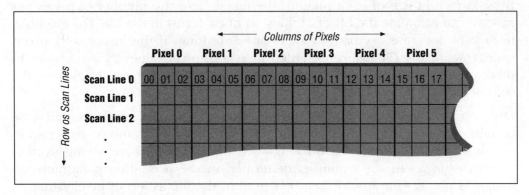

FIGURE 3-1: *Organization of pixel data into scan lines*

not one single color). Under this definition, most normal colored images that you are familiar with are composite images.

A composite image, then, can be represented by three blocks of bitmap data, each block containing just one of the component colors making up the image. Constructing each block is akin to the photographic process of making a separation—using filters to break up a color photograph into a set of component colors, usually three in number. The original photograph can be reconstructed by combining the three separations. Each block is composed of rows laid end to end, as in the simpler storage method explained above; in this case, more than one block is now needed to reconstruct the image. The blocks may be stored consecutively or may be physically separated from one another in the file.

Planar format data is usually a sign that the format designer had some particular display device in mind, one that constructed composite color pixels from components routed through hardware designed to handle one color at a time. For reasons of efficiency, planar format data is usually read one plane at a time in blocks, although an application may choose to laboriously assemble composite pixels by reading data from the appropriate spot in each plane sequentially.

As an example, a 24-bit image two rows by three columns wide might be represented in RGB format as six RGB pixel values:

```
(00, 01, 02) (03, 04, 05) (06, 07, 08)
(09, 10, 11) (12, 13, 14) (15, 16, 17)
```

but be written to the file in planar format as:

```
(00) (03) (06) (red plane)   (09) (12) (15)
(01) (04) (07) (green plane)  (10) (13) (16)
(02) (05) (08) (blue plane)   (11) (14) (17)
```

Notice that the exact same data is being written; it's just arranged differently. In the first case, an image consisting of six 24-bit pixels is stored as six 3-byte pixel values arranged in a single plane. In the second, planar, method, the same image is stored as 18 1-byte pixel values arranged in three planes, each plane corresponding to red, green, and blue information, respectively. Each method takes up exactly the same amount of space, 18 bytes, at least in this example.

It's pretty safe to say that most bitmap files are stored in non-planar format. Supporting planar hardware, then, usually means disassembling the pixel data and creating multiple color planes in memory, which are then presented to the planar rendering subroutine or the planar hardware.

Planar files may need to be assembled in a third buffer or, as mentioned above, laboriously set (by the routine servicing the output device) one pixel at a time.

Figure 3-2 illustrates the organization of pixel data into color planes.

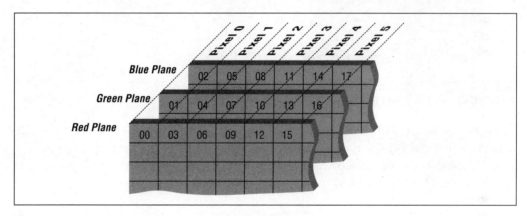

FIGURE 3-2: *Organization of pixel data into color planes*

Different Approaches to Bitmap Data Organization

Normally, we consider an image to be made up of a number of rows, each row a certain number of pixels wide. Pixel data representing the image can be stored in the file in three ways: as *contiguous data*, as *strips* or as *tiles*. Figure 3-3 illustrates these three representations.

Contiguous data

The simplest method of row organization is where all of the image data is stored contiguously in the file, one row following the last. To retrieve the data you read the rows in file order, which delivers the rows in the order in which they were written. The data in this organizational scheme is stored in the file

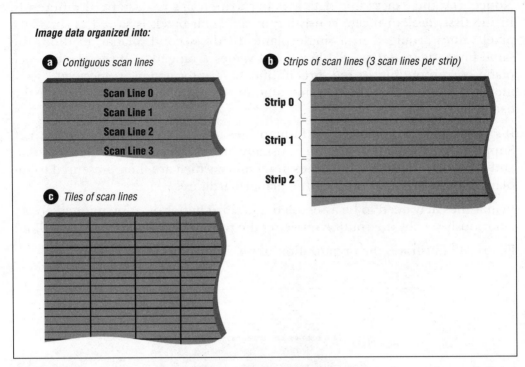

FIGURE 3-3: *Examples of bitmap data organization (contiguous scan lines, strips, and tiles)*

equivalent of a two-dimensional array. You can index into the data in the file knowing the width of the row in pixels and the storage format and size of the pixel values. Data stored contiguously in this manner can be read quickly, in large chunks, and assembled in memory quite easily.

Strips

In the second method of file organization, images are stored in strips, which also consist of rows stored contiguously. The total image, however, is represented by more than one strip, and the individual strips may be widely separated in the file. Strips divide the image into a number of segments, which are always just as wide as the original image.

Strips make it easier to manage image data on machines with limited memory. An image 1024 rows long, for instance, can be stored in the file as eight strips, each strip containing 128 rows. Arranging a file into strips facilitates buffering. If this isn't obvious, consider an uncompressed 8-bit image 1024 rows long and 10,000 pixels wide, containing 10 megabytes of pixel data. Even dividing the data into eight strips of 128 rows leaves the reading application with the job of handling 1.25 megabytes of data per strip, a chore even for a machine with a lot of flat memory and a fast disk. Dividing the data into 313 strips, however, brings each strip down to a size which can be read and buffered quickly by machines capable of reading only 32K of data per file read pass.

Strips also come into play when pixel data is stored in a compressed or encoded format in the file. In this case, an application must first read the compressed data into a buffer and then decompress or decode the data into another buffer the same size as, or larger than, the first. Arranging the compression on a per-strip basis greatly eases the task of the file reader, which need handle only one strip at a time.

You'll find that strips are often evidence that a file format creator has thought about the limitations of the possible target platforms being supported and has wanted to not limit the size of images that can be handled by the format. Image file formats allowing or demanding that data be stored in strips usually provide for the storage of information in the file header such as the number of strips of data, the size of each strip, and the offset position of each strip within the file.

Tiles

A third method of bitmap data organization is tiling. Tiles are similar to strips in that each is a delineation of a rectangular area of an image. However, unlike strips, which are always the width of the image, tiles can have any width at all, from a single pixel to the entire image. Thus, in one sense, a contiguous image is actually one large tile. In practice, however, tiles are arranged so that the pixel data corresponding to each is between 4Kb and 64Kb in size and is usually of a height and width divisible by 16. These limits help increase the efficiency with which the data can be buffered and decoded.

When an image is tiled, it is generally the case that all the tiles are the same size, that the entire image is tiled, that the tiles do not overlap, and that the tiles are all encoded using the same encoding scheme. One exception is the CALS Raster Type II format, which allows image data to be composed of both encoded and unencoded image tiles. Tiles are usually left unencoded when such encoding would cause the tile data to increase in size (negative compression) or when an unreasonable amount of time would be required to encode the tile.

Dividing an image into tiles also allows different compression schemes to be applied to different parts of an image to achieve an optimal compression ratio. For example, one portion of an image (a very busy portion) could be divided into tiles that are compressed using JPEG, while another portion of the same image (a portion containing only one or two colors) could be stored as tiles that are run-length encoded. In this case, the tiles in the image would not all be the same uniform size; the smallest would be only a few pixels, and the largest would be hundreds or thousands of pixels on a side.

Tiling sometimes allows faster decoding and decompression of larger images than would be possible if the pixel data were organized as lines or strips. Because tiles can be individually encoded, file formats allowing the use of tiles will contain tile quantity, size, and offset information in the header specifications. Using this information, a reader that needs to display only the bottom-right corner of a very large image would have to read only the tiles for that area of the image; it would not have to read all of the image data that was stored before it.

Certain newer tile-oriented compression schemes, such as JPEG, naturally work better with file formats capable of supporting tiling. A good example of this is the incorporation of JPEG in later versions of the TIFF file format. For more information about the use of tiles, see the article on the TIFF file format in Part II of this book.

Palette
Many bitmap file formats contain a color palette. For a discussion of palettes of different kinds, see "Pixel Data and Palettes" in Chapter 2.

Footer

The *footer*, sometimes called the *trailer*, is a data structure similar to a header and is often an addition to the original header, but appended to the end of a file. A footer is usually added when the file format is upgraded to accommodate new types of data and it is no longer convenient to add or change information in the header. It is mainly a result of a desire to maintain backward compatibility with previous versions of the format. An example of this is the TGA format, later revisions of which contain a footer that enables applications to identify the different versions of its format and to access special features available only in the later version of the format.

Because by definition it appears after the image data, which is usually of variable length, a footer is never found at a fixed offset from the beginning of an image file unless the image data is always the same size. It is, however, usually located at a specified offset from the end of an image file. Like headers, footers are usually a fixed size. The offset value of the footer may also be present in the header information, provided there was reserved space or padding available in the header. Also like a header, a footer may contain an identification field or magic number which can be used by a rendering application to differentiate it from other data structures in the file.

Other Bitmap File Data Structures

Besides headers, footers, and palettes, bitmap files may contain additional data structures, which are usually added to aid manipulation of the image data by the rendering application.

A file format which allows more than one image in the file needs to provide some method of identifying the start of each image. Thus, an *image offset table*, sometimes called an *image file index* or *page table*, may be used to store the offset values of the start of each image from the beginning of the file.

A *scan-line table* may be provided for locating the start of each image scan line in the pixel data. This can be useful if the image data is compressed and pixel data corresponding to individual scan lines must be accessed randomly; the pixels in the image data cannot be counted until the image data is decoded. Scan-line tables contain one entry per image scan line. Variants of this idea include strip location tables (one entry per group of scan lines) and tile location tables (one entry for each rectangular subarea of the image).

Other Bitmap File Features

Several formats incorporate unique or unusual data structures in their design. These are usually to accomplish the specific purpose of the format or to create as much generality as possible.

A common file format that comes to mind under the heading of "unusual" is TIFF. TIFF contains a rudimentary header, but stores much of its data in a series of tags called Image File Directories, which are fixed in neither size nor position. They are instead like an in-memory list data structure in that they are linked by a series of file offset values. Data can be found by seeking to the next offset from the current offset. While this arrangement can lead to confusion (and indeed TIFF has many times been called a "write-only" format), it allows a programmer to construct a header-like structure that can contain any information at all, thus adding to its versatility.

Unusual or unique features of other formats include the storing of image data and palette information in separate files (the Dr. Halo CUT and PAL files, for example) and the storing of monochrome bitmaps as blocks of ASCII format 1's and 0's (as in the PBM format), designed perhaps with interplatform portability in mind.

Pros and Cons of Bitmap File Formats

Bitmap files are especially suited for the storage of real-world images; complex images can be rasterized in conjunction with video, scanning, and photographic equipment and stored in a bitmap format.

Advantages of bitmap files include the following:

- Bitmap files may be easily created from existing pixel data stored in an array in memory.

- Retrieving pixel data stored in a bitmap file may often be accomplished by using a set of coordinates that allows the data to be conceptualized as a grid.

- Pixel values may be modified individually or as large groups by altering a palette if present.

- Bitmap files may translate well to dot-format output devices such as CRTs and printers.

Bitmap files, however, do have drawbacks:

- They can be very large, particularly if the image contains a large number of colors. Data compression can shrink the size of pixel data, but the data must be expanded before it can be used, and this can slow down the reading and rendering process considerably. Also, the more complex a bitmap image (large number of colors and minute detail), the less efficient the compression process will be.

- They typically do not scale very well. Shrinking an image by decimation (throwing away pixels) can change the image in an unacceptable manner, as can expanding the image through pixel replication. Because of this, bitmap files must usually be printed at the resolution in which they were originally stored.

CHAPTER 4

Vector Files

In this chapter we'll be talking about vector files. Because we've already introduced bitmap files in Chapter 3, *Bitmap Files*, we'll be contrasting selected features of vector files with their bitmap counterparts.

Vector Versus Bitmap Files

A bitmap file in some sense contains an exact pixel-by-pixel mapping of an image, which can then be reconstructed by a rendering application on the display surface of an output device. Rendering applications seldom have to take into account any structural elements other than pixels, scan lines, strips, and tiles—subdivisions of the image which were made without reference to the content of the image.

Vector files contain, instead, mathematical descriptions of one or more *image elements*, which are used by the rendering application to construct a final image. Vector files are thus said to be made up of descriptions of image elements or *objects*, rather than pixel values. Although the term object has a modern meaning, you will find vector format specifications adhering to the older usage.

What Is Vector Data?

Vectors are line segments minimally defined as a starting point, a direction, and a length. They can, however, be much more complex and can include various sorts of lines, curves, and splines. Straight and curved lines can be used to define geometrical shapes, such as circles, rectangles, and polygons, which then can be used to create more complex shapes, such as spheres, cubes, and polyhedrons.

Vector file formats have been around since computers were first used to display lines on an output device. CRTs, for example, were first used as computer-driven output devices in the 1950s. The first CRT displays were random scan devices similar to oscilloscopes, capable of producing images of mathematical and geometrical shapes. Vector display devices provided output sufficient for the needs of computer users for many years after their introduction, due to the limited range of tasks computers were called upon to perform.

At some point the need to store vector data arose, and portable storage media such as punch cards or paper tape were pressed into use. Prior to rendering time, an image was logically subdivided into its simplest elements. At rendering time, the image was produced and maintained by drawing each of its elements repeatedly in a specified order. At storage time, data was readily exported as a list of drawing operations, and mathematical descriptions of the image elements—their size, shape, and position on the display screen—were written to the storage device in the order in which they were displayed.

Vector Files and Device Independence

As mentioned above, vector images are collections of device-independent mathematical descriptions of graphical shapes.

More so than their bitmap counterparts, various vector formats differ primarily because each was designed for a different purpose. While the conceptual differences between the designs of formats supporting 1-bit and 24-bit bitmap data may be small, the differences between vector formats used with CAD applications and those used for general data interchange can be formidable. Thus, it is difficult to generalize about vector formats in the same way we did when discussing bitmap formats.

On the other hand, most output devices are point-addressable, providing a grid of pixels which can be addressed individually, as if the surface of the device were graph paper made of discrete elements. This means that an application can always find a way to draw vector-format image elements on the device.

Sources of Vector Format Files

The simplest vector formats are those used by spreadsheet applications. These normally contain numerical data meant to be displayed on a two-dimensional grid on an output device. Some non-spreadsheet applications use spreadsheet file formats to store data that can alternately be interpreted as either bitmap or vector data.

Examples of common spreadsheet formats include those associated with the programs Lotus 1-2-3 (.WKS and .WK1), Excel (.XLS), and Quattro Pro. Although these originated on Intel-based PCs, the respective vendors now support multiple platforms. Several spreadsheet formats have been developed explicitly to support portable data interchange between different spreadsheet applications; as a result, these are now also found on multiple platforms. These include Lotus DIF (Data Interchange Format) and Microsoft SYLK (SYmbolic LinK Format).

The majority of vector formats, however, are designed for storing line drawings created by CAD applications. CAD packages are used to create mechanical, electrical, and architectural drawings, electronic layouts and schematics, maps and charts, and artistic drawings. The complexity of information needed to support the needs of a major CAD application is considerably greater than that needed to support a spreadsheet and generally requires a more complicated vector format.

CGM (Computer Graphics Metafile) is an example of a general format designed with data interchange in mind, a format that is defined in a published standard. All elements in a CGM-format file are constructed of simple objects such as lines and polygons, primitives assumed to be available in every rendering application. Very complex objects are broken down into the simplest possible shapes.

Autodesk's AutoCAD DXF (Data eXchange Format) was also designed with vector data interchange in mind but is vendor-controlled and originated as a format supporting a single application. In addition, DXF was specifically tailored for CAD information useful in the construction of mechanical, electrical, and architectural drawings. DXF therefore supports not only common vector elements such as circles and polygons, but also complex objects frequently used in CAD renderings, such as three-dimensional objects, labels, and hatching.

How Vector Files Are Organized

Although vector files, like bitmap files, vary considerably in design, most contain the same basic structure: a header, a data section, and an end-of-file marker. Some structure is needed in the file to contain information global to the file and to correctly interpret the vector data at render time. Although most vector files place this information in a header, some rely solely on a footer to perform the same task.

Vector files on the whole are structurally simpler than most bitmap files and tend to be organized as data streams. Most of the information content of the file is found in the image data.

The basic components of a simple vector file are the following:

Header
Image Data

If a file contains no image data, only a header will be present. If additional information is required that does not fit in the header, you may find a footer appended to the file, and a palette may be included as well:

Header
Palette
Image Data

Header

The header contains information that is global to the vector file and must be read before the remaining information in the file can be interpreted. Such information can include a file format identification number, a version number, and color information.

Headers may also contain default attributes, which will apply to any vector data elements in the file lacking their own attributes. While this may afford some reduction in file size, it does so at the cost of introducing the need to cache the header information throughout the rendering operation.

Headers and footers found in vector-format files may not necessarily be a fixed size. For historical reasons mentioned above, it is not uncommon to find vector formats which use streams of variable-length records to store all data. If this is the case, then the file must be read sequentially and will normally fail to provide offset information that is necessary to allow the rendering application to subsample the image.

The type of information stored in the header is governed by the types of data stored in the file. Basic header information contains the height and width of the image, the position of the image on the output device, and possibly the number of layers in the image. Thus, the size of the header may vary from file to file within the same format.

Vector Data

The bulk of all but tiny files consists of vector element data that contain information on the individual objects making up the image. The size of the data used to represent each object will depend upon the complexity of the object and how much thought went into reducing the file size when the format was designed.

Following the header is usually the image data. The data is composed of *elements*, which are smaller parts that comprise the overall image. Each element is either explicitly associated with default information, or inherits information, that specifies its size, shape, position relative to the overall image, color, and possibly other attribute information. An example of vector data in ASCII format containing three elements (a circle, a line, and a rectangle), might appear as:

```
;CIRCLE,40,100,100,BLUE;LINE,200,50,136,227,BLACK;RECT,80,65,25,78,RED;
```

Although this example is a simple one, it illustrates the basic problem of deciphering vector data, which is the existence of multiple levels of complexity. When deciphering a vector format, you not only must find the data, but you also must understand the formatting conventions and the definitions of the individual elements. This is hardly ever the case in bitmap formats; bitmap pixel data is all pretty much the same.

In this example, elements are separated by semicolons, and each is named, followed by numerical parameters and color information. Note, however, that consistency of syntax across image elements is never guaranteed. We could have just as easily defined the format in such a way as to make blocks of unnamed numbers signify lines by default:

```
;CIRCLE,40,100,100,BLUE;200,50,136,227,BLACK;RECT,80,65,25,78,RED;
```

and the default color black if unspecified:

```
;CIRCLE,40,100,100,BLUE;200,50,136,227;RECT,80,65,25,78,RED;
```

Many formats allow abbreviations:

```
;C,40,100,100,BL;200,50,136,227;R,80,65,25,78,R;
```

Notice that the R for RECT and R for RED are distinguished by context. You will find that many formats have opted to reduce data size at the expense of conceptual simplicity. You are free to consider this as evidence of flawed reasoning on the part of the format designer. The original reason for choosing ASCII was for ease of reading and parsing. Unfortunately, using ASCII may make the data too bulky. Solution: reduce the data size through implied rules and conventions and allow abbreviation (in the process making the format unreadable). The format designer would have been better off using a binary format in the first place.

After the image data is usually an end-of-section or end-of-file marker. This can be as simple as the string EOF at the end the file. For the same reasons discussed in Chapter 3, *Bitmap Files*, some vector formats also append a footer to the file. Information stored in a footer is typically not necessary for the correct interpretation of the rendering and may be incidental information such as the time and date the file was created, the name of the application used to create the file, and the number of objects contained in the image data.

Palettes and Color Information

Like bitmap files, vector files can contain palettes. (For a full discussion of palettes, see the discussion in Chapter 2.) Because the smallest objects defined in vector format files are the data elements, these are the smallest features for which color can be specified. Naturally, then, a rendering application must look up color definitions in the file palette before rendering the image. Our example above, to be correct, would thus need to include the color definitions, which take the form of a palette with associated ASCII names:

```
RED,255,0,0,
BLACK,0,0,0,
BLUE,0,0,255
;C,40,100,100,BL;200,50,136,227;R,80,65,25,78,R;
```

Some vector files allow the definition of enclosed areas, which are considered outlines of the actual vector data elements. Outlines may be drawn with variations in thickness or by using what are known as different *pen styles,* which are typically combinations of dots and dashes and which may be familiar from technical and CAD drawings. Non-color items of information necessary for the reproduction of the image by the rendering application are called *element attributes.*

Fills and color attributes

Enclosed elements may be designed to be filled with color by the rendering application. The filling is usually allowed to be colored independently from the element outline. Thus, each element may have two or more colors associated with it, one for the element outline and one for the filling. *Fill colors* may be transparent, for instance, and some formats define what are called *color attributes.* In addition to being filled with solid colors, enclosed vector elements may contain hatching or shading, which are in turn called *fill attributes.* In some cases, fill and color attributes are lumped together, either conceptually in the format design, or physically in the file.

Formats that do not support fill patterns must simulate them by drawing parts of the pattern (lines, circles, dots, etc.) as separate elements. This not only introduces an uneven quality to the fill, but also dramatically increases the number of objects in the file and consequently the file size.

Gradient fills

An enclosed vector element may also be filled with more than one color. The easiest way is with what is called a *gradient fill,* which appears as a smooth transition between two colors located in different parts of the element fill area. Gradient fills are typically stored as a starting color, an ending color, and the direction and type of the fill. A rendering application is then expected to construct the filled object, usually at the highest resolution possible. CGM is an example of a format that supports horizontal, vertical, and circular gradient fills. Figure 4-1 illustrates a gradient fill.

Footer

A footer may contain information that can be written to the file only after all the object data is written, such as the number of objects in the image. The footer in most vector formats, however, is simply used to mark the end of the object data.

Vector File Size Issues

Not counting palette and attribute information, the size of a vector file is directly proportional to the number of objects it contains. Contrast this with a complex bitmap file, which stays the same size no matter how complex the image described within. The only impact complexity has on bitmap files is on the degree of compression available to the file creator.

Vector files thus can vary greatly in size. A format can store images efficiently by using some form of shorthand notation to allow the compact definition of complex elements. A vector format rich in objects might be able to represent a

dark blue

gradient

light blue

FIGURE 4-1: *Gradient fill*

single complex element using a Bezier curve, for instance. Another format not supporting Bezier curves would need to represent the same curve inefficiently, perhaps using a series of lines. Each line, in this case, would be a separate element, producing a file much larger than one supporting Bezier curves directly.

A format creator was probably addressing the problem of file size when he or she decided to support the creation and naming of complex elements. Great size savings come about when elements are repeated in the image; all that needs to be stored after the original element definition is a pointer to that definition, as well as attribute and position information specific to each individual repeated element.

Size savings may also come about from the way in which a format stores information. Different formats may support identical information in widely varying ways. For example, in the CGM format a hatch pattern is represented as a single object. In the PIC and Autodesk DXF formats, however, each line in the hatch pattern is stored as a separate element.

Because vector data is stored as numbers, it can be scaled, rotated, and otherwise manipulated easily and quickly, at least compared to bitmap data. Also, because scaling is so easy, vector files are not subject to image size limitations in the same way as bitmap files.

Vector formats normally do not support data compression as most bitmap formats do. Some formats, however, support an alternate encoding method that produces smaller data files, but contains the same information. CGM, for instance, normally stores vector information in a clear-text ASCII format that is human-readable, as does the example we presented earlier in this chapter. It also allows the storage of information in a binary format, however, which results in smaller files at the cost of readability and cross-platform portability. The DXF format also has a binary analog called DXB (Data eXchange Binary) which is not only smaller, but faster to load into its parent application (Auto-CAD). It is, however, not portable to other applications.

Scaling Vector Files

A vector element may be scaled to any size. Precision, overflow, and underflow problems may occur, however, if vector data is scaled too large or too small, "large" and "small" being relative to the intrinsic data size of the hardware and software platform supporting the rendering application. Although these problems are well known in numerical analysis, they are not generally recognized by the majority of programmers, and it pays to keep them in mind.

Another common problem occurs when apparently enclosed elements are enlarged and then rendered. Two lines meant to be joined may have endpoints slightly misaligned, and this misalignment may show up as a gap when the element is enlarged or rotated. When a rendering application attempts to display the element on an output device, fill colors or patterns may inexplicably "leak." Many applications that allow the creation of vector files have tools to prevent this, but they may not be applied automatically before the file is saved.

Text in Vector Files

Vector formats that allow the storage of text strings do so in one of two ways. The simplest approach is to store the text as a literal ASCII string along with font, position, color, and attribute information. Although the text is provided in a compact form, this scheme requires the rendering application to have a knowledge of the font to be used, which is always problematic. Because font names are for the most part vendor-controlled, it is sometimes difficult to even specify the font to be drawn. The CGM format addresses this problem through the use of an international registry of font names and associated descriptive data. Any rendering application supporting CGM must have access to this data, or it must use the font metric data supplied in the CGM file's header. Text, however, because it is stored in human-readable format, can be edited.

The second approach, and by far the most flexible, is to store the characters making up the text string as outlines constructed from a series of primitive vector data elements. Under this scheme each creator application must have access to font outline data; because it is stored like any other vector data, font outline data can be scaled at will, rotated, and otherwise manipulated. Until recently, access to outline data has been a problem, but vendors have realized the importance of support for outline fonts and are now routinely supplying this capability at the operating system level.

Because the graphics industry at large and the font industry have grown up in parallel, there are naturally some incompatibilities between data storage models. Most fonts, for instance, are stored as a series of splines joined end-to-end, and a particular spline type may not be supported by the file format in use. In this case, the creator application may choose to convert the splines to arcs or lines and store these instead. This may or may not have an effect on the appearance of the text.

Creator applications may even incorporate vector or stroke fonts, which are usually primitive sets of character outlines with an angular or mechanical look, designed to be drawn with a minimum of fuss. Although many vendors have chosen to make their own, one widely available source is the Hershey fonts. Hershey data is available commercially, but is no longer considered adequate for general use.

The use of vector, stroke, or outline fonts usually increases the size of a file dramatically, but this may be offset by an increase in visual quality in the case of spline-based outline fonts. Text stored in outline format cannot easily be edited.

Pros and Cons of Vector Files

Advantages of vector files include the following:

- Vector files are useful for storing images composed of line-based elements such as lines and polygons, or those that can be decomposed into simple geometrical objects, such as text. More sophisticated formats can also store three-dimensional objects such as polyhedrons and wire-frame models.

- Vector data can be easily scaled and otherwise manipulated to accommodate the resolution of a spectrum of output devices.

- Many vector files containing only ASCII-format data can be modified with simple text editing tools. Individual elements may be added, removed, or changed without affecting other objects in the image.

- It is usually easy to render vector data and save it to a bitmap format file, or, alternately, to convert the data to another vector format, with good results.

Some drawbacks of vector files include the following:

- Vector files cannot easily be used to store extremely complex images, such as some photographs, where color information is paramount and may vary on a pixel-by-pixel basis.

- The appearance of vector images can vary considerably depending upon the application interpreting the image. Factors include the rendering application's compatibility with the creator application and the sophistication of its toolkit of geometric primitives and drawing operations.

- Vector data also displays best on vectored output devices such as plotters and random scan displays. High-resolution raster displays are needed to display vector graphics as effectively.

- Reconstruction of vector data may take considerably longer than that contained in a bitmap file of equivalent complexity, because each image element must be drawn individually and in sequence.

## CHAPTER 5

Metafiles

Metafiles can contain both bitmap and vector data.

When the term *metafile* first appeared, it was used in discussions of device- and machine-independent interchange formats. In the mid-1970's, the National Center for Atmospheric Research (NCAR), along with several other research institutions, reportedly used a format called metacode, which was device- and platform-independent to a certain degree. What is known for certain is that in 1979, the SIGGRAPH Graphics Standards and Planning Committee used the term, referring to a part of their published standards recommendations. These early attempts at defining device- and platform-independent formats mainly concerned themselves with vector data. Although work has continued along this line, we will refer to formats that can accommodate both bitmap and vector data as metafiles, because for all practical purposes the interchange formats in widespread use in the marketplace handle both types of data.

Although metafile formats may be used to store only bitmap or only vector information, it is more likely that they will contain both types of data. From a programmer's point of view, bitmap and vector data are two very different problems. Because of this, supporting both bitmap and vector data types adds to the complexity of a format. Thus, programmers find themselves avoiding the use of metafile formats unless the added complexity is warranted—either because they need to support multiple data types or for external reasons.

The simplest metafiles closely resemble vector format files. Historically, limitations of vector formats were exceeded when the data that needed to be stored became complex and diverse. Vector formats were extended conceptually, allowing the definition of vector data elements in terms of a language or grammar, and also by allowing the storage of bitmap data. In a certain sense, the resulting formats went beyond the capabilities of both bitmap and vector formats—hence the term *metafile.*

Platform Independence?

Metafiles are widely used to transport bitmap or vector data between hardware platforms. The character-oriented nature of ASCII metafiles, in particular, eliminates problems due to byte ordering. It also eliminates problems encountered when transferring binary files across networks where the eighth bit of each byte is stripped off, which can leave files damaged beyond repair. Also, because a metafile supports both bitmap and vector data, an application designer can kill two birds with one stone by providing support for one metafile rather than two separate bitmap and vector formats.

Metafiles are also used to transfer image data between software platforms. A creator application, for instance, can save an image in both bitmap and vector form in a metafile. This file may then be read by any bitmap-capable or vector-capable application supporting the particular metafile format. Many desktop publishing programs, for instance, can manipulate and print vector data, but are unable to display that same data on the screen for various reasons. To accommodate this limitation, a bitmap representation of the image is often included along with the vector data in a metafile. The application can read the bitmap representation of the image from the metafile, which serves as a reduced-quality visual representation of the image that will eventually appear on the printed page. When the page is actually printed, however, the vector data from the metafile is used to produce the image on the printer. Display PostScript files are an example of this type of arrangement.

How Metafiles Are Organized

Metafiles vary so widely in format that it is pointless to attempt to construct a hierarchical explanation of their general construction. Most metafiles contain some sort of header, followed by one or more sections of image data. Some metafiles contain nothing but bitmap data, and still others contain no data at all, opting instead for cryptic drawing instructions, or numerical data similar to that found in vector files.

Pros and Cons of Metafiles

Because metafiles are in a sense a combination of bitmap and vector formats, many of the pros and cons associated with these formats also apply to metafiles. Your decision to choose one particular metafile format over another will thus depend on what kind of data (bitmap or vector) makes up the bulk of the file, and on the strengths and weaknesses of that particular type of data. With that said, we can safely generalize as follows:

- Although many metafile formats are binary, some are character-oriented (ASCII), and these are usually very portable between computer systems.

- Metafiles containing mixtures of vector and bitmap data can in some cases be smaller than fully-rendered bitmap versions of the same image.

- Because they can contain high-redundancy ASCII-encoded data, metafiles generally compress well for file transfer.

- Most metafiles are very complex, because they are usually written by one application for another application. Although their ASCII nature means that theoretically they may be modified with a text editor, modification of a metafile by hand generally requires a skilled eye and special knowledge.

## CHAPTER 6

Platform Dependencies

One of our criteria for choosing the formats discussed in this book was whether they are used for data exchange (both between applications and across platforms). This analysis necessarily ruled out formats incorporating hardware-specific instructions (for example, printer files). Although the formats we discuss here do not raise many hardware issues, several machine dependency issues do come up with some regularity. Two of these issues have some practical implications beyond being simply sources of annoyance. This chapter describes those issues. It also touches on differences between filenames among different platforms. These are significant only because filenames may offer clues about the origins of files you may receive and need to convert.

Byte Order

We generally think of information in memory or on disk as being organized into a series of individual bytes of data. The data is read sequentially in the order in which the bytes are stored. This type of data is called byte-oriented data and is typically used to store character strings and data created by 8-bit CPUs.

Not all computers look at the universe through an 8-bit window, however. For reasons of efficiency, 16- and 32-bit CPUs prefer to work with bytes, organized into 16- and 32-bit cells, which are called words and doublewords respectively. The order of the bytes within word-oriented and doubleword-oriented data is not always the same; it varies depending upon the CPU that created it. (Note, however, that CPUs do exist in which byte ordering can be changed; Digital Equipment Corporation's Alpha chip is a recent example.)

Byte-oriented data has no particular order and is therefore read the same on all systems. But, word-oriented data does present a potential problem—probably the most common portability problem you will encounter when moving files between platforms. The problem arises when binary data is written to a file on a machine with one byte order and is then read on a machine assuming a different byte order. Obviously, the data will be read incorrectly.

It is the order of the bytes within each word and doubleword of data that determine the "endianness" of the data. The two main categories of byte-ordering schemes are called *big-endian* and *little-endian.* * Big-endian machines store the most significant byte (MSB) at the lowest address in a word, usually referred to as byte 0. Big-endian machines include those based on the Motorola MC68000A series of CPUs (the 68000, 68020, 68030, 68040, and so on), including the Commodore Amiga, the Apple Macintosh, and some UNIX machines.

Little-endian machines store the least significant byte (LSB) at the lowest address in a word. The two-byte word value, 1234h, written to a file in little-endian format, would be read as 3412h on a big-endian system. This occurs because the big-endian system assumes that the MSB, in this case the value 12h, is at the lowest address within the byte. The little-endian system, however, places the MSB at the highest address in the byte. When read, the position of the bytes in the word are effectively flipped in the file-reading process by the big-endian machine. Little-endian machines include those based on the Intel iAPX86 series of CPUs (the 8088, 80286, 80386, 80486, and so forth), including the IBM PC and clones.

A third term, *middle-endian,* has been coined to refer to all byte-ordering schemes that are neither big-endian nor little-endian. Such middle-endian ordering schemes include the 3-4-1-2, 2-1-4-3, 2-3-0-1, and 1-0-3-2 packed-decimal formats. The Digital Equipment Corporation PDP-11 is an example of a middle-endian machine. The PDP-11 has a DWORD byte-ordering scheme of 2-3-0-1.

The I/O routines in the C standard library always read word data in the native byte order of the machine hosting the application. This means that functions such as *fread*() and *fwrite*() have no knowledge of byte order and cannot provide needed conversions. Most C libraries, however, contain a function named *swab*(), which is used to swap the bytes in an array of bytes. While *swab*() can be used to convert words of data from one byte order to another, doing so can be inefficient, due to the necessity of making multiple calls for words greater than two bytes in size.

---

* The terms big-endian and little-endian were originally found in Jonathan Swift's book, *Gulliver's Travels,* as satirical descriptions of politicians who disputed whether eggs should be broken at their big end or their little end. This term was first applied to computer architecture by Danny Cohen. (See "For Further Information" below.)

Programmers working with bitmap files need to be concerned about byte order, because many popular formats such as Macintosh Paint (MacPaint), Interchange File Format (IFF or AmigaPaint), and Sun Raster image files are always read and written in big-endian byte order. The TIFF file format is unique, however, in that any TIFF file can be written in either format, and any TIFF reader must be able to read either byte order correctly regardless of the system on which the code is executing.

File Size and Memory Limitations

The second most common problem, after byte-ordering differences, is the handling of large files. Many systems have limited memory, as is the case with MS-DOS-based, early Macintosh, and other desktop machines. As a consequence of this limitation, two problems can arise. The first is that buffer memory available on a small machine may not be adequate to handle chunks of data deemed reasonable on a larger machine. Fortunately, this is a rare occurrence, but it is something to be aware of. Some formats are designed with the limitations of small machines in mind. A prudent thing to do is to avoid forcing the rendering application to buffer more than 32K of data at a time.

The second problem is absolute file size. As suggested above, an uncompressed 24-bit bitmap file 1024 pixels square will be a minimum of 3,145,728 bytes in size. While this much memory may be available on a workstation, it may not be on a smaller machine. In this case, the rendering application will not be able to assemble the data in memory. If any alteration to the image must be done, extraordinary measures may need to be taken by the application prior to rendering. Thus, it is prudent to take advantage of the file "chunking" features available in many formats. Although it may take more programming effort to accommodate smaller machines, the effort also guarantees portability to future platforms.

Floating-point Formats

Vector file formats occasionally store key points in floating-point format, and a number of different floating-point formats are in common use. Most floating-point data, however, is stored in a portable manner. The least common denominator approach is to store floating-point numbers as ASCII data, as a series of point pairs:

```
1234.56 2345.678 987.65 8765.43
```

The main problems you will encounter with floating-point data stored in ASCII format are with formatting conventions—how the numbers are delimited (comma, whitespace, etc.), and how many digits of precision need to be handled by your parsing routines. Library routines are readily available to handle conversion from ASCII to native binary floating-point formats.

Floating-point numbers stored in binary format present different problems. There are a number of floating-point binary formats in common use, including IEEE, Digital Equipment Corporation, and Microsoft Basic. Library routines are available for these conversions, but it may take some searching to find the correct one for your application. Sometimes, however, the hardest part of the job is identifying the formats you are trying to convert from and to.

Bit Order

Bit order refers to the direction in which bits are represented in a byte of memory. Just as words of data may be written with the most significant byte or the least significant byte first (in the lowest address of the word), so too can bits within a byte be written with the most significant bit or the least significant bit first (in the lowest position of the byte).

The bit order we see most commonly is the one in which the zeroth, or least-significant bit, is the first bit read from the byte. This is referred to as *up bit ordering* or normal bit direction. When the seventh, or most significant, bit is the first one stored in a byte, we call this *down bit ordering* , or reverse bit direction.

The terms big-endian and little-endian are sometimes erroneously applied to bit order. These terms were specifically adopted as descriptions of differing byte orders only and are not used to differentiate bit orders (see the section called "Byte Order" earlier in this chapter).

Normal bit direction, least significant bit to most significant bit, is often used in transmitting data between devices, such as FAX machines and printers, and for storing unencoded bitmapped data. Reverse bit direction, most significant bit to least significant bit, is used to communicate data to display devices and in many data compression encoding methods. It is therefore possible for a bitmap image file to contain data stored in either or both bit directions if both encoded and unencoded data is stored in the file (as can occur in the TIFF and CALS Raster image file formats).

Problems that occur in reading or decoding data stored with a bit orders that is the reverse of the expected bit order are called *bit sex* problems. When the bit order of a byte must be changed, we commonly refer to this as reversing the bit sex.

Color sex problems result when the value of the bits in a byte are the inverse of what we expect them to be. Inverting a bit (also called flipping or toggling a bit) is to change a bit to its opposite state. A 1 bit becomes a 0 and a 0 bit becomes a 1. If you have a black-on-white image and you invert all the bits in the image data, you will have a white-on-black image. In this regard, inverting the bits in a byte of image data is normally referred to as inverting the color sex.

It is important to realize that inverting and reversing the bits in a byte are not the same operation and rarely produce the same results. Note the different resulting values when the bits in a byte are inverted and reversed:

    Original Bit Pattern: 10100001
    Inverted Bit Pattern: 01011110

    Original Bit Pattern: 10100001
    Reversed Bit Pattern: 10000101

There are, however, cases when the inverting or reversing of a bit pattern will yield the same value:

    Original Bit Pattern: 01010101
    Inverted Bit Pattern: 10101010

    Original Bit Pattern: 01010101
    Reversed Bit Pattern: 10101010

Occasionally, it is necessary to reverse the order of bits within a byte of data. This most often occurs when a particular hardware device, such as a printer, requires that the bits in a byte be sent in the reverse order in which they are stored in the computer's memory. Because it is not possible for most computers to directly read a byte in a reversed bit order, the byte value must be read and its bits rewritten to memory in reverse order.

Reversing the order of bits within a byte, or changing the bit sex, may be accomplished by calculation or by table look-up. A function to reverse the bits within a byte is shown below:

```
//
// Reverse the order of bits within a byte.
// Returns: The reversed byte value.
//
BYTE ReverseBits(BYTE b)
{
  BYTE c;
  c  = ((b >>  1) & 0x55) | ((b <<  1) & 0xaa);
  c |= ((b >>  2) & 0x33) | ((b <<  2) & 0xcc);
  c |= ((b >>  4) & 0x0f) | ((b <<  4) & 0xf0);
    return(c);
}
```

If an application requires more speed in the bit-reversal process, the above function can be replaced with the REVERSEBITS macro and look-up table below. Although the macro and look-up table is faster in performing bit reversal than the function, the macro lacks the prototype checking that ensures that every value passed to the function *ReverseBits*() is an 8-bit unsigned value. An INVERTBITS macro is also included for color sex inversion.

```
#define INVERTBITS(b)    (~(b))
#define REVERSEBITS(b)   (BitReverseTable[b])

static BYTE BitReverseTable[256] =
{
0x00, 0x80, 0x40, 0xc0, 0x20, 0xa0, 0x60, 0xe0,
0x10, 0x90, 0x50, 0xd0, 0x30, 0xb0, 0x70, 0xf0,
0x08, 0x88, 0x48, 0xc8, 0x28, 0xa8, 0x68, 0xe8,
0x18, 0x98, 0x58, 0xd8, 0x38, 0xb8, 0x78, 0xf8,
0x04, 0x84, 0x44, 0xc4, 0x24, 0xa4, 0x64, 0xe4,
0x14, 0x94, 0x54, 0xd4, 0x34, 0xb4, 0x74, 0xf4,
0x0c, 0x8c, 0x4c, 0xcc, 0x2c, 0xac, 0x6c, 0xec,
0x1c, 0x9c, 0x5c, 0xdc, 0x3c, 0xbc, 0x7c, 0xfc,
0x02, 0x82, 0x42, 0xc2, 0x22, 0xa2, 0x62, 0xe2,
0x12, 0x92, 0x52, 0xd2, 0x32, 0xb2, 0x72, 0xf2,
0x0a, 0x8a, 0x4a, 0xca, 0x2a, 0xaa, 0x6a, 0xea,
0x1a, 0x9a, 0x5a, 0xda, 0x3a, 0xba, 0x7a, 0xfa,
0x06, 0x86, 0x46, 0xc6, 0x26, 0xa6, 0x66, 0xe6,
0x16, 0x96, 0x56, 0xd6, 0x36, 0xb6, 0x76, 0xf6,
0x0e, 0x8e, 0x4e, 0xce, 0x2e, 0xae, 0x6e, 0xee,
0x1e, 0x9e, 0x5e, 0xde, 0x3e, 0xbe, 0x7e, 0xfe,
0x01, 0x81, 0x41, 0xc1, 0x21, 0xa1, 0x61, 0xe1,
0x11, 0x91, 0x51, 0xd1, 0x31, 0xb1, 0x71, 0xf1,
0x09, 0x89, 0x49, 0xc9, 0x29, 0xa9, 0x69, 0xe9,
0x19, 0x99, 0x59, 0xd9, 0x39, 0xb9, 0x79, 0xf9,
0x05, 0x85, 0x45, 0xc5, 0x25, 0xa5, 0x65, 0xe5,
0x15, 0x95, 0x55, 0xd5, 0x35, 0xb5, 0x75, 0xf5,
0x0d, 0x8d, 0x4d, 0xcd, 0x2d, 0xad, 0x6d, 0xed,
0x1d, 0x9d, 0x5d, 0xdd, 0x3d, 0xbd, 0x7d, 0xfd,
0x03, 0x83, 0x43, 0xc3, 0x23, 0xa3, 0x63, 0xe3,
0x13, 0x93, 0x53, 0xd3, 0x33, 0xb3, 0x73, 0xf3,
0x0b, 0x8b, 0x4b, 0xcb, 0x2b, 0xab, 0x6b, 0xeb,
0x1b, 0x9b, 0x5b, 0xdb, 0x3b, 0xbb, 0x7b, 0xfb,
0x07, 0x87, 0x47, 0xc7, 0x27, 0xa7, 0x67, 0xe7,
0x17, 0x97, 0x57, 0xd7, 0x37, 0xb7, 0x77, 0xf7,
0x0f, 0x8f, 0x4f, 0xcf, 0x2f, 0xaf, 0x6f, 0xef,
0x1f, 0x9f, 0x5f, 0xdf, 0x3f, 0xbf, 0x7f, 0xff
};
```

Filenames

Whether you are writing a file or reading one written by another user, you need to be aware of the differences among filenames on various platforms.

Filename Structure

By number of installed machines, the three most popular platforms at the time of this writing are MS-DOS, Macintosh, and UNIX, roughly in the ratio of 100:10:5. All three support the *name.extension* filenaming convention (although this is mostly true of the MS-DOS and UNIX systems). Applications occasionally use the extension portion of the filename for file type identification.

Other systems with a large installed user base (such as OS/2, Amiga, Atari, and VMS) have roughly similar naming conventions. VMS, for instance, uses as a default the format:

> *name1.name2;version*

where *version* is an integer denoting the revision number of the file. In any case, files are likely to come from anywhere, and examination of the extension portion of a filename, if present, may help you to identify the format.

Filename Length

UNIX and Macintosh users are accustomed to long filenames:

> *ThisIsAMacFilename*
> *This is also a Mac Filename*
> *This.Is.A.Unix.Filename*

The MS-DOS, Windows NT, and OS/2 FAT filesystems, on the other hand, limit filenames to the 8.3 format (eight characters per filename, three per extension):

> *msdosnam.ext*

For interplatform portability, we suggest that you consider using the 8.3 convention. Be aware, if you are using MS-DOS, that you may get filename duplication errors when you convert multiple files from other platforms. Depending on the application doing the filename conversion, the following files from a typical UNIX installation:

> *thisis.file.number.1*
> *thisis.file.number.2*

are both converted to the following filename under MS-DOS, and the second
file will overwrite the first:

thisis.fil

Case Sensitivity

Users on Macintosh and UNIX systems are accustomed to the fact that filenames are case-sensitive, and that filenames can contain mixed uppercase and
lowercase. Filenames on MS-DOS systems, however, are case-insensitive, and
the filesystem effectively converts all names to uppercase before manipulating
them. Thus:

AMacFile.Ext
AUnixFile.Ext

become:

AMACFILE.EXT
AUNIXFIL.EXT

under MS-DOS and other similar filesystems. Similarly:

Afile.Ext
AFile.Ext

are both converted to:

AFILE.EXT

For Further Information

For an excellent description of the war between the byte orders, see Danny
Cohen's paper, cited below. A good description of the original of the "endian"
terms may be found in Eric Raymond's monumental work, also cited below.
Both publications are also widely available via the Internet.

Cohen, Danny. "On Holy Wars and a Plea for Peace," *IEEE Computer
Magazine*, Volume 14, October 1981, pp. 48-54.

Raymond, Eric. *The New Hacker's Dictionary*, MIT Press, Cambridge, MA,
1991.

## CHAPTER 7

Format Conversion

Is It Really Possible?

Programmers of all kinds always ask for information on how to convert between file formats, and graphics programmers are no exception. You must realize, however, that not every format can be converted to every other format, and this is doubly so if you wish to preserve image quality. The biggest problems occur when you attempt to convert between files of different basic format types—bitmap to vector, for instance. Successful conversion between basic format types is not always possible due to the great differences in the ways data is stored.

File conversion is a thankless task for any number of reasons. No vendor, for instance, feels obligated to disclose revisions to proprietary formats, or even to publish accurate and timely specifications for the ones already in common use. Many formats also have obscure variants which may be difficult to track down. At any moment, too, a revision to a major application may appear, containing a bug which makes it produce incorrect files. These files will ever after need to be supported. For all these reasons, think long and hard about any decision you make about whether to include file conversion features in your application. Remember, too, that a format that is reasonably well designed for a particular intended application cannot necessarily be converted for use with another application. Interchange between devices and applications is only as good as the software components (readers and writers) which generate and interpret the format, whether it is CGM, PostScript, or any other format.

Don't Do It If You Don't Need to ...

If you do need to convert image files between formats, consider using one or more of the software packages written especially for file format conversion. UNIX systems, in particular, have a number of extraordinarily good tools for format conversion, which are freely available and distributed in source form; *pbmplus* is a particularly good tool, and we've included it on the CD-ROM that accompanies this book. We have also included conversion tools for other platforms, including a *pbmplus* port (MS-DOS), Conversion Assistant for Windows (Windows), GBM (OS/2), and Graphics Converter (Macintosh). Inset Systems' HiJaak, a commercial product that we are not able to include on the CD-ROM, is an excellent product as well.

You should consider writing your own conversion program only if you have very specific conversion needs not satisfied by the many publicly available and commercial applications—for example, to accommodate a proprietary format. If you do decide to write your own converter, you will need to know a bit about what to expect when converting from one format type to another.

... But If You Do

In what follows we will call the file to be converted (which already exists in one format) the *original*, and the file produced in the second format (after the conversion operation) the *converted* file. A *conversion application* acts upon an *original file* to produce a *converted file*.

If you remember our terminology, an application renders a graphics file to an output device or file. By extension, then, we will say that a conversion application *renders* an original file to a converted file. We will also use the term *translation* as a synonym for *conversion*.

Bitmap to Bitmap

Converting one bitmap format to another normally yields the best results of all the possible conversions between format types. All bitmap images consist of pixels, and ultimately all bitmap data is converted one pixel value at a time. Bitmap headers and the data contained in them can vary considerably, but the data contained in them can be added or discarded at the discretion of the conversion software to make the best conversion possible.

Usually, some rearrangement of the color data is necessary. This might take the form of separation of pixel data into color plane data, or the addition or removal of a palette. It might even entail conversion from one color model to another.

Unsuccessful bitmap-to-bitmap conversions occur most often when translating a file written in a format supporting deep pixel data to one written in a lesser-color format, for example, one supporting only palette color. This can occur when you are converting between a format supporting 24-bit data and one supporting only 8-bit data. The palette color format may not support the storage of enough data necessary to produce an accurate rendering of the image. Usually, some image-processing operations (*quantization* or *dithering*, most likely) are needed to increase the apparent quality of the converted image. Operations of this sort will necessarily make the converted image appear different from the original, and thus technically the image will not have been preserved in the conversion process.

The other main problem comes about when the converted image must be made smaller or larger than the original. If the converted image is smaller than the original, information in the original image must be thrown away. Although various image-processing strategies can be used to improve image quality, some of the information is nonetheless removed when the original file is shrunk. If the converted image is larger than the original, however, information must be created to fill in the spaces that appear between formerly adjacent pixels when the original image is enlarged. There is no completely satisfactory way to do this, and the processes currently used typically give the enlarged image a block-pixel look.

An example of a bitmap-to-bitmap conversion that is almost always successful is PCX to Microsoft Windows Bitmap.

Vector to Vector

Conversion between vector formats—for example, from AutoCAD DXF to Lotus DIF—is possible and sometimes quite easy. Two serious problems can occur, though. The first comes about due to differences in the number and type of objects available in different vector formats. Some formats, for instance, provide support for only a few simple image elements, such as circles and rectangles. Richer formats may also provide support for many additional complex elements, such as pattern fills, drop shadowing, text fonts, b-splines, and Bezier curves. Attempting to convert a file written in a complex format rich in elements to a simpler format will result in an approximation of the original image.

The second problem comes from the fact that that each vector format has its own interpretation of measurements and the appearance of image elements and primitives. Rarely do two formats agree exactly on the placement and appearance of even simple image elements. Common problems are those related to line joint styles and end styles, and to centerline and centerpoint locations. For example, the Macintosh PICT format assumes that lines are drawn with a pen point that is below and to the right of the specified coordinates, while most other formats center their pens directly on the coordinates. Another example is the GEM VDI format, which assumes that a line should be drawn so that it extends one-half of the width of the line past the end coordinate. Lines in other formats often stop exactly at the end of the coordinate pixel.

It is quite difficult to generalize further than this. If you write a vector-to-vector format converter, you must be aware of the peculiarities of each vector format and the problems of conversion between one specific format and the other.

Metafile to Metafile

Because metafiles can contain both bitmap and vector image data in the same file, problems inherent in bitmap and vector conversion apply to metafiles as well. Generally, the bitmap part of the metafile will convert with success, but the accuracy of the conversion of the vector part will depend on the match to the format to which you are converting. An example of a metafile-to-metafile conversion is Microsoft Windows Metafile (WMF) to CGM.

Vector and Metafile to Bitmap

Converting vector and metafile format files to bitmap format files is generally quite easy. A vector image can be turned into a bitmap simply by dividing it up into component pixels and then writing those pixels to an array in memory in the memory equivalent of a contrasting color. The array can then be saved in a bitmap format file. This process is familiar to users of paint programs, where a mouse or stylus is used to draw geometrical shapes which appear as series of lines on the screen. When the data is written out to disk, however, it is stored in a bitmap file as a series of colored pixels rather than as mathematical data describing the position of the lines making up the image. The ultimate quality of the resulting bitmap image will depend on the resolution of the bitmap being rendered to and the complexity (color, pixel depth, and image features) of the original vector image.

The most common problem occurring with this type of conversion is *aliasing*, sometimes known as the *jaggies*. This is where arcs and diagonal lines take on a staircase appearance, partly due to the relatively low resolution of the output bitmap compared to that necessary to adequately support rendering of the output image.

The conversion of ASCII metafile data to binary bitmap data is usually the most complicated and time-consuming part of metafile conversion. As mentioned above in the section discussing the three basic formats, many metafile formats also contain a bitmap image. If conversion from vector to bitmap data achieves poor results, then converting the bitmap data to the desired format may not only result in a better job, but may also be a much quicker process.

A metafile-to-bitmap conversion that is almost always successful is Microsoft Windows Metafile to Microsoft Windows Bitmap.

Bitmap and Metafile to Vector

Converting bitmap and metafile format files to vector format files is usually the hardest of all to perform, and rarely does it achieve any kind of usable results. This is due to the fact that complex image processing algorithms and heuristics are necessary to find all the lines and edges in bitmap images. Once the outlines are found, they must be recognized and converted to their vector element equivalents, and each step is prone to error. Simple bitmap images may be approximated as vector images, usually as black-and-white line drawings, but more complex photographic-type images are nearly impossible to reproduce accurately. Nevertheless, commercial applications exist to provide various types of *edge detection* and *vectorization*. Edge detection remains an active area of research.

Another problem inherent in the conversion of bitmap format files to vector is that of color. Although most bitmap files incorporate many colors, vector formats seldom provide support for more than a few. The conversion of an original bitmap file to a vector file can result in a loss of color in the converted image.

Metafiles also have the same problems associated with the conversion of their bitmap components, although many metafile formats are capable of handling the colors found in the original raster image data. Close vector reproductions of bitmap images are not usually possible unless the bitmap data is very simple.

Bitmap and Vector to Metafile

Converting bitmap format files to metafiles can be quite accurate because most metafile format files can contain a bitmap image as well. Vector format source files have a more limited range of metafile target formats to which they can successfully convert. Problems encountered in this type of conversion are the same as those occurring in bitmap-to-vector conversions.

A common process conversion of this type is the conversion of binary bitmap or vector image files to an ASCII metafile format such as PostScript. Although PostScript is covered only briefly in this book, it is widely used for file interchange, particularly on the Macintosh platform. Such conversions lend portability to image data designed to be moved between machines or which may be directed to a number of different output devices.

Other Format Conversion Considerations

There are other problems that occur when converting from one file format to another. One of the most vexing comes up when converting to a destination format that supports fewer colors than are contained in the original image.

Also, the number of colors in an image may not be a problem, but the specific colors contained in the original image may be. For example, consider the conversion of a 256-color image from one format to another. Both formats support images with up to 256 different colors in the bitmap, so the number of colors is not a problem. What is a problem, however, is that the source format chooses the colors that can go in the palette from a field of 16 million (24-bit palette), while the target format can store colors only from a range of 65,535 (16-bit palette). It is quite likely that the source image will contain colors not defined in the palette of the target image. The application doing the conversion will have to rely on some color aliasing scheme, which usually fails to provide satisfactory results.

## CHAPTER 8

Working With Graphics Files

This chapter provides some general guidance on reading and writing graphics files stored in the various formats described in this book, as well as examples of code you can use in your own programs. (For many additional code examples for specific file formats, see the CD that accompanies this book.) In this chapter we also discuss the use of test files, and we touch upon what it means to develop your own file format (if you dare!).

Reading Graphics Data

A graphics format file reader is responsible for opening and reading a file, determining its validity, and interpreting the information contained within it. A reader may take, as its input, source image data either from a file or from the data stream of an input device, such as a scanner or frame buffer.

There are two types of reader designs in common use. The first is the *filter*. A filter reads a data source one character at a time and collects that data for as long as it is available from the input device or file. The second type is the *scanner* (also called a *parser*). Scanners are able to randomly access across the entire data source. Unlike filters, which cannot back up or skip ahead to read information, scanners can read and reread data anywhere within the file. The main difference between filters and scanners is the amount of memory they use. Although filters are limited in the manner in which they read data, they require only a small amount of memory in which to perform their function. Scanners, on the other hand, are not limited in how they read data, but as a tradeoff may require a large amount of memory or disk space in which to store data.

Because most image files are quite large, make sure that your readers are highly optimized to read file information as quickly as possible. Graphics and imaging applications are often harshly judged by users based on the amount of time it takes them to read and display an image file. One curiosity of user interface lore states that an application that renders an image on an output device one scan line at a time will be perceived as slower than an application that waits to paint the screen until the entire image has been assembled, even though in reality both applications may take the same amount of time.

Binary Versus ASCII Readers

Binary image readers must read binary data written in 1-, 2-, and 4-byte word sizes and in one of several different byte-ordering schemes. Bitmap data should be read in large chunks and buffered in memory for faster performance, as opposed to reading one pixel or scan line at a time.

ASCII-format image readers require highly optimized string reader and parser functions capable of quickly finding and extracting pertinent information from a string of characters and converting ASCII strings into numerical values.

Reading a Graphics File Header

The type of code you use to implement a reader will vary greatly, depending upon how data is stored in a graphics file. For example, PCX files contain only little-endian binary data; Encapsulated PostScript files contain both binary and ASCII data; TIFF files contain binary data that may be stored in either the big- or little-endian byte order; and AutoCAD DXF files contain only ASCII data.

Many graphics files that contain only ASCII data may be parsed one character at a time. Usually, a loop and a series of rather elaborate nested case statements are used to read through the file and identify the various tokens of keywords and values. The design and implementation of such a text parser is not fraught with too many perils.

Where you can find some real gotchas is in working with graphics files containing binary data, such as the contents of most bitmap files. A few words of advice are in order, so that when you begin to write your own graphics file readers and writers you don't run into too many problems (and inadvertently damage your fists with your keyboard!).

When you read most bitmap files, you'll find that the header is the first chunk of data stored in the file. Headers store attributes of the graphics data that may change from file to file, such as the height and width of the image and the number of colors it contains. If a format always stored images of the same size, type, and number of colors, a header wouldn't be necessary. The values for that format would simply be hard-coded into the reader.

As it is, most bitmap file formats have headers, and your reader must know the internal structure of the header of each format it is to read. A program that reads a single bitmap format may be able to get away with seeking to a known offset location and reading only a few fields of data. However, more sophisticated formats containing many fields of information require that you read the entire header.

Using the C language, you might be tempted to read in a header from a file using the following code:

```
typedef struct _Header
{
    DWORD FileId;
    BYTE  Type;
    WORD  Height;
    WORD  Width;
    WORD  Depth;
    CHAR  FileName[81];
    DWORD Flags;
    BYTE  Filler[32];
} HEADER;

HEADER header;
FILE *fp = fopen("MYFORMAT.FOR", "rb");
if (fp)
    fread(&header, sizeof(HEADER), 1, fp);
```

Here we see a typical bitmap file format header defined as a C language structure. The fields of the header contain information on the size, color, type of image, attribute flags, and name of the image file itself. The fields in the header range from one to 80 bytes in size, and the entire structure is padded out to a total length of 128 bytes.

The first potential gotcha may occur even before you read the file. It lies waiting for you in the *fopen*() function. If you don't indicate that you are opening the graphics file for reading as a binary file (by specifying the "rb" in the second argument of the *fopen*() parameter list), you may find that extra carriage returns and/or line feeds appear in your data in memory that are not in the graphics file. This is because *fopen*() opens files in text mode by default.

In C++, you need to OR the ios::binary value into the mode argument of the fstream or ifstream constructor:

```
fstream *fs = new fstream ("MYFORMAT.FOR", ios::in|ios::binary);
```

After you have opened the graphics file successfully, the next step is to read the header. The code we choose to read the header in this example is the *fread*() function which is most commonly used for reading chunks of data from a file stream. Using *fread*(), you can read the entire header with a single function call. A good idea, except that in using *fread*() you are likely to encounter problems. You guessed it, the second gotcha!

A common problem you may encounter when reading data into a structure is that of the boundary alignment of elements within the structure. On most machines, it is usually more efficient to align each structure element to begin on a 2-, 4-, 8-, or 16-byte boundary. Because aligning structure elements is the job of the compiler, and not the programmer, the effects of such alignment are not always obvious.

The compiler word-aligns structure elements in the same way. By adding padding, we increased the length of the header so it ends on a 128-byte boundary. Just as we added padding at the end of the header, compilers add invisible padding to structures to do the following:

- Start the structure on a word boundary (an even memory address).

- Align each element on the desired word or doubleword boundary.

- Ensure that the size of the structure is an even number of bytes in size (16-bit machines) or is divisible by four (32-bit machines).

The padding takes the form of invisible elements that are inserted between the visible elements the programmer defines in the structure. Although this invisible padding is not directly accessible, it is as much a part of the structure as any visible element in the structure. For example, the following structure will be five, six, or eight bytes in size if it is compiled using a 1-, 2-, or 4-byte word alignment:

```
typedef struct _test
{
    BYTE  A;    /* One byte */
    DWORD B;    /* Four bytes */
} TEST;
```

With 1-byte alignment, there is no padding, and the structure is five bytes in size, with element B beginning on an odd-byte boundary. With 2-byte alignment, one byte of padding is inserted between elements A and B to allow element B to begin on the next even-byte boundary. With 4-byte alignment, three bytes of padding are inserted between A and B, allowing element B to begin on the next even-word boundary.

Determining the Size of a Structure

At runtime, you can use the sizeof() operator to determine the size of a structure:

```
typedef struct _test
{
    BYTE  A;
    DWORD B;
} TEST;
printf("TEST is %u bytes in length\n", sizeof(TEST));
```

Because most ANSI C compilers don't allow the use of sizeof() as a pre-processor statement, you can check the length of the structure at compile time by using a slightly more clever piece of code:

```
/*
** Test if the size of TEST is five bytes or not. If not, the array
** SizeTest[] will be declared to have zero elements, and a
** compile-time error will be generated on all ANSI C compilers.
** Note that the use of a typedef causes no memory to be allocated
** if the sizeof() test is true. And please, document all such
** tests in your code so other programmer will know what the heck
** you are attempting to do.
*/
typedef char CHECKSIZEOFTEST[sizeof(TEST) == 5];
```

The gotcha here is that the *fread*() function will write data into the padding when you expected it to be written to an element. If you used *fread*() to read five bytes from a file into our 4-byte-aligned TEST structure, you would find that the first byte ended up correctly in element A, but that bytes 2, 3, and 4 were stored in the padding and not in element B as you had expected. Element B will instead store only byte 5, and the last three bytes of B will contain garbage.

There are several steps involved in solving this problem.

First, attempt to design a structure so each field naturally begins on a 2-byte (for 16-bit machines) or 4-byte (for 32-bit machines) boundary. Now if the compiler's byte-alignment flag is turned on or off, no changes will occur in the structure.

When defining elements within a structure, you also want to avoid using the INT data type. An INT is two bytes on some machines and four bytes on others. If you use INTs, you'll find that the size of a structure will change between 16- and 32-bit machines even though the compiler is not performing any word alignment on the structure. Always use SHORT to define a 2-byte integer element and LONG to specify a four-byte integer element, or use WORD and DWORD to specify their unsigned equivalents.

When you read an image file header, you typically don't have the luxury of being the designer of the file's header structure. Your structure must exactly match the format of the header in the graphics file. If the designer of the graphics file format didn't think of aligning the fields of the header, then you're out of luck.

Second, compile the source code module that contains the structure with a flag indicating that structure elements should not be aligned (/Zp1 for Microsoft C++ and –a1 for Borland C++). Optionally, you can put the #pragma directive for this compiler option around the structure; the result is that only the structure is affected by the alignment restriction and not the rest of the module.

This, however, is not a terribly good solution. As we have noted, by aligning all structure fields on a 1-byte boundary, the CPU will access the structure data in memory less efficiently. If you are reading and writing the structure only once or twice, as is the case with many file format readers, you may not care how quickly the header data is read.

You must also make sure that, whenever anybody compiles your source code, they use the 1-byte structure alignment compiler flag. Depending on which machine is executing your code, failure to use this flag may cause problems reading image files. Naming conventions may also differ for #pragma directives between compiler vendors; on some compilers, the byte-alignment #pragma directives might not be supported at all.

Finally, we must face the third insidious gotcha—the native byte order of the CPU. If you attempt to *fread*() a graphics file header containing data written in the little-endian byte order on a big-endian machine (or big-endian data in a file on a little-endian machine), you will get nothing but byte-twiddled garbage. The *fread*() function cannot perform the byte-conversion operations necessary to read the data correctly, because it can only read data using the native byte order of the CPU.

At this point, if you are thinking "But, I'm not going to read in each header field separately!" you are in for a rather rude change of your implementation paradigm!

Reading each field of a graphics file header into the elements of a structure, and performing the necessary byte-order conversions, is how it's done. If you are worried about efficiency, just remember that a header is usually read from a file and into memory only once, and you are typically reading less than 512 bytes of data—in fact, typically much less than that. We doubt if the performance meter in your source code profiler will show much of a drop.

So, how do we read in the header fields one element at a time? We could go back to our old friend *fread*():

```
HEADER header;
fread(&header.FileId,   sizeof(header.FileId),   1, fp);
fread(&header.Height,   sizeof(header.Height),   1, fp);
fread(&header.Width,    sizeof(header.Width),    1, fp);
fread(&header.Depth,    sizeof(header.Depth),    1, fp);
fread(&header.Type,     sizeof(header.Type),     1, fp);
fread(&header.FileName, sizeof(header.FileName), 1, fp);
fread(&header.Flags,    sizeof(header.Flags),    1, fp);
fread(&header.Filler,   sizeof(header.Filler),   1, fp);
```

While this code reads in the header data and stores it in the structure correctly (regardless of any alignment padding), *fread*() still reads the data in the native byte order of the machine on which it is executing. This is fine if you are reading big-endian data on a big-endian machine, or little-endian data on a little-endian machine, but not if the byte order of the machine is different from the byte order of the data being read. It seems that what we need is a filter that can convert data to a different byte order.

If you have ever written code that diddled the byte order of data, then you have probably written a set of *SwapBytes* functions to exchange the position of bytes with a word of data. Your functions probably looked something like this:

```
/*
** Swap the bytes within a 16-bit WORD.
*/
WORD SwapTwoBytes(WORD w)
{
    register WORD tmp;
    tmp =  (w & 0x00FF);
    tmp = ((w & 0xFF00) >> 0x08) | (tmp << 0x08);
    return(tmp);
}
/*
** Swap the bytes within a 32-bit DWORD.
*/
DWORD SwapFourBytes(DWORD w)
```

```
{
    register DWORD tmp;
    tmp =  (w & 0x000000FF);
    tmp = ((w & 0x0000FF00) >> 0x08) | (tmp << 0x08);
    tmp = ((w & 0x00FF0000) >> 0x10) | (tmp << 0x08);
    tmp = ((w & 0xFF000000) >> 0x18) | (tmp << 0x08);
    return(tmp);
}
```

Because words come in two sizes, you need two functions: *SwapTwoBytes*() and *SwapFourBytes*()—for those of you in the C++ world, you'll just write two over-loaded functions, or a function template, called *SwapBytes*(). Of course you can swap signed values just as easily by writing two more functions which substitute the data types SHORT and LONG for WORD and DWORD.

Using our *SwapBytes* functions, we can now read in the header as follows:

```
HEADER header;
fread(&header.FileId,    sizeof(header.FileId),    1, fp);
header.FileId = SwapFourBytes(header.FileId);
fread(&header.Height,    sizeof(header.Height),    1, fp);
header.Height = SwapTwoBytes(header.Height);
fread(&header.Width,     sizeof(header.Width),     1, fp);
header.Width = SwapTwoBytes(header.Width);
fread(&header.Depth,     sizeof(header.Depth),     1, fp);
header.Depth = SwapTwoBytes(header.Depth);
fread(&header.Type,      sizeof(header.Type),      1, fp);
fread(&header.FileName, sizeof(header.FileName),  1, fp);
fread(&header.Flags,     sizeof(header.Flags),     1, fp);
header.Flags = SwapFourBytes(header.Flags);
fread(&header.Filler,    sizeof(header.Filler),    1, fp);
```

We can read in the data using *fread*() and can swap the bytes of the WORD and DWORD-sized fields using our *SwapBytes* functions. This is great if the byte order of the data doesn't match the byte order of the CPU, but what if it does? Do we need two separate header reading functions, one with the *SwapBytes* functions and one without, to ensure that our code will work on most machines? And, how do we tell at runtime what the byte-order of a machine is? Take a look at this example:

```
#define LSB_FIRST        0
#define MSB_FIRST        1
/*
** Check the byte-order of the CPU.
*/
int CheckByteOrder(void)
{
```

```
    SHORT  w = 0x0001;
    CHAR  *b = (CHAR *) &w;
    return(b[0] ? LSB_FIRST : MSB_FIRST);
}
```

The function *CheckByteOrder*() returns the value LSB_FIRST if the machine is little-endian (the little end comes first) and MSB_FIRST if the machine is big-endian (the big end comes first). This function will work correctly on all big- and little-endian machines. Its return value is undefined for middle-endian machines (like the PDP-11).

Let's assume that the data format of our graphics file is little-endian. We can check the byte order of the machine executing our code and can call the appropriate reader function, as follows:

```
int byteorder = CheckByteOrder();
if (byteorder == LSB_FIRST)
    ReadHeaderAsLittleEndian();
else
    ReadHeaderAsBigEndian();
```

The function *ReadHeaderAsLittleEndian*() would contain only the *fread*() functions, and *ReadHeaderAsBigEndian*() would contain the *fread*() and *SwapBytes*() functions.

But this is not very elegant. What we really need is a replacement for both the *fread*() and *SwapBytes* functions that can read WORDs and DWORDs from a data file, making sure that the returned data are in the byte order we specify. Consider the following functions:

```
/*
** Get a 16-bit word in either big- or little-endian byte order.
*/
WORD GetWord(char byteorder, FILE *fp)
{
    register WORD w;

    if (byteorder == MSB_FIRST)
    {
        w =  (WORD) (fgetc(fp) & 0xFF);
        w = ((WORD) (fgetc(fp) & 0xFF)) | (w << 0x08);
    }
    else            /* LSB_FIRST */
    {
        w  =  (WORD) (fgetc(fp) & 0xFF);
        w |= ((WORD) (fgetc(fp) & 0xFF) << 0x08);
    }
```

```
        return(w);
}


/*
** Get a 32-bit word in either big- or little-endian byte order.
*/
DWORD GetDword(char byteorder, FILE *fp)
{
    register DWORD w;

    if (byteorder == MSB_FIRST)
    {
        w =  (DWORD) (fgetc(fp) & 0xFF);
        w = ((DWORD) (fgetc(fp) & 0xFF)) | (w << 0x08);
        w = ((DWORD) (fgetc(fp) & 0xFF)) | (w << 0x08);
        w = ((DWORD) (fgetc(fp) & 0xFF)) | (w << 0x08);
    }
    else            /* LSB_FIRST */
    {
        w |=   (DWORD) (fgetc(fp) & 0xFF);
        w |= (((DWORD) (fgetc(fp) & 0xFF)) << 0x08);
        w |= (((DWORD) (fgetc(fp) & 0xFF)) << 0x10);
        w |= (((DWORD) (fgetc(fp) & 0xFF)) << 0x18);
    }
    return(w);
}
```

The *GetWord*() and *GetDword*() functions will read a word of data from a file stream in either byte order (specified in their first argument). Valid values are LSB_FIRST and MSB_FIRST.

Now, let's look at what reading a header is like using the *GetWord*() and *GetDword*() functions. Notice that we now read in the single-byte field Type using *fgetc*() and that *fread*() is still the best way to read in blocks of byte-aligned data:

```
HEADER header;

int byteorder = CheckByteOrder();

header.FileId  = GetDword(byteorder, fp);
header.Height  = GetWord(byteorder, fp);
header.Width   = GetWord(byteorder, fp);
header.Depth   = GetWord(byteorder, fp);
header.Type    = fgetc(fp);
```

```
fread(&header.FileName, sizeof(header.FileName), 1, fp);
header.Flags    = GetDword(byteorder, fp);
fread(&header.Filler, sizeof(header.Filler), 1, fp);
```

All we need to do now is to pass the byte order of the data being read to the *GetWord*() and *GetDword*() functions. The data is then read correctly from the file stream regardless of the native byte order of the machine on which the functions are executing.

The techniques we've explored for reading a graphics file header can also be used for reading other data structures in a graphics file, such as color maps, page tables, scan-line tables, tags, footers, and even pixel values themselves.

Reading Graphics File Data

In most cases, you will not find any surprises when you read image data from a graphics file. Compressed image data is normally byte-aligned and is simply read one byte at a time from the file and into memory before it is decompressed. Uncompressed image data is often stored only as bytes, even when the pixels are two, three, or four bytes in size.

You will also usually use *fread*(), to read a block of compressed data into a memory buffer that is typically 8K to 32K in size. The compressed data is read from memory a single byte at a time, is decompressed, and the raw data is written either to video memory for display, or to a bitmap array for processing and analysis.

Many bitmap file formats specify that scan lines (or tiles) of 1-bit image data should be padded out to the next byte boundary. This means that, if the width of an image is not a multiple of eight, then you probably have a few extra zeroed bits tacked onto the end of each scan line (or the end and/or bottom of each tile). For example, a 1-bit image with a width of 28 pixels will contain 28 bits of scan-line data followed by four bits of padding, creating a scan line 32 bits in length. The padding allows the next scan line to begin on a byte boundary, rather than in the middle of a byte.

You must determine whether the uncompressed image data contains scan line padding. The file format specification will tell you if padding exists. Usually, the padding is loaded into display memory with the image data, but the size of the display window (the part of display memory actually visible on the screen) must be adjusted so that the padding data is not displayed.

Writing Graphics Data

As you might guess, writing a graphics file is basically the inverse of reading it. Writers may send data directly to an output device, such as a printer, or they may create image files and store data in them.

Writing a Graphics File Header

When you write a graphics file header, you must be careful to initialize all of the fields in the header with the correct data. Initialize reserved fields used for fill and padding with the value 00h, unless the file format specification states otherwise. You must write the header data to the graphics files using the correct byte order for the file format as well.

Because the *GetWord*() and *GetDword*() functions were so handy for correctly reading a header, their siblings *PutWord*() and *PutDword*() must be just as handy for writing one:

```
/*
** Put a 16-bit word in either big- or little-endian byte order.
*/
void PutWord(char byteorder, FILE *fp, WORD w)
{
    if (byteorder == MSB_FIRST)
    {
        fputc((w >> 0x08) & 0xFF, fp);
        fputc( w          & 0xFF, fp);
    }
    else            /* LSB_FIRST */
    {
        fputc( w          & 0xFF, fp);
        fputc((w >> 0x08) & 0xFF, fp);
    }
}


/*
** Put a 32-bit word in either big- or little-endian byte order.
*/
void PutDword(char byteorder, FILE *fp, DWORD w)
{
    if (byteorder == MSB_FIRST)
    {
        fputc((w >> 0x18) & 0xFF, fp);
        fputc((w >> 0x10) & 0xFF, fp);
        fputc((w >> 0x08) & 0xFF, fp);
        fputc( w          & 0xFF, fp);
```

```
    }
    else            /* LSB_FIRST */
    {
        fputc( w           & 0xFF, fp);
        fputc((w >> 0x08) & 0xFF, fp);
        fputc((w >> 0x10) & 0xFF, fp);
        fputc((w >> 0x18) & 0xFF, fp);
    }
}
```

In the following example, we use *fwrite()*, *PutWord()*, and *PutDword()* to write out our header structure. Note that the byteorder argument in *PutWord()* and *PutDword()* indicates the byte order of the file we are writing (in this case, little-endian), and not the byte order of the machine on which the functions are being executed. Also, we indicate in *fopen()* that the output file is being opened for writing in binary mode (wb):

```
typedef struct _Header
{
    DWORD FileId;
    BYTE  Type;
    WORD  Height;
    WORD  Width;
    WORD  Depth;
    CHAR  FileName[81];
    DWORD Flags;
    BYTE  Filler[32];
} HEADER;

int WriteHeader()
{
    HEADER header;
    FILE *fp = fopen("MYFORMAT.FOR", "wb");

    if (fp)
    {
        header.FileId  = 0x91827364;
        header.Type    = 3;
        header.Depth   = 8;
        header.Height  = 512;
        header.Width   = 512;
        strncpy((char *)header.FileName, "MYFORMAT.FOR",
sizeof(header.FileName));
        header.Flags   = 0x04008001;
        memset(&header.Filler, 0, sizeof(header.Filler));
```

```
        PutDword(MSB_FIRST, fp, header.FileId);
        fputc(header.Type, fp);
        PutWord(MSB_FIRST, fp, header.Height);
        PutWord(MSB_FIRST, fp, header.Width);
        PutWord(MSB_FIRST, fp, header.Depth);
        fwrite(&header.FileName, sizeof(header.FileName), 1, fp);
        PutDword(MSB_FIRST, fp, header.Flags);
        fwrite(&header.Filler, sizeof(header.Filler), 1, fp);

        fclose(fp);
        return(0);
    }
    return(1);
}
```

Writing Graphics File Data

Writing binary graphics data can be a little more complex than just making sure you are writing data in the correct byte order. Many formats specify that each scan line is to be padded out to end on a byte or word boundary if they do not naturally do so. When the scan-line data is read from the file, this padding (usually a series of zero bit values) is thrown away, but it must be added again later if the data is written to a file.

Image data that is written uncompressed to a file may require a conversion before it is written. If the data is being written directly from video memory, it may be necessary to convert the orientation of the data from pixels to planes, or from planes to pixels, before writing the data.

If the data is to be stored in a compressed format, the quickest approach is to compress the image data in memory and use *fwrite()* to write the image data to the graphics file. If you don't have a lot of memory to play with, then write out the compressed image data as it is encoded, usually one scan line at a time.

Test Files

How can you be sure that your application supports a particular file format? Test, test, test...

Files adhering to the written format specification, and software applications that work with them, are called *fully conforming*, or just *conforming*. Fully conforming software should always make the conservative choice if there is any ambiguity in the format specification. Of course it's not always clear what conservative means in any specified context, but the point is to not extend the format if given the chance, no matter how tempting the opportunity. In any case, if you write software to manipulate graphics files, you'll need some fully conforming files to test the code.

If you happen to be working with TIFF, GIF, or PCX, files in these formats are often just a phone call away, but beware. Files are not necessarily fully conforming, and there is no central registry of conforming files. In some cases, effort has gone into making sets of canonical test files; for example, some are included in the TIFF distribution.

The trick is to get a wide spectrum of files from a number of sources and to do extensive testing on everything you find—every size, resolution, and variant that can be found. Another strategy is to acquire files created by major applications and test for compatibility. For example, Aldus PageMaker files are often used to test TIFF files. Unfortunately, PageMaker has historically been the source of undocumented de facto TIFF revisions, and testing compatibility with PageMaker-produced TIFF files does not produce wholly accurate results.

Any number of graphics file conversion programs exist which can do screen captures, convert files, and display graphics and images in many different formats. Once again, you are at the mercy of the diligence of the application author.

Remember, too, that it's your responsibility to locate the latest format revisions. We still see new GIF readers, for instance, on all platforms, which fail to support the latest specification. If you simply cannot locate an example of the format you need, your last resort will always be the format creator or caretaker. While this approach is to be used with discretion, and is by no means guaranteed, it sometimes is your only recourse, particularly if the format is very new.

In any case, don't stop coding simply because one variation of an image file format can be read and converted successfully by your application. Test your application using as many variations of the format, and from as many different sources as possible. Have your application do its best to support the image format fully.

Designing Your Own Format

We find it hard to imagine why anyone would think that the world needs another graphics file format. And, in fact, we don't want to give the impression that we're encouraging such behavior. But given the fact that people can and will create new formats, we'd like to leave you with some pointers.

Why Even Consider It?

The truth is that this book does not even begin to include all of the hundreds of more obscure formats, some of which are used only privately and remain inside company walls. Companies wishing the output of their products to remain proprietary will always find a way to do so and thus will continue to develop new formats.

Designing your own format also will help you avoid trouble should use of someone else's format one day be restricted through legal action. Kodak has taken steps to ensure that its Photo CD format remains proprietary, for instance. It has also been active in enforcing that protection through the threat of legal action. Something to remember is that even though many formats may appear to be publicly available, very few actually are.

Of course there are functional reasons for designing your own format. You may decide that an appropriate format doesn't yet exist, for instance, and thus feel compelled to create a new one. Reasoning leading to this decision is always suspect, however, and sending yet another format out into the world might even decrease your market share in this era of increasing interoperability and file sharing. The unfortunate reality is that file formats are usually created to support applications after the fact. In the modern world, marketing decisions and speculation about the future evolution of the supporting operating system and hardware platform play large parts in the development of program specifications from the very start. So we urge you to consider designing your application around a set of existing formats, or at least a format model.

But If You Must . . .

With that said, consider the following guidelines if you persist in designing your own:

- Study everybody else's mistakes. No matter what you think, you're not smart enough to avoid them all, unless you see them first.

- Plan for future revisions. Give plenty of room for future expansion of, and changes to, data. Avoid building limitations into your format that will one day force you to make kludges to support further revisions.

- Keep it simple. The last thing the world needs is another "write-only" format. The object is to make it easy to read, not easy to write.

- Document everything! Use consistent terminology that everyone understands and will continue to understand until the end of time. Number your documentation revisions with the format revisions; that way, it will be obvious if you "forget" to document a new feature.

- Write the format before, not after, your application. Build the application around it. Don't make convenience revisions no matter what the provocation.

- Avoid machine dependencies; at the same time, don't add complications designed to support portability.

- Find some unambiguous means by which a reading application can identify the format.

- Make the specification available. Do not discourage people interested in your format by refusing to supply them with information simply because they are not a registered user of your product. Charge a nominal fee, if you must, but make it available to all. Make identical electronic and printed versions of the specification in some common format like ASCII or PostScript. Place electronic versions on BBSs and FTP sites.

- If your format is truly superior, market, market, market! Write software applications that use your format. Formats gain currency almost entirely through the marketing power of companies and their software. If your format is unique in the way it stores information, and you feel that it fills a niche that other formats don't, then advertise that fact.

- Explicitly place the format in the public domain. If that is too threatening in the context of your company model, allow use with attribution. Do not discourage the spread of your format by including threats about copyright infringement and proprietary information in the specification. This only prevents your format from becoming widely accepted, and it alienates programmers who would otherwise be happy to further your company's plan of world domination for free.

- Develop canonical test files and make them freely available. Mark them as such *in the image*, with your company name, the format type, color model, resolution, and pixel depth at the very least. They will be a good form of advertising for you and your company, and are sure to be widely distributed with no effort on your part.

One Last Word

Remember that there is a lot of code already out there and that there are plenty of libraries available in source form that may be able to supply your needs. Consider this statement from the FAQ (Frequently Asked Questions list) from the *comp.graphics* newsgroup on the Internet:

> Format documents for TIFF, IFF, BIFF, NFF, OFF, FITS, etc. You almost certainly don't need these. Read the [section] on free image manipulation software. Get one or more of these packages and look through

them. Chances are excellent that the image converter you were going to write is already there.

For Further Information

An excellent article concerning the solution to byte-order conversion problems appeared in the now-extinct magazine, *C Gazette*. It was written by a fellow named James D. Murray!

Murray, James D. "Which Endian is Up?," *C Gazette*, Summer, 1990.

## CHAPTER 9

Data Compression

Introduction

Compression is the process used to reduce the physical size of a block of information. In computer graphics, we're interested in reducing the size of a block of graphics data so we can fit more information in a given physical storage space. We also might use compression to fit larger images in a block of memory of a given size. You may find when you examine a particular file format specification that the term *data encoding* is used to refer to algorithms that perform compression. Data encoding is actually a broader term than data compression. Data compression is a type of data encoding, and one that is used to reduce the size of data. Other types of data encoding include encryption (cryptography) and data transmission (e.g., Morse code).

A *compressor*, naturally enough, performs compression, and a *decompressor* reconstructs the original data. Although this may seem obvious, a decompressor can operate only by using knowledge of the compression algorithm used to convert the original data into its compressed form. What this means in practice is that there is no way for you to avoid understanding the compression algorithms in the market today if you are interested in manipulating data files. At a minimum, you need a good general knowledge of the conceptual basis of the algorithms.

If you read through a number of specification documents, you'll find that almost every format incorporates some kind of compression method, no matter how rudimentary. You'll also find that only a few different compression schemes are in common use throughout the industry. The most common of these schemes are variants of the following methods, which we discuss in the sections below.

- Run-length Encoding (RLE)

- Lempel-Ziv-Welch (LZW)

- CCITT (one type of CCITT compression is a variant on Huffman encoding)

- Discrete Cosine Transform (DCT) (used in the JPEG compression we discuss in this chapter)

In addition, we discuss pixel packing, which is not a compression method per se, but is an efficient way to store data in contiguous bytes of memory.

Data compression works somewhat differently for the three common types of graphics data: bitmap, vector, and metafile. In bitmap files, *only* the image data is compressed; the header and any other data (color map, footer, and so on) are always left uncompressed. This uncompressed data makes up only a small portion of a typical bitmap file.

Vector files normally do not incorporate a native form of data compression. Vector files store a mathematical description of an image rather than the image data itself. There are reasons why vector files are rarely compressed:

- The expression of the image data is already compact in design, so data compression would have little effect.

- Vector images are typically slow to read in the first place; adding the overhead of decompression would make ending them still slower.

If a vector file is compressed at all, you will usually find the entire file compressed, header and all.

In metafiles, data compression schemes often resemble those used to compress bitmap files, depending upon the type of data the metafiles contain.

It's important to realize that compression algorithms do not describe a specific disk file format. Many programmers ask vendors or newsgroups for specifications for the CCITT or JPEG file formats. There are no such specifications. Compression algorithms define only how data is encoded, not how it is stored on disk. For detailed information on how data is stored on disk, look to an actual image file format specification, such as BMP or GIF, which will define file headers, byte order, and other issues not covered by discussions of compression algorithms. More complex formats, such as TIFF, may incorporate several different compression algorithms.

The following sections introduce the terms used in discussions of data compression and each of the main types of data compression algorithms used for graphics file formats today.

Data Compression Terminology

This section describes the terms you'll encounter when you read about data compression schemes in this chapter and in graphics file format specifications.

The terms *unencoded data* and *raw data* describe data before it has been compressed, and the terms *encoded data* and *compressed data* describe the same information after it has been compressed.

The term *compression ratio* is used to refer to the ratio of uncompressed data to compressed data. Thus, a 10:1 compression ratio is considered five times more efficient than 2:1, and data through 100 of the image before finding the ten lines it needed. Of course compressed using an algorithm yielding 10:1 compression is five times smaller than the same data compressed using an algorithm yielding 2:1 compression. In practice, because only image data is normally compressed, analysis of compression ratios provided by various algorithms must take into account the absolute sizes of the files tested.

Physical and Logical Compression

Compression algorithms are often described as squeezing, squashing, crunching, or imploding data, but these are not very good descriptions of what is actually happening. Although the major use of compression is to make data use less disk space, compression does not actually physically cram the data into a smaller size package in any meaningful sense.

Instead, compression algorithms are used to reencode data into a different, more compact representation conveying the same information. In other words, fewer words are used to convey the same meaning, without actually saying the same thing.

The distinction between *physical* and *logical compression* methods is made on the basis of how the data is compressed, or, more precisely, how the data is rearranged into a more compact form. Physical compression is performed on data exclusive of the information it contains; it only translates a series of bits from one pattern to another, more compact one. While the resulting compressed data may be related to the original data in a mechanical way, that relationship will not be obvious to us humans.

Physical compression methods typically produce strings of gibberish, at least relative to the information content of the original data. The resulting block of compressed data is smaller than the original because the physical compression algorithm has removed the redundancy that existed in the data itself. All the compression methods discussed in this chapter are physical methods.

Logical compression is accomplished through the process of logical substitution—that is, replacing one alphabetic, numeric, or binary symbol with another. Changing "United States of America" to "USA" is a good example of logical substitution, because "USA" is derived directly from the information contained in the string "United States of America," and retains some of its meaning. In a similar fashion "can't" can be logically substituted for "cannot." Logical compression works only on data at the character level or higher and is based exclusively on information contained within the data. Logical compression itself is not used in image data compression.

Symmetrical and Asymmetrical Compression

Compression algorithms can also be divided into two categories: *symmetric* and *asymmetric*. A symmetric compression method uses roughly the same algorithms, and performs the same amount of work, for compression as it does for decompression. For example, a data transmission application where compression and decompression are both being done on the fly will usually require a symmetric algorithm for the greatest efficiency.

Asymmetric methods require substantially more work to go in one direction than they require in the other. Usually, the compression step takes far more time and system resources than the decompression step. In the real world this makes sense. For example, if we are making an image database in which an image will be compressed once for storage, but decompressed many times for viewing, then we can probably tolerate a much longer time for compression than for decompression. An asymmetric algorithm which uses much CPU time for compression, but is quick to decode, would work well in this case.

Algorithms which are asymmetric in the other direction are less common but have some applications. In making routine backup files, for example, we fully expect that many of the backup files will never be read. A fast compression algorithm that is expensive to decompress might be useful in this case.

Adaptive, Semi-adaptive, and Non-adaptive Encoding

Certain dictionary-based encoders, such as CCITT compression algorithms (see the section later in this chapter called "CCITT (Huffman) Encoding") are designed to compress only specific types of data. These *non-adaptive encoders* contain a static dictionary of predefined substrings that are known to occur with high frequency in the data to be encoded. A non-adaptive encoder designed specifically to compress English language text would contain a dictionary with predefined substrings such as "and", "but", "of", and "the", because these substrings appear very frequently in English text.

An *adaptive encoder*, on the other hand, carries no preconceived heuristics about the data it is to compress. Adaptive compressors, such as LZW, achieve data independence by building their dictionaries completely from scratch. They do not have a predefined list of static substrings and instead build phrases dynamically as they encode.

Adaptive compression is capable of adjusting to any type of data input and of returning output using the best possible compression ratio. This is in contrast to non-adaptive compressors, which are capable of efficiently encoding only a very select type of input data for which they are designed.

A mixture of these two dictionary encoding methods is the *semi-adaptive encoding method*. A *semi-adaptive encoder* makes an initial pass over the data to build the dictionary and a second pass to perform the actual encoding. Using this method, an optimal dictionary is constructed before any encoding is actually performed.

Lossy and Lossless Compression

The majority of compression schemes we deal with in this chapter are called *lossless*. What does this mean? When a chunk of data is compressed and then decompressed, the original information contained in the data is preserved. No data has been lost or discarded; the data has not been changed in any way.

Lossy compression methods, however, throw away some of the data in an image in order to achieve compression ratios better than that of most lossless compression methods. Some methods contain elaborate heuristic algorithms that adjust themselves to give the maximum amount of compression while changing as little of the visible detail of the image as possible. Other less elegant algorithms might simply discard a least-significant portion of each pixel, and, in terms of image quality, hope for the best.

The terms lossy and lossless are sometimes erroneously used to describe the quality of a compressed image. Some people assume that if any image data is lost, this could only degrade the image. The assumption is that we would never want to lose any data at all. This is certainly true if our data consists of text or numerical data that is associated with a file, such as a spreadsheet or a chapter of our great American novel. In graphics applications, however, there are circumstances where data loss may be acceptable, and even recommended.

In practice, a small change in the value of a pixel may well be invisible, especially in high-resolution images where a single pixel is barely visible anyway. Images containing 256 or more colors may have selective pixel values changed with no noticeable visible effect on the image.

In black-and-white images, however, there is obviously no such thing as a small change in a pixel's value: each pixel can only be black or white. Even in black-and-white images, however, if the change simply moves the boundary between a black and a white region by one pixel, the change may be difficult to see and therefore acceptable.

As mentioned in Chapter 2, *Computer Graphics Basics,* the human eye is limited in the number of colors it can distinguish simultaneously, particularly if those colors are not immediately adjacent in the image or are sharply contrasting. An intelligent compression algorithm can take advantage of these limitations, analyze an image on this basis, and achieve significant data size reductions based on the removal of color information not easily noticed by most people.

In case this sounds too much like magic, rest assured that much effort has gone into the development of so-called lossy compression schemes in recent years, and many of these algorithms can achieve substantial compression ratios while retaining good quality images. This is an active field of research, and we are likely to see further developments as our knowledge of the human visual system evolves, and as results from the commercial markets regarding acceptance of lossy images make their way back to academia.

For more information about lossy compression, see the JPEG section later in this chapter.

Pixel Packing

Pixel packing is not so much a method of data compression as it is an efficient way to store data in contiguous bytes of memory. Most bitmap formats use pixel packing to conserve the amount of memory or disk space required to store a bitmap. If you are working with image data that contains four bits per pixel, you might find it convenient to store each pixel in a byte of memory, because a byte is typically the smallest addressable area of memory on most computer systems. You would quickly notice, however, that by using this arrangement, half of each byte is not being used by the pixel data (shown in Figure 9-1, a). Image data containing 4096 4-bit pixels will require 4096 bytes of memory for storage, half of which is wasted.

To save memory, you could resort to pixel packing; instead of storing one 4-bit pixel per byte, you could store two 4-bit pixels per byte (shown in Figure 9-1, b). The size of memory required to hold the 4-bit, 4096-pixel image drops from 4096 bytes to 2048 bytes, only half the memory that was required before.

Pixel packing may seem like common sense, but it is not without cost. Memory-based display hardware usually organizes image data as an array of bytes, each storing one pixel or less. If this is the case, it will actually be faster to store only

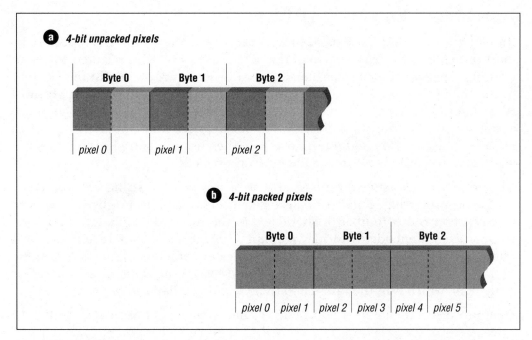

a *4-bit unpacked pixels*

Byte 0　　Byte 1　　Byte 2

pixel 0　　pixel 1　　pixel 2

b *4-bit packed pixels*

Byte 0　　Byte 1　　Byte 2

pixel 0 | pixel 1 | pixel 2 | pixel 3 | pixel 4 | pixel 5

FIGURE 9-1:　*Pixel packing*

one 4-bit pixel per byte and read this data directly into memory in the proper format rather than to store two 4-bit pixels per byte, which requires masking and shifting each byte of data to extract and write the proper pixel values. The tradeoff is faster read and write times versus reduced size of the image file. This is a good example of one of the costs of data compression.

Compression always has a cost. In this case, the cost is in the time it takes to unpack each byte into two 4-bit pixels. Other factors may come into play when decompressing image data: buffers need to be allocated and managed; CPU-intensive operations must be executed and serviced; scan line bookkeeping must be kept current. If you are writing a file reader, you usually have no choice; you *must* support all compression schemes defined in the format specification. If you are writing a file writer, however, you always need to identify the costs and tradeoffs involved in writing compressed files.

At one time in the history of computing, there was no decision to be made; disk space was scarce and expensive, so image files needed to be compressed. Now, however, things are different. Hard disks are relatively inexpensive, and alternate distribution and storage media (CD-ROM for instance) are even more so. More and more applications now write image files uncompressed by default. You need to examine carefully the target market of your application before deciding whether to compress or not.

Run-length Encoding (RLE)

Run-length encoding is a data compression algorithm that is supported by most bitmap file formats, such as TIFF, BMP, and PCX. RLE is suited for compressing any type of data regardless of its information content, but the content of the data will affect the compression ratio achieved by RLE. Although most RLE algorithms cannot achieve the high compression ratios of the more advanced compression methods, RLE is both easy to implement and quick to execute, making it a good alternative to either using a complex compression algorithm or leaving your image data uncompressed.

RLE works by reducing the physical size of a repeating string of characters. This repeating string, called a *run*, is typically encoded into two bytes. The first byte represents the number of characters in the run and is called the *run count* In practice, an encoded run may contain 1 to 128 or 256 characters which is often stored in the run count as the number of characters minus one (a value in the range of 0 to 127 or 255). The second byte is the value of the character in the run, which is in the range of 0 to 255, and is called the *run value*

Uncompressed, a character run of 15 A characters would normally require 15 bytes to store:

    AAAAAAAAAAAAAAA

The same string after RLE encoding would require only two bytes:

    15A

The 15A code generated to represent the character string is called an *RLE packet*. Here, the first byte, 15, is the run count and contains the number of repetitions. The second byte, A, is the run value and contains the actual repeated value in the run.

A new packet is generated each time the run character changes, or each time the number of characters in the run exceeds the maximum count. Assume that our 15-character string now contains four different character runs:

    AAAAAAbbbXXXXXt

Using run-length encoding this could be compressed into four 2-byte packets:

    6A3b5X1t

Thus, after run-length encoding, the 15-byte string would require only eight bytes of data to represent the string, as opposed to the original 15 bytes. In this case, run-length encoding yielded a compression ratio of almost 2 to 1.

Long runs are rare in certain types of data. For example, ASCII plaintext (such as the text on the pages of this book) seldom contains long runs. In the previous example, the last run (containing the character t) was only a single character in length; a 1-character run is still a run. Both a run count and a run value must be written for every 2-character run. To encode a run in RLE requires a minimum of two characters worth of information; therefore, a run of single characters actually takes more space. For the same reasons, data consisting entirely of 2-character runs remains the same size after RLE encoding.

In our example, encoding the single character at the end as two bytes did not noticeably hurt our compression ratio because there were so many long character runs in the rest of the data. But observe how RLE encoding doubles the size of the following 14-character string:

```
Xtmprsqzntwlfb
```

After RLE encoding, this string becomes:

```
1X1t1m1p1r1s1q1z1n1t1w1l1f1b
```

RLE schemes are simple and fast, but their compression efficiency depends on the type of image data being encoded. A black-and-white image that is mostly white, such as the page of a book, will encode very well, due to the large amount of contiguous data that is all the same color. An image with many colors that is very busy in appearance, however, such as a photograph, will not encode very well. This is because the complexity of the image is expressed as a large number of different colors. And because of this complexity there will be relatively few runs of the same color.

Variants on Run-length Encoding

There are a number of variants of run-length encoding. Image data is normally run-length encoded in a sequential process that treats the image data as a 1-dimensional stream, rather than as a 2-dimensional map of data. In sequential processing, a bitmap is encoded starting at the upper left corner and proceeding from left to right across each scan line (the X axis) to the bottom right corner of the bitmap (shown in Figure 9-2, a). But, alternative RLE schemes can also be written to encode data down the length of a bitmap (the Y axis) along the columns (shown in Figure 9-2, b), to encode a bitmap into 2-dimensional tiles (shown in Figure 9-2, c), or even to encode pixels on a diagonal in a zig-zag fashion (shown in Figure 9-2, d). Odd RLE variants such as this last one might be used in highly specialized applications, but are usually quite rare.

Another seldom-encountered RLE variant is a lossy run-length encoding algorithm. RLE algorithms are normally lossless in their operation. However, discarding data during the encoding process, usually by zeroing-out one or two least significant bits in each pixel, can increase compression ratios without adversely affecting the appearance of very complex images. This RLE variant

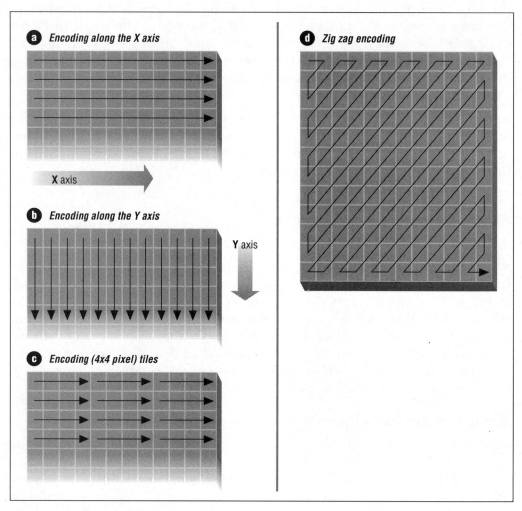

FIGURE 9-2: *Run-length encoding variants*

works well only with real-world images that contain many subtle variations in pixel values.

Make sure that your RLE encoder always stops at the end of each scan line of bitmap data that is being encoded. There are several benefits to doing so. Encoding only a simple scan line at a time means that only a minimal buffer size is required. Encoding only a simple line at a time also prevents a problem known as *cross-coding*.

Cross-coding is the merging of scan lines that occur when the encoded process loses the distinction between the original scan lines. If the data of the individual scan lines is merged by the RLE algorithm, the point where one scan line stopped and another began is lost, or at least is very hard to detect quickly.

Cross-coding is sometimes done, although we advise against it. It may buy a few extra bytes of data compression, but it complicates the decoding process, adding time cost. For bitmap file formats, this technique defeats the purpose of organizing a bitmap image by scan lines in the first place. Although many file format specifications explicitly state that scan lines should be individually encoded, many applications encode image data as a continuous stream, ignoring scan line boundaries.

If you have ever encountered an RLE-encoded image file that could be displayed using one application but not using another, cross-coding is typically the problem. To be safe, decoding and display applications must take cross-coding into account and not assume that an encoded run will always stop at the end of a scan line.

When an encoder is encoding an image, an end-of-scan-line marker is placed in the encoded data to inform the decoding software that the end of the scan line has been reached. This marker is usually a unique packet, explicitly defined in the RLE specification, which cannot be confused with any other data packets. End-of-scan-line markers are usually only one byte in length, so they don't adversely contribute to the size of the encoded data.

Encoding scan lines individually has advantages when an application needs to use only part of an image. Let's say that an image contains 512 scan lines, and we need to display only lines 100 to 110. If we did not know where the scan lines started and ended in the encoded image data, our application would have to decode lines one through 100 of the image before finding the ten lines it needed. Of course, if the transitions between scan lines were marked with some sort of easily recognizable delimiting marker, the application could simply read through the encoded data, counting markers until it came to the lines it needed. But this approach would be a rather inefficient one.

Another option for locating the starting point of any particular scan line in a block of encoded data is to construct a scan-line table. A scan-line table usually contains one element for every scan line in the image, and each element holds the offset value of its corresponding scan line. To find the first RLE packet of scan line 10, all a decoder needs to do is seek to the offset position value stored in the tenth element of the scan-line lookup table. A scan-line table could also hold the number of bytes used to encode each scan line. Using this method, to find the first RLE packet of scan line 10, your decoder would add together the values of the first nine elements of the scan-line table. The first packet for scan line 10 would start at this byte offset from the beginning of the RLE-encoded image data.

Bit-, Byte-, and Pixel-level RLE Schemes

The basic flow of all RLE algorithms is the same, as illustrated in Figure 9-3.

The parts of run-length encoding algorithms that differ are the decisions that are made based on the type of data being decoded (such as the length of data runs). RLE schemes used to encode bitmap graphics are usually divided into classes by the type of atomic (that is, most fundamental) elements that they encode. The three classes used by most graphics file formats are bit-, byte-, and pixel-level RLE.

Bit-level RLE schemes encode runs of multiple bits in a scan line and ignore byte and word boundaries. Only monochrome (black and white), 1-bit images contain a sufficient number of bit runs to make this class of RLE encoding efficient. A typical bit-level RLE scheme encodes runs of one to 128 bits in length in a single-byte packet. The seven least significant bits contain the run count minus one, and the most significant bit contains the value of the bit run, either 0 or 1 (shown in Figure 9-4, a). A run longer than 128 pixels is split across several RLE-encoded packets.

Byte-level RLE schemes encode runs of identical byte values, ignoring individual bits and word boundaries within a scan line. The most common byte-level RLE scheme encodes runs of bytes into 2-byte packets. The first byte contains the run count of 0 to 255, and the second byte contains the value of the byte run. It is also common to supplement the 2-byte encoding scheme with the ability to store literal, unencoded runs of bytes within the encoded data stream as well.

In such a scheme, the seven least significant bits of the first byte hold the run count minus one, and the most significant bit of the first byte is the indicator of the type of run that follows the run count byte (shown in Figure 9-4, b). If the most significant bit is set to 1, it denotes an encoded run (shown in Figure 9-4, c). Encoded runs are decoded by reading the run value and repeating it the number of times indicated by the run count. If the most significant bit is set to 0, a *literal run* is indicated, meaning that the next run count bytes are read literally from the encoded image data (shown in Figure 9-4, d). The run count byte then holds a value in the range of 0 to 127 (the run count minus one). Byte-level RLE schemes are good for image data that is stored as one byte per pixel.

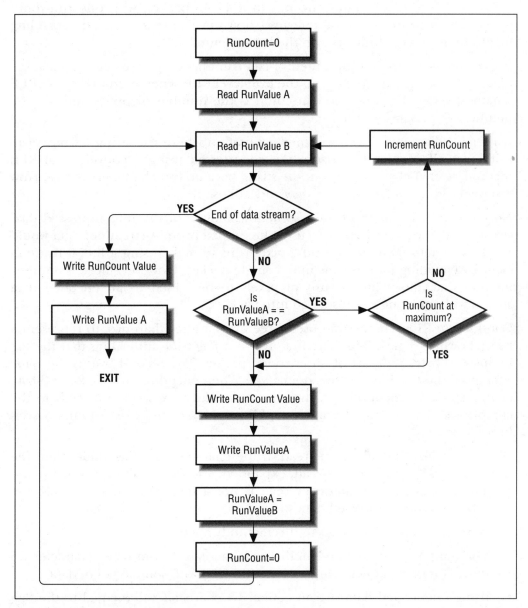

FIGURE 9-3: *Basic run-length encoding flow*

Pixel-level RLE schemes are used when two or more consecutive bytes of image data are used to store single pixel values. At the pixel level, bits are ignored, and bytes are counted only to identify each pixel value. Encoded packet sizes vary depending upon the size of the pixel values being encoded. The number of bits or bytes per pixel is stored in the image file header. A run of image data stored as 3-byte pixel values encodes to a 4-byte packet, with one run-count byte followed by three run-value bytes (shown in Figure 9-4, e). The encoding method remains the same as with the byte-oriented RLE.

It is also possible to employ a literal pixel run encoding by using the most significant bit of the run count as in the byte-level RLE scheme. In pixel-level RLE schemes, remember that the run count is the number of pixels and not the number of bytes in the run.

Earlier in this section, we examined a situation where the string "Xtmprsqzntwlfb" actually doubled in size when compressed using a conventional RLE method. Each 1-character run in the string became two characters in size. How can we avoid this *negative compression* and still use RLE?

Normally, an RLE method must somehow analyze of the uncompressed data stream to determine whether to use a literal pixel run. A stream of data would need to contain many on 1- and 2-pixel runs to make using a literal run efficient by encoding all the runs into a single packet. However, there is another method that allows literal runs of pixels to be added to an encoded data stream without being encapsulated into packets.

Consider an RLE scheme that uses three bytes, rather than two, to represent a run (shown in Figure 9-5). The first byte is a *flag value* indicating that the following two bytes are part of an encoded packet. The second byte is the *count value*, and the third byte is the *run value*.e When encoding, if a 1-, 2-, or 3-byte character run is encountered, the character values are written directly to the compressed data stream. Because no additional characters are written, no overhead is incurred.

When decoding, a character is read; if the character is a flag value, then the run count and run values are read, expanded, and the resulting run written to the data stream. If the character read is not a flag value, then it is written directly to the uncompressed data stream.

There two potential drawbacks to this method:

- The minimum useful run-length size is increased from three characters to four. This could affect compression efficiency with some types of data.

- If the unencoded data stream contains a character value equal to the flag value, it must be compressed into a 3-byte encoded packet as a run length of one. This prevents erroneous flag values from occurring in the compressed data stream. If many of these flag value characters are present, then poor compression will result. The RLE algorithm must therefore use a flag value that rarely occurs in the uncompressed data stream.

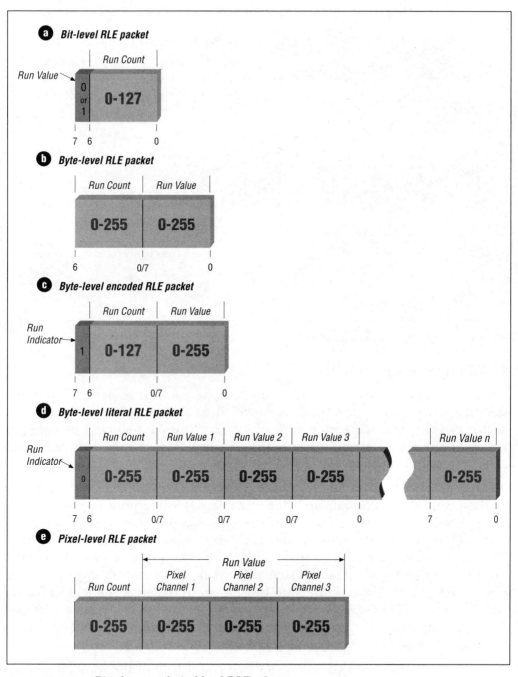

FIGURE 9-4: *Bit-, byte-, and pixel-level RLE schemes*

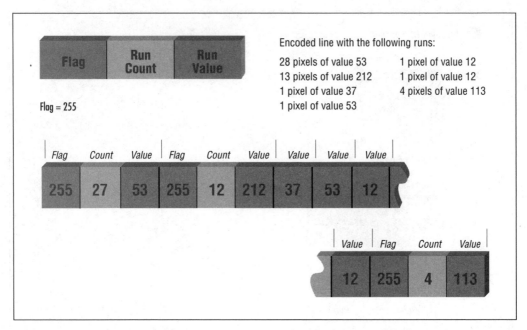

Flag = 255

Encoded line with the following runs:

28 pixels of value 53	1 pixel of value 12
13 pixels of value 212	1 pixel of value 12
1 pixel of value 37	4 pixels of value 113
1 pixel of value 53	

FIGURE 9-5: *RLE scheme with three bytes*

Vertical Replication Packets

Some RLE schemes use other types of encoding packets to increase compression efficiency. One of the most useful of these packets is the *repeat scan line packet*, also known as the *vertical replication packet*. This packet does not store any real scan-line data; instead, it just indicates a repeat of the previous scan line. Here's an example of how this works.

Assume that you have an image containing a scan line 640 bytes wide and that all the pixels in the scan line are the same color. It will require 10 bytes to run-length encode it, assuming that up to 128 bytes can be encoded per packet and that each packet is two bytes in size. Let's also assume that the first 100 scan lines of this image are all the same color. At 10 bytes per scan line, that would produce 1000 bytes of run-length encoded data. If we instead used a vertical replication packet that was only one byte in size (possibly a run-length packet with a run count of 0) we would simply run-length encode the first scan line (10 bytes) and follow it with 99 vertical replication packets (99 bytes). The resulting run-length encoded data would then only be 109 bytes in size.

If the vertical replication packet contains a count byte of the number of scan lines to repeat, we would need only one packet with a count value of 99. The resulting 10 bytes of scan-line data packets and two bytes of vertical replication packets would encode the first 100 scan lines of the image, containing 64,000 bytes, as only 12 bytes—a considerable savings.

Figure 9-6 illustrates 1- and 2-byte vertical replication packets.

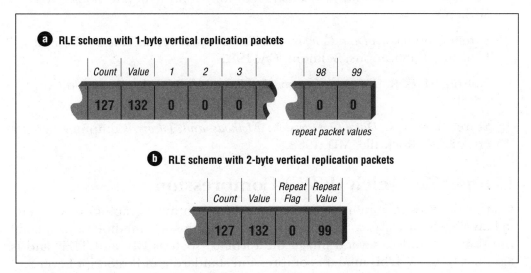

FIGURE 9-6: *RLE scheme with 1- and 2-byte vertical replication packets*

Unfortunately, definitions of vertical replication packets are application dependent. At least two common formats, WordPerfect Graphics Metafile (WPG) and GEM Raster (IMG), employ the use of repeat scan line packets to enhance data compression performance. WPG uses a simple 2-byte packet scheme, as previously described. If the first byte of an RLE packet is zero, then this is a vertical replication packet. The next byte that follows indicates the number of times to repeat the previous scan line.

The GEM Raster format is more complicated. The byte sequence, 00h 00h FFh, must appear at the beginning of an encoded scan line to indicate a vertical replication packet. The byte that follows this sequence is the number of times to repeat the previous scan line minus one.

NOTE

Many of the concepts we have covered in this section are not limited to RLE. All bitmap compression algorithms need to consider the concepts of cross-coding, sequential processing, efficient data encoding based on the data being encoded, and ways to detect and avoid negative compression.

For Further Information About RLE

Most books on data compression have information on run-length encoding algorithms. The following references all contain information on RLE:

Held, Gilbert. *Data Compression: Techniques and Applications, Hardware and Software Considerations*, second edition, John Wiley & Sons, New York, NY, 1987.

Lynch, Thomas D. *Data Compression Techniques and Applications*, Lifetime Learning Publications, Belmont, CA, 1985.

Nelson, Mark R. *The Data Compression Book*, M&T Books, Redwood City, CA, 1991.

Storer, James A. *Data Compression: Methods and Theory*, Computer Science Press, Rockville, MD, 1988.

Lempel-Ziv-Welch (LZW) Compression

One of the most common algorithms used in computer graphics is the Lempel-Ziv-Welch, or LZW, compression scheme. This lossless method of data compression is found in several image file formats, such as GIF and TIFF, and is also part of the V.42bis modem compression standard and PostScript Level 2.

In 1977, Abraham Lempel and Jakob Ziv created the first of what we now call the LZ family of substitutional compressors. The LZ77 compression algorithms are commonly found in text compression and archiving programs, such as *compress, zoo, lha, pkzip,* and *arj*. The LZ78 compression algorithms are more commonly used to compress binary data, such as bitmaps.

In 1984, while working for Unisys, Terry Welch modified the LZ78 compressor for implementation in high-performance disk controllers. The result was the LZW algorithm that is commonly found today.

LZW is a general compression algorithm capable of working on almost any type of data. It is generally fast in both compressing and decompressing data and does not require the use of floating-point operations. Also, because LZW writes compressed data as bytes and not as words, LZW-encoded output can be identical on both big-endian and little-endian systems, although you may still encounter bit order and fill order problems. (See Chapter 6, *Platform Dependencies,* for a discussion of such systems.)

LZW is referred to as a *substitutional* or *dictionary-based encoding algorithm.* The algorithm builds a *data dictionary* (also called a *translation table* or *string table*) of data occurring in an uncompressed data stream. Patterns of data (*substrings*) are identified in the data stream and are matched to entries in the dictionary.

If the substring is not present in the dictionary, a code phrase is created based on the data content of the substring, and it is stored in the dictionary. The phrase is then written to the compressed output stream.

When a reoccurrence of a substring is identified in the data, the phrase of the substring already stored in the dictionary is written to the output. Because the phrase value has a physical size which is smaller than the substring it represents, data compression is achieved.

Decoding LZW data is the reverse of encoding. The decompressor reads a code from the encoded data stream and adds the code to the data dictionary if it is not already there. The code is then translated into the string it represents and is written to the uncompressed output stream.

LZW goes beyond most dictionary-based compressors in that it is not necessary to preserve the dictionary to decode the LZW data stream. This can save quite a bit of space with storing the LZW-encoded data. When compressing text files, LZW initializes the first 256 entries of the dictionary with the 8-bit ASCII character set (values 00h through FFh) as phrases. These phrases represent all possible single-byte values that may occur in the data stream, and all substrings are in turn built from these phrases. Because both LZW encoders and decoders begin with dictionaries initialized to these values, a decoder need not have the original dictionary and instead will build a duplicate dictionary as it decodes.

TIFF, among other file formats, applies the same method for graphic files. In TIFF, the pixel data is packed into bytes before being presented to LZW, so an LZW source byte might be a pixel value, part of a pixel value, or several pixel values, depending on the image's bit depth and number of color channels.

GIF requires each LZW input symbol to be a pixel value. Because GIF allows 1- to 8-bit deep images, there are between two and 256 LZW input symbols in GIF, and the LZW dictionary is initialized accordingly. It is irrelevant how the pixels might have been packed into storage originally; LZW will deal with them as a sequence of symbols.

The TIFF approach does not work very well for odd-size pixels, because packing into bytes creates byte sequences that do not match the original pixel sequences, so any patterns in the pixels are obscured. If pixel boundaries and byte boundaries agree (e.g. two 4-bit pixels per byte, or one 16-bit pixel every two bytes), then TIFF's method works well.

The GIF approach works better for odd-size bit depths, but it is difficult to extend it to more than eight bits per pixel because the LZW dictionary must become very large to achieve useful compression on large input alphabets.

Noise Removal and Differencing

LZW does a very good job of compressing image data with a wide variety of pixel depths. 1-, 8-, and 24-bit images all compress at least as well as they do using RLE encoding schemes. Noisy images, however, can degrade the compression effectiveness of LZW significantly. Removing noise from an image, usually by zeroing out one or two of the least significant bit planes of the image, is recommended to increase compression efficiency. In other words, if your data does not compress well in its present form, then transform it to a different form that does compress well.

One method that is used to make data more "compressible" by reducing the amount of extraneous information in an image is called *differencing*. The idea is that unrelated data may be easily converted by an invertible transform into a form that can be more efficiently compressed by an encoding algorithm. Differencing accomplishes this using the fact that adjacent pixels in many continuous-tone images vary only slightly in value. If we replace the value of a pixel with the difference between the pixel and the adjacent pixel, we will reduce the amount of information stored, without losing any data.

With 1-bit monochrome and 8-bit gray-scale images, the pixel values themselves are differenced. RGB pixels must have each of their color channels differenced separately, rather than the absolute value of the RGB pixels' differences (difference red from red, green from green, and blue from blue).

Differencing is usually applied in a horizontal plane across scan lines. In the following code example, the algorithm starts at the last pixel on the first scan line of the bitmap. The difference between the last two pixels in the line is calculated, and the last pixel is set to this value. The algorithm then moves to the next to last pixel and continues up the scan line and down the bitmap until finished, as shown in the following pseudo-code:

```
/* Horizontally difference a bitmap */
for (Line = 0; Line < NumberOfLines; Line++)
    for (Pixel = NumberOfPixelsPerLine - 1; Pixel >= 1; Pixel—)
        Bitmap[Line][Pixel] -= Bitmap[Line][Pixel-1];
```

Vertical and 2-dimensional differencing may also be accomplished in the same way. The type of differencing used will have varied effectiveness depending upon the content of the image. And, regardless of the method used, differenced images compress much more efficiently using LZW.

Variations on the LZW Algorithm

Several variations of the LZW algorithm increase its efficiency in some applications. One common variation uses index pointers that vary in length, usually starting at nine bits and growing upward to 12 or 13 bits. When an index pointer of a particular length has been used up, another bit is tacked on to increase precision.

Another popular variation of LZW compressors involves constantly monitoring the compression process for any drop in efficiency. If a drop is noted, the least recently used (LRU) phrases in the dictionary are discarded to make room for new phrases, or the entire dictionary is discarded and rebuilt.

The LZMW variant on the LZW compression method builds phrases by concatenating two phrases together, rather than by concatenating the current phrase and the next character of data. This causes a quicker buildup of longer strings at the cost of a more complex data dictionary.

LZW is a simple algorithm that is difficult to implement efficiently. Deciding when to discard phrases from the dictionary and even how to search the data dictionary during encoding (using a hashing or tree-based scheme) is necessary to improve efficiency and speed.

Variations on the standard LZW algorithm are more common than a programmer may realize. For example, the TIFF and GIF formats use the standard features of the LZW algorithm, such as a Clear code (the indication to discard the string table), EOF code (End Of File), and a 12-bit limit on encoded symbol width. However, GIF treats each pixel value as a separate input symbol. Therefore, the size of the input alphabet, the starting compressed-symbol width, and the values of the Clear and EOF codes will vary depending on the pixel depth of the image being compressed.

GIF also stores compressed codes with the least significant bit first, regardless of the native bit order of the machine on which the algorithm is implemented. When two codes appear in the same byte, the first code is in the lower bits. When a code crosses a byte boundary, its least significant bits appear in the earlier bytes.

TIFF's LZW variation always reads 8-bit input symbols from the uncompressed data regardless of the pixel depth. Each symbol may therefore contain one pixel, more than one pixel, or only part of a pixel, depending upon the depth of the pixels in the image. TIFF always stores compressed codes with the most significant bit first, the opposite of GIF. (Don't confuse the byte-order indicator in the TIFF header, or the value of the FillOrder tag, with the bit order of the LZW compressed data. In a TIFF file, LZW-compressed data is always stored most significant bit first.)

TIFF LZW also contains a bit of a kludge. Compressed code widths are required to be incremented one code sooner than is really necessary. For example, the compressor changes from 9-bit to 10-bit codes after adding code 511 to its table rather than waiting until code 512 is added, thus wasting one bit.

We understand that the explanation for this practice is that the LZW implementation supplied by Aldus in Revision 5.0 of the TIFF Developer's Toolkit contained this bug, although the TIFF 5.0 specification itself specified the LZW algorithm correctly. By the time the problem was identified (by Sam Leffler, the head of the TIFF Advisory Committee), too many applications existed that used the erroneous implementation, and there was no way to identify incorrectly-encoded LZW data. The solution was simply to change the TIFF specification to require this "variation" in the TIFF algorithm, rather than to change the code and break all existing TIFF LZW applications and regard all previously created TIFF 5.0 LZW images as incorrect and useless.

Patent Restrictions

The LZW compression method is patented both by Unisys (4,558,302) and by IBM (4,814,746). Unisys requires that all hardware developers who wish to use LZW purchase a one-time licensing fee for its use. How Unisys or IBM enforces the use of LZW in software-only applications is not clear. Further information on this subject can be obtained from the following source:

> Welch Licensing Department
> Office of the General Counsel
> M/S C1SW19
> Unisys Corporation
> Blue Bell, PA 19424 USA

The LZ77 algorithm is subject to a number of patents. Several of these patents overlap, or even duplicate, other patents pertaining to LZ77. Here is some history in case you need it:

- The original LZ77 algorithm was patented (4,464,650) in 1981 by Lempel, Ziv, Cohen, and Eastman.

- A patent (4,906,991) was obtained by E.R. Fiala and D.H. Greene in 1990 for a variation of LZ77 using a tree data dictionary structure.

- IBM obtained a patent (5,001,478) in 1991 for a variation combining the LZ77 history buffer with the LZ78 lexicon buffer.

- Phil Katz (of pkzip fame) owns a 1991 patent (5,051,745) on LZ77 using sorted hash tables when the tables are smaller than the window size.

- Various patents for LZ77 using hashing are also held by Robert Jung (5,140,321), Chambers (5,155,484), and Stac Inc. (5,016,009).

- Stac also owns the patent (4,701,745) for the LZ77 variant LZRW1. Both of the Stac patents are the basis of the lawsuit between Stac and Microsoft over the file compression feature found in MS-DOS 6.0.

For Further Information About LZW

Many books on data compression contain information on the LZ and LZW compression algorithms. The first reference below is the definitive source for a very general explanation about the LZW algorithm itself and does not focus specifically on bitmap image data:

Welch, T. A. "A Technique for High Performance Data Compression," *IEEE Computer*, Volume 17, Number 6, June 1984.

The TIFF specification (both revisions 5.0 and 6.0) contains an explanation of the TIFF variation on LZW compression. Refer to the "For Further Information" section of the TIFF article in Part II of this book for information and see the CD-ROM for the specification itself.

The following articles and manuscripts are also specifically related to LZW:

Bell, Timothy C. "Better OPM/L Text Compression," *IEEE Transactions on Communications*, V34N12 (December 1986): 1176-1182.

Bernstein, Daniel J. *Y coding, Draft 4b*, March 19, 1991. Manuscript part of the Yabba Y Coding package.

Blackstock, Steve. *LZW and GIF Explained*, Manuscript in the public domain, 1987.

Montgomery, Bob. *LZW Compression Used to Encode/Decode a GIF File*, Manuscript in the public domain, 1988.

Nelson, Mark R. "LZW Data Compression," *Dr. Dobbs Journal*, 156, October 1989, pp. 29-36.

Phillips, Dwayne. "LZW Data Compression," *The Computer Applications Journal*, Circuit Cellar Ink, 27, June/July 1992, pp. 36-48.

Thomborson, Clark. "The V.42bis standard for data-compressing modems,"*IEEE Micro*, October, 1992, pp. 41-53.

Ziv, J. and A. Lempel. "A Universal Algorithm for Sequential Data Compression," *IEEE Transactions on Information Theory*, 23(3), 1977, pp. 337-343.

Ziv, J. and A. Lempel (1978). "Compression of Individual Sequences via Variable-Rate Coding," *IEEE Transactions on Information Theory*, 24(5), September, 1978.

CCITT (Huffman) Encoding

Many facsimile and document imaging file formats support a form of lossless data compression often described as CCITT encoding. The CCITT (International Telegraph and Telephone Consultative Committee) is a standards organization that has developed a series of communications protocols for the facsimile transmission of black-and-white images over telephone lines and data networks. These protocols are known officially as the CCITT T.4 and T.6 standards, but are more commonly referred to as CCITT Group 3 and Group 4 compression, respectively.

Sometimes, CCITT encoding is referred to, not entirely accurately, as Huffman encoding. Huffman encoding is a simple compression algorithm introduced by David Huffman in 1952. CCITT 1-dimensional encoding, described in a subsection below, is a specific type of Huffman encoding. The other types of CCITT encodings are not, however, implementations of the Huffman scheme.

Group 3 and Group 4 encodings are compression algorithms that are specifically designed for encoding 1-bit image data. Many document and FAX file formats support Group 3 compression and several, including TIFF, also support Group 4.

Group 3 encoding was designed specifically for bilevel, black-and-white image data telecommunications. All modern FAX machines and FAX modems support Group 3 facsimile transmissions. Group 3 encoding and decoding is fast, maintains a good compression ratio for a wide variety of document data, and contains information which aids a Group 3 decoder in detecting and correcting errors without special hardware.

Group 4 is a more efficient form of bilevel compression which has almost entirely replaced the use of Group 3 in many conventional document image storage systems. (An exception is facsimile document storage systems where original Group 3 images are required to be stored in an unaltered state.)

Group 4 encoded data is approximately half the size of 1-dimensional Group 3-encoded data. Although Group 4 is fairly difficult to implement efficiently, it encodes at least as fast as Group 3 and in some implementations decodes even faster. Also, Group 4 was designed for use on data networks, so it does not contain the synchronization codes used for error detection that Group 3 does, making it a poor choice for an image transfer protocol.

Group 4 is sometimes confused with the IBM MMR (Modified Modified Read) compression method. In fact, Group 4 and MMR are almost exactly the same algorithm and achieve almost identical compression results. IBM released MMR in 1979 with the introduction of its Scanmaster product before Group 4 was standardized. MMR became IBM's own document compression standard and is still used in many IBM imaging systems today.

Document-imaging systems that store large amounts of facsimile data have adopted these CCITT compression schemes to conserve disk space. CCITT-encoded data can be decompressed quickly for printing or viewing (assuming that enough memory and CPU resources are available). The same data can also be transmitted using modem or facsimile protocol technology without needing to be encoded first.

The CCITT algorithms are non-adaptive. That is, they do not adjust the encoding algorithm to encode each bitmap with optimal efficiency. They use a fixed table of code values that were selected according to a reference set of documents containing both text and graphics that were considered to be representative of documents that would be transmitted by facsimile.

Group 3 normally achieves a compression ratio of 5:1 to 8:1 on a standard 200-dpi (204x196 dpi), A4-sized, document. Group 4 results are roughly twice as efficient as Group 3, achieving compression ratios upwards of 15:1 with the same document. Claims that the CCITT algorithms are capable of far better compression on standard business documents are exaggerated—largely by hardware vendors.

Because the CCITT algorithms have been optimized for type and handwritten documents, it stands to reason that images radically different in composition will not compress very well. This is all too true. Bilevel bitmaps which contain a high frequency of short runs, as typically found in digitally half-toned continuous-tone images, do not compress as well using the CCITT algorithms. Such images will usually result in a compression ratio of 3:1 or even lower, and many will actually compress to a size larger than the original.

The CCITT actually defines three algorithms for the encoding of bilevel image data:

- Group 3 One-Dimensional (G31D)
- Group 3 Two-Dimensional (G32D)
- Group 4 Two-Dimensional (G42D)

G31D is the simplest of the algorithms and the easiest to implement. For this reason, it is discussed in its entirety in the first subsection below. G32D and

G42D are much more complex in their design and operation, and are described only in general terms below.

The Group 3 and Group 4 algorithms are standards and therefore produce the same compression results for everybody. If you have heard any claims made to the contrary, it is for one of these reasons:

• Non-CCITT test images are being used as benchmarks.

• Proprietary modifications have been made to the algorithm.

• Pre- or post-processing is being applied to the encoded image data.

• You have been listening to a misinformed salesperson.

Group 3 One-Dimensional (G31D)

Group 3 one-dimensional encoding (G31D) is a variation of the Huffman keyed compression scheme. A bilevel image is composed of a series of black-and-white 1-bit pixel runs of various lengths (1 = black and 0 = white). A Group 3 encoder determines the length of a pixel run in a scan line and outputs a variable-length binary code word representing the length and color of the run. Because the code word output is shorter than the input, pixel data compression is achieved.

The run-length code words are taken from a predefined table of values representing runs of black or white pixels. This table is part of the T.4 specification and is used to encode and decode all Group 3 data.

The size of the code words were originally determined by the CCITT, based statistically on the average frequency of black-and-white runs occurring in typical type and handwritten documents. The documents included line art and were written in several different languages. Run lengths that occur more frequently are assigned smaller code words while run lengths that occur less frequently are assigned larger code words.

In printed and handwritten documents, short runs occur more frequently than long runs. Two- to 4-pixel black runs are the most frequent in occurrence. The maximum size of a run length is bounded by the maximum width of a Group 3 scan line.

Run lengths are represented by two types of code words: *makeup* and *terminating*. An encoded pixel run is made up of zero or more *makeup code words* and a *terminating code word*. Terminating code words represent shorter runs, and makeup codes represent longer runs. There are separate terminating and makeup code words for both black and white runs.

Pixel runs with a length of 0 to 63 are encoded using a single terminating code. Runs of 64 to 2623 pixels are encoded by a single makeup code and a terminating code. Run lengths greater than 2623 pixels are encoded using one or more makeup codes and a terminating code. The run length is the sum of the length values represented by each code word.

Here are some examples of several different encoded runs:

- A run of 20 black pixels would be represented by the terminating code for a black run length of 20. This reduces a 20-bit run to the size of an 11-bit code word, a compression ratio of nearly 2:1. This is illustrated in Figure 9-7, a.

- A white run of 100 pixels would be encoded using the makeup code for a white run length of 64 pixels followed by the terminating code for a white run length of 36 pixels (64 + 36 = 100). This encoding reduces 100 bits to 13 bits, or a compression ratio of over 7:1. This is illustrated in Figure 9-7, b.

- A run of 8800 black pixels would be encoded as three makeup codes of 2560 black pixels (7680 pixels), a makeup code of 1088 black pixels, followed by the terminating code for 32 black pixels (2560 + 2560 + 2560 + 1088 + 32 = 8800). In this case, we will have encoded 8800 run-length bits into five code words with a total length of 61 bits, for an approximate compression ratio of 144:1. This is illustrated in Figure 9-7, c.

The use of run lengths encoded with multiple makeup codes has become a de facto extension to Group 3, because such encoders are necessary for images with higher resolutions. And while most Group 3 decoders do support this extension, do not expect them to do so in all cases.

Decoding Group 3 data requires methods different from most other compression schemes. Because each code word varies in length, the encoded data stream must be read one bit at a time until a code word is recognized. This can be a slow and tedious process at best. To make this job easier, a state table can be used to process the encoded data one byte at a time. This is the quickest and most efficient way to implement a CCITT decoder.

All scan lines are encoded to begin with a white run-length code word (most document image scan lines begin with white run lengths). If an actual scan line begins with a black run, a zero-length white run-length code word will be prepended to the scan line.

A decoder keeps track of the color of the run it is decoding. Comparing the current bit pattern to values in the opposite color bit table is wasteful. That is, if a black run is being decoded, then there is no reason to check the table for white run-length codes.

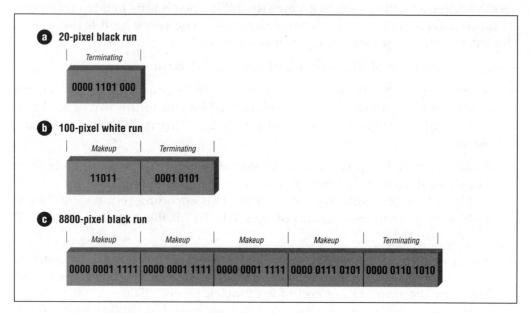

a **20-pixel black run**

Terminating

0000 1101 000

b **100-pixel white run**

Makeup | Terminating

11011 | 0001 0101

c **8800-pixel black run**

Makeup | Makeup | Makeup | Makeup | Terminating

0000 0001 1111 | 0000 0001 1111 | 0000 0001 1111 | 0000 0111 0101 | 0000 0110 1010

FIGURE 9-7: *CCITT Group 3 encoding*

Several special code words are also defined in a Group 3-encoded data stream. These codes are used to provide synchronization in the event that a phone transmission experiences a burst of noise. By recognizing this special code, a CCITT decoder may identify transmission errors and attempt to apply a recovery algorithm that approximates the lost data.

The EOL code is a 12-bit codeword that begins each line in a Group 3 transmission. This unique code word is used to detect the start/end of a scan line during the image transmission. If a burst of noise temporarily corrupts the signal, a Group 3 decoder throws away the unrecognized data it receives until it encountered an EOL code. The decoder would then start receiving the transmission as normal again, assuming that the data following the EOL is the beginning of the next scan line. The decoder might also replace the bad line with a predefined set of data, such as a white scan line.

A decoder also uses EOL codes for several purposes. It uses them to keep track of the width of a decoded scan line (an incorrect scan-line width may be an error, or it may be an indication to pad with white pixels to the EOL). In addition, it uses EOL codes to keep track of the number of scan lines in an image, in order to detect a short image. If it finds one, it pads the remaining length with scan lines of all white pixels. A Group 3 EOL code is illustrated in Figure 9-8.

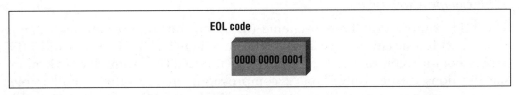

EOL code

```
0000 0000 0001
```

FIGURE 9-8: *CCITT Group 3 encoding (EOL code)*

Most FAX machines transmit data of an "unlimited length," in which case the decoder cannot detect how long the image is supposed to be. Also, it is faster not to transmit the all-white space at the end of a page, and many FAX machines stop when they detect that the rest of a page is all white; they expect the receiver to do white padding to the end of the negotiated page size.

When Group 3 data is encapsulated in an image file, information regarding the length and width of the image is typically stored in the image file header and is read by the decoder prior to decoding.

Group 3 message transmissions are terminated by a Return To Control (RTC) code that is appended to the end of every Group 3 data stream and is used to indicate the end of the message transmission. An RTC code word is simply six EOL codes occurring consecutively. The RTC is actually part of the facsimile protocol and not part of the encoded message data. It is used to signal the receiver that it should drop the high-speed message carrier and listen on the low-speed carrier for the post-page command. A Group 3 RTC code is illustrated in Figure 9-9.

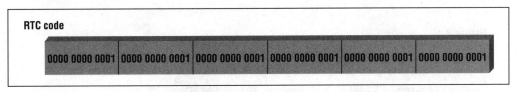

RTC code

```
0000 0000 0001 | 0000 0000 0001 | 0000 0000 0001 | 0000 0000 0001 | 0000 0000 0001 | 0000 0000 0001
```

FIGURE 9-9: *CCITT Group 3 encoding (RTC code)*

A Fill (FILL) is not actually a code word, but instead is a run of one or more zero bits that occurs between the encoded scan-line data and the EOL code (but never in the encoded scan line itself). Fill bits are used to pad out the length of an encoded scan line to increase the transmission time of the line to a required length. Fill bits may also be used to pad the RTC code word out to end on a byte boundary.

TIFF Compression Type 2

The TIFF compression Type 2 scheme (in which the compression tag value is equal to 2) is a variation of CCITT G31D encoding. The TIFF Type 3 and TIFF Type 4 compression methods follow exactly the CCITT Group 3 and Group 4 specifications, respectively. Type 2 compression, on the other hand, implements Group 3 encoding, but does not use EOL or RTC code words. For this reason, TIFF Type 2 compression is also called "Group 3, No EOLs." Also, fill bits are never used except to pad out the last byte in a scan line to the next byte boundary.

These modifications were incorporated into the TIFF specification because EOL and RTC codes are not needed to read data stored on tape or disk. A typical letter-size image (1728x2200 pixels) would contain 26,484 bits (3310.5 bytes) of EOL and RTC information. When storing Group 3 data to a file, the following are not needed:

- The initial 12-bit EOL
- The 12 EOL bits per scan line
- The 72 RTC bits tacked onto the end of each image

Conventional Group 3 decoders cannot handle these modifications and either will refuse to read the TIFF Type 2-encoded data or will simply return a stream of decoded garbage. However, many decoders have been designed to accept these Group 3 trivial "modifications" and have no problems reading this type of data. Group 3 encoding is illustrated in Figure 9-10.

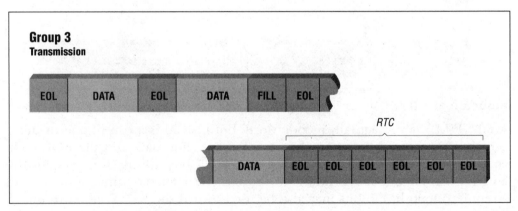

FIGURE 9-10: *Group 3 CCITT encoding (TIFF Compression Type 2)*

TIFF Class F

There is nearly one facsimile file format for every brand of computer FAX hardware and software made. Many compress the facsimile data using RLE (presumably so it will be quicker to display) or store it in its original Group 3 encoding. Perhaps the most widely used FAX file format is the unofficial TIFF Class F format. (See the TIFF article in Part II of this book for more information about TIFF Class F.)

Even with the latest release of TIFF, revision 6.0, Class F has never been officially included in the standard, despite the wishes of the TIFF Advisory Council. The reason for this is that Aldus feels that supporting applications which require facsimile data storage and retrieval is outside of the scope of TIFF. (TIFF was designed primarily with scanner and desktop publishing in mind.) This is too bad, considering that one of TIFF's main goals is to aid in promoting image data interchangeability between hardware platforms and software applications.

Group 3 Two-Dimensional (G32D)

Group 3 one-dimensional (G31D) encoding, which we've discussed above, encodes each scan line independent of the other scan lines. Only one run length at a time is considered during the encoding and decoding process. The data occurring before and after each run length is not important to the encoding step; only the data occurring in the present run is needed.

With two-dimensional encoding (G32D), on the other hand, the way a scan line is encoded may depend on the immediately preceding scan-line data. Many images have a high degree of vertical coherence (redundancy). By describing the differences between two scan lines, rather than describing the scan line contents, 2-dimensional encoding achieves better compression.

The first pixel of each run length is called a changing element. Each changing element marks a color transition within a scan line (the point where a run of one color ends and a run of the next color begins).

The position of each changing element in a scan line is described as being a certain number of pixels from a changing element in the current, coding line (horizontal coding is performed) or in the preceding, reference line (vertical coding is performed). The output codes used to describe the actual positional information are called Relative Element Address Designate (READ) codes.

Shorter code words are used to describe the color transitions that are less than four pixels away from each other on the code line or the reference line. Longer code words are used to describe color transitions laying a greater distance from the current changing element.

Two-dimensional encoding is more efficient than 1-dimensional because the usual data that is compressed (typed or handwritten documents) contains a high amount of 2-dimensional coherence.

Because a G32D-encoded scan line is dependent on the correctness of the preceding scan line, an error, such as a burst of line noise, can affect multiple, 2-dimensionally encoded scan lines. If a transmission error corrupts a segment of encoded scan line data, that line cannot be decoded. But, worse still, all scan lines occurring after it also decode improperly.

To minimize the damage created by noise, G32D uses a variable called a K factor and 2-dimensionally encodes K-1 lines following a 1-dimensionally encoded line. If corruption of the data transmission occurs, only K-1 scan lines of data will be lost. The decoder will be able to resync the decoding at the next available EOL code.

The typical value for K is 2 or 4. G32D data that is encoded with a K value of 4 appears as a single block of data. Each block contains three lines of 2-dimensional scan-line data followed by a scan line of 1D encoded data.

The K variable is not normally used in decoding the G32D data. Instead, the EOL code is modified to indicate the algorithm used to encode the line following it. If a 1 bit is appended to the EOL code, the line following is 1-dimensionally encoded; if a 0 bit is appended, then the line following the EOL code is 2-dimensionally encoded. All other transmission code word markers (FILL and RTC) follow the same rule as in G31D encoding. K is only needed in decoding if regeneration of the previous 1-dimensionally encoded scan line is necessary for error recovery.

Group 4 Two-Dimensional (G42D)

Group 4 two-dimensional encoding (G42D) was developed from the G32D algorithm as a better 2-dimensional compression scheme—so much better, in fact, that Group 4 has almost completely replaced G32D in commercial use.

Group 4 encoding is identical to G32D encoding except for a few modifications. Group 4 is basically the G32D algorithm with no EOL codes and a K variable set to infinity. Group 4 was designed specifically to encode data residing on disk drives and data networks. The built-in transmission error detection/correction found in Group 3 is therefore not needed by Group 4 data.

The first reference line in Group 4 encoding is an imaginary scan line containing all white pixels. In G32D encoding, the first reference line is the first scan line of the image. In Group 4 encoding, the RTC code word is replaced by an End of Facsimile Block (EOFB) code, which consists of two consecutive Group 3 EOL code words. Like the Group 3 RTC, the EOFB is also part of the transmission protocol and not actually part of the image data. Also, Group 4-encoded image data may be padded out with FILL bits after the EOFB to end on a byte boundary.

Group 4 encoding will usually result in an image compressed twice as small as if it were done with G31D encoding. The main tradeoff is that Group 4 encoding is more complex and requires more time to perform. When implemented in hardware, however, the difference in execution speed between the Group 3 and Group 4 algorithms is not significant, which usually makes Group 4 a better choice in most imaging system implementations.

Tips for Designing CCITT Encoders and Decoders

Here are some general guidelines to follow if you are using the CCITT encoding method code to encode or decode.

- Ignore bits occurring after the RTC or EOFB markers. These markers indicate the end of the image data, and all bits occurring after them can be considered filler.

- You must know the number of pixels in a scan line before decoding. Any row that decodes to fewer or greater pixels than expected is normally considered corrupt, and further decoding of the image block (2-dimensional encoding only) should not be attempted. Some encoding schemes will produce short scan lines if the line contains all white pixels. The decoder is expected to realize this and pad the entire line out as a single white run.

- Be aware that decoded scan-line widths will not always be a multiple of eight, and decoders should not expect byte-boundary padding to always occur. Robust decoders should be able to read non-byte-aligned data.

- If a decoder encounters an RTC or EOFB marker before the expected number of scan lines has been decoded, assume that the remaining scan lines are all white. If the expected number of scan lines has been decoded, but an RTC or EOFB has not been encountered, stop decoding. A decoder should then produce a warning that an unusual condition has been detected.

- Note that a well-designed CCITT decoder should be able to handle the typical color-sex and bit-sex problems associated with 1-bit data, as described below:

The CCITT defines a pixel value of 0 as white and a pixel value of 1 as black. Many bitmaps, however, may be stored using the opposite pixel color values and the decoder would interpret a "negative" of the image in this case (a color-sex problem). Different machine architectures also store the bits within a byte in different ways. Some store the most significant bit first, and some store the least significant bit first. If bitmap data is read in the opposite format from the one in which it was stored, the image will appear fragmented and disrupted (a bit-sex problem). To prevent these problems, always design a CCITT decoder that is capable of reading data using either of the color-sex and bit-sex schemes to suit the requirements of the user.

For Further Information About CCITT

The original specifications for the CCITT Group 3 and Group 4 algorithms are in CCITT (1985) Volume VII, Fascicle VII.3, Recommendations T.4 and T.6:

> "Standardization of Group 3 Facsimile Apparatus for Document Transmission," *Recommendation T.4, Volume VII, Fascicle VII.3, Terminal Equipment and Protocols for Telematic Services,* The International Telegraph and Telephone Consultative Committee (CCITT), Geneva, Switzerland, 1985, pp. 16-31.

> "Facsimile Coding Schemes and Coding Control Functions for Group 4 Facsimile Apparatus," *Recommendation T.6, Volume VII, Fascicle VII.3, Terminal Equipment and Protocols for Telematic Services,* The International Telegraph and Telephone Consultative Committee (CCITT), Geneva, Switzerland, 1985, pp. 40-48.

The latest specification is CCITT (1992) Volume VII, Fascicle VII.3, Recommendations T.0 through T.63.

Both the CCITT and ANSI documents may be obtained from the following source:

> American National Standards Institute, Inc.
> Attn: Sales
> 1430 Broadway
> New York, NY 10018 USA
> Voice: 212-642-4900

See also the following references. (For information on getting RFCs (Requests for Comments), send email to *rfc-info@isi.edu* with a subject line of "getting rfcs" and a body of "help: ways _to_get_rfcs".)

> R. Hunter and A.H. Robinson. "International Digital Facsimile Coding Standards," *Proceedings of the IEEE,* Volume 68, Number 7, July 1980, pp. 854-867.

> *RFC 804—CCITT Draft Recommendation T.4 (Standardization of Group 3 Facsimile Apparatus for Document Transmission).*

RFC 1314—A File Format for the Exchange of Images in the Internet.

FAX: Digital Facsimile Technology & Applications, McConnell, Artech House, Norwood, MA; second edition, 1992.

Marking, Michael P. "Decoding Group 3 Images," *The C Users Journal,* June 1990, pp. 45-54.

Information on MMR encoding may be found in the following references:

"Binary-image-manipulation Algorithms in the Image View Facility," *IBM Journal of Research and Development,* Volume 31, Number 1, January 1987.

Information on Huffman encoding may be found in the following references:

Huffman, David. "A Method for the Construction of Minimum Redundancy Codes," *Proceedings of the IRE,* Volume 40, Number 9, 1952, pp. 1098-1101.

Kruger, Anton (1991). "Huffman Data Compression." *C Gazette,* Volume 5, Number 4, pp.71-77.

JPEG Compression

One of the hottest topics in image compression technology today is JPEG. The acronym JPEG stands for the Joint Photographic Experts Group, a standards committee that had its origins within the International Standard Organization (ISO).

In 1982, the ISO (the European equivalent of ANSI, the American National Standards Institute) formed the Photographic Experts Group (PEG) to research methods of transmitting video, still images, and text over ISDN (Integrated Services Digital Network) lines. PEG's goal was to produce a set of industry standards for the transmission of graphics and image data over digital communications networks.

In 1986, a subgroup of the CCITT began to research methods of compressing color and gray-scale data for facsimile transmission. The compression methods needed for color facsimile systems were very similar to those being researched by PEG. It was therefore agreed that the two groups should combine their resources and work together towards a single standard.

In 1987, the ISO and CCITT combined their two groups into a joint committee that would research and produce a single standard of image data compression for both organizations to use. This new committee was JPEG.

Although the creators of JPEG might have envisioned a multitude of commercial applications for JPEG technology, a consumer public made hungry by the marketing promises of imaging and multimedia technology are benefiting greatly as well. Most previously developed compression methods do a relatively poor job of compressing continuous-tone image data; that is, images containing hundreds or thousands of colors taken from real-world subjects. And very few file formats can support 24-bit raster images.

GIF, for example, can store only images with a maximum pixel depth of eight bits, for a maximum of 256 colors. And its LZW compression algorithm does not work very well on typical scanned image data. The low-level noise commonly found in such data defeats LZW's ability to recognize repeated patterns.

Both TIFF and BMP are capable of storing 24-bit data, but in their pre-JPEG versions are capable of using only encoding schemes (LZW and RLE, respectively) that do not compress this type of image data very well.

JPEG provides a compression method that is capable of compressing continuous-tone image data with a pixel depth of six to 24 bits with reasonable speed and efficiency. And although JPEG itself does not define a standard image file format, several have been invented or modified to fill the needs of JPEG data storage.

JPEG in Perspective

Unlike all of the other compression methods described so far in this chapter, JPEG is not a single algorithm. Instead, it may be thought of as a toolkit of image compression methods that may be altered to fit the needs of the user. JPEG may be adjusted to produce very small, compressed images that are of relatively poor quality in appearance, but still suitable for many applications. Conversely, JPEG is capable of producing very high quality compressed images that are still far smaller than the original uncompressed data.

JPEG is also different in that it is primarily a lossy method of compression. Most popular image format compression schemes, such as RLE, LZW, or the CCITT standards, are lossless compression methods. That is, they do not discard any data during the encoding process. An image compressed using a lossless method is guaranteed to be identical to the original image when uncompressed.

Lossy schemes, on the other hand, throw useless data away during encoding. This is, in fact, how lossy schemes manage to obtain superior compression ratios over most lossless schemes. JPEG was designed specifically to discard information that the human eye cannot easily see. Slight changes in color are not perceived well by the human eye, while slight changes in intensity (light and dark) are. Therefore JPEG's lossy encoding tends to be more frugal with the gray-scale part of an image and to be more frivolous with the color.

JPEG was designed to compress color or gray-scale continuous-tone images of real-world subjects: photographs, video stills, or any complex graphics that resemble natural subjects. Animations, ray tracing, line art, black-and-white documents, and typical vector graphics don't compress very well under JPEG, and shouldn't be expected to. And, although JPEG is now used to provide motion video compression, the standard makes no special provision for such an application.

The fact that JPEG is lossy and works only on a select type of image data might make you ask "Why bother to use it?" It depends upon your needs. JPEG is an excellent way to store 24-bit photographic images, like those used in imaging and multimedia applications. JPEG 24-bit (16 million color) images are superior in appearance to 8-bit (256 color) images on a VGA display and are at their most spectacular when using 24-bit display hardware (which is now quite inexpensive).

The amount of compression achieved depends upon the content of the image data. A typical photographic-quality image may be compressed from 20:1 to 25:1 without experiencing any noticeable degradation in quality. Higher compression ratios will result in image files that differ noticeably from the original image, but that still have an overall good image quality. And achieving a 20:1 or better compression ratio in many cases not only saves disk space, but also reduces transmission time across data networks and phone lines.

An end user can "tune" the quality of a JPEG encoder using a parameter sometimes called a "quality setting" or a "Q factor." Although different implementations have varying scales of Q factors, a range of 1 to 100 is typical. A factor of 1 produces the smallest, worst quality images; a factor of 100 produces the largest, best quality images. The optimal Q factor depends on the image content and is therefore different for every image. The art of JPEG compression is finding the lowest Q factor that produces an image that is visibly acceptable, and preferably as identical to the original as possible.

The JPEG library supplied by the Independent JPEG Group (included on the CD-ROM that accompanies this book) uses a quality setting scale of 1 to 100. To find the optimal compression for an image using the JPEG library, follow these steps:

1. Encode the image using a quality setting of 75 (–Q 75).

2. If you observe unacceptable defects in the image, increase the value and re-encode the image.

3. If the image quality is acceptable, decrease the setting until the image quality is barely acceptable. This will be the optimal quality setting for this image.

4. Repeat this process for every image you have (*or just encode them all using a quality setting of 75*).

JPEG isn't always an ideal compression solution. There are several reasons:

- As we have said, JPEG doesn't fit every compression need. Images containing large areas of a single color do not compress very well. In fact, JPEG will introduce "artifacts" into such images that are visible against a flat background, making them considerably worse in appearance than if you used a conventional lossless compression method was used. Images of a "busier" composition contain even worse artifacts, but they are considerably less noticeable against the image's more complex background.

- JPEG can be rather slow when it is implemented only in software. If fast decompression is required, a hardware-based JPEG solution is your best bet, unless you are willing to wait for a faster software-only solution to come along or buy a faster computer.

- JPEG is not trivial to implement. It is not likely you will be able to sit down and write your own JPEG encoder/decoder in a few evenings. We recommend that you obtain a third-party JPEG library, rather than writing your own.

- JPEG is not supported by very many file formats. The formats that do support JPEG are all fairly new and can be expected to be revised at frequent intervals.

Baseline JPEG

The JPEG specification defines a minimal subset of the standard called baseline JPEG, which all JPEG-aware applications are required to support. This baseline uses an encoding scheme based on the Discrete Cosine Transform (DCT) to achieve compression. DCT is a generic name for a class of operations identified and published some years ago. DCT-based algorithms have since made their way into various compression methods.

DCT-based encoding algorithms are always lossy by nature. DCT algorithms are capable of achieving a high degree of compression with only minimal loss of data. This scheme is effective only for compressing continuous-tone images, in which the differences between adjacent pixels are usually small. In practice, JPEG works well only on images with depths of at least four or five bits per color channel. The baseline standard actually specifies eight bits per input sample. Data of lesser bit depth can be handled by scaling it up to eight bits per sample, but the results will be bad for low-bit-depth source data, because of the large jumps between adjacent pixel values. For similar reasons, colormapped source data does not work very well, especially if the image has been dithered.

The JPEG compression scheme is divided into the following stages:

1. Transform the image into an optimal color space.

2. Down-sample chrominance components by averaging groups of pixels together.

3. Apply a Discrete Cosine Transform (DCT) to blocks of pixels, thus removing redundant image data.

4. Quantize each block of DCT coefficients using weighting functions optimized for the human eye.

5. Encode the resulting coefficients (image data) using a Huffman variable word-length algorithm to remove redundancies in the coefficients.

Figure 9-11 summarizes these steps, and the following subsections look at each of them in turn. Note that JPEG decoding performs the reverse of these steps.

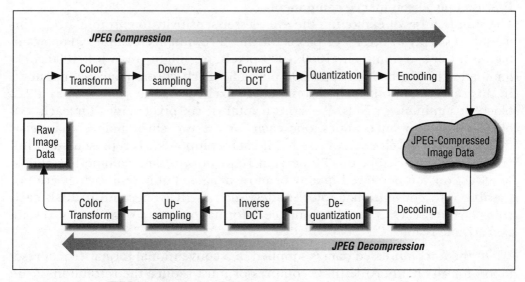

FIGURE 9-11: *JPEG compression and decompression*

Transform the image

The JPEG algorithm is capable of encoding images that use any type of color space. JPEG itself encodes each component in a color model separately, and it is completely independent of any color-space model, such as RGB, HSI, or CMY. The best compression ratios result if a luminance/chrominance color space, such as YUV or YCbCr, is used (see "A Word About Color Spaces" in Chapter 2, *Computer Graphics Basics*, for a description of these color spaces).

Most of the visual information to which human eyes are most sensitive is found in the high-frequency, gray-scale, luminance component (Y) of the YCbCr color space. The other two chrominance components (Cb and Cr) contain high-frequency color information to which the human eye is less sensitive. Most of this information can therefore be discarded.

In comparison, the RGB, HSI, and CMY color models spread their useful visual image information evenly across each of their three color components, making the selective discarding of information very difficult. All three color components would need to be encoded at the highest quality, resulting in a poorer compression ratio. Gray-scale images do not have a color space as such and therefore do not require transforming.

Downsample chrominance components

The simplest way of exploiting the eye's lesser sensitivity to chrominance information is simply to use fewer pixels for the chrominance channels. For example, in an image nominally 1000x1000 pixels, we might use a full 1000x1000 luminance pixels, but only 500x500 pixels for each chrominance component. In this representation, each chrominance pixel covers the same area as a 2x2 block of luminance pixels. We store a total of six pixel values for each 2x2 block (four luminance values, one each for the two chrominance channels), rather than the twelve values needed if each component is represented at full resolution. Remarkably, this 50 percent reduction in data volume has almost no effect on the perceived quality of most images. Equivalent savings are not possible with conventional color models such as RGB, because in RGB each color channel carries some luminance information and so any loss of resolution is quite visible.

When the uncompressed data is supplied in a conventional format (equal resolution for all channels), a JPEG compressor must reduce the resolution of the chrominance channels by *downsampling*, or averaging together groups of pixels. The JPEG standard allows several different choices for the sampling ratios, or relative sizes, of the downsampled channels. The luminance channel is always left at full resolution (1:1 sampling). Typically both chrominance channels are downsampled 2:1 horizontally and either 1:1 or 2:1 vertically, meaning that a chrominance pixel covers the same area as either a 2x 1 or a 2x2 block of luminance pixels. JPEG refers to these downsampling processes as 2h1v and 2h2v sampling respectively.

Another notation commonly used is 4:2:2 sampling for 2h1v, and 4:2:0 sampling for 2h2v; this notation derives from television customs (color transformation and downsampling have been in use since the beginning of color TV transmission). 2h1v sampling is fairly common because it corresponds to National Television Standards Committee (NTSC) standard TV practice, but it offers less compression than 2h2v sampling, with hardly any gain in perceived quality.

Apply a Discrete Cosine Transform

The image data is divided up into 8x8 blocks of pixels (from this point on, each color component is processed independently, so a "pixel" means a single value, even in a color image). A DCT is applied to each 8x8 block. DCT converts the spatial image representation into a frequency map: the low-order or "DC" term represents the average value in the block, while successive higher-order ("AC") terms represent the strength of more and more rapid changes across the width or height of the block. The highest AC term represents the strength of a cosine wave alternating from maximum to minimum at adjacent pixels.

The DCT calculation is fairly complex; in fact, this is the most costly step in JPEG compression. The point of doing it is that we have now separated out the high- and low-frequency information present in the image. We can discard high-frequency data easily without losing low-frequency information. The DCT step itself is lossless except for roundoff errors.

Quantize each block

To discard an appropriate amount of information, the compressor divides each DCT output value by a "quantization coefficient" and rounds the result to an integer. The larger the quantization coefficient, the more data is lost, because the actual DCT value is represented less and less accurately. Each of the 64 positions of the DCT output block has its own quantization coefficient, with the higher-order terms being quantized more heavily than the low-order terms (that is, the higher-order terms have larger quantization coefficients). Furthermore, separate quantization tables are employed for luminance and chrominance data, with the chrominance data being quantized more heavily than the luminance data. This allows JPEG to exploit further the eye's differing sensitivity to luminance and chrominance.

It is this step that is controlled by the "quality" setting of most JPEG compressors. The compressor starts from a built-in table that is appropriate for a medium-quality setting, and increases or decreases the value of each table entry in inverse proportion to the requested quality. The complete quantization tables actually used are recorded in the compressed file so that the decompressor will know how to (approximately) reconstruct the DCT coefficients.

Selection of an appropriate quantization table is something of a black art. Most existing compressors start from a sample table developed by the ISO JPEG committee. It is likely that future research will yield better tables that provide more compression for the same perceived image quality. Implementation of improved tables should not cause any compatibility problems, because decompressors merely read the tables from the compressed file; they don't care how the table was picked.

Encode the resulting coefficients

The resulting coefficients contain a significant amount of redundant data. Huffman compression will losslessly remove the redundancies, resulting in smaller JPEG data. An optional extension to the JPEG specification allows arithmetic encoding to be used instead of Huffman for an even greater compression ratio (see the section called "JPEG Extensions" below). At this point, the JPEG data stream is ready to be transmitted across a communications channel or encapsulated inside an image file format.

JPEG Extensions

What we have examined thus far is only the baseline specification for JPEG. A number of extensions have been defined in the JPEG specification that provide progressive image buildup, improved compression ratios using arithmetic encoding, and a lossless compression scheme. These features are beyond the needs of most JPEG implementations and have therefore been defined as "not required to be supported" extensions to the JPEG standard.

Progressive image buildup

Progressive image buildup is an extension for use in applications that need to receive JPEG data streams and display them on the fly. A baseline JPEG image can be displayed only after all of the image data has been received and decoded. But, some applications require that the image be displayed after only some of the data is received. Using a conventional compression method, this means displaying the first few scan lines of the image as it is decoded. In this case even if the scan lines were interlaced, you would need at least 50 percent of the image data to get a good clue as to the content of the image. The progressive buildup extension of JPEG offers a better solution.

Progressive buildup allows an image to be sent in layers rather than scan lines. But instead of transmitting each bitplane or color channel in sequence (which wouldn't be very useful), a succession of images built up from approximations of the original image are sent. The first scan provides a low-accuracy representation of the entire image—in effect, a very low-quality JPEG compressed image. Subsequent scans gradually refine the image by increasing the effective quality factor. If the data is displayed on the fly, you would first see a crude, but recognizable, rendering of the whole image. This would appear very quickly because only a small amount of data would need to be transmitted to produce it. Each subsequent scan would improve the displayed image's quality one block at a time.

A limitation of progressive JPEG is that each scan takes essentially a full JPEG decompression cycle to display. Therefore, with typical data transmission rates, a very fast JPEG decoder (probably specialized hardware) would be needed to make effective use of progressive transmission.

A related JPEG extension provides for hierarchical storage of the same image at multiple resolutions. For example, an image might be stored at 250x250, 500x500, 1000x1000, and 2000x2000 pixels, so that the same image file could support display on low-resolution screens, medium-resolution laser printers, and high-resolution imagesetters. The higher-resolution images are stored as differences from the lower-resolution ones, so they need less space than they would need if they were stored independently. This is not the same as a progressive series, because each image is available in its own right at the full desired quality.

Arithmetic encoding

The baseline JPEG standard defines Huffman compression as the final step in the encoding process. A JPEG extension replaces the Huffman engine with a binary arithmetic entropy encoder. The use of an arithmetic coder reduces the resulting size of the JPEG data by a further 10 percent to 15 percent over the results that would be achieved by the Huffman coder. With no change in resulting image quality, this gain could be of importance in implementations where enormous quantities of JPEG images are archived.

Arithmetic encoding has several drawbacks:

- Not all JPEG decoders support arithmetic decoding. Baseline JPEG decoders are required to support only the Huffman algorithm.

- The arithmetic algorithm is slower in both encoding and decoding than Huffman.

- The arithmetic coder used by JPEG (called a Q Coder) is owned by IBM and AT&T (Mitsubishi also holds patents on arithmetic coding.) You must obtain a license from the appropriate vendors if their Q coders are to be used as the back end of your JPEG implementation.

Lossless JPEG compression

A question that commonly arises is "At what Q factor does JPEG become lossless?" The answer is "never." Baseline JPEG is a lossy method of compression regardless of adjustments you may make in the parameters. In fact, DCT-based encoders are always lossy, because roundoff errors are inevitable in the color conversion and DCT steps. You can suppress deliberate information loss in the downsampling and quantization steps, but you still won't get an exact recreation of the original bits. Further, this minimum-loss setting is a very inefficient way to use lossy JPEG.

The JPEG standard does offer a separate lossless mode. This mode has nothing in common with the regular DCT-based algorithms, and it is currently implemented only in a few commercial applications. JPEG lossless is a form of Predictive Lossless Coding using a 2-dimensional Differential Pulse Code Modulation (DPCM) scheme. The basic premise is that the value of a pixel is combined with the values of up to three neighboring pixels to form a predictor value. The predictor value is then subtracted from the original pixel value. When the entire bitmap has been processed, the resulting predictors are compressed using either the Huffman or the binary arithmetic entropy encoding methods described in the JPEG standard.

Lossless JPEG works on images with two to 16 bits per pixel, but performs best on images with six or more bits per pixel. For such images, the typical compression ratio achieved is 2:1. For image data with fewer bits per pixels, other compression schemes do perform better.

For Further Information About JPEG

The JPEG standard itself is not available electronically; you must order a paper copy through ISO (but see the Pennebaker and Mitchell book below). In the United States, copies of the standard may be ordered from:

American National Standards Institute, Inc.
Attn: Sales
1430 Broadway
New York, NY 10018
Voice: 212-642-4900

The standard is divided into two parts; Part 1 is the actual specification, and Part 2 covers compliance-testing methods. Part 1 of the draft has now reached International Standard status. See this document:

Digital Compression and Coding of Continuous-tone Still Images, Part 1: Requirements and Guidelines. Document number ISO/IEC IS 10918-1.

Part 2 is still at Committee Draft status. See this document:

> *Digital Compression and Coding of Continuous-tone Still Images, Part 2: Compliance Testing.* Document number ISO/IEC CD 10918-2.

New information on JPEG and related algorithms is appearing constantly. The majority of the commercial work for JPEG is being carried out at companies such as the following:

Eastman Kodak Corporation
343 State Street
Rochester, NY 14650
Voice: 800-242-2424

C-Cube Microsystems
1778 McCarthy Boulevard
Milpitas, CA 95035
Voice: 408-944-6300

See the article about the JFIF (JPEG File Interchange Format) supported by C-Cube in Part II of this book.

The JPEG FAQ (Frequently Asked Questions) article is a useful source of general information about JPEG. This FAQ is included on the CD-ROM that accompanies this book; however, because the FAQ is updated frequently, the CD-ROM version should be used only for general information. The FAQ is posted every two weeks to Usenet newsgroups *comp.graphics*, *news.answers*, and other groups. You can get the latest version of this FAQ from the *news.answers* archive at *rtfm.mit.edu* in */pub/usenet/news.answers/jpeg-faq*. You can also get this FAQ by sending email to *mail-server@rtfm.mit.edu* with the message "send usenet/news.answers/jpeg-faq" in the body.

A consortium of programmers, the Independent JPEG Group (IJG), has produced a public-domain version of a JPEG encoder and decoder in C source code form. We have included this code on the CD-ROM that accompanies this book. See Appendix A, *What's On the CD-ROM?* for information on how you can obtain the IJG library from the CD-ROM and from various FTP sites, information services, and computer bulletin boards.

The best short technical introduction to the JPEG compression algorithm is:

> Wallace, Gregory K. "The JPEG Still Picture Compression Standard," *Communications of the ACM*, April 1991 (Volume 34, Number 4), pp. 30-44.

A more complete explanation of JPEG can be found in the following texts:

Pennebaker, William B. and Mitchell, Joan L, *JPEG Still Image Data Compression Standard*, Van Nostrand Reinhold, New York, 1992.

This book includes the complete text of the ISO JPEG standards (DIS 10918-1 and draft DIS 10918-2). This is by far the most complete exposition of JPEG in existence and is highly recommended.

Nelson, Mark, *The Data Compression Book*, M&T Books, Redwood City, CA, 1991.

This book provides good explanations and example C code for a multitude of compression methods including JPEG. It is an excellent source if you are comfortable reading C code but don't know much about data compression in general. The book's JPEG sample code is incomplete and not very robust, but the book is a good tutorial.

For Further Information About Data Compression

On Usenet the *comp.compression* newsgroup FAQ article provides a useful source of information about a variety of different compression methods, including JPEG, MPEG, Huffman, and the various LZ algorithms. Also included is information on many archiving programs (pkzip, lzh, zoo, etc.) and patents pertaining to compression algorithms. This FAQ is included on the CD-ROM that accompanies this book; however, because the FAQ is updated frequently, the CD-ROM version should be used only for general information. You can get the latest version of this FAQ from the *news.answers* newsgroup at *rtfm.mit.edu*, where it is stored in the directory */pub/usenet/comp.compression/compression-faq* in three parts: *part1*, *part2*, and *part3*. This FAQ may also be obtained by sending email to the address *mail-server@rtfm.mit.edu* with the message "send usenet/comp.compression/compression-faq/part1", etc., in the body.

There are many books on data encoding and compression. Most older books contain only mathematical descriptions of encoding algorithms. Some newer books, however, have picked up the highly desirable trend of including working (we hope) C code examples in their text and even making the code examples available online or on disk.

The following references contain good general discussions of many of the compression algorithms discussed in this chapter:

Bell, T.C, I.H. Witten, and J.G. Cleary. "Modeling for Text Compression," *ACM Computing Surveys*, Volume 21, Number 4, December, 1989, p.557.

Bell, T.C, I.H. Witten, J.G. Cleary. *Text Compression*, Prentice-Hall, Englewood Cliffs, N.J, 1990.

Huffman, D.A. "A Method for the Construction of Minimum-Redundancy Codes," *Communications of the ACM*, Volume 40, Number 9, September, 1952, pp. 1098-1101.

Jain, Anil K., Paul M. Farrelle, and V. Ralph Angazi. *Image Data Compression: Digital Image Processing Techniques*, Academic Press, San Diego, CA, 1984, pp. 171-226.

Lelewer, D.A, and Hirschberg, D.S. "Data Compression," *ACM Computing Surveys*, Volume 19, Number 3, September, 1987, p. 261.

Storer, James A. *Data Compression: Methods and Theory*, Computer Science Press, Rockville, MD, 1988.

Storer, James A., ed. *Image and Text Compression*, Kluwer Books, Boston, MA, 1992.

Williams, R. *Adaptive Data Compression*, Kluwer Books, Boston, MA, 1990.4, Number 4), pp. 30-44.

## CHAPTER 10

Multimedia

Beyond Traditional Graphics File Formats

Most of this book describes image file formats and the types of data compression they employ. However, still images are not the only type of data that can be stored in a file. This chapter describes the other types of graphics data that are becoming popular.

A hot topic in the world of personal computers today is multimedia. Multimedia applications combine text, graphics, audio, and video in much the same way a motion picture film combines sound and motion photography. But, unlike motion pictures, multimedia can be interactive through the use of a keyboard, mouse, joystick, or other input device to control the behavior of the multimedia presentation. The output from a multimedia application can be through conventional speakers or a stereo system, a music or voice synthesizer, or other types of output devices.

A conventional stereo system or television and video tape recorder (VCR) are *passive information devices*. You can raise and lower the volume of a stereo, change the color of a television picture, or fast-forward a VCR, but this type of control is very limited in capability and is used only intermittently. When you use a passive information device, you normally just sit and watch the picture and listen to the sound.

Anyone who has played a computer or video arcade game has experienced an *active information device*. The games at your local video arcade, or hooked up to your living room television (and therefore permanently attached to your eight-year-old's hands), require constant input in order to function properly. And, although the sights and sounds of such a game might be staggering, the control and utility a user gains from an active information device is only slightly more than is gained using a passive one.

Personal computers are not only active information devices, but also interactive devices. A computer itself does very little unless a user interacts with it. Computers are, as you would expect, excellent platforms for interactive multimedia applications.

Interactive multimedia provides more than just the stimulus-response reaction of a video game. It also allows a collection of complex data to be manipulated with a much finer control than is possible using non-interactive devices. Sample multimedia applications in existence today include:

- Online, multimedia dictionaries and encyclopedias containing text, sounds, and images. These allow the instant lookup of word definitions and provide video playback, in addition to pictures.

- Games that respond to hand movements and that talk back to the user

Computerized multimedia is still in its infancy. It is currently a tool used for educational and entertainment purposes and is expanding out into the commercial world. There probably isn't a complex computerized control system that wouldn't be easier to learn or to use if it had a standardized, multimedia front end. And one day you might even see multimedia applications with heuristic algorithms that will allow your computer to learn as much from you as you will from your computer.

Multimedia File Formats

Multimedia data and information must be stored in a disk file using formats similar to image file formats. Multimedia formats, however, are much more complex than most other file formats because of the wide variety of data they must store. Such data includes text, image data, audio and video data, computer animations, and other forms of binary data, such as Musical Instrument Digital Interface (MIDI), control information, and graphical fonts. (See the "MIDI Standard" section later in this chapter.) Typical multimedia formats do not define new methods for storing these types of data. Instead, they offer the ability to store data in one or more existing data formats that are already in general use.

For example, a multimedia format may allow text to be stored as PostScript or Rich Text Format (RTF) data rather than in conventional ASCII plain text format. Still-image bitmap data may be stored as BMP or TIFF files rather than as raw bitmaps. Similarly, audio, video, and animation data can be stored using industry-recognized formats specified as being supported by that multimedia file format.

Multimedia formats are also optimized for the types of data they store and the format of the medium on which they are stored. Multimedia information is commonly stored on CD-ROM. Unlike conventional disk files, CD-ROMs are limited in the amount of information they can store. A multimedia format must therefore make the best use of available data storage techniques to efficiently store data on the CD-ROM medium.

There are many types of CD-ROM devices and standards that may be used by multimedia applications. If you are interested in multimedia, you should become familiar with them.

The original Compact Disc first introduced in early 1980s was used for storing only audio information using the CD-DA (Compact Disc-Digital Audio) standard produced by Phillips and Sony. CD-DA (also called the Red Book) is an optical data storage format that allows the storage of up to 74 minutes of audio (764 megabytes of data) on a conventional CD-ROM.

The CD-DA standard evolved into the CD-XA (Compact Disc-Extended Architecture) standard, or what we call the CD-ROM (Compact Disc-Read Only Memory). CD-XA (also called the Yellow Book) allows the storage of both digital audio and data on a CD-ROM. Audio may be combined with data, such as text, graphics, and video, so that it may all be read at the same time. An ISO 9660 file system may also be encoded on a CD-ROM, allowing its files to be read by a wide variety of different computer system platforms. (See Appendix A, *What's On the CD-ROM?*, for a discussion of the ISO 9660 standard.)

The CD-I (Compact Disc-Interactive) standard defines the storage of interactive multimedia data. CD-I (also called the Green Book) describes a computer system with audio and video playback capabilities designed specifically for the consumer market. CD-I units allow the integration of fully interactive multimedia applications into home computer systems.

A still-evolving standard is CD-R (Compact Disc-Recordable or Compact Disc-Write Once), which specifies a CD-ROM that may be written to by a personal desktop computer and read by any CD-ROM player. CD-R (also called the Orange Book) promises to turn any home computer into a CD-ROM publishing facility within the next few years.

For more specific information on multimedia, refer to the articles on the RIFF, DVI, QuickTime, and MPEG multimedia formats in Part II of this book.

Types of Data

The following sections describe various types of data that you might find, in addition to static graphics data, in multimedia files.

Animation

Somewhere between the motionless world of still images and the real-time world of video images lies the flip-book world of computer animation. All of the animated sequences seen in educational programs, motion CAD renderings, and computer games are computer-animated (and in many cases, computer-generated) animation sequences.

Traditional cartoon animation is little more than a series of artwork cells, each containing a slight positional variation of the animated subjects. When a large number of these cells is displayed in sequence and at a fast rate, the animated figures appear to the human eye to move.

A computer-animated sequence works in exactly the same manner. A series of images is created of a subject; each image contains a slightly different perspective on the animated subject. When these images are displayed (played back) in the proper sequence and at the proper speed (frame rate), the subject appears to move.

Computerized animation is actually a combination of both still and motion imaging. Each frame, or cell, of an animation is a still image that requires compression and storage. An animation file, however, must store the data for hundreds or thousands of animation frames and must also provide the information necessary to play back the frames using the proper display mode and frame rate.

Animation file formats are only capable of storing still images and not actual video information. It is possible, however, for most multimedia formats to contain animation information, because animation is actually a much easier type of data than video to store.

The image-compression schemes used in animation files are also much simpler than most of those used in video compression. Most animation files use a delta compression scheme, which is a form of Run-Length Encoding that stores and compresses only the information that is different between two images (rather than compressing each image frame entirely). (See Chapter 9, *Data Compression*, for a description of RLE compression.)

Storing animations using a multimedia format also produces the benefit of adding sound to the animation (what's a cartoon without sound?). Most animation formats cannot store sound directly in their files and must rely on storing the sound in a separate disk file which is read by the application that is playing back the animation.

Animations are not only for entertaining kids and adults. Animated sequences are used by CAD programmers to rotate 3D objects so they can be observed from different perspectives; complex, ray-traced objects may be sent into movement so their behavior can be seen; mathematical data collected by an aircraft or satellite may be rendered into an animated fly-by sequence; and movie special effects benefit greatly by computer animation.

For more specific information on animation, refer to the articles on the FLI and GRASP animation formats in Part II of this book.

Digital Video

One step beyond animation is broadcast video. Your television and video tape recorder are a lot more complex than an 8mm home movie projector and your kitchen wall. There are many complex signals and complicated standards that are involved in transmitting those late-night reruns across the airwaves and cable. Only in the last few years has a personal computer been able to work with video data at all.

Video data normally occurs as continuous, analog signals. In order for a computer to process this video data, we must convert the analog signals to a non-continuous, digital format. In a digital format, the video data can be stored as a series of bits on a hard disk or in computer memory.

The process of converting a video signal to a digital bitstream is called analog-to-digital conversion (A/D conversion), or digitizing. A/D conversion occurs in two steps:

1. Sampling captures data from the video stream.

2. Quantizing converts each captured sample into a digital format.

Each sample captured from the video stream is typically stored as a 16-bit integer. The rate at which samples are collected is called the *sampling rate*. The sampling rate is measured in the number of samples captured per second (samples/second). For digital video, it is necessary to capture millions of samples per second.

Quantizing converts the level of a video signal sample into a discrete, binary value. This value approximates the level of the original video signal sample. The value is selected by comparing the video sample to a series of predefined threshold values. The value of the threshold closest to the amplitude of the sampled signal is used as the digital value.

A video signal contains several different components which are mixed together in the same signal. This type of signal is called a composite video signal and is not really useful in high-quality computer video. Therefore, a standard composite video signal is usually separated into its basic components before it is digitized.

The composite video signal format defined by the NTSC (National Television Standards Committee) color television system is used in the United States. The PAL (Phase Alternation Line) and SECAM (Sequential Coleur Avec Memoire) color television systems are used in Europe and are not compatible with NTSC. Most computer video equipment supports one or more of these system standards.

The components of a composite video signal are normally decoded into three separate signals representing the three channels of a color space model, such as RGB, YUV, or YIQ. Although the RGB model is quite commonly used in still imaging, the YUV, YIQ, or YCbCr models are more often used in motion-video imaging. TV practice uses YUV or similar color models because the U and V channels can be downsampled to reduce data volume without materially degrading image quality.

The three composite channels mentioned here are the same channels used in the downsampling stage of JPEG compression; for more information, see the discussion of JPEG in Chapter 9, *Data Compression.*)

Once the video signal is converted to a digital format, the resulting values can be represented on a display device as pixels. Each pixel is a spot of color on the video display, and the pixels are arranged in rows and columns just as in a bitmap. Unlike a static bitmap, however, the pixels in a video image are constantly being updated for changes in intensity and color. This updating is called scanning, and it occurs 60 times per second in NTSC video signals (50 times per second for PAL and SECAM).

A video sequence is displayed as a series of frames. Each frame is a snapshot of a moment in time of the motion-video data, and is very similar to a still image. When the frames are played back in sequence on a display device, a rendering of the original video data is created. In real-time video the playback rate is 30 frames per second. This is the minimum rate necessary for the human eye to successfully blend each video frame together into a continuous, smoothly moving image.

A single frame of video data can be quite large in size. A video frame with a resolution of 512 x 482 will contain 246,784 pixels. If each pixel contains 24 bits of color information, the frame will require 740,352 bytes of memory or disk space to store. Assuming there are 30 frames per second for real-time video, a 10-second video sequence would be more than 222 megabytes in size! It is clear there can be no computer video without at least one efficient method of video data compression.

There are many encoding methods available that will compress video data. The majority of these methods involve the use of a transform coding scheme, usually employing a Fourier or Discrete Cosine Transform (DCT). These transforms physically reduce the size of the video data by selectively throwing away unneeded parts of the digitized information. Transform compression schemes usually discard 10 percent to 25 percent or more of the original video data, depending largely on the content of the video data and upon what image quality is considered acceptable.

Usually a transform is performed on an individual video frame. The transform itself does not produce compressed data. It discards only data not used by the human eye. The transformed data, called coefficients, must have compression applied to reduce the size of the data even further. Each frame of data may be compressed using a Huffman or arithmetic encoding algorithm, or even a more complex compression scheme such as JPEG. (See Chapter 9, *Data Compression*, for a discussion of these compression methods.) This type of intraframe encoding usually results in compression ratios between 20:1 to 40:1 depending on the data in the frame. However, even higher compression ratios may result if, rather than looking at single frames as if they were still images, we look at multiple frames as temporal images.

In a typical video sequence, very little data changes from frame to frame. If we encode only the pixels that change between frames, the amount of data required to store a single video frame drops significantly. This type of compression is known as interframe delta compression, or in the case of video, motion compensation. Typical motion compensation schemes that encode only frame deltas (data that has changed between frames) can, depending on the data, achieve compression ratios upwards of 200:1.

This is only one possible type of video compression method. There are many other types of video compression schemes, some of which are similar and some of which are different. For more information on compression methods, refer to Chapter 9 and to the articles in Part II that describe multimedia file formats.

Digital Audio

All multimedia file formats are capable of storing sound information. Sound data, like graphics and video data, has its own special requirements when it is being read, written, interpreted, and compressed. Before looking at how sound is stored in a multimedia format we must look at how sound itself is stored as digital data.

All of the sounds that we hear occur in the form of analog signals. An analog audio recording system, such as a conventional tape recorder, captures the entire sound wave form and stores it in analog format on a medium such as magnetic tape.

Because computers are now digital, and not analog, devices it is necessary to store sound information in a digitized format that computers can readily use. A digital audio recording system does not record the entire wave form as analog systems do (the exception being Digital Audio Tape [DAT] systems). Instead, a digital recorder captures a wave form at specific intervals, called the sampling rate. Each captured wave-form snapshot is converted to a binary integer value and is then stored on magnetic tape or disk.

Storing audio as digital samples is known as Pulse Code Modulation (PCM). PCM is a simple quantizing or digitizing (audio to digital conversion) algorithm, which linearly converts all analog signals to digital samples. This process is commonly used on all audio CD-ROMs.

Differential Pulse Code Modulation (DPCM) is an audio encoding scheme that quantizes the difference between samples rather than the samples themselves. Because the differences are easily represented by values smaller than those of the samples themselves, fewer bits may be used to encode the same sound (for example, the difference between two 16-bit samples may only be four bits in size). For this reason, DPCM is also considered an audio compression scheme.

One other audio compression scheme, which uses difference quantization, is Adaptive Differential Pulse Code Modulation (ADPCM). DPCM is a non-adaptive algorithm. That is, it does not change the way it encodes data based on the content of the data. DPCM uses the sample number of bits to represent every signal level. ADPCM, however, is an adaptive algorithm and changes its encoding scheme based on the data it is encoding. ADPCM specifically adapts by using fewer bits to represent lower-level signals than it does to represent higher-level signals. Many of the most commonly used audio compression schemes are based on ADPCM.

Digital audio data is simply a binary representation of a sound. This data can be written to a binary file using an audio file format for permanent storage much in the same way bitmap data is preserved in an image file format. The data can be read by a software application, can be sent as data to a hardware device, and can even be pressed into a plastic medium and stored as a CD-ROM.

The quality of an audio sample is determined by comparing it to the original sound from which it was sampled. The more identical the sample is to the original sound, the higher the quality of the sample. This is similar to comparing an image to the original document or photograph from which it was scanned.

The quality of audio data is determined by three parameters:

- Sample resolution
- Sampling rate
- Number of audio channels sampled

The *sample resolution* is determined by the number of bits per sample. The larger the sampling size, the higher the quality of the sample. Just as the apparent quality (resolution) of an image is reduced by storing fewer bits of data per pixel, so is the quality of a digital audio recording reduced by storing fewer bits per sample. Typical sampling sizes are eight bits and 16 bits.

The *sampling rate* is the number of times per second the analog wave form was read to collect data. The higher the sampling rate, the greater the quality of the audio. A high sampling rate collects more data per second than a lower sampling rate, therefore requiring more memory and disk space to store. Common sampling rates are 44.100 kHz (higher quality), 22.254 kHz (medium quality), and 11.025 kHz (lower quality). Sampling rates are usually measured in the signal processing terms hertz (Hz) or kilohertz (kHz), but the term samples per second (samples/second) is more appropriate for this type of measurement.

A sound source may be sampled using one channel (monaural sampling) or two channels (stereo sampling). Two-channel sampling provides greater quality than mono sampling and, as you might have guessed, produces twice as much data by doubling the number of samples captured. Sampling one channel for one second at 11,000 samples/second produces 11,000 samples. Sampling two channels at the same rate, however, produces 22,000 samples/second.

The amount of binary data produced by sampling even a few seconds of audio is quite large. Ten seconds of data sampled at the lowest quality (one channel, 8-bit sample resolution, 11.025 samples/second sampling rate) produces about 108K of data (88.2 Kbits/second). Adding a second channel doubles the amount of data to produce nearly a 215K file (176 Kbits/second). If we increase the sample resolution to 16 bits, the size of the data doubles again to 430K (352 Kbits/second). If we now increase the sampling rate to 22.05 Ksamples/second, the amount of data produced doubles again to 860K (705.6 Kbits/second). At the highest quality (two channels, 16-bit sample resolution, 44.1 Ksamples/second sampling rate), our 10 seconds of audio now requires 1.72 megabytes (1411.2 Kbits/second) of disk space to store.

Consider how little information can really be stored in 10 seconds of sound. The typical musical song is at least three minutes in length. Music videos are from five to 15 minutes in length. A typical television program is 30 to 60 minutes in length. Movie videos can be three hours or more in length. We're talking a lot of disk space here.

One solution to the massive storage requirements of high-quality audio data is data compression. For example, the CD-DA (Compact Disc-Digital Audio) standard performs mono or stereo sampling using a sample resolution of 16 bits and a sampling rate of 44.1 samples/second, making it a very high-quality format for both music and language applications. Storing five minutes of CD-DA information requires approximately 25 megabytes of disk space—only half the amount of space that would be required if the audio data were uncompressed.

Audio data, in common with most binary data, contains a fair amount of redundancy that can be removed with data compression. Conventional compression methods used in many archiving programs (zoo and pkzip, for example) and image file formats don't do a very good job of compressing audio data (typically 10 percent to 20 percent). This is because audio data is organized very differently from either the ASCII or binary data normally handled by these types of algorithms.

Audio compression algorithms, like image compression algorithms, can be categorized as lossy and lossless. Lossless compression methods do not discard any data. The decompression step produces exactly the same data as was read by the compression step. A simple form of lossless audio compression is to Huffman-encode the differences between each successive 8-bit sample. Huffman encoding is a lossless compression algorithm and, therefore the audio data is preserved in its entirety.

Lossy compression schemes discard data based on the perceptions of the psychoacoustic system of the human brain. Parts of sounds that the ear cannot hear, or the brain does not care about, can be discarded as useless data.

An algorithm must be careful when discarding audio data. The ear is very sensitive to changes in sound. The eye is very forgiving about dropping a video frame here or reducing the number of colors there. The ear, however, notices even slight changes in sounds, especially when specifically trained to recognize audial infidelities and discrepancies. However, the higher the quality of an audio sample, the more data will be required to store it. As with lossy image compression schemes, at times you'll need to make a subjective decision between quality and data size.

Audio

There is currently no "audio file interchange format" that is widely used in the computer-audio industry. Such a format would allow a wide variety of audio data to be easily written, read, and transported between different hardware platforms and operating systems.

Most existing audio file formats, however, are very machine-specific and do not lend themselves to interchange very well. Several multimedia formats are capable of encapsulating a wide variety of audio formats, but do not describe any new audio data format in themselves.

Many audio file formats have headers just as image files do. Their header information includes parameters particular to audio data, including sample rate, number of channels, sample resolution, type of compression, and so on. An identification field ("magic" number) is also included in several audio file format headers.

Several formats contain only raw audio data and no file header. Any parameters these formats use are fixed in value and therefore would be redundant to store in a file header. Stream-oriented formats contain packets (chunks) of information embedded at strategic points within the raw audio data itself. Such formats are very platform-dependent and would require an audio file format reader or converter to have prior knowledge of just what these parameter values are.

Most audio file formats may be identified by their file types or extensions. Some common sound file formats are:

.AU	Sun Microsystems
.SND	NeXT
HCOM	Apple Macintosh
.VOC	SoundBlaster
.WAV	Microsoft Waveform
AIFF	Apple/SGI
8SVX	Apple/SGI

A multimedia format may choose to either define its own internal audio data format or simply encapsulate an existing audio file format. Microsoft Waveform files are RIFF files with a single Waveform audio file component, while Apple QuickTime files contain their own audio data structures unique to QuickTime files.

MIDI Standard

Musical Instrument Digital Interface (MIDI) is an industry standard for representing sound in a binary format. MIDI is not an audio format, however. It does not store actual digitally sampled sounds. Instead, MIDI stores a description of sounds, in much the same way that a vector image format stores a description of an image and not image data itself.

Sound in MIDI data is stored as a series of control messages. Each message describes a sound event using terms such as pitch, duration, and volume. When these control messages are sent to a MIDI-compatible device (the MIDI standard also defines the interconnecting hardware used by MIDI devices and the communications protocol used to interchange the control information) the information in the message is interpreted and reproduced by the device.

MIDI data may be compressed, just like any other binary data, and does not require special compression algorithms in the way that audio data does.

For Further Information

Information about multimedia products from Microsoft may be obtained from the following address:

Microsoft Corporation
Multimedia Systems Group
Product Marketing
One Microsoft Way
Redmond, WA 98052-6399

The following documents, many of which are included in the Microsoft Multimedia Development Kit (MDK), contain information on multimedia applications and file formats:

Microsoft Windows Multimedia Development Kit (MDK) 1.0 Programmers Reference

Microsoft Windows 3.1 Software Development Kit (SDK) Multimedia Programmer's Reference

Microsoft Windows Multimedia Programmer's Guide

Microsoft Windows Multimedia Programmer's Reference

Multimedia Developer Registration Kit (MDRK)

Multimedia Programming Interface and Data Specification 1.0, August 1991

Microsoft Multimedia Standards Update March 13, 1993, 2.0.0

A great deal of useful information about multimedia files and applications may be found at the following FTP site:

ftp.microsoft.com (in the *developer/drg/Multimedia* directory)

The specification for MIDI may be obtained from:

International MIDI Association (IMA)
5316 West 57th Street
Los Angles, CA 90056
213-649-6434

Refer to the articles on Microsoft RIFF, Intel DVI, MPEG, and QuickTime in Part II of this book for specific information on multimedia file formats.

Graphics File Formats

NAME:	Adobe Photoshop
ALSO KNOWN AS:	Photoshop 2.5
TYPE:	Bitmap
COLORS:	See article
COMPRESSION:	Uncompressed, RLE
MAXIMUM IMAGE SIZE:	30,000x30,000
MULTIPLE IMAGES PER FILE:	No
NUMERICAL FORMAT:	Big-endian
ORIGINATOR:	Adobe
PLATFORM:	Macintosh, MS Windows
SUPPORTING APPLICATIONS:	Photoshop, others
SPECIFICATION ON CD:	Yes
CODE ON CD:	No
IMAGES ON CD:	No
SEE ALSO:	None

USAGE: Storage and interchange of files for use with Adobe's Photoshop application.

COMMENTS: A simple yet well-thought-out bitmap format notable for the large number of colors supported.

Overview

The Adobe Photoshop format was created to support Adobe's Photoshop application, which is currently in revision 2.5. Photoshop is a highly regarded professional application with tools for bitmap editing, color, and image manipulation. It is widely distributed and used primarily in the commercial sector. There are versions which run under both the Apple Macintosh and Microsoft Windows. A previous version of the format, version 2.0, suffered from several shortcomings, including a lack of compression and dependence on the Macintosh file system. These problems have been eliminated in version 2.5.

File Organization

Files in the Photoshop format consist of the following:

- A fixed-length header, which may include color information

- A variable-length mode block

- A variable-length image resources block

- A reserved block

- A word indicating the compression type

- The image data

On the Macintosh platform, files are identified by the filetype code 8BPS, which is contained in the signature string of the header. Under MS Windows, on the IBM PC platform, files are saved with the extension .PSD.

File Details

The Adobe Photoshop header has the following format:

```
typedef struct _PSHOP_HEADER
{
    CHAR Signature[4];          /* signature string */
    WORD Version;               /* version number */
    CHAR Reserved[6];           /* reserved data */
    WORD Channels;              /* number of color channels */
    DWORD Rows;                 /* number of rows in image */
    DWORD Columns;              /* number of columns in image */
    WORD Depth;                 /* bits per channel */
    WORD Mode;                  /* color mode */
} PSHOP_HEADER;
```

Signature contains the four bytes 8BPS, which also identifies the filetype on the Macintosh system.

Version is currently always 1. Adobe advises rejecting the image if the version number is anything but 1.

Reserved is six bytes of reserved data following the version number; these should be filled with zeros.

Channels is the number of color channels in the image. Between one and 16 color channels are supported in Photoshop 2.5.

Rows and Columns indicate the size of the image.

Depth supplies the number of bits per color channel, which currently may be either 1 or 8.

Mode is the color mode of the file, which provides information about how the image data should be interpreted. Possible values are:

0	Bitmap
1	Gray scale
2	Palette color
3	RGB color
4	CMYK color
7	Multi-channel color
8	Duotone
9	Lab color

The above header is followed by the mode data. This consists of a 4-byte length field and subsequent data. If the mode field indicates that palette data is contained in the file, the length is 768 bytes. If the mode field indicates that duotone data is contained in the file, the mode data contains undocumented duotone specification information, and the uninitiated reader may treat the duotone data as gray-scale information. If the mode field indicates any other type of data (not palette or duotone), the length field is zero, and mode data is not present.

Following the mode data is another variable-length image resources block. This consists of a 4-byte length field, followed by a Photoshop 2.5 image resources block, which contains information on the image's resolution and data relevant to the application. For more information about the Photoshop 2.5 image resources block, contact Adobe.

Following the image resources block is a reserved block, consisting of a 4-byte length and data. Currently this is reserved for future use, and the length is zero.

The reserved block is followed by two bytes of compression data, for which two values are currently defined:

0	Uncompressed
1	Run length each codeup (RLE)

The RLE algorithm used is the same as that used by the Macintosh PackBits system routine and in the TIFF file format.

The image data follows and is planar; each plane is in scanline order. There are no pad bytes. If the data is RLE compressed, the image data is preceded by the byte counts for all the scan lines. Each count is stored as a 2-byte value. This is followed by the RLE compressed data. Each line is compressed separately.

For Further Information

For further information about the Adobe Photoshop format, see the specification included on the CD-ROM that accompanies this disk. You can also contact Adobe Systems at:

Adobe Systems Inc.
Attn: Adobe Systems Developer Support
1585 Charleston Rd.
P.O. Box 7900
Mountain View, CA 94039-7900

Voice: 415-961-4400
Voice: 800-344-8335
FAX:　415-961-3769

NAME:	Atari ST graphics file formats
ALSO KNOWN AS:	.ANI, .ANM, .CE1, .CE2, .CE3, .FLM, .UC1, .UC2, .UC3., NEO, .PAC, .PC1, .PC2, .PC3, PC3, .PI1, .PI2, .PI3, .RGB, .SEQ, .TNY, .TN1, .TN2, .TN3
TYPE:	Bitmap and animation
COLORS:	Typically 16
COMPRESSION:	None and RLE
MAXIMUM IMAGE SIZE:	Typically 320x200 pixels
MULTIPLE IMAGES PER FILE:	Yes (animation formats only)
NUMERICAL FORMAT:	Big-endian
ORIGINATOR:	Various Atari ST software developers
PLATFORM:	Atari ST
SUPPORTING APPLICATIONS:	Many
SPECIFICATION ON CD:	Yes (third-party description)
CODE ON CD:	No
IMAGES ON CD:	No
SEE ALSO:	IFF

USAGE: All of these formats are used by paint and animation packages found on the Atari ST.

COMMENTS: The Atari ST, with its superior graphics capabilities, was a natural platform for development of multimedia, so much of the multimedia developments of today are based on these formats.

Overview

The Atari ST computer is the home of many sparsely documented image file formats. Many of these formats are used specifically for storing animation images and dumps of images displayed on the screen. Although the Electronic Arts IFF format is used by most Atari ST paint and animation programs, many software developers have devised their own special-purpose formats to fill their needs.

File Organization and Details

This section contains a brief description of each of the Atari ST file formats; each format has its own file extension.

Animatic Film Format (.FLM)

The Animatic Film file format (file extension .FLM) stores a sequence of low-resolution 16-color images, which are displayed as an animation. Files in the .FLM format are stored as a header followed by one or more frames of image data. The header is 26 bytes in length and has the following format:

```
typedef struct _AnimaticFilmHeader
{
    WORD NumberOfFrames;         /* Number of frames in the animation */
    WORD Palette[16];            /* Color palette */
    WORD FilmSpeed;              /* Speed of playback */
    WORD PlayDirection;          /* Direction of play */
    WORD EndAction;              /* Action to take after last frame */
    WORD FrameWidth;             /* Width of frame in pixels */
    WORD FrameHeight;            /* Height of frame in pixels */
    WORD MajorVersionNumber;     /* Animatic major version number */
    WORD MinorVersionNumber;     /* Animatic minor version number */
    LONG MagicNumber;            /* ID number (always 27182818h) */
    LONG Reserved[3];            /* Unused (all zeros) */
} ANIMATICFILMHEADER;
```

NumberOfFrames specifies the total number of frames in the animation.

Palette is the color palette for the animation, stored as an array of 16 WORD values.

FilmSpeed is the number of delay (vblank) frames to display between each animation frame. The value of this field may be in the range 0 to 99.

PlayDirection is the direction the animation is played. Values for this field are 00h for forwards and 01h for backwards.

EndAction specifies the action to take when the last frame of the animation is reached during playback. A value of 00h indicates that the player should pause and then repeat the animation from the beginning. A value of 01h indicates that the animation should immediately repeat from the beginning (loop). A value of 03h indicates that playback should repeat in the reverse direction.

FrameWidth and FrameHeight are the size of the animation frames in pixels.

MajorVersionNumber and MinorVersionNumber contain the version number of the Animatic software that created the animation.

MagicNumber contains an identification value for Animatic Film files. This value is always 27182818h.

Reserved is 12 bytes of space reserved for future header fields. All bytes in this field have the value 00h.

ComputerEyes Raw Data Format (.CE1 and .CE2)

The ComputerEyes Raw Data Format is found in a low-resolution (file extension .CE1) and a medium-resolution (file extension .CE2) format. The header is 10 bytes in length and has the following format:

```
typedef struct _ComputerEyesHeader
{
    LONG Id;           /* Identification value (always 45594553h) */
    WORD Resolution;   /* Image data resolution */
    BYTE Reserved[8];  /* Miscellaneous data */
} COMPUTEREYESHEAD;
```

Id is a value used to identify a file as containing ComputerEyes-format data. The value of this field is always 45594553h or "EYES" as an ASCII string.

Resolution is the resolution of the image data stored in the file. This value is 00h for low-resolution data and 01h for high-resolution data.

Reserved is eight bytes of additional information, which is not needed for decoding the image data.

If the Resolution field value is 00h (low resolution), then the image data will be divided into three 320x220 RGB planes. Each plane is 64,000 bytes in size and is stored in red, green, blue order. The image data stores one pixel per byte, and only the lower six bits of each byte are used. Low-resolution image data is stored vertically, so rows of data are read along the Y-axis and not along the X-axis as in most other formats.

If the Resolution field value is 01h (high resolution), then the image data is stored in a single 640x480 plane, which is always 256,000 bytes in size. The image data stores one pixel per WORD, with the red value stored in bits 0 through 4, green in bits 5 through 9, and blue in bits 10 through 14. Bit 15 is not used. High-resolution image data is also stored along the vertical, rather than the horizontal, axis of the bitmap.

Cyber Paint Sequence Format (.SEQ)

The Cyber Paint Sequence file format (file extension .SEQ) is used for storing sequences of 16-color low-resolution images used in animations. Cyber Paint also supports an efficient form of delta-encoded data compression.

```
typedef struct _CyberPaintHeader
{
    WORD MagicNumber;                           /* Identification number */
    WORD VersionNumber;                         /* Version number */
    LONG NumberOfFrames;                        /* Total number of frames */
    WORD DisplayRate;                           /* Display speed */
    BYTE Reserved[118];                         /* Unused */
    LONG FrameOffsets[NumberOfFrames];  /* Array of frame offsets */
} CUVERPAINTHEAD;
```

MagicNumber is an identification number used to indicate that the file contains Cyber Paint Sequence data. This value is typically FEDBh or FEDCh.

VersionNumber is the version number of the format.

NumberOfFrames specifies the number of data frames stored.

DisplayRate is the number of delay (vblank) frames to display between each animation frame.

Reserved is a 118-byte field reserved for future header fields. This field is set to a value of 00h.

FrameOffsets is an array of LONG offset values with a number of elements equal to the value stored in the NumberOfFrames field. Each offset value indicates the starting position of each frame, calculated from the beginning of the file.

Each frame contains a header of descriptive information in the following format:

```
typedef struct _CyberPaintFrame
{
    WORD Type;                /* Frame type */
    WORD Resolution;          /* Frame Resolution */
    WORD Palette[16];         /* Color palette */
    BYTE FileName[12];        /* Name of frame data file */
    WORD Limits;              /* Color animation limits */
    WORD Speed;               /* Color animation speed and direction */
    WORD NumberOfSteps;       /* Number of color steps */
    WORD XOffset;             /* Left position of frame on display */
```

```
       WORD YOffset;          /* Top position of frame on display */
       WORD FrameWidth;       /* Width of the frame in pixels */
       WORD FrameHeight;      /* Height of the frame in pixels */
       BYTE Operation;        /* Graphics operation */
       BYTE Compression;      /* Data storage method */
       LONG DataSize;         /* Length of the frame data in bytes */
       BYTE Reserved[60];     /* Unused */
   } CYBERPAINTFRAME;
```

Type is an identification value identifying the header as belonging to a frame.

Resolution is the resolution of the frame data and is usually 00h.

Palette is an array of values for the 16-color palette for this frame.

FileName stores the name of the disk file in which the frame data is stored. The default string stored in this field is "   . ", which indicates no filename.

Limits is the color animation limits of the frame.

Speed specifies the speed and direction of the playback.

NumberOfSteps is the number of color steps in the image data.

XOffset is the left position of the frame on the display. This value may be in the range of 0 to 319.

YOffset is the top position of the frame on the display. This value may be in the range of 0 to 199.

FrameWidth and FrameHeight are the size of the frame in pixels.

Operation is the graphics operation to perform on the frame data. A value of 00h indicates copy, and a value of 01h indicates an exclusive OR.

Compression indicates whether the frame data is compressed (a value of 01h) or uncompressed (a value of 00h).

DataSize is the actual size of the data (compressed or uncompressed) stored in the frame.

Reserved is a 60-byte field reserved for future header fields. All bytes in this field have the value 00h.

Frame data stored in a Sequence file is always 320x200 pixels. The frame data is stored as four bitplanes, with one pixel stored per WORD. Pixels are always stored along the vertical (Y) axis of the bitmap. Therefore, the first 200 bytes of frame data are the first pixels of the first bitplane of the frame, and so on.

Frame data may be compressed using a delta-encoding algorithm. Using this technique, only the changes between frames are actually encoded. Interframe data that does not change is not saved.

The first frame in a sequence is always stored in its entirety. You have to start someplace. Each frame thereafter is compared to the previous frame, and only the X and Y coordinates of rectangular regions of pixel values (called *change boxes*) that have changed are saved. Only one change box is stored per frame.

Each change box may be stored in one of five different variations, always using the variation that yields the best compression for a particular change box. These variations are:

- Uncompressed Copy, where the frame data is uncompressed and is simply copied onto the screen at coordinates specified in the XOffset and YOffset header fields.

- Uncompressed EOR, where the frame data is exclusive ORed with the data already at XOffset,YOffset.

- The frame data is compressed and must be uncompressed before copying to the screen.

- Compressed EOR, where the frame data must be uncompressed before it is exclusive ORed with the screen data.

- Null Frame, which contains no data (height and width are 00h) and is treated as the previous frame.

Compressed data contains a sequence of control WORDs (16-bit signed WORDs) and data. A control WORD with a value between 1 and 32,767 indicates that the next WORD is to be repeated a number of times equal to the control WORD value. A control WORD with a negative value indicates that a run of bytes equal to the absolute value of the control WORD value is to be read from the compressed data.

DEGAS Format (.PI1, .PI2, .PI3, .PC1, .PC2, .PC3)

The DEGAS animation file format actually occurs in three different variations. The DEGAS and DEGAS Elite formats support low, medium, and high-resolution graphics data (files have the extension .PI1, .PI2, and .PI3 respectively). The DEGAS Elite Compressed format supports low, medium, and high-resolution graphics data (files have the extension .PC1, .PC2, and .PC3 respectively), and it also supports data compression.

The DEGAS format stores only a single image of the display. The header is 34 bytes long and is followed by 32,000 bytes of image data:

```
typedef struct _DegasHeader
{
     WORD Resolution;      /* Image resolution */
     WORD Palette[16];     /* Color palette */
} DEGASHEAD;
```

Resolution is the resolution of the image data stored as a bit-field. Valid values are:

00h	Left
01h	Off
02h	Right

Palette is an array of 16 WORD values that holds the color palette for the image.

The DEGAS Elite format contains the same header and image data structure as the DEGAS format. It differs form the DEGAS format in that it has a 32-byte footer containing additional information:

```
typedef struct _DegasEliteFooter
{
     WORD LeftColor[4];    /* Left color animation limit table */
     WORD RightColor[4];   /* Right color animation limit table */
     WORD Direction[4];    /* Animation channel direction flag */
     WORD Delay[4];        /* Animation channel delay */
} DEGASELITEFOOT;
```

LeftColor stores the left color animation limit table containing the starting color numbers for the animation.

RightColor stores the right color animation limit table containing the ending color numbers for the animation.

Direction contains the animation channel direction bit-field flag. Valid values are:

00h	Left
01h	Off
02h	Right

Atari ST Graphics Formats (cont'd)

Delay is the animation channel delay rate between frames. This value is measured in 1/60 of a second and is subtracted from the constant 128 to calculate this value.

The DEGAS Elite Compressed format contains the same header and footer as the DEGAS Elite format, with one variation in the header data.

The Resolution field uses the following bit values to indicate the resolution of the image data:

8000h   Low resolution
8001h   Medium resolution
8002h   High resolution

The compression algorithm used is identical to RLE scheme found in the Interchange file format (IFF); see the article on the Interchange format for details.

RGB Intermediate Format (.RGB)

The RGB Intermediate Format (file extension .RGB) is actually three low-resolution DEGAS .PI1 files concatenated into a single file. The pixel data in each plane contains an actual red, green, or blue color-channel value rather than an index into the 16-color palette. On the Atari ST, there are only three bits per color channel. The Atari ST with the extended color palette uses four bits per color channel.

The structure of an entire RGB file is shown here:

```
struct _RgbFile
{
    WORD RedResolution;      /* Red plane resolution (ignored) */
    WORD RedPalette[16];     /* Red plane palette (ignored) */
    WORD RedPlane[16000];    /* Red plane data */
    WORD GreenResolution     /* Green plane resolution (ignored) */
    WORD GreenPalette        /* Green plane palette (ignored) */
    WORD GreenPlane[16000];  /* Green plane data */
    WORD BlueResolution;     /* Blue plane resolution (ignored) */
    WORD BluePalette;        /* Blue plane palette (ignored) */
    WORD BluePlane[16000];   /* Blue plane data */
}
```

Imagic Film/Picture Format (.IC1, .IC2, .IC3)

The Imagic Format stores low-, medium-, and high-resolution image data using the file extensions .IC1, .IC2, and .IC3 respectively. The header is 49 bytes long and is formatted as follows:

```
typedef struct _ImagicHeader
{
    BYTE Id[4];               /* File identification value */
    WORD Resolution;          /* Image resolution */
    WORD Palette[16];         /* Color palette */
    WORD Date;                /* Date stamp */
    WORD Time;                /* Time stamp */
    BYTE Name[8];             /* Base file name */
    WORD Length;              /* Length of data */
    LONG Registration;        /* Registration number */
    BYTE Reserved[8];         /* Unused */
    BYTE Compression;         /* Data compression flag */
} IMAGICHEAD;
```

Id is the identification value for this format and contains the characters IMDC.

Resolution specifies the resolution of the image data. Values are:

00h	Low resolution
01h	Medium resolution
02h	High resolution

Palette is an array of 16 elements storing the color palette for this image.

Date and Time contain a date and time stamp indicating when the file was created. These stamps are in GEMDOS (Atari native operating system) format.

Name is the base filename of the image file.

Length is the length of the image data stored in the file.

Registration is the registration number of the Imagic application program which created the image file.

Reserved is an 8-byte field which is unused and set to a value of 00h.

Compression indicates whether the image data is compressed. A value of 00h indicates no compression, while a value of 01h indicates that the image data is compressed.

Image data may be run-length encoded (RLE) or delta compressed. Delta compression results in smaller animation files than RLE, although on complex images RLE works better.

NEOchrome Format (.NEO)

NEOchrome image files have the file extension .NEO and contain a 79-byte header followed by 16,000 bytes of image data. The format of the header is as follows:

```
typedef struct _NeochromeHeader
{
    WORD Flag;                /* Flag byte (always 00h) */
    WORD Resolution;          /* Image resolution */
    WORD Palette[16];         /* Color palette */
    CHAR FileName[12];        /* Name of image file */
    WORD Limits;              /* Color animation limits */
    WORD Speed;               /* Color animation speed and direction */
    WORD NumberOfSteps;       /* Number of color steps */
    WORD XOffset;             /* Image X offset (always 00h) */
    WORD YOffset;             /* Image Y offset (always 00h) */
    WORD Width;               /* Image width (always 320) */
    WORD Height;              /* Image height (always 200) */
    WORD Reserved[33];        /* Reserved (always 00h) */
} NEOCHROMEHEAD;
```

Flag is a collection of flag bits and is always set to a value of 00h.

Resolution specifies the resolution of the image data. Values are:

00h   Low resolution
01h   Medium resolution
02h   High resolution

Palette is the color palette for this image stored as an array of 16 WORD values.

FileName is the name of the image file. The default string for this field is " . " .

Limits specifies the color animation limits of the image. Bits 0 through 3 specify the value of the upper-right limit, and bits 4 through 7 specify the value of the lower-left limit. Bit 15 is set to 1 if the animation data is valid.

Speed specifies the color animation speed and direction. Bits 0 through 7 specify the speed of the playback in number of blank frames displayed per animation frame. Bit 15 indicates the direction of playback. A value of 0 indicates normal and a value of 1 indicates reversed.

NumberOfSteps is the number of frames in the animation.

XOffset and YOffset are the starting coordinates of the image on the display. These values are always 00h.

Width is the width of the image in pixels. This value is always 320.

Height is the height of the image in pixels. This value is always 200.

Reserved is a field of 33 bytes reserved for future header fields. All bytes in this field are set to 00h.

NEOchrome Animation Format (.ANI)

NEOchrome Animation files have the file extension .ANI and contain a header followed by a sequence of one or more frames of animation data stored in their playback order. The header is 22 bytes and is formatted as follows:

```
typedef struct _NewchromeAniHeader
{
    LONG MagicNumber;        /* ID value (always BABEEBEAh) */
    WORD Width;              /* Width of image in bytes */
    WORD Height;             /* Height of image in scan lines */
    WORD Size;               /* Size of image in bytes + 10 */
    WORD XCoord;             /* X coordinate of image */
    WORD YCoord;             /* Y coordinate of image - 1 */
    WORD NumberOfFrames;     /* Total number of frames */
    WORD Speed;              /* Animation playback speed */
    LONG Reserved;           /* Reserved (always 00h) */
} NEWCHROMEANIHEAD;
```

MagicNumber is the identification value for Neochrome animation files. This value is always BABEEBEAh.

Width is the width of the animation in pixels. This value must always be divisible by 8.

Height is the height of the animation frames in pixels (scan lines).

Size is the total size of a frame in bytes, plus 10.

XCoord specifies the left position of the image in pixels, minus one. This value must be divisible by 16.

YCoord specifies the top position of the image in pixels, minus one.

NumberOfFrames specifies the number of image frames in the animation.

Speed specifies the playback speed of the animation in number of blank frames displayed per image frames.

Reserved is an unused field, which is set to 00h.

STAD Format (.PAC)

The STAD image file format has the file extension .PAC. It contains a header followed by a single block of RLE-compressed image data. The header is seven bytes in size and contains only information necessary to decompress the image data. The format of the header is as follows:

```
typedef struct _StadHeader
{
    CHAR Packed[4];       /* Packing orientation of image data */
    BYTE IdByte;          /* RLE ID value of a 'PackByte' run */
    BYTE PackByte;        /* The value of a 'PackByte' run */
    BYTE SpecialByte;     /* RLE ID value of a non-'PackByte' run */
} STADHEADER;
```

Packed contains the characters pM86 if the image data in the file is vertically packed, or pM85 if it is horizontally packed.

IdByte is a value used to indicate an RLE byte run that uses the PackByte value.

PackByte is the most frequently occurring byte value in the image data.

SpecialByte is a value used to indicate an RLE byte run using a value stored in the image data.

The image data in a STAD file is always compressed using a simple RLE algorithm. STAD is a bit unique in that it allows the option of packing image data either horizontally along the bitmap (with the scan lines), or vertically down the bitmap (across the scan lines). The direction of the encoding is specified in the Packed field in the header.

The most frequently occurring byte value in the image data is stored in the PackByte field of the header. This reduces the size of the compressed data by not requiring this value to be redundantly stored in the compressed image data itself.

The STAD RLE algorithm uses three types of packets:

• The first type of packet is two bytes in length and contains an Id value and a run-count value. If the ID matches the value stored in the IdByte field of the header, then the value in the PackByte header field is repeated "run count + 1" times. This packet is used only to encode byte runs of the value stored in the PackByte header field.

- The second type of packet is three bytes in length and is used to store a run of a value other than that in the PackByte field. The first byte is an ID matching the SpecialByte field in the header. The second byte is the value of the run, and the third byte is the number of bytes in the run.

- The third type of packet is a single literal byte. If an ID byte is read, and it does not match either the IdByte or SpecialByte value, then this byte is simply written literally to the output.

Following is a simple, pseudo-code description of the RLE decoding process:

```
Read a byte
    If the byte is the IdByte value
        Read a byte (the RunCount)
        Repeat the PackByte value RunCount + 1 times else
    If the byte is the SpecialByte value
        Read a byte (the RunValue)
        Read a byte (the RunCount)
        Repeat the RunValue RunCount times
    else
        Use the byte value literally.
```

Tiny Format (.TNY, .TN1, .TN2, .TN3)

The Tiny format (.TNY) is similar to the NEOchrome formats. Tiny files may contain low (.TN1), medium (.TN2), or high (.TN3) resolution image data.

Tiny files may have one of two different header formats. The most common is 37 bytes in length and is formatted as follows:

```
typedef struct _TinyHeader
{
    BYTE Resolution;        /* Resolution of the image data */
    WORD Palette[16];       /* Color palette */
    WORD ControlBytes;      /* Number of control bytes */
    WORD DataWords;         /* Number of data words */
} TINYHEAD;
```

Resolution specifies the resolution of the image data. Values are:

00h	Low resolution
01h	Medium resolution
02h	High resolution

Palette is the 16-color palette of the image data.

ControlBytes is the number of control bytes found in the image data. This value is in the range of 3 to 10,667.

DataWords is the number of WORDs of image data stored in the file. This value is in the range of 1 to 16,000.

If the value of the Resolution field is 03h or greater, the Tiny header has the following format:

```
typedef struct _TinyHeader
{
    BYTE Resolution;            /* Resolution of the image data */
    BYTE Limits;                /* Color animation limits */
    BYTE Speed;                 /* Speed and direction of playback */
    WORD Duration;              /* Color rotation duration */
    WORD Palette[16];           /* Color palette */
    WORD ControlBytes;          /* Number of control bytes */
    WORD DataWords;             /* Number of data words */
} TINYHEAD;
```

Limits specifies the left and right color animation limits. Bits 0 through 3 store the right (end) limit value, and bits 4 through 7 store the left (start) limit value.

Speed specifies the speed and direction of the animation playback. A negative value indicates left playback, and a positive value indicates right playback. The absolute value is the speed (delay between frames) in increments of 1/60 of a second.

Duration specifies the color rotation duration (number of iterations).

ControlBytes specifies the size of a BYTE array that follows the header. This array contains control values used to specify how the Tiny image data is to be uncompressed.

DataWords specifies the number of data words in the image data. The run-length encoded image data follows the control-value array. Tiny image data is uncompressed by reading a control value and then, based on the control value, performing an action on the encoded data.

If a control value is negative, then the absolute value of the control value indicates the number of WORDs to read literally from the compressed data. If a control value is equal to zero, another control value is read, and its value (128 to 32767) is used to specify the number of times to repeat the next data WORD. If a control value is equal to one, another control value is read and its value (128 to 32767) is used to specify the number of literal WORDs to read from the data section. And a control value greater than one specifies the number of times to repeat the next WORD read from the data section (two to 127).

The uncompressed image data is stored along its Y-axis in a fashion identical to many other Atari image file formats.

For Further Information

Although we have not been able to obtain an official specification document from Atari, the article included on the CD that accompanies this book contains detailed information about the Atari ST graphics file formats. See the following:

Baggett, David M., *Atari ST Picture Formats.*

The author has also kindly agreed to be a resource for information about the Atari ST format files. Contact:

David M. Baggett
dmb@ai.mit.edu

AutoCAD DXF

NAME:	AutoCAD DXF
ALSO KNOWN AS:	AutoCAD Drawing Exchange Format, DXF, .DXB, .SLD, .ADI
TYPE:	Vector
COLORS:	256
COMPRESSION:	None
MAXIMUM IMAGE SIZE:	NA
MULTIPLE IMAGES PER FILE:	No
NUMERICAL FORMAT:	Multiple
ORIGINATOR:	Autodesk
PLATFORM:	MS-DOS
SUPPORTING APPLICATIONS:	AutoCad, many CAD programs, Corel Draw, others
SPECIFICATION ON CD:	Yes
CODE ON CD:	No
IMAGES ON CD:	No
SEE ALSO:	None
USAGE:	Storage and exchange of CAD and vector information.
COMMENTS:	A difficult format, mainly because it is controlled by a single vendor, but one that is in wide use, both for the exchange of CAD information and simple line-oriented vector information. It has two twin binary formats, one with the same file extension as the non-binary version and one tailored to the originating application (AutoCad). Data is stored as 7-bit text.

Overview

The AutoCAD DXF (Drawing eXchange Format) and the AutoCAD DXB (Drawing eXchange Binary) formats are associated with the CAD application AutoCAD, created and maintained by Autodesk. DXB is a binary version of a DXF file used for faster loading and is apparently tailored for use by AutoCAD. The DXB format first appeared in AutoCAD in Release 10. Other file formats associated with AutoCAD are the slide (.SLD) and plot (.ADI) formats. DXF supports many features not found in most other vector formats, including the ability to store three-dimensional objects and to handle associative dimensioning.

One curiosity of the format is that each object in a DXF file can be assigned a color value, but because the file contains no palette information, there is no way to associate the color values with any external referent. Because DXF was created in support of a CAD program, there is good support for included text. Although DXF is widely used as a least-common-denominator format for the exchange of simple line data, an application designer wishing to support DXF must consider that fact that AutoCAD can store curves and 3-D objects as well as 2-D. Although there is a provision in AutoCAD (and other programs) for writing only the simplest vector data, providing full support for DXF is a huge task. Many application designers ultimately decide to write, but not read, DXF files, preferring to leave the hard part to others.

Because the DXF format is quite complex and is fully and concisely documented in about 40 pages, we will simply outline some of the information necessary to understand the file. Please refer to the original specification document on the CD-ROM included with this book.

File Organization

Each DXF file consists of five sections: a header; tables, blocks, and entities sections; and an end-of-file marker.

- The header contains zero or more groups of header variables that contain information applying to the entire image.

- The tables section contains organized data that is referenced by other sections of data. Table data may include information on font sizes and styles, line type descriptions, and layer information.

- The blocks section describes each block of information that is found in the image.

- The entities section contains the actual object data of the image.

- The end-of-file marker is the string EOF; it appears as the last line in the file.

Each section contains zero or more groups of data; there is no minimum set of groups that is required to appear in any section. Each group occupies two lines in the file in the following format:

```
GROUP CODE
GROUP VALUE
```

The first line is the group code, which identifies the type of data found within the group. It is a numeric field, three bytes, and is padded with spaces if it consists of less than three characters. Group codes are followed by a carriage return/linefeed pair. Some common group codes include:

0	The start of a section
1	A text value
2	A section name identifier
9	A header variable name identifier
10	X coordinate
20	Y coordinate
30	Z coordinate
62	color value
999	Comment

The second line of a group is the group value. This is a label, similar to a variable name, which identifies how the value of a group is to be used. There is no minimum set of header variables required to appear in all DXF headers. Of the more than 100 defined header variables, only the ones necessary to render the image are actually found in a DXF header. A DXF header with no header variable would appear as:

```
0 SECTION 2 HEADER 999 [header variables would appear here.] 0 ENDSEC
```

Normally, a DXF file contains only 7-bit ASCII characters, but a binary version of the format exists, which also has the extension .DXF. Binary DXF files are smaller (by 20-30 percent), load faster into AutoCAD, and preserve floating-point data more accurately than the ASCII DXF format. Release 10 was the first version of AutoCAD to support binary-format DXF files.

File Details

Binary DXF files always begin with a specific 22-byte identification string:

```
AutoCAD Binary DXF<0Dh><0Ah><1Ah><00h>
```

The format is the same as the ASCII DXF file, but all numeric values are re-encoded in binary form. All group codes are 2-byte little-endian words; all floating-point numbers are 8-byte double precision words; and all ASCII strings are NULL-terminated. In addition, there are no comments in binary DXF files.

The Drawing Interchange Binary (DXB) format is a subset of the DXF format that is also binary encoded. The DXB files are much smaller than binary DXF format files and load very quickly. DXB format also supports fewer entities than the DXF format.

A DXB file can be distinguished from a binary DXF file by the file extension .DXB, and by the fact that it always begins with a 19-byte identification string:

```
AutoCAD DXB 1.0<0Dh><0Ah><1Ah><00h>
```

For Further Information

For further information about the AutoCAD DXF format, see the DXF specification included on the CD that accompanies this book.

The AutoCAD Manual Release 12 also contains complete information on the DXF format; see:

> *AutoCAD Customization Manual*, Release 12, Autodesk Inc., 1992, pp.241-281.

Autodesk has also released an electronic document describing the DXF format, which may be found on many online services and BBSs.

Many books on AutoCAD have been published, and several include in-depth information on the DXF format, including the following:

> Jones, Frederick H. and Martin, Lloyd. *The AutoCAD Database Book*, Ventana Press, Chapel Hill, NC, 1989.

> Johnson, N. *AutoCAD, The Complete Reference*, second edition, McGraw-Hill, New York, NY, 1991.

For additional information about this format, you may also contact:

> Autodesk, Inc.
> Attn: Neele Johnston
> Autodesk Developer Marketing
> 2320 Marinship Way
> Sausalito, CA 94965
> Voice: 415-491-8719
> *neele@autodesk.com*

BDF

NAME:	BDF
ALSO KNOWN AS:	Bitmap Distribution Format
TYPE:	Bitmap
COLORS:	Mono
COMPRESSION:	None
MAXIMUM IMAGE SIZE:	Unlimited
MULTIPLE IMAGES PER FILE:	Yes
NUMERICAL FORMAT:	ASCII
ORIGINATOR:	X Consortium
PLATFORM:	Any supporting X Window System
SUPPORTING APPLICATIONS:	Many X applications
SPECIFICATION ON CD:	Yes
CODE ON CD:	No
IMAGES ON CD:	Yes
SEE ALSO:	None
USAGE:	Used to store and exchange font information.
COMMENTS:	Can be used to store arrays of ornamental glyph and other bitmap data.

Overview

BDF (Bitmap Distribution Format) is used by the X Window System as a method of storing and exchanging font data with other systems. The current version of BDF is 2.1; it is part of X11 Release 5. BDF is similar in concept to the PostScript Page Description Language. Both formats store data as printable ASCII characters, using lines of ASCII text that vary in length. Each line is terminated by an end-of-line character that may be a carriage return (ASCII 0Dh), a linefeed (ASCII 0Ah), or both.

Each BDF file stores information for exactly one typeface at one size and orientation (in other words, a font). A typeface is the name of the type style, such as Goudy, Courier, or Helvetica. A font is a variation in size, style, or orientation of a typeface, such as Goudy 10 Point, Courier Italic, or Helvetica Reversed. A glyph is a single character of a font, such as the letter "j". A BDF file therefore contains the data for one or more glyphs of a single font and typeface.

File Organization

A BDF file begins with information pertaining to the typeface as a whole, followed by the information on the font, and finally by the bitmapped glyph information itself. The information in a BDF file is stored in a series of records. Each record begins with an uppercase keyword, followed by one or more fields called tokens:

```
KEYWORD <token> <token> . . .
```

All records, keywords, and information fields contain only ASCII characters and are separated by spaces. Lines are terminated by a <CR>, <LF>, or <CR/LF> pair. More than one record may appear on a physical line.

File Details

Following are some of the more common records found in BDF files:

```
STARTFONT <version>
ENDFONT
```

All BDF files begin with the STARTFONT record. This record contains a single information field indicating the version of the BDF format used in the file. The STARTFONT record contains all of the information within the BDF file and is terminated by the ENDFONT keyword as the last record in the file.

```
COMMENT <text>
```

COMMENT records may be found anywhere between the STARTFONT and ENDFONT records. They usually contain human-readable text that is ignored by font-reader applications.

```
FONT <fontname>
```

The FONT record specifies the name of the font contained within the BDF file. The name is specified using either the XFD font name or a private font name. The name may contain spaces, and the line containing the FONT record must be terminated by an end-of-line character.

```
SIZE <pointsize> <x resolution> <y resolution>
```

SIZE specifies the size of the font in points and the resolution of the output device that is to support the font.

```
FONTBOUNDINGBOX <width> <height> <x offset> <y offset>
```

The FONTBOUNDINGBOX record stores the size and the position of the font's bounding box as an offset from the origin (the lower-left corner of the bitmap).

```
STARTPROPERTIES <number of properties>
ENDPROPERTIES
```

The STARTPROPERTIES record contains subrecords that define the characteristics of the font. The STARTPROPERTIES keyword is followed by the number of properties defined within this record. The subrecords specify information such as the name of the font's creator, the typeface of the font, kerning and other rendering information, and copyright notices. The ENDPROPERTIES record always terminates the STARTPROPERTIES record. Following the ENDPROPERTIES record is the actual font data.

Following are descriptions of some common record keywords that may be used to describe the font data:

```
CHARS <number of segments>
```

The CHARS record indicates the number of font character (glyph) segments stored in the file.

```
STARTCHAR <glyphname>
ENDCHAR
```

The STARTCHAR record contains subrecords that store each glyph's information and data. The STARTCHAR keyword is followed by the name of the glyph. This name can be up to 14 characters in length and may not contain any spaces. The subrecords specify the index number of the glyph, the scalable width, and the position of the character.

The BITMAP record contains the actual glyph data encoded as 4-digit hexadecimal values. All bitmapped lines are padded on the right with zeros out to the nearest byte boundary. All of the glyph information is contained between the STARTCHAR record and the terminating ENDCHAR record. There is one STARTCHAR/ENDCHAR section per glyph stored in the BDF file.

Refer to the BDF documentation included with the X11R5 distribution for more information about the BDF information records.

Following is an example of a BDF file containing the characters j and quoteright ('). Note that more than one record appears per physical line:

```
STARTFONT 2.1 COMMENT This is a sample font in 2.1 format.
FONT -Adobe-Helvetica-Bold-R-Normal—24-240-75-75-
P-65-ISO8859-1 SIZE 24 75 75 FONTBOUNDINGBOX 9 24 -2 -6
STARTPROPERTIES 19 FOUNDRY "Adobe" FAMILY "Helvetica"
WEIGHT_NAME "Bold" SLANT "R" SETWIDTH_NAME "Normal"
ADD_STYLE_NAME "" PIXEL_SIZE 24 POINT_SIZE 240 RESOLUTION_X
75 RESOLUTION_Y 75 SPACING "P" AVERAGE_WIDTH 65
CHARSET_REGISTRY "ISO8859" CHARSET_ENCODING "1" MIN_SPACE 4
FONT_ASCENT 21 FONT_DESCENT 7 COPYRIGHT "Copyright (c) 1987
Adobe Systems, Inc." NOTICE "Helvetica is a registered
trademark of Linotype Inc." ENDPROPERTIES CHARS 2 STARTCHAR
j ENCODING 106 SWIDTH 355 0 DWIDTH 8 0 BBX 9 22 -2 -6 BITMAP
0380 0380 0380 0380 0000 0700 0700 0700 0700 0E00 0E00 0E00
0E00 0E00 1C00 1C00 1C00 1C00 3C00 7800 F000 E000 ENDCHAR
STARTCHAR quoteright ENCODING 39 SWIDTH 223 0 DWIDTH 5 0 BBX
4 6 2 12 ATTRIBUTES 01C0 BITMAP 70 70 70 60 E0 C0 ENDCHAR
ENDFONT
```

The following is the same BDF file with each of the records stored on separate lines and indented to illustrate the layering of BDF records and subrecords:

```
STARTFONT 2.1
    COMMENT This is a sample font in 2.1 format.
    FONT -Adobe-Helvetica-Bold-R-Normal—24-240-75-75-P-65-ISO8859-1
    SIZE 24 75 75
    FONTBOUNDINGBOX 9 24 -2 -6
    STARTPROPERTIES 19
        FOUNDRY "Adobe"
        FAMILY "Helvetica"
        WEIGHT_NAME "Bold"
        SLANT "R"
        SETWIDTH_NAME "Normal"
        ADD_STYLE_NAME ""
        PIXEL_SIZE 24
        POINT_SIZE 240
        RESOLUTION_X 75
        RESOLUTION_Y 75
        SPACING "P"
        AVERAGE_WIDTH 65
        CHARSET_REGISTRY "ISO8859"
        CHARSET_ENCODING "1"
```

```
        MIN_SPACE 4
        FONT_ASCENT 21
        FONT_DESCENT 7
        COPYRIGHT "Copyright (c) 1987  Adobe Systems, Inc."
        NOTICE "Helvetica is a registered trademark of Linotype Inc."
    ENDPROPERTIES
    CHARS 2
    STARTCHAR j
        ENCODING 106
        SWIDTH 355 0
        DWIDTH 8 0
        BBX 9 22 -2 -6
        BITMAP 0380 0380 0380 0380 0000 0700 0700 0700 0700 0E00 0E00
0E00 0E00 0E00 1C00 1C00 1C00 1C00 3C00 7800 F000 E000
    ENDCHAR
    STARTCHAR quoteright
        ENCODING 39
        SWIDTH 223 0
        DWIDTH 5 0
        BBX 4 6 2 12
        ATTRIBUTES 01C0
        BITMAP 70 70 70 60 E0 C0
    ENDCHAR
ENDFONT
```

For Further Information

For further information, see the BDF specification on the CD that accompanies this book. You may also find information about the BDF format in the X11R5 distribution of the X Window System, available via FTP from *ftp.x.org*.

NAME:	BRL-CAD
ALSO KNOWN AS:	Ballistic Research Laboratory CAD Package
TYPE:	See article
COLORS:	NA
COMPRESSION:	NA
MAXIMUM IMAGE SIZE:	NA
MULTIPLE IMAGES PER FILE:	NA
NUMERICAL FORMAT:	See article
ORIGINATOR:	US Army Advanced Communication Systems
PLATFORM:	UNIX
SUPPORTING APPLICATIONS:	BRL-CAD
SPECIFICATION ON CD:	Yes (summary only; specification is too lengthy)
CODE ON CD:	No
IMAGES ON CD:	No
SEE ALSO:	None
USAGE:	Solid modeling, network-distributed image processing.
COMMENTS:	A massive, polymorphic system consisting of several standards.

Overview

BRL-CAD (Ballistic Research Laboratory CAD) is a solid-modeling system that originated at the Advanced Computing Systems Group of the U.S. Army Ballistic Research Laboratory. It was originally designed to provide an interactive editor for use in conjunction with a vehicle-description database. In the U.S. Army, "vehicle" often means "tank," and the documention contains many interesting and high-quality renderings of tank-like objects.

BRL-CAD is massive, consisting of more than 100 programs, and includes about 280,000 lines of C source code. It is extraordinarily well-documented and has been distributed to at least 800 sites worldwide.

Conceptually, BRL-CAD implements several subsystems:

- Solid geometry editor
- Ray tracer and ray tracing library
- Image-processing utilities
- General utilities

Data in the current release of BRL-CAD can be in several forms:

- BRL-specific CSG (Constructive Solid Geometry) database
- Uniform B-Spline and NURB surfaces
- Faceted data
- NMG (n-manifold geometry)

For Further Information

The BRL-CAD documentation is extensive and well-written, and we found it a pleasure to work with. Unfortunately, it is too extensive to be included on the CD, so we have elected to include only a summary description there. The full documentation is readily available in *The Ballistic Research Laboratory CAD Package*, Release 4.0, December 1991, albeit in paper form. Our copy came in a box weighing about ten pounds! It consists of five volumes:

Volume I	The BRL-CAD Philosophy
Volume II	The BRL-CAD User's Manual
Volume III	The BRL-CAD Applications Manual
Volume IV	The MGED User's Manual
Volume V	The BRL-CAD Analyst's Manual

This is an extraordinary document set, and not only in contrast to the rest of the documention we've run across in the research for this book. It's just a great job. If the application is one-tenth as well-crafted as the documentation, it must be a marvel.

For general information about BRL-CAD, contact:

Attn: Mike Muuss
BRL-CAD Architect
U.S. Army Research Laboratory
Aberdeen Proving Ground, MD 21005-5068
mike@brl.mil

BRL-CAD is distributed in two forms:

1. Free distribution with no ongoing support. You must complete and return an agreement form; in return, you will be given instructions on how to obtain and decrypt the files via FTP. Files are archived at a number of sites worldwide. One copy of the printed documentation will be sent at no cost.

   For further information about this distribution, contact:

   BRL-CAD Distribution
   Attn: SCLBR-LV-V
   Aberdeen Proving Ground, MD 21005-5066
   FAX: 410-278-5058
   keith@brl.mil

2. Full-service distribution with support. Items provided are similar to those mentioned in the free distribution described above, except that it costs U.S. $500 and may include the software on magnetic tape.

   For further information about this distribution, contact:

   BRL-CAD Distribution
   Attn: Mrs. Carla Moyer
   SURVIAC Aberdeen Satellite Office
   1003 Old Philadelphia Road, Suite 103
   Aberdeen, MD 21001
   Voice: 410-273-7794
   FAX: 410-272-6763
   cad_dist@brl.mil

NAME:	BUFR
ALSO KNOWN AS:	Binary Universal Form for the Representation of Meteorological Data
TYPE:	Various
COLORS:	NA
COMPRESSION:	Uncompressed
MAXIMUM IMAGE SIZE:	NA
MULTIPLE IMAGES PER FILE:	NA
NUMERICAL FORMAT:	Binary bit-oriented
ORIGINATOR:	World Meteorological Organization
PLATFORM:	All
SUPPORTING APPLICATIONS:	Unknown
SPECIFICATION ON CD:	Yes (summary description)
CODE ON CD:	No
IMAGES ON CD:	No
SEE ALSO:	GRIB

USAGE: Designed to convey meteorological data, it can be used for any other kind of data.

COMMENTS: The BUFR format is outside the scope of this book, but we include a brief description because it is likely to be more useful in the future as interest in geographical information systems increases.

Overview

BUFR (Binary Universal Form for the Representation of Meteorological Data) was created by the World Meteorological Organization (WMO). Technically it is known as WMO Code Form FM 94-IX Ext. BUFR. It is the result of a committee, which produced the first BUFR documents in 1988. The current revision of the format, Version 2, dates from 1991. Work on the format is ongoing. It is a code in the sense that it defines a protocol for the transmission of quantitative data, one of a number of codes created by the WMO.

BUFR was designed to convey generalized meteorological data, but due to its flexibility it can be used for almost anything. BUFR files, in fact, were designed to be infinitely extensible, and to this end are written in a unique data description language.

We've included BUFR in this book because it can and has been used for transmission and exchange of graphics data, although that is not its primary purpose. It also is associated with observational data obtained from weather satellites.

BUFR data streams and files adhere to the specification called *WMO Standard Formats for Weather Data Exchange Among Automated Weather Information Systems*.

File Organization

BUFR files are stream-based and consist of a number of consecutive records. The format documentation describes BUFR records as self-descriptive. Records, or messages, make up the BUFR data stream, and each always contains a table consisting of a complete description of the data contained in the record, including data type identification, units, scaling, compression, and bits per data item.

File Details

Detailing the data definition language implemented in BUFR is beyond the scope of this article. It is extremely complex and is, at this point, used in a narrow area of technology.

For Further Information

For detailed information about BUFR, see the summary description included on the CD that accompanies this book:

> Thorpe, W., "Guide to the WMO Code Form FM 94-IX EXT. BUFR," Fleet Numerical Oceanography Center, Monterey, California.

Although there are a number of documents on BUFR available from meteorological sources, this article is the most useful that we have found. Additional information about WMO data specifications can be found in the following official specification:

> *Standard Formats for Weather Data Exchange Among Automated Weather Information Systems*, Document Number FCM-S2-1990.

This document is available from:

> U.S. Department of Commerce/National Oceanic and
> Atmospheric Administration
> Attn: Ms. Lena Loman
> Office of the Federal Coordinator for Meteorological Services
> and Supporting Research (OFCM)
> 6010 Executive Blvd, Suite 900
> Rockville, MD 20852
> Voice: 301-443-8704

For more information about the BUFR format, contact:

> U.S. Department of Commerce/National Oceanic and
> Atmospheric Administration
> (NOAA)
> Attn: Dr. John D. Stackpole
> Chief, Production Management Branch, Automation Division
> National Meteorological Center
> WINMC42, Room 307, WWB
> 5200 Auth Road
> Camp Springs, MD 20746
> Voice: 301-763-8115
> FAX: 301-763-8381
> *jstack@sun1.wwb.noaa.gov*

NAME:	CALS Raster
ALSO KNOWN AS:	CALS, CAL, RAS
TYPE:	Bitmap
COLORS:	Mono
COMPRESSION:	CCITT Group 4, uncompressed
MAXIMUM IMAGE SIZE:	Unlimited
MULTIPLE IMAGES PER FILE:	Yes (Type II only)
NUMERICAL FORMAT:	NA
ORIGINATOR:	U.S. Department of Defense
PLATFORM:	All
SUPPORTING APPLICATIONS:	Too numerous to list
SPECIFICATION ON CD:	No
CODE ON CD:	No
IMAGES ON CD:	Yes
SEE ALSO:	None

USAGE: Compound document exchange, DTP, CAD/CAM, image processing.

COMMENTS: A well-documented, though cumbersome, format that attempts to do many things. If you are unfamiliar with U.S. government specification documents, you will probably find working with this format a complicated and challenging task. CALS raster is mandatory for use in most U.S. government document-handling applications. Because all data is byte-oriented, big-endian versus little-endian problems never arise.

Overview

The CALS raster format is a standard developed by the Computer Aided Acquisition and Logistics Support (CALS) office of the United States Department of Defense to standardize graphics data interchange for electronic publishing, especially in the areas of technical graphics, CAD/CAM, and image processing applications.

CALS is also an Office Document Interchange Format (ODIF) used in the Office Document Architecture (ODA) system for the exchange of compound document data between multiple machine platforms and software applications. CALS is an attempt to integrate text, graphics, and image data into a standard document architecture. Its ultimate goal is to improve and integrate the logistics functions of the military and its contractors.

All technical publications for the federal government must conform to the CALS standard. Many other government organizations are also quickly adopting CALS. Commercial businesses, such as the medical, telecommunications, airline, and book publishing industries have also standardized on CALS.

CALS has also come into wide use in the commercial computer industry, such as in CAD/CAM applications, and in the aerospace industry, which owes a large part of its business to government and military contracts. CALS-compliant technical illustration systems also use the PostScript Page Description Language and Encapsulated PostScript files to exchange data between themselves and commercial systems.

File Organization

There are two types of CALS raster formats as defined by MIL-STD-28002A. They are specified as the Type I and Type II raster formats. Type I raster data files contain a single, monochrome image compressed using the CCITT Group 4 (T.6) encoding algorithm and appended to a CALS raster header record data block.

Type II image files contain one or more monochrome images that are also stored using the CCITT Group 4 encoding algorithm. In addition, the Type II format supports the encoding of image data as a collection of pel tiles. Each tile of image data is either separately encoded using CCITT Group 4 or is stored in its raw, unencoded format. The location of each tile within the image is stored in a tile offset index, for convenient retrieval of individual tiles. For further detail on the CALS Type II raster graphics format, refer to MIL-R-28002A.

The structures of the two CALS variants, Type I and Type II, are shown below.

The Type I file format consists of the following:

    Header
    Image Data

The Type II file format looks like this:

    Header
    Document Profile
    Presentation Styles
    Document Layout

Root Layout
  Layout Object Page 1
    Tile Index
    Image Data
  Layout Object Page 2
    Tile Index
    Image Data
  Layout Object Page N
    Tile Index
    Image Data

As you can see, the Type II format is considerably more complex than the Type I. Each Type II file may contain one or more pages of image data. There is also a considerable amount of page and document formatting data present in a Type II file. But by far the most common use of the Type II format is simply to store a collection of Type I CALS raster images in the same physical file. In such an arrangement, all the image pages are untiled, CCITT Group 4 encoded, and the profile, style, and layout information are omitted.

The raster data in a Type I file is always encoded using the CCITT Group 4 encoding method. CCITT Group 3 encoded and unencoded data is not supported. Type II files may contain tiles that are either CCITT Group 4 encoded or raw, unencoded data. Both raw and encoded tiles may occur in the same Type II CALS file and are always 512 pels in size. If the end of the image is reached before a tile is completely encoded, then this partial tile is completed by adding padding.

Two other types of tiles found in Type II images are null foreground and null background tiles. Null tiles are entirely white or entirely black, depending upon the designated background and foreground colors. They are actually pseudo-tiles that are not present in the image data and have no tile offset value.

Tile data is stored in the image data along the pel path (rows) and down the line progression (columns). Storage of randomly distributed tiles is possible, but discouraged. Tiles are normally encoded, unless the image data is so complex that the time required to encode the image is too great or unless very little reduction in the size of the data would result if the tile were encoded. The inclusion of unencoded data in a T.6-encoded data stream is not supported by the CALS raster format.

File Details

This section contains detailed information about the components of a CALS raster file.

Header Record Data Block

The CALS raster header is different from most other graphics file format headers in that it is composed entirely of 7-bit ASCII characters in a human-readable format. When most graphics image files are displayed as a text file, seemingly random garbage is displayed on the screen. Listing a CALS raster file, however, will reveal ASCII information which is quite understandable to a human reader. The unintelligible garbage following the header is the compressed image data.

The CALS raster data file header is 1408 bytes and is divided into eleven 128-byte records. Each record begins with a predefined 7-bit ASCII record identifier that is followed by a colon. The remaining part of the 128-byte record is the record information. If a record contains no information, the character string NONE is found in the record. The remainder of the bytes in each record contain space characters (ASCII 32) as filler. All data in the header block is byte-oriented, so no adjustments need to be made for byte order.

Following the last record in the header is 640 bytes of padding that rounds the header out to a full 2048 bytes in length. In fact, the raster image data always begins at offset 2048. Although this padding is not actually defined as part of the header, additional records added to future versions of the CALS header would be placed in this area. The byte value used for the padding is usually a space character (ASCII 20h), but any ASCII character can be used.

The structure for the CALS raster header block is shown below.

```
typedef struct _CalsHeader
{
CHAR   SourceDocId[128];          /* Source Document Identifier   */
CHAR   DestDocId[128];            /* Destination Document ID  */
CHAR   TextFileId[128];           /* Text File Identifier   */
CHAR   FigureId[128];             /* Table Identifier   */
CHAR   SourceGraph[128];          /* Source System Filename   */
CHAR   DocClass[128];             /* Data File Security Label   */
CHAR   RasterType[128];           /* Raster Data Type   */
CHAR   Orientation[128];          /* Raster Image Orientation   */
CHAR   PelCount[128];             /* Raster Image Pel Count   */
```

```
CHAR   Density[128];          /* Raster Image Density   */
CHAR   Notes[128];            /* Notes   */
CHAR   Padding[640];          /* Pad header out to 2048-bytes   */
} CALSHEAD;
```

Image record identifiers

Each record in a CALS raster file starts with a record identifier, which is a string of ASCII characters followed by a colon and a single space. Record data immediately follows the record identifier. If the record does not contain any relevant data, then the ASCII string NONE is written after the identifier.

SourceDocId:

SourceDocId starts with the source system document identifier (srcdocid). This record is used by the source system (the system on which the document was created) to identify the document to which the image is attached. This identifier can be a document title, publication number, or other similar information.

DestDocId:

DestDocId starts with the destination system document identifier (dstdocid). This record contains information used by the destination organization to identify the document to which the image is attached. This record may contain the document name, number or title, the drawing number, or other similar information.

TextFileId:

TextFileId starts with the text file identifier (txtfilid). This record contains a string indicating the document page that this image page contains. A code is usually found in this record that identifies the section of the document to which the image page belongs. Such codes may include:

COV	Cover or title page
LEP	List of effective pages
WRN	Warning pages
PRM	Promulgation pages
CHR	Change record
FOR	Forword or preface
TOC	Table of contents
LOI	Lists of illustrations and tables
SUM	Safety Summary

PTn	Part number n
CHn	Chapter number n
SEn	Section number n
APP-n	Appendix n
GLS	Glossary
INX	Index
FOV	Foldout section

FigureId:

FigureId starts with the figure or table identifier (figid). This is the number by which the image page figure is referenced. A sheet number is preceded by the ASCII string –S and followed by the drawing number. A foldout figure is preceded by the ASCII string –F and followed by the number of pages in the foldout.

SourceGraph:

SourceGraph starts with the source system graphics filename (srcgph). This record contains the name of the image file.

DocClass:

DocClass starts with the data file security label (doccls). This record identifies the security level and restrictions that apply to this image page and/or associated document.

RasterType:

RasterType starts with the raster data type (rtype). This is the format of raster image data that follows the header record data block in this file. This record contains the character 1 for Type I raster data and 2 for Type II raster data.

Orientation:

Orientation starts with the raster image orientation identifier (rorient). This record indicates the the proper visual orientation of the displayed image. This data is represented by two strings of three numeric characters separated by a comma. The first three characters are the direction of the pel path of the image page. Legal values are 0, 90, 180, and 270 representing the number of degrees the image was rotated clockwise from the origin when scanned. A page scanned normally has a pel path of 0 degrees, while an image scanned in upside-down has a pel path of 180 degrees.

The second three characters represent the direction of line progression of the document. Allowed values are 90 and 270 representing the number of degrees clockwise of the line progression from the pel path direction. A normal image has a line progression of 270, while a mirrored image has a line progression of 90.

PelCount:

PelCount starts with the raster image pel count identifier (rpelcnt). This record indicates the width of the image in pels and the length of the image in scan lines. This data is represented by two strings of six numeric characters separated by a comma. Typical values for this record are shown in Table CALS-1.

TABLE CALS RASTER-1: *Typical CALS Raster Pel Count Values*

Drawing Size	Pels Per Line, Number of Lines
A	001728,002200
B	002240,003400
C	003456,004400
D	004416,006800
E	006848,008800
F	005632,008000

Density:

Density starts with the raster image density identifier (rdensity). This density is a single four-character numeric string representing the numerical density value of the image. This record may contain the values 200, 240, 300, 400, 600, or 1200 pels per inch, with 300 pels per inch being the default.

Notes:

Notes starts with the notes identifier (notes). This is a record used to contain miscellaneous information that is not applicable to any of the other records in the CALS raster file header.

Example

This section contains an example of a CALS raster file header data block created by a facsimile (FAX) software application. This image file contains a single page of a facsimile document received via a computer facsimile card and stored to disk as a CALS raster image file.

The source of the document is identified as FAX machine number one. The destination is an identification number used to index the image in a database. The ID number is constructed from the date the FAX was received, the order in which it was received (e.g., it was the third FAX received that day), and the total number of pages. The text file identifier indicates that this file is page three of a seven-page facsimile document, for example.

The figure record is not needed, so the ASCII string NONE appears in this field. The source graphics filename contains the MS-DOS filename of the CALS raster file in which the page is stored. The remaining records indicate that the FAX document is unclassified, contains Type I CALS raster image data, has a normal orientation, and that the size and density of the image correspond to that of a standard facsimile page. The Notes field contains a time stamp showing when the FAX was actually received.

Please note that this is only one possible way that data may appear in a CALS header block. Most government and military software applications create CALS header blocks that are far more cryptic and confusing than this example. On the other hand, several CAD packages create simpler CALS headers.

Following is an example of a CALS header record data block:

```
srcdocid:    Fax machine #1
dstdocid:    910814-003.007
txtfilid:    003,007
figid:       NONE
srcgph:      F0814003.007
doccls:      Unclass
rtype:       1
rorient:     000,270
rpelcnt:     001728,002200
rdensity:    0200
notes:       Fri Aug 14 12:21:43 1991 PDT
```

For Further Information

Information about the CALS raster format is found primarily in the following military standards documents:

> *Automated Interchange of Technical Information*, MIL-STD-1840A. This document contains a description of the header (called a header record data block) in the CALS format.

Requirements for Raster Graphics Representation in Binary Format, MIL-R-28002A. This document contains a description of the image data in the CALS format.

The CALS raster file format is supported through the following office of the Department of Defense:

CALS Management Support Office (DCLSO)
Office of the Assistant Director for Telecommunications
    and Information Systems
Headquarters Defense Logistics Agency
Cameron Station
Alexandria, VA 22314

The documents MIL-STD-1840 and MIL-R-28002A may be obtained from agencies that distribute military specifications standards, including the following:

Standardization Documents Ordering Desk
Building 4D
700 Robbins Avenue
Philadelphia, PA 19111-5094

Global Engineering Documents
2805 McGaw Avenue
Irvine, CA 92714

Voice: 800-854-7179
Voice: 714-261-1455

Useful and readily available periodical articles on CALS and ODA include the following:

Dawson, F., and Nielsen, F., "ODA and Document Interchange," *UNIX Review,* Volume 8, Number 3, 1990, p. 50.

Hobgood, A., "CALS Implementation—Still a Few Questions," *Advanced Imaging,* April 1990, pp. 24-25.

CGM

NAME:	CGM
ALSO KNOWN AS:	Computer Graphics Metafile
TYPE:	Metafile
COLORS:	Unlimited
COMPRESSION:	RLE, CCITT Group3 and Group4
MAXIMUM IMAGE SIZE:	Unlimited
MULTIPLE IMAGES PER FILE:	Yes
NUMERICAL FORMAT:	NA
ORIGINATOR:	ANSI, ISO
PLATFORM:	All
SUPPORTING APPLICATIONS:	Too many to list
SPECIFICATION ON CD:	No
CODE ON CD:	No
IMAGES ON CD:	Yes
SEE ALSO:	None

USAGE: Standardized platform-independent format used for the interchange of bitmap and vector data.

COMMENTS: CGM is a very feature-rich format which attempts to support the graphic needs of many general fields (graphic arts, technical illustration, cartography, visualization, electronic publishing, and so on). While the CGM format is rich in features (many graphical primitives and attributes), it is less complex than PostScript, produces much smaller (more compact) files, and allows the interchange of very sophisticated and artistic images. In fact, so many features are available to the software developer that a full implementation of CGM is considered by some to be quite difficult. Nevertheless, CGM use is spreading quickly.

Overview

CGM (Computer Graphics Metafile) was developed by experts working on committees under the auspices of the International Standards Organization (ISO) and the American Standards National Institute (ANSI). It was specifically designed as a common format for the platform-independent interchange of bitmap and vector data, and for use in conjunction with a variety of input and output devices. Although CGM incorporates extensions designed to support bitmap (called raster in the CGM specification) data storage, files in CGM format are used primarily to store vector information. CGM files typically contain either bitmap or vector data, but rarely both.

The newest revision of CGM is the CGM:1992 standard, which defines three upwardly compatible levels of increasing capability and functionality. Version 1 is the original CGM:1987 standard, a collection of simple metafile primitives. Version 2 metafiles may contain Closed Figures (a filled primitive comprised of other primitives). Version 3 is for advanced applications, and its metafiles may contain Beziers, NURBS, parabolic and hyperbolic arcs, and the Tile Array compressed tiled raster primitive.

CGM uses three types of syntactical encoding formats. All CGM files contain data encoded using one of these three methods:

- Character-based, used to produce the smallest possible file size for ease of storage and speed of data transmission

- Binary encoded, which facilitates exchange and quick access by software applications

- Clear-text encoded, designed for human readability and ease of modification using an ASCII text editor

CGM is intended for the storage of graphics data only. It is sometimes (erroneously) thought to be a data transfer standard for CAD/CAM data, like IGES, or a three-dimensional graphic object model data storage standard. However, CGM is quite suited for the interchange of renderings from CAD/CAM systems, but not for the storage of the engineering model data itself.

CGM supports and is used by the Graphical Kernel System (GKS) standard, but is something completely different. GKS, which is in fact an API graphics library specification, is often mistaken for a graphics file format. CGM has found a role on most platforms as a method for the transfer of graphics data between applications. Programs that support CGM include most business graphics and visualization packages and many word processing and CAD applications.

Vector primitives supported by Version 1 CGM metafiles include lines, polylines, arcs, circles, rectangles, ellipses, polygons, and text. Each primitive may have one or more attributes, including fill style (hatch pattern), line or edge color, size, type, and orientation. CGM supports bitmaps in the form of *cell arrays* and *tile arrays*. The logical raster primitives of CGM are device-independent.

A minor point, but one worth noting, is that the three flavors of encoding supported by CGM may not all be readable by all software applications that import CGM files. Despite the existence of a solid body of rules and encoding schemes, CGM files are not universally interchangeable.

Many CGM file-writing applications support different subsets of standard features, often leaving some features out that may be required by other CGM readers. Also, because CGM allows vendor-specific extensions, many (such as custom fills) have been added, making full CGM support by an application difficult.

The CGM:1987 standard included a "Minimum Recommended Capabilities" list to aid developers in implementing a CGM application capable of reading and writing CGM metafiles correctly. Unfortunately, some of the big manufacturers chose to ignore even these modest requirements. Therefore, because it is impossible to police everyone who implements CGM in an application, many incompatibilities do exist.

In an effort to improve compatibility, the CGM:1992 standard has removed the "Minimum Recommended Capabilities" list in anticipation of the publication of the pending CGM Amendment 1, which defines more stringent conformance requirements and a "Model Profile," which could be considered a minimal useful implementation level.

File Organization and Details

All CGM files start with the same identifier, the BEGIN METAFILE statement, but its actual appearance in the file depends on how the file is encoded. In clear-text encoding, the element is simply the ASCII string BEGMF. If the file is binary encoded, you must read in the first two bytes as a word; the most significant byte (MSB) is followed in the file by the least significant byte (LSB). Bits in this word provide the following information:

15-12:	Element class
11-05:	Element ID
04-00:	Parameter list length

BEGIN METAFILE is a "Delimiter Element," making it class 0. The element ID within that class is 1. The parameter list length is variable, so it must be ANDed out when comparing. The bit pattern is then:

```
0 0 0 0 0 0 0 0 0 0 1 X X X X X
```

To check it, simply AND the word with 0XFFE0 and compare it with 0X0020. In reading the standard, we get the impression that it is actually legal to add padding characters (nulls) to the beginning of the file. We rather doubt that anyone would actually do this, but it may be appropriate to read in words until a non-zero word is read and compare this word. You can read in full words because all elements are constrained to start on a word boundary.

For Further Information

CGM is both an ANSI and an ISO standard and has been adopted by many countries, such as Australia, France, Germany, Japan, Korea, and the United Kingdom. The full ANSI designation of the current version of CGM is:

> *Information Processing Systems—Computer Graphics Metafile for the Storage and Transfer of Picture Description Information*, ANSI/ISO 8632-1992 (commonly called CGM:1992).

Note that CGM:1992 is the current standard. Be careful not to obtain the earlier ANSI X3.122-1986 if you need the latest standard. This earlier document, CGM:1986, defining the Version 1 metafile, was superseded by ISO/IEC 8632:1992. ANSI adopted CGM:1992 without modification and replaced ANSI X3.122-1986 with it. The CGM standard is contained in four ISO standards documents:

    ISO 8632-1 Part 1: Functional Specification
    ISO 8632-2 Part 2: Character Encoding
    ISO 8632-3 Part 3: Binary Encoding
    ISO 8632-4 Part 4: Clear Text Encoding

These may be purchased from any of the following organizations:

    International Standards Organization (ISO)
    1 rue de Varembe
    Case Postal 56
    CH-1211 Geneva 20 Switzerland
    Voice: +41 22 749 01 11
    FAX: +41 22 733 34 30

American National Standards Institute (ANSI)
Sales Department
1430 Broadway
New York, NY, 10018
Voice: 212-642-4900

Canadian Standards Association (CSA)
Sales Group
178 Rexdale Blvd.
Rexdale, Ontario, M9W 1R3
Voice: 416-747-4044

Other countries also make the CGM specification available through their standards organizations; these include DIN (Germany), BSI (United Kingdom), AFNOR (France), and JIS (Japan).

The National Institute of Standards and Technology (NIST) has set up a CGM Testing Service for testing CGM metafiles, generators, and interpreters. The Testing Service examines binary-encoded CGM files for conformance to Version 1 CGM, as defined in the application profiles of FIPS 128-1 and the DoD CALS CGM AP military specification MIL-D-28003A. You can purchase the testing tool used by NIST so you can do internal testing on various PC and UNIX systems.

For more information about the CGM Testing Service, contact:

National Institute of Standards and Technology (NIST)
Computer Systems Laboratory
Information Systems Engineering Division
Gaithersburg, MD 20899
Voice: 301-975-3265

You can also obtain information about CGM from the following references:

Henderson. L.R. and Mumford, A.M., *The CGM Handbook*, Academic Press, San Diego, CA, 1993.

Arnold, D.B. and Bono, P.R., *CGM and CGI: Metafile and Interface Standards for Computer Graphics*, Springer-Verlag, New York, NY, 1988.

Arnold, D.B. and Bono, P.R., *CGM et CGI: normes de metafichier et d'interfaces pour l'infographie*, French translation and updating of the above reference, Masson, 1992.

P.R. Bono, J.L. Encarnacao, L.M. Encarnacao, and W.R. Herzner, *PC Graphics With GKS*, Prentice-Hall, Englewood Cliffs, NJ, 1990.

CMU Formats

NAME:	CMU Formats
ALSO KNOWN AS:	Andrew Formats, CMU Bitmap
TYPE:	Multimedia
COLORS:	NA
COMPRESSION:	Uncompressed
MAXIMUM IMAGE SIZE:	NA
MULTIPLE IMAGES PER FILE:	NA
NUMERICAL FORMAT:	NA
ORIGINATOR:	Carnegie Mellon University
PLATFORM:	All
SUPPORTING APPLICATIONS:	Andrew Toolkit
SPECIFICATION ON CD:	Yes
CODE ON CD:	No
IMAGES ON CD:	No
SEE ALSO:	None

USAGE: Used primarily at Carnegie Mellon University in conjunction with the Andrew Toolkit.

COMMENTS: Included mainly for its architectural uniqueness.

Overview

The Andrew Consortium at Carnegie Mellon University is the source of the Andrew Toolkit, which is associated with the Andrew User Interface System. The Toolkit API is the basis for applications in the Andrew User Interface System. Data objects manipulated by the Andrew Toolkit must adhere to conventions crystallized in the Andrew Data Stream specification, a draft of which is included on the CD accompanying this book. The system was designed to support multimedia data from a variety of programs and platforms.

We understand that there is a bitmap format which originated at Carnegie Mellon University, but were unable to locate information prior to publication. The PBM utilities may include some support for converting and manipulating a CMU Bitmap, however.

File Organization

In the CMU formats, data is organized into streams and is written in 7-bit ASCII text. This is an interesting idea—nearly unique in the graphics file format world—which appears designed to enhance the portability of the format, at some cost in file size. Text may include tabs and newline characters and is limited to 80 characters of data per line.

Note that Andrew Toolkit files assume access by the user to the Andrew Toolkit. In the words of the documentation authors:

> As usual in ATK, the appropriate way to read or write the data stream is to call upon the corresponding Read or Write method from the AUIS distribution. Only in this way is your code likely to continue to work in the face of changes to the data stream definition. Moreover, there are a number of special features—mostly outdated data streams—that are implemented in the code, but not described here.

File Details

Data files used by the Andrew Toolkit consist of data objects, which are marked in the file by a begin/end marker pair. The initial marker associated with each data object must include information denoting the object type, as well as a unique identifier, which may be used as a reference ID by other objects.

The following is an example from the documentation:

```
\begindata{text,1}
<text data>
\begindata{picture,2}
<picture data>
\enddata{picture,2}
\view {pictureview,2}
<more text data>
\enddata{text,1}
```

Text Data Streams

Text data streams are similar to other data streams. Their structure is as follows:

```
\begindata line
\textdsversion line
\template line
```

```
definitions of additional styles
the text body itself
styled text
embedded objects in text body
\enddata line
```

Each of these elements is described below.

\begindata

This line has the form:

```
\begindata{text,99999}
```

where 99999 is a unique identifier.

\textdsversion

This line has the form:

```
\textdsversion{12}
```

There are apparently files written with data stream versions other than 12.

\template

A file may use a style template, in which case there will be a line of the form:

```
\template{default}
```

where default is the name of the template used and is the prefix of a filename. The system appends a suffix .tpl and looks for the template along file paths defined in the Andrew Toolkit installation. Please see the specification for further information.

Definitions of additional styles

Additional styles may be defined and used on the fly; each style consists of two or more lines:

```
\define{internalstylename
menuname
attribute
. . .
attribute}
```

internalstylename is always written in lowercase and may not contain spaces.

The menuname line is optional. If it is missing, there must be an empty line in its place. If present, it has the form:

```
menu:[Menu card name,Style name]
```

Attributes are also optional; if they are missing, the closing } appears at the end of the menuname line. Attribute lines are of the form:

```
attr:[attributename basis units value]
```

where value is a signed integer.

Text body
Text consists of any number of consecutive lines, each terminated by a newline character.

Styled text
Text in the body may be displayed in a style, in which case it is preceded by a previously defined name:

```
\internalstylename{
```

and is followed by the corresponding closing brace.

Embedded objects
Objects may be embedded in the text body. The documentation for the CMU formats describes the use of embedded objects as follows:

> When an object is embedded in a text body, two items appear: the data stream for the object and a \view line. The \begindata for the object is always at the beginning of a line. (The previous line is terminated with a backslash if there is to be no space before the object.) The \enddata line for the object always ends with a newline (which is not treated as a space).

> The \view line has the form:

```
\view{rasterview,8888,777,0,0}
```

\enddata
The \enddata line has the form:

```
\enddata{text,99999}
```

Bitmap Images

A bitmap image is a standard data stream beginning with a \begindata line and ending with a \enddata line. These generally surround a header and an image body.

The first line of the header consists of the following:

```
2 0 65536 65536 0 0 484 603
```

The following describes the numbers in this header:

Raster version	2	Denotes the second version of this encoding
Options	0	This field may specify changes to the image before displaying it:

```
raster_INVERT(1<<0) /* exchange black and white */
raster_FLIP(1<<1)   /* exch top and bottom */
raster_FLOP(1<<2)   /* exch left and right */
raster_ROTATE(1<<3) /* rotate 90 clockwise */
```

xScale, yScale:	65536 65536	Affects the size at which the image is printed. The value raster_UNITSCALE (136535) prints the image at approximately the size on the screen. The default scale of 65,536 is approximately half the screen size.
x, y, width, height:	0 0 484 603	It is possible for a raster object to display a portion of an image. These fields select this portion by specifying the index of the upper-left pixel and the width and height of the image in pixels. In all instances so far, x and y are both zero, and the width and height specify the entire image.

The second header line has three possible variations. Currently, only the first is used.

Variation 1: bits 10156544 484 603

RasterType:	bits
RasterId:	10156544
Width, Height:	484 603

Width and Height describe the width of each row and the number of rows.

Variation 2: refer 10135624

RasterType:	refer
RasterId:	10135624

The current data object refers to the bits stored in another data object that appears earlier in the same data stream.

Variation 3: file 10235498 filename path

RasterType:	file
RasterId:	10235498

The bit data is found in the file <filename>.

Please check the specification document on the CD-ROM for subtleties and further details of the format.

For Further Information

For further information about the CMU formats and the Andrew Toolkit, contact:

Andrew Consortium
Attn: Andrew Plotkin, Fred Hansen
Carnegie Mellon University
Pittsburgh, PA 15213-3890
info-andrew+@andrew.cmu.edu

NAME:	DKB
ALSO KNOWN AS:	None
TYPE:	Scene format
COLORS:	NA
COMPRESSION:	Uncompressed
MAXIMUM IMAGE SIZE:	NA
MULTIPLE IMAGES PER FILE:	NA
NUMERICAL FORMAT:	NA
ORIGINATOR:	David K. Buck
PLATFORM:	All
SUPPORTING APPLICATIONS:	DKB Ray Trace application
SPECIFICATION ON CD:	No
CODE ON CD:	No
IMAGES ON CD:	No
SEE ALSO:	POV

USAGE: Designed to support the widely-distributed, but now obsolete, DKB ray trace application.

COMMENTS: The DKB ray tracer preceded, and has influenced, the development of the POV ray tracer.

Overview

The DKB ray trace application was created by David K. Buck, for whom it is named. DKB has enjoyed wide distribution, particularly in the PC/MS-DOS BBS world.

Mr. Buck declined our request for information on the format and permission to reprint the relevant documentation. He feels that there is no interest in the program, and that it has been superseded by the POV ray tracer, which is based in part on DKB. We think otherwise, of course. Once a format is out there—especially if it is distributed as freeware or shareware—it is out there, and there is no practical way to stop people from using it. Our survey of some of the large BBSs in the U.S. showed that DKB, along with other, older ray trace programs, is being downloaded with some regularity, despite the availability of POV. Unfortunately, we are not able to describe the DKB format in any detail here.

For Further Information

The DKB ray trace package is available for download from Internet archive sites and BBS systems running on a number of platforms.

Dore Raster File Format

NAME:	Dore Raster File Format
ALSO KNOWN AS:	Dore, RFF
TYPE:	Bitmap
COLORS:	Unlimited
COMPRESSION:	None
MAXIMUM IMAGE SIZE:	Unlimited
MULTIPLE IMAGES PER FILE:	No
NUMERICAL FORMAT:	Any
ORIGINATOR:	Kubota Pacific Computers
PLATFORM:	UNIX
SUPPORTING APPLICATIONS:	AVS visualization package, many others
SPECIFICATION ON CD:	Yes
CODE ON CD:	No
IMAGES ON CD:	No
SEE ALSO:	None

USAGE: Storage and interchange of 2D and 3D image data.

COMMENTS: The Dore Raster File Format is one of the rare formats that combines both ASCII and binary information within the same image file. Dore lacks a native method of data compression, but does support the storage of voxel data.

Overview

The Dore Raster File Format (Dore RFF) is used by the Dore graphics library for storing two- and three-dimensional image data. Once stored, the data may be retrieved or the RFF files may be used to interchange the image information with other software packages.

Dore itself is an object-oriented 3D graphics library used for rendering 2D and 3D near-photographic quality images and scenes. Dore supports features such as texture and environment mapping, 2D and 3D filtering, and storage of 3D raster data.

Most raster (bitmap) file formats are only capable of storing two-dimensional pixels (picture elements). Dore RFF is capable of storing three-dimensional pixels called voxels (volume elements). A voxel contains standard pixel information, such as color and alpha channel values, plus Z-depth information, which describes the relative distance of the voxel from a point of reference. The Dore RFF format defines Z-depth data as a 32-bit integer value in the range of 00h to FFFFFFFFh (2^32 - 1). A value of 00h places a voxel at the farthest possible point from the point of reference, and a value of FFFFFFFFh places a voxel at the closest possible point.

The Dore Raster File Format is the underlying API for the AVS visualization package.

File Organization

Dore RFF is a rather simple, straightforward format that contains primarily byte-oriented data. All Dore RFF files contain an ASCII header, followed by binary image data.

Following is an example of a Dore RFF file. The position of the binary image data is indicated by the label in brackets. The <FF> symbols are formfeed (ASCII 0Ch) characters:

```
# # Dore Raster File Example
#
  rastertype = image
  width = 1280
  height = 1024
  depth = 2
  pixel = r8g8b8a8z32
  wordbyteorder = big-endian
<FF><FF>
[Binary Image Data]
<EOF>
```

The header may contain up to six fields. Each field has the format *keyword = value* and is composed entirely of ASCII characters. There is typically one field per line, although multiple fields may appear on a single line if they are separated by one or more white-space characters. Comments begin with the # character and continue to the end of the line.

The header fields are summarized below:

rastertype Type of raster image contained in the file. The only supported value for this keyword is image. This field must appear first in all RFF headers and has no default value.

width 2-byte WORD value that indicates the width of the image in pixels or voxels. The width field must appear in all RFF headers and has no default value.

height 2-byte WORD value that indicates the height of the image in pixels or voxels. The height field must appear in all RFF headers and has no default value.

depth 2-byte WORD value that indicates the depth of the raster. 2D raster images always contain pixels, and therefore the depth value is 1. 3D raster images always contain voxels, and therefore the depth value is always greater than 1. The depth field is optional and has a default value of 1.

pixel String indicating the data format of each pixel or voxel. The pixel field has no default value and must appear in all RFF headers. The possible values for this field are as follows:

r8g8b8 Pixels are three bytes in size and stored as three separate 8-bit RGB values.

r8g8b8a8 Pixels are four bytes in size and stored as three separate 8-bit RGB values and a single 8-bit alpha channel value in RGBA order.

a8b8g8r8 Pixels are four bytes in size and stored as three separate 8-bit RGB values and a single 8-bit alpha channel value in ABGR order.

a8g8b8a8z32
Voxels are eight bytes in size and stored as three separate 8-bit RGB values, a single 8-bit alpha channel value, and a single 32-bit DWORD containing the Z-depth value in RGBAZ order.

a8 Pixels or voxels are a single byte in size and only contain a single 8-bit alpha channel value.

z32 Voxels are a single byte in size and only contain a single 32-bit Z-depth value.

wordbyteorder

> Indicates the byte-order of the Z-depth values in the binary image data. The value of this field may be either the string big-endian or little-endian. The appearance of the wordbyteorder field in the header is optional, and the value defaults to big-endian.

The order of the fields within the header is not significant, except for the rastertype field. rastertype must always appear in every RFF header and must always be the first field. The width, height, and pixel fields must appear in every header as well. All other fields are optional; if not present, their default values are assumed.

The End Of Header marker is two formfeed characters. If it is necessary to pad out the header to end on a particular byte boundary, you can place any number of ASCII characters, except formfeeds, between these two formfeed characters. See the example below:

```
# # Example of using the End Of Header marker to pad out the header
# # to a byte boundary
#
  rastertype = image
  width = 64
  height = 64
  depth = 1
  pixel = r8g8b8
  wordbyteorder = little-endian
<FF>
  [ ASCII data used to extend the length of the header ]
<FF>
[Binary Image Data]
<EOF>
```

File Details

The image data immediately follows the End OF Header maker and is always stored in an uncompressed binary form. The format of the image data depends upon the format of the pixel (or voxel) data indicated by the value of the pixel field in the header.

The image data is always stored as contiguous pixels or voxels organized within scan lines. All RGB and alpha channel values are stored as bytes. Z-depth values are stored as 32-bit DWORDs, with the byte-order of the Z-depth values being indicated by the value of the wordbyteorder field in the header. Any pixel containing a Z-depth value is regarded as a voxel.

The format of each possible type of pixel or voxel is illustrated using C language structures as follows:

```
/* Pixel - Simple RGB triple */
typedef struct _r8g8b8
{
  BYTE red;
  BYTE green;
  BYTE blue;
} R8G8B8;
/* Pixel - RGB triple with alpha channel value */
typedef struct _r8g8b8a8
{
  BYTE red;
  BYTE green;
  BYTE blue;
  BYTE alpha;
} R8G8B8A8;
/* Pixel - RGB triple with alpha in reverse order */
typedef struct _a8b8g8r8
{
  BYTE alpha;
  BYTE blue;
  BYTE green;
  BYTE red;
} A8B8G8R8;
/* Voxel - RGB triple, alpha, and Z-depth */
typedef struct _a8g8b8a8z32
{
  BYTE red;
  BYTE green;
  BYTE blue;
  BYTE alpha
  DWORD zdepth;
} R8G8B8A8Z32;
/* Pixel or voxel mask - Only an alpha channel value */
typedef struct _a8 {
        BYTE alpha;
```

```
} A8;
/* Voxel mask - Only a Z-depth value */
typedef struct _z32
{
   DWORD zdepth;
} Z32;
```

For Further Information

For further information about the Dore Raster File Format, see the specification included on the CD-ROM that accompanies this book. You can also contact:

Kubota Pacific Computer, Inc.
Attn: Steve Hollasch
2630 Walsh Avenue
Santa Clara, CA 95051
Voice: 408-727-8100
hollasch@kpc.com

You can also contact:

Lori Whippler
loriw@kpc.com

Dr. Halo

NAME:	Dr. Halo
ALSO KNOWN AS:	CUT, PAL
TYPE:	Bitmap
COLORS:	8-bit maximum
COMPRESSION:	RLE, uncompressed
MAXIMUM IMAGE SIZE:	64KbX64Kb pixels
MULTIPLE IMAGES PER FILE:	No
NUMERICAL FORMAT:	Little-endian
ORIGINATOR:	Media Cybernetics
PLATFORM:	MS-DOS
SUPPORTING APPLICATIONS:	Dr. Halo
SPECIFICATION ON CD:	Yes
CODE ON CD:	No
IMAGES ON CD:	Yes
SEE ALSO:	None

USAGE: Used in device independent file interchange

COMMENTS: A well-defined, well-documented format in wide use, which is quick and easy to read and decompress. It lacks, however, a superior compression scheme, making it unsuited for the storage of deep-pixel images.

Overview

The Dr. Halo file format is a device-independent interchange format used for transporting image data from one hardware environment or operating system to another. This format is associated with the HALO Image File Format Library, the Dr. Halo III paint program, and other software applications written and marketed by Media Cybernetics.

Dr. Halo images may contain up to 256 colors, selectable from an 8-bit palette. Only one image may be stored per file. The Dr. Halo format is unusual in that it is divided into two separate files. The first file has the extension .CUT and contains the image data; the second has the extension .PAL and contains the color palette information for the image.

File Organization

The Dr. Halo header is shown below:

```
typedef struct _HaloHeader
{
WORD        Width;          /* 00h   Image Width in Pixels */
WORD        Height;         /* 02h   Image Height in Scan Lines */
WORD        Reserved;       /* 04h   Reserved Field (set to 0) */
} HALOHEAD;
```

Width and Height represent the size of the image data.

Reserved is set to zero to allow for possible future expansion of the header.

Following the header is the image data. Each scan line is always encoded using a simple byte-wise run length encoding (RLE) scheme.

File Details

The .CUT file contains image data in the form of a series of scan lines. The first two bytes of each encoded scan line form a Run Count value, indicating the number of bytes in the encoded line. Each encoded run begins with a one-byte Run Count value. The number of pixels in the run is the seven least significant bits of the Run Count byte and ranges in value from 1 to 127. If the most significant bit of the Run Count is 1, then the next byte is the Run Value and should be repeated Run Count times. If the most significant bit is zero, then the next Run Count bytes are read as a literal run. The end of every scan line is marked by a Run Count byte, which may be 00h or 80h.

The following pseudocode illustrates the decoding process:

```
ReadScanLine:
    Read a WORD value of the number of encoded bytes in this scan line
ReadRunCount:
    Read a BYTE value as the Run Count
        If the value of the seven Least Significant Bits (LSB)
            If the Most Significant Bit (MSB)
                Read the next byte as the Run Value and repeat it Run
                    Count times
        else
            If the MSB of the Run Count is 0
            Read the next Run Count bytes
    Goto ReadRunCount:
```

        else
    If the value of the seven LSB of the Run Count is 0
        The end of the scan line has been reached
        Goto ReadScanLine:

The second Dr. Halo image file usually has the extension .PAL and contains the color palette information for the image. Having a separate color palette file offers the advantage of being able to change the stored colors of an image without re-encoding the image data. The PAL file header is 40 bytes in length and has the following format:

```
typedef struct _HaloPalette
{
BYTE  FileId[2];          /* 00h   File Identifier - always "AH" */
WORD  Version;            /* 02h   File Version */
WORD  Size;               /* 04h   File Size in Bytes minus header */
CHAR  FileType;           /* 06h   Palette File Identifier   */
CHAR  SubType;            /* 07h   Palette File Subtype   */
WORD  BoardId;            /* 08h   Board ID Code */
WORD  GraphicsMode;       /* 0Ah   Graphics Mode of Stored Image   */
WORD  MaxIndex;           /* 0Ch   Maximum Color Palette Index   */
WORD  MaxRed;             /* 0Eh   Maximum Red Palette Value   */
WORD  MaxGreen;           /* 10h   Maximum Green Palette Value   */
WORD  MaxBlue;            /* 12h   Maximum Blue Color Value   */
CHAR  PaletteId[20];      /* 14h   Identifier String "Dr. Halo" */

} HALOPAL;
```

There are actually two types of .PAL files: generic and video hardware-specific. The header shown above is for the generic type. A hardware-specific palette file may contain additional information in the header.

FileId always contains the byte values 41h and 48h.

Version indicates the version of the HALO format to which the palette file conforms.

Size is the total size of the file minus the header. This gives the total size of the palette data in bytes.

FileType, the palette file identifier, is always set to 0Ah.

Subtype, the palette file subtype, is set to 00h for a generic palette file and to 01h for hardware-specific.

BoardId and GraphicsMode indicate the type of hardware and the mode that created and displayed the palette data.

MaxIndex, MaxRed, MaxGreen, and MaxBlue describe the palette data.

PaletteId contains up to a 20-byte string with an ASCII identifier. Unused string elements are set to 00h.

Palette data is written as a sequence of three-byte triplets of red, green, and blue values in 512-byte blocks. If a triplet does not fit at the end of a block, the block is padded and the triplet used to start the next block. All RGB values are in the range of 0 to 255.

For Further Information

For further information about the Dr. Halo format, see the specification included on the CD-ROM that accompanies this book. For additional information, contact:

Media Cybernetics
Attn: Bill Shotts
Technical Support Manager
8484 Georgia Avenue
Silver Spring, MD 20910
Voice: 301-495-3305, extension 235
FAX: 301-495-5964

Encapsulated PostScript

NAME:	Encapsulated PostScript
ALSO KNOWN AS:	EPS, EPSF, EPSI
TYPE:	Page Description Language (PDL); used as metafile (see article)
COLORS:	Mono
COMPRESSION:	See article
MAXIMUM IMAGE SIZE:	NA
MULTIPLE IMAGES PER FILE:	No
NUMERICAL FORMAT:	NA
ORIGINATOR:	Adobe
PLATFORM:	Macintosh, MS-DOS, MS Windows, UNIX, others
SUPPORTING APPLICATIONS:	Too numerous to list
SPECIFICATION ON CD:	Yes
CODE ON CD:	No
IMAGES ON CD:	Yes
SEE ALSO:	None

USAGE: Illustration and DTP applications, bitmap and vector data interchange.

COMMENTS: A file format with wide support associated with the PostScript PDL. Although complex, internal language features are well-documented in Adobe's excellent PostScript publications and elsewhere. Many applications, however, write but do not read EPSF-format files, preferring to avoid supporting PostScript rendering to the screen.

Overview

Data in an Encapsulated PostScript (EPSF) file is encoded in a subset of the PostScript Page Description Language (PDL) and then "encapsulated" in the EPS standard format for portable interchange between applications and platforms. An EPSF file is also a special PostScript file that may be included in a larger PostScript language document.

EPSF files are commonly used to contain the graphics and image portions of a document. The main body of the document is defined in one or more PostScript files, but each piece of line art or photographic illustration embedded in the document is stored in a separate EPSF file. This scheme offers several advantages, including the ability to alter illustrations in a document without having to edit the document file itself.

EPSF also provides the ability to store image data in a 7-bit ASCII form, which is occasionally more convenient than the 8-bit binary format used by most bitmap formats.

Although we choose not to discuss PostScript itself in detail, because it is described so extensively elsewhere, we must look briefly at it in order to understand EPSF, which implements a subset of the language.

PostScript was created in 1985 by Adobe Systems and is most often described as a PDL. It is used mainly as a way to describe the layout of text, vector graphics, and bitmap images on a printed or displayed page. Text, color, black-and-white graphics, or photographic-quality images obtained from scanners or video sources can all be described using PostScript. PostScript, however, is a versatile general-purpose computer language, similar in some respects to Forth.

Partly because it is a language, PostScript is device-independent and provides portability and consistent rendering of images across a wide range of platforms. It also implements a de facto industry-standard imaging model for communicating graphics information between applications and hardware devices, such as between word processors and printers. In addition to general-purpose language features, however, PostScript includes commands used for drawing.

A PostScript output device typically contains an interpreter designed to execute PostScript programs. An application sends a stream of PostScript commands (or copies a file to) the device, which then renders the image by interpreting the commands. In the case of printers, typesetters, imagesetters, and film recorders, their main function is to interpret a stream of PostScript language code and render the encoded graphical data onto a permanent medium, such as paper or photographic film. PostScript is capable of handling monochrome, gray-scale, or color images at resolutions ranging from 75 to over 3000 DPI.

PostScript files are written in 7-bit ASCII and can be created using a conventional text editor. Although PostScript can be written by hand, the bulk of the PostScript code produced today comes from applications, which include illustration packages, word processors, and desktop publishing programs. Files produced in this manner are often quite large; it is not unusual to see files in the range of several megabytes.

The PostScript specification is constantly evolving, and two fairly recent developments include Display PostScript and PostScript Level 2. Display PostScript is used for on-screen imaging and is binary-encoded. It is used to drive window-oriented PostScript interpreters for the display of text, graphics, and images. PostScript Level 2 adds additional features to the PostScript Level 1 language, including data compression (including JPEG), device-independent color, improved halftoning and color separation, facsimile compatibility, forms and patterns caching, improved printer support, automatic stroke adjustment, step and repeat capability, and higher operational speeds. PostScript Level 2 code is completely compatible with PostScript Level 1 devices.

File Organization

As we mentioned at the beginning of this section, the EPS format is designed to encapsulate PostScript language code in a portable manner. To accomplish this, an EPS file normally contains nothing but 7-bit ASCII characters, except for the Display EPS format discussed later. An example of a small EPS file is shown in the section called "EPS Files."

File Details

This section contains information about, and examples of, EPS, EPSI, and EPSF files.

EPS Files

An EPS file contains a PostScript header, which is a series of program comments, and may appear as:

```
%!PS-Adobe-3.0 EPSF-3.0
%%Title: Figure 1-1, Page 34
%%Creator: The Image Encapsulator
%%CreationDate: 12/03/91 13:48:04
%%BoundingBox:126 259 486 534
%%EndComments
```

Any line beginning with a percent sign (%) in a PostScript file is a comment. Normally, comments are ignored by PostScript interpreters, but comments in the header have special meanings. Encapsulated PostScript files contain two comments that identify the EPS format. The EPS identification comment appears as the first line of the file:

```
%!PS-Adobe-3.0 EPSF-3.0
```

The version number following the "PS-Adobe-" string indicates the level of conformance to the PostScript Document Structuring Conventions. This number will typically be either 2.0 or 3.0. The version number following the "EPSF-" indicates the level of conformance to the Encapsulated PostScript Files Specification and is typically 1.2, 2.0, or 3.0.

The next EPS-specific comment line is:

```
%%BoundingBox:
```

followed by four numeric values, which describe the size and the position of the image on the printed page. The origin point is at the lower-left corner of the page, so a 640x480 image starting at coordinates 0,0 would contain the following comment:

```
%%BoundingBox: 0 0 640 480
```

Both the %%PS-Adobe- and the %%BoundingBox: lines must appear in every EPS file. Ordinary PostScript files may formally be changed into EPS files by adding these two lines to the PostScript header. This, however, is a kludge and does not always work, especially if certain operators are present in the PostScript code (such as initgraphics, initmatrix, initclip, setpageparams, framedevice, copypage, erasepage, and so forth) which are not part of the EPSF subset.

The other comment lines in the header, %%Title:, %%Creator:, and %%CreationDate: are used to identify the name, creator, and creation date of the EPS file. The header is always terminated by the %%EndComments comment. Other comments may also appear in the header, such as %%IncludeFile, %%IncludeFont, and %%Page.

Encapsulated PostScript (EPS) Example
The following shows an example of an EPS file:

```
%!PS-Adobe-2.0 EPSF-1.2
%%Creator: O'Reilly 2.1
%%CreationDate: 12/12/91 14:12:40
%%BoundingBox:126 142 486 651
%%EndComments
/ld {load def} bind def
/s /stroke ld /f /fill ld /m /moveto ld /l /lineto ld /c /curveto ld /rgb
{255 div 3 1 roll 255 div 3 1 roll 255 div 3 1 roll setrgbcolor} def
126 142 translate
```

```
360.0000 508.8000 scale
/picstr 19 string def
152 212 1[152 0 0 -212 0 212]{currentfile picstr readhexstring pop}image
FFFFFFFFFFFFFFFFFFFFFFFFFFFFFFFFFFFFFFFF
FFFFFFFFFFFFFFFFFFFFFFFFFFFFFFFFFFFFFFFF
FFFFFFFFFFFFFFFFFFFFFFFFFFFFFFFFFFFFFFFF
FFFFFFFFFFFFFFFFFFFFFFFFFFFFFFFFFFFFFFFF
FFFFFFFFFFFFFFFFFFFFFFFFFFFFFFFFFFFFFFFF
FFFFFFFFFFFFFFFFFFFFFFFFFFFFFFFFFFFFFFFF
FFFFFFFFFFFFFFFFFFFFFFFFFFFFFFFFFFFFFFFF
FFFFFFFFFFFFFFFFFFFFFFFFFFFFFFFFFFFFFFFF
FFFF8000EE614FFFFFFFFFFFFFFFFFFFFFFFFFFFF
FFFF0000000000000000000000000FFFFFFFF
FFFF000000000000000000000000000000FFFF
FFFF000000000000000000000000000800FFFF
FFFF80000000435C7FFFFFFF600001FFFFFFFF
FFFF0000000000000FFFFFFF700047FFFFFFFF
FFFF0000000000000000000000000000001FFFF
```

```
%%  Thousands of lines deleted to save space in this book.
```

```
FFFF0000000000000000000000000000000FFFF
FFFF80000000001DF7E61000000001FFFFFFFF
FFFF00000000391FFFFFFFFFE70003FFFFFFFF
FFFF000000000000000000000001FFFFFFFF
FFFF00000000000000000000000000000FFFF
FFFF80000000000000000000000000837DFFFF
FFFF8000000067DFFCF0000000001FFFFFFFFF
FFFF00000000000000000000000FFFFFFFFF
FFFF0000000000000000000000000001FFFF
FFFFFFFFFFFFFFFFFFFFFFFFFFFFFFFFFFFFFFFF
FFFFFFFFFFFFFFFFFFFFFFFFFFFFFFFFFFFFFFFF
FFFFFFFFFFFFFFFFFFFFFFFFFFFFFFFFFFFFFFFF
showpage
^D
```

Looking at the EPS example, we can see the comments header at the start of the file. Following the header there is a short block of PostScript code, which does the actual drawing, scaling, cropping, rotating, and so on of the image. This block is sometimes all that needs to be changed in order to alter the appearance of the image.

Following the PostScript code block is bitmap data, which in an EPS file is called a graphics screen representation. This consists of hexadecimal digits. Each byte of image data contains eight pixels of information and is represented by two bytes of hexadecimal data in the bitmap. Image line widths are always a multiple of eight bits and are padded when necessary. Only black-and-white, 1-bit per pixel images are currently supported by EPS.

At the end of the EPS file is the showpage operator, which normally indicates a PostScript output device on which to print or display the completed image or page. In EPS files embedded in other documents, however, showpage is not really needed. Sometimes an EPS file fails to display or import properly because the PostScript interpreter reading the file does not expect to encounter a showpage and becomes confused. You can solve the problem either by disabling the showpage operator in the interpreter or by removing the showpage operator from the EPS files.

If you look at a PostScript file in a editor, you may find that the very last character in the file is a CTRL-D (ASCII 04h) character. This control code has a special meaning to a PostScript device; it is an End-Of-Job marker and signals that the PostScript code stream has ended. When a PostScript device reads this character, it may perform an end-of-file terminate-and-reset operation in preparation for the next PostScript data stream. The presence of this character can sometimes be a source of problems to applications that are not expecting or equipped to handle a non-printable ASCII character in the data stream. On the other hand, problems can occur in PostScript output devices if a file does not have this character at the end of the code stream. And if spurious CTRL-D characters appear in the data stream, not much will come out of your printer at all.

EPS files (as opposed to normal PostScript) are generally created exclusively by code generators and not by hand. Each line is a maximum of 255 characters wide and is terminated with a carriage return (ASCII 0Dh) on the Macintosh, a linefeed (ASCII 0Ah) under UNIX, and a newline (ASCII 0Dh/0Ah) under MS-DOS. A PostScript interpreter should be able to recognize files using any of these line-termination conventions.

EPS files may also be in preview format. In this format, an actual image file is appended to the end of the file. This provides a quick method of viewing the image contents of the EPS file without having to actually translate the PostScript code. This is handy for applications that cannot handle PostScript interpretation, but which can display bitmap graphics and wish to import EPS files. Previews are typically scaled down (but not cropped), lower-resolution versions of the image. EPS previews are similar to postage stamp images found in the Truevision TGA and Lumena bitmap formats.

Four file formats may be used as EPS preview images: TIFF, Microsoft Windows Metafile (WMF), Macintosh PICT, and EPSI (Encapsulated PostScript Interchange format). In the Macintosh environment, an EPS file is stored only in the file data fork. A PICT preview is stored in the resource fork of the EPS file and will have a resource number of 256. PostScript Level 2 supports JPEG-compressed images as well. TIFF and WMF files are appended to EPS files in their entirety. Because MS-DOS files do not have a resource fork or similar mechanism, a binary header must be prepended to the EPS file containing information about the appended image file.

EPS Preview Header
The EPS preview header is 32 bytes in length and has the following format:

```
typedef struct EPSHeader
{
  BYTE Id[4];                 /* Magic Number (always C5D0D3C6h) */
  DWORD PostScriptOffset;     /* Offset of PostScript code */
  DWORD PostScriptLength;     /* Size of PostScrip code */
  DWORD WMFOffset;            /* Offset of WIndows Metafile */
  DWORD WMFSize;             /* Size of Windows Metafile */
  DWORD TIFOffset;           /* Offset of TIFF file */
  DWORD TIFSize;             /* Size of TIFF file */
  DWORD CheckSum;            /* Checksum of previous header fields */
} EPSHEADER;
```

Id, in the first four bytes of the header, contains an identification value. To detect whether an MS-DOS EPS file has a preview section, read the first four bytes of the file. If they are the values C5h D0h D3h C6h, the EPS file has a preview section. Otherwise, the first two bytes of an EPS file will always be 25h 21h (%!).

PostScriptOffset and PostScriptLength point to the start of the PostScript language section of the EPS file. The PostScript code begins immediately after the header, so its offset is always 32.

WMFOffset and WMFSize point to the location of the WMF data if a WMF file is appended for preview; otherwise, these fields are zero.

The same is true for TIFOffset and TIFSize. Because either a TIFF or a WMF file (but not both) can be appended, at least one, and possibly both, sets of the fields will always be zero. If the checksum field is set to zero, ignore it. Offsets are always measured from the beginning of the file.

The three preview formats detailed are only somewhat portable and are fairly device dependent; not all environments can make use of the TIFF and WMF image file formats and fewer still of PICT. For one thing, the addition of 8-bit binary data to the EPS file prevents the file from being transmitted via a 7-bit data path without special encoding. The EPSI format, described in the next section, however, is designed as a completely device-independent method of image data interchange.

EPSI Files

EPSI bitmap data is the same for all systems. Its device independence makes its use desirable in certain situations where it is inconvenient to store preview data in 8-bit TIFF, WMF, or PICT format. EPSI image data is encoded entirely in printable 7-bit ASCII characters and requires no uncompression or decoding.

EPSI is similar to EPS bitmap data except that each line of the image begins with a comment % token. In fact, nearly every line in the EPSI preview is a comment; this is to keep a PostScript interpreter from reading the EPSI data as if it were part of the EPS data stored in the file.

Typically, an application will support one or more of the device-dependent preview formats. An application should also support the EPSI format for the export of EPS data to environments that cannot use one of the other preview formats.

The following shows an example of an EPSI file:

```
%%Title: EPSI Sample Image
%%Creator: James D. Murray
%%CreationDate: 12/03/91 13:56:24
%%Pages: 0
%%BoundingBox: 0 0 80 24
%%EndComments
%%BeginPreview: 80 24 1 24
% C0FFFFFFFFFFFFFFFFFFFF
% 0007F1E18F80FFFFFFFF
% 0007F1C000000001FFFF
% 001FFFE78C01FFFFFFFF
% E7FFFFFFFFFFFFFFFFFF
% 000FFFFF81FFFFFFFFFF
% 0007F38000000001FFFF
```

```
% 000FFFCE00000001FFFF
% E1FFFFFFFFC7FFFFFFFF
% 00FFFFFFFFFEFFFFFFFFF
% 0003FFCF038008EFFFFF
% 0003FFCF00000000FFFF
% 007FFFFFFFCFFFFFFFFF
% 40FFFFFFFFFFFFFFFFFF
% 0003FFFFFFFBFFFFFFFF
% 00003FFFFFE00001FFFF
% 0001FFFFFFF00031FFFF
% 00FFFFFFFFFFFFFFFFFF
% 0003FFFFFFFFFFFFFFFF
% 00000E000FF80073FFFF
% 00000E000FF80001FFFF
% 0003FFCFFFFFFFFFFFFF
% 0007FFFFFFFFFFFFFFFF
% 000003800071FFFFFFFF
%%EndPreview
%%EndProlog
%%Page: "one: 1
4 4 moveto 72 0 rlineto 0 16 rlineto -72 0 rlineto closepath
8 setlinewidth stroke
%%Trailer
```

EPSF Files

A question that is frequently asked is "What is the difference between an EPS file and an EPSF file?" The answer is that there is no difference; they are the same format. The actual designation, EPSF, is often shortened to EPS, which is also the file extension used for EPSF files on operating systems such as MS-DOS and UNIX.

EPSF files come in two flavors. The first is a plain EPSF file that contains only PostScript code. The second is a Display or Preview EPSF file that has a TIFF, WMF, PICT, or EPSI image file appended to it. Under MS-DOS, Encapsulated PostScript files have the extension .EPS, and Encapsulated PostScript Interchange files have the extension .EPI. On the Macintosh, all PostScript files have the file type EPSF. Also on the Macintosh, a file type of TEXT is allowed for PostScript files created in an editor. Such files should have the extension .EPSF or .EPSI. All other systems should use the filename extensions .EPSF and .EPSI.

For Further Information

PostScript was created and is maintained by Adobe Systems Inc. For specific information about PostScript, contact:

Adobe Systems Inc.
Attn: Adobe Systems Developer Support
1585 Charleston Rd.
P.O. Box 7900
Mountain View, CA 94039-7900
Voice: 415-961-4400
Voice: 800-344-8335
FAX: 415-961-3769

Adobe Systems distributes and supports a PostScript Language Software Development Kit to help software developers create applications that use PostScript. The kit includes technical information on PostScript Level 1 and Level 2 compatibility, optimal use of output devices, font software, and file format specifications. Also included are sample fonts, source code, and many PostScript utilities.

There are also numerous books written on PostScript. The fundamental reference set consists of the blue, green, and red books available in bookstores or directly from Adobe Systems or Addison-Wesley:

Adobe Systems, *PostScript Language Tutorial and Cookbook*, Addison-Wesley, Reading, MA, 1985.

Adobe Systems, *PostScript Language Program Design*, Addison-Wesley, Reading, MA, 1988.

Adobe Systems, *PostScript Language Reference Manual*, Second Edition, Addison-Wesley, Reading, MA, 1990.

Other excellent and readily available books about PostScript include:

Braswell, Frank Merritt, *Inside PostScript*, Peachpit Press, Atlanta, GA, 1989.

Glover, Gary, *Running PostScript from MS-DOS*, Wincrest Books, 1989. Reid, Glenn C., *Thinking in PostScript*. Addison-Wesley, Reading, MA, 1990.

Roth, Stephen F., *Real World PostScript*, Addison-Wesley, Reading, MA, 1988.

Smith, Ross, *Learning PostScript, A Visual Approach*, Peachpit Press, 1990.

A very helpful PostScript resource also exists in the form of a gentleman named Don Lancaster. Mr. Lancaster is the author of more than two dozen books on PostScript, laser printers, and desktop publishing. His articles can be read regularly in *Computer Shopper* magazine. His company, Synergetics, offers many PostScript products and information as well as a free technical support hotline for PostScript users. Contact:

Synergetics
Attn: Don Lancaster
Box 809-PCT
Thatcher, AZ 85552
Voice: 602-428-4073

NAME:	FaceSaver
ALSO KNOWN AS:	None
TYPE:	Bitmap
COLORS:	8-bit
COMPRESSION:	Uncompressed
MAXIMUM IMAGE SIZE:	NA
MULTIPLE IMAGES PER FILE:	No
NUMERICAL FORMAT:	NA
ORIGINATOR:	Metron Computerware, Ltd.
PLATFORM:	UNIX
SUPPORTING APPLICATIONS:	FaceSaver
SPECIFICATION ON CD:	Yes
CODE ON CD:	No
IMAGES ON CD:	No
SEE ALSO:	None

USAGE: A little-used format, but extremely simple and well-known, in part due to the fact that there is support for this format in the PBM utilities.

COMMENTS: This is an interesting format to examine if you are implementing an ID card system or a similar type of system that deals with the storage of small images (e.g., people's faces).

Overview

The FaceSaver format was created by Lou Katz, and FaceSaver is a registered trademark of Metron Computerware, Ltd. It was created to hold video facial portrait information in a compact, portable, and easy to use form. It is intended to be printed on a PostScript printer. Outside the UNIX graphics world, it is known chiefly because it is supported by the widely used PBM utilities included on the CD-ROM that comes with this book.

The original FaceSaver images were digitized using a Truevision TGA M8 video board.

File Organization

Each FaceSaver file consists of several lines of personal information in ASCII format, followed by bitmap data. There must be at least two lines of personal information, and they must include at least the PicData and Image fields.

File Details

The personal information in a FaceSaver file can consist of the following fields:

```
FirstName:
LastName:
E-mail:
Telephone:
Company:
Address1:
Address2:
CityStateZip:
Date:
PicData:      width - height - image bits/pixel
Image:        width - height - bits/pixel
```

Following these fields is a blank line, which is required, and which separates the personal information from the bitmap data that follows it.

The bitmap data consists of ASCII-encoded hexadecimal information, suitable for printing on a PostScript printer. The data is stored in scanline order, starting from the bottom and continuing to the top of the image, and from left to right. The image data comes originally from a video camera, and is first rotated 90 degrees before being written to a file.

Each pixel is transformed before it's written to the file by multiplying its value by the factor:

```
256 / (max - min)
```

where max and min are the maximum and minimum pixel values found in the image, respectively.

The Image field in the personal information above is used to correct for non-square pixels. The author writes:

In most cases, there are 108 (non-square) pixels across in the data, but they would have been 96 pixels across if they were square. Therefore, Image says 96; PicData says 108.

For Further Information

For further information about FaceSaver, see the file format specification included on the CD-ROM that accompanies this book. You may also contact the author directly for additional information.

Lou Katz
lou@orange.metron.com

FAX Formats

NAME:	FAX Formats
ALSO KNOWN AS:	FAX, Facsimile File Formats
TYPE:	Bitmap
COLORS:	Mono
COMPRESSION:	RLE, CCITT Group 3, CCITT Group 4
MAXIMUM IMAGE SIZE:	1728x2200 pixels (typical)
MULTIPLE IMAGES PER FILE:	No
NUMERICAL FORMAT:	NA
ORIGINATOR:	Many
PLATFORM:	All
SUPPORTING APPLICATIONS:	Too numerous to list
SPECIFICATION ON CD:	No
CODE ON CD:	No
IMAGES ON CD:	No
SEE ALSO:	TIFF, PCX, Chapter 9, *Data Compression* (CCITT Group 3 and CCITT Group 4 compression)
USAGE:	Storage of FAX images received through computer-based FAX and FAX-modem boards.
COMMENTS:	There is no one single FAX format. The closest to standard are the formats based on a proprietary specification, such as PCX or TIFF. Consider yourself blessed if the format you need to support is one of these.

Overview

There are many facsimile (FAX) file formats, almost as many as there are FAX add-in boards. The PC-based HiJaak Graphics File Conversion Utility (by Inset Systems), as of version 2.1, supports no fewer than 22 different FAX file formats. Each format, however, is basically the same, and consists of a binary header, followed by one or more sections of compressed image data. The data encoding is usually a variant of RLE, CCITT Group 3 or CCITT Group 4. Several FAX formats, in fact, are proprietary variants of better-known formats, such as TIFF and PCX.

Even though all of these FAX file formats were created to store the same kind of image data obtained from the same type of hardware device (i.e., FAX cards), each one is slightly different from all the others. This is problematic.

The evolution of the FAX card industry in some ways recapitulates the early evolution of the computer industry as a whole. Each company perhaps imagined it was working alone, or, if not, would quickly come to dominate the market. As the presence of competition became clear, a mad scramble to ship products ensued, and corners were cut. Because companies making FAX cards are by definition hardware-oriented, you can guess where the corners were cut: software.

As the industry started to mature, companies realized that competition was a fact of life, and tried to differentiate their products. One way to do so was through the promulgation of proprietary "standards," designed to keep the originator company one jump ahead of any competition unlucky enough not to be able to push their own specification. Add an unhealthy glop of NIH ("not invented here") spread liberally over the entire FAX board industry, and you have the present situation.

Recently, there have been signs of true maturity in the FAX card industry, with the emergence of the realization that all companies benefit by standardization, and an effort in this direction has been underway for some time. An extension of the TIFF file format, called TIFF Class F, would add the necessary tag extensions to allow easier storage and manipulation of FAX images stored in TIFF format files. (For further information, see the article on TIFF.) At the time of this writing, only one company, Everex, has adopted the unofficial TIFF Class F as its FAX file format standard (perhaps because a now-dead subsidiary of Everex, Cygnet Technologies, pioneered TIFF Class F).

If you need to need to convert FAX file formats, you will need a very versatile conversion utility, such as HiJaak. If you need to write code for an application that reads and writes one or more FAX file formats, you will ordinarily need to contact the manufacturer of the FAX card and obtain any information they are willing to release. If your FAX format is a common one and worth supporting, you should find that you are able to obtain the specifications you need from the manufacturer.

For Further Information

As mentioned above, the best source of information on FAX file formats is from the manufacturer of the FAX card you wish to support. Some FAX card companies publish developers' toolkits for designing software to work with their FAX cards. Unless a company considers its format proprietary, it will have some sort of specification available for their FAX file format.

For more information about TIFF Class F, see the TIFF article. You may also be able to obtain the following document:

> Campbell, Joe. *The Spirit of TIFF Class F*, Cygnet Technologies, Berkeley, CA, April 1990.

Cygnet is no longer in business, and Aldus now supports the TIFF Class F specification. You contact Aldus at:

> Aldus Corporation
> Attn: Aldus Developers Desk
> 411 First Avenue South
> Seattle, WA 98104-2871
> Voice: 206-628-6593
> Voice: 800-331-2538
> FAX: 206-343-4240

NAME:	FITS
ALSO KNOWN AS:	Flexible Image Transport System, FTI
TYPE:	General data format
COLORS:	Unlimited gray scale
COMPRESSION:	Uncompressed
MAXIMUM IMAGE SIZE:	NA
MULTIPLE IMAGES PER FILE:	Yes
NUMERICAL FORMAT:	Two's complement/big-endian
ORIGINATOR:	NOST
PLATFORM:	All
SUPPORTING APPLICATIONS:	IMDISP, xv, pbmplus, SAOImage
SPECIFICATION ON CD:	Yes
CODE ON CD:	No
IMAGES ON CD:	Yes
SEE ALSO:	VICAR2, PDS

USAGE:	FITS is a general-purpose data storage format used primarily for the interchange of data between hardware platforms and software applications.
COMMENTS:	FITS is the standard image data storage format for many astronomical organizations, including the astrophysics branch of NASA.

Overview

The FITS image file format is used primarily as a method of exchanging bitmap data between different hardware platforms and software applications that do not support a common image file format. FITS is used mostly by scientific organizations and government agencies that require the storage of astronomical image data (e.g., image data returned by orbital satellites, manned spacecraft, and planetary probes) and ground-based image data (e.g., data obtained from CCD imagery, radio astronomy, and digitized photographic plates).

Although the I in FITS stands for Image, FITS is actually a general-purpose data interchange format. In fact, there is nothing in the FITS specification that limits its use to bitmapped image data.

FITS was originally designed explicitly to facilitate the interchange of data between different hardware platforms, rather than between software applications. Much of the FITS data in existence today is (and traditionally, always has been) ground-based and most, if not all, of the agencies and organizations requiring the use of FITS are astronomical in nature.

FITS was originally created by Eric Greisen, Don Wells, Ron Harten, and P. Grosbol and described in a series of papers published in the journal *Astronomy & Astrophysics Supplement*. The NASA/OSSA Office of Standards and Technology (NOST) codified FITS by consolidating these papers into a draft standard of a format for the interchange of astronomical data between scientific organizations. Many such organizations use proprietary imaging software and image file formats not supported by other organizations. FITS, along with VICAR2 and PDS, became a standard interchange format that allows the successful exchange of image data.

FITS is supported by all astronomical image processing facilities and astrophysics data archives. Much of the solar, lunar, and planetary data that is retrieved by the Astrophysics branch of the National Aeronautics and Space Administration (NASA) is distributed using the FITS file format. FITS is currently maintained by a Working Group of the International Astronomical Union (IAU).

Image data normally is converted to FITS not to be stored, but to be imported into another image processing system. Astronomical image data is generally stored in another format, such as the VICAR2 (Video Image Communication and Retrieval) format used by the Multi-Mission Image Processing Laboratory (MIPL).

FITS itself is a very general format capable of storing many types of data, including bitmaps, ASCII text, multidimensional matrices, and binary tables. The simplest FITS file contains a header and a single data stream, called a multidimensional binary array. This is the type of FITS image file we will be examining in this article.

File Organization

In FITS terminology, a basic FITS file contains a primary header and single primary data array. This data structure is known collectively as a Header and Data Unit (HDU). An HDU may contain a header followed by data records, or may contain only a header. All data in a FITS file is organized into logical records 2880 bytes in length.

Basically, a FITS file is a header, normally followed by a data stream. Every FITS file begins with an ASCII header which contains one or more logical records. Each logical record is 2880 bytes in size. The last logical record in the header must be padded to 2880 bytes with spaces (ASCII 32).

Each logical record contains 36 records, called card images. A card image is a logical field similar to a data field in a binary image file header. Each card image contains 80 bytes of ASCII data, which describes some aspect of the organization of the FITS image file data. Card images are padded with spaces when necessary to fill out the 80 bytes and do not have delimiters. Card images that are not needed for the storage of a particular set of data contain only spaces.

Most card images may appear in any order within the header, with a few exceptions. The SIMPLE card image must always be first, followed by BITPIX second, NAXIS third, and END last.

Every card image has the following syntax:

```
keyword = value /comment
```

keyword is a 1- to 8-character, left-justified ASCII string that specifies the format and use of the data stored in the card image. If a keyword contains fewer than eight characters, it is padded with spaces. A keyword always occupies columns one through eight in a card image. Only uppercase alphanumerics, hyphens (-), and underscores (_) may be used as characters in a keyword. No lowercase characters, other punctuation, or control codes may be used. If a card image does not have a keyword (the keyword is all spaces), then the card image is treated as a comment.

If the keyword has an associated value, it is then followed by a two-character value indicator (=). This indicator always occupies columns nine and ten in the card image, and if it is present, a value follows the keyword. If the keyword does not have an associated value, then any other ASCII characters may appear in place of the value indicator.

value is an ASCII representation of the numerical or string data associated with the keyword. The value is an ASCII representation of boolean, string, integer, or real (floating-point) data.

comment is an optional field which may follow any value within a card image. A comment is separated from the value by a slash (/) or a space and a slash (/); the latter is recommended. A comment may contain any ASCII characters.

The data in a card image is stored in specific columns. For example, the keyword identifier always occupies columns one through seven in a card image. The keyword value indicator, if present, always occupies columns eight and nine. A boolean value always occupies column 30. And a complex-integer value always occupies columns 31 through 50. Columns that do not contain data are filled with spaces.

Character strings are contained within single quotes. If a string contains a single quote, then it is represented by two consecutive single quotes ('O'Reilly' becomes 'O"Reilly'). All strings contain only 7-bit ASCII values and must be at least eight characters in length, padded with spaces, if necessary. Strings may contain a maximum of 68 characters. Strings may begin with leading spaces, but trailing spaces are considered padding.

All boolean, integer, and floating-point values are represented by their ASCII string equivalents. Boolean variables are represented by the value T or F and are always found in column 30 of the card image. Integer and floating-point values are located in columns 11 through 30 and are right-justified with spaces, if necessary. Complex integers and complex floating-point values are located in columns 31 through 50 and are also right-justified when necessary. All letters used in exponential forms are uppercase.

Examples of valid values are shown below.

Name	Size in bits	Example
ASCII character	8	'Saturn'
Integer		
Unsigned, one byte	8	127
Unsigned, two bytes	16	32767
Unsigned, four bytes	32	1451342181
Single-precision real		
Fixed-point notation	32	3.14159
Exponential notation	32	0.314159E+01
Double-precision real		
Exponential notation	64	0.3141592653525D+01

File Details

This section describes FITS headers and image data.

Keywords

There are many keywords that may be included in FITS headers, and it is unlikely that any FITS reader will understand them all (unrecognized keywords are treated as comments by FITS readers). There are five keywords that are required in every FITS file: SIMPLE, BITPIX, NAXIS, NAXISn, and END. (EXTEND is also a required keyword if extensions are present in the file.) These mandatory keywords are described below:

SIMPLE

The SIMPLE keyword always appears first in any FITS header. The value of this keyword is a boolean value indicating the conformance level of the file to the FITS specification. If the file conforms to the FITS standard, this value is T. If the value is F, then the file differs in some way from the requirements specified in the FITS standard.

BITPIX

The BITPIX card image contains an integer value which specifies the number of bits used to represent each data value. For image data, this is the number of bits per pixel.

BITPIX Value	Data
8	Character or unsigned binary integer
16	16-bit two's complement binary integer
32	32-bit two's complement binary integer
-32	32-bit floating point, single precision
-64	64-bit floating point, double precision

NAXIS

The NAXIS card image contains an integer value in the range of 0 to 999, indicating the number of axes in the data array. Conventional bitmaps have an NAXIS value of 2. A value of 0 signifies that no data follows the header, although an extension may be present.

NAXISn

The NAXISn card image indicates the length of each axis in BITPIX units. No NAXISn card images are present if the NAXIS value is 0. The value field of this indexed keyword contains a non-negative integer, representing the number of positions along axis n of an ordinary data array. The NAXISn card image must be present for all values n = 1, ..., NAXIS. A value of 0 for any of the NAXISn card images signifies that no data follows the header in the HDU. If NAXIS is equal to 0, there should not be any NAXISn keywords.

EXTEND

The EXTEND card image may be included if there are extensions in the FITS file. If there are no extensions, there are no EXTEND card images.

END

The END keyword indicates the end of the header and is always the last card image in a header. END has no value. The card image contains spaces in columns 9 though 80 and is padded out with spaces so that the length of the header is a multiple of 2880 bytes.

Sample Header

The header of a basic FITS image file might appear as follows (the first two lines are for positional information only and are not included in the FITS file):

```
          1         2         3         4         5         6         7         8
12345678901234567890123456789012345678901234567890123456789012345678901234567890
SIMPLE  =                    T
BITPIX  =                    8/ 8 bits per pixel
NAXIS   =                    2/ Table is a two-dimensional matrix
NAXIS1  =                  168/ Width of table row in bytes
NAXIS2  =                    5/ Number of rows in table
DATE    = '09/17/93'
ORIGIN  = 'O''Reilly & Associates'/ Publisher
AUTHOR  = 'James D. Murray'/ Creator
REFERENC= 'Graphics File Formats'/ Where referenced
COMMENT = 'Sample FITS header'
END
```

For a description of all other valid FITS header keywords, refer to the FITS specification.

FITS Image Data

Immediately following the header is the binary image data. This data is stored in 8-bit bytes and is currently never compressed. At the time of this writing, an extension to the FITS standard has been proposed to the FITS community, so future revisions to the FITS standard may incorporate data compression.

The presence or absence of a primary data array is indicated by the values of either the NAXIS or the NAXISn keyword in the primary header.

Data in a FITS file may be stored as bytes, 16- or 32-bit words, and 32- or 64-bit floating-point values that conform to the ANSI/IEEE-754 standard. Fill (ASCII 00h) is added to the data to pad the data out to end on a 2880-byte boundary.

The number of bits of image data, not including the padding added to the end of the image data, may be calculated from the BITPIX, NAXIS, and NAXISn card image values:

```
NumberOfBits = BITBIX * (NAXIS1 * NAXIS2 * ... * NAXIS[NAXIS])
```

For Further Information

The specification for FITS is contained in the NOST document included on the CD-ROM that accompanies this book:

> *Implementation of the Flexible Image Transport System (FITS)*, Draft Implementation Standard NOST 100-0.3b., December 1991.

A tutorial and historical guide to FITS is included in the following document, also on the CD-ROM:

> *A User's Guide for FITS*, January 1993.

Both of these documents are also available from the NASA/OSSA Office of Standards and Technology (NOST) FITS Support Office:

NASA/OSSA Office of Standards and Technology
Code 633.2
Goddard Space Flight Center
Greenbelt, MD 20771
Voice: 301-441-4189
Voice: 301-513-1634
Internet: *nost@nssdca.gsfc.nasa.gov*
          fits@nssdca.gsfc.nasa.gov

The FITS standard is also described in the following references, known collectively as the "Four FITS Papers:"

Wells, D. C., Greisen, E. W., and Harten, R. H. "FITS: a flexible image transport system," *Astronomy and Astrophysics Supplement Series*, Volume 44, 1981, pp. 363-370.

Greisen, E. W. and Harten, R. H. "An extension of FITS for small arrays of data," *Astronomy and Astrophysics Supplement Series*, Volume 44, 1981, pp. 371-374.

Grosbol, P., Harten, R. H., Greisen, E. W., and Wells, D. C. "Generalized extensions and blocking factors for FITS,"*Astronomy and Astrophysics Supplement Series*, Volume 73, 1988, pp. 359-364.

Harten, R. H., Grosbol. P., Greisen, E. W., and Wells, D. C. "The FITS tables extension," *Astronomy and Astrophysics Supplement Series*, Volume 73, 1988, pp. 365-372.

Updated information on FITS, including new software applications, frequently appears on the Usenet newsgroups *sci.astro.fits* and *sci.data.formats*. Additional software and information on FITS may also be obtained from the following FTP sites:

fits.cv.nrao.edu:FITS
ames.arc.nasa.gov:pub/SPACE/SOFTWARE
hypatia.gsfc.nasa.gov:pub/software

FITS is also one of the primary responsibilities of the Working Group on Astronomical Software (WGAS) of the American Astronomical Society. The North American FITS Committee (Dr. Robert J. Hanisch at Space Telescope Science Institute is the chairman) is appointed under the auspices of the WGAS. The WGAS also has a list server, which may be reached by sending a mail message to the following for information on the WGAS mail exploder:

listserv@hypatia.gsfc.nasa.gov

The IMDISP program displays FITS images on MS-DOS machines and is maintained, enhanced, and distributed free of charge by Archibald Warnock, Ron Baalke, and Mike Martin. It is included on the CD-ROM. (See Appendix A, *What's On the CD-ROM?* for information about obtaining IMDISP via FTP as well.)

The NSSDC Coordinated Request and Support Office (CRUSO) will provide IMDISP on floppy for a nominal fee. Contact them at:

Voice: 301-286-6695
request@nssdc.gsfc.nasa.gov

The FITSIO package contains a collection of subroutines for reading and writing data in the FITS format. This library supports most machines, including Sun, VAX/VMS, Amiga, and the IBM PC and mainframes. It is available via FTP from:

tetra.gsfc.nasa.gov:pub/fitsio

FLI

NAME:	FLI
ALSO KNOWN AS:	FLI Animation, Flic, FLC, FII
TYPE:	Animation
COLORS:	64, 256
COMPRESSION:	Raw, RLE, and delta
MAXIMUM IMAGE SIZE:	320x200, 64Kx64K
MULTIPLE IMAGES PER FILE:	Yes
NUMERICAL FORMAT:	Little-endian
ORIGINATOR:	Autodesk
PLATFORM:	Intel
SUPPORTING APPLICATIONS:	Autodesk Animator and Animator Pro
SPECIFICATION ON CD:	Yes (summary description by its author)
CODE ON CD:	No
IMAGES ON CD:	Yes
SEE ALSO:	GRASP
USAGE:	Used to store animation sequences found in graphics applications, CAD systems, and computer games.
COMMENTS:	Currently occupies a market niche being colonized by video.

Overview

The FLI file format (sometimes called Flic) is one of the most popular animation formats found in the MS-DOS and Windows environments today. FLI is used widely in animation programs, computer games, and CAD applications requiring 3D manipulation of vector drawings. Flic, in common with most animation formats, does not support either audio or video data, but instead stores only sequences of still image data.

FLI is popular because of its simple design. It easy to implement FLI readers and writers in software-only applications. FLI also enables quick animation playback and does not require special hardware to encode or decode its data.

FLI is best suited for computer-generated or hand-drawn animation sequences, such as those created using animation and CAD programs. These images achieve the best compression ratios when stored using the FLI format.

Natural, real-world images may also be animated by FLI, but such images usually contain a fair amount of noise that will degrade the ability of the FLI encoding algorithms to compress the data and will therefore possibly affect the speed of the animation playback. Also, the fewer the colors in the animation, the better the compression ratio will typically be.

There are two types of FLI animation files. The original FLI format has an extension of .FLI, has a maximum display resolution of 320x200 pixels, and is only capable of supporting 64 colors. This format was created for use by the Autodesk Animator application.

The new FLI format has the extension .FLC, has a maximum display resolution of 64Kx64K pixels, and supports up to 256 colors. The data compression scheme used by .FLC files is also more efficient than the scheme used by .FLI files. Applications such as the IBM Multimedia Tool Series, Microsoft Video for Windows, and Autodesk Animator Pro all support .FLC files.

Any application capable of reading the newer .FLC files should be able to read and play back the older .FLI files as well. However, most newer FLI file writers may only have the capability of creating .FLC files. There is really no reason to create .FLI files, unless the animations you are producing must run under software that reads only the .FLI format.

File Organization

FLI animations are sequences of still images called frames. Each frame contains a slice of the animation data. The speed of the animation playback is controlled by specifying the amount of delay that is to occur between each frame.

The data in each frame is always color mapped. Each pixel in a frame contains an index value into a color map defined for that frame. The colors in the map may change from frame to frame as required. And, although the FLI file is limited to displaying a maximum of 256 colors per frame, each pixel is 24 bits in depth, resulting in a palette of more than 16 million colors from which to choose.

The FLI format also supports several types of data compression. Each frame of a FLI animation is typically compressed using an interframe delta encoding scheme. This scheme encodes only the differences between adjacent image frames and not the frames themselves. This strategy results in significantly smaller files than if each frame were independently encoded (intraframe encoding). Interframe encoded data is also very fast to uncompress and display.

FLI *(cont'd)*

The first frame of every FLI animation is compressed in its entirety, using a simple run-length encoding algorithm. Because only the differences between each successive frame are encoded, you have to start somewhere. If a frame is delta encoded and the resulting compressed data is larger than the original uncompressed data (quite possible with noisy, natural images), then the frame may be stored uncompressed.

File Details

The header of a FLI file is 128 bytes in length. The first nine fields (22 bytes) are the same for both .FLI and .FLC files. The last ten fields (106 bytes) contain valid data only in .FLC files and are set to 00h in .FLI files.

The FLI file header has the following format:

```
typedef struct _FlicHeader
{
  DWORD FileSize;        /* Total size of file */
  WORD  FileId;          /* File format indicator */
  WORD  NumberOfFrames;  /* Total number of frames */
  WORD  Width;           /* Screen width in pixels */
  WORD  Height;          /* Screen height in pixels */
  WORD  PixelDepth;      /* Number of bits per pixel */
  WORD  Flags;           /* Set to 03h */
  DWORD FrameDelay;      /* Time delay between frames */
  WORD  Reserved1;       /* Not used (Set to 00h) */

  // The following fields are set to 00h in a .FLI file

  DWORD DateCreated;     /* Time/Date the file was created */
  DWORD CreatorSN;       /* Serial number of creator program */
  DWORD LastUpdated;     /* Time/Date the file last changed */
  DWORD UpdaterSN;       /* Serial number of updater program */
  WORD  XAspect;         /* X-axis of display aspect ratio */
  WORD  YAspect;         /* Y-axis of display aspect ratio */
  BYTE  Reserved2[38];   /* Not used (Set to 00h) */
  DWORD Frame1Offset;    /* Offset of first frame */
  DWORD Frame2Offset;    /* Offset of second frame */
  BYTE  Reserved3[40];   /* Not used (Set to 00h) */

} FLICHEADER;
```

FileSize contains the total size of the FLI file in bytes.

FileId contains a value identifying the type of Flic file. A value of AF11h indicates an .FLI file, and a value of AF12h indicates an .FLC file.

NumberOfFrames contains the total number of frames of animation data. A .FLC file may contain a maximum of 4000 frames; this does not include the ring frame.

Width and Height specify the size of the animation in pixels.

PixelDepth indicates the number of bits per pixel; the value of this field is always 08h.

Flags is always set to 03h, as an indication that the file was properly updated.

FrameDelay indicates the amount of time delay between frames and is used to control the speed of playback. For .FLI files, this value is interpreted in units of 1/70 of a second. For .FLC files, this value is in units of 1/1000 of a second.

Reserved1 is not used and is set to 00h.

DateCreated is an MS-DOS date stamp (the number of seconds occurring since midnight, January 1, 1970) of the date the FLI file was created.

CreatorSN contains the serial number of the Animator Pro application program that created the FLI file. If the file was created by an application using the FlicLib development library, the value of this field will be 46h 4Ch 49h 42h ("FLIB").

LastUpdated is an MS-DOS date stamp indicating the last time the FLI file was modified (also in number of seconds since midnight January 1, 1970).

UpdaterSN contains the serial number of the program that last modified the Flic file.

XAspect and YAspect contain the aspect ratio of the display used to create the animation. For a display with a resolution of 320x200, the aspect ratio is 6:5, and these fields contain the values 6 and 5 respectively. For all other resolutions, the aspect ratio is typically 1:1.

Reserved2 is not used and is set to 00h.

Frame1Offset and Frame2Offset contain the offset of the first and second frames, respectively, of the animation from the beginning of the file. The first

FLI (cont'd)

frame offset is used to identify the beginning of the animation. The second offset is used as the starting point when the animation loops back to the beginning of the animation from the ring frame.

Reserved3 is not used and is set to 00h.

Chunks

All of the data in a FLI file is encapsulated into chunks. Each chunk is a collection of data beginning with a header and followed by the data for that chunk. Chunks may also contains subchunks of data with the same basic format. If a Flic reader encounters a chunk it does not recognize, it should simply skip over it.

Each chunk in a FLI file begins with a 16-byte header that contains the following format:

```
format:
typedef struct _ChunkHeader
{
    DWORD ChunkSize;         /* Total size of chunk */
    WORD  ChunkType;         /* Chunk identifier */
    WORD  NumberOfChunks;    /* Number of subchunks in this chunk */
    BYTE  Reserved[8];       /* Not used (Set to 00h) */

} CHUNKHEADER;
```

ChunkSize is the size of the chunk in bytes. This value includes the size of the header itself and any subchunks contained within the chunk.

ChunkType is an identification value indicating the format of the chunk and the type of data it contains.

NumberOfChunks specifies the number of subchunks contained within this chunk.

Reserved is not used and is set to 00h.

As we have said, a chunk may contain subchunks. In fact, the entire FLI file itself is a single chunk that begins with the FLICHEADER structure. In .FLC files, an optional CHUNKHEADER structure may follow the FLICHEADER structure. This secondary header is called a *prefix header*. If present, this header contains information specific to the Animator Pro application that is not used during the playback of the animation. Other applications can safely skip over the prefix header and ignore the information it contains. Applications other than Animator Pro should never include a prefix header in any .FLC files they create.

For the prefix header, ChunkSize is the size of the entire FLI file minus the 128 bytes of the FLICHEADER. ChunkType is F100h. NumberOfChunks contains the total number of subchunks in the file.

Following the prefix header is a series of frame chunks. Each frame chunk contains a single frame of data from the animation. For the frame chunk, ChunkSize is the total number of bytes in the frame, including the header and all subchunks. ChunkType is always F1FAh. NumberOfChunks contains the total number of subchunks in the frame. If the NumberOfChunks value is 0, then this frame is identical to the previous frame, so no color map or frame data is stored, and the previous frame is repeated with the delay specified in the header.

The following lists all the subchunks that may be found in a frame chunk.

ChunkType Value	Chunk Name	Chunk Data Description
04h	COLOR_256	256-level color palette (.FLC files only)
07h	DELTA_FLC	Delta-compressed frame data (.FLC files only)
0Bh	COLOR_64	64-level color palette (.FLI files only)
0Ch	DELTA_FLI	Delta-compressed frame data (.FLI files only)
0Dh	BLACK	Black frame data
0Fh	BYTE_RUN	RLE-compressed frame data
10h	FLI_COPY	Uncompressed frame data
12h	PSTAMP	Postage stamp image (.FLC files only)

The following lists the general internal arrangement of a FLI file:

    FLI header
    Prefix header (optional)
    Frame 1 (RLE compressed)
        PSTAMP subchunk (optional)
        COLOR_256 subchunk (256 colors)
        BYTE_RUN subchunk

    COLOR_256 subchunk (256 colors)
    BYTE_RUN subchunk
Frame 2 (Delta compressed)
    COLOR_256 subchunk (colors different from previous map
    DELTA_FLC subchunk
Frame 3 (Uncompressed)
    COLOR_256 subchunk (colors different from previous map)
    FLI_COPY subchunk
Frame 4 (Black)
    BLACK subchunk
Frame *n* (Delta compressed)
    COLOR_256 subchunk (colors different from previous map)
    DELTA_FLC subchunk

Each frame chunk contains at least two subchunks: a color map and the data for the frame. The frame data may be stored in one of several different compressed or uncompressed formats. The first frame of a Flic animation may also contain an additional postage stamp subchunk.

Following is an explanation of each subchunk:

DELTA_FLI chunk

The DELTA_FLI chunk contains a single frame of data, which is compressed using delta encoding. The data in this chunk contains the pixel value differences between the current frame and the previous frame. Each scan line of the frame which contains pixel changes is encoded into packets, and only the values of the pixels in the line that have changed are stored.

The DELTA_FLI encoding scheme is an older scheme found mostly in .FLI files, although .FLC files may also contain DELTA_FLI chunks.

The format of a DELTA_FLI chunk is as follows:

```
typedef struct _DeltaFliChunk
{
  CHUNKHEADER Header;      /* Header for this chunk */
  WORD LinesToSkip;       /* Number of initial lines to skip */
  WORD NumberOfLines;     /* Number of encoded lines */

  /* Encoded line (one per 'NumberOfLines') */
  struct _Line
  {
   BYTE NumberOfPackets; /* Number of packets in this line */
```

```
      BYTE LineSkipCount;      /* Number of lines to skip */
      struct _Packet           /* Encoded packet (one/NumberOfPackets) */
        {
        BYTE SkipCount;        /* Number of pixels to skip */
        BYTE PacketType;       /* Type of encoding used on this packet */
        BYTE PixelData[];      /* Pixel data for this packet */
        } Packet[NumberOfPackets];

      } Lines[NumberOfLines];

  } DELTAFLICHUNK;
```

LinesToSkip contains the number of lines down from the top of the image that are unchanged from the prior frame. This value is used to find the first scan line which contains deltas.

NumberOfLines indicates the number of encoded scan lines in this chunk.

NumberOfPackets indicates the number of packets used to encode this scan line. Each encoded scan line begins with this value.

LineSkipCount is the number of lines to skip to locate the next encoded line.

Each packet in every encoded line contains two values. SkipCount indicates the location of the pixel deltas in this line that are encoded in this packet. PacketType specifies the type of encoding used in this packet. A positive value indicates that the next "PacketType" pixels should be literally read from the chunk and written to the display. A negative value indicates that the absolute value of "PacketType" pixels are to be read literally from the encoded data.

For example, suppose that we have a frame with three encoded scan lines. The first is line number 25, which contains deltas at pixels 4, 22, 23, 24, and 202. The second is line number 97, which contains deltas at pixels 20 and 54 through 67. The third is line number 199, in which all 320 pixels of the line have changed to the same color. The sequence of line and packet field values is shown below:

LinesToSkip	24	Skip 24 lines to first encoded line
NumberOfLines	3	Three encoded lines in this frame
Line		Line 1
NumberOfPackets	3	Three encoded packets in this line
LineSkipCount	71	Skip 71 lines to the next encoded line
Packet		Packet 1

SkipCount	4	Skip 4 pixels
PacketType	1	Read one pixel literally
PixelData	23	New value of pixel 4 is 23
Packet		Packet 2
SkipCount	17	Skip 17 pixels
PacketType	−3	Read one pixel and repeat 3 times
PixelData	65	New value of pixels 22, 23, and 24 is 65
Packet		Packet 3
SkipCount	176	Skip 176 pixels
PacketType	1	Read one pixel literally
PixelData	17	New value of pixel 202 is 17
Line		Line 2
NumberOfPackets	2	Two encoded packets in this line
LineSkipCount	102	Skip 102 lines to the next encoded line
Packet		Packet 1
SkipCount	20	Skip 20 pixels
PacketType	1	Read one pixel literally
PixelData	121	New value of pixel 20 is 121
Packet		Packet 2
SkipCount	32	Skip 32 pixels
PacketType	13	Read next 13 pixels literally
PixelData	255	New value of pixels 54 through 67 is 255
Line		Line 3
NumberOfPackets	2	Two encoded packets in this line
LineSkipCount	0	Last encoded line in frame
Packet		Packet 1
SkipCount	0	Start at first pixel in line
PacketType	−256	Read one pixel and repeat 256 times
PixelData	0	New value of pixels 0 though 255 is 0
Packet		Packet 2
SkipCount	256	Skip 256 pixels
PacketType	−64	Read one pixel and repeat 64 times
PixelData	0	New value of pixels 256 though 319 is 0

DELTA_FLC chunk

The DELTA_FLC chunk is a newer version of the DELTA_FLI chunk and is found in all .FLC files. This chunk is essentially the same as the DELTA_FLI chunk with a few field modifications. The PixelData values stored in a

DELTA_FLC chunk are 16 bits in size rather than the 8-bit pixel size found in the DELTA_FLI chunk.

The structure of a DELTA_FLC chunk is as follows:

```
typedef struct _DeltaFlcChunk
{
CHUNKHEADER Header;         /* Header for this chunk */
WORD NumberOfLines;         /* Number of encoded lines in chunk */

struct _Line                /* Encoded line (one/'NumberOfLines') */
  {
  WORD PacketCount;         /* Packet count, skip count,
                                 or last byte value */
  /*
  ** Additional WORDs of data may appear in this location
  */
  struct _Packet            /* Encoded packet (one per 'Count') */
    {
    BYTE SkipCount;         /* Number of pixels to skip */
    BYTE PacketType;        /* Type of encoding used on this packet */
    WORD PixelData[];       /* Pixel data for this packet */
    } Packet[NumberOfPackets];

  } Lines[NumberOfLines];

} DELTAFLCCHUNK;
```

The number of fields occurring between the PacketCount and the first packet will vary depending upon the value stored in PacketCount. The two most significant bits in PacketCount determine the interpretation of the value stored in this field. If these two bits are 0, then the value is the number of packets occurring in this line. Packet data immediately follows this field and there are no additional WORD values following.

A value of 0 in this field indicates that only the last pixel on the line has changed.

If the most significant bit (bit 15) is 1 and the next bit (bit 14) is 0, the low byte in this WORD is to be stored in the last byte of the current line. A WORD field containing the number of packets in this line follows this value.

If both bits 14 and 15 are set to 1, PacketCount contains a skip count to the next encoded line. PacketCount may then be followed by additional WORD values containing a packet count, skip counts, or last byte values.

BYTE_RUN chunk

When a frame is run-length encoded, the data is stored in a BYTE_RUN chunk. Normally, only the data in the first frame of an animation is encoded using this scheme.

The structure of a BYTE_RUN chunk is as follows:

```
typedef struct _ByteRunChunk
{
  CHUNKHEADER Header;    /* Header for this chunk */
  BYTE PixelData[];      /* RLE pixel data */

} BYTERUNCHUNK;
```

Each line in the frame is individually encoded into a series of one or more RLE packets. In the original .FLI format, the first byte of each encoded line was the count of the number of packets used to encode that line, with a packet maximum of 255. The .FLC format, however, allows much longer lines to be used in an animation, and more than 255 packets may be used to encode a line. Therefore, in both .FLC and .FLI files, this initial count byte is read and ignored. Instead, a FLI reader should keep track of the number of pixels decoded to determine when the end of a scan line has been reached.

The RLE scheme used in the BYTE_RUN packet is fairly simple. The first byte in each packet is a type byte that indicates how the packet data is to be interpreted. If the value of this byte is a positive number then the next byte is to be read and repeated "type" times. If the value is negative then it is converted to its absolute value and the next "type" pixels are read literally from the encoded data.

FLI_COPY chunk

This chunk contains a single, uncompressed frame of data. When a frame is stored uncompressed, the FLI_COPY chunk is used. Data is only stored uncompressed when delta or RLE encoding would result in negative compression.

The structure of a FLI_COPY chunk is as follows:

```
typedef struct _CopyChunk
{
  CHUNKHEADER Header;              /* Header for this chunk */
  BYTE PixelData[];                /* Raw pixel data */

} COPYCHUNK;
```

The number of pixels in this chunk is equal to the product of the Width and Height fields (Width*Height) in the FLI file header. FLI_COPY chunks usually result when very complex or noisy images cause the compressed frames to be larger than the uncompressed originals.

PSTAMP chunk

The PSTAMP is a postage stamp of a FLI animation found in the first frame chunk only in .FLC files. This stamp may be a reduced-sized copy of a frame from the animation, possibly from the title screen, that is used as an icon. The size of the stamp is usually 100x63 pixels, but will vary to match the aspect ratio of the frame. This chunk is skipped by FLI readers that do not support the use of PSTAMP chunks.

The PSTAMP chunk contains a CHUNKHEADER and two subchunks:

```
typedef struct _PstampChunk
{
    DWORD ChunkSize;              /* Total size of chunk */
    WORD  ChunkType;              /* Chunk identifier */
    WORD  Height;                 /* Height of stamp in pixels */
    WORD  Width;                  /* Width of stamp in pixels */
    WORD  ColorType;              /* Color translation type */
    BYTERUNCHUNK  PixelData;      /* Postage stamp data */

} PSTAMPCHUNK;
```

ChunkSize is the total size of the PSTAMP chunk.

ChunkType value is 0fh, 10h, or 12h.

Height and Width are the height and width of the stamp in pixels.

ColorType indicates the type of color space used by the postage stamp image. This value is always 01h, indicating a six-cube colorspace (see the FLI file format specification for more information on six-cube color space).

Following this header is the postage stamp data chunk.

ChunkType of this header indicates the format of the pixel data. Values are:

0Fh   Indicates run-length encoding (a BYTE_RUN chunk)
10h   Indicates uncompressed data (a FLI_COPY chunk)
12h   Indicates a six-cube color translation table

BLACK chunk

The BLACK chunk represents a single frame of data in which all pixels are set to the color index 0 (normally black) in the color map for this frame. This chunk itself contains no data and has a ChunkType of 0Dh.

The BLACK chunk contains only a CHUNKHEADER:

```
typedef struct _BlackChunk
{
  CHUNKHEADER Header;        /* Header for this chunk */
} BLACKCHUNK;
```

COLOR_64 and COLOR_256 chunks

The FLI file format uses a color map to define the colors in an animation. The older .FLI format may have a maximum of 64 colors and stores its color map in a COLOR_64 chunk. A .FLC file may have up to 256 colors and stores its color map in a COLOR_256 chunk. Both of these chunks have the same format:

```
typedef struct _ColormapChunk
{
  CHUNKHEADER Header;        /* Header for this chunk */
  WORD NumberOfElements;     /* Number of color elements in map */
  struct _ColorElement       /* Color element (one per
                                  NumberOfElements) */

  {
   BYTE SkipCount;           /* Color index skip count */
   BYTE ColorCount;          /* Number of colors in this element */
   struct _ColorComponent    /* Color component
                                  (one /'ColorCount') */

   {
    BYTE Red;                /* Red component color */
    BYTE Green;              /* Green component color */
    BYTE Blue;               /* Blue component color */
   } ColorComponents[ColorCount];

  } ColorElements[NumberOfElements];

} COLORMAPCHUNK;
```

The value of ChunkSize in the Header varies depending upon the number of elements in this color map. A chunk containing a color map with 256 elements is 788 bytes in size and therefore ChunkSize contains the value 788.

ChunkType contains a value of 04h for a COLOR_256 chunk or a value of 0Bh for a COLOR_64 chunk.

NumberOfChunks always contains a value of 00h, indicating that this chunk contains no subchunks.

NumberOfElements indicates the number of ColorElement structures in the COLORMAPCHUNK structure. Following this value are the actual ColorElement structures themselves. Each structure contains two fields and one or more ColorComponent structures.

SkipCount indicates the number of color elements to skip when locating the next color map element.

ColorCount indicates the number of ColorComponents structures contained within this ColorElement structure. Following the ColorCount field are the actual ColorComponents structures. Each structure is three bytes in size and contains three fields.

The Red, Green, and Blue fields of each ColorComponents structure contain the component values for this color. The range of these field values is 0 to 63 for a COLOR_64 chunk and 0 to 255 for a COLOR_256 chunk.

Normally, an image file contains only one color map. A FLI file, however, allows a color map to be defined for each frame in the animation. Storing a complete color map for each frame would normally require quite a bit of data (768 bytes per frame). FLI files, however, have the capability of storing color maps that contain only the colors that change from frame to frame.

Storing only the deltas in a color map requires that not only the color values be stored, but also their locations in the map. This is accomplished by using a color index value and a skip count. Before a color map value is written, the skip count of the packet is added to the current color index. This sum is the location of the next color map value to write. The number of entries in the packet are written across the same number of entries in the color map. The color index for each color map always starts with the value 0.

For example, the first frame of a .FLC animation always contains a full, 256-element color map. This map is represented by a NumberOfElements value of 1 followed by a single ColorElements structure. This structure will contain a SkipCount value of 0, a ColorCount value of 256, and 256 ColorComponents structures defining the colors in the map. This chunk is 788 bytes in size.

Now, let's say that in the next frame the colors 2, 15, 16, 17, and 197 in the color map are different from those in the first frame. Rather than storing another 788-byte color map chunk, with 251 elements identical to the color map in the previous chunk, we will store only the values and positions of the five color components that changed in the color map.

The color map chunk for the second frame will then contain a NumberOfElements value of 3, followed by three ColorElements structures:

- The first structure will have a SkipCount value of 2, a ColorCount value of 1, and one ColorComponents structure defining the new color values of element 2.

- The second structure will have a SkipCount value of 14, a ColorCount value of 3, and three ColorComponents structures defining the new color values of elements 15, 16, and 17.

- The third structure will have a SkipCount value of 180, a ColorCount value of 1, and one ColorComponents structure defining the new color value of element 197. This chunk will be only 39 bytes in size.

The sequence of fields and values for this map is the following:

```
NumberOfElements      3
ColorElement
 SkipCount            2
 ColorCount           1
  ColorComponent      R,G,B
ColorElement
 SkipCount            14
 ColorCount           3
  ColorComponent      R,G,B
  ColorComponent      R,G,B
  ColorComponent      R,G,B
ColorElement
 SkipCount            180
 ColorCount           1
  ColorComponent      R,G,B
```

As you can see, the location of changed color elements is determined by their relative position from the previous changed elements and from their absolute position in the color map. The SkipCount value of the first element is always calculated from the 0th index position. To change the value of element 2, we skip two places, from element 0 to element 2, and change a single component value. To change the values of elements 17, 18, and 19, we make 14 skips from element 2 to element 17 and change the next three component values. We then make 180 skips to element 197 and change the final component value.

Note that if the color map for the current frame is identical to the color map of the previous frame, the color map subchunk need not appear in the current frame chunk.

For Further Information

Autodesk no longer maintains the FLI format and does not distribute information about it. For further information about FLI, see the articles by Jim Kent and John Bridges (the author of the format,) that are included on the CD that accompanies this book. In addition, see the following article for information on FLI:

Kent, Jim. "The Flic File Format," *Dr. Dobbs Journal*, March 1993.

GEM Raster

NAME:	GEM Raster
ALSO KNOWN AS:	IMG
TYPE:	Bitmap
COLORS:	16,384
COMPRESSION:	RLE, uncompressed
MAXIMUM IMAGE SIZE:	64Kx64K
MULTIPLE IMAGES PER FILE:	No
NUMERICAL FORMAT:	Big-endian
ORIGINATOR:	Digital Research, now part of Novell
PLATFORM:	GEM, MS-DOS, Atari ST
SUPPORTING APPLICATIONS:	GEM-based applications. Versions of the MS-DOS-based Ventura Publisher were distributed bound to GEM that served mainly to provide GUI services to the application. Many programs on the Atari ST.
SPECIFICATION ON CD:	No
CODE ON CD:	No
IMAGES ON CD:	Yes
SEE ALSO:	None

USAGE: Primarily useful in GEM-based application environments.

COMMENTS: A poorly documented format (in the sense that documentation is hard to come by) in wide use only on the Atari ST platform. It lacks a superior compression scheme and support for included color information. There are at least two versions in existence.

Overview

GEM Raster (also known as IMG) is the native image storage format for the Graphical Environment Manager (GEM), developed and marketed by Digital Research. GEM made its way into the market through OEM bundling deals, special runtime versions bound to products, and as the native operating environment of at least one system, the Atari ST. GEM image files have been important in the PC desktop publishing community due to the bundling deal between Digital Research and the creators of Ventura Publisher, a widely used desktop publishing application.

Although GEM was a contender in the GUI wars some years back, Digital Research's fortunes in this arena declined and the company was eventually purchased by Novell. Prior to this, however, GEM was distributed by a number of PC hardware manufacturers along with their systems, and thus enjoyed a certain currency. GEM raster images may be color, gray scale, or black and white and are always read and written in the big-endian format. Note that several different file formats use the file extension .IMG, a fact which causes confusion in some applications designed to read only GEM raster (IMG) files.

File Organization

Like many other simple bitmap formats, GEM raster files start with a fixed-length header, followed by bitmap data.

File Details

GEM raster files use a 16- or 18-byte header in the following format:

```
typedef struct _GemRaster
{
WORD    Version;          /* Image File Version (Always 1h)    */
WORD    HeaderLength;     /* Size of Header in WORDs    */
WORD    NumberOfPlanes;   /* Number of Planes    */
WORD    PatternLength;    /* Pattern Definition Length    */
WORD    PixelWidth;       /* Pixel Width in Micros    */
WORD    PixelHeight;      /* Pixel Height in Micros    */
WORD    ScanLineWidth;    /* Image Width in Pixels    */
WORD    NumberOfLines     /* Image Height in Scan Lines    */
WORD    BitImageFlag;     /* Multi-plane GrayColor Flag    */

} GEMHEAD;
```

Version always has a value of one.

HeaderLength is either be 8 or 9; if the value is 8, then there is no BitImageFlag field in the header.

NumberOfPlanes contains the number of bits per pixel of the image source device (a scanner, for instance). This value is typically 1.

PatternLength contains a run count value, which is usually 1. Any pattern code found in the encoded image data is repeated this number of times.

PixelHeight and PixelWidth are the pixel size in microns and are often 85 (55h), corresponding to 1/300 inch, or 300 dpi. The scale of the image may also be determined by using these pixel size values.

ScanLineWidth and NumberOfScanLines describe the size of the image in lines and pixels.

BitImageFlags indicates whether a multi-plane image is color or gray scale. If the BitImageFlags field is present in the header (indicated by a value of 9 in the HeaderLength field), and the image data contains multiple planes (indicated by a value of 2 or greater in the NumberOfPlanes field), a value of 0 indicates color image data and a value of 1 indicates gray-scale image data. If a multi-plane image has an 8-field header, then the image is displayed in gray-scale from a fixed, 16-color palette by default. If the image has a 9-field header and only a single plane, the value in the BitImageFlag field is ignored.

Image data in GEM raster files is always encoded using a simple run-length encoding (RLE) scheme. Data is always encoded and decoded one byte at a time, and there are always eight bits of image data per pixel. For this reason, scan lines are always a multiple of eight pixels in width and are padded when necessary. If the image data contains two or more bits per pixel, then the image will have multiple bit planes.

There are four types of codes in the GEM raster RLE format: vertical replication codes, literal run codes, pattern codes, and encoded runs. Complicating this RLE scheme is the fact that each of these four codes is a different size, as shown below.

```
Vertical Replication Code    00 00 FF <Run Count>
Literal Run Code             80 <Run Count 1 to 7F>
                                <'Run Count' Bytes>
Pattern Code                 00 <Pattern Length>
Black Run Code               <MSB = 1> <7 LSB = RunCount>
White Run Code               <MSB = 0> <7 LSB = RunCount>
```

A vertical replication code contains the values 00h 00h FFh, followed by a 1-byte count. The count is the number of times to repeat the line that is about to be decoded. A count of one indicates two identical, consecutive lines. A vertical replication code may only appear at the beginning of a scan line. If a replication code is not present at the beginning of a scan line, the line is not repeated.

Literal runs are contiguous lines of pixels that are not encoded. They are written to the encoded data stream as they appear in the bitmap. Literal runs usually appear in encoded image data because data compression had little effect on the pixel data, and it was not efficient to encode the pixels as a run. A literal run code begins with the byte value 80h and is followed by a byte that holds the count value. Following the count are a number of bytes equal to the count value that should be copied literally from the encoded data to the decoded data.

A pattern code begins with the byte 00h and is followed by a byte containing the pattern length. That length is followed by the pattern itself, replicated the number of times specified by the Pattern Length field in the header. Pattern codes are similar to literal run codes, in that the data they contain is not actually compressed in the encoded image data.

Encoded run codes contain only runs of either black or white pixels and are by far the most numerous of all the codes in IMG RLE image data. Black-and-white runs are encoded as a 1-byte packets. Encoded run packets are never 00h or 80h in value. These values are reserved to mark the start of vertical replication codes, pattern codes, and literal run codes. If a byte is read and is not equal to 00h or 80h, the most significant bit indicates the color of the run. If the most significant bit is 1, all the pixels in the run are set to 1 (black). If the most significant bit is 0, the pixels in the run are set to 0 (white). The seven least significant bits in the encoded run are the number of bits in the run. The run may contain 1 to 127 bits.

If an image contains multiple planes, each plane is encoded as the next consecutive scan line of data. One scan line of a four-plane image is encoded as four scan lines of data. The order of the planes is red, green, blue, and intensity value.

The following segment of an encoded scan line:

```
00 00 FF 05  07  8A  02  80 04 2A 14 27 C9  00 03 AB CD EF
```

represents a vertical replication code of five scan lines, a run of seven white bytes (56 pixels), a run of 10 black bytes, (80 pixels), a run of two white bytes (16 pixels), a literal run of four bytes, and pattern code three bytes in length.

For Further Information

The GEM raster format originated at Digital Research, which is now owned by Novell, and is currently being supported by DISCUS Distribution Services, a service organization. Note that DISCUS will provide support only if you have first purchased the GEM Programmers's Toolkit from Digital Research.

Contact DISCUS at:

DISCUS Distribution Services, Inc.
8020 San Miguel Canyon Road
Salinas, CA 93907-1208
Voice: 408-663-6966

You may be able to get some information from Novell/Digital Research at:

Novell/Digital Research, Inc.
P.O. Box DRI
Monterey, CA 93942
Voice: 408-649-3896
Voice: 800-848-1498
BBS: 408-649-3896

NAME:	GEM VDI
ALSO KNOWN AS:	GEM Vector, VDI, .GDI
TYPE:	Metafile
COLORS:	256
COMPRESSION:	Uncompressed
MAXIMUM IMAGE SIZE:	32Kx32K
MULTIPLE IMAGES PER FILE:	No
NUMERICAL FORMAT:	Big-endian
ORIGINATOR:	Digital Research
PLATFORM:	GEM GUI running under MS-DOS, some Ataris
SUPPORTING APPLICATIONS:	GEM Artline, GEM Draw Plus, GEM Scan, others
SPECIFICATION ON CD:	No
CODE ON CD:	No
IMAGES ON CD:	No
SEE ALSO:	GEM Raster

USAGE: Illustration, drawing, and desktop publishing applications, and some data interchange.

COMMENTS: A vector format with good support at one time, associated with the GEM GUI from Digital Research. If you are thinking of supporting this format, be prepared to draw Bezier curves. It also has support for embedded bitmaps.

Overview

Although often called the GEM Vector Format, GEM VDI is actually a metafile format and is closely associated with the functioning of the GEM user interface. The GEM system provides a metafile driver which is accessed from within the GEM programming system through a documented API. Display requests to the driver result in items being written to a metafile buffer in GEM's standard metafile format. Metafile elements thus consist of calls to the GEM display system.

Supporting GEM VDI is similar to supporting many other metafile formats. Be prepared to duplicate the functionality of the host system, in this case GEM, or at least a reasonable subset of it, before you're through.

File Organization

We would like to have more information on this format. Information provided by DISCUS (see "For Further Information" below) indicates that the file consists of a header, followed by a stream of standard-format metafile items.

File Details

The structure for the GEM VDI header is shown below.

```
typedef struct _GemVdiHeader
{
    WORD Identifier;       /* Magic number. Always FFFFh */
    WORD LengthOfHeader    /* Length of the header in 16-bit WORD */
    WORD Version;          /* Format version number */
    WORD Transform;        /* Image origin */
    WORD Coords[4];        /* Size and position of image */
    WORD PageSize[2];      /* Physical page size */
    WORD Bounds[4];        /* Limits of coordinate system */
    WORD Flags;            /* Bit image opcode flag */
} GEMVDIHEADER;
```

Identifier is the magic number of GEM VDI image files. This value is always FFFFh.

LengthOfHeader is the size of the header described as the number of 16-bit WORDs it contains. This value is typically 0Fh.

Version is the version number of the file format. This value is calculated using the formula: 100 * major version number + minor version number.

Transform is the NDC/RC transformation mode flag. This value is 00h if the origin of the image is in the lower-left corner of the display and 02h if the origin is in the upper-left corner.

Coords are four WORDs indicating the minimum and maximum coordinate values of data in the file. These values indicate the size of the image and its position on the display and are stored as: minimum X, minimum Y, maximum X, maximum Y.

PageSize is the size of the physical printed page the image will cover in 1/10 of millimeters. This value is 00h if the page size is undefined by the application creating the image.

Bounds are four WORDs which described the maximum extent of the coordinate system used by the image and defined by the application. These values are stored as: lower-left X, lower-left Y, upper-right X, upper-right Y.

Flags contains the bit image opcode flag. The values for this field are 00h if no bit image is included in the file and 01h if a bit image is included. Bits 2 through 15 in Flags should always be set to 0.

Standard format metafile items consist of control, integer, and vertex parameters. This structure is described below.

Word	Value	Description
0	control[0]	Opcode
1	control[1]	Vertex count
2	control[3]	Integer parameter count
3	control[5]	Sub-opcode or zero
4	ptsin[0-n]	Input vertex list (if provided)
. . .		
n+4	intin[0-m]	Input integer (if provided)
. . .		

The following shows the correspondence of standard metafile items to the display commands accepted by the GEM display subsystem. Arguments appear to be documented only in the GEM Programmer's Toolkit, but you might be able to recover them through diligent application of trial and error.

v_alpha_text	Output Printer Alpha Text
v_arc	Arc GDP
v_bar	Bar GDP
v_bit_image	Output Bit Image File
v_circle	Circle GDP
v_clear_disp_list	Clear Display List
v_clrwk	Clear Workstation
v_ellarc	Elliptical Arc GDP
v_ellipse	Ellipse GDP
v_ellpie	Elliptical Pie Slice GDP
v_entercur	Enter Alpha Mode
v_exitcur	Exit Alpha Mode
v_fillarea	Fill Area

v_form_adv	Form Advance
v_justified	Justified Graphics Text GDP
v_line	Polyline
v_output_window	Output Window
v_pieslice	Pie GDP
v_pmarker	Polymarker
v_qtext	Text
v_rbox	Rounded Rectangle GDP
v_rfbox	Filled, Rounded Rectangle GDP
v_updwk	Update Workstation
vr_recfl	Fill Rectangle
vs_clip	Set Clipping Rectangle
vs_color	Set Color Representation
vsf_color	Set Fill Color Index
vsf_interior	Set Fill Interior Style
vsf_perimeter	Set Fill Perimeter Visibility
vsf_style	Set Fill Style Index
vsf_updat	Set User-defined Fill Pattern
vsl_color	Set Polyline Color Index
vsl_ends	Set Polyline End Styles
vsl_type	Set Polyline Line Type
vsl_udsty	Set User-defined Line Style Pattern
vsl_width	Set Polyline Line Width
vsm_color	Set Polymarker Color Index
vsm_height	Set Polymarker Height
vsm_type	Set Polymarker Type
vst_alignment	Set Graphic Text Alignment
vst_color	Set Text Color Index
vst_effects	Set Graphic Text Special Effects
vst_font	Set Text Font
vst_height	Set Character Height, Absolute Mode
vst_point	Set Character Height, Points Mode
vst_rotation	Set Character Baseline Vector
vswr_mode	Set Writing Mode

There are also two non-standard metafile items:

v_opnwk	Open Workstation
v_clswk	Close Workstation

There are three metafile escape functions:

v_meta_extents	Update Metafile Extents
v_write_meta	Write Metafile Item
vm_filename	Change GEM VDI Filename

There are several inquire functions:

vq_chcells	Inquire Addressable Character Cells
vq_color	Inquire Color Representation
vq_attributes	Inquire Current Polyline Attributes
vq_extnd	Extended Inquire

There are several metafile sub-opcodes reserved for the Digital Research GEM Output application:

Physical Page Size
Coordinate Window

There are also several metafile sub-opcodes reserved for the Digital Research GEM Draw Plus application:

Group
Set No Line Style
Set Attribute Shadow On
Set Attribute Shadow Off
Start Draw Area Type Primitive
End Draw Area Type Primitive

Also associated with the GEM VDI format is a standard keyboard mapping.

For Further Information

The GEM VDI format originated at Digital Research, which is now owned by Novell, and GEM VDI is currently being supported by DISCUS Distribution Services, a service organization. Note that DISCUS will provide support only if you have first purchased the GEM Programmer's Toolkit from Digital Research. Contact DISCUS at:

DISCUS Distribution Services, Inc.
8020 San Miguel Canyon Road
Salinas, CA 93907-1208
Voice: 408-663-6966

You may still be able to get some information from Novell/Digital Research at:

Novell/Digital Research, Inc.
P.O. Box DRI
Monterey, CA 93942
Voice: 408-649-3896
Voice: 800-848-1498
BBS: 408-649-3896

NAME:	GIF
ALSO KNOWN AS:	Graphics Interchange Format
TYPE:	Bitmap
COLORS:	1 to 8 bit
COMPRESSION:	LZW
MAXIMUM IMAGE SIZE:	64Kb X 64Kb pixels
MULTIPLE IMAGES PER FILE:	Yes
NUMERICAL FORMAT:	Little-endian
ORIGINATOR:	CompuServe Inc.
PLATFORM:	MS-DOS, Macintosh, UNIX, Amiga, others
SUPPORTING APPLICATIONS:	Too numerous to list
SPECIFICATION ON CD:	Yes
CODE ON CD:	Yes
IMAGES ON CD:	Yes
SEE ALSO:	Chapter 9, *Data Compression* (Lempel-Ziv-Welch Compression)
USAGE:	Originally designed to facilitate image transfer and online storage for use by CompuServe and its customers, GIF is primarily an exchange and storage format, although it is based on, and is supported by, many applications.
COMMENTS:	A well-defined, well-documented format in wide use, which is quick and easy to read and reasonably easy to uncompress. It lacks, however, support for the storage of deep-pixel images.

Overview

GIF (Graphics Interchange Format) is a creation of CompuServe Inc., and is used to store multiple bitmap images in a single file for exchange between platforms and systems. In terms of number of files in existence, GIF is perhaps the most widely used format for storing multibit graphics and image data. Even a quick peek into the graphics file section of most BBSs and file archives seems to prove this true. Many of these are high-quality images of people, landscapes, cars, astrophotographs, and anthropometric gynoidal data (you guess what that is). Shareware libraries and BBSs are filled with megabytes of GIF images.

The vast majority of GIF files contain 16-color or 256-color near-photographic quality images. Gray-scale images, such as those produced by scanners, are also commonly stored using GIF, although monochrome graphics, such as clip art and document images, rarely are.

Although the bulk of GIF files are found in the Intel-based MS-DOS environment, GIF is not associated with any particular software application. GIF also was not created for any particular software application need, although most software applications that read and write graphical image data, such as paint programs, scanner and video software, and most image file display and conversion programs usually support GIF. GIF was instead intended to allow the easy interchange and viewing of image data stored on local or remote computer systems.

Although CompuServe allows unrestricted use, provided that you give the appropriate credit to CompuServe as the originator of the format, the compression used by GIF, Lempel-Ziv-Welch (LZW), has been the subject of much legal battle. Therefore, while reading and possessing GIF files (or any other graphics files containing LZW-compressed image data) provides no legal problems, writing software which creates GIF, or other LZW files, may.

File Organization

GIF is different from many other common bitmap formats in the sense that it is stream-based. It consists of a series of data packets, called blocks, along with additional protocol information. Because of this arrangement, GIF files must be read as if they are a continuous stream of data. The various blocks and sub-blocks of data defined by GIF may be found almost anywhere within the file. This uncertainty makes it difficult to encapsulate every possible arrangement of GIF data in the form of C structures.

There are a number of different data block categories, and each of the various defined blocks falls into one of these categories. In GIF terminology, a Graphics Control Extension block is a type of Graphics Control block, for instance. In like manner, Plain Text Extension blocks and the Local Image Descriptor are types of Graphic Rendering blocks. The bitmap data is an Image Data block. Comment Extension and Application Extension blocks are types of Special Purpose blocks.

Blocks, in addition to storing fields of information, can also contain sub-blocks. Each data sub-block begins with a single count byte, which can be in the range of 1 to 255, and which indicates the number of data bytes that follow the count byte. Multiple sub-blocks may occur in a contiguous grouping (count byte, data bytes, count byte, data bytes, and so on). A sequence of one or more data sub-blocks is terminated by a count byte with a value of zero.

The GIF format is capable of storing bitmap data with pixel depths of 1 to 8 bits. Images are always stored using the RGB color model and using palette data. GIF is also capable of storing multiple images per file, but this capability is rarely utilized, and the vast majority of GIF files contain only a single image. Most GIF file viewers do not, in fact, support the display of multiple image GIF files, or may display only the first image stored in the file. For these reasons, we recommend not creating applications that rely on multiple images per file, even though the specification allows this.

The image data stored in a GIF file is always LZW compressed. (See Chapter 9, *Data Compression*, for a discussion of LZW and other compression methods.) This algorithm reduces strings of identical byte values into a single code word and is capable of reducing the size of typical 8-bit pixel data by 40 percent or more. The ability to store uncompressed data, or data encoded using a different compression algorithm, is not supported in the current version of the GIF format.

There are two revisions of the GIF specification, both of which have been widely distributed. The original revision was GIF 87a, and many images were created in this format. The current revision, GIF 89a, adds several capabilities, including the ability to store text and graphics data in the same file. If you are supporting GIF, you should include support for both the 87a and 89a revisions. It is a mistake to support only the 89a version, because many applications continue to produce only 87a version files for backward compatibility.

File Details

The "GIF87a" section below discusses features common to both versions; the "GIF89a" section describes only the features added in GIF89a.

GIF87a

Version 87a is the original GIF format introduced in May 1987 and is read by all major software applications supporting the GIF format.

Figure GIF-1 illustrates the basic layout of a GIF87a file. Each file always begins with a Header and a Logical Screen Descriptor. A Global Color Table may optionally appear after the Logical Screen Descriptor. Each of these three sections is always found at the same offset from the start of the file. Each image stored in the file contains a Local Image Descriptor, an optional Local Color Table, and a block of image data. The last field in every GIF file is a Terminator character, which indicates the end of the GIF data stream.

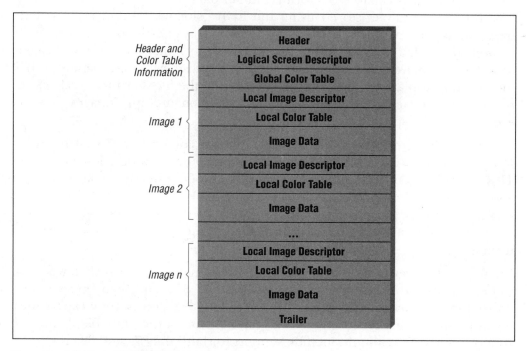

FIGURE GIF-1: *GIF87a file layout*

Header

The Header is six bytes in size and is used only to identify the file as type GIF. The Logical Screen Descriptor, which may be separate from the actual file header, may be thought of as a second header. We may therefore store the Logical Screen Descriptor information in the same structure as the Header:

```
typedef struct _GifHeader
{
  // Header
  BYTE Signature[3];    /* Header Signature (always "GIF")  */
  BYTE Version[3];      /* GIF format version("87a" or "89a")*/

  // Logical Screen Descriptor
  WORD ScreenWidth;     /* Width of Display Screen in Pixels */
  WORD ScreenHeight;    /* Height of Display Screen in Pixels */
```

```
    BYTE Packed;            /* Screen and Color Map Information */
    BYTE BackgroundColor;   /* Background Color Index */
    BYTE AspectRatio;       /* Pixel Aspect Ratio */

} GIFHEAD;
```

Signature is three bytes in length and contains the characters GIF as an identifier. All GIF files start with these three bytes, and any file that does not should not be read by an application as a GIF image file.

Version is also three bytes in length and contains the version of the GIF file. There are currently only two versions of GIF: 87a (the original GIF format) and 89a (the new GIF format). Some GIF 87a file viewers may be able to read GIF 89a files, although the stored image data may not display correctly.

Logical Screen Descriptor
The Logical Screen Descriptor contains information describing the screen and color information used to create and display the GIF file image.

ScreenHeight and ScreenWidth fields contain the minimum screen resolution required to display the image data. If the display device is not capable of supporting the specified resolution, some sort of scaling will be necessary to properly display the image.

Packed contains the following four subfields of data (bit 0 is the least significant bit, or LSB):

Bits 0-2	Size of the Global Color Table
Bit 3	Color Table Sort Flag
Bits 4-6	Color Resolution
Bit 7	Global Color Table Flag

The Size of the Global Color Table subfield contains the number of bits in each Global Color Table entry minus one. For example, if an image contains 8 bits per pixel, the value of this field is 7. The total number of elements in the Global Color Table is calculated by shifting the value one to the left by the value in this field:

```
NumberOfGlobalColorTableEntries =
                    (1L << (SizeOfTheGlobalColorTable + 1));
```

The Size of the Global Color Table subfield is always set to the proper size even if there is no Global Color Table (i.e., the Global Color Table Flag subfield is set to 0). If the Color Table Sort Flag subfield is 1, then the Global Color Table entries are sorted from the most important (most frequently occurring color in the image) to the least important. Sorting the colors in the color table aids an application in choosing the colors to use with display hardware that has fewer available colors than the image data. The Sort flag is only valid under version 89a of GIF. Under version 87a, this field is reserved and is always set to 0.

The Color Resolution subfield is set to the number of bits in an entry of the original color palette minus one. This value equates to the maximum size of the original color palette. For example, if an image originally contained eight bits per primary color, the value of this field would be 7. The Global Color Table Flag subfield is set to 1 if a Global Color Table is present in the GIF file, and 0 if one is not. Global Color Table data, if present, always follows the Logical Screen Descriptor header in the GIF file.

BackgroundColor in the Logical Screen Descriptor contains an index value into the Global Color Table of the color to use for the border and background of the image. The background is considered to be the area of the screen not covered by the GIF image. If there is no Global Color Table (i.e., the Global Color Table Flag subfield is set to 0), this field is unused and should be ignored.

AspectRatio contains the aspect ratio value of the pixels in the image. The aspect ratio is the width of the pixel divided by the height of the pixel. This value is in the range of 1 to 255 and is used in the following calculation:

```
PixelAspectRatio = (AspectRatio + 15) / 64;
```

If this field is 0, then no aspect ratio is specified.

Global Color Table
The Logical Screen Descriptor may be followed by an optional Global Color Table. This color table, if present, is the color map used to index the pixel color data contained within the image data. If a Global Color Table is not present, each image stored in the GIF file contains a Local Color Table that it uses in place of a Global Color Table. If every image in the GIF file uses its own Local Color Table, then a Global Color Table may not be present in the GIF file. If neither a Global nor a Local Color Table is present, make sure your application supplies a default color table to use. It is suggested that the first entry of a default color table be the color black and the second entry be the color white.

Global Color Table data always follows the Logical Screen Descriptor information and varies in size depending upon the number of entries in the table. The

Global Color Table is a series of three-byte triples making up the elements of the color table. Each triple contains the red, green, and blue primary color values of each color table element:

```
typedef struct _GifColorTable
{
  BYTE Red;          /* Red Color Element     */
  BYTE Green;        /* Green Color Element   */
  BYTE Blue;         /* Blue Color Element    */

} GIFCOLORTABLE;
```

The number of entries in the Global Color Table is always a power of two (2, 4, 8, 16, and so on), up to a maximum of 256 entries. The size of the Global Color Table in bytes is calculated by using bits 0, 1, and 2 in the Packed field of the Logical Image Descriptor in the following way:

```
ColorTableSize = 3L * (1L << (SizeOfGlobalColorTable + 1));
```

The Header, Logical Screen Descriptor, and Global Color Map data are followed by one or more sections of image data. Each image in a GIF file is stored separately, with an Image Descriptor and possibly a Local Color Table. The Image Descriptor is similar to a header and contains information only about the image data that immediately follows it. The Local Color Table contains color information specific only to that image data and may or may not be present.

Local Image Descriptor

The Local Image Descriptor appears before each section of image data and has the following structure:

```
typedef struct _GifImageDescriptor
{
  BYTE Separator;    /* Image Descriptor identifier */
  WORD Left;         /* X position of image on the display */
  WORD Top;          /* Y position of image on the display */
  WORD Width;        /* Width of the image in pixels */
  WORD Height;       /* Height of the image in pixels */
  BYTE Packed;       /* Image and Color Table Data Information */

} GIFIMGDESC;
```

Separator contains the value 2Ch and denotes the beginning of the Image Descriptor data block.

Left and Top are the coordinates in pixels of the upper-left corner of the image on the logical screen. The upper-left corner of the screen is considered to be coordinates 0,0.

Width and Height are the size of the image in pixels.

Packed contains the following five subfields of data (bit 0 is the LSB):

Bit 0	Local Color Table Flag
Bit 1	Interlace Flag
Bit 2	Sort Flag
Bits 3-4	Reserved
Bits 5-7	Size of Local Color Table Entry

The Local Color Table Flag subfield is 1 if there is a Local Color Table associated with this image. If the value of this subfield is 0, then there is no Local Color Table present, and the Global Color Table data should be used instead.

The Interlace Flag subfield is 1 if the image is interlaced and 0 if it is non-interlaced (see the description of Image Data for an explanation of interlaced image data).

The Sort Flag subfield indicates whether the entries in the color table have been sorted by their order of importance. Importance is usually decided by the frequency of occurrence of the color in the image data. A value of 1 indicates a sorted color table, while a value of 0 indicates a table with unsorted color values. The Sort Flag subfield value is valid only under version 89a of GIF. Under version 87a, this field is reserved and is always set to 0.

The Size of Local Color Table Entry subfield is the number of bits per entry in the Local Color Table. If the Local Color Table Flag subfield is set to 0, then this subfield is also set to 0.

Local Color Table

If a Local Color Table is present, it immediately follows the Local Image Descriptor and precedes the image data with which it is associated. The format of all Local Color Tables is identical to that of the Global Color Table. Each element is a series of 3-byte triples containing the red, green, and blue primary color values of each element in the Local Color Table:

```
typedef struct _GifColorTable
{
   BYTE Red;              /* Red Color Element        */
   BYTE Green;            /* Green Color Element       */
   BYTE Blue;             /* Blue Color Element        */

} GIFCOLORTABLE;
```

The number of entries and the size in bytes of the Local Color Table is calculated in the same way as the Global Color Table:

```
ColorTableSize = 3L * (1L << (SizeOfLocalColorTable + 1));
ColorTableNumberOfEntries = 1L << (SizeOfLocalColorTable + 1);
```

A Local Color Table only affects the image it is associated with and, if it is present, its data supersedes that of the Global Color Table. Each image may have no more than one Local Color Table.

Image data

GIF files do not compress well when stored using file archivers such as pkzip and zoo. This is because the image data found in every GIF file is always compressed using the LZW (Lempel-Ziv-Welch) encoding scheme (described in Chapter 9), the same compression algorithm used by most file archivers. Compressing a GIF file is therefore a redundant operation, which rarely results in smaller files and is usually not worth the time and effort involved in the attempt.

Normally when LZW-encoded image data is stored in a graphics file format, it is arranged as a continuous stream of data that is read from beginning to end. The GIF format, however, stores encoded image data as a series of data sub-blocks.

Each data sub-block begins with a count byte. The value of the count byte may range from 1 to 255 and indicates the number of data bytes in the sub-block. The data blocks immediately follow the count byte. A contiguous group of data blocks is terminated by a byte with a zero value. This may be viewed as either a terminator value or as a sub-block with a count byte value of zero; in either case, it indicates that no data bytes follow.

Because GIF files do not contain a contiguous stream of LZW-encoded data, each sub-block must be read and the data sent to an LZW decoder. Most sub-blocks storing image data will be 255 bytes in length, so this is an excellent maximum size to use for the buffer that will hold the encoded image data. Also, the LZW encoding process does not keep track of where each scan line begins and ends. It is therefore likely that one scan line will end and another begin in the middle of a sub-block of image data.

The format of the decoded GIF image data is fairly straightforward. Each pixel in a decoded scan line is always one byte in size and contains an index value into either a Global or Local Color Table. Although the structure of the GIF format is quite capable of storing color information directly in the image data (thus bypassing the need for a color table), the GIF specification does not specify this as a possible option. Therefore, even 1-bit image data must use 8-bit index values and a 2-entry color table.

GIF image data is always stored by scan line and by pixel. GIF does not have the capability to store image data as planes, so when GIF files are displayed using plane-oriented display adapters, quite a bit of buffering, shifting, and masking of image data must first occur before the GIF image can be displayed.

The scan lines making up the GIF bitmap image data are normally stored in consecutive order, starting with the first row and ending with the last. The GIF format also supports an alternate way to store rows of bitmap data in an interlaced order. Interlaced images are stored as alternating rows of bitmap data. If you have ever viewed a GIF file that appeared on the screen as a series of four "wipes" that jumped across the screen as the image is displayed, you were viewing an interlaced GIF file.

Figure GIF-2 compares the order of rows stored in an interlaced and non-interlaced format. In the non-interlaced format, the rows of bitmap data are stored starting with the first row and continuing sequentially to the last row. This is the typical storage format for most bitmap file formats. The interlaced format, however, stores the rows out of the normal sequence. All the even rows are stored first and all the odd rows are stored last. We can also see that each successive pass usually encodes more rows than the previous pass.

GIF uses a 4-pass interlacing scheme. The first pass starts on row 0 and reads every eighth row of bitmap data. The second pass starts on the fourth row and reads every eighth row of data. The third pass starts on the second row and reads every fourth row. The final pass begins on the first row and reads every second row. Using this scheme, all of the rows of bitmap data are read and stored.

Why interlace a GIF image? Interlacing might seem to make the reading, writing, and displaying of the image data more difficult, and of course it does. Does this arrangement somehow make the image easier to display on interlaced monitors? The answer lies in one of the original purposes of GIF.

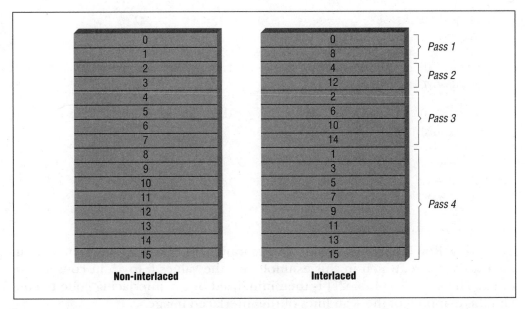

FIGURE GIF-2: *Arrangement of interlaced and non-interlaced scan lines*

GIF was designed as an image communications protocol used for the interactive viewing of online images. A user connected to an information service via a modem could not only download a GIF image, but could also see it appear on his or her display screen as it was being downloaded. If a GIF image were stored in a non-interlaced format, the GIF image would display in a progressive fashion starting at the top of the screen and ending at the bottom. After 50 percent of the download was completed, only the top half of the GIF image would be visible. An interlaced image, however, would display starting with every eighth row, then every fourth row, then every second row, and so on. When the download of an interlaced GIF image was only 50 percent complete. the entire contents of the image could be discerned even though only half the image had been displayed. The viewer's eye and brain would simply fill in the missing half.

Interlacing presents a problem when converting a GIF image from one format to another. A scan-line table must be created to write out the scan lines in their proper, non-interlaced order. The following sample code is used to produce a scan-line table of an interlaced image:

```
WORD i, j;
WORD RowTable1[16];
WORD RowTable2[16];
WORD ImageHeight = 16;   /* 16 lines in the GIF image */
for (i = 0; i < ImageHeight; i++) /* Initialize source array */
    RowTable1[i] = i;
j = 0;
for (i = 0; i < ImageHeight; i += 8, j++)   /* Interlace Pass 1 */
    RowTable2[i] = RowTable1[j];
for (i = 4; i < ImageHeight; i += 8, j++)   /* Interlace Pass 2 */
    RowTable2[i] = RowTable1[j];
for (i = 2; i < ImageHeight; i += 4, j++)   /* Interlace Pass 3 */
    RowTable2[i] = RowTable1[j];
for (i = 1; i < ImageHeight; i += 2, j++)   /* Interlace Pass 4 */
    RowTable2[i] = RowTable1[j];
```

The array RowTable1[] contains the mapping of the scan lines in a non-interlaced image, which in this example are the values 0 to 15 in consecutive order. The array RowTable2[] is then initialized by the interlacing code to contain the mapping of the scan lines of the interlaced image:

RowTable1[]	RowTable2[]
0	0
1	8
2	4
3	9
4	2
5	10
6	5
7	11
8	1
9	12
10	6
11	13
12	3
13	14
14	7
15	15

We can restore the non-interlaced image by stepping through the values stored in RowTable2[]. The 0th row of the non-interlaced image is the 0th row of the interlaced image. The first row of the non-interlaced image is the eighth row of the interlaced image. The second row of the non-interlaced image is the fourth row of the interlaced image, and so on.

Trailer

The Trailer is a single byte of data that occurs as the last character in the file. This byte value is always 3Bh and indicates the end of the GIF data stream. A trailer must appear in every GIF file.

GIF 89a

Version 89a is the most recent revision of the GIF image file format and was introduced in July of 1989. Although the GIF 89a format is very similar to GIF 87a, it contains several additional blocks of information not defined in the 87a specification. For this reason GIF 89a image files may not be read and displayed properly by applications that read only GIF 87a image files. Many of these programs do not not attempt to display an 89a image file, because the version number "89a" will not be recognized. Although changing the version number from "89a" to "87a" will solve this problem, the GIF image data may still not display properly, for reasons we shall soon see.

Figure GIF-3 illustrates the basic layout of a GIF 89a image file. Just as with version 87a, the 89a version also begins with a Header, a Logical Screen Descriptor, and an optional Global Color Table. Each image also contains a Local Image Descriptor, an optional Local Color Table, and a block of image data. The trailer in every GIF 89a file contains the same values found in 87a files.

Version 89a added a new feature to the GIF format called Control Extensions. These extensions to the GIF 87a format are specialized blocks of information used to control the rendering of the graphical data stored within a GIF image file. The design of GIF 87a only allowed the display of images one at a time in a "slide show" fashion. Through the interpretation and use of Control Extension data, GIF 89a allows both textual and bitmap-based graphical data to be displayed, overlaid, and deleted as in an animated multimedia presentation.

The four Control Extensions introduced by GIF 89a are the Graphics Control Extension, the Plain Text Extension, the Comment Extension, and the Application Extension, summarized here and described in greater detail in the sections below.

Graphics Control Extension blocks control how the bitmap or plain text data found in a Graphics Rendering block is displayed. Such control information includes whether the graphic is to be overlaid in a transparent or opaque fashion over another graphic, whether the graphic is to be restored or deleted, and whether user input is expected before continuing with the display of the GIF file data.

Plain Text Extension blocks allow the mixing of plain text ASCII graphics with bitmapped image data. Many GIF images contain human-readable text that is actually part of the bitmap data itself. Using the Plain Text Extension, captions that are not actually part of the bitmapped image may be overlaid onto the image. This can be invaluable when it is necessary to display textual data over an image, but it is inconvenient to alter the bitmap to include this information. It is even possible to construct an 89a file that contains only plain-text data and no bitmap image data at all.

Application Extension blocks allow the storage of data that is understood only by the software application reading the GIF file. This data could be additional information used to help display the image data or to coordinate the way the image data is displayed with other GIF image files.

Comment Extension blocks contain human-readable ASCII text embedded in the GIF data stream that is used in a manner similar to program comments in C language code.

With only a few restrictions, any number of Control Extension blocks may appear almost anywhere in a GIF data stream following the Global Color Table. All Extension blocks begin with the Extension Introducer value 21h, which identifies the block of data as an Extension block. This value is followed by a Block Label, which identifies the type of extension information contained within the block. Block Label identification values range from 00h to FFh. The Plain Text, Application, and Comment Extension blocks may also contain one or more sub-blocks of data.

Interestingly enough, all of the Control Extension features added by 89a are optional and are not required to appear in a GIF data stream. The only other difference between 87a and 89a is that at least one of the Image Descriptor and Logical Screen Descriptor fields, which are reserved under 87a, is used under 89a. In fact, any GIF files which are written under Version 89a, but which do not use any of the 89a features, should use the version number GIF87a.

Graphics Control Extension block

The information found in a Graphics Control block is used to modify the data in the Graphical Rendering block that immediately follows it. A Graphics Control block may modify either bitmap or plain text data. It must also occur in the GIF stream before the data it modifies, and only one Graphic Control block may appear per Graphics Rendering block.

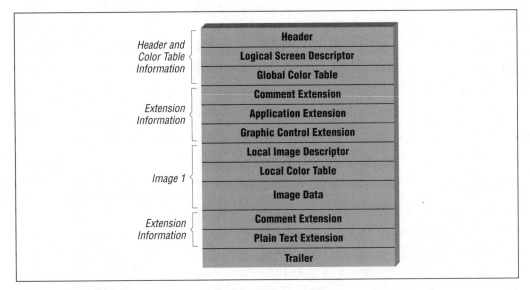

FIGURE GIF-3: *Layout of a GIF 89a file*

The Graphics Control Extension block is eight bytes in length and has the following structure:

```
typedef struct _GifGraphicsControlExtension
{
   BYTE  Introducer;    /* Extension Introducer (always 21h)*/
   BYTE  Label;         /* Graphic Control Label (always F9h) */
   BYTE  BlockSize;     /* Size of remaining fields (always 04h) */
   BYTE  Packed;        /* Method of graphics disposal to use */
   WORD  DelayTime;     /* Hundredths of seconds to wait */
   BYTE  ColorIndex;    /* Transparent Color Index */
   BYTE  Terminator;    /* Block Terminator (always 0) */

} GIFGRAPHICCONTROL;
```

Introducer contains the value 21h and is used to identify the start of a Extension data block.

Label contains the value F9h and is used to identify this block of data as a Graphics Control Extension.

BlockSize contains the value 04h which is the number of bytes in the Packed, DelayTime, and ColorIndex fields.

Packed contains the following four subfields of information (bit 0 is the LSB):

Bit 0	Transparent Color Flag
Bit 1	User Input Flag
Bits 2-4	Disposal Method
Bits 5-7	Reserved

If the Transparent Color Flag subfield is set to 1, the ColorIndex field of this extension contains a color transparency index. If no index is present, this bit is set to 0.

The User Input Flag subfield is set to 1 if user input (key press, mouse click, and so forth) is expected before continuing to the next graphic sequence; otherwise, this bit is set to zero.

The Disposal Method subfield contains a value indicating how the graphic is to be disposed of once it has been displayed. The currently defined values for this field are 00h (disposal method not specified), 01h (do not dispose of graphic), 02h (overwrite graphic with background color), and 04h (overwrite graphic with previous graphic).

The Reserved subfield is not used in GIF 89a and is always set to 0.

DelayTime in the Graphics Control Extension block contains a value equal to the number of hundredths of a second that must elapse before the graphics presentation continues. If this field is 0, then no delay is used. If both this delay and the user input bit is set, the graphic continues when either the delay expires or user input is received.

ColorIndex is the color transparency index. This field contains a value only if the Transparent Color Flag subfield in the Packed field is set to 1.

Terminator contains the value 0 and marks the end of the Graphics Control Extension block.

Plain Text Extension block

GIF 87a files may contain bitmapped data only in the form of a Graphical Rendering block. GIF 89a adds the ability to store textual information that may be rendered as a graphical image.

Any number of Plain Text Extension blocks may appear in a GIF file. To display plain-text data, a grid is described that contains the data. The height, width, and position of the grid on the display screen are specified. The size of each cell in the grid is also described, and one character is displayed per cell.

The foreground and background color of the text are taken from the Global Color Table and are also described in the Plain Text Extension block. The actual Plain Text data is a simple string of ASCII characters.

The Plain Text Extension block is 15 bytes in length and has the following structure:

```
typedef struct _GifPlainTextExtension
{
  BYTE Introducer;          /* Extension Introducer (always 21h)*/
  BYTE Label;               /* Extension Label (always 01h)*/
  BYTE BlockSize;           /* Size of Extension Block (always
                               0Ch) */
  WORD TextGridLeft;        /* X position of text grid in pixels */
  WORD TextGridTop;         /* Y position of text grid in pixels */
  WORD TextGridWidth;       /* Width of the text grid in pixels */
  WORD TextGridHeight;      /* Height of the text grid in pixels */
  BYTE CellWidth;           /* Width of a grid cell in pixels */
  BYTE CellHeight;          /* Height of a grid cell in pixels */
  BYTE TextFgColorIndex;    /* Text foreground color index value */
  BYTE TextBgColorIndex;    /* Text background color index value */
  BYTE *PlainTextData;      /* The Plain Text data      */
  BYTE Terminator;          /* Block Terminator (always 0)*/

} GIFPLAINTEXT;
```

Introducer contains the value 21h and is used to identify the start of a Extension data block.

Label contains the value 01h and is used to identify this block of data as a Plain Text Extension.

BlockSize contains the value 0Ch, which is the number of bytes contained in the fields following the BlockSize field.

TextGridLeft and TextGridTop contain the X and Y coordinate position of the text grid with respect to the upper-left corner of the display screen (coordinate 0,0).

TextGridWidth and TextGridHeight contain the size of the text grid in pixels.

CellWidth and CellHeight contain the size in pixels of each character cell in the grid.

TextFgColorIndex contains an index into the Global Color Table to retrieve the color of the text.

TextBgColorIndex contains a Global Color Table index value to be used as the color for the background of the text.

PlainTextData contains the actual textual information that is to be rendered as a graphic. This field contains one or more sub-blocks of data. Each sub-block begins with a byte that indicates the number of data bytes that follow. From 1 to 255 data bytes may follow this byte. There may be any number of sub-blocks in this field.

Terminator contains the value zero and marks the end of the Plain Text Extension block.

Application Extension block

Application Extension blocks contain application-specific information in a way similar to the way tags are used in the TIFF and TGA image file formats. Information not normally found in a GIF-format file may be stored in an Application Extension block and then read by any application which understands how to interpret the data. Any number of Application Extension blocks may appear in a GIF file.

Application Extension data is application-readable only. All data stored in this extension is designed to be acted upon by the software application that is reading and processing the GIF data stream. To store human-readable data the Comment Extension block is used instead (see the "Comment Extension block" section).

Examples of data stored in an Application Extension block include instructions on changing video modes, applying special processing to displayed image data, and storing additional color tables. Information used to control the computer platform executing the application can also be stored. This can include information on how to manipulate files, how to access peripheral devices such as modems and printers, and how to send audible signals to the audio speaker.

The Application Extension block is 14 bytes in length and has the following structure:

```
typedef struct _GifApplicationExtension
{
    BYTE Introducer;        /* Extension Introducer (always 21h)*/
    BYTE Label;             /* Extension Label (always FFh) */
    BYTE BlockSize;         /* Size of Extension Block (always
                               0Bh) */
    CHAR Identifier[8];     /* Application Identifier */
    BYTE AuthentCode[3];    /* Application Authentication
```

```
                                        Code        */
    BYTE *ApplicationData;      /* Point to Application Data sub-
                                   blocks */
    BYTE Terminator;            /* Block Terminator (always 0) */

    } GIFAPPLICATION;
```

Introducer contains the value 21h and is used to identify the start of a Extension data block.

Label contains the value FFh and is used to identify this block of data as an Application Extension.

BlockSize contains the value 0Bh, which is the number of bytes in the Identifier and AuthentCode fields.

Identifier may contain up to eight printable 7-bit ASCII characters. These characters are used to identify the application that wrote the Application Extension block. If this identifier value is recognized, the remaining portion of the block is read and its data acted upon. If the identifier value is not recognized, the remaining portion of the block is read and its data is discarded.

AuthentCode contains a value that is used to uniquely identify a software application that created the Application Extension block. This field may contain a serial number, a version number, or a unique binary or ASCII code used to identify an individual software application or computer platform. This field may be used to allow only specific copies or revisions of a particular software application to access the data in certain Application Extension blocks. ApplicationData contains the information that is used by the software application. This field is structured in a series of sub-blocks identical to the data found in a Plain Text Extension block.

Terminator contains the value zero and marks the end of the Application Extension block.

To understand how a GIF reader could interpret Application Extension block information, consider the following example:

An application reading a GIF file comes across an Application Extension. The Identifier field contains the characters "CHKDATE". This identifier is recognized by the application reading the GIF file. The AuthentCode field contains the value "UNX", which is an indication that only versions of this software application running under the UNIX operating system should use the data in this block. All versions of the program not running under UNIX should ignore this block.

The application reading this GIF file knows that a CHKDATE block holds a 2-byte date stamp in the ApplicationCode field. If the current system date is not the same as this date stamp value, the next Graphics Rendering block should not be displayed. The count byte is read from the data sub-block and then the two-byte stamp value. The Terminator field value follows this stamp value.

A second Application Extension is read containing the identifier "CLRSCRN". The application recognizes this identifier and knows that it is an instruction for the display screen to be cleared immediately. The AuthentCode field is not used in this block and its value is read and ignored. This block also does not contain any data sub-blocks, and therefore the block terminator value occurs immediately.

A third Application Extension is read containing the identifier "SOUNDBYT". This identifier informs the application that this block contains audio data that should be sent to the sound card driver installed in the system. The Authent-Code field contains the code CDI, which indicates the format of the audio data stored in this block. If the AuthentCode field is recognized, then the data sub-blocks are read, and the data is sent to the computer platform's audio system until a zero count byte is read.

Finally, a fourth Application Extension is read containing the identifier "SPE-CIAL". This particular identifier is not recognized by the application reading the GIF file, so the AuthentCode field and the ApplicationData field are read and ignored.

The above examples are only a few of the hundreds of ways Application Extension blocks may be used to provide control over a computer system and the way GIF images are displayed. The GIF 89a specification does not list any specific examples of the use of Application Extension blocks, nor does it include a standard list of identifiers; presumably, this is left up to the ingenuity of the developer.

Comment Extension block

The Comment Extension block is used to insert a human-readable string of text into a GIF file or data stream. Each comment may contain up to 255 7-bit ASCII characters, including all the ASCII control codes. Any number of Comment Extension blocks may occur in a GIF file and they may appear anywhere after the Global Color Table. It is suggested, however, that comments should appear before or after all image data in the GIF file.

All data stored in the Comment Extension is designed to be read only by the human user examining a GIF file or data stream. All comment data should be ignored by the application reading the GIF data stream. To store computer-readable data and instructions, use the Application Extension block. (See the section called "Application Extension block" earlier in this article).

Comments are typically used to identify the source of the GIF image, its author, the creating software, the creation time and date, the copyright notice for the image data, and so on. Several image display programs that accommodate version 89a images also have the capability of displaying comment data stored within the GIF files.

Comment Extension blocks must always remain independent of all other data in a GIF file. Comment Extension data is not modified by the information in any other Extension blocks, and comments should not contain data that is intended to be read and interpreted as instructions by software applications.

The Comment Extension block may vary from 5 to 259 bytes in length and has the following structure:

```
typedef struct _GifCommentExtension
{
    BYTE Introducer;        /* Extension Introducer (always 21h)*/
    BYTE Label;             /* Comment Label (always FEh) */
    BYTE *CommentData;      /* Pointer to Comment Data sub-blocks */
    BYTE Terminator;        /* Block Terminator (always 0) */

} GIFCOMMENT;
```

Introducer contains the value 21h and is used to identify the start of a Extension data block.

Label contains the value FEh and is used to identify this block of data as a Comment Extension.

CommentData contains one or more sub-blocks of ASCII string data. The character strings stored in the CommentData field sub-blocks are not required to be NULL-terminated.

Terminator contains the value 0 and marks the end of the Comment Extension block. The value of the Terminator field may be used as a NULL-terminator if "size + 1" bytes of comment data is read from the block.

For Further Information

For further information about GIF, see the specifications included on the CD-ROM that accompanies this book:

> CompuServe Incorporated, *GIF Graphics Interchange Format: A standard defining a mechanism for the storage and transmission of bitmap-based graphics information.* Columbus, OH, 1987.

> CompuServe Incorporated, *Graphics Interchange Format: Version 89a.* Columbus, OH, 1990.

You can also obtain a copy of the GIF89a specification from many BBSs and online services, or directly from CompuServe at:

CompuServe Incorporated
Attn: Graphics Technology Department
5000 Arlington Center Boulevard
Columbus, OH 43220
Voice: 614-457-8600
Voice: 800-848-8199

NAME:	GRASP
ALSO KNOWN AS:	Graphical System for Presentation, .GL, .CLP, .FNT, .PIC, .SET, TXT
TYPE:	Animation
COLORS:	256
COMPRESSION:	RLE
MAXIMUM IMAGE SIZE:	Variable
MULTIPLE IMAGES PER FILE:	Yes
NUMERICAL FORMAT:	Little-endian
ORIGINATOR:	Microtex Industries
PLATFORM:	MS-DOS
SUPPORTING APPLICATIONS:	GRASP
SPECIFICATION ON CD:	Yes (summary description)
CODE ON CD:	No
IMAGES ON CD:	No
SEE ALSO:	Microsoft RIFF, FLI
USAGE:	GRASP is a simple animation format capable of displaying low- and medium-resolution images, text, and simple sounds.
COMMENTS:	At one time the most widely used animation format around, GRASP's fortunes have been declining, perhaps because of increased interest in digital video formats such as AVI and QuickTime.

Overview

GRASP (GRAphical System for Presentation) is an MS-DOS application used to create and play back simple animated sequences. Such animations are incorporated into other applications, such as graphical presentations, educational tutorials, and games.

GRASP is a simple toolkit of utilities used to create and play back animations. The basic tool found in GRASP is the editor (*GRASP.EXE* under MS-DOS). The editor program organizes graphics and command information together into a GRASP animation. An animation may contain both text and images, which can be presented in a variety of ways. Simple sounds may be generated from the PC's speaker, and the animation may be controlled via user input.

GRASP supports all standard EGA and VGA display modes.

Most GRASP animations that you will encounter are stored in a GRASP library file (with a .GL extension). A .GL file is actually a library of separate files that contain information required to display a GRASP animation. These files are normally stored as separate disk files when used by GRASP. But when an animation must be transported to another environment or incorporated into another application, the GRASP Library Manager (*GLIB.COM* under MS-DOS) combines all the necessary files into a single .GL library file.

A GRASP library may contain four different types of information files; the formats of these files are discussed later in this article. When these files are stored separately on disk, their types can be identified by their file extensions:

.TXT	Command file
.PIC	Picture file
.CLP	Clip file (picture file without a color map)
.FNT	Font character information (also *.SET)
.SET	Font character information

A GRASP animation is played back using the GRASP run-time display program (*GRASPRT.EXE* under MS-DOS). All applications playing back .GL animation files will call this program to display the animation. The GRASPRT program is capable of reading the animation from a single .GL file or from each information file stored separately on disk.

A .GL file is created as follows:

1. Using a paint or imaging program, create or capture the individual frames you want animated. The images must be saved to disk using the PCPAINT/Pictor file format.

2. Use the GRASP editor program to create a sequence of commands that will be used to display the animation.

3. Combine all the resulting data files into a single .GL file using the GRASP Library Manager. The resulting .GL file may be played back using the GRASP run-time display engine.

File Organization

All GRASP library files begin with a header. The header is a directory of the separate files stored in the .GL file. The header varies in size depending on the number of files stored. The format of the header is shown below:

```
typedef struct _GLHeader
{
  WORD DirectorySize;              /* Size of header in bytes */
  struct _FileEntry
  {
    DWORD FileOffset;              /* Offset of file in the .GL file */
    CHAR  FileName[13];            /* Name of the file */
  } FileDirectory[DirectorySize];

} GLHEADER;
```

DirectorySize is the size of the .GL header in bytes.

The FileDirectory contains one FileEntry structure for each file stored in the .GL.

FileOffset contains the offset location of the file within the .GL file. If a FileOffset value is 00h, then the end of the file directory has been reached.

FileName contains the original disk filename of the file. Each file in a .GL library file is stored as a 4-byte value indicating the size of the file, followed by the file data itself. A structure representing this arrangement appears as follows:

```
typedef struct _FileData
{
  DWORD FileLength;                /* Size of the file data in bytes */
  BYTE  FileData[FileLength];      /* File data */

} FILEDATA;
```

File Details

This section describes the types of files contained in a GRASP library.

Command File

A command (.TXT) file is simply a script of GRASP commands read by the .GL playback program and used to display the animation. A command file is an ordinary ASCII text file and usually begins with a few comment lines identifying the name of the file and author, title of the animation, date of creation, and so on. There is one command file per .GL file.

A number of commands allow GRASP animations to have many special operations and effects. Some of the commands are:

- Load image files and fonts

- Execute MS-DOS programs

- Receive input from the user

- Draw geometric shapes

- Change video modes

- Change color maps

- Create sound

- Display text

- Perform fades

Each command is a keyword followed by zero or more arguments delimited by commas. All commands are case-insensitive except for literal strings which must appear in double quotes. All comments begin with a semicolon and are ignored during playback.

Consider the following example. A .GL file which contains a simple, five-frame animation that displays in an infinite loop might contain the following command file:

```
video L               ; Set video mode to 320x200x256 VGA
pload PALETTE,1       ; Load palette.pic into picture buffer 1
palette 1             ; Set the palette
pfree 1               ; Free picture buffer 1
cload CLP0,1          ; Load clp0.pic into buffer 1
cload CLP1,2          ; Load clp1.pic into buffer 2
cload CLP2,3          ; Load clp2.pic into buffer 3
cload CLP3,4          ; Load clp3.pic into buffer 4
cload CLP4,5          ; Load clp4.pic into buffer 5
forever:              ; Label
putup 80,50,1,10      ; Display buffer 1
putup 80,50,2,10      ; Display buffer 2
putup 80,50,3,10      ; Display buffer 3
putup 80,50,4,10      ; Display buffer 4
putup 80,50,5,10      ; Display buffer 5
putup 80,50,5,10      ; Display buffer 5
putup 80,50,4,10      ; Display buffer 4
putup 80,50,3,10      ; Display buffer 3
putup 80,50,2,10      ; Display buffer 2
goto forever          ; GOTO 'forever' label (and repeat
                      ; display of buffers)
```

Image Files

Each frame in a GRASP animation is stored using the Pictor PC Paint file format. Files with the .PIC extension contain a color map, whereas files with the .CLP extension do not. It is common for a GRASP animation to include a single .PIC file that contains only a color map and to store all of its animation frames as mapless .CLP files.

For more information about it the Pictor PC Paint file format, refer to the article about it later in this book.

Font File

Text is displayed in a GRASP animation by first loading a font and then displaying it using the TEXT command. Fonts are stored with the extension .FNT or .SET. A font file may contain data for up to 256 font characters. The header for the font file is shown below:

```
typedef struct _FontHeader
{
  WORD FileLength;            /* Size of font file in bytes */
  BYTE NumberOfCharacters;    /* Number of characters in file */
  BYTE FirstCharacterValue;   /* ASCII value of first character */
  BYTE CharacterWidth;        /* Width of character in pixels */
  BYTE CharacterHeight;       /* Height of character in pixels */
  BYTE CharacterSize;         /* Size of character in bytes */

} FONTHEADER;
```

FileLength is the size of the font file in bytes, including header.

NumberOfCharacters is the number of font character defined in this file. This number may be 0 through 255, with 0 representing 256 characters stored.

FirstCharacterValue is the ASCII value of the first font character appearing in the data (font characters are arranged in ASCII value order). Most fonts start with the space character (ASCII value 20h).

CharacterWidth and CharacterHeight represent the size of the font in pixels.

CharacterSize is the number of bytes required to store each font character. This value is usually calculated from the pixel size of the font (CharacterWidth * CharacterHeight / 8).

The font data immediately follows the header. Each character is stored by row, and each row is padded out to the nearest byte boundary. An 8x16 font contains sixteen rows by eight columns of 1-bit pixels. A 0 bit indicates black and a 1 bit indicates color.

An 8x16 font requires 16 bytes of data per character to store. A full 256-character font is then 4096 bytes in size. The maximum size of a font file is 64K.

For Further Information

For further information about GRASP, see the article included on the CD that accompanies this book.

GRASP was originally created by Microtext Incorporated of Irvine, CA. It was bought in 1988 by Paul Mace software, where it is maintained today. Information on GRASP and GRASP Multimedia may be obtained directly from Paul Mace Software:

> Paul Mace Software, Inc.
> Attn: Steven Belsky
> 400 Williamson Way
> Ashland, Oregon 97520
> Voice: 503-488-2322
> FAX: 503-488-1549
> BBS: 503-482-7435

NAME:	GRIB
ALSO KNOWN AS:	Gridded Binary
TYPE:	Various
COLORS:	NA
COMPRESSION:	Uncompressed
MAXIMUM IMAGE SIZE:	NA
MULTIPLE IMAGES PER FILE:	NA
NUMERICAL FORMAT:	Binary bit-oriented
ORIGINATOR:	World Meteorological Organization
PLATFORM:	All
SUPPORTING APPLICATIONS:	Unknown
SPECIFICATION ON CD:	Yes (summary description)
CODE ON CD:	No
IMAGES ON CD:	No
SEE ALSO:	BUFR
USAGE:	Transfer and transmission of weather and other data.
COMMENTS:	The GRIB format is outside the scope of this book, but we include a brief description because it is likely to be more useful in the future as interest in geographical information systems increases.

Overview

GRIB was created by the World Meteorological Organization (WMO) and is officially designated as FM 92-VIII Ext. GRIB (GRIdded Binary). It is designed to support fast computer-to-computer transmission of large volumes of data. Speed and efficiency are the key words here.

Data in GRIB files, as the name suggests, is expected to be in gridded form, that is, arrayed in a rectilinear fashion. That this suggests our idea of a bitmap is no coincidence, although the WMO and its affiliates normally use the format for the transmission of observational data such as air pressure and temperature.

GRIB *(cont'd)*

GRIB data streams and files adhere to the specification called "WMO Standard Formats for Weather Data Exchange Among Automated Weather Information Systems."

File Organization

GRIB files consist of a number of records, each of which may contain the following information:

- Indicator section
- Product definition section (PDS)
- Optional grid description section (GDS)
- Otional bitmap section (BMS)
- Binary data section (BDS)
- ASCII characters 7777

File Details

Detailing the internals of GRIB is beyond the scope of this article. GRIB is extremely complex and is, at this point, used in a narrow area of technology.

For Further Information

For detailed information about GRIB, see the paper included on the CD-ROM that accompanies this book:

> Stackpole, John D., "The WMO Format For the Storage of Weather Product Information and the Exchange of Messages in Gridded Binary Form."

Additional information on WMO data specifications can also be found in the following document:

> *Standard Formats for Weather Data Exchange Among Automated Weather Information Systems*, Document Number FCM-S2-1990.

This document is available from:

> U.S. Department of Commerce/National Oceanic and Atmospheric Administration
> Attn: Ms. Lena Loman

Office of the Federal Coordinator for Meteorological Services
and Supporting Research (OFCM)
6010 Executive Blvd, Suite 900
Rockville, MD 20852
Voice: 301-443-8704

For more information about the GRIB format, contact:

U.S. Department of Commerce/National Oceanic and Atmospheric
Administration (NOAA)
National Meteorological Center
Attn: Dr. John D. Stackpole
Chief, Production Management Branch, Automation Division
WINMC42, Room 307, WWB
5200 Auth Road
Camp Springs, MD 20746
Voice: 301-763-8115
FAX: 301-763-8381
jstack@sun1.wwb.noaa.gov

Harvard Graphics

NAME:	Harvard Graphics
ALSO KNOWN AS:	None
TYPE:	Metafile
COLORS:	NA
COMPRESSION:	None
MAXIMUM IMAGE SIZE:	NA
MULTIPLE IMAGES PER FILE:	No
NUMERICAL FORMAT:	Little-endian
ORIGINATOR:	Software Publishing
PLATFORM:	MS-DOS
SUPPORTING APPLICATIONS:	Harvard Graphics, other presentation graphics
SPECIFICATION ON CD:	No
CODE ON CD:	No
IMAGES ON CD:	No
SEE ALSO:	None

USAGE: Proprietary to Software Publishing; used by Harvard Graphics business graphics application.

COMMENTS: Software Publishing considers the format proprietary, but will consider a license arrangement.

Overview

Software Publishing, the originator of the Harvard Graphics format, considers this format to be proprietary. Although we wish this were not the case, we can hardly use our standard argument—that documenting and publicizing file formats make sales by seeding the aftermarket. Harvard Graphics has been the top, or one of the top, sellers in the crowded and cutthroat MS-DOS business graphics market, and has remained so despite the lack of cooperation of Software Publishing with external developers.

While we would be happy to provide information about the format if it were available, we have failed to find any during our research for this book, so it appears that Software Publishing has so far been successful in their efforts to restrict information flow from their organization.

To be fair, Software Publishing appeared to consider our request to include the Harvard Graphics format in this book. Although the organization wishes to continue to exert some measure of control over information about the format, they are willing to enter into license arrangements with third-party developers that include nondisclosure agreements. We got the impression that reasonable requests would not be refused.

For Further Information

To obtain further information about obtaining the Harvard Graphics file format under distribution license, contact Software Publishing at:

Software Publishing Inc.
P.O. Box 54983
3165 Kifer Road
Santa Clara, CA 95056-0983
Voice: 408-986-9800

Hierarchical Data Format

NAME:	Hierarchical Data Format
ALSO KNOWN AS:	HDF
TYPE:	Metafile
COLORS:	NA
COMPRESSION:	NA
MAXIMUM IMAGE SIZE:	NA
MULTIPLE IMAGES PER FILE:	Yes
NUMERICAL FORMAT:	NA
ORIGINATOR:	National Center for Supercomputer Applications (NCSA)
PLATFORM:	All
SUPPORTING APPLICATIONS:	Various
SPECIFICATION ON CD:	Yes
CODE ON CD:	No
IMAGES ON CD:	No
SEE ALSO:	FITS

USAGE: Transport and exchange of scientific data, including images, between different applications and platforms.

COMMENTS: A tremendously versatile format that supports the inclusion of various types of "metadata" while continuing to provide support for more mundane data objects, such as images. Used by applications associated with scientific visualization, and well-supported by a portable library of functions from the NCSA Software Tools Group.

Overview

The Hierarchical Data Format (HDF) was created by a group at the National Center for Supercomputer Applications (NCSA) to support the needs of the scientific community with respect to scientific data management. The format was designed to provide support for the following:

- Scientific data and metadata
- Multiple diverse platforms

- Support for a range of software tools
- Rapid and efficient data transfer
- Extensibility

The format is, in the words of Mike Folk at NCSA, a "self-describing extensible file format based on the use of tagged objects that have standard meanings." The specification is extremely complete and is included on the CD, so we will confine ourselves to some introductory remarks. We include the format in this book because we feel that data visualization will be increasingly important in the future.

HDF supports lower-level data types such as multidimensional gridded data, 2D and 3D bitmap images, polygonal mesh data, multivariate datasets, sparse matrices, finite element (FE) data, spreadsheets, splines, non-Cartesian coordinate data, and text.

The file structure is entirely tag-based and is founded on the assumption that the needs of scientists are unknowable in advance. While this might result in anarchy in another situation, manipulation of data associated with public tags is supported by a portable, publicly available library maintained by NCSA. Note that the HDF Project at NCSA is closely associated with the NCSA Software Tools group, which works to support the scientific community, especially in the area of scientific visualization.

Tags are grouped under the unifying concept of a Vset, which is a hierarchical grouping structure flexible enough to support multiple views, useful for data analysis and retrieval.

For Further Information

For further information about the HDF format, see the specification included on the CD that accompanies this book. You can also contact NCSA, the organization responsible for maintaining the spec, at:

National Center for Supercomputer Applications
Attn: Michael Folk
University of Illinois
605 East Springfield Avenue
Champaign, IL 61820
Voice: 217-244-0072
FAX: 217-244-1987
mfolk@ncsa.uiuc.edu

The latest HDF specification is also available via FTP. You must sign a license and then download from *ftp.ncsa.uiuc.edu* in directories *Documentation/HDF3.2* and *Documentation/HDF.Vset2.1.*

NAME:	IGES
ALSO KNOWN AS:	Initial Graphics Exchange Specification
TYPE:	Data transfer protocol
COLORS:	NA
COMPRESSION:	Uncompressed
MAXIMUM IMAGE SIZE:	NA
MULTIPLE IMAGES PER FILE:	NA
NUMERICAL FORMAT:	NA
ORIGINATOR:	National Computer Graphics Association (NCGA)
PLATFORM:	All
SUPPORTING APPLICATIONS:	NA
SPECIFICATION ON CD:	No
CODE ON CD:	No
IMAGES ON CD:	No
SEE ALSO:	None

USAGE: Graphics data transfer over phone lines and other narrow-bandwidth channels.

COMMENTS: IGES is a format that has a lot of technical merit. It would be more popular if it were not so expensive, especially because equivalent or technically superior formats are more readily available.

Overview

IGES (Initial Graphics Exchange Specification) is a set of protocols for the transfer and display of graphics information and is designed primarily to support graphics display on remote terminals and similar equipment.

IGES is associated with NCGA (National Computer Graphics Association) as part of the U.S. Product Data Association (USPRO) and the IGES/PDES Organization (IGO). NCGA administers the National IGES User Group (NIUG), which provides access to information and is a place to exchange information on IGES.

For Further Information

To obtain the IGES file format specification, you must be a member of both NIUG and a Regional Interest Group (RIG). Membership in the NIUG costs $49 dollars per year, and gives you access to a BBS, a bimonthly newsletter, and discounts on various user group activities. Becoming a member in the national organization automatically enrolls you as a member of a Regional Interest Group, if one exists in your area. The IGES specification itself is available through NCGA and costs $100, although a discount is reportedly available if you are a NIUG member.

For information about the NIUG and the IGES specification contact:

> National Computer Graphics Association
> 2722 Merrilee Drive
> Suite 3200
> Fairfax, VA 22031
> Voice: 703-698-9600

NCGA can give you information about the National Institute for Standards and Technology (NIST) testing for IGES.

Inset PIX

NAME:	Inset PIX
ALSO KNOWN AS:	PIX
TYPE:	Bitmap
COLORS:	Up to 16
COMPRESSION:	Proprietary, documented
MAXIMUM IMAGE SIZE:	64Kx64K
MULTIPLE IMAGES PER FILE:	No
NUMERICAL FORMAT:	Little-endian
ORIGINATOR:	Inset Systems
PLATFORM:	MS-DOS
SUPPORTING APPLICATIONS:	InSet Versions 1 and 2, HiJaak, WordStar, Multimate
SPECIFICATION ON CD:	Yes
CODE ON CD:	No
IMAGES ON CD:	Yes
SEE ALSO:	None

USAGE: Neutral common format for Inset Systems' products. Also used for graphics storage by the WordStar and Multimate word processors.

COMMENTS: A great little format marred by lack of support for more than 16 colors. It would be a good model for a deep-pixel format, however.

Overview

Inset PIX is an intermediate graphic format created by Inset Systems, which sells the InSet and HiJaak applications for use on Intel-based PCs. HiJaak is a widely used and highly regarded screen-capture and graphics file conversion utility. Version 2 of the package supports the graphics, printer, and FAX formats listed below:

ASCII
AT&T Group 4
AutoCAD DXF
CALS raster
CGM

Inset IGF
Kofax Group 4
Lotus Picture
Macintosh Paint
Macintosh PICT

GIF	MathCAD
DataBeam DBX	Microsoft Paint
Dr. Halo	Microsoft Windows Bitmap
Encapsulated PostScript	Microsoft Windows Metafile
FAX formats (various)	PCX
GEM raster	Presentation Manager Metafile
GEM VDI	Tektronix P10
HPPCL	TGA
HPGL	TIFF
ILBM	WordPerfect Graphics Metafile
Inset PIX	

As you might imagine, Inset has a great deal of experience with graphics file formats. The design of PIX reflects this experience, and is a well thought-out and flexible format. If you need to convert a file from an odd format to one on the above list, you might consider converting to PIX as an intermediate step and then using the application to do the rest. (And, no, we don't have any financial or personal interest in Inset Systems!)

PIX was designed as an extensible, device-independent format which would allow random access of portions of a compressed image. Although nominally a bitmap format, the file structure supports the future addition of other data types.

File Organization

Inset documentation describes a PIX file as, "an indexed database of data items." A table of the size and location of data items is included in the beginning of each file. Data items can include information on the following:

- Image attributes, including dimensions, type, origin, and colors
- Information relevant at print time, such as clipping, size, and rotation
- Palette information
- Compressed sections of bitmap data ("image tiles")
- Bitmap tile-sectioning information

File Details

This section describes the header, index table, and different types of image data in a PIX file.

Header

PIX files always have a short header:

```
typedef struct _PIX_HEADER
{
  WORD RevisionLevel;      // currently 3
  WORD DataItemsInTable;   // number of data items in the index table

} PIX_HEADER;
```

RevisionLevel is the version number for the format; this level is currently 3.

DataItemsInTable is the number of items in the PIX file's index table, described in the next section.

Index Table

Following the header is an index table containing an array of data item information structures of the following form:

```
typedef struct DATA_ITEM_INFO
{
  WORD DataID;          // Data item ID
  WORD DataLength;      // Length of data item
  LONG DataLocation;    // Location of data item in file

} DATA_ITEM_INFO;
```

DataID values may be any of the following:

00	Image information
11	Printing options
01	Palette
02	Tile information

Empty data items have DataID values of -1.

DataLength is the length of this item in the index table.

DataLocation is the location of the item in the file.

Image Information

The following information is extracted from the specification document supplied by Inset Systems:

The application ID for the image structure is 0. This data item contains information on the overall image size, type, and origin of the image. The structure (in C) of this data item is:

```
struct mode_data
{
    BYTE     hmode;
    BYTE     htype;
    BYTE     cfore;
    BYTE     cback;
    BYTE     tattr;
    BYTE     tcpr;
    BYTE     trows;
    BYTE     thfnts;
    BYTE     tlfnts;
    BYTE     tcpf;
    BYTE     tfsize[4];
    WORD     gcols;
    WORD     grows;
    BYTE     gfore;
    BYTE     prepal;
    BYTE     lodpal;
    BYTE     lintens;
    BYTE     lred;
    BYTE     lgreen;
    BYTE     lblue;
    BYTE     pages;
    BYTE     haspect;
    BYTE     vaspect;
}
```

Following is a description of each member of this structure:

hmode   Hardware-specific mode. 0 if not specifically related to a particular hardware mode of a board.

htype   Hardware type. Bit 0 is zero if alphanumeric and 1 if bitmap graphics. Board types are ORed into this byte. Board types include:

8 = CGA
16 = Hercules
24 = EGA

cfore   Text foreground color bits (ignore if graphics) 4 for CGA

tattr   Text background color bits (ignore if graphics) 3 for CGA

tcpr   Text characters per row (ignore if graphics)

trows   Text rows (ignore if graphics)

thfnts   Text hardware fonts (not used)

tlfnts   Text loadable fonts (not used)

tcpf   Text characters per font (not used)

tfsize   Font size (not used)

gcols   Graphics columns

grows   Graphics rows

gfore   Graphics foreground color bits

prepal   Number of preset palettes (default to 0)

lodpal   Number of loadable palettes

lintens   Number of palette bits for intensity

lred   Number of palette bits for red

lgreen   Number of palette bits for green

lblue   Number of palette bits for blue

pages   Number of possible pages (not used)

haspect   Horizontal component of aspect ratio (number of horizontal pixels to fit
             in a square)

vaspect   Vertical component of aspect ratio (number of vertical pixels to fit in a
             square)

A sample image structure for a 600-row-by-800-column single-bit plane image
might be initialized as follows:

```
struct mode_data
{
    BYTE    hmode;      /* 0 */
    BYTE    htype;      /* 1 */
    BYTE    cfore;      /* 0 */
    BYTE    cback;      /* 0 */
    BYTE    tattr;      /* 0 */
    BYTE    tcpr;       /* 80 */
    BYTE    trows;      /* 25 */
    BYTE    thfnts;     /* 0 */
    BYTE    tlfnts;     /* 0 */
    BYTE    tcpf;       /* 0 */
    WORD    tfsize[4];  /* 0,0,0,0 */
    WORD    gcols;      /* 800 */
    WORD    grows;      /* 500 */
    BYTE    gfore;      /* 1 */
    BYTE    prepal;     /* 0 */
    BYTE    lodpal;     /* 0 */
    BYTE    lintens;    /* 1 */
    BYTE    lred;       /* 0 */
    BYTE    lgreen;     /* 0 */
    BYTE    lblue;      /* 0 */
    BYTE    pages;      /* 0 */
    BYTE    haspect;    /* 1 */
    BYTE    vaspect;    /* 1 */
}
```

Printing Options

The application ID for Inset Printing options is 11h. The C structure containing these items follows:

```
struct prt_options
{
    SHORT       pitch;
    SHORT       scol;
    SHORT       ecol;
    SHORT       srow;
    SHORT       erow;
    SHORT       p_wid;
    SHORT       siz;
    SHORT       rotat;
    SHORT       do_sw;
    SHORT       res_1;
    SHORT       res_2;
    SHORT       pcolor;
    SHORT       row_dp;
    SHORT       col_dp;
    SHORT       flags;
    CHAR ink_tab[16];
}
```

Following is a description of each member of this structure:

pitch   Printer Pitch divided by 10 (e.g., 100 = 10 pitch); not required, set to 100

scol   Start column clip boundary

ecol   End column clip boundary

srow   Start row clip boundary

erow   End row clip boundary

p_wid   Printer width (not required, set to 0)

size   Size (not used, set to 0)

rotat   Rotation (0 = horizontal, -1 = left, 1=right)

do_sw   Option bits ORed. Applicable bits to set include:

                Double Pass | = 2
                Letter Quality | = 4
                Border On | = 10 (hex)

res_1

res_2   Internal use (don't use, set to 0)

pcolor   Low-order byte indicates whether the image settings are intended for color printer (true = 1, false = 0)

          High-order byte indicates which dither pattern type to use (0 = old, 1 = gray, 2 = contrast).

row_dp   Height of image in decipoints (1/720 inches)

col_dp   Width of image in decipoints (1/720 inches)

flags   Modify flags

          Size option bits:

                #define INDATA_USE_COL 0x1
                #define INDATA_USE_INCH 0x2
                #define INDATA_USE_DP   0x3

          Modify ink selection:

                #define INDATA_INK_INV 0x8
                #define INDATA_INK_BW   0x10
                #define INDATA_INK_TAB 0x18
                #define INDATA_VDISK   0x20
                #define INDATA_VSIZE   0x40
                #define INDATA_DYNAMIC 0x80

ink_tab   Sixteen-byte table mapping screen colors to printer colors/gray patterns (see the MODIFY/INKS section of the Inset manual for more information on ink tables). If you want to select your own Ink table mapping, the flags variable must have a 0x18 OR'ed in. Preset Inset Ink tables are set as follows:

Color Number 0 1 2 3 4 5 6 7 8 9 A B C D E F

Standard	F 1 2 3 4 5 6 7 8 9 A B C D E 0
Invert	0 1 2 3 4 5 6 7 8 9 A B C D E F
B&W	F 0 0 0 0 0 0 0 F 0 0 0 0 0 0 0

Palette Data

Application ID = 1 contains display palette information. Palette information is stored in an array of palette structures of the following form:

```
struct pallette
{
   CHAR intens, red, green, blue;
}
```

The number of significant palette items in the array is determined by the number of available colors (the "gfore" member in the image data structure) in the image. The significant bits are determined by the lintens lred, lgreen, and lblue items in the mode_data structure.

Tile Information

Application ID = 2 contains information as to how the image is broken down into tiles. The Tile_Data structure follows:

```
struct Tile_Data
{
   WORD    page_rows;
   WORD    page_cols;
   WORD    stp_rows;
   WORD    stp_cols;
}
```

Following is a description of each member of this structure:

page_rows	Number of rows within each tile
page_cols	Number of columns in each tile (must be divisible by 8)
stp_rows	Number of horizontal tile strips within the image
stp_cols	Number of vertical tile strips

Each tile is limited to a maximum of 4096 bytes of uncompressed data. The actual tiles are numbered starting with the upper left row as tile 0 and incremented from left to right as illustrated below.

0	1	2	3
4	5	6	7
8	9	A	B

The ID of a tile is the tile number ORed with a 8000h. For example, the lower-right tile can be found by finding the record with ID=800Bh.

Images may be broken down into checkerboard sections or horizontal strips. However, if an image is broken into horizontal strips for processing, the image as rotated by Inset will be slowed.

Pixel Tiles

Each individual pixel tile ID is determined by ORing in 8000h with the tile number, as described in the preceding section on tile information.

The image is organized into bit planes with eight pixels per byte; the most significant bit contains the leftmost pixel. For multiple-bit plane images, all scan lines for a plane are written out before the scan lines in the next plane.

If the actual column boundary of the tile exceeds the column boundary of the image, the image is padded with blank bytes to fill out the tile. If the actual row boundary of the tile exceeds that of the image, the extra rows are not present.

When the tile is stored on disk, it is in a vertically compressed format. The first scan line of each tile is written out with no modification. Then, before the following scan lines, there are compression bytes that indicate which bytes in the scan line are different from the preceding line. Each bit in the compression byte indicates whether a particular byte in that scan has changed (1 if changed, 0 if not). Then, following the compression bytes, only the modified scan bytes are written to the file.

For example, suppose we have a tile that is eight columns wide, the first scan line is all blank, and there is a dot at the beginning and end of the second scan line. This tile would be written to disk as follows:

```
    00 00 00 00 00 00 00 00 <- First scan line
 81 80                   01 <- changed bytes
  ^
  |
  Compression Byte
```

In multiple-bit plane images, the first scan is uncompressed, and the following lines are compressed in the same manner as described above.

Character Tiles

Alphanumeric images can be generally described as two-plane images with the first plane containing the alphanumeric character data and the second containing the attribute information. Alphanumeric characters are presumed to correspond to the IBM extended ASCII character set, with attribute information corresponding to the IBM CGA standard.

The character and text planes are compressed in the same manner as image bit planes with one caveat. The text scan-line length is twice what it should be (i.e., 160 bytes go out uncompressed for an 80-column screen).

For Further Information

For further information about Inset PIX, see the specification included on the CD-ROM that accompanies this book. You can also contact:

Inset Systems
Attn: Mike Kaltschnee
Developer Relations
71 Commerce Drive
Brookfield, CT 06804
Voice: 203-740-2400

Intel DVI

NAME:	Intel DVI
ALSO KNOWN AS:	DVI, Digital Video Interface, Intel Real-Time Video
TYPE:	Multimedia
COLORS:	16 million
COMPRESSION:	JPEG, proprietary
MAXIMUM IMAGE SIZE:	256x240
MULTIPLE IMAGES PER FILE:	Yes
NUMERICAL FORMAT:	NA
ORIGINATOR:	Intel Corporation
PLATFORM:	Intel-based PCs
SUPPORTING APPLICATIONS:	MS-DOS and Microsoft Windows Multimedia
SPECIFICATION ON CD:	Yes
CODE ON CD:	No
IMAGES ON CD:	No
SEE ALSO:	Microsoft RIFF, Apple QuickTime
USAGE:	A format designed to support Intel's bid to establish a hardware standard in the Intel-based PC marketplace.
COMMENTS:	At the time of this writing, it's too early to decide whether this format will ever see the light of day in a commercial product. If it ever does, you'll find the specification on the CD-ROM useful.

Overview

Intel is the current owner of DVI, which was one of the first systems that provided practical full-motion video incorporating real-time decompression technology. DVI originated in 1984 at the David Sarnoff Research Center in Princeton, New Jersey, which was the central research facility for RCA Corporation. Ownership of DVI changed in 1986 when RCA was acquired by GE. The official unveiling of GE DVI occurred in March 1987 at the Second Microsoft CD-ROM Conference in Seattle, Washington. GE later sold DVI Technology to Intel Corporation in October 1988.

DVI is actually both the name of the Digital Video Interactive hardware system sold by Intel and the file format associated with that system. DVI technology is essentially a PC-based interactive audio/video system used for multimedia applications. The DVI system consists of a board for use in an Intel-based PC, drivers, and associated software. The four components of DVI technology are:

- DVI hardware chipset
- Runtime software interface
- Data compression and decompression schemes
- Data file formats

The heart of the DVI system is the hardware architecture based on the video display processor (VDP) chipset. DVI technology was originally designed for implementation on the IBM PC AT platform. A collection of three 16-bit, ISA-bus DVI interface boards (audio, video, and CD-ROM) were plugged into the AT, and all of the hardware capabilities were accessed through the runtime software interface. The functions in the interface were called by writing a software program using a programming language such as assembly or C.

Today, Intel distributes licenses to third-party developers who want to incorporate DVI technology into their platforms and multimedia products. All of IBM's multimedia hardware platforms (such as the ActionMedia II boards), and software applications are based upon DVI technology. This is logical, because Intel is partly owned by IBM.

DVI is a major competitor of both QuickTime and MPEG for market share in digital audio/video applications. Although QuickTime is a versatile method of storing multimedia data on both the Macintosh and the PC, and MPEG is now a solid standard with further extensions nearing completion, DVI became available first, and many people who faithfully follow the trends set forth by Intel and IBM continue to choose DVI technology.

Like many of the multimedia systems available today, the current version of DVI allows the storage and playback of audio and video information. All DVI images have a 5:4 pixel aspect ratio and are 256x240 pixels in size. DVI is also capable of storing still images and supports both a lossy and a lossless native compression method for such images. DVI works across all MS-DOS, Microsoft Windows, and OS/2 platforms and supports the capability of using its own proprietary compression scheme, or using user-definable algorithms, such as JPEG, as well. Audio compression is achieved using either the ADPCM or PCM8 algorithms.

File Organization

The DVI file format is extremely flexible in its design and is used to store a wide variety of data. This format is capable of storing both still-image and motion-video/audio data. The type of data a DVI file contains is described by its file extension. The common extensions for DVI files containing still-image data are the following:

Uncompressed, 8-bit data

.IMR	Red channel
.IMG	Green channel
.IMB	Blue channel
.IMY	Y luminance channel
.IMI	I color channel
.IMQ	Q color channel
.IMM	Monochrome or gray scale
.IMA	Alpha channel
.IMC	Color map
.I8	Device-dependent data

Uncompressed, 16-bit data

.I16	Device-dependent data

Compressed, 8-bit data

.CMY	Y luminance channel
.CMI	I color channel
.CMQ	Q color channel

Compressed, 16-bit data

.C16	Device-dependent data

As you can see, a common practice of DVI is to store each color plane of an image in a separate disk file. This allows the easy reading and writing of bitmap information, without the need to buffer data to read or write a single file.

A still image is saved using three color-channel files and possibly a color map and alpha channel file as well. Motion-video/audio data is stored using the Audio/Video Support System (AVSS) file format. AVSS (pronounced "avis") allows audio and video data to be stored in the same file and played back in a synchronized manner. All AVSS files have the extension .AVS or the file type AVSS.

File Details

The data in AVSS files is primarily stream-based, and there is at least one data stream per AVSS file. Each file contains a standard header, an AVL file header, one stream header per data stream, one substream header per substream, frame data, and a frame directory.

DVI File Header

The standard header of a DVI file is 12 bytes long and has the following structure:

```
typedef _DviStandardHeader
{
   DWORD FileId;            /* Magic number (56445649h) of DVI file */
   SHORT HeaderSize;        /* Size of this header structure */
   SHORT HeaderVersion;     /* Version of this header structure */
   DWORD AnnotationOffset;  /* Location of annotation data */

} DVISTANDARDHEADER;
```

FileId contains the characters VDVI and identifies the file as containing DVI information. If the file contains still-image information, this field contains the characters VIM.

HeaderSize contains the number of bytes found in the header, which is currently 12. Older versions of the DVI format may contain a value of 1 in this field. In this case, this value should be ignored and treated as if it were 12.

HeaderVersion indicates the format of the header and is currently 1.

AnnotationOffset is used to point at additional, unstructured data, such as a title or copyright notice, which is normally placed at the end of the file. If no annotation exists, then this field is set to 0.

AVL File Header

The AVL file header immediately follows the standard header and is a directory of all the other data structures within the DVI file. This header is 120 bytes in length and has the following format:

```
typedef struct _AvlHeader
{
  DWORD HeaderId;               /* Header ID value (41565353h) */
  SHORT HeaderSize;             /* Size of this header structure */
  SHORT HeaderVersion;          /* Format of this header structure */
  SHORT StreamGroupCount;       /* Number of stream groups in the
                                   file */
  SHORT StreamGroupSize;        /* Size of each stream group */
  DWORD StreamGroupOffset;      /* Location of the first stream
                                   group */
  SHORT StreamGroupVersion;     /* Format of each stream group */
  SHORT StreamSize;             /* Size of the stream header */
  SHORT StreamVersion;          /* Format of the stream header */
  SHORT StreamCount;            /* Number of stream headers in the
                                   file */
  DWORD StreamOffset;           /* Location of stream structures
                                   array */
  DWORD HeaderPoolOffset;       /* Location of substream headers */
  LONG  LabelCount;             /* Number of labels in the file */
  DWORD LabelOffset;            /* Location of the first label */
  SHORT LabelSize;              /* Size of each label */
  SHORT LabelVersion;           /* Format of each label */
  DWORD VideoSeqHeaderOffset;     /* Location of video sequence
                                   header */
  WORD  VideoSeqHeaderSize;     /* Size of video sequence header */
  SHORT FrameVersion;           /* Version of frame headers in file */
  LONG  FrameCount;             /* Number of frame headers in file */
  LONG  FrameSize;              /* Size of frame header and data */
  DWORD FirstFrameOffset;       /* Location of the first frame */
  DWORD EndOfFrameOffset;       /* Location of last frame byte + 1 */
  SHORT FrameHeaderSize;        /* Size of frame header */
  SHORT FrameDirectorySize;     /* Size of the frame directory */
  DWORD FrameDirectoryOffset;     /* Location of the frame
                                   directory */
  SHORT FrameDirectoryVersion;    /* Format of the frame
                                   directory */
  SHORT FramesPerSecond;        /* Frame rate of the data */
  DWORD UpdateFlag;             /* Data is updating or complete */
  DWORD FreeBlockOffset;        /* Not used */
  BYTE  Patch[32];              /* Not used */

} AVLHEADER;
```

HeaderId contains the characters AVSS and identifies the header as containing AVL file information.

HeaderSize contains the number of bytes found in the header. This value is currently 120.

HeaderVersion contains a value that specifies the format of the header based on a version control rating. Each modification to the header structure increments the header version. The current HeaderVersion value for the AVL-HEADER structure is 3.

If the streams within a DVI file are organized as groups, then the Stream-GroupCount value indicates the number of groups; the StreamGroupSize value specifies the size of each group; the StreamGroupOffset value points to the location of the first group; and the StreamGroupVersion specifies the format of the group. If no stream groups are present in the file, then the value of these fields will be 00h.

The next four fields contain information on the array of STREAMHEADER structures stored in the DVI file. StreamSize indicates the size of each structure, which is currently 44. StreamVersion specifies the format of each structure, which is currently a value of 3. StreamCount is the number of streams in the file and structures in the array. StreamOffset contains the offset value to the beginning of the array.

HeaderPoolOffset points to the first substream header. This value is 00h if there are no substreams present in the file.

If the DVI file contains labels, then LabelCount indicates the number of labels; LabelOffset points to the location of the first label; LabelSize specifies the size of each label; and LabelVersion specifies the format of the label. If no labels are present in the file, then the values of these fields are all 00h.

VideoSeqHeaderOffset and VideoSeqHeaderSize describe the location and size of the video sequence header, if one is present in the file.

FrameVersion indicates the format of the data frames and is currently 3. FrameCount is the number of frames in the file, and FrameSize is the size of a frame, including its header. FirstFrameOffset is the location of the first frame header.

EndOfFrameOffset points to the location of the first byte after the frame data.

FrameHeaderSize value is the size of the frame header.

Intel DVI (cont'd)

The FrameDirectorySize specifies the size of the frame directory and is currently 4.

FrameDirectoryOffset points to the location of the frame directory.

FrameDirectoryVersion specifies the format of the frame directory.

FramesPerSecond contains the frame rate of the data for playback, rounded to the nearest integer.

UpdateFlag is a non-zero value if the file is in the process of being updated. A value of 00h indicates that the file is not currently being modified.

FreeBlockOffset and Patch[32] are set to 00h.

Stream Header

Each DVI file contains one or more data streams. Each stream is identified by an associated **STREAMHEADER** structure, which contains detailed information about the stream data. This header is four bytes in length and has the following format:

```
typedef struct _StreamHeader
{
DWORD HeaderId;                 /* Header ID value (5354524Dh) */
WORD  Type;                     /* The type of data stream */
WORD  SubType;                  /* The subtype of data stream */
SHORT HeaderCount;              /* Number of substream headers */
SHORT NextStreamNumber;         /* ID of the next stream */
SHORT StreamGroupNumber;        /* The group ID for this stream */
SHORT Pad;                      /* Pad value */
DWORD Flag;                     /* Variable frame size flag */
LONG  FrameSize;                /* Maximum amount of data per frame */
DWORD FirstHeaderOffset;        /* Location of first substream header */
BYTE  StreamName[16];           /* Name of the stream */

} STREAMHEADER;
```

HeaderId contains the characters STRM and identifies the header as containing AVL file information.

HeaderSize contains the number of bytes found in the header. This value is currently 120.

Type and SubType indicate the type of data that is stored in this stream. Valid Type values are:

02h	Compressed audio stream

02h   Compressed audio stream
03h   Compressed image stream
05h   Associated per-frame data
06h   Uncompressed image stream
07h   Pad stream

SubType indicates a variation of each of these stream types and is described for different types of streams (e.g., video) in the following sections.

HeaderCount indicates the number of substreams associated with this stream.

NextStreamNumber is not used and is set to -1.

StreamGroupNumber indicates the ID of the group this stream is associated with.

Pad is not used and is set to 00h.

Flag is 04h if the stream contains frames that vary in size; otherwise, the value will be 00h.

FrameSize field specifies the maximum number of bytes per frame in the stream.

FirstHeaderOffset points to the location of the first substream header.

StreamName is the name of the stream in the form of a NULL-terminated ASCII string.

Audio Substream Header
Each type of data stream has a substream header. The audio substream header describes the attributes of an audio stream. The type of audio stream is indicated by the SubType field in the STREAMHEADER structure. For audio streams, this value is always 0. The AUDIOSUBSTREAMHEADER header is 168 bytes in length and is formatted as follows:

```
typedef struct _AudioSubStreamHeader
{
    DWORD HeaderId;          /* Header ID value (41554449h) */
    SHORT HeaderSize;        /* Size of this header structure */
    SHORT HeaderVersion;     /* Format of this header structure */
    BYTE  OriginalFile[80];  /* Name of file stream is derived
                                from */
    LONG  OriginalFrame;     /* Original frame ID */
    SHORT OriginalStream;    /* Original stream ID */
    SHORT Pad;               /* Pad value */
```

```
        LONG   FrameCount;              /* The number of frames */
        DWORD  NextHeaderOffset;        /* Location of next substream header */
        BYTE   LibraryName[16];         /* Name of library stream if from */
        BYTE   AlgorithmName[16];       /* Audio compression algorithm used */
        LONG   DataRate;                /* Audio data rate in bits/sec */
        SHORT  CutoffFrequency;         /* Filter cutoff frequency */
        SHORT  Parameter3;              /* Not used */
        SHORT  LeftVolum rate;          /* Loudness of left audio channel */
        SHORT  RightVolume;             /* Loudness of right audio channel */
        LONG   LoopOffset;              /* Not used */
        LONG   StartingFrame;           /* ID of the first frame in the
                                           stream */
        DWORD  Flag;                    /* Mono/Stereo flag */
        SHORT  FrameRate;               /* The playback rate for this stream */
        SHORT  Pad2                     /* Pad value */
        LONG   DCFId;                   /* Digital Compression Facility ID */

} AUDIOSUBSTREAMHEADER;
```

HeaderId contains the characters AUDI and identifies the header as containing audio stream information.

HeaderSize contains the number of bytes found in this header. This value is currently 168.

HeaderVersion indicates the version number of the header. The current HeaderVersion field value is 5.

OriginalFile contains a NULL-terminated ASCII string identifying the name and path of the file, from which the audio information is derived.

OriginalFrame, OriginalStream, and Pad are not used and are set to 0.

FrameCount indicates the number of frames in the audio stream.

NextHeaderOffset specifies the location of the next audio substream header. This value is always 00h.

LibraryName is not used and should be set to all NULL values.

AlgorithmName contains a NULL-terminated ASCII string that identifies the name of the compression method used on the audio data stream. This string is apdcm4e or pcm8 for the ADPCM and PCM8 algorithms respectively.

DataRate is the data rate of the audio stream in bits per second.

CutoffFrequency indicates the maximum filter cutoff frequency for the sample.

Parameter3 is not used and is set to 0.

LeftVolume and RightVolume specify the volume level of the left and right audio channels respectively. These numbers are a percentage of the total volume; the default value is 100.

LoopOffset has a default value of -1.

StartFrame normally has a value of 0.

Flag has a value of 4000h, indicating that the audio stream is stereophonic, or 8000h, indicating that it is monophonic.

FrameRate is the data rate of the audio stream.

Pad2 is not used and is set to 0.

DCFId contains a value indicating the software service that compressed the data. The value of this field is -1 if the ID of the service is not known or is unimportant.

Video substream header

The video substream header describes the attributes of a video or compressed image stream. The type of video stream is indicated by the SubType field in the STREAMHEADER structure, which may have the following values for a video stream:

1	Y-channel data only
11	U-channel data only
12	V-channel data only
13	YVU data
14	YUV data

All images are stored in YVU format, except for JPEG-compressed images, which are stored using YUV.

The VIDEOSUBSTREAMHEADER header is 136 bytes in length and is formatted as follows:

```
typedef struct _VideoSubStreamHeader
{
    DWORD HeaderId;          /* Header ID value (h) */
    SHORT HeaderSize;        /* Size of this header structure */
    SHORT HeaderVersion;     /* Format of this header structure */
    BYTE  OriginalFile[80];  /* Name of file stream is derived
                                from */
```

```
        LONG  OriginalFrame;       /* Original frame ID */
        SHORT OriginalStream;      /* Original stream ID */
        SHORT Pad;                 /* Pad value */
        LONG  FrameCount;          /* Number of frames until next header */
        DWORD NextHeaderOffset;    /* Location of next substream header */
        SHORT XPosition;           /* X coordinate top-left corner of
                                      image */
        SHORT YPosition;           /* Y coordinate top-left corner of
                                      image */
        SHORT XLength;             /* Width of image */
        SHORT YLength;             /* Height of image */
        SHORT XCrop;               /* X cropping coordinate */
        SHORT YCrop;               /* Y cropping coordinate */
        SHORT DropFrame;           /* Not used */
        SHORT DropPhrase;          /* Not used */
        LONG  StillPeriod;         /* Frequency of intraframe images */
        SHORT BufferMinimum;       /* Minimum buffer size required */
        SHORT BufferMaximum;       /* Maximum buffer size required */
        SHORT DecodeAlgorithm;     /* ID of the decompression algorithm */
        SHORT Pad2;                /* Pad value */
        LONG  DCFId;               /* Digital Compression Facility ID */

    } VIDEOSTREAMHEADER;
```

HeaderId contains the characters CMIG and identifies the header as containing audio stream information.

HeaderSize contains the number of bytes found in this header. This value is currently 136.

HeaderVersion currently has a value of 4.

OriginalFile contains a NULL-terminated ASCII string identifying the name and path of the file from which the video or image information is derived.

OriginalFrame, OriginalStream, and Pad are not used and are set to 0.

FrameCount indicates the number of frames in the current substream.

NextHeaderOffset specifies the location of the next video substream header. This field value is always 00h.

XPosition and YPosition indicate the position of the top-left corner of the image. These fields are normally 0.

XLength and YLength specify the maximum width and height of the images stored in this stream.

XCrop and YCrop specify alternate length values used to crop the image. These values are 0 by default.

DropFrame and DropPhrase are not used and are set to 0.

StillPeriod indicates the interval at which intraframe encoding occurs. For example, a value of 12 in this field indicates that every 12th frame in this video stream is intraframe-encoded. A value of 1 indicates that every frame is intraframe encoded. The default value of -1 indicates that the intraframe interval is unknown.

BufferMinimum and BufferMaximum indicate the extremes of the buffer sizes required for decompressing the image. These fields are normally set to 00h.

DecodeAlgorithm contains a value identifying the algorithm, needed to decompress the stream. Pad2 is not used and is set to 0.

DCFId contains a value indicating the software service that compressed the data. The value of this field is -1 if the ID of the service is unknown or not important.

For information on other substream header formats, refer to the DVI specifications on the CD-ROM.

Frames

Each section of frame data in a DVI file is preceded by a header describing the data in the frame. The structure of this header is shown below.

```
typedef struct _FrameHeader
{
    LONG FrameNumber;          /* Sequence number of this frame */
    LONG PreviousOffset;       /* Location of previous frame */
    LONG Checksum;             /* Checksum value for this frame */
    LONG StreamFrameSize[];    /* Array of all frame sizes */

} FRAMEHEADER;
```

FrameNumber stores the sequence number of the frame. PreviousOffset points to the location of the previous frame. This value is 00h if it is the first frame.

Checksum contains a checksum value of the frame header.

StreamFrameSize is an array of byte count values, one for each frame stored in the stream.

Intel DVI (cont'd)

The location of each frame is stored in a directory of offset values. There will be one FRAMEDIRECTORY structure per frame stored in the stream. The format of this structure is shown below.

```
typedef struct _FrameDirectory
{
DWORD FrameOffset;          /* Location of the frame for this directory */

} FRAMEDIRECTORY;
```

FrameOffset points to the location of its associated frame. If the most significant bit of this value is set to 1, this offset may be used for access to the frame data of every stream in the file. Typically, only audio streams are suitable for random access.

For Further Information

For further information about the Intel DVI format, see the specification included on the CD-ROM that accompanies this book. The specifications for DVI and the AVSS file format may also be found in the reference material from the DVI Developer's Kit available from Intel:

Intel Corporation
Attn: Intel Action Media Support
6505 West Chandler Blvd
Chandler, AZ 85226
Voice: 602-554-4231

See the following books and articles for additional information about Intel DVI:

Luther, Arch C. *Digital Video in the PC Environment: Featuring DVI Technology*, McGraw-Hill, New York, NY, 1989

Dixon, D.F., Golkin, S.J., and Hashfield, I.H. "DVI Video Graphics," *Computer Graphics World*, July 1987.

Hurst, R.N. and Luther, A.C. "DVI: Digital Video from a CD-ROM," *Information Display*, April 1988.

NAME:	Interchange File Format
ALSO KNOWN AS:	IFF, ILM, Amiga Paint, ILBM
TYPE:	Bitmap
COLORS:	24-bit maximum
COMPRESSION:	RLE, uncompressed
MAXIMUM IMAGE SIZE:	64Kx64K pixels
MULTIPLE IMAGES PER FILE:	No
NUMERICAL FORMAT:	Big-endian
ORIGINATOR:	Commodore Amiga, Inc.
PLATFORM:	Amiga, others
SUPPORTING APPLICATIONS:	Too numerous to list
SPECIFICATION ON CD:	Yes
CODE ON CD:	Yes (in FBM and pbmplus packages)
IMAGES ON CD:	Yes
SEE ALSO:	Microsoft RIFF

USAGE: Widely used in desktop publishing, paint, and image processing applications, particularly on the Amiga.

COMMENTS: A well-defined, well-documented format in wide use, which is quick and easy to read and uncompress. It lacks, however, a superior compression scheme, making it unsuited for the storage of deep-pixel images when file size is an issue. Numbers in the file are stored in big-endian format.

Overview

The Interchange File Format (IFF) is most often associated with the Commodore Amiga and its graphics, imaging, and animation applications.

File Organization

Each IFF file consists of a series of sections called chunks. The first chunk is a 40-byte header. The header is followed by one or more sections of data. Each chunk, including the header, is preceded by a 4-byte identifier; common identifiers are:

BMHD   Header
CAMG   Amiga view modes
CMAP   Color map
BODY   Image data itself

File Details

This section contains the types of chunks that may be found in an Interchange File Format file.

Header Chunk

An IFF file begins with a 40-byte header chunk in the following format:

```
typedef struct _IffHeader
{
  BYTE  Id[4];              /* Identification value   */
  DWORD FileLength;         /* Size of the File in Bytes    */
  BYTE  FileType[8];        /* Bitmap Header Chunk Identifier   */
  DWORD HeaderLength;       /* Size of the Header    */
  WORD  Width;              /* Width of the Image in Pixels    */
  WORD  Length;             /* Length of the Image in Pixels    */
  WORD  XOffset;            /* X Origin of Image on the Display   */
  WORD  YOffset;            /* Y Origin of Image on the Display   */
  BYTE  NumberOfPlanes;     /* Number of Planes of Image Data    */
  BYTE  Mask;               /* Mask Type to Use with Image Data   */
  BYTE  Encoding;           /* Data Encoding \ 0=No, 1=Yes\     */
  BYTE  Padding;            /* Alignment Padding \ not used\     */
  WORD  Transparent;        /* Transparent Bit Patterns    */
  BYTE  XAspectRatio;       /* Horizontal Pixel Aspect Ratio   */
  BYTE  YAspectRatio;       /* Vertical Piexel Aspect Ratio   */
  WORD  PageWidth;          /* Source Page Width in Pixels    */
  WORD  PageHeight;         /* Source Page Height in Pixels    */

} IFFHEAD;
```

ID is the text string FORM.

FileLength is the size of the file in bytes.

FileType contains the header chunk identifier, the string ILBMBMHD.

HeaderLength contains the size of the remaining part of the header after this field and is usually 14h.

Width and Length represent the size of the image. Width is the number of pixels in a row and is always a multiple of two.

XOffset and YOffset represent the origin of the image on the display.

NumberOfPlanes is the number of interleaved planes used to store the image data.

Mask indicates the transparency of the image.

Encoding contains a value which specifies the type of encoding used. A value of 0 indicates that no encoding is used.

Padding is not used and is always set to 0.

Transparent contains the bit pattern if a transparency mask is used; otherwise, this field is set to 0.

XAspectRatio and YAspectRatio indicate the size of the pixels in the image in microns.

PageWidth and PageHeight represent the physical size of the image source (such as the display) in pixels.

Following the header are one or more data chunks. As mentioned above, each chunk is preceded by a chunk identifier. Following each chunk identifier is a four-byte value that is the length of each chunk in bytes. Chunks follow each other in the file; that is, following one complete chunk will be another chunk identifier, or the end of the file. Usually, the BODY chunk is the last to appear in an IFF file.

CAMG Chunk

The Commodore Amiga is the native platform for the IFF format, and the CAMG chunk contains attributes specific to the display hardware of the Amiga. The following values may be specified:

HIRES	High resolution	8000h
HAM	Hold and modify	800h
HALFBRIT	Half bright	80h
LACE	Interlaced	4h

The HAM (hold and modify) mode allows an image to be displayed in up to 4096 colors. HAM images contain six planes. Planes 0 through 3 contain the index of the color value in the color map (CMAP chunk). Planes 4 and 5 contain the HAM bits and may be set as follows:

00	No modify. Planes 0 through 3 hold the pixel colors.
10	Hold previous pixel and modify blue using planes 0-3.
01	Hold previous pixel and modify red using planes 0-3.
11	Hold previous pixel and modify green using planes 0-3.

A pixel is modified by taking the color of the previous pixel (hold) and substituting the bits in planes 0 through 3 for the current pixel index value (modify).

The HALFBRITE mode allows images to be displayed using a palette of 64 fixed colors. When the HALFBRITE bit is set in the CAMG chunk, the last bit in each color plane is the HALFBRITE flag. If this flag is set to 1, then that pixel is displayed at half brightness.

CMAP Chunk

The CMAP chunk contains the color map used to display the image. Each IFF color map is a palette of RGB values. Each value is stored in a three-byte triplet in the order R, G, and B; each primary color is one byte in size.

BODY Chunk

The image data (BODY chunk) is stored in an interleaved format by plane. The first scan line is actually the first plane of the first scan line. Consecutive lines are read until the number of planes in a scan line have been read. The planes are then reassembled into the complete scan line. IFF is designed to handle up to three planes of image data, each plane having a maximum depth of eight bits, for a total of 24 bits of image data. All scan lines are padded out to an even-byte boundary.

The image data in an IFF image file may also be compressed, using a simple byte-wise RLE scheme. Runs of identical byte values are encoded into a single two-byte packet. The first packet is the number of bytes in the run minus one. This value, called the Run Count, may be from 0 to 127 and may encode runs from 1 to 128 bytes in length. The second byte, called the Run Value, contains the actual byte value of the run.

Normally, only runs of three or more identical byte values are stored as encoded runs. If the image data contains very few runs, then the image data may be stored using a literally encoded run. A literal run begins with a Run Count byte and is followed by a number of bytes equal to the Run Count value.

Although no actual data compression is achieved by using a literal run, it prevents negative compression from occurring when the image data being encoded is quite busy in its appearance.

The following pseudocode illustrates the decoding process:

Read a BYTE value
   If the Most Significant Bit (MSB)
      The Run Count is the value of the seven Least Significant Bits plus one
      Read the next byte as the Run Value and repreat it Run Count times
   If the MSB is 0
      The Run Count is this value plus one
      Read the next Run Count bytes

The most significant bit of the Run Count indicates whether the run is encoded or literal. The Run Count is the seven least significant bits of the Run Count byte plus one.

For Further Information

For further information about the Interchange File Format, see the specification included on the CD that accompanies this book. You can also contact Electronic Arts, the creator of the format, at:

Electronic Arts
1820 Gateway Drive
San Mateo, CA 94404
Voice: 415-571-7171
Voice: 415-572-2787

The following documents about the IFF format are available from Electronic Arts and from many online services and BBSs:

Morrison, Jerry. *EA IFF 85 Standard for Interchange Format Files*. Electronic Arts. January 14, 1985.

Morrison, Jerry. *ILBM IFF Interleaved Bitmap*. Electronic Arts. January 17, 1986.

Commodore Amiga also supports the Interchange File Format and may be reached at:

Commodore Business Machines, Inc.
1200 Wilson Drive
West Chester, PA 19380
Voice: 215-431-9262
Voice: 215-431-9100

The following document from Commodore is widely available online:

Scheppner, Carolyn. *Introduction to Amiga IFF ILBM Files and Amiga View-modes*, Commodore Amiga Technical Support.

The following book also discusses the IFF file format:

Commodore Amiga, Inc. *Amiga ROM KERNEL Reference Manual: Includes and Autodocs*, Addison-Wesley, Reading, MA, 1989.

NAME:	JPEG File Interchange Format
ALSO KNOWN AS:	JFIF, JFI, JPG, JPEG
TYPE:	Bitmap
COLORS:	Up to 24-bit
COMPRESSION:	JPEG
MAXIMUM IMAGE SIZE:	64Kx64K pixels
NUMERICAL FORMAT:	Big-endian
MULTIPLE IMAGES PER FILE:	No
ORIGINATOR:	C-Cube Microsystems
PLATFORM:	All
SUPPORTING APPLICATIONS:	Too numerous to list
SPECIFICATION ON CD:	Yes
CODE ON CD:	Yes (in JPEG package)
IMAGES ON CD:	Yes
SEE ALSO:	Chapter 9, *Data Compression* (JPEG section)
USAGE:	Used primarily in graphics and image manipulation programs
COMMENTS:	One of the few formats incorporating JPEG compression and as such offers superior compression for deep-pixel images.

Overview

JPEG (Joint Photographic Experts Group) refers to a standards organization, a method of file compression, and sometimes a file format. In fact, the JPEG specification itself, which we describe in terms of compression in Chapter 9, *Data Compression*, does not itself define a common file interchange format to store and transport JPEG data between computer platforms and operating systems. The JPEG File Interchange Format (JFIF) is a development of C-Cube Microsystems for the purpose of storing JPEG-encoded data. JFIF is designed to allow files containing JPEG-encoded data streams to be exchanged between otherwise incompatible systems and applications.

A JFIF file is basically a JPEG data stream with a few restrictions and an identfying marker. In order to understand the JFIF format, you'll need to understand

JPEG; in addition to Chapter 9, see the JPEG FAQ (Frequently Asked Questions) document included on the CD-ROM and available on the Internet.

File Organization

Both JPEG and JFIF data are byte streams, always storing 16-bit word values in big-endian format. JPEG data in general is stored as a stream of blocks, and each block is identified by a marker value.

The first two bytes of every JPEG stream are the Start Of Image (SOI) marker values FFh D8h. In a JFIF-compliant file there is a JFIF APP0 (Application) marker, immediately following the SOI, which consists of the marker code values FFh E0h and the characters JFIF in the marker data, as described in the next section. In addition to the JFIF marker segment, there may be one or more optional JFIF extension marker segments, followed by the actual image data.

File Details

Although JFIF files do not possess a formally-defined header, the SOI and JFIF APP0 markers taken together act as a header in the following marker segment structure:

```
typedef struct _JFIFHeader
{
  BYTE SOI[2];         /* 00h  Start of Image Marker   */
  BYTE APP0[2];        /* 02h  Application Use Marker   */
  BYTE Length[2];      /* 04h  Length of APP0 Field     */
  BYTE Identifier[5];  /* 06h  "JFIF" (zero terminated) Id
                               String */
  BYTE Version[2];     /* 07h  JFIF Format Revision     */
  BYTE Units;          /* 09h  Units used for Resolution */
  BYTE Xdensity[2];    /* 0Ah  Horizontal Resolution    */
  BYTE Ydensity[2];    /* 0Ch  Vertical Resolution      */
  BYTE XThumbnail;     /* 0Eh  Horizontal Pixel Count   */
  BYTE YThumbnail;     /* 0Fh  Vertical Pixel Count     */

} JFIFHEAD;
```

SOI is the start of image marker and always contains the marker code values FFh D8h.

APP0 is the Application marker and always contains the marker code values FFh E0h.

Length is the size of the JFIF (APP0) marker segment, including the size of the Length field itself and any thumbnail data contained in the APP0 segment. Because of this, the value of Length equals 16 + 3 * XThumbnail * YThumbnail.

Identifier contains the values 4Ah 46h 49h 46h 00h (JFIF) and is used to identify the code stream as conforming to the JFIF specification.

Version identifies the version of the JFIF specification, with the first byte containing the major revision number and the second byte containing the minor revision number. For version 1.02, the values of the Version field are 01h 02h; older files contain 01h 00h or 01h 01h.

Units, Xdensity, and Ydensity identify the unit of measurement used to describe the image resolution. Units may be 01h for dots per inch, 02h for dots per centimeter, or 00h for none (use measurement as pixel aspect ratio). Xdensity and Ydensity are the horizontal and vertical resolution of the image data, respectively. If the Units field value is 00h, the Xdensity and Ydensity fields will contain the pixel aspect ratio (Xdensity : Ydensity) rather than the image resolution. Because non-square pixels are discouraged for portability reasons, the Xdensity and Ydensity values normally equal 1 when the Units value is 0.

XThumbnail and YThumbnail give the dimensions of the thumbnail image included in the JFIF APP0 marker. If no thumbnail image is included in the marker, then these fields contain 0. A thumbnail image is a smaller representation of the image stored in the main JPEG data stream (some people call it an icon or preview image). The thumbnail data itself consists of an array of XThumbnail * YThumbnail pixel values, where each pixel value occupies three bytes and contains a 24-bit RGB value (stored in the order R,G,B). No compression is performed on the thumbnail image.

Storing a thumbnail image in the JFIF APP0 marker is now discouraged, though it is still supported for backward compatibility. Version 1.02 of JFIF defines extension markers that allow thumbnail images to be stored separately from the identification marker. This method is more flexible, because multiple thumbnail formats are permitted and because multiple thumbnail images of different sizes could be included in a file. Version 1.02 allows color-mapped thumbnails (one byte per pixel plus a 256-entry colormap) and JPEG-compressed thumbnails, in addition to the 24-bit RGB thumbnail format. In any case, a thumbnail image is limited to less than 64K bytes because it must fit in an APP0 marker.

Following the JFIF marker segment, there may be one or more optional JFIF extension marker segments. Extension segments are used to store additional information and are found only in JFIF version 1.02 and later. The structure of these extension segments is shown below:

```
typedef struct _JFIFExtension
{
BYTE    APP0[2];          /* 00h  Application Use Marker */
BYTE    Length[2];        /* 02h  Length of APP0 Field   */
BYTE    Identifier[5];    /* 04h  "JFXX" (zero terminated) Id String */
BYTE    ExtensionCode;    /* 09h  Extension ID Code       */

} JFIFEXTENSION;
```

APP0 contains the values FFh E0h.

Length stores the length in bytes of the extension segment.

Identifier contains the values 4Ah 46h 58h 58h 00h (JFXX).

ExtensionCode indicates the type of information this extension marker stores. For version 1.02, the only extension codes defined are 10h (thumbnail encoded using JPEG), 11h (thumbnail stored using 1-byte pixels and a palette) and 13h (thumbnail stored using 3-byte RGB pixels).

The extension data follows the extension segment information and varies in size and content depending upon the ExtensionCode value. (Refer to the current JFIF specification for the possible formats of the extension marker segment.)

JFIF decoders must be prepared to ignore unrecognized extension markers and APPn segments. Application-specific APPn markers not recognized by a JPEG decoder can be simply skipped over by using the data length field of the marker.

The JFIF marker is essentially a guarantee that the file conforms to the JFIF conventions. Most JFIF decoders therefore regard the JFIF marker segment as optional, and are quite capable of reading a raw JPEG data stream that complies with the JFIF conventions regarding color space and sample alignment. (There are many such files out there, because JFIF merely formalized common practice in these areas.) A robust decoder will treat a JFIF file as a stream of blocks, with no assumptions about block order beyond those mandated by the JPEG standard. This makes it possible to read many non-standard and incorrect JFIF file variations, such as a COM marker inserted between the SOI and JFIF APP0 markers (there are a fair number of these in existence too). We also recommend that a decoder should accept any JFIF file with a known major version number, even if the minor version number is newer than those known to the decoder.

The actual JPEG data in a JFIF file follows all APP0 markers and adheres to the format defined in the JPEG documentation. The baseline JPEG process is the recommended type of image data encoding to be used in JFIF files. This is to ensure maximum compatibility of JFIF files for data interchange.

To identify a JFIF file or data stream, scan for the values FFh D8h FFh. This will identify the SOI marker, followed by another marker. In a proper JFIF file, the next byte will be E0h, indicating a JFIF APP0 marker segment. However, it is possible that one or more other marker segments may be erroneously written between the SOI and JFIF APP0 markers (a violation of the JFIF specification). As previously mentioned, a decoder should still attempt to read the file.

The next two bytes (the APP0 segment length) vary in value, but are typically 00h 10h, and these are followed by the five byte values 4Ah 46h 49h 46h 00h (JFIF). If these values are found, the SOI marker (FFh D8h) marks the beginning of a JFIF data stream. If only the FFh D8h FFh values are found, but not the remaining data, then a "raw" JPEG data stream has been found. All JFIF and JPEG data streams end with the End Of Image (EOI) marker values FFh D9h.

There are many proprietary image file formats which contain JPEG data. Many simply encapsulate a JPEG or JFIF data stream within their own file format wrapper. Scanning for the JPEG SOI marker and reading until the EOI marker is encountered will usually allow you to extract the JPEG/JFIF data stream. At least one proprietary image file format, the .HSI format by Handmade Software, contains JPEG data, but cannot be successfully read or uncompressed without using special software, due to proprietary modifications of the JPEG encoding process. (All .HSI files begin with the values 68h 73h 69h 31h and should not be considered normal JPEG files.)

Only two non-proprietary formats, other than JFIF, currently support JPEG-encoded data. The latest version of the Macintosh PICT format prepends a PICT header to a JFIF file stream. Strip off the PICT header (everything before the SOI marker) and any trailing data (everything after the EOI marker) and you have the equivalent of a JFIF file. The other format, TIFF 6.0, also supports JPEG and is discussed in depth in the article on TIFF.

For Further Information

For further information about the JFIF file format, see the specification included on the CD-ROM that accompanies this book. You may also contact C-Cube Microsystems at:

C-Cube Microsystems
Attn: Scott St. Clair
Corporate Communications
1778 McCarthy Blvd.
Milpitas, CA 95035
Voice: 408-944-6300
FAX: 408-944-6314

See also Chapter 9, *Data Compression*, for information about JPEG compression. The JPEG FAQ, also included on the CD-ROM, contains background information about JPEG.

The JPEG standard itself is not available electronically; you must order a paper copy through ISO. In the United States, copies of the standard may be ordered from:

American National Standards Institute, Inc.
Attn: Sales
1430 Broadway
New York, NY 10018
Voice: 212-642-4900

The standard is divided into two parts; Part 1 is the actual specification, and Part 2 covers compliance-testing methods. Part 1 of the draft has now reached International Standard status. See this document:

Digital Compression and Coding of Continuous-tone Still Images, Part 1: Requirements and Guidelines. Document number ISO/IEC IS 10918-1.

Part 2 is still at Committee Draft status. See this document:

Digital Compression and Coding of Continuous-tone Still Images, Part 2: Compliance Testing. Document number ISO/IEC CD 10918-2.

See the discussion of JPEG in Chapter 9 for a list of additional references, including commercially available books that contain the JPEG specification and the JPEG FAQ (Frequently Asked Questions). That chapter and Appendix

A, *What's On the CD-ROM*, also describe how to obtain JPEG code used to read and write JFIF files from the Independent JPEG Group (IJG) from the CD-ROM and from many FTP sites, information services, and computer bulletin boards.

Kodak Photo CD

NAME:	Kodak Photo CD
ALSO KNOWN AS:	Photo CD
TYPE:	Bitmap
COLORS:	24-bit
COMPRESSION:	Proprietary
MAXIMUM IMAGE SIZE:	2048x3072
MULTIPLE IMAGES PER FILE:	No
NUMERICAL FORMAT:	NA
ORIGINATOR:	Eastman Kodak
PLATFORM:	All
SUPPORTING APPLICATIONS:	Photo CD Access, Shoebox, Photoshop, others
SPECIFICATION ON CD:	No
CODE ON CD:	No
IMAGES ON CD:	Yes
SEE ALSO:	None

USAGE: Static data storage of multi-resolution deep-pixel images.

COMMENTS: Kodak will not divulge information on the format that would enable developers to directly access the image data.

Overview

Photo CD is actually the name of a CD-ROM-based storage and retrieval system from Eastman Kodak. Most people in the development community use the name Photo CD to refer to the files associated with the system, however, and we will conform to this usage.

A Photo CD CD-ROM is intended for the storage of conventional film-based photographic images which have been converted to digital form, using a slide or flatbed scanner, for instance. This is apparently part of Kodak's strategy for the product: to serve as an adjunct to their conventional film business. There are no technical restrictions on the source of the data, however.

Unfortunately, we cannot describe the Kodak Photo CD format in any detail because Kodak will not divulge the details of the format, and, in fact, has threatened legal action to those who would seek to reverse-engineer the product. This decision on the part of Kodak has enraged members of the development community who have an interest in the future of imaging technology. Cooler heads see Photo CD as a transitional technology. Our own opinion is that a large company with a sufficient presence in the market and a long-term view could have used a system like Photo CD as a way of capturing a major share of the disc-based multimedia market. However, Kodak seems to have taken the more conservative course of protecting their traditional film-based business.

Kodak does, however, sell a shrink-wrapped Photo CD development kit for a reasonable fee, which provides an API of sufficient richness for almost any developer need. At the time of this writing, there are Microsoft Windows, Macintosh, and UNIX versions of the toolkit available. Obviously, developers on other platforms are out of luck, unless Kodak sees fit to accommodate their needs. Toolkits are closely coupled to the platform supported.

As a result of the situation we have described, we are obviously able in this article to provide only information about the Photo CD system and format that is publicly available from Kodak.

File Organization

In the Kodak Photo CD environment, groups of images and associated information written at one time is called a session. The original Photo CD specification called for hardware that supported a single session per disc. Later versions of the Photo CD system allow multiple sessions per disc, which requires special hardware, firmware revisions, or a combination of both to read. As a consequence of this, many older CD-ROM drives will not read multi-session Photo CD discs, so you might make sure that yours does before you get involved with the Photo CD system.

Taking advantage of the storage capacity of CD-ROMs (more than 600 megabytes), images are stored on disc at multiple resolutions, in an arrangement called pyramid encoding. This accomplishes the same thing as the common strategy of storing a "postage stamp," or reduced version of the main image in the same file, albeit carried to a logical extreme. At the time of this writing, six resolutions are normally stored for each image:

Base Over 64	64x96
Base Over 16	128x192
Base Over 4	256x384

Base   512x768
Base Times 4   1024x1536
Base Times 16   2048x3072

Another version of the Photo CD product, called Photo CD PRO, may contain higher resolutions, including:

Base Times 16   2048x3072

Multiple versions of the image are grouped into a file that Kodak calls an Image Pac. A copy of at least one of the two lowest-resolution versions of the image in the Image Pac in the current sessions is stored in another file called the Overview Pac. These are used for the display of postage stamp images, which might be used by an application for quick display of the images in the Image Pac, for selection purposes, perhaps.

File Details

In the Kodak Photo CD format, Image data is compressed using a proprietary algorithm. Data is stored in what Kodak calls PhotoYCC format. The developer toolkit delivers color in several formats, depending on the platform. These include 256-level gray-scale and various palette-based formats, in addition to 24-bit YCC and RGB.

In the 24-bit YCC format, 24 bits of data per pixel are distributed among three color components, called Y (luminance information), C1, and C2 (two chrominance channels). Each channel occupies eight bits of data. Although the YCC format has some advantages, most developers choose RGB as the preferred model in which they want the toolkit to deliver the image data.

For Further Information

More details about the Photo CD format are available in descriptive documentation from Kodak marketing sources and in the Kodak Photo CD Access Developer Toolkit for your platform, which contains the following:

- A disc full of sample images

- The Access Developer Toolkit Programmer's Guide

- A disk containing the library and associated files needed to compile your application, including a sample application with source code included

For information about obtaining these, contact:

Eastman Kodak Corporation
343 State Street
Rochester, NY 14650
Voice: 800-242-2424

As mentioned above, Kodak has threatened legal action against developers who have tried to make details of the Photo CD format public, although the organization has not been completely successful in suppressing information. Source code has been posted to the Internet that will convert Photo CD files to PBM format (used by the pbmplus utilities described in Appendix A, *What's On the CD-ROM?*) and presumably remains available at many sites. As a consequence of this posting of information and source code, you may run across an application which reads and manipulates Photo CD format files, but which may not be properly licensed from Kodak. Always check to see if the application vendor is properly licensed.

Kodak YCC

NAME:	Kodak YCC
ALSO KNOWN AS:	YCC, ICC
TYPE:	Bitmap
COLORS:	8-bit, 24-bit
COMPRESSION:	Uncompressed
MAXIMUM IMAGE SIZE:	NA
MULTIPLE IMAGES PER FILE:	No
NUMERICAL FORMAT:	Big-endian
ORIGINATOR:	Eastman Kodak
PLATFORM:	All
SUPPORTING APPLICATIONS:	Unknown
SPECIFICATION ON CD:	Yes (summary description by third party)
CODE ON CD:	Yes
IMAGES ON CD:	No
SEE ALSO:	Kodak Photo CD

USAGE: Unknown

COMMENTS: Included because YCC files had some currency in high-end graphics and because of its relevance to the Photo CD format.

Overview

We have been unable to find information on the origin of what has come to be called the Kodak YCC format. Obviously, it originated at Eastman Kodak, in one of the company's graphics-related divisions, but whether it is a "real" format or just a printer dump format, we are unable to tell. We have included it because we have been able to obtain some information on the format and because it may be of interest to people involved with Photo CD or 24-bit color applications in general.

The Kodak YCC format provides data in a format compatible with Kodak's XL7700 printer, which produces truecolor and gray-scale output.

File Organization

A Kodak YCC file consists of a header followed by bitmap data. The bitmap data is organized into three planes in the order red, green, and blue.

File Details

The Kodak YCC has the following structure:

```
LONG Magic;          /* Magic number = 5965600 */
LONG HSize;          /* Header Size, in bytes */
CHAR Un01[n];        /* Unused (n = Header Size - 4 bytes) */
LONG HSize;          /* File header length */
LONG FSize;          /* File size */
CHAR FName[16]       /* Filename */
LONG FType;          /* File Type (= 7) */
CHAR Un02[8];        /* Unused */
LONG XSize;          /* Image X size */
LONG YSize;          /* Image Y size */
CHAR Un03[12];       /* Unused */
LONG Planes;         /* Number of image planes (usually 1 or 3) */
CHAR Un04[8];        /* Unused */
```

Following the header is the image data. If the image is composed of gray-scale data, one plane of 8-bit gray-scale data is present. If the image is truecolor, then there are three planes in the sequence red, green, blue. Each plane consists of 8-bit data. If the data is to be interpreted otherwise, for example, as Y,C,C (luminance followed by two chrominance channels), each channel is eight bits in length, but the rendering application must interpret the data according to the appropriate color model.

For Further Information

For further information about the Kodak YCC format, see the summary description (a newsgroup posting) included on the CD-ROM that accompanies this book. We have tried unsuccessfully to obtain information from Kodak about this format, so we don't believe you will be able to get any help from them.

Lotus DIF

NAME:	Lotus DIF
ALSO KNOWN AS:	DIF, Data Interchange Format
TYPE:	Vector
COLORS:	NA
COMPRESSION:	None
MAXIMUM IMAGE SIZE:	Unknown
MULTIPLE IMAGES PER FILE:	No
NUMERICAL FORMAT:	NA
ORIGINATOR:	Software Arts
PLATFORM:	MS-DOS
SUPPORTING APPLICATIONS:	Spreadsheets, others
SPECIFICATION ON CD:	No
CODE ON CD:	No
IMAGES ON CD:	No
SEE ALSO:	Microsoft SYLK

USAGE: Exchange of numerical data often associated with spreadsheets

COMMENTS: Not usually considered a graphics format, but is often a carrier of graphics data. Big- and little-endian issues are moot because data is stored as 7-bit ASCII.

Overview

The Lotus DIF (Data Interchange Format) is used for the storage and exchange of numeric data between applications such as spreadsheets. Although DIF is not usually considered a graphics file format, it is vector-based and often carries information used to generate both bitmap and vector images.

DIF was developed by Software Arts and originally appeared along with the VisiCalc spreadsheet program, which was first released in 1979. Because most spreadsheet applications have their own native file format for storing information, it is usually not possible for a single application to support every other format. DIF has become one of the commonly used interchange formats, perhaps because it has been around so long.

Logically, a spreadsheet is a two-dimensional matrix of storage cells, each of which contains numeric and text data, and formulas. Stored along with the data item in each cell is a unique identifier, usually the coordinates of the cell itself. Creating a file format from spreadsheet data in memory is often merely a matter of writing out each cell in some predefined order. Spreadsheet files also may contain information relevant only to the originating application, which is normally ignored by an application seeking to extract the data for other uses.

Popular software applications that support DIF include Lotus 1-2-3 and Borland's Quattro Pro. DIF files contain only 7-bit ASCII characters and therefore can be edited using a simple text editor. DIF is also independent of any hardware issues.

For Further Information

For further information about the Lotus DIF file format, you might try contacting Lotus at:

> Lotus Development Corporation
> 55 Cambridge Parkway
> Cambridge, MA 02142
> Voice: 617-577-8500
> Voice: 800-831-9679
> FAX: 617-225-1197

The following publications also contain information about DIF:

> Beil, Donald H., *The DIF File*, Reston Publishing Co., Reston, VA, 1983.

> Walden, Jeffrey B., *File Formats for Popular PC Software*, John Wiley & Sons, New York, NY, 1986.

Lotus PIC

NAME:	Lotus PIC
ALIAS:	Lotus Picture, PIC
TYPE:	Vector
COLORS:	6
COMPRESSION:	NA
MAXIMUM IMAGE SIZE:	Apparently 64Kx64K
MULTIPLE IMAGES PER FILE:	No
NUMERICAL FORMAT:	NA
ORIGINATOR:	Lotus Development
PLATFORM:	MS-DOS
SUPPORTING APPLICATIONS:	Lotus 1-2-3 and competing programs, word-processing and desktop-publishing applications, others
SPECIFICATION ON CD:	No
CODE ON CD:	No
IMAGES ON CD:	No
SEE ALSO:	Microsoft SYLK

USAGE: Used by the graphing program associated with Lotus 1-2-3

COMMENTS: A widely used format for interchange of data, primarily business graphics. Somewhat dated. Big-endian in format, although originating under MS-DOS on Intel-based machines.

Overview

Lotus PIC appeared in support of early versions of Lotus 1-2-3; files in PIC format were generated by the main application for use by an auxiliary program called Lotus Print Graph. Although recent versions of the application still support PIC, they have started using the Computer Graphics Metafile (CGM) as well, and we can safely assume that the days of PIC are numbered. Nevertheless, a great deal of data still exists in PIC format.

File Organization and Details

The file is very simple and consists of a header, vector data, and an end-of-file indicator. The header appears to be arbitrary and contains the following hex string:

```
01 00 00 00 01 00 08 00 44 00 00 00 0C 7F 09 06
```

Following the header is a list of encoded drawing commands, stored either as byte pairs or as 16-bit values. Either form may be followed by arguments. Commands are recognized by reading data either one byte at a time, assembling 16 bits of data in memory, or reading data 16 bits at a time and examining the first byte of each item. Coordinate values are always stored as 16-bit signed integers. Although positional data can theoretically be in the range -32,767 to 32,767, Lotus Print Graph always scales data to fit into the rectangle 0, 0, 3200, 2311.

Drawing commands supported by PIC are listed below:

BN	color	N is an 8-bit color value
A0 *XX YY*	move	Move drawing cursor to XX,YY
A2 *XX YY*	draw	Draw to XX,YY, update cursor
30 *N-1 X1 Y1 ... XN YN*	fill	Filled polygon of N vertices
D0 *N-1 X1 Y1 ... XN YN*	fill outlined	Filled polygon with outline
AC *XX YY*	text size	XX and YY are char cell size
A7 *N*	font	Set font: type 0 or 1 only
A8 *N STRING*	text	Draw NULL-terminated text string STRING, N contains direction and alignment information:

00	horizontal
10	vertical up
20	upside down
30	vertical down
00	center aligned
01	left center aligned
02	top center aligned
03	right center aligned
04	bottom center aligned
05	top left aligned
06	top right aligned

		07 bottom left aligned
		08 bottom right aligned
60-6F	end	End of image

The following example draws a line from 0,0 to 100,100 and draws the string "text" with characters fitting into an 8 by 10 cell:

```
A0 00 00 00 00 A2 00 64 00 64 AC 00 08 00 0A A8 00 74 65 78 74 60
```

For Further Information

Lotus no longer supports PIC, so it is difficult to get information about it. You might try contacting Lotus at:

Lotus Development Corporation
55 Cambridge Parkway
Cambridge, MA 02142
Voice: 617-577-8500
Voice: 800-831-9679
FAX: 617-225-1197

The following book, available in bookstores or from Lotus, provides additional information about Lotus PIC:

Lotus Development Corporation, *Lotus File Formats for 1-2-3, Symphony, & Jazz,* Lotus Books, Cambridge, MA, 1986.

NAME:	Lumena Paint
ALSO KNOWN AS:	.PIX, .BPX
TYPE:	Bitmap
COLORS:	24-bit maximum
COMPRESSION:	RLE, uncompressed
MAXIMUM IMAGE SIZE:	Unlimited
MAXIMUM IMAGE SIZE:	Unlimited
NUMERICAL FORMAT:	Little-endian
ORIGINATOR:	Time Arts Inc.
PLATFORM:	MS-DOS
SUPPORTING APPLICATIONS:	Lumena, others
SPECIFICATION ON CD:	Yes
CODE ON CD:	No
IMAGES ON CD:	No
SEE ALSO:	TGA

USAGE: Used mainly in conjunction with Time Arts programs, particularly Lumena Paint.

COMMENTS: This format is used frequently by production houses for data interchange.

Overview

Lumena Paint is a 24-bit paint program for the PC that uses the TGA, TIFF, and EPS file formats to import and export images. Lumena also uses its own native bitmap formats, which often have the extension .PIX (Time Arts Picture Format) and .BPX (Time Arts Big Picture Format), and which are also referred to as the Lumena 16 and Lumena 32 formats, respectively.

Lumena sold into what was known as the Targa market, centered around compatibility with truecolor display adapters for the PC sold by Truevision and its competitors. This was a small niche market in the PC world, and at its peak consisted of about 50,000 sites. Increased interest in truecolor on PCs led Hercules to introduce a relatively inexpensive display adapter (Hercules Graphics Station) supporting 24-bit color, and as part of its marketing effort Hercules entered into an OEM arrangement with Time Arts to bundle Lumena with the boards.

File Organization

Besides the depth of the pixel data, the main difference between the Lumena 16 and the Lumena 32 formats is in the header. Both formats have the same file header. In the Lumena 16 format, four of the header fields associated with pixel values are two bytes in size, while the same fields are four bytes in size for the Lumena 32 format. Lumena 16 files may also contain a postage stamp image, while Lumena 32 files may not.

Following the common file header may be a descriptor header; this header is different for the two formats. Lumena 16 files have a PIX header, whereas Lumena 32 files have a BPX header.

File Details

Each pixel value in the Lumena 16 image is two bytes in size (five bits each of red, green, and blue, and one overlay bit), and each pixel value in a Lumena 32 file is 32 bits (eight bits each of red, green, blue, and alpha channel). Both the alpha channel and the overlay bits occupy the most significant bits of each pixel value. Image data always follows the postage stamp data, or a feature called the descriptor header, if no postage stamp image is present in the file.

The largest size of a typical Lumena 16 image is 512x482 pixels. Larger images are stored using the Lumena 32 format and at a size that is an exact multiple of the display resolution (for example 1024x768x32 bits).

Both Lumena file types start with the same file header:

```
typedef struct _LumenaHeader
{
    BYTE  DescriptorSize;       /* Size of Image Descriptor   */
    BYTE  IsImageStamp;         /* Image Stamp Present   */
    BYTE  FileType;             /* File Encoding Type   */
    WORD  StampWidth;           /* Stamp Width in Pixels   */
    WORD  StampHeight;          /* Stamp Length in Pixels   */
    BYTE  StampBPP;             /* Bits per Pixel in Stamp   */
    WORD  XOrigin;              /* X Origin of Image   */
    WORD  YOrigin;              /* Y Origin of Image   */
    WORD  ImageWidth;           /* Image Width in Pixels   */
    WORD  ImageHeight;          /* Image Height in Pixels   */
```

```
    BYTE   BitsPerPixel;      /* Number of Bits Per Pixel   */
    BYTE   AlphaMaskBPP;      /* Alpha Bits Per Pixel   */

  } LUMENAHEAD;
```

DescriptorSize is the size of the descriptor header in bytes. The descriptor header is a second header that may follow the file header and that differs in size between the two Lumena formats.

IsImageStamp field is set to 1h if there is a postage-stamp image included in the file, otherwise it is set to 0h. The postage-stamp image always follows the descriptor header.

A postage-stamp image is a smaller version of the primary image stored in the Lumena file. Postage stamps are used to preview the contents of an image file without taking the time to display the original image. Postage-stamp images may be very quickly displayed because of their small size. Typically, postage stamps are one-eight the height and width of the original image, with 64x64 pixels being a typical maximum size. A typical 512x482-pixel Lumena image would then contain a 64x60-pixel postage-stamp image. Although postage stamps are useful, not every Lumena image file will contain one. (See the article on the TGA format for information on ways to create postage-stamp images.)

FileType indicates the type of data compression algorithm used on the image data. A value of 02h indicates a standard file with uncompressed image data; the image data is arranged just as it is in the TGA Type 2 data format. A value of 0Ah indicates run-length encoded image data the same as found in TGA Type 10 image data. A value of 8Eh indicates an older style of data compression that is no longer used by applications supporting the Lumena image file formats.

StampWidth, StampHeight, and StampBPP all store information about the postage stamp image. Only Lumena 16 image files may contain postage-stamp images; Lumena 32 image files never contain these images. The StampWidth and StampHeight are in pixels, and the StampBPP field contains the number of bits per pixel in the postage-stamp data, including alpha channel bits, if any.

XOrigin and YOrigin are the starting coordinates of the image on the display with 0,0 being the lower-left corner of the screen.

ImageHeight and ImageWidth represent the size of the image in pixels.

BitsPerPixel contains the number of bits in each pixel of image data. This value is 16 for Lumena 16 images and 32 for Lumena 32 images and includes any alpha bits present in the pixel data.

AlphaMaskBPP contains the number of bits in each pixel used for alpha channel data. This value is 0 for Lumena 16 images and 8 for Lumena 32 images.

Lumena 16 files also have a PIX descriptor header in the following format:

```
typedef struct _Lumena16Descriptor
{
WORD   Identifier;      /* Descriptor Identifier   */
WORD   RedMask;         /* Mask for Red Bits    */
WORD   GreenMask;       /* Mask for Green Bits   */
WORD   BlueMask;        /* Mask for Blue Bits    */
WORD   XAspectRatio;    /* X Axis Image Aspect Ratio   */
WORD   YAspectRatio;    /* Y Axis Image Aspect Ratio   */
WORD   Background;      /* Background Color (Black = 0)   */
BYTE   Comment[40];     /* Text Comment    */

} LUM16DESCRP;
```

Lumena 32 files have a BPX descriptor header instead of a PIX header. The BPX descriptor header is identical to the PIX descriptor header except for four fields that are four bytes in size rather than two:

```
typedef struct _Lumena32Descriptor
{
WORD    Identifier;     /* Descriptor Identifier   */
DWORD   RedMask;        /* Mask for Red Bits    */
DWORD   GreenMask;      /* Mask for Green Bits   */
DWORD   BlueMask;       /* Mask for Blue Bits    */
WORD    XAspectRatio;   /* X Axis Image Aspect Ratio   */
WORD    YAspectRatio;   /* Y Axis Image Aspect Ratio   */
DWORD   Background;     /* Background Color (Black = 0)    */
BYTE    Comment[40];    /* Text Comment    */

} LUM32DESCRP;
```

Identifier always contains the value 8Eh and is used to identify the start of the descriptor header.

RedMask, GreenMask, and BlueMask contain the values used to mask and shift out the separate red, green, and blue values from the pixel data. The code to do so is shown below:

```
RedValue    = (PixelValue & RedMaskValue) >> (BitsPerPixel * 2);
GreenValue  = (PixelValue & GreenMaskValue) >> (BitsPerPixel * 1);
BlueValue   = (PixelValue & BlueMaskValue) >> (BitsPerPixel * 0);
```

XAspectRatio and YAspectRatio contain the horizontal and vertical aspect ratios of the image.

Background indicates the background color of the display not covered by the image. The default is 0 for black, and this value may be any valid screen color value.

Comment is a NULL-terminated string of ASCII characters. Images created using the Lumena Paint program typically contain the comment "Time Arts Lumena file."

For Further Information

For further information about the Lumena Paint format and application, see the specification included on the CD-ROM that accompanies this book. You may also contact:

Time Arts Inc.
Attn: Scott Gross
Vice-President, Engineering
1425 Corporate Center Parkway
Santa Rosa, CA 95407
Voice: 800-959-0509
FAX: 707-576-7731
BBS: 707-576-7352

You might also be able to obtain information about Lumena from Hercules Computer, which bundles Lumena Paint with its PCs and graphics boards. Contact:

Hercules Computer Inc.
Attn: Lumena/Hercules Art Department
921 Parker Street
Berkeley, CA 94710
Voice: 510-540-6000
Voice: 800-532-0600
FAX: 510-540-6621
BBS: 510-540-0621

Macintosh Paint

NAME:	Macintosh Paint
ALSO KNOWN AS:	PNTG, MAC, MacPaint
TYPE:	Bitmap
COLORS:	Mono
COMPRESSION:	RLE, uncompressed
MAXIMUM IMAGE SIZE:	576x720 pixels
MULTIPLE IMAGES PER FILE:	No
NUMERICAL FORMAT:	Big-endian
ORIGINATOR:	Apple Computer Inc.
PLATFORM:	Macintosh
SUPPORTING APPLICATIONS:	Too numerous to list
SPECIFICATION ON CD:	No
CODE ON CD:	Yes, (in FBM, pbmplus, Xli, and xloadimage packages)
IMAGES ON CD:	Yes
SEE ALSO:	Macintosh PICT
USAGE:	Clip art, screen dumps, monochrome artwork
COMMENTS:	A well-defined, well-documented format in use on the Macintosh platform. MacPaint is quick and easy to read and decompress, but it lacks support for more than monochrome images. Numbers in the file are stored in big-endian format.

Overview

Macintosh Paint (MacPaint) is the original and most common graphics file format used on the Apple Macintosh. Most Macintosh applications that use graphics are able to read and write the MacPaint format. MacPaint files on the Macintosh have the file type PNTG, while on the PC they usually have the extension .MAC. The first real image files widely available to PC users were MacPaint files. PC users usually obtained them from BBSs or shareware disks, and a number of programs exist that allow MacPaint files to be displayed and printed using a PC under MS-DOS. Today, extensive black-and-white clip art and graphics are available in the MacPaint format. MacPaint files are also used to store line drawings, text, and scanned images.

MacPaint images are always black and white and are a fixed size (576 pixels wide by 720 scan lines high) and fixed resolution (75 dpi). Uncompressed, the image data is always 51,840 bytes in size. Because the Apple Macintosh is based on the Motorola 68000 series of CPUs, most files are stored in big-endian format, and MacPaint files are no exception. They are always read and written in big-endian format, no matter what the host platform. The ENDIANIO library can be used to read and write MacPaint files on non-big-endian systems.

Files are stored differently on the Macintosh than they are on most other systems in common use. Every Macintosh file consists of two parts, called forks. Although a user sees only a single file, data is actually stored as two physical files on disk. The first file is called the data fork, which stores program information. The second file is called the resource fork, and it stores program code. Data associated with a MacPaint file occupies only the data fork of the file pair; its companion resource fork is always empty.

Outside the Macintosh environment a MacPaint file is stored as a single file, with the two forks combined into one file, allowing it to reside on foreign file systems not adhering to the Macintosh conventions. A MacBinary header is prepended to the file. The MacBinary header is a structure which allows a Macintosh file to be copied or otherwise transported between a Macintosh and another system, and which contains the information required to reconstruct the two forks when the file is returned to the Macintosh environment. It is necessary to preserve the MacBinary header only if the file will one day be returned to a Macintosh environment; otherwise, it can be stripped from the file.

There are actually two MacBinary standards, the original MacBinary and MacBinary II. Both standards have a header that is 128 bytes in length. The MacBinary II header contains additional information not found in the original MacBinary header.

File Organization

The structure of a MacBinary II header is shown below:

```
typedef struct _MacBinaryIIHeader
{
BYTE    Version;             /* Always set to 0    */
BYTE    FileNameLength;      /* Size of file name (0 to 31)    */
BYTE    FileName[63];        /* File name    */
DWORD   FileType;            /* Type of macintosh mile    */
DWORD   FileCreator;         /* ID of program that created file    */
```

```
    BYTE    FileFlags;              /* File attribute flags    */
    BYTE    Reserved1;              /* Reserved field    */
    WORD    FileVertPos;            /* File vertical position in window */
    WORD    FileHorzPos;            /* File horizontal position in
                                       window  */
    WORD    WindowId;               /* Window or folder ID    */
    BYTE    Protected;              /* File protection (1 = protected) */
    BYTE    Reserved2;              /* Reserved field    */
    DWORD   SizeOfDataFork;         /* Size of file data fork in bytes   */
    DWORD   SizeOfResourceFork;     /* Size of file resource fork in
                                       bytes  */
    DWORD   CreationStamp;          /* Time and date file created    */
    DWORD   ModificationStamp;      /* Time and date file last modified */
    WORD    GetInfoLength;          /* GetInfo message length    */

    /* The following fields were added for MacBinary II */

    WORD    FinderFlags;            /* Finder flags    */
    BYTE    Reserved3[14];          /* Reserved field    */
    DWORD   UnpackedLength;         /* Total unpacked file length    */
    WORD    SecondHeadLength;       /* Length of secondary header    */
    BYTE    UploadVersion;          /* MacBinary version used with
                                       uploader */
    BYTE    ReadVersion;            /* MacBinary version needed to read */
    WORD    CrcValue;               /* CRC value of previous 124 bytes */
    BYTE    Reserved4[2];           /* Reserved field    */

} MACBIN2HEAD;
```

Before extracting the image data from a MacPaint file in a non-Macintosh environment, you must determine if a MacBinary header is prepended. This is best done by reading the bytes at offsets 101 through 125 and checking to see if they are all zero. The byte at offset 2 should be in the range of 1 to 63, and the DWORDs at offsets 83 and 87 should be in the range of 0 to 007FFFFFh. If all of these checks are true, then a MacBinary header is present.

It is not necessary for a non-Macintosh application to modify the MacBinary header unless the image data is changed or the MacPaint file has been created outside of the Macintosh environment with the intent of one day being returned to the Mac. However, it is good general practice to assume that your image file will one day return to the originator platform. Because any application reading a MacPaint file must be prepared to decode the MacBinary header anyway, there is no good reason for omitting it or for failing to update its fields when the file is changed.

File Details

Version, the first byte of a MacBinary header, is always zero; MacPaint files with or without a MacBinary header, always start with a zero byte. In fact, if the first byte is not zero, do not treat the file as a MacPaint file.

FileNameLength stores the length of the Macintosh-format filename, which can be from 1 to 63.

FileName stores the actual filename, and only the first "FileNameLength" characters are significant. Note that the filename is not NULL-terminated. Because the Macintosh can accommodate longer filenames than are found on some systems, a certain amount of intelligence is needed when you copy MacPaint files to filesystems that cannot accommodate the full filename. UNIX and Macintosh programmers, in particular, should be wary of copying files to MS-DOS systems and are advised to keep the filenames limited to eight characters or less. Files destined only for UNIX systems should limit names to 14 or fewer characters.

FileType contains up to four ASCII characters indicating the type of file that is attached to the header. A MacPaint file has a type of PNTG; a PICT file (another Macintosh file type) has type PICT; a TIFF file has type TIFF; and so on.

FileCreator also contains a 4-character ASCII identifier that identifies the creator application. The creator identifier is MPNT for MacPaint files created by the MacPaint paint program, for instance.

FileFlags contains file attributes specific to the Macintosh environment; these are represented by the following bits in the field:

Bit 0	Inited
Bit 1	Changed
Bit 2	Busy
Bit 3	Bozo
Bit 4	System
Bit 5	Bundle
Bit 6	Invisible
Bit 7	Locked

FileVertPos and FileHorzPos contain the position of the file on the display screen.

The WindowID and Protected bit flags are specific to the Macintosh environment.

SizeOfDataFork is the size of the MacPaint file minus the size of the MacBinary header.

SizeOfResourceFork is always zero for MacPaint files.

CreationStamp and ModificationStamp contain the time and date the Mac-Paint file was first created and last modified, respectively. The stamp values are stored as the number of seconds since January 1, 1904.

GetInfoLength contains the length of the Get Info comment and is set to zero in MacPaint files.

The following fields were added by the MacBinary II standard:

FinderFlags contains the first eight bit flags of the Finder. Finder bit flags 8 through 15 are stored in the FileFlags field.

UnpackedLength is the uncompressed size of the file.

SecondHeadLength holds the length of any additional header following the MacBinary header; this value is for future expansion of the MacBinary header and is currently set to zero.

UploadVersion and ReadVersion contain version numbers of the programs required to transmit and read the MacBinary II header.

CrcValue contains a value that may be used to check the validity of the first 124 bytes of the header and needs to be recalculated if the header is changed. If this field is set to zero, ignore it.

There are four fields in the MacBinary II header marked as reserved. They are used for padding and as space for additional fields in future revisions of the MacBinary header. They should be set to zero, as should all unused fields in the header.

The MacBinary header is followed by four bytes of data (00h, 00h, 00h, 02h) signaling the start of the actual MacPaint file. Following these four bytes are 304 bytes of pattern data. This data is used and modified by paint programs such as MacPaint as pattern palette data and is not used for the reconstruction or display of MacPaint images themselves. There is always data for 38 patterns, and each pattern is eight bytes in length.

Following the pattern data are 204 bytes of zero-byte data used for padding. The MacPaint image data follows this padding and always starts at file offset 640 when a MacBinary header is present. Image data in a MacPaint file is always compressed using a simple byte-wise run-length encoding (RLE) scheme. Each scan line is always 72 bytes in length and there are always 720 scan lines per MacPaint image.

A byte is read and used as the run count. If the most significant bit is set to 1, the byte is converted to its two's-complement value, and the next byte is repeated RunCount times. If the most significant bit is zero, then one is added to the count and the next RunCount bytes are read. We can use the steps shown in the following pseudocode to decode a scan line:

```
Read a byte value
   If high bit is one
      Count is two's complement of byte (count = ~byte value)
      Read a byte
      Write this byte 'count' times
   If high bit is zero
      Count is byte value plus one (count = byte value + 1)
      Read and copy the next 'count' bytes
   If 72 bytes have been written, the scan line is done
```

Note that the Macintosh displays black characters on a white background, as opposed to the PC and other systems, which display white characters on a black background; for this reason, it may be necessary to flip the bit values of the image data to obtain the proper color orientation.

For Further Information

For further information about the Macintosh Paint format, see the code examples included on the CD-ROM that accompanies this book. You can also contact:

Apple Computer Inc.
20525 Mariani Avenue
Cupertino, CA 95104
Voice: 408-996-1010
Voice: 800-538-9696
Fax: 408-974-1725

Additional information on this format can be found in:

Apple Computer, *Inside Macintosh: Imaging*, Volumes I and V, Addison-Wesley, Reading, MA, 1985.

These volumes are also available on the Apple Developer CDs.

Additional references include:

"MacPaint Documents Format," *Macintosh Technical Note #86*, Apple Computer Developer Technical Support.

Birse, Cameron, Guillermo Ortiz, and Jon Zap. "Things You Wanted to Know About PackBits," *Macintosh Technical Note #71*, Apple Computer Developer Technical Support.

NAME:	Macintosh PICT
ALSO KNOWN AS:	PICT, Macintosh Picture, .PCT, QuickDraw Picture Format
TYPE:	Metafile
COLORS:	Up to 24-bit
COMPRESSION:	PackBits, JPEG
MAXIMUM IMAGE SIZE:	NA
MULTIPLE IMAGES PER FILE:	No
NUMERICAL FORMAT:	Big-endian
ORIGINATOR:	Apple Computer Inc.
PLATFORM:	Apple Macintosh
SUPPORTING APPLICATIONS:	Most Macintosh programs
SPECIFICATION ON CD:	Yes
CODE ON CD:	Yes
IMAGES ON CD:	Yes
SEE ALSO:	Macintosh Paint
USAGE:	Desktop publishing, paint, and imaging applications using QuickDraw calls
COMMENTS:	A versatile format in wide use on the Macintosh by applications having anything to do with graphics. Because of its complexity, however, it is seldom supported on other platforms.

Overview

The Macintosh PICT (Macintosh Picture) format is associated with applications on the Macintosh and is one of the best supported formats on that platform. PICT files are meant to encapsulate the functionality of QuickDraw, the native graphics drawing protocol on the Macintosh, and consist mainly of QuickDraw calls arranged in no particular order. There have been two major releases of QuickDraw, Version 1 and Version 2 (Color QuickDraw). There have also been numerous minor QuickDraw revisions, each associated with a corresponding Macintosh PICT version.

QuickDraw Version 1 supports monochrome bitmaps up to 32K in size. Image resolution is fixed at the original Macintosh display resolution, or 72 dpi.

QuickDraw Version 2, sometimes known as Color QuickDraw, supports 8-bit bitmaps as well as monochrome. There is no compression available for 8-bit Version 2.0 PICT files.

All information in Macintosh PICT files is stored in the data fork of the Macintosh file pair. Although the resource fork may be present, it is left empty. Image data is stored in binary format and consists of a series of operators and associated data.

High-level routines in the Macintosh ToolKit are available to read and write PICT files and are often used when writing applications that translate PICT files to other image file formats.

File Organization

All Macintosh PICT files start with a 512-byte header, which contains information that the Macintosh uses to keep track of the file. This is followed by three fields describing the image size, the image frame, and a version number. In Version 2 files, another header follows. In both versions, the preceding information is followed by the image data. In all versions, the end of the file is signalled by an end-of-file operator.

File Details

QuickDraw, and consequently the Macintosh PICT format, is far too complex for us to do justice to it here, so we will merely note some details of the start of the file. A good deal of information and codes are included on the CD-ROM. Note that most secondary references only give examples of bitmap encoding and ignore the vector nature of the format.

The information following the platform-specific 512-byte header is in the following format:

```
SHORT     File size in bytes
SHORT     Frame x-value of top left of image (at 72 dpi)
SHORT     Frame y-value of top left of image (at 72 dpi)
SHORT     Frame x-value of lower right of image (at 72 dpi)
SHORT     Frame y-value of lower right of image (at 72 dpi)
```

in Version 1 files, this is followed by:

```
BYTE      Version operator(0x11)
BYTE      Version number(0x01)
```

or, in Version 2 files, by:

```
SHORT      Version operator (0x0011)
SHORT      Version number (0x02ff)
```

Version 2 files also have a 26-byte header following the version information:

```
SHORT      Header opcode for Version 2 (0C00)
SHORT      FFEF or FFEE
SHORT      Reserved (0000)
LONG       Original horizontal resolution in pixels/inch
LONG       Original vertical resolution in pixels/inch
SHORT      Frame upper left x at original resolution
SHORT      Frame upper left y original resolution
SHORT      Frame lower right x at original resolution
SHORT      Frame lower right y at original resolution
LONG       Reserved
```

For Further Information

For further information about the Macintosh PICT format, see the documentation and sample code included on the CD-ROM that accompanies this book.

Additional information on the Macintosh PICT format may be obtained from Claris Corporation, a software spinoff from Apple, in the form of an update to Apple Technical Note #27. Apple Technical Notes may be obtained from Apple Computer and from many online information services. Contact:

Apple Computer Inc.
20525 Mariani Avenue
Cupertino, CA 95104
Voice: 408-996-1010
Voice: 800-538-9696
FAX: 408-974-1725

Claris Corporation
5201 Patrick Henry Drive
P.O. Box 58168
Santa Clara, CA 95052-8168
Technical Support: 408-727-9054
Customer Relations: 408-727-8227

Other Apple Technical Notes related to Macintosh PICT and other Apple formats include:

TN #021 *QuickDraw Picture Definitions*

TN #041 *Offscreen Bitmaps*

TN #091 *Optimizing of the LaserWriter—Picture Comments*

TN #119 *Color QuickDraw*

TN #120 *Offscreen PixMap*

TN #171 *Things You Wanted to Know About PackBits*

TN #181 *Every Picture (Comment) Tells Its Story, Don't It?*

TN #154 *Displaying Large PICT Files*

TN #275 *32-Bit Quickdraw Version 1.2 Features*

Addtional information on the PICT format can be found in:

Apple Computer, *Inside Macintosh*, Volumes I, V, and VI, Addison-Wesley, Reading, MA, 1985.

These volumes are also available on the Apple Developer CDs.

NAME:	Microsoft Paint
ALSO KNOWN AS:	MSP
TYPE:	Bitmap
COLORS:	Mono
COMPRESSION:	RLE, uncompressed
MAXIMUM IMAGE SIZE:	64Kx64K pixels
MULTIPLE IMAGES PER FILE:	No
NUMERICAL FORMAT:	Little-endian
ORIGINATOR:	Microsoft Corporation
PLATFORM:	Microsoft Windows, MS-DOS
SUPPORTING APPLICATIONS:	Microsoft Paint, others
SPECIFICATION ON CD:	No
CODE ON CD:	No
IMAGES ON CD:	Yes
SEE ALSO:	Microsoft Windows Bitmap
USAGE:	Black-and-white drawings, clip art
COMMENTS:	A format that was in wider use in the early days of Microsoft Windows. It is a simple format that is not currently suitable for deep pixel or truecolor images.

Overview

The Microsoft Paint (MSP) image file format is used exclusively for storing black-and-white images. The vast majority of MSP files contain line drawings and clip art. MSP is used most often by Microsoft Windows applications, but may be used by MS-DOS-based programs as well. The Microsoft Paint format is apparently being replaced by the more versatile Microsoft Windows BMP format; it contains information specifically for use in the Microsoft Windows operating environment. For information on the Windows-specific use of the header information, refer to the Microsoft Paint format specification available from Microsoft.

File Organization

The Microsoft Paint header is 32 bytes in length and has the following structure. In the discussion that follows, a WORD is a 16-bit unsigned value.

```
typedef struct _MicrosoftPaint
{
WORD  Key1;              /* Magic number    */
WORD  Key2;              /* Magic number    */
WORD  Width;             /* Width of the bitmap in pixels   */
WORD  Height;            /* Height of the bitmap in pixels   */
WORD  XARBitmap;         /* X Aspect ratio of the bitmap   */
WORD  YARBitmap;         /* Y Aspect ratio of the bitmap   */
WORD  XARPrinter;        /* X Aspect ratio of the printer   */
WORD  YARPrinter;        /* Y Aspect ratio of the printer   */
WORD  PrinterWidth;      /* Width of the printer in pixels   */
WORD  PrinterHeight;     /* Height of the printer in pixels   */
WORD  XAspectCorr;       /* X aspect correction (unused)    */
WORD  YAspectCorr;       /* Y aspect correction (unused)    */
WORD  Checksum;          /* Checksum of previous 24 bytes   */
WORD  Padding[3];        /* Unused padding    */

}MSPHEAD;
```

File Details

In the Microsoft Paint header, Key1 and Key2 contain identification values used to determine the version of the file format. For version 1.x of the Microsoft Paint format, the values of the Key1 and Key2 fields are 6144h and 4D6Eh respectively. For version 2.0, the Key1 and Key2 field values are 694Ch and 536Eh respectively.

Width and Height are the size of the bitmap in pixels. The size of the bitmap in bytes is calculated by dividing Width by 8 and multiplying it by Height.

XARBitmap and YARBitmap contain the aspect ratio in pixels of the screen used to create the bitmapped image.

XARPrinter and YARPrinter contain the aspect ratio in pixels of the output device used to render the bitmapped image. When an MSP file is created by a non-Windows application, these four fields typically contains the same values as the Width and Height fields.

PrinterWidth and PrinterHeight contain the size in pixels of the output device for which the image is specifically formatted. Typical values for these fields are the same values as those stored in Width and Height.

XAspectCorr and YAspectCorr are used to store aspect ratio correction information, but are not used in version 2.0 or earlier versions of the Microsoft Paint format and should be set to 0.

Checksum contains the XORed values of the first 12 WORDs of the header. When an MSP file is read, the first 13 WORDs, including the Checksum field, are XORed together, and if the resulting value is 0, the header information is considered valid.

Padding extends the header out to a full 32 bytes in length and is reserved for future use.

The image data directly follows the header. The format of this image data depends upon the version of the Microsoft Paint file. For image files prior to version 2.0, the image data immediately follows the header. There are eight pixels stored per byte, and the data is not encoded.

Each scan line in a version 2.0 or later Microsoft Paint bitmap is always RLE-encoded to reduce the size of the data. Each encoded scan line varies in size depending upon the bit patterns it contains. To aid in the decoding process, a scan-line map immediately follows the header. The scan-line map is used to seek to a specific scan line in the encoded image data without needing to decode all image data prior to it. There is one element in the map per scan line in the image. Each element in the scan-line map is 16 bits in size and contains the number of bytes used to encode the scan line it represents. The scan-line map starts at offset 32 in the MSP file and is sizeof(WORD).

Consider the following example. If an application needs to seek directly to the start of scan-line 20, it adds together the first 20 values in the scan-line map. This sum is the offset from the beginning of the image data of the 20th encoded scan line. The scan-line map values can also be used to double-check that the decoding process read the proper number of bytes for each scan line.

Following the scan-line map is the run-length encoded monochrome bitmapped data. A byte-wise run-length encoding scheme is used to compress the monochrome bitmapped data contained in an MSP-format image file. Each scan line is encoded as a series of packets containing runs of identical byte values. If there are very few runs of identical byte values, or if all the runs are very small, then a way to encode a literal run of different byte values may be used.

The following pseudocode illustrates the decoding process:

```
Read a BYTE value as the RunType
    If the RunType value is zero
        Read next byte as the RunCount
        Read the next byte as the RunValue
        Write the RunValue byte RunCount times
    If the RunType value is non-zero
        Use this value as the RunCount
        Read and write the next RunCount bytes literally
```

As you can see, this is yet another variation of a simple run-length encoding scheme. A byte is read, and if it contains a value of 0, then the following byte is the RunCount (the number of bytes in the run). The byte following the Run-Count is the RunValue (the value of the bytes in the run). If the byte read is non-zero, then the byte value is used as the RunCount and the next RunCount bytes are read literally from the encoded data stream.

For Further Information

For further information about Microsoft Paint, contact:

Microsoft Corporation
One Microsoft Way
Redmond, WA 98052-6399
Voice: 206-882-8080
Fax: 206-936-7329
BBS: 206-637-9009

The Microsoft Windows Programmer's Reference Library is the master reference for programmers working with all aspects of Microsoft Windows. The books in this library are supplied with the Microsoft Windows Software Development Kit (SDK). The manuals supplied with the Microsoft C 7.0 Professional Development Systems are also very helpful. You can get information about obtaining these products from:

Microsoft Information Center
Voice: 800-426-9400

You may also be able to get information via FTP through the Developer Relations Group at:

ftp.microsoft.com (in the */developer/drg* directory)

Microsoft RIFF

NAME:	Microsoft RIFF
ALSO KNOWN AS:	RIFF, Resource Interchange File Format, RIFX, .WAV, .AVI, .BND, .RMI, .RDI
TYPE:	Multimedia
COLORS:	24-bit
COMPRESSION:	RLE, uncompressed, audio, video
MAXIMUM IMAGE SIZE:	Varies
MULTIPLE IMAGES PER FILE:	No
NUMERICAL FORMAT:	Little- and big-endian
ORIGINATOR:	Microsoft Corporation
PLATFORM:	Microsoft Windows 3.x, Windows NT
SUPPORTING APPLICATIONS:	Microsoft Windows and OS/2 multimedia applications
SPECIFICATION ON CD:	Yes
CODE ON CD:	No
IMAGES ON CD:	No
SEE ALSO:	Interchange File Format, Chapter 10, *Multimedia*
USAGE:	RIFF is a device control interface and common file format native to the Microsoft Windows system. It is used to store audio, video, and graphics information used in multimedia applications.
COMMENTS:	A complex format designed to accommodate various types of data for multimedia applications. Because it is quite new and vendor-controlled, the specification is likely to change in the future.

Overview

Microsoft RIFF (Resource Interchange File Format) is a multimedia file format created by Microsoft for use with the Windows GUI. RIFF itself does not define any new methods of storing data, as many of the bitmap formats described in this book do. Instead, RIFF defines a structured framework, which may contain existing data formats. Using this concept, you can create new, composite formats consisting of two or more existing file formats.

Multimedia applications require the storage and management of a wide variety of data, including bitmaps, audio data, video data, and peripheral device control information. RIFF provides an excellent way to store all these varied types of data. The type of data a RIFF file contains is indicated by the file extension. Examples of data that may be stored in RIFF files are:

- Audio/visual interleaved data (.AVI)
- Waveform data (.WAV)
- Bitmapped data (.RDI)
- MIDI information (.RMI)
- A bundle of other RIFF files (.BND)

NOTE

At this point, AVI files are the only type of RIFF files that have been fully implemented using the current RIFF specification. Although WAV files have been implemented, these files are very simple, and their developers typically use an older specification in constructing them.

Because RIFF is an umbrella name for a variety of multimedia files, RIFF files are referred to by the type of data they contain, rather than by the actual format name of RIFF. For this reason, you may find RIFF files rather confusing when you start to use them. For example, a RIFF file containing Audio/Visual Interleaved data is normally referred to simply as an "AVI file" and not as a "RIFF Audio/Visual Interleaved Format File." Only a programmer might ever realize that all of these different files are the same format, or even care.

There is another area of potential confusion. Some people think that RIFF files are somehow similar in design to TIFF (Tag Image File Format) files. While it is true that both formats contain data structures that may be added or deleted to a file ("tags" in TIFF and "chunks" in RIFF), the internal concept and design of these structures within RIFF and TIFF differ greatly. Unlike TIFF, the RIFF file format is based on the Electronic Arts Interchange File Format (IFF) structure (see the article describing this format). And, although both formats use the same concept of data storage, they are not compatible in their design.

File Organization

RIFF is a binary file format containing multiple nested data structures. Each data structure within a RIFF file is called a *chunk*. Chunks do not have fixed positions within a RIFF file, and therefore standard offset values cannot be used to locate their fields. A chunk contains data such as a data structure, a data stream, or another chunk called a *subchunk*. Every RIFF chunk has the following basic structure:

```
typedef struct _Chunk
{
    DWORD ChunkId;                  /* Chunk ID marker */
    DWORD ChunkSize;                /* Size of the chunk data in bytes */
    BYTE ChunkData[ChunkSize];      /* The chunk data */

} CHUNK;
```

ChunkId contains four ASCII characters that identify the data the chunk contains. For example, the characters RIFF are used to identify chunks containing RIFF data. If an ID is smaller than four characters, it is padded on the right using spaces (ASCII 32). Note that RIFF files are written in little-endian byte order. Files written using the big-endian byte ordering scheme have the identifier RIFX.

ChunkSize is the length of the data stored in the ChunkData field, not including any padding added to the data. The size of the ChunkId and ChunkSize fields are not themselves included in this value.

ChunkData contains data that is WORD-aligned within the RIFF file. If the data is an odd length in size, an extra byte of NULL padding is added to the end of the data. The ChunkSize value does not include the length of the padding.

Subchunks also have the same structure as chunks. A subchunk is simply any chunk that is contained within another chunk. The only chunks that may contain subchunks are the RIFF file chunk RIFF and the list chunk, LIST (explained in the next section). All other chunks may contain only data.

A RIFF file itself is one entire RIFF chunk. All other chunks and subchunks in the file are contained within this chunk. If you are decoding, your RIFF reader should ignore any chunks that the reader does not recognize or it cannot use. If you are encoding, your RIFF writer will write out all unknown and unused chunks that were read. Do not discard them.

File Details

RIFF files that are used to store audio and video information are called AVI files. The RIFF AVI file format normally contains only a single AVI chunk; however, other types of chunks may also appear. An AVI reader should ignore all chunks it does not need or recognize that are stored within a RIFF AVI file.

Although Microsoft uses a standard notation to describe the internal arrangement of data structures within RIFF files, we believe it is clearer to use our own C-like syntax to illustrate the placement of chunks and subchunks within a RIFF AVI file. The ChunkId for each chunk is listed in the comments:

```
struct _RIFF    /* "RIFF" */
{
    struct _AVICHUNK    /* "AVI " */
    {
        struct _LISTHEADERCHUNK    /* "hdrl" */
        {
            AVIHEADER AviHeader;       /* "avih" */
            struct _LISTHEADERCHUNK    /* "strl" */
            {
                AVISTREAMHEADER    StreamHeader; /* "strh" */
                AVISTREAMFORMAT    StreamFormat; /* "strf" */
                AVISTREAMDATA      StreamData;   /* "strd" */
            }
        }
        struct _LISTMOVIECHUNK    /* "movi" */
        {
            struct _LISTRECORDCHUNK    /* "rec " */
            {
                /* Subchunk 1 */
                /* Subchunk 2 */
                /* Subchunk N */
            }
        }
        struct _AVIINDEXCHUNK    /* "idx1" */
        {
            /* Index data */
        }
    }
}
```

The above structure represents the internal data layout of a RIFF file containing only one AVI chunk. This chunk follows the format of the chunk data structure previously described. The AVI chunk is identified by the 4-character chunk identifier "AVI " (note the final blank character). The AVI chunk contains two mandatory LIST subchunks, which indicate the format of the data stream(s) stored in the file.

AVI Header Subchunk

The first mandatory LIST chunk contains the main AVI header subchunk and has the identifier hdrl. The information in the header subchunk defines the format of the entire AVI chunk. The hdrl chunk must appear as the first chunk within the AVI chunk. The format of the header subchunk is the following:

```
typedef struct _AVIHeader
{
    DWORD TimeBetweenFrames;       /* Time delay between frames */
    DWORD MaximumDataRate;         /* Data rate of AVI data */
    DWORD PaddingGranularity;      /* Size of single unit of padding */
    DWORD Flags;                   /* Data parameters */
    DWORD TotalNumberOfFrames;     /* Number of video frame stored */
    DWORD NumberOfInitialFrames;   /* Number of preview frames */
    DWORD NumberOfStreams;         /* Number of data streams in chunk*/
    DWORD SuggestedBufferSize;     /* Minimum playback buffer size */
    DWORD Width;                   /* Width of video frame in pixels */
    DWORD Height;                  /* Height of video frame in pixels*/
    DWORD TimeScale;               /* Unit used to measure time */
    DWORD DataRate;                /* Data rate of playback */
    DWORD StartTime;               /* Starting time of AVI data */
    DWORD DataLength;              /* Size of AVI data chunk */

} AVIHEADER;
```

TimeBetweenFrames contains a value indicating the amount of delay between frames in microseconds.

MaximumDataRate value indicates the data rate of the AVI data in bytes per second.

PaddingGranularity specifies the multiple size of padding used in the data in bytes. When used, the value of this field is typically 2048.

Flags contains parameter settings specific to the AVI file and its data. The parameters correspond to the bit values of the Flags field as follows:

Bit 4   AVI chunk contains an index subchunk (idx1).

Bit 5   Use the index data to determine how to read the AVI data, rather than the physical order of the chunks with the RIFF file.

Bit 8   AVI file is interleaved.

Bit 16   AVI file is optimized for live video capture.

Bit 17   AVI file contains copyrighted data.

TotalNumberOfFrames indicates the total number of frames of video data stored in the movi subchunk.

NumberOfInitialFrames specifies the number of frames in the file before the actual AVI data. For non-interleaved data this value is 0.

NumberOfStreams holds the number of data streams in the chunk. A file with an audio and video stream contains a value of 2 in this field, while an AVI file containing only video data has 1. In the current version of the RIFF format, one audio and one video stream are allowed.

SuggestedBufferSize is the minimum size of the buffer to allocate for playback of the AVI data. For non-interleaved AVI data, this value is at least the size of the largest chunk in the file. For interleaved AVI files, this value should be the size of an entire AVI record.

Width and Height values indicate the size of the video image in pixels.

TimeScale is the unit used to measure time in this chunk. It is used with DataRate to specify the time scale that the stream will use. For video streams, this value should be the frame rate and typically has a value of 30. For audio streams, this value is typically the audio sample rate.

DataRate is divided by the TimeScale value to calculate the number of samples per second.

StartTime is the starting time of the AVI data and is usually 0.

DataLength is the size of the AVI chunk in the units specified by the TimeScale value.

The hdrl subchunk also contains one or more LIST chunks with the identifier strl. There will be one of these LIST chunks per data stream stored in the AVI chunk.

Three subchunks are stored within the strl LIST chunk. The first is the Stream Header subchunk, which has the identifier strh. This header contains information specific to the data stream stored in the strl LIST chunk. A stream header is required and has the following format:

```
typedef struct _StreamHeader
{
        char  DataType[4];               /* Chunk identifier ("strl") */
        char  DataHandler[4];            /* Device handler identifier */
        DWORD Flags;                     /* Data parameters */
        DWORD Priority;                  /* Set to 0 */
        DWORD InitialFrames;             /* Number of initial audio frames */
        DWORD TimeScale;                 /* Unit used to measure time */
        DWORD DataRate;                  /* Data rate of playback */
        DWORD StartTime;                 /* Starting time of AVI data */
        DWORD DataLength;                /* Size of AVI data chunk */
        DWORD SuggestedBufferSize;       /* Minimum playback buffer size */
        DWORD Quality;                   /* Sample quailty factor */
        DWORD SampleSize;                /* Size of the sample in bytes */

} STREAMHEADER;
```

DataType contains a 4-character identifier indicating the type of data the stream header refers to. Identifiers supported by the current version of the RIFF format are: vids for video data and auds for audio data.

DataHandler may contain a 4-character identifier specifying the preferred type of device to handle the data stream.

Flags contains a set of bit flags use to indicate parameter settings related to the data.

Priority is set to 0.

InitialFrames indicates in seconds how far the audio is placed ahead of the video in interleaved data.

TimeScale, DataRate, StartTime, DataLength, and SuggestedBufferSize all have the same function as the fields of the same names in the hdr1 chunk.

Quality is an integer in the range of 0 to 10,000, indicating the quality factor used to encode the sample.

SampleSize is the size of a single sample of data. If this value is 0, the sample varies in size and each sample is stored in a separate subchunk. If this value is non-zero, then all the samples are the same size and are stored in a single sub-chunk.

Immediately following the stream header is a stream format subchunk with the identifier strf. This header describes the format of the stream data. Its format varies depending on the type of data that is stored (audio or video). This sub-chunk is also required.

Another stream data subchunk with the identifier strd can optionally follow the stream format subchunk. The data in this chunk is used to configure the drivers required to interpret the data. The format of this chunk also varies depending upon the type of compression used on the stream data.

AVI Data Subchunk

The second mandatory LIST chunk contains the actual AVI data, has the identifier movi, and must appear as the second chunk within the AVI chunk.

The data in the movi chunk may be grouped in the form of LIST records (a LIST chunk containing one or more subchunks each with the identifier "rec "). Only data that is interleaved to be read from a CD-ROM is stored as a series of LIST records (data is read more efficiently from a CD-ROM when it is interleaved). If the data is not interleaved, it is stored as a single block of data within the movi chunk itself.

Index Chunk

The AVI chunk may also contain a third chunk, called an index chunk. An index chunk has the identifier idx1 and must appear after the hdrl and movi chunks. This chunk contains a list of all chunks within the AVI chunk, along with their locations, and is used for random access of audio and video data. The index chunk has the following format:

```
typedef struct _AviIndex
{
    DWORD Identifier;      /* Chunk identifier reference */
    DWORD Flags;           /* Type of chunk referenced */
    DWORD Offset;          /* Position of chunk in file */
    DWORD Length;          /* Length of chunk in bytes */

} AVIINDEX;
```

Identifier contains the 4-byte identifier of the chunk it references (strh, strf, strd, and so on).

Flags bits are used to indicate the type of frame the chunk contains or to identify the index structure as pointing to a LIST chunk.

Offset indicates the start of the chunk in bytes relative to the movi list chunk.

Length is the size of the chunk in bytes.

The idx1 chunk contains one of these structures for every chunk and subchunk in the AVI chunk. The structures need not index each chunk in the order in which they occur within the AVI chunk. The order of the index structures in the idx1 may also be used to control the presentation order of the data stored in the AVI chunk. If an index is included in an AVI chunk, the appropriate indication bit must be set in the Flags field of the AVI header chunk. If an application reading a RIFF file decides to use the information in the index chunk, it must first find the hdrl chunk and determine if an index chunk exists by examining the Flags field value in the AVI header. If it does exist, the reader will skip past all the chunks in the AVI chunk until it encounters the idx1 chunk.

JUNK Chunk

One other type of chunk that is commonly encountered in an AVI chunk is the padding or JUNK chunk (so named because its chunk identifier is JUNK). This chunk is used to pad data out to specific boundaries (for example, CD-ROMs use 2048-byte boundaries). The size of the chunk is the number of bytes of padding it contains. If you are reading AVI data, do not use use the data in the JUNK chunk. Skip it when reading and preserve it when writing. The JUNK chunk uses the standard chunk structure:

```
typedef struct _JunkChunk
{
    DWORD ChunkId;              /* Chunk ID marker (JUNK)*/
    DWORD PaggingSize;          /* Size of the padding in bytes */
    BYTE Padding[ChunkSize];    /* Padding */

} JUNKCHUNK;
```

For Further Information

For further information about the Microsoft RIFF format, see the specification included on the CD-ROM that accompanies this book.

If you write an application that recognizes the RIFF file format, you will need to get a copy of the Microsoft Multimedia Development Kit (MDK). The MDK contains all the tools and documentation necessary to work with RIFF files, as well as with the other details of Microsoft Windows multimedia.

For information about Microsoft multimedia products, including the MDK, contact Microsoft:

Microsoft Corporation
Attn: Multimedia Systems Group
Product Marketing
One Microsoft Way
Redmond, WA 98052-6399

For specific information about Microsoft AVI and the RIFF file formats, see the following Microsoft documents:

Microsoft Corporation. *Microsoft Windows Multimedia Programmer's Guide,* Microsoft Press, Redmond, WA.

Microsoft Corporation. *Microsoft Windows Multimedia Programmer's Reference,* Microsoft Press, Redmond, WA.

See also the discussion and additional references in Chapter 10, *Multimedia,* in this book.

You may also be able to get information via FTP through the Developer Relations Group at:

ftp.microsoft.com (in the */developer/drg* directory)

Microsoft RTF

NAME:	Microsoft RTF
ALSO KNOWN AS:	Rich Text Format
TYPE:	Metafile
COLORS:	256
COMPRESSION:	None
MAXIMUM IMAGE SIZE:	NA
MULTIPLE IMAGES PER FILE:	No
NUMERICAL FORMAT:	Little-endian
ORIGINATOR:	Microsoft Corporation
PLATFORM:	MS-DOS
SUPPORTING APPLICATIONS:	Most word processing, some spreadsheet
SPECIFICATION ON CD:	Yes
CODE ON CD:	No
IMAGES ON CD:	No
SEE ALSO:	None

USAGE: Used for document data interchange.

COMMENTS: A least-common-denominator format used mainly in word-processor documents.

Overview

Microsoft RTF (Rich Text Format) is a metafile standard developed by Microsoft Corporation to encode formatted text and graphics for interchange between applications. Normally, exporting a formatted file from one word processor to another requires that the file be converted from its original format to the format supported by the target application. This conversion almost never produces a target document that is an exact functional duplicate of the original. This is due both to the different features present in the word processor formats, and to limitations of the format converters. If a document is stored as an RTF file, however, and the reading application can also handle RTF files also, no intermediate conversion is necessary and therefore no data is misinterpreted or lost.

RTF has excellent font-handling capabilities and bitmap storage features. RTF files contain only 7-bit ASCII characters, so the format can support documents formatted using the ANSI, MS-DOS, and Macintosh character sets. These features and others make the RTF format a good choice for use as a multi-platform interchange format.

File Organization

The encoded data in RTF files is arranged more like a stream than a fixed data structure, so there is no definite information header that is the same in all RTF files. Instead, an RTF code stream consists of variable-sized fields called *control words*, *control symbols*, and *groups*. Each of these three types of fields begins with a backslash character (\), followed by one or more ASCII characters. A control word is an RTF code that contains special formatting and printing instructions.

File Details

Looking at the 22 lines of RTF code included in this section, we see the following control codes at the beginning of the file:

```
\rtf1\ansi
```

These control codes indicate that this data stream is an RTF document, that the code conforms to version 1 of the RTF specification, and that the document uses the ANSI (\ansi) rather than the PC (\pc), PS/2 (\pca), or Macintosh (\mac) character sets.

Control symbols are special escape character sequences consisting of a backslash that is followed by a single, nonalphabetic character. RTF control symbols include:

```
\~     Nonbreaking space
\_     Nonbreaking hyphen
\:     Index subentry
\'     Hexadecimal value xx
```

A group is a collection of text, control words, and control symbols, enclosed in a set of braces ({}). In fact, the entire RTF code stream is considered a group and is always enclosed in braces. The first control word in the group identifies the group type. Both the backslash (\) and the brace characters ({}) have special meanings in RTF and should be preceded by a backslash if they are to be interpreted as text.

```
{\rtf1\ansi \deff0\deflang1024
{\fonttbl{\f0\froman Tms Rmn;}{\f1\froman Symbol;}{\f2\fswiss Helv;}}
{\colortbl;\red0\green0\blue0;\red0\green0\blue255;\red0\green255\blue255;
\red0\green255\blue0;\red255\green0\blue255;\red255\green0\blue0;
\red255\green255\blue0;\red255\green255\blue255;\red0\green0\blue127;
\red0\green127\blue127;\red0\green127\blue0;\red127\green0\blue127;
\red127\green0\blue0;\red127\green127\blue0;\red127\green127\blue127;
\red192\green192\blue192;}
{\stylesheet{\fs20\lang1033 \snext0 Normal;}}
{\info{\author \'00\'00\'00\'00\'00\'00\'00\'00\'00\'00\'00\'00\'00\'00\'00}
{\operator \'00\'00\'00\'00\'00\'00\'00\'00\'00\'00\'00\'00\'00\'00\'00}
{\creatim\yr1992\mo1\dy9\hr12\min53}
{\revtim\yr1992\mo1\dy9\hr12\min53}{\version1}{\edmins3}{\nofpages0}
{\nofwords0}{\nofchars0}{\vern16504}}
\paperw12240\paperh15840\margl1800\margr1800\margt1440\margb1440\gutter0
\widowctrl\ftnbj \sectd \linex0\endnhere \pard\plain \fs20\lang1033
Four Basic Principles to Unify Mind and Body.
\par \tab 1. Keep one point.
\par \tab 2. Relax completely.
\par \tab 3. Keep weight underside.
\par \tab 4. Extend Ki.
\par }
```

Looking again at the RTF code in the figure, we can see a number of groups. The first group is obviously the \rtf group, which contains the code for the entire file.

The \fonttbl group contains the descriptions of the fonts used within the document. This document defines Times Roman, Symbol, and Helvetica font sets.

The next group, \colortbl, is a color table used to control screen and printer colors. This file defines a basic palette of 16 colors, with each color channel containing an 8-bit index value in the range of 0 to 255.

The \stylesheet group contains descriptions and definitions of the various styles and formats used in the document. In this example, we can see that Normal is the only style defined in this document.

The \info group contains one or more pieces of information about the documents, such as title, subject, author, version, keywords, and comments. In this example, the author and operator (the person who made the last change to the document) are blank. The remaining fields identify the creation time and last revision time of the document and its application version number.

After the groups, we see a series of control words that define the document, section, and paragraph formats, including the width, height, and margins. Following these control words is the actual text, which is one line of text followed by four lines of tab-indented text.

RTF can also handle bitmap images encoded in either a hexadecimal or binary format. The control word \pict always begins a group containing bitmapped data. A \pict group might appear in an RTF code stream as follows:

```
{\pict\wmetafile8\picw23918\pich14552\picwgoal13562\pichgoal8251
\picscalex63\piccaley63
```

The control words are the following:

- Source file type
- Image width and height
- Picture width and height
- Horizontal scaling value
- Vertical scaling value

If the image source is a bitmap (\wbitmap), then the following additional control words may appear:

- Bits per pixel
- Number of pixel planes
- Picture width in bytes

Source images may also be Macintosh PICT files.

Following the \pict group is the actual bitmap data, which is hexadecimal in format by default (as shown in the example below). If the data is in binary format, it is preceded by the \bin control word, followed by the number of bytes of binary data that follow.

```
{\rtf1\ansi \deff0\deflang1024
{\fonttbl{\f0\froman CG Times (WN);}{\f1\fdecor Symbol;}{\f2\fswiss Univers (WN);}}
{\colortbl;\red0\green0\blue0;\red0\green0\blue255;\red0\green255\blue255;
\red0\green255\blue0;\red255\green0\blue255;\red255\green0\blue0;
\red255\green255\blue0;\red255\green255\blue255;\red0\green0\blue127;
\red0\green127\blue127;\red0\green127\blue0;\red127\green0\blue127;
\red127\green0\blue0;\red127\green127\blue0;\red127\green127\blue127;
\red192\green192\blue192;}
{\stylesheet{\fs20\lang1033 \snext0 Normal;}}
```

```
{\info{\author James D. Murray}
{\creatim\yr1992\mo1\dy9\hr15\min31}{\printim\yr1992\mo1\dy9\hr15\min32}
{\version1}{\edmins2}{\nofpages1}{\nofwords0}{\nofchars2}{\vern16504}}
\paperw12240\paperh15840\margl1800\margr1800\margt1440\margb1440\gutter0
\widowctrl\ftnbj \sectd \linex0\endnhere \pard\plain \fs20\lang1033
{\pict\wmetafile8\picw23918\pich14552\picwgoal13562\pichgoal8251
\picscalex63\picscaley63
01000900000328ea01000000fee901000000050000000b0200000000050000000c024c0410070500
00000b0200000000050000000c024c0410070500000009020000000005000000102fffffff00fee9
0100430f2000cc0000004c041007000000004c041007000000002800000010070000 4c0400000100
0100000000000000000000000000000000000000000000000000000000ffffff00ffffffffffffff
ffffffffffffffffffffffffffffffffffffffffffffffffffffffffffffffffffffffffffffffffff
ffffffffffffffffffffffffffffffffffffffffffffffffffffffffffffffffffffffffffffffffff
ffffffffffffffffffffffffffff00000300000000000000000000000000000000000000000000000
0000}\par}
```

For Further Information

For further information, see the specification included on the CD-ROM that accompanies this book. You may be able to get additional information by contacting Microsoft:

Microsoft Corporation
Attn: Department RTF
16011 N.E. 36th Way
Box 97017
Redmond, WA 98073-9717

The RTF file format is also documented in the following reference:

Microsoft Corporation. *Microsoft Word Technical Reference Manual,* Microsoft Press, Redmond, WA.

This book is available in bookstores or from:

Microsoft Press
Voice: 800-677-7377

You may also be able to get information via FTP through the Developer Relations Group at:

ftp.microsoft.com (in the */developer/drg* directory)

NAME:	Microsoft SYLK
ALSO KNOWN AS:	Symbolic Link Format, SLK
TYPE:	Vector
COLORS:	NA
COMPRESSION:	NA
MAXIMUM IMAGE SIZE:	NA
MULTIPLE IMAGES PER FILE:	No
NUMERICAL FORMAT:	NA
ORIGINATOR:	Microsoft Corporation
PLATFORM:	MS-DOS, others
SUPPORTING APPLICATIONS:	Spreadsheets, business graphics applications
SPECIFICATION ON CD:	No
CODE ON CD:	No
IMAGES ON CD:	No
SEE ALSO:	Lotus DIF

USAGE: Interchange of spreadsheet information.

COMMENTS: Yet another format used to share spreadsheet information with business graphics applications.

Overview

The Microsoft SYLK (Symbolic Link) format is used mainly for the interchange of spreadsheet data between applications such as Microsoft Multiplan and Excel. Files in this format might also be imported directly by business graphics applications. SYLK files are written entirely in ASCII and, like Lotus DIF and SDI, are application-independent. SYLK, however, incorporates several features not found in other spreadsheet data interchange formats.

File Organization

Records in a SYLK file contain three fields: a Record Type Descriptor (RTD), a Field Type Descriptor (FTD), and a variable amount of data.

An SYLK record has the following format:

```
<RTD>;<FTD>;<data> . . .
```

File Details

The following Record Type Descriptors (RTDs) are currently defined by SYLK:

RTD	Description
B	Cell boundary
C	A data cell
E	End of file
F	Cell formatting parameter
ID	SYLK file identification record
NE	Link to an inactive spreadsheet file
NN	Name given to a rectangluar area of cells
NU	Substitute filename
P	Time and date stamp formats

Each Record Type Decriptor may be followed by a single Field Type Descriptor (FTD) if needed. Most field type descriptors have meanings unique to each record, but a few, listed below, have meanings global to all record types:

FTD	Description
W	Column width
X	Horizontal cell coordinate
Y	Vertical cell coordinate

The SYLK file format does not contain a header and resembles a data stream in its design. Except for the ID record, which must be the first record in every SYLK file, RTDs may appear anywhere in the file with the following exceptions:

- The first record must be an ID record (the RTD is ID)
- All P records follow the ID record.
- All B records follow the P records.
- A ;D or ;G FTD must appear in a C record prior to a reference to that FTD by another record.

- NE records always follow NU records.

- The final record must be an E record.

For Further Information

SYLK was created and is maintained by Microsoft Corporation. You may be able to get information by contacting:

Microsoft Corporation
One Microsoft Way
Redmond, WA 98052-6399
Voice: 206-882-8080
Voice: 800-426-9400
Fax: 206-883-8101

The following reference also contains information about the SYLK format:

Walden, Jeffrey B. *File Formats for Popular PC Software*, John Wiley & Sons, New York, NY, 1986.

You may also be able to get information via FTP through the Developer Relations Group at:

ftp.microsoft.com (in the */developer/drg* directory)

Microsoft Windows Bitmap

NAME:	Microsoft Windows Bitmap
ALSO KNOWN AS:	BMP, DIB, Windows Bitmap, Windows DIB
TYPE:	Bitmap
COLORS:	Mono, 4-bit, 8-bit, 24-bit
COMPRESSION:	RLE, uncompressed
MAXIMUM IMAGE SIZE:	64Kx64K pixels
MULTIPLE IMAGES PER FILE:	No
NUMERICAL FORMAT:	Little-endian
ORIGINATOR:	Microsoft Corporation
PLATFORM:	Intel machines running Microsoft Windows, Windows NT
SUPPORTING APPLICATIONS:	Too numerous to list
SPECIFICATION ON CD:	Yes
CODE ON CD:	Yes
IMAGES ON CD:	Yes
SEE ALSO:	OS/2 Bitmap

USAGE: Used along with several variations in Microsoft Windows and Windows-based products. It is primarily an exchange and storage format. Although it is based on Windows internal bitmap data structures, it is supported by many non-Windows and non-PC applications.

COMMENTS: A well-defined, well-documented format in wide use that is quick and easy to read and uncompress. It lacks, however, a superior compression scheme, making it unsuited for the storage of deep-pixel images. Applications on non-Intel machines need to pay attention to byte-ordering of 16-bit numerical data, because data is stored in little-endian format.

Overview

The Microsoft Windows Bitmap (BMP) file format is one of several supported by Microsoft Windows. Most graphics and imaging applications operating in the Microsoft Windows environment support creation and display of BMP format files.

Microsoft shared responsibility with IBM for the development of early versions of IBM's OS/2 operating system. Thus, versions of the BMP format exist on both the Microsoft Windows and the OS/2 platforms and are similar in many respects. There are currently four variations of the BMP format, each associated with an operating system version. In historical order of appearance, they are:

Microsoft Windows	1.X and 2.X
OS/2	1.X
Microsoft Windows	3.X
OS/2	2.X

This article discusses the two versions from Microsoft, corresponding to Microsoft Windows Version 1.x/2.x (Version 1 bitmaps), and Version 3.x (Version 3 bitmaps). Rumors of further revisions to the Microsoft versions of the BMP format were circulating at the time of this writing.

For a discussion of the OS/2 variants, see the article about the OS/2 Bitmap format.

An early version of the BMP format was device-dependent—a simple bitmap format with no palette and no support for data compression. It was designed to support the most popular IBM PC graphics cards in use at the time (CGA, EGA, Hercules, and others). A refinement of the original BMP format, the DIB (device-independent bitmap), was developed partially in support of IBM's OS/2 Presentation Manager. It gained device-independent information in the header, a color palette, and RLE data compression. The current version of the DIB format made its first official appearance in Microsoft products with the release of Windows 3.0, and differs only slightly from the OS/2 Presentation Manager bitmap format that preceded it. Note that later revisions designed to support IBM OS/2 Presentation Manager 2.X have resulted in further divergence between the Microsoft Windows and IBM OS/2 bitmap formats. Windows BMP files are now assumed to be written in the DIB format, although a defensively-coded application might attempt to support all variants, including those supported by IBM.

All of the BMP versions originated on Intel-based machines, and thus share a common little-endian heritage. The current BMP format is otherwise hardware-independent and can accommodate images with up to 24-bit color. Its basic design makes it a good general-purpose format that can be used for color or black-and-white image storage if file size is not a factor. Its main virtues are its simplicity and widespread support in the PC marketplace.

The compression method used is a type of run-length encoding (RLE), although most BMP files to date have been stored uncompressed. A notable exception is the Microsoft Windows signon screen shipped with all copies of the product. Although RLE is lossless and easily and quickly decompressed, it is not considered a superior compression method.

Although the BMP format is well-defined, there is no actual format specification document published by Microsoft. Information about structure and data encoding methods is contained in a number of programmer's references, manuals, on-line help facilities, and include files associated with the Microsoft Windows Software Development Kit (SDK), available for purchase from Microsoft.

We recommend that, if you are writing an application that will run on a non-Intel platform, you take pains to write 16-bit numerical data in little-endian order, that is, low byte first. Note also that long data words are not aligned in the header and palette sections.

File Organization

Version 1 of the BMP format contains two sections: a file header and bitmap data. The file header is 16 bytes in length.

Version 3 bitmaps contain four sections: a bitmap header, the information header, a palette, and the bitmap data. Of these four sections only the palette is ever optional. The Version 3 bitmap header is 14 bytes in length and is nearly identical to the Version 1 file header. This is followed by a second header, called the information header, which is 40 bytes in length, a variable-sized palette, and the bitmap data.

File Details

This section describes BMP Version 1 and Version 3 in greater detail.

Version 1 (Microsoft Windows 1.x and 2.x)

BMP Version 1 files contain only a file header followed by uncompressed bitmap data. The following shows the structure of the Version 1 file header. For information about the bitmap data, see the discussion of Version 3 data in the following section.

```
typedef struct _Win1xBitmapHeader
{
  WORD Type;          /*  File type identifier (always 0)  */
  WORD Width;         /*  Width of bitmap in pixels  */
  WORD Height;        /*  Height of bitmap in scanlines  */
```

```
    WORD ByteWidth;     /* Width of bitmap in bytes */
    BYTE Planes;        /* Number of color planes */
    BYTE BitsPerPixel;  /* Number of bits per pixel */

} WIN1XHEAD;
```

Type indicates the file type and, for Version 1 file headers, is always 0.

Width and Height represent the size of the bitmap in pixels (Width) and scan lines (Height).

ByteWidth shows the width of the bitmap (in bytes).

Planes is the number of color planes represented by the bitmap.

BitsPerPixel is the number of bits per pixel in the bitmap.

Version 3 (Microsoft Windows 3.x)

BMP Version 3 files contain a bitmap header, an information header, a palette (optional), and bitmap data.

Bitmap Header

The following shows the bitmap header used by Version 3 BMP files.

```
    typedef struct _Win3xBitmapHeader
    {
    WORD  ImageFileType;    /* Image file type, always 4D42h ("BM") */
    DWORD FileSize;         /* Physical file size in bytes */
    WORD  Reserved1;        /* Always 0 */
    WORD  Reserved2;        /* Always 0 */
    DWORD ImageDataOffset;  /* Start of image data offset in bytes */

} WIN3XHEAD;
```

ImageFileType holds a 2-byte magic value used to identify the file type; it is always 4D42h or BM in ASCII. If your application reads Windows bitmap files, make sure that it always checks this field before attempting to use any of the data read from the file.

FileSize is the total size of the file in bytes and should agree with the file size reported by the file system.

Reserved1 and Reserved2 are not used and should both be set to zero.

ImageDataOffset is the offset starting from the beginning of the file to the start of the image data, in bytes.

Bitmap information header

In Version 3 BMP files, the bitmap header is followed by a bitmap information header. The structure of this header is shown below.

```
typedef struct _Win3xBitmapInfoHeader
{
    WORD   HeaderSize;              /* Size of this header */
    DWORD  ImageWidth;             /* Image width in pixels */
    DWORD  ImageHeight;            /* Image height in pixels */
    WORD   NumberOfImagePlanes;    /* Number of planes (alwaays 1) */
    WORD   BitsPerPixel;           /* Bits per pixel (1, 4, 8, or 24) */
    DWORD  CompressionMethod       /* Compression method used (0, 1,
                                      or 2) */
    DWORD  SizeOfBitmap;           /* Size of the bitmap in bytes */
    DWORD  HorzResolution;         /* Horizontal resolution in pixels
                                      per meter */
    DWORD  VertResolution;         /* Vertical resolution in pixels
                                      per meter */
    DWORD  NumColorsUsed;          /* Number of colors in the image */
    DWORD  NumSignificantColors;   /* Number of important colors in
palette */

} WIN3XINFOHEAD;
```

HeaderSize is the size of the information header in bytes, and is the value read to identify the bitmap variant. For Microsoft Windows 3.X, the value is 40.

ImageWidth and ImageHeight are the the width and height of the image in pixels, respectively.

NumberOfImagePlanes is always 1, because BMP image files always contain a single color plane.

BitsPerPixel can be 1, 4, 8, or 24.

CompressionMethod indicates the type of encoding method used on the bitmap data. 0 indicates that the data is uncompressed; 1 indicates that 8-bit RLE was used; and 2 indicates that 4-bit RLE was used. (See the section called "Bitmap Data" below for more information on BMP RLE encoding.)

SizeofBitmap is the size of the compressed data in bytes. This value is typically 00h when the bitmap is uncompressed; in this case, the decoder computes the size from the image dimensions.

HorzResolution and VertResolution are the horizontal and vertical resolutions in pixels per meter, respectively, and are used to help you choose a proper mode to use when printing or displaying the image.

NumColorsUsed is the number of colors present in the palette. If this value is zero, then the number of entries is equal to the maximum size possible for the color map. The value is calculated by shifting 1 in the BitsPerPixel field:

```
NumColorsUsed = 1 << bmp.BitsPerPixel
```

NumSignificantColors is the number of significant colors in the palette, determined by their frequency of appearance in the image; the more frequent the occurrence of a color, the more significant it is. This field is used to provide as accurate a display as possible when using graphics hardware supporting fewer colors than defined in the image. An 8-bit image with 142 colors, for instance, might have only a dozen or so colors comprising the bulk of the image. If these colors are known, a display adapter with only 16-color capability would be able to display the image more accurately by using the 16 most frequently occurring colors in the image. NumSignificantColors is 0 if all the colors in the color map are significant.

Palette

All 1-, 4-, and 8-bit BMP image files have a palette. The size of the palette is dependent upon the number of colors in the image and can be determined by the value in the NumColorsUsed field in the bitmap information header described in the previous section.

The Version 3 palette has the following format:

```
typedef struct _Win3xPalette
{
  RGBQUAD Palette[];          /* 2, 16, or 256 elements */

} WIN3XPALETTE;
```

Palettes, like the bitmap information header, are different in files created under OS/2 1.x, Microsoft Windows, and OS/2 2.0. In Microsoft Windows Version 3 of the format, palettes consist of 4-byte values, each of which is called a RGBQUAD in Microsoft literature. The first three bytes are color information; the fourth reserved byte is always set to 0.

The RGBQUAD structure has the following format:

```
typedef struct _Win3xRgbQuad
{
  BYTE Blue;          /* 8-bit blue component */
  BYTE Green;         /* 8-bit green component */
  BYTE Red;           /* 8-bit red component */
  BYTE Reserved;      /* 8-bit reserved value (always 0) */

} RGBQUAD;
```

The first two colors defined in the palette are normally white (entry 0) and black (entry 1). Remaining colors usually appear in random order. If the image data stored in the file is less than 16 colors, however, it is usually best to sort the colors in the color table and place the colors occurring with the greatest frequency in the image first. A value can then be stored in the NumSignificantColors field (typically a value of 8 or 16) in the bitmap information header to help display hardware with a small color palette correctly display the colors in the image.

Some applications creating 1-bit files invert the color sense of the image data, causing color reversal (i.e., white becomes black, and black becomes white). This usually occurs in operating environments where the normal display consists of black characters on a white background (found on the Apple Macintosh and Microsoft Windows). Artificially inverting the data—interpreting all 1 bits as 0 and all 0 bits as 1—fixes this problem.

Image Data

The remainder of the BMP file consists of the actual bitmap data, which can be either uncompressed or in RLE format.

Image data in a BMP file is always byte-oriented. How the data is read, however, depends on the number of bits per pixel and whether the image data is compressed.

In 1-bit image data, each byte represents eight pixels, and the most significant bit in the byte is the first pixel value. Four-bit images contain two pixel values per byte, and the most significant nibble is the first pixel value; the least significant nibble is the next pixel value. Eight-bit images, of course, contain one pixel value per byte. Twenty four-bit image data uses three bytes per pixel, stored in blue, green, and red order. Each scan line in a BMP image file is always a multiple of four bytes in length and is padded when necessary.

Because all 1-, 4-, and 8-bit images use palettes, the pixel values read from the image data are index values into the palette that hold the actual pixel color.

Twenty-four-bit images, however, never use a palette, because their pixel color data is stored directly in the image data. Image data is always displayed starting at the lower-left corner of the screen; that is, pixel coordinate 0,0 is at the lower-left corner of the image.

Image data encoding

The vast majority of BMP files written to date have been uncompressed, which makes for larger BMP files (300K to 500K is not uncommon), but which also allows the files to load and save quickly. Compression is accomplished by a type of run-length encoding (RLE) scheme.

The BMP compression scheme allows for the compression of image data stored at four or eight bits per pixel. Because this is a byte-oriented RLE, 1- and 24-bit images may not compress well and may even grow in size due to the absence of repetitive character data. Exceptions to this are 24-bit gray-scale image data and 1-bit image data with long runs of a single color. BMP readers should always support RLE. Runs of identical bytes in the image data are encoded as packets, which are of two types: encoded and literal (or absolute).

An encoded run contains two bytes; the first byte is the number of pixels in the run, and the second byte is the pixel value. The first byte is always non-zero and ranges in value from 1 to 255.

A literal run contains five or more bytes of data. The first byte is always set to zero, and signals the start of a literal run. The second byte ranges in value from 3 to 255 and indicates the number of bytes to follow, which are to be read as literal pixel values. Literal runs must always end on a 2-byte word boundary. Both literal and encoded runs stop at the end of scan lines. Normally, most of the runs in an RLE-compressed file are encoded. Very complex or noisy images containing many colors, however, may not compress well using run encoding. An image must contain pixel runs of three or more bytes long for encoding to be effective.

Escape sequences are composed of two bytes; the first byte is always zero, as in a literal run, and the second byte may be 0, 1, or 2. A value of 0 in the second byte signals the end of the image; a value of 1 indicates the end of a scan line; and a value of 2 is a delta escape sequence, indicating a change in the coordinates of the encoded image data.

RLE methods normally encode a bitmap one scan line at a time, starting at the first byte of the image data and ending with the last. The delta escape sequence allows the encoding process to skip around in the image, however, encoding parts of the image in chunks without regard to scan lines. When a delta escape code is detected, the following two bytes signify the horizontal and vertical offsets of the start of the next run. When the run at the new point is read, the decoding continues from that point.

Delta escape codes make decoding the BMP image data much more difficult. Normally, decoding is provided by a simple function that reads and decodes a single scan line at a time. Thus, a temporary buffer need only be large enough to hold a single decoded scan line before it is copied to a file or output device. The presence of delta escape codes, however, may force the use of a buffer large enough to hold the entire decoded image, so that the decoded data may be written to any part of the decoded image at any time.

Fortunately, delta escape codes are seldom used. Delta encoding does, however, offer several advantages over the other forms of encoding. The most important is that an area of an image that is a single color can be compressed with greater efficiency using deltas than with the use of single scan-line encoding. Deltas can also be used to encode image data into a series of tiles, rather than into scan lines or strips.

For Further Information

For further information about the Microsoft Windows Bitmap format, see the documentation and sample code included on the CD-ROM that accompanies this book. You may also be able to get information from Microsoft at:

Microsoft Corporation
One Microsoft Way
Redmond, WA 98052-6399
Voice: 206-882-8080
FAX: 206-936-7329
BBS: 206-637-9009

Information about the BMP format can also be found in the following references:

Microsoft Corporation. *Microsoft Windows Programmer's Reference,* Microsoft Press, Redmond, WA, 1990.

Petzold, Charles. "What's New in Bitmap Formats: A Look at Windows and OS/2," *PC Magazine,* September 11, 1990, pp. 403-410.

Petzold, Charles. "The Windows 3.0 Device-Independent Bitmap," *PC Magazine,* June 25, 1991, pp. 397-401.

Petzold, Charles. "Preserving a Device-Independent Bitmap: The Packed-DIB Format." *PC Magazine,* July 1991, pp. 433-39.

The Microsoft Windows Programmer's Reference Library is the master reference for programmers working with all aspects of Microsoft Windows. The books in this library are supplied with the Microsoft Windows Software Development Kit (SDK). The manuals supplied with the Microsoft C 7.0 Professional Development Systems are also very helpful. You can get information about obtaining these products from:

Microsoft Information Center
Voice: 800-426-9400

You may also be able to get information via FTP through the Developer Relations Group at:

ftp.microsoft.com (in the */developer/drg* directory)

Microsoft Windows Metafile

NAME:	Microsoft Windows Metafile
ALSO KNOWN AS:	Windows Metafile, WMF
TYPE:	Metafile
COLORS:	24-bit maximum
COMPRESSION:	NA
MAXIMUM IMAGE SIZE:	NA
MULTIPLE IMAGES PER FILE:	No
NUMERICAL FORMAT:	Little-endian
ORIGINATOR:	Microsoft Corporation
PLATFORM:	Microsoft Windows
SUPPORTING APPLICATIONS:	Numerous Microsoft Windows-based graphics applications
SPECIFICATION ON CD:	Yes
CODE ON CD:	No
IMAGES ON CD:	No
SEE ALSO:	Encapsulated PostScript, Microsoft Windows Bitmap
USAGE:	Used for file interchange, device support.
COMMENTS:	A widely used format associated with Microsoft Windows, although applications on other platforms may provide support.

Overview

Microsoft Windows Metafile (WMF) files are used to store vector and bitmap-format image data in memory or in disk files for later playback to an output device. Although Windows Metafile is specific to Microsoft Windows, many non-Windows-based applications support this format as a method for interchanging data with Windows applications. Because of the widespread popularity of the Microsoft Windows GUI, the Windows Metafile format has become a staple format for graphical applications and is supported on all platforms. Encapsulated PostScript (EPSF) supports the use of an included Windows Metafile when required to store vector-based data. The logical unit of measurement used in Windows Metafiles is the *twip*. A twip (meaning "twentieth of a point") is equal to 1/1440 of an inch. Thus 720 twips equal 1/2 inch, while 32,768 twips is 22.75 inches.

File Organization

Windows Metafile format files contain a header, followed by one or more records of data. The header contains a description of the record data stored in the metafile. Each record is a binary-encoded Microsoft Windows Graphics Device Interface (GDI) function call. The GDI is used by Windows to perform all output to a screen window or other output device. When the metafile data is rendered (or played back, in Microsoft terminology), the data from each record is used to perform the appropriate function call to render each object in the image. The last record in the file contains information indicating that the end of the record data has been reached.

File Details

The header is 18 bytes in length and is structured as follows:

```
typedef struct _WindowsMetaHeader
{
    WORD   FileType;        /* Type of metafile (1=memory, 2=disk) */
    WORD   HeaderSize;      /* Size of header in WORDS (always 9) */
    WORD   Version;         /* Version of Microsoft Windows used */
    DWORD  FileSize;        /* Total size of the metafi+le in WORDs */
    WORD   NumOfObjects;    /* Number of objects in the file */
    DWORD  MaxRecordSize;   /* The size of largest record in WORDs */
    WORD   NoParameters;    /* Not Used (always 0) */

} WMFHEAD;
```

FileType contains a value which indicates the location of the metafile data. A value of 1 indicates that the metafile is stored in memory, while a 2 indicates that it is stored on disk.

HeaderSize contains the size of the metafile header in WORDs.

Version stores the version number of Microsoft Windows that created the metafile. This value is always read in hexadecimal format. For example, in a metafile created by Windows 3.0, this item would have the value 300h.

FileSize specifies the total size of the metafile in 16-bit WORDs.

NumOfObjects specifies the number of objects that are in the metafile.

MaxRecordSize specifies the size of the largest record in the metafile in WORDs.

NumOfParams is not used and is set to a value of 0.

Following the header is a series of data records. The basic format of each record is shown below:

```
typedef struct _WindowsMetaRecord
{
DWORD Size;         /* Total size of the record in WORDs */
WORD  Function;     /* Function number (defined in WINDOWS.H) */
WORD  Parmeters[];  /* Parameter values passed to function */

} WMFRECORD;
```

Size is the total size of the records in WORDs, including the Size field itself. The minimum possible size for a record is 3.

Function is the GDI number of the function.

Parameters is an array of the parameters used by the function. The parameters are stored in the reverse order in which they are passed to the function.

When a Windows Metafile format file is played back, each record is read and the function call it contains is executed in the sequence in which it is read. The last record in every metafile always has a function number of zero and is used to indicate the end of the record data.

There are several important considerations that must be observed when reading WMF record data.

First, not all of the records in a Windows Metafile have the above format, although most do. The GDI function calls that do follow the basic record format are the following:

Arc	ScaleViewportExt
Chord	ScaleWindowExt
Ellipse	SetBkColor
ExcludeClipRect	SetBkMode
FloodFill	SetMapMode
IntersectClipRect	SetMapperFlags
LineTo	SetPixel
MoveTo	SetPolyFillMode
OffsetClipRgn	SetROP2
OffsetViewportOrg	SetStretchBltMode
OffsetWindowOrg	SetTextAlign

PatBlt
Pie
RealizePalette
Rectangle
ResizePalette
RestoreDC
RoundRect
SaveDC

SetTextCharExtra
SetTextColor
SetTextJustification
SetViewportExt
SetViewportOrg
SetWindowExt
SetWindowOrg

Second, several record formats deviate from this basic record format by containing a data structure, rather than a data array, in the Parameters field. These are:

AnimatePalette
BitBlt
CreateBrushIndirect
CreateFontIndirect
CreatePalette
CreatePatternBrush
CreatePenIndirect
CreateRegion

DeleteObject
DrawText
Escape
ExtTextOut
Polygon
PolyPolygon
Polyline

Consult the Microsoft Windows Programmer's Reference Library for the internal structure of each of these special records.

Third, several GDI function calls were added or had their parameters changed with the release of Microsoft Windows 3.0. GDI function calls in this category include:

AnimatePalette
BitBlt
CreatePalette
Record
CreatePatternBrush

Record
DeleteObject
RealizePalette
ResizePalette

Note that not all GDI function calls can appear in a metafile. The only calls that are valid are those that take a handle to a device context as their first parameter. A complete list of all of the GDI function calls is documented in Chapter 9 of *Microsoft Windows Programmer's Reference*. They are also found in the *WINDOWS.H* header file. These GDI function calls are the directives that begin with the characters META. There are more than 70 different GDI function calls defined for Windows 3.0.

Porting WMF Files Between Applications

Most Microsoft Windows applications that create metafiles prepend a 22-byte header to the file. This header contains information not found in the metafile header, but which is needed to move the metafile information between applications. The structure of this header is as follows:

```
typedef struct _WmfSpecialHeader
{
  DWORD Key;           /* Magic number (always 9AC6CDD7h) */
  WORD  Handle;        /* Metafile HANDLE number (always 0) */
  SHORT Left;          /* Left coordinate in metafile units */
  SHORT Top;           /* Top coordinate in metafile units */
  SHORT Right;         /* Right coordinate in metafile units */
  SHORT Bottom;        /* Bottom coordinate in metafile units */
  WORD  Inch;          /* Number of metafile units per inch */
  DWORD Reserved;      /* Reserved (always 0) */
  WORD  Checksum;      /* Checksum value for previous 10 WORDs */

} WMFSPECIAL;
```

Key contains a special identification value that indicates the presence of a special header and is always 9AC6CDD7h.

Handle is not used and always contains the value 0.

Left, Top, Right, and Bottom contain the coordinates of the upper-left and lower-right corners of the image on the output device. These are measured in twips. These four fields also correspond to the RECT structure used in Microsoft Windows and found in the file *WINDOWS.H.*

Inch contains the number of twips per inch used to represent the image. Normally, there are 1440 twips per inch; however, this number may be changed to scale the image. A value of 720 indicates that the image is double its normal size, or scaled to a factor of 2:1. A value of 360 indicates a scale of 4:1, while a value of 2880 indicates that the image is scaled down in size by a factor of two. A value of 1440 indicates a 1:1 scale ratio.

Reserved is not used and is always set to 0.

Checksum contains a checksum value for the previous 10 WORDs in the header, calculated by XORing each WORD value to 0:

```
WMFSPECIAL wmfspecial; wmfspecial.
Checksum = 0;

wmfspecial.Checksum ^= (wmfspecial.Key & 0x0000FFFFL);
wmfspecial.Checksum ^= ((wmfspecial.Key & 0xFFFF0000L) >> 16);
wmfspecial.Checksum ^= wmfspecial.Handle; wmfspecial.Checksum ^=
wmfspecial.Left;
wmfspecial.Checksum ^= wmfspecial.Top; wmfspecial.Checksum ^=
wmfspecial.Right;
wmfspecial.Checksum ^= wmfspecial.Bottom; wmfspecial.Checksum ^=
wmfspecial.Inch;
wmfspecial.Checksum ^= (wmfspecial.Reserved & 0x0000FFFFL);
wmfspecial.Checksum ^= ((wmfspecial.Reserved & 0xFFFF0000L) >> 16);
```

An alternative way to step through the header structure one WORD at a time is to use a pointer as shown below:

```
WMFSPECIAL *wmfspecial;
WORD *ptr;
wmfspecial->Checksum = 0;
for(ptr = (WORD *) wmfspecial;
    ptr < (WORD *)wmfspecial->Checksum;
    ptr++)
        wmfspecial->Checksum ^= *ptr;
```

Storing Bitmaps in a WMF File

The BitBlt function (GDI function number 940h) is used to store device-independent bitmaps in a Windows Metafile. This record was modified for Windows 3.0, so metafiles created under earlier versions of Windows may not be suitable for playback on all graphics output devices.

For Further Information

For further information about the Microsoft Windows Metafile format, see the specification included on the CD-ROM that accompanies this book. You may also obtain information by contacting Microsoft at:

Microsoft Corporation
One Microsoft Way
Redmond, WA 98052-6399
Voice: 206-882-8080
FAX: 206-936-7329
BBS: 206-637-9009

Additional information about the Windows Metafile Format and the Microsoft Windows Graphics Device Interface can also be found in the following references:

Petzold, Charles. *Programming Windows: the Microsoft Guide to Writing Applications for Windows 3*, Second Edition, Microsoft Press, Redmond, WA, 1990.

Microsoft Corporation. *Microsoft Windows: A Guide to Programming*, Microsoft Windows Programmer's Reference Library, Microsoft Press, Redmond, WA, 1990.

Microsoft Corporation. *Microsoft Windows: Programmer's Reference*, Microsoft WIndows Programmer's Reference Library, Microsoft Press, Redmond, WA, 1990.

Microsoft Corporation. *Microsoft Windows: Programming Tools*, Microsoft Windows Programmer's Reference Library, Microsoft Press, Redmond, WA, 1990.

The Microsoft Windows Programmer's Reference Library is the master reference for programmers working with all aspects of Microsoft Windows. The books in this library are supplied with the Microsoft Windows Software Development Kit (SDK). The manuals supplied with the Microsoft C 7.0 Professional Development Systems are also very helpful. You can get information about obtaining these products from:

Microsoft Information Center
Voice: 800-426-9400

You may also be able to get information via FTP through the Developer Relations Group at:

ftp.microsoft.com (in the */developer/drg* directory)

NAME:	MIFF
ALSO KNOWN AS:	Machine Independent File Format
TYPE:	Bitmap
COLORS:	16 million
COMPRESSION:	RLE, Q-coder, JPEG predictive arithmetic compression
MAXIMUM IMAGE SIZE:	Unlimited
MULTIPLE IMAGES PER FILE:	No
NUMERICAL FORMAT:	NA
ORIGINATOR:	John Cristy
PLATFORM:	X Window System
SUPPORTING APPLICATIONS:	ImageMagick
SPECIFICATION ON CD:	Yes
CODE ON CD:	Yes (in ImageMagick package)
IMAGES ON CD:	Yes
SEE ALSO:	JFIF
USAGE:	Bitmap still image and animation storage format.
COMMENTS:	MIFF is the native image file format for the X Window System-based ImageMagick utilities.

Overview

MIFF (Machine Independent File Format) is a platform-independent format for storing bitmap images. MIFF is part of the ImageMagick toolkit of image manipulation utilities for the X Window System. ImageMagick is capable of converting many different image file formats to and from MIFF, in addition to creating and displaying animated bitmap image presentations.

File Organization

The MIFF header is composed entirely of ASCII characters. The fields in the header are keyword and value combinations in the *keyword=value* format, with each keyword and value separated by an equal sign (=).

Each *keyword=value* combination is delimited by at least one control or whitespace character. Comments may appear in the header section and are always delimited by braces. The MIFF header always ends with a colon (:) character, followed by a newline character. It is also common for a formfeed and a newline character to appear before the colon.

The following is a list of *keyword=value* combinations that may be found in a MIFF file:

class=DirectClass or class=PseudoClass

> class indicates the type of binary image data stored in the MIFF file. If this keyword is not present, DirectClass image data is assumed.

colors=value

> colors specifies the number of colors in a DirectClass image. For a Pseudo-Color image this keyword specifies the size of the colormap. If this keyword is not present in the header, and the image is PseudoColor, then a linear colormap is used with the image data.

columns=value

> columns indicates the width of the image in pixels. This is a required keyword and has no default.

compression=QEncoded or compression=RunlengthEncoded

> compression indicates the type of algorithm used to compress the image data. If this keyword is not present, the image data is assumed to be uncompressed.

id=ImageMagick

> The id keyword identifies the file as a MIFF-format image file. This keyword is required and has no default.

packets=value

> packets specifies the number of compressed color packets in the image data section. This keyword is optional for RunlengthEncoded images, mandatory for QEncoded images, and not used for uncompressed images.

rows=value

> rows indicates the height of the image in pixels. This is a required keyword and has no default.

scene=value

> scene indicates the sequence number for this MIFF image file. This optional keyword is used when a MIFF image file is one in a sequence of files used in an animation.

signature=value

> The optional keyword signature contains a string that uniquely identifies the image colormap. Unique colormap identifiers are normally used when animating a sequence of PseudoClass images.

The following is a sample MIFF header. In this example, <FF> is a formfeed character:

```
{
    A sample MIFF header
}
id=ImageMagick
class=PseudoClass  colors=256
compression=RunlengthEncoded  packets=10672
columns=800  rows=600 {size of the image}
scene=1  signature=d79e1c308aa5bbcdeea8ed63df412da9
<FF>
:
```

Note that *keyword=value* combinations may be separated by newlines or spaces and may occur in any order within the header. Comments (within braces) may appear anywhere before the colon.

Following the header is the binary image data itself. How the image data is formatted depends upon the class of the image as specified (or not specified) by the value of the class keyword in the header.

File Details

DirectClass images (class=DirectClass) are continuous tone, RGB images stored as intensity values in red-green-blue order. Each color value is one byte in size and there are three bytes per pixel. The total number of pixels in a DirectClass image is calculated by multiplying the rows value by the columns value in the header.

PseudoClass images (class=PseudoClass) are colormapped RGB images. The colormap is stored as a series of red-green-blue pixel values, each value being a byte in size. The number of map entries is indicated by the colors keyword in the header, with a maximum of 65,535 total entries allowed. The colormap data occurs immediately following the header.

PseudoClass image data is an array of index values into the color map. If there are 256 or fewer colors in the image, each byte of image data contains an index value. If the image contains more than 256 colors, then the index value is stored in two contiguous bytes with the most significant byte being first. The total number of pixels in a PseudoClass image is calculated by multiplying the rows value by the columns value in the header.

MIFF is capable of storing a digital signature for colormapped images. This signature was developed for use when animating a sequence of images on a colormapped X server. All of the signatures in a sequence of MIFF files are checked, and if they all match, you do not need to compute a global colormap.

The default colormap identifier is a digital signature computed using the RSA Data Security MD4 Digest Algorithm. (See a description of this algorithm in RFC 1186, October 1990.) The colormap signature is computed if the MIFF file is part of a scene (i.e., the scene value does not equal 0).

The image data in a MIFF file may be uncompressed or may be compressed using one of two algorithms. The predictive arithmetic compression algorithm found in the JPEG compression scheme (described in Chapter 9, *Data Compression*) may be used to encode either DirectColor or PseudoColor image data into packets of compressed data. Older MIFF files will use the IBM Q-coder algorithm to QEncode image data. The number of Q-encoded packets stored in the file is specified by the packets keyword in the header.

A less costly alternative to the Q-coder algorithms is a simple, run-length encoding (RLE) algorithm. For DirectColor images, runs of identical pixel values (not BYTE values) are encoded into a series of four-byte packets. The first three bytes of the packet contain the red, green, and blue values of the pixel in the run. The fourth byte contains the number of pixels in the run. This value many be in the range of 0 to 255 and is one less than the actual number of pixels in the run. For example, a value of 147 indicates that there are 148 pixels in the run.

For PseudoColor images, the same RLE algorithm is used. Runs of identical index values are encoded into packets. Each packet contains the colormap index value followed by the number of index values in the run. The number of bytes in a PseudoColor RLE packet will be either two or three, depending upon the size of the index values. The number of RLE packets stored in the file is specified by the packets keyword in the header, but is not required.

For Further Information

For further information about MIFF, see the specification included on the CD that accompanies this book.

ImageMagick was created by John Cristy, of E.I. duPont de Nemours & Company, and is copyright by duPont.

ImageMagick is included on the CD-ROM that accompanies this book. See Appendix A, *What's on the CD-ROM?*, for a description of the package and how you can obtain it via FTP.

For more information about MIFF, you can contact:

duPont de Nemour & Company
Attn: John Cristy
Central Research and Development
Experimental Station
P.O. Box 80328
Room 162-A
Wilmington, DE 19880-0328
Voice: 302-695-1159
cristy@dupont.com

For information about the JPEG predictive arithmetic compression algorithm, see the section called "JPEG" in Chapter 9, *Data Compression*.

For information about the IBM-patented Q-coder compression algorithm, see the following reference:

Mitchell, J. L. and Pennebaker, W.B., "Software implementations of the Q-Coder," *IBM Journal of Research Development*, Volume 32, Number 6, November, 1988, pp. 753-74.

MPEG

NAME:	MPEG
ALSO KNOWN AS:	MPG, MPEG-1, MPEG-2
TYPE:	Audio/video data storage
COLORS:	Up to 24-bits (4:2:0 YCbCr color space)
COMPRESSION:	DCT and block-based scheme with motion compensation
MAXIMUM IMAGE SIZE:	4095x4095x30 frames/second
MULTIPLE IMAGES PER FILE:	Yes (multiple program multiplexing)
NUMERICAL FORMAT:	NA
ORIGINATOR:	Motion Picture Experts Group (MPEG) of the International Standards Organization (ISO)
PLATFORM:	All
SUPPORTING APPLICATIONS:	Xing Technologies MPEG player, others
SPECIFICATION ON CD:	Yes (FAQ)
CODE ON CD:	Yes (in ISO MPEG-2 Codec package)
IMAGES ON CD:	Yes
SEE ALSO:	JPEG File Interchange Format, Intel DVI

USAGE: Stores an MPEG-encoded data stream on a digital storage medium. MPEG is used to encode audio, video, text, and graphical data within a single, synchronized data stream.

COMMENTS: MPEG-1 is a finalized standard in wide use. MPEG-2 is still in the development phase and continues to be revised for a wider base of applications. Currently, there are few stable products available for making practical use of the MPEG standard, but this is changing.

Overview

MPEG (pronounced "em-peg") is an acronym for the Motion Picture Experts Group, a working group of the International Standards Organization (ISO) that is responsible for creating standards for digital video and audio compression.

The MPEG specification is a specification for an encoded data stream which contains compressed audio and video information. MPEG was designed specifically to store sound and motion-video data on standard audio Compact Discs (CD) and Digital Audio Tapes (DAT).

The main application for MPEG is the storage of audio and video data on CD-ROMs for use in multimedia systems, such as those found on the Apple Macintosh platform and in the Microsoft Windows environment. Such systems require the ability to store and play back high-quality audio and video material for commercial, educational, and recreational applications. The new MPEG-2 standard allows the transmission of MPEG data across television and cable network systems.

On most systems, you use special hardware to capture MPEG data from a live video source at a real-time sampling rate of 30 frames per second. Each frame of captured video data is then compressed and stored as an MPEG data stream. If an audio source is also being sampled, it too is encoded and multiplexed in with the video stream, with some extra information to synchronize the two streams together for playback.

To play back MPEG data, you use either a hardware/software or software-only player. The player reads in the MPEG data stream, decompresses the information, and sends it to the display and audio systems of the computer. Speed of the playback depends upon how quickly the resources of the computer allow the MPEG data to be read, decompressed, and played. Available memory, CPU speed, and disk I/O throughput are all contributing factors. The quality of the MPEG stream is determined during encoding, and there are typically no adjustments available to allow an application to "tweak" the apparent quality of the MPEG output produced during playback.

MPEG is based on digital television standards (specified in CCIR-601) used in the United States. In its initial form, MPEG is not actually capable of storing CCIR-601 images. The typical resolution of 720x576 requires more bandwidth than the maximum MPEG data rate of 1.86Mbits/second allows. Standard television images must therefore be decimated by 2:1 into lower resolution SIF format data (352x240) to be stored.

European (PAL and SECAM) and Japanese standards are different in many respects, including the display rate (30 frames/second U.S., 25 frames/second European) and the number of lines per field (240 U.S., 288 European). Therefore, an MPEG player must be able to recognize a wide variety of variations possible in the encoded video signal itself.

Constrained Parameters Bitstreams (CPB) are a complex aspect of MPEG. CPBs are those bitstreams that are limited in terms of picture size, frame rate, and coded bit-rate parameters. These limitations normalize the computation complexity required of both hardware and software, thus guaranteeing a reasonable, nominal subset of MPEG that can be decoded by the widest possible range of applications while still remaining cost-effective. MPEG bitstreams for video are limited to 1.86 Mbits/second if they meet constrained parameters. If it were not for the constrained parameters, the MPEG syntax could specify a data rate of more than 100 Mbits/second.

File Organization

No actual structured MPEG file format has been defined. Everything required to play back MPEG data is encoded directly in the data stream. Therefore, no header or other type of wrapper is necessary. It is likely that when needed, a multimedia standards committee—perhaps MHEG or the DSM (Digital Storage Medium) MPEG subgroup—will one day define an MPEG file format.

File Details

This section describes the relationship between MPEG, JPEG, and MJPEG, the type of compression used for MPEG files, and the MPEG-2 standard.

Relationship Between MPEG, JPEG, and MJPEG

Some people are confused about the relationship between MPEG and JPEG. The MPEG and JPEG (Joint Photographic Experts Group) committees of the ISO originally started as the same group, but with two different purposes. JPEG focused exclusively on still-image compression, while MPEG focused on the encoding/synchronization of audio and video signals within a single data stream. Although MPEG employs a method of spatial data compression similar to that used for JPEG, they are not the same standard nor were they designed for the same purpose.

Another acronym you may hear is MJPEG (Motion JPEG). Several companies have come out with an alternative to MPEG—a simpler solution (but not yet a standard) for how to store motion video. This solution, called Motion JPEG, simply uses a digital video capture device to sample a video signal, to capture frames, and to compress each frame in its entirety using the JPEG compression method. A Motion JPEG data stream is then played back by decompressing and displaying each individual frame. A standard audio compression method is usually included in the Motion JPEG data stream.

There are several advantages to using Motion JPEG:

*   Fast, real-time compression rate

*   No frame-to-frame interpolation (motion compensation) of data is required.

But there are also disadvantages:

*   Motion JPEG files are considerably larger than MPEG files.

*   They are somewhat slower to play back (more information per frame then MPEG).

*   They exhibit poor video quality if a higher JPEG compression ratio (quality factor) is used.

On average, the temporal compression method used by MPEG provides a compression ratio three times that of JPEG for the same perceived picture quality.

MPEG Compression

MPEG uses an asymmetric compression method. Compression under MPEG is far more complicated than decompression, making MPEG a good choice for applications that need to write data only once, but need to read it many times. An example of such an application is an archiving system. Systems that require audio and video data to be written many times, such as an editing system, are not good choices for MPEG; they will run more slowly when using the MPEG compression scheme.

MPEG uses two types of compression methods to encode video data: interframe and intraframe encoding. Interframe encoding is based upon both predictive coding and interpolative coding techniques, as described below.

When capturing frames at a rapid rate (typically 30 frames/second for real time video) there will be a lot of identical data contained in any two or more adjacent frames. If a motion compression method is aware of this "temporal redundancy," as many audio and video compression methods are, then it need not encode the entire frame of data, as is done via *intraframe encoding*. Instead, only the differences (deltas) in information between the frames is encoded. This results in greater compression ratios, with far less data needing to be encoded. This type of *interframe encoding* is called *predictive encoding*.

A further reduction in data size may be achieved by the use of bi-directional prediction. Differential predictive encoding encodes only the differences between the current frame and the previous frame. Bi-directional prediction encodes the current frame based on the differences between the current, previous, and next frame of the video data. This type of interframe encoding is called motion-compensated interpolative encoding.

To support both interframe and intraframe encoding, an MPEG data stream contains three types of coded frames:

*   I-frames (intraframe encoded)
*   P-frames (predictive encoded)
*   B-frames (bi-directional encoded)

An *I-frame* contains a single frame of video data that does not rely on the information in any other frame to be encoded or decoded. Each MPEG data stream starts with an I-frame.

A *P-frame* is constructed by predicting the difference between the current frame and closest preceding I- or P-frame. A *B-frame* is constructed from the two closest I- or P-frames. The B-frame must be positioned between these I- or P-frames.

A typical sequence of frames in a MPEG stream might look like this:

```
IBBPBBPBBPBBIBBPBBPBBPBBI
```

In theory, the number of B-frames that may occur between any two I- and P-frames is unlimited. In practice, however, there are typically twelve P- and B-frames occurring between each I-frame. One I-frame will occur approximately every 0.4 seconds of video runtime.

Remember that the MPEG data is not decoded and displayed in the order that the frames appear within the stream. Because B-frames rely on two reference frames for prediction, both reference frames need to be decoded first from the bitstream, even though the display order may have a B-frame in between the two reference frames.

In the previous example, the I-frame is decoded first. But, before the two B-frames can be decoded, the P-frame must be decoded, and stored in memory with the I-frame. Only then may the two B-frames be decoded from the information found in the decoded I- and P-frames. Assume, in this example, that you are at the start of the MPEG data stream. The first ten frames are stored in the sequence IBBPBBPBBP (0123456789), but are decoded in the sequence:

```
IPBBPBBPBB (0312645978)
```

and finally are displayed in the sequence:

```
IBBPBBPBBP (0123456789)
```

Once an I-, P-, or B-frame is constructed, it is compressed using a DCT compression method similar to JPEG. Where interframe encoding reduces temporal redundancy (data identical over time), the DCT-encoding reduces spatial redundancy (data correlated within a given space). Both the temporal and the spatial encoding information are stored within the MPEG data stream.

By combining spatial and temporal subsampling, the overall bandwidth reduction achieved by MPEG can be considered to be upwards of 200:1. However, with respect to the final input source format, the useful compression ratio tends to be between 16:1 and 40:1. The ratio depends upon what the encoding application deems as "acceptable" image quality (higher quality video results in poorer compression ratios). Beyond these figures, the MPEG method becomes inappropriate for an application.

In practice, the sizes of the frames tend to be 150 Kbits for I-frames, around 50 Kbits for P-frames, and 20 Kbits for B-frames. The video data rate is typically constrained to 1.15 Mbits/second, the standard for DATs and CD-ROMs.

The MPEG standard does not mandate the use of P- and B-frames. Many MPEG encoders avoid the extra overhead of B- and P-frames by encoding I-frames. Each video frame is captured, compressed, and stored in its entirety, in a similar way to Motion JPEG. I-frames are very similar to JPEG-encoded frames. In fact, the JPEG Committee has plans to add MPEG I-frame methods to an enhanced version of JPEG, possibly to be known as JPEG-II.

With no delta comparisons to be made, encoding may be performed quickly; with a little hardware assistance, encoding can occur in real time (30 frames/second). Also, random access of the encoded data stream is very fast because I-frames are not as complex and time-consuming to decode as P- and B-frames. Any reference frame needs to be decoded before it can be used as a reference by another frame.

There are also some disadvantages to this scheme. The compression ratio of an I-frame-only MPEG file will be lower than the same MPEG file using motion compensation. A one-minute file consisting of 1800 frames would be approximately 2.5Mb in size. The same file encoded using B- and P-frames would be considerably smaller, depending upon the content of the video data. Also, this scheme of MPEG encoding might decompress more slowly on applications that allocate an insufficient amount of buffer space to handle a constant stream of I-frame data.

MPEG-2

The original MPEG standard is now referred to as MPEG-1. The MPEG-1 Video Standard is aimed at small-scale systems using CD-ROM storage and small, lower resolution displays. Its 1.5-Megabit/second data rate, however, limits MPEG-1 from many high-power applications. The next phase in MPEG technology development is MPEG-2.

The new MPEG-2 standard is a form of digital audio and video designed for the television industry. It will be used primarily as a way to consolidate and unify the needs of cable, satellite, and television broadcasts, as well as computing, optical storage, Ethernet, VCR, CD-I, HDTV, and blue-laser CD-ROM systems.

MPEG-2 is an extension of the MPEG-1 specification and therefore shares many of the same design features. The baseline part of MPEG-2 is called the Video Main Profile and provides a minimum definition of data quality. This definition fills the needs of high-quality television program distribution over a wide variety of data networks. Video Main Profile service over cable and satellite systems could possibly start in 1994. Consumers who need such features as interactive television and vision phones will benefit greatly from this service.

Features added by MPEG-2 include:

- Interlaced video formats

- Multiple picture aspect ratios (such as 4:3 and 16:9, as required by HDTV)

- Conservation of memory usage (by lowering the picture quality below the Video Main Profile definition)

- Increased video quality over MPEG-1 (when coding for the same target arbitrates)

- Ability to decode MPEG-1 data streams.

MPEG-2 can also multiplex audio, video, and other information into a single data stream and provides 2- to 15-Mbits/second data rates while maintaining full CCIR-601 image quality. MPEG-2 achieves this by the use of two types of data streams: the Program stream and the Transport stream.

The Program stream is similar to the MPEG-1 System stream, with extensions for encoding program-specific information, such as multiple language audio channels. The Transport stream was newly added to MPEG-2 and is used in broadcasting by multiplexing multiple programs comprised of audio, video, and private data, such as combining standard-definition TV and HDTV signals on the same channel. MPEG-2 supports multi-program broadcasts, storage of programs on VCRs, error detection and correction, and synchronization of data streams over complex networks.

Just as MPEG-1 encoding and decoding hardware has appeared, so will the same hardware for MPEG-2. With its broad range of applications and its toolkit approach, MPEG-2 encoding and decoding is very difficult to implement fully in a single chip. A "do everything" MPEG-2 chipset is not only difficult to design, but also expensive to sell. It is more likely that MPEG-2 hardware designed for specific applications will appear in the near future, with much more extensible chipsets to come in the more distant future.

The compression used on the MPEG audio stream data is based on the European MUSICAM standard, with additional pieces taken from other algorithms. It is similar in conception to the method used to compress MPEG video data. It is a lossy compression scheme, which throws away (or at least assigns fewer bits of resolution to) audio data that humans cannot hear. It is also a temporal-based compression method, compressing the differences between audio samples rather than the samples themselves. At this writing, a publicly available version of the audio code was due to be released by the MPEG audio group.

The typical bandwidth of a CD audio stream is 1.5 Mbits/second. MPEG audio compression can reduce this data down to approximately 256 Kbits/second for a 6:1 compression ratio with no discernible loss in quality (lower reductions are also possible). The remaining 1.25 Mbits/second of the bandwidth contain the MPEG-1 video and system streams. And using basically the same MPEG-1 audio algorithm, MPEG-2 audio will add discrete surround sound channels.

For Further Information

For further information about MPEG, see the MPEG Frequently Asked Questions (FAQ) document included on the CD-ROM that accompanies this book. Note, however, that this FAQ is included for background only; because it is constantly updated, you should obtain a more recent version. The MPEG FAQ on Usenet is posted monthly to the newsgroups *comp.graphics*, *comp.compression*, and *comp.multimedia*. The FAQ is available by using FTP from *rtfm.mit.edu* and is located in the directories that are called */pub/usenet/comp.graphics* and */pub/usenet/comp.compression.*

To obtain the full MPEG draft standard, you will have to purchase it from ANSI. The MPEG draft ISO standard is ISO CD 11172. This draft contains four parts:

11172.1	Synchronization and multiplexing of audio-visual information
11172.2	Video compression
11172.3	Audio compression
11172.4	Conformance testing

Contact ANSI at:

American National Standards Institute
Sales Department
1430 Broadway
New York, NY, 10018
Voice: 212-642-4900

Drafts of the MPEG-2 standard are expected to be available in 1994. For more information about MPEG, see the following article:

Le Gall, Didier, "MPEG: A Video Compression Standard for Multimedia Applications," *Communications of the ACM*, April, 1991, Volume 3, Number 4, pp. 46-58.

On the CD-ROM you will find several pieces of MPEG software. The ISO MPEG-2 Codec software, which converts uncompressed video frames into MPEG-1 and MPEG-2 video-coded bitstream sequences, and vice versa, is included in source code form and as a precompiled MS-DOS binary. The Sparkle MPEG player is also included for Macintosh platforms.

NAME:	MTV
ALSO KNOWN AS:	None
TYPE:	Scene description
COLORS:	NA
COMPRESSION:	Uncompressed
MAXIMUM IMAGE SIZE:	NA
MULTIPLE IMAGES PER FILE:	Yes
NUMERICAL FORMAT:	ASCII
ORIGINATOR:	Mark VandeWettering
PLATFORM:	All
SUPPORTING APPLICATIONS:	MTV, various conversion utilities
SPECIFICATION ON CD:	Yes
CODE ON CD:	Yes (in pbmplus package)
IMAGES ON CD:	No
SEE ALSO:	NFF, PBM

USAGE: Used by the MTV ray tracer, although numerous conversion utilities, usually associated with other ray tracers, exist.

COMMENTS: One of the early ray tracers, still in use because of its easy availability, wide distribution, and simplicity.

Overview

The MTV formats were created to support Mark VandeWettering's MTV ray tracer and are named for the author. The MTV application has been ported to many platforms and has enjoyed wide distribution, through the *comp.graphics* newsgroup on the Internet and through the network of private (primarily PC-based) BBSs. Although the author considers both the program and the format to be dead, the format still enjoys a certain degree of currency, mainly due to its understandable design and simplicity. MTV is still being downloaded with some regularity from a number of bulletin boards and information services.

File Organization and Details

Both the MTV input format and the output format are based on other formats that are described in this book. The following sections provide summary information only.

Input Format

The MTV input format is identical to the Neutral File Format (NFF) developed by Eric Haines and described in detail in the NFF article.

NFF files consist of lines of ASCII text. Each line describes an object called an entity. The first field of each line describes the entity's type, and subsequent fields on the same line, and possibly subsequent lines, contain further information about the entity. The following entities are currently supported:

- Simple perspective frustum

- Background color description

- Positional (versus directional) light-source description

- Surface-properties description

- Polygon, polygonal patch, cylinder/cone, and sphere descriptions

Entities are coded as follows:

"v"	Viewpoint location (viewing vectors and angles)
"b"	Background color
"l"	Positional light location
"f"	Object material properties
"c"	Cone or cylinder primitive
"s"	Sphere primitive
"p"	Polygon primitive
"pp"	Polygonal patch primitive

See the NFF article for a discussion of each entity.

Output Format

The MTV output format is based on the PPM format, a part of the pbmplus package of utilities developed by Jef Poskanzer. PPM is described in the PBM article in this book, and the utilities are included on the CD that accompanies this book and are described in Appendix A, *What's On The CD-ROM?* The MTV output format differs only trivially from the PPM format. The author of the MTV format describes the output format as follows:

> An MTV format image consists of an ASCII header followed directly by the image data bytes. The ASCII header is merely a string containing the width and height followed by a newline character. The following C statement will print out the ASCII header:
>
> ```
> fprintf(fp, "%d %d\n", width, height) ;
> ```
>
> This is followed directly by the image data, which is written out as three unsigned bytes per pixel, originating at the upper left of the image. This is identical to how the bytes are written out in the PPM image format.
>
> If you desire to write PPM format files, you merely need to change the line which outputs the ASCII header to the following:
>
> ```
> fprintf(fp, "P6\n%d %d\n255\n", width, height) ;
> ```
>
> Here is an example of a small pixmap in this format:
>
> ```
> P3
> # feep.ppm
> 4 4
> 15
>  0  0  0    0  0  0    0  0  0   15  0 15
>  0  0  0    0 15  7    0  0  0    0  0  0
>  0  0  0    0  0  0    0 15  7    0  0  0
> 15  0 15    0  0  0    0  0  0    0  0  0
> ```
>
> Programs that read this format should be as lenient as possible, accepting anything that looks remotely like a pixmap.

The PBM article provides additional information about the PPM output format.

For Further Information

For further information about the MTV format, see the specification included on the CD that accompanies this book, as well as the specifications for NFF and PBM.

The MTV ray tracer is no longer being maintained by Mr. VandeWettering, who considers it dead. Ample documentation is provided with the package, however, should the need ever arise. You may also be able to get additional information from:

Mark VandeWettering
Pixar
1001 West Cutting
Richmond, CA 94804
Voice: 510-236-4000
FAX: 510-236-0388
markv@pixar.com

You can also contact:

Tony Apodaca
aaa@pixar.com

NAME:	NAPLPS
ALSO KNOWN AS:	North American Presentation Layer Protocol Syntax
TYPE:	Graphics Protocol/Metafile
COLORS:	NA
COMPRESSION:	None
MAXIMUM IMAGE SIZE:	NA
MULTIPLE IMAGES PER FILE:	Yes
NUMERICAL FORMAT:	ASCII
ORIGINATOR:	ISO/ANSI/CSA
PLATFORM:	All
SUPPORTING APPLICATIONS:	Videotex services, Prodigy
SPECIFICATION ON CD:	Yes (summary description by third party)
CODE ON CD:	No
IMAGES ON CD:	Yes
SEE ALSO:	None
USAGE:	Transfer of graphics information to devices such as modems and terminals.
COMMENTS:	Although not strictly a file format, NAPLPS is likely to become the basis of one, because it is in wide use in a rapidly growing segment of the computer communications industry.

Overview

NAPLPS (North American Presentation Layer Protocol Syntax) was designed as an information transfer protocol rather than as a file format. However, because NAPLPS data is occasionally written to disk and saved in file form, it is only a matter of time before an actual format stabilizes. For this reason, we are including summary information about NAPLPS in this book.

NAPLPS is used by a number of Videotex services, is supported by special NAPLPS terminals, and is used by Prodigy, a well-known commercial online service. Data is sent as a stream of either 7- or 8-bit ASCII characters. It was specifically designed to provide usable information transfer rates, even at 2400 baud. As such, it services the low end of the market and for this reason should be more important in the future.

For Further Information

For further information about NAPLPS, see the excellent article by Michael Dillon included on the CD that accompanies this book. This article provides an overview and some detailed information about NAPLPS. You can also contact Mr. Dillon at:

Michael Dillon
CompuServe: 71532,137
Internet: *mpdillon@halcyon.com*

NAPLPS is formally defined in standards documents available for purchase from the International Standards Organization (ISO), the American National Standards Association (ANSI), and the Canadian Standards Association (CSA). Note that information contained in the CSA supplement (see below) is not included in the ANSI version of the document.

International Standards Organization (ISO)
1 rue de Varembe
Case Postal 56
CH-1211 Geneva 20 Switzerland
Voice: +41 22 749 01 11
FAX: +41 22 733 34 30

Ask ISO for the NAPLPS specification.

American National Standards Institute (ANSI)
Attn: Sales Department
1430 Broadway
New York, NY, 10018
Voice: 212-642-4900

Ask ANSI for document number X3.110-1983.

Canadian Standards Association (CSA)
Attn: Sales Group
178 Rexdale Blvd.
Rexdale, Ontario, M9W 1R3
Voice: 416-747-4044

Ask CSA for document number T500-1983 and supplement number 1-1991.

Further information about the NAPLPS format can be found in the February, March, April, and May 1983 issues of *Byte* magazine.

NAME:	NFF
ALSO KNOWN AS:	Neutral File Format
TYPE:	Scene description
COLORS:	NA
COMPRESSION:	Uncompressed
MAXIMUM IMAGE SIZE:	NA
MULTIPLE IMAGES PER FILE:	NA
NUMERICAL FORMAT:	NA
ORIGINATOR:	Eric Haines
PLATFORM:	All
SUPPORTING APPLICATIONS:	Standard Procedural Database (SPD), MTV, others
SPECIFICATION ON CD:	Yes
CODE ON CD:	No
IMAGES ON CD:	No
SEE ALSO:	MTV, Pixar RIB, POV, PRT, QRT, Radiance, Rayshade, RTrace
USAGE:	Modelling of rendering algorithms, ray-trace applications.
COMMENTS:	A simple scene description language incorporating most of the basics, which would be informative for anyone thinking about designing yet another ray-trace scene-description format.

Overview

NFF (Neutral File Format) is the creation of Eric Haines. Mr. Haines, the publisher of *Ray Tracing News*, has been active in the high-end graphics community for a number of years, He is well-known through these efforts, particularly on the Internet. As a consequence of Mr. Haines' visibility, although NFF was originally designed to test rendering algorithms, the format has played a role in the evolution of other, more sophisticated, scene description languages and formats.

Eric Haines describes NFF as follows:

> The NFF (Neutral File Format) is designed as a minimal scene description language. The language was designed in order to test various

rendering algorithms and efficiency schemes. It is meant to describe the geometry and basic surface characteristics of objects, the placement of lights, and the viewing frustum for the eye. Some additional information is provided for aesthetic reasons (such as the color of the objects, which is not strictly necessary for testing the efficiency of rendering algorithms).

Note that NFF has minimal support for lighting and shading.

File Organization

NFF files consist of lines of ASCII text. Each line describes an object called an entity. The first field of each line describes the entity's type, and subsequent fields on the same line, and possibly subsequent lines, contain further information on the entity.

File Details

The information in this section is extracted from the NFF documentation kindly provided by Eric Haines.

By providing a minimal interface, NFF is meant to act as a simple format to allow the programmer to quickly write filters to move from NFF to the local file format. Presently, the following entities are supported:

- Simple perspective frustum

- Background color description

- Positional (versus directional) light-source description

- Surface-properties description

- Polygon, polygonal patch, cylinder/cone, and sphere descriptions

Entities are coded as follows:

"v"	Viewpoint location (viewing vectors and angles)
"b"	Background color
"l"	Positional light location
"f"	Object material properties
"c"	Cone or cylinder primitive
"s"	Sphere primitive

"p"   Polygon primitive
"pp"   Polygonal patch primitive

These are explained in the following sections.

Viewpoint Location

The viewpoint location entity is coded as follows:

"v"
"from" Fx Fy Fz
"at" Ax Ay Az
"up" Ux Uy Uz
"angle" angle
"hither" hither
"resolution" xres yres

Format:

v
from %g %g %g
at %g %g %g
up %g %g %g
angle %g
hither %g
resolution %d %d

Parameters:

from   Eye location in XYZ

at   Position to be at the center of the image, in XYZ world coordinates (AKA "lookat")

up   Vector defining which direction is up, as an XYZ vector

angle   In degrees, defined as the angle from the center of top pixel row to bottom pixel row and left column to right column hither   Distance of the hither plane (if any) from the eye. Mostly needed for hidden surface algorithms.

resolution In pixels, in x and in y

Note that no assumptions are made about normalizing the data (e.g., the from-at distance does not have to be 1). Also, vectors are not required to be perpendicular to each other.

For all databases, some viewing parameters are always the same:

yon is "at infinity."
aspect ratio is 1.0.

A view entity must be defined before any objects are defined. (This requirement is so that NFF files can be displayed on-the-fly by hidden-surface machines.)

Background Color

A color is simply RGB, with values between 0 and 1:

"b" R G B

Format:

b %g %g %g

If no background color is set, assume that RGB = [0,0,0].

Positional Light Location

A light is defined by XYZ position:

"l" X Y Z [R G B]

Format:

l %g %g %g [%g %g %g]

All light entities must be defined before any objects are defined. (This requirement is so that NFF files can be used by hidden surface machines). Lights have a non-zero intensity of no particular value, if not specified (i.e., the program can determine a useful intensity as desired); the red/green/blue color of the light can optionally be specified.

Object Material Properties (Fill Color and Shading Parameters)

Object material properties (fill color and shading parameters) are coded as follows:

"f" red green blue Kd Ks Shine T index_of_refraction

Format:

f %g %g %g %g %g %g %g %g

RGB is in terms of 0.0 to 1.0.

Parameters:

Kd	Diffuse component
Ks	Specular
Shine	Phong cosine power for highlights
T	Transmittance (fraction of contribution of the transmitting ray).

Usually, $0 <= Kd <= 1$ and $0 <= Ks <= 1$, though it is not required that Kd + Ks = 1. Note that transmitting objects (T > 0) are considered to have two sides for algorithms that need these (normally, objects have one side).

The fill color is used to color the objects following it until a new color is assigned.

Objects (Cone or Cylinder Primitive)

All objects are considered one-sided, unless the second side is needed for transmittance calculations (e.g., you cannot throw out the second intersection of a transparent sphere in ray tracing).

A cylinder is defined as having a radius and an axis defined by two points, which also define the top and bottom edge of the cylinder.

A cone is defined in similar fashion; the difference is that the apex and base radii are different. The apex radius is defined as being smaller than the base radius. Note that the surface exists without endcaps. The cone or cylinder description is shown below:

"c"
base.x base.y base.z base_radius
apex.x apex.y apex.z apex_radius

Format:

    c
    %g %g %g %g
    %g %g %g %g

A negative value for both radii means that only the inside of the object is visible (objects are normally considered one-sided, with the outside visible). Note that the base and apex cannot be coincident for a cylinder or cone. Making them coincident could be used to define endcaps, but none of the SPD scenes currently make use of this definition.

Sphere

A sphere is defined by a radius and center position, as shown below:

"s" center.x center.y center.z radius

Format:

    s %g %g %g %g

If the radius is negative, then only the sphere's inside is visible (objects are normally considered one-sided, with the outside visible). Currently none of the SPD scenes makes use of negative radii.

Polygon

A polygon is defined by a set of vertices. With these databases, a polygon is defined to have all points coplanar. A polygon has only one side; the order of the vertices is counterclockwise as you face the polygon (right-handed coordinate system). The first two edges must form a non-zero convex angle, so that the normal and side visibility can be determined by using just the first three vertices.

A polygon is defined as shown below:

    "p" total_vertices
    vert1.x vert1.y vert1.z
    [etc. for total_vertices vertices]

Format:

    p %d
    [%g %g %g] <— for total_vertices vertices

Polygonal Patch

A patch is defined by a set of vertices and their normals. With these databases, a patch is defined to have all points coplanar. A patch has only one side, with the order of the vertices being counterclockwise as you face the patch (right-handed coordinate system). The first two edges must form a non-zero convex angle, so that the normal and side visibility can be determined.

A polygonal patch is defined as shown below:

    "pp" total_vertices
    vert1.x vert1.y vert1.z norm1.x norm1.y norm1.z
    [etc. for total_vertices vertices]

Format:

    pp %d
    [%g %g %g %g %g %g] <— for total_vertices vertices

Comment

A comment is defined as shown below:

    "#" [string]

Format:

    # [string]

As soon as a # character is detected, the rest of the line is considered a comment.

For Further Information

For further information about the NFF format, see the specification included on the CD that accompanies this book. You can also contact the NFF author:

Eric Haines
3D/Eye Inc.
2359 North Triphammer Road
Ithaca, NY 14850
erich@eye.com

NFF is also used in conjunction with the Standard Procedural Database (SPD) software, a package designed to create a variety of databases for testing rendering schemes. For more information about SPD, see the following paper:

"A Proposal for Standard Graphics Environments," *IEEE Computer Graphics and Applications*, Volume 7, Number 11, November, 1987, pp. 3-5.

SPD is available by anonymous FTP from:

wuarchive.wustl.edu in directory */graphics/graphics/objects*
princeton.edu in directory */pub/Graphics*

Images of the databases are available from (among other places):

ftp.ipl.rpi.edu in directory */sigma/erich*
gondwana.ecr.mu.oz.au in directory */pub/images/haines*

NAME:	OFF
ALSO KNOWN AS:	Object File Format
TYPE:	Scene description
COLORS:	NA
COMPRESSION:	Uncompressed
MAXIMUM IMAGE SIZE:	NA
MULTIPLE IMAGES PER FILE:	NA
NUMERICAL FORMAT:	NA
ORIGINATOR:	Randi Rost
PLATFORM:	UNIX
SUPPORTING APPLICATIONS:	dxmodel, others
SPECIFICATION ON CD:	Yes
CODE ON CD:	Yes
IMAGES ON CD:	No
SEE ALSO:	MTV, Pixar RIB, POV, PRT, QRT, Radiance, RTrace
USAGE:	Description of 3D scenes for later rendering.
COMMENTS:	The OFF format is designed to support easy and flexible description of 3D objects for later manipulation and rendering.

Overview

OFF (Object File Format) was developed in 1986 at Digital Equipment Corporation's Workstations Systems Engineering by Randi Rost and was subsequently made available for public distribution. OFF is partly derived from an object file format used at Ohio State University. OFF was designed from the start to support data interchange and archiving; in this case, the interchange and archiving of 3D objects. Although this plan originally bore fruit inside Digital, OFF has seen use in the 3D modeling community, partly because of its wide availability on the Internet.

The OFF author thought carefully about how to establish libraries of laboriously-produced 3D objects so that the labor that went into construction of the objects could be amortized through reuse. OFF files consist of lines of ASCII text describing objects, implementing part of the author's goal of making OFF independent of language, device, and operating system.

The format is well described in the original specification documents included on the CD-ROM, and only a summary of that format is included here.

File Organization and Details

An OFF file consists of a number of ASCII lines. The following are usually found at the beginning of these lines:

Name   Short descriptive name of object defined in the file.

Description
            Fuller description of the object defined in the file.

Author   Actual author or company owner.

Copyright   Distribution information.

Type   Object type; currently, only polygons are supported.

Following this information is a series of lines, each defining an object attribute. Each attribute consists of:

Property name
            Uniquely describes the property; currently, conventions exist for geometry, polygon colors, vertex colors, back faces, vertex order, diffusion coefficients, specular coefficients, and specular power.

Property types
            One of the following: default, generic, indexed, or indexed_poly.

Data format
            String of characters indicating the order and type of the data to follow.

Filename or data
            The file indicated here may contain more elaborate data than might be appropriate in this file.

Associated with the original OFF system are an include file, *objects.h,* and a library file, *off.a* (on UNIX systems). Together, these implement a subroutine library for reading and writing OFF files. You can adapt these for operating systems other than UNIX.

For Further Information

For further information about the OFF format, see the specification included on the CD-ROM that accompanies this book:

Rost, Randi, *OFF—A 3D Object File Format,* November 6, 1986, updated October 12, 1989.

You can also obtain the OFF archive (containing the distribution format, tools, and objects) via FTP from:

gatekeeper.dec.com (in the *pub/DEC* directory)

The OFF author, Randi Rost, is not currently supporting OFF or enhancing its tools (nor is Digital Equipment, where Mr. Rost developed OFF). The archive can be used freely, but comes with no express or implied warranties. You must adhere to the usage guidelines outlined in the copyright sections of the individual files.

For further information, contact:

Randi Rost
Kubota Pacific Computer, Inc.
2630 Walsh Avenue
Santa Clara, CA 95051
rost@kpc.com

OS/2 Bitmap

NAME:	OS/2 Bitmap
ALSO KNOWN AS:	BMP, DIB, Presentation Manager Bitmap, PM Bitmap, PM BMP, PM DIB
TYPE:	Bitmap
COLORS:	Mono, 4-bit, 8-bit, 24-bit
COMPRESSION:	RLE, uncompressed
MAXIMUM IMAGE SIZE:	64KbX64Kb pixels
MULTIPLE IMAGES PER FILE:	No
NUMERICAL FORMAT:	Little-endian
ORIGINATOR:	Microsoft Inc, IBM Inc.
PLATFORM:	Intel machines running OS/2, Microsoft Windows, MS-DOS, Windows NT
SUPPORTING APPLICATIONS:	Too numerous to list
SPECIFICATION ON CD:	Yes (part of Presentation Manager Metafile specification)
CODE ON CD:	Yes
IMAGES ON CD:	No
SEE ALSO:	Microsoft Windows Bitmap

USAGE: Used along with several variations in IBM OS/2, Microsoft Windows, and OS/2- and Windows-based products. OS/2 Bitmap is primarily a storage format. Although it is based on OS/2 internal bitmap data structures; it is supported by many non-OS/2 and non-PC applications.

COMMENTS: A well-defined, well-documented format, with fairly good distribution, which is quick and easy to read and uncompress. It lacks, however, a superior compression scheme, making it unsuited for the storage of deep-pixel images. Applications on non-Intel machines need to pay attention to byte-ordering of 16-bit numerical data.

Overview

The OS/2 Bitmap file format is supported primarily by applications running under IBM OS/2 Presentation Manager, and secondarily by applications running under Microsoft Windows. Most graphics and imaging applications that operate under the OS/2 Presentation Manager environment support creation and display of OS/2 Bitmap format files.

IBM shared responsibility with Microsoft for the development of early versions of IBM's OS/2 operating system. Thus, versions of the BMP format exist on both the Microsoft Windows and the OS/2 platforms and are similar in many respects. There are currently four variations of the BMP format, each associated with an operating system version. In historical order of appearance, they are:

- Microsoft Windows 1.X and 2.X

- OS/2 1.X

- Microsoft Windows 3.X

- OS/2 2.X

This article discusses the two versions from IBM, corresponding to OS/2 Version 1.X and Version 2.X. For a discussion of the Microsoft Windows variants, see the Microsoft Windows Bitmap article.

An early version of Microsoft's Windows Bitmap format (BMP) was device-dependent—a simple bitmap format with no palette or data compression. A refinement of the original BMP format, the DIB (device-independent bitmap), was developed partially in support of IBM's OS/2 Presentation Manager Version 1.x. It gained device-independent information in the header, a color palette, and RLE data compression. Revisions designed to support IBM OS/2 Presentation Manager 2.X have resulted in further changes.

All of the OS/2 Bitmap variants originated on Intel-based machines and thus share a common little-endian heritage. The current format is otherwise hardware-independent, however, and can accommodate images with up to 24-bit color. Its basic design makes it a good general-purpose format that can be used for color or black-and-white image storage if file size is not a factor. Its main virtues are its simplicity and its relatively widespread support in the PC marketplace.

Although the OS/2 Bitmap format is well-defined, there is no actual format specification document available for reprint from IBM. Information about structure and data encoding methods is contained in a number of programmer's references, manuals, and include files.

The compression method used is a type of run-length encoding (RLE). Although RLE is lossless and is easily and quickly uncompressed, it is not considered a superior compression method.

We recommend that applications running on non-Intel platforms take pains to write 16-bit numerical data in little-endian order, that is, low byte first. Note also that long data words are not aligned in the header and palette sections.

File Organization

An OS/2 Bitmap file is organized into four sections: the bitmap header, the information header, the palette, and the bitmap data. Of these four sections, only the palette is optional. This structures for Versions 1.X and 2.X are shown below.

OS/2 1.x	OS/2 2.x
Bitmap Header	Bitmap Header
Core Information Header	Bitmap Information Header
Palette	Palette
Bitmap Data	Bitmap Data

The OS/2 bitmap header is 14 bytes in length and has remained unchanged through several revisions of the format.

The bitmap header is followed by a second header, called the information header, which has grown in size with each new version of the format. OS/2 1.x files have a 12-byte information header; Windows 3.0 files add an additional 28 bytes, bringing its total length to 40 bytes. OS/2 2.0 adds still another 24 bytes, increasing the size to 64 bytes. In fact, the usual way to tell the difference between versions of the format is by the size of the information header.

File Details

This section describes the details of the bitmap file header, bitmap information header, palette, and image data.

Bitmap File Header

The OS/2 Bitmap format actually contains two headers; the first is usually referred to as the bitmap file header, is 14 bytes in length, and always occurs at the beginning of the file (this is true for both variants of the OS/2 format). The structure of the file header is shown below.

```
typedef struct _Os2BitmapHeader
{
  WORD   ImageFileType;        /* Image file type, always 4D42h ("BM")*/
  DWORD  FileSize;             /* Physical file size in bytes */
  WORD   Reserved1;            /* Always 0 */
  WORD   Reserved2;            /* Always 0 */
  DWORD  ImageDataOffset;      /* Start of image data offset in bytes */
} OS2HEAD;
```

ImageFileType holds a 2-byte magic value used to identify the file type, and is always 4D42h, or BM in ASCII. Applications reading OS/2 Bitmap files should always check this field before attempting to use any of the data read from the file.

FileSize is the total size of the file in bytes and should agree with the file size reported by the file system.

Reserved1 and Reserved2 are not used and should be set to zero.

ImageDataOffset is the offset starting from the beginning of the file to the start of the image data in bytes.

Bitmap Information Header (for Version 1.x)

Following the bitmap file header is a second header called the bitmap information header, which varies in size depending on the format variant. The following shows the structure for Presentation Manager Version 1.X files:

```
typedef struct _Os21xBitmapInfoHeader
{
  WORD   HeaderSize;           /* Size of this header */
  DWORD  ImageWidth;           /* Image width in pixels */
  DWORD  ImageHeight;          /* Image height in pixels */
  WORD   NumberOfImagePlanes;  /* Number of planes (alwaays 1) */
  WORD   BitsPerPixel;         /* Bits per pixel (1, 4, 8, or 24) */
  DWORD  CompressionMethod     /* Compression method used (0, 1,
                                  or 2) */
  DWORD  SizeOfBitmap;         /* Size of the bitmap in bytes */
  DWORD  HorzResolution;       /* Horizontal resolution in pixels per
                                  meter */
  DWORD  VertResolution;       /* Vertical resolution in pixels per
                                  meter */
  DWORD  NumColorsUsed;        /* Number of colors in the image */
```

```
    DWORD NumSignificantColors;      /* Number of important colors in
                                        palette */

  } OS21XINFOHEAD;
```

HeaderSize is the size of the information header in bytes, and is the value read to identify the bitmap variant. For OS/2 1.x, the value is 12, and for OS/2 2.0, the value is 64.

ImageWidth and ImageHeight are the height and width of the image, respectively, in pixels.

NumberOfImagePlanes is always 1 because OS/2 Bitmap files always contain only a single plane.

BitsPerPixel is the number of bits per pixel and can be 1, 4, 8, or 24.

CompressionMethod indicates the type of compression used on the bitmap data. A 0 indicates no compression; 1 indicates that the 8-bit RLE method was used; and 2 indicates that 4-bit RLE was used. (See Chapter 9, *Data Compression*, for more information on OS/2 RLE encoding.)

SizeOfBitmap is the size of the unencoded bitmap in bytes.

HorzResolution and VertResolution are the horizontal and vertical resolutions in pixels per meter, used to help choose a proper mode to use when printing or displaying the image.

NumColorsUsed is the number of colors present in the palette. If this value is 0, then the number of entries is equal to the maximum size possible for the color map. The value is calculated by shifting 1 in the BitsPerPixel field:

```
    NumColorsUsed = 1 << bmp.BitsPerPixel
```

NumSignificantColors denotes the number of significant colors in the color map, determined by their frequency of appearance in the image. The more frequent the occurrence of a color, the more significant it is. This value is used to provide as accurate display as possible when using graphics hardware that supports fewer colors than defined in the image. An 8-bit image with 142 colors, for instance, might only have a dozen or so colors comprising the bulk of the image. If these colors are known, a display adapter with only 16 colors is able to display the image more accurately by using the 16 most frequently occurring colors in the image. This value is 0 if all the colors in the color map are significant.

Bitmap Information Header (for Version 2.x)

The following shows the eight additional fields included for Presentation Manager 2.X. (Note that all fields shown for Version 1.X are also included for 2.X files.) The additional header structure is shown below:

Version 2.X:

```
typedef struct _Os22xBitmapInfoHeader
{
    WORD   Resolution;        /* Units used for resolution */
    WORD   Reserved;          /* Always 0 */
    WORD   Recording;         /* Bitmap orientation */
    WORD   Rendering;         /* Halftone algorithm */
    DWORD  Size1;             /* Halftone algorithm data */
    DWORD  Size2;             /* Halftone algorithm data */
    DWORD  ColorEncoding;     /* Palette format */
    DWORD  Identifier;        /* For user application use */

} OS22XINFOHEAD;
```

Resolution refers to two fields, horizontal resolution and vertical resolution. In the OS/2 2.0 variant, the unit of measure used in the two resolution fields may be specified. Currently there is only one value defined, which is 0 for the default unit of pixels per meter.

Reserved is reserved and is always set to 0.

Recording indicates how the bitmap data is stored. The only value currently defined is 0, meaning that the image is stored starting with the bottom line of the image.

Rendering, Size1, and Size2 refer to the digital halftoning algorithm that was used on the image data, if any. If no algorithm was used, these fields are set to 0.

ColorEncoding denotes the type of color model used by the image data. The only value currently defined is 0 for RGB data.

Identifier is a 4-byte field for use by an application creating the file, which may contain information such as an image identification number or a 4-character ASCII string.

Palette

All 1-, 4-, and 8-bit files have a palette, the size of which is dependent upon the number of colors in the image. The number of colors can be determined by the value in the NumColorsUsed field in the bitmap information header. Palettes, like the bitmap information headers, are different in files created under OS/2 1.x and OS/2 2.0. In OS/2 1.x the palette is a sequence of three 1-byte values, each representing the blue, green, and red color components in each palette entry. (Microsoft Windows Bitmap palettes also contain a 3-byte sequence of color information, which is, however, followed by a fourth reserved byte always set to the value 0.)

The first two colors defined in the table are normally white and black as entries 0 and 1 respectively. Remaining colors are usually appear in random order. If the image data stored in the file has less than 16 colors, however, it is usually best to sort the colors in the color table and place the colors occurring with the greatest frequency in the image first. A value can then be stored in the Num-SignificantColors field (typically a value of 8 or 16) in the information header to aid display hardware with a small color palette to correctly display the colors in the image.

Some applications creating 1-bit files invert the color sense of the image data, causing color reversal (i.e., white becomes black, and black becomes white). This usually occurs in operating environments where the normal display consists of black characters on a white background (found on the Apple Macintosh and Microsoft Windows). Artificially inverting the data—interpreting all 1 bits as 0 and all 0 bits as 1—fixes this problem.

Image Data

The image data in an OS/2 Bitmap is always byte-oriented. How the data is read, however, depends on the number of bits per pixel and whether the image data is compressed.

In 1-bit image data, each byte represents eight pixels, and the most significant bit in the byte is the first pixel value. 4-bit images contain two pixel values per byte, and the most significant nibble is the first pixel value; the least significant nibble is the next pixel value. 8-bit images, of course, contain one pixel value per byte. 24-bit image data uses three bytes per pixel, stored in blue, green, and red order.

Each scan line in an OS/2 Bitmap file is always a multiple of 4 bytes in length and is padded when necessary. Because all 1-, 4-, and 8-bit images use palettes, the pixel values read from the image data are index values into the palette which hold the actual pixel color. 24-bit images, however, never use a palette, because their pixel color data is stored directly in the image data. Image data is always displayed starting at the lower left corner of the screen; that is, pixel coordinate 0,0 is at the lower-left corner of the image. The OS/2 2.0 variant added a flag allowing this orientation to be changed, but currently no other orientation values have been defined.

Image Data Encoding

The vast majority of OS/2 Bitmap files are uncompressed, which makes for larger files (300K to 500K is not uncommon), but which also allows the files to load and save quickly. Compression is accomplished by a type of run-length encoding (RLE).

The OS/2 Bitmap RLE compression scheme allows for the compression of image data stored at four or eight bits per pixel. Because this is a byte-oriented RLE 1-bit and 24-bit images may not compress well and may even grow in size, due to the absence of repetitive character data. Exceptions to this are 24-bit gray-scale image data and 1-bit image data with long runs of a single color. OS/2 Bitmap readers should always support RLE. Runs of identical bytes in the image data are encoded as packets, which are of two types: encoded and literal (or absolute). An encoded run contains two bytes; the first byte is the number of pixels in the run and the second byte is the pixel value. The first byte is always non-zero and ranges in value from 1 to 255.

Literal runs contain five or more bytes of data. The first byte is always set to zero, and signals the start of a literal run. The second byte ranges in value from 3 to 255 and indicates the number of bytes to follow which are to be read as literal pixel values. Literal runs should always end on a 2-byte word boundary. Both literal and encoded runs stop at the end of scan lines. Normally, most of the runs in an RLE-compressed file are encoded. Very complex or noisy images containing many colors, however, may not compress well using run encoding; an image must contain pixel runs of three or more bytes long for encoding to be effective.

Escape sequences are composed of two bytes; the first byte is always zero, as in a literal run, and the second byte may be 0, 1, or 2. A value of 0 in the second byte signals the end of the image; a value of 1 indicates the end of a scan line; and a value of 2 is a delta escape sequence, indicating a change in the coordinates of the encoded image data.

RLE methods ordinarily encode a bitmap one scan line at a time, starting at the first byte of the image data and ending with the last. The delta escape sequence allows the encoding process to skip around in the image, however, encoding parts of the image in chunks without regard to scan lines. When a delta escape code is detected, the following two bytes signify the horizontal and vertical offsets of the start of the next run. When the run at the new point is read, the decoding continues from that point.

Delta escape codes make decoding the OS/2 Bitmap image data much more difficult. Normally, decoding is provided by a simple function that reads and decodes a single scan line at a time. Thus, a temporary buffer need only be large enough to hold a single decoded scan line before it is copied to a file or output device. The presence of delta escape codes, however, may force the use of a buffer large enough to hold the entire decoded image, so that the decoded data may be written to any part of the decoded image at any time.

Fortunately delta escape codes are seldom used. Delta encoding does, however, offer several advantages over the other forms of encoding. The most important is that an area of an image that is a single color can be compressed with greater efficiency using deltas than with the use of single scan-line encoding. Deltas can also be used to encode image data into a series of tiles, rather than into scan lines or strips.

For Further Information

The OS/2 Bitmap file format is maintained by IBM, and primary information is contained in the Presentation Manager System Development Kit (SDK). We have included that information on the CD-ROM that accompanies this book. For further information, contact:

IBM Corporation
Attn: Independent Vendor League
Mail Stop 147
150 Kettletown Road
Southbury, CT 06488
Voice: 203-266-2000

See also the following references:

Microsoft Corporation, *Microsoft Windows Programmer's Reference,* Microsoft Press, Redmond, WA, 1990.

Petzold, Charles, "What's New in Bitmap Formats: A Look at Windows and OS/2," *PC Magazine*, September 11, 1990, pp. 403-410.

Petzold, Charles, "The Windows 3.0 Device-Independent Bitmap," *PC Magazine*, June 25, 1991, pp. 397-401.

Petzold, Charles, "Preserving a Device-Independent Bitmap: The Packed-DIB Format," *PC Magazine*, July 1991, pp. 433-439.

P3D

NAME:	P3D
ALSO KNOWN AS:	Pittsburgh Supercomputer Center 3D Metafile
TYPE:	3D scene description
COLORS:	NA
COMPRESSION:	Uncompressed
MAXIMUM IMAGE SIZE:	NA
MULTIPLE IMAGES PER FILE:	NA
NUMERICAL FORMAT:	NA
ORIGINATOR:	Carnegie Mellon University
PLATFORM:	All
SUPPORTING APPLICATIONS:	P3D
SPECIFICATION ON CD:	Yes
CODE ON CD:	No
IMAGES ON CD:	No
SEE ALSO:	None

USAGE: Description and storage of 3D objects.

COMMENTS: A powerful format that implements its own language and provides support for a number of common and useful renderers.

Overview

P3D is a system that originated at Carnegie Mellon University's Pittsburgh Supercomputing Center, which retains the copyright for the system. The P3D format used by the P3D system was intended for the storage of 3D models and was designed to be portable, flexible, compact, and extensible. The authors wished to create a format that would be compatible with applications, renderers in particular, on a number of platforms.

The P3D format implements a sophisticated description language, which consists of a set of extensions to Common Lisp. Perhaps to avoid implementation dependencies, only a subset of Common Lisp, called Alisp, is used. While this can be a boon to developers who already know a Lisp dialect, it provides a barrier to entry to those who don't. As a consequence, the P3D format has not been used much outside academic circles, which is a shame, because it is otherwise a powerful model and a well-thought-out specification.

File Organization

A P3D file consists of a number of ASCII lines that are usually Common Lisp statements. Extensions to the language are mainly in an idiosyncratic terminology that is unfortunately at odds with most of the rest of the computer graphics world.

File Details

A P3D file stores a model, which is a set of objects; these may be geometrical structures or things more like architectural primitives, such as directed acyclic graphs. P3D normally supports the specification of spheres, cylinders, tori, polygons, polylines, polymarkers, lists of triangles, meshes, spline surfaces, font objects, and lighting objects. Various attributes may be associated with objects.

There are also procedural features designed to trigger actions in the application processing a P3D file. An example is the snap function, which can be used to trigger rendering.

A P3D file contains descriptions of one or more graphical objects, called *gobs* in the documentation. These may be primitive objects, like spheres or triangle lists, or they may consist of numbers of primitive objects. A gob is generally a directed acyclic graph, the nodes of which may be other gobs.

The P3D documentation describes gobs as follows:

> Gobs are defined either by invoking a function which returns a primitive gob, or by listing the "children" and possibly the attributes the new gob is to have. A gob can be saved either by binding it to a name (for example, via a Lisp setq function) or by including it directly into the list of children of another gob. Color, material type, and backface cullability are examples of attributes which might be associated with a gob.

There is intrinsic support in P3D for mathematical entities such as vectors, points, and lines, which may be manipulated in an arbitrary fashion. After the initial definition, a gob may be referenced repeatedly. Each reference instance may be associated with attributes and transformations independent of the those inherent in the original definition. It is the programmer's responsibility to make sure that no gob is its own descendent.

Coordinate System

The P3D system assumes a right-hand coordinate system. Coordinate transformations are effected by manipulation with 4x4 matrices as follows:

Rotation:

```
[ R11 R12 R13 0 ]
[ R21 R22 R23 0 ]
[ R31 R32 R33 0 ]
[  0   0   0  1 ]
```

Translation:

```
[ 1  0  0  Tx ]
[ 0  1  0  Ty ]
[ 0  0  1  Tz ]
[ 0  0  0  1  ]
```

Scale:

```
[ Sx  0   0  0 ]
[  0  Sy  0  0 ]
[  0  0  Sz  0 ]
[  0  0   0  1 ]
```

Points are defined in the following manner:

```
(defstruct point
   (x 0.0)      ;x coordinate
   (y 0.0)      ;y coordinate
   (z 0.0))     ;z coordinate
```

They can also be made with the function make-point, which takes three floating-point arguments (x,y,z) that default to zero.

```
(setq origin (make-point))
```

is the definition of the standard symbol "origin."

Vectors are defined as follows:

```
(defstruct vector
   (x 0.0)      ;x coordinate
   (y 0.0)      ;y coordinate
   (z 0.0))     ;z coordinate
```

and can also be created through the function make-vector. Thus:

```
(setq x-vec (make-vector :x 1.0 :y 0.0 :z 0.0))
```

is the definition of the standard symbol "x-vec."

The structure holding a color is as follows:

```
(defstruct color
   (r 0.8)      ;red intensity
   (g 0.8)      ;green intensity
   (b 0.8)      ;blue intensity
   (a 1.0))     ;opacity
```

The color "red," for instance, can be made as follows:

```
(setq red (make-color :r 1.0 :g 0.0 :b 0.0))
```

A vertex may be formed in a similar manner:

```
(defstruct vertex
   (x 0.0)         ;x coordinate
   (y 0.0)         ;y coordinate
   (z 0.0)         ;z coordinate
   (clr nil)       ;local color
   (normal nil))   ;local surface normal
```

For example:

```
(setq red-origin (make-vertex :clr red))
```

creates vertex "red-origin."

Structured Fields

This discussion of structured fields in a P3D file is extracted from the P3D documentation.

The structure used to hold a material (a set of properties used with attributes like color to determine the appearance of an object) is represented as a structure with at least the following fields:

Field	Type	Meaning
:ka	float	Ambient light weighting factor
:kd	float	Diffuse light weighting factor
:ks	float	Specular light weighting factor
:exp	float	Specular exponent
:reflect	float	Reflection coefficient

:refract	float	Index of refraction
:energy	color	Energy density (for radiosity)

Other structure fields may exist, but they are maintained by P3D and should not be modified by the programmer. A material should always be created with the "def-material" function:

```
( def-material :ka ka-value :kd kd-value :ks ks-value
    :exp exp-value :reflect reflect-value
    :refract refract-value :energy energy-color )
```

Parameters are listed below:

:ka ka-value	optional	Ambient light weighting factor
:kd kd-value	optional	Diffuse light weighting factor
:ks ks-value	optional	Specular light weighting factor
:exp exp-value	optional	Specular exponent
:reflect reflect-value	optional	Reflection coefficient
:refract refract-value	optional	Index of refraction
:energy energy-color	optional	Energy density for radiosity

This function returns material with the given characteristics.

All of the keyword-field pairs are optional. Fields that are not specified are assigned specific default values; see the specification for the 'default-material' predefined symbol at the end of this document for the default values of each field.

Cameras

Cameras are defined as follows:

```
(defstruct camera
  (lookfrom origin)        ;eye point
  (lookat origin)          ;point to look at
  (up y-vec)               ;view's 'up' direction
  (fovea 56.0)             ;view included angle
  (hither -0.01)           ;hither clipping distance
  (yon -100.0)             ;yon clipping distance
  (background black))      ;background color
```

Gob Structures

A gob is represented as a structure with at least the following options:

Option	Type	Meaning
:attr	assoc-list	Attribute-value pairs for this gob
:transform	transformation	Coordinate transformation
:children	list	List of gobs to be children

Other structure slots may exist, but they are maintained by P3D and should not be modified by the programmer. All of the fields default to nil.

A gob should always be created with "def-gob," or with one of the geometrical primitive generators (see below). If "def-gob" is used, the definition should include a ":children" option or the gob will have no descendents in the DAG and thus be useless.

```
( def-gob :attr attrlist
  :transform transformation
  :children childlist )
```

Parameters are the following:

:children childlist	required	List of children of this gob
:transform transformation	optional	Coordinate transformation for this gob
:attr attrlist	optional	Association list of attribute and value pairs for this gob

This function returns a gob with the given children, coordinate transformation, and attributes.

For Further Information

For further information about the P3D format, see the P3D specification on the CD-ROM that accompanies this book. You can also contact:

Joel Welling
Pittsburgh Supercomputer Center
4400 Fifth Avenue
Pittsburgh, PA 15213
welling@psc.edu

PBM, PGM, PNM, and PPM

NAME:	PBM, PGM, PNM, PPM
ALSO KNOWN AS:	Portable Bitmap Utilities, pbmplus
TYPE:	Bitmap
COLORS:	Up to 24-bit
COMPRESSION:	None
MAXIMUM IMAGE SIZE:	NA
MULTIPLE IMAGES PER FILE:	NA
NUMERICAL FORMAT:	NA
ORIGINATOR:	Jef Poskanzer
PLATFORM:	UNIX, Intel-based PCs
SUPPORTING APPLICATIONS:	pbmplus, others
SPECIFICATION ON CD:	Yes (man pages)
CODE ON CD:	Yes (in pbmplus package)
IMAGES ON CD:	No
SEE ALSO:	Most of the formats in this book
USAGE:	File format conversion through an intermediary least-common-denominator format.
COMMENTS:	PBM, PGM, PNM, and PPM are intermediate formats used in the conversion of many little known formats via pbmplus, the Portable Bitmap Utilities. These formats are mainly available under UNIX and on Intel-based PCs.

Overview

The Portable Bitmap Utilities (PBM) is a collection of programs organized, maintained, and primarily written by Jef Poskanzer. Although owned and copyrighted by Mr. Poskanzer, they are freely available in both source and executable form on the Internet and on many BBS systems. The "bitmap" in PBM is used in the older sense to refer to monochrome images. There are actually three other sets of programs encompassed by the PBM utilities. These are the Portable Greymap Utilities (PGM), the Portable Pixmap Utilities (PPM), and the Portable Anymap Utilities (PNM). PBM programs manipulate monochrome bitmaps, and PGM and PPM programs manipulate gray-scale bitmaps and color bitmaps, respectively. PNM programs operate on all of the bitmaps produced by the other programs. There is no file format associated with PNM itself. Most people call the overall set of programs PBM and the newer version pbmplus, however, and we'll follow this convention.

Associated with pbmplus are three least-common-denominator intermediate formats. When converting a graphics file from one format to another, we speak of the *source file* (in the current format) and the *destination file* (in the desired new format). pbmplus works by taking a source file and converting it into one of the intermediate formats. That intermediate format file is then converted into the destination format.

To see how this works, here are the steps necessary to convert a Microsoft Windows Bitmap (BMP) format file named *testfile.bmp* to a GIF format file. These are 256-color files, so we use the PPM utilities bmptoppm and ppmtogif:

bmptoppm testfile.bmp	This produces *testfile.ppm*
ppmtogif testfile.ppm	This produces *testfile.gif*

The latest version of pbmplus is available on the CD-ROM that accompanies this book.

File Organization

The PBM, PGM, and PPM formats are each designed to be as simple as possible. Each starts out with a header, and the bitmap data follows immediately after. The header is always written in ASCII, and data items are separated by white space (blanks, tabs, carriage returns, or linefeeds). The data portion of each file type can be written in either ASCII or binary form.

File Details

There are two versions of each of the the PBM, PGM, and PPM headers. Although all the headers are in ASCII format, one is used for the ASCII version of the format, and the other is used for the binary version.

PBM Header

A PBM header consists of the following entries, each separated by white space:

MagicValue	Literally P1 for ASCII version, P4 for binary
ImageWidth	Width of image in pixels (ASCII decimal value)
ImageHeight	Height of image in pixels (ASCII decimal value)

PGM Header

A PGM header consists of the following entries, each separated by white space:

MagicValue	Literally P2 for ASCII version, P5 for binary
ImageWidth	Width of image in pixels (ASCII decimal value)
ImageHeight	Height of image in pixels (ASCII decimal value)
MaxGrey	Maximum gray value (ASCII decimal value)

PPM Header

A PPM header consists of the following entries, each separated by white space:

MagicValue	Literally P3 for ASCII version, P6 for binary
ImageWidth	Width of image in pixels (ASCII decimal value)
ImageHeight	Height of image in pixels (ASCII decimal value)
MaxGrey	Maximum color value (ASCII decimal value)

Image Data

After the header is a series of lines describing width * height pixels. For PPM, each pixel contains three ASCII decimal values between 0 and the specified maximum value, starting at the top-left corner of the pixmap, proceeding in normal English reading order. The three values for each pixel represent red, green, and blue, respectively; a value of 0 means that color is turned off, and the maximum value means that color is "maxxed out."

For PBM and PGM, there is only one ASCII decimal value per pixel. For PBM, the maximum value is implicitly 1.

Here is an example of a small pixmap in this format:

```
P3
# feep.ppm
4 4
15
 0  0  0    0  0  0    0  0  0   15  0 15
 0  0  0    0 15  7    0  0  0    0  0  0
 0  0  0    0  0  0    0 15  7    0  0  0
15  0 15    0  0  0    0  0  0    0  0  0
```

You can include comments in the PBM file. Characters from a # character to the next end-of-line are ignored. There is a suggested maximum of 70 characters per line, but this is not an actual restriction.

Mr. Poskanzer cautions that programs that read this format should be as lenient as possible, accepting anything that looks remotely like a pixmap.

RAWBITS Variant

There is also a variant on the format, available by setting the RAWBITS option at compile time. This variant differs from the traditional format in the following ways:

- The "magic numbers" are as follows:

Format	Normal	RAWBITS Variant
PBM	P1	P4
PGM	P2	P5
PPM	P3	P6

- The pixel values are stored as plain bytes, instead of ASCII decimal:

PBM	RAWBITS is eight pixels per byte
PGM	RAWBITS is one pixel per byte
PPM	RAWBITS is three bytes per pixel

- White space is not allowed in the pixel area, and only a single character of white space (typically a newline) is allowed after the MaxGrey value.

- The files are smaller and many times faster to read and write.

- Bit order within the byte is most significant bit (MSB) first.

Note that this raw format can only be used for maximum values less than or equal to 255. If you use the PPM library and try to write a file with a larger maximum value, it automatically uses the slower, but more general, plain format.

For Further Information

For further information about the PBM, PGM, PNM, and PPM utilities, see the documentation on the CD-ROM that accompanies this book. See also the code and documentation for the pbmplus utilities, also included on the CD-ROM. See Appendix A, "What's on the CD-ROM," for a description of the package and how you can obtain it via FTP.

PBM, PGM, PNM, and PPM *(cont'd)*

For more information about PBM, PGM, PNM, and PPM, you can contact:

Jef Poskanzer
jef@well.sf.ca.us

NAME:	PCX
ALSO KNOWN AS:	PC Paintbrush File Format, DCX, PCC
TYPE:	Bitmap
COLORS:	Mono, 4-bit, 8-bit, 24-bit
COMPRESSION:	RLE, uncompressed
MAXIMUM IMAGE SIZE:	64Kbx64Kb pixels
MULTIPLE IMAGES PER FILE:	No
NUMERICAL FORMAT:	Little-endian
ORIGINATOR:	ZSoft, Microsoft Inc.
PLATFORM:	MS-DOS, Windows, UNIX, others
SUPPORTING APPLICATIONS:	Too numerous to list
SPECIFICATION ON CD:	Yes
CODE ON CD:	Yes
IMAGES ON CD:	No
SEE ALSO:	FAX formats

USAGE:
PCX is used in Microsoft Windows and Windows-based products, but has found wide acceptance, mainly in the MS-DOS world. It is mainly an exchange and storage format.

COMMENTS:
A partially-documented format in wide use, which is quick and easy to read and decompress. It lacks, however, a superior compression scheme, making it unsuited for the storage of deep-pixel images.

Overview

PCX is one of the most widely used storage formats. It originated with ZSoft's MS-DOS-based PC Paintbrush, and because of this, PCX is sometimes referred to as the PC Paintbrush format. ZSoft entered into an OEM arrangement with Microsoft, which allowed Microsoft to bundle PC Paintbrush with various products, including a version called Microsoft Paintbrush for Windows; this product was distributed with every copy of Microsoft Windows sold. This distribution established the importance of PCX, not only on Intel-based MS-DOS platforms, but industry-wide.

PCX has been used by manufacturers of computer-based FAX boards, and also as a general format for the storage of clip-art targeted at the desktop publishing aftermarket.

The original PCX format (starting with version 2.5 of PC Paintbrush) stored graphics and images with no more than 16 colors, due to limitations of Enhanced Graphics Adapter (EGA) display technology produced by IBM. When IBM introduced the VGA display adapter, the PCX format was revised to store graphics and images with up to 256 colors.

The latest revision of the PCX format now includes the ability to store 24-bit color images. This allows the PCX format to be used for the storage of images created by the most advanced graphics, imaging, and video technology available today.

PCX is hardware-dependent in the sense that it was originally designed to accommodate a specific type of display hardware. Data may be stored either plane- or pixel-oriented, to accommodate the hardware design of the plane-oriented IBM EGA or the pixel-oriented IBM Virtual Graphics Array display adapters.

Image data is encoded using an RLE variant, which is simple and somewhat quick in its operation, if not terribly efficient in actually reducing the size of the data. As with other RLE schemes, how much the PCX compression scheme reduces the size of a given image is difficult to say, because the reduction factor is dependent largely upon the content of the image (how "busy" the image is) and how many colors are actually used. Generally, an image incorporating 16 or fewer colors will be reduced by 40 to 70 percent from the original data, whereas a 64- to 256-color image from a scanner or video source may be reduced by only 10 to 30 percent. It is possible for an image to be so complex that the PCX compression scheme actually causes the data to increase in size after compression. (For further discussion of these and other topics please see Chapter 9, *Data.*)

File Organization

PCX files are organized into three major sections: the header, the image data, and the color palette. The color palette normally contains entries for 256 colors and is associated with the VGA display adapter. This VGA color palette is only found in later versions of the PCX image file format.

File Details

This section describes the major sections of PCX files and methods of reading, compressing, encoding, and decoding these files.

Header

The first 128 bytes of every PCX file is the header, which has the following format:

```
typedef struct _PcxHeader
{
    BYTE Identifier;            /* PCX Id Number (Always 0x0A) */
    BYTE Version;               /* Version Number */
    BYTE Encoding;              /* Encoding Format */
    BYTE BitsPerPixel;          /* Bits per Pixel */
    WORD XStart;                /* Left of image */
    WORD YStart;                /* Top of Image */
    WORD XEnd;                  /* Right of Image
    WORD YEnd;                  /* Bottom of image */
    WORD HorzRes;               /* Horizontal Resolution */
    WORD VertRes;               /* Vertical Resolution */
    BYTE Palette[48];           /* 16-Color EGA Palette */
    BYTE Reserved1;             /* Reserved (Always 0) */
    BYTE NumBitPlanes;          /* Number of Bit Planes */
    WORD BytesPerLine;          /* Bytes per Scanline */
    WORD PaletteType;           /* Palette Type */
    WORD HorzScreenSize;        /* Horizontal Screen Size */
    WORD VertScreenSize;        /* Vertical Screen Size */
    BYTE Reserved2[54];         /* Reserved (Always 0) */
} PCXHEAD;
```

Identifier is an identification value defined by the PCX specification as always being 10h. This value has no real meaning other than to indicate that the file is a ZSoft PCX file. PCX readers should always check that this byte contains the proper value, even though the file may have the extension PCX. However, it is possible that a non-PCX format file might also begin with the value 10h, so the remainder of the header information should be read, and the information fields be checked for the proper values before trying to decode any image data in the file. In other words, don't just jump to byte offset 128 and start decoding what you think is encoded image data.

Version contains the version of Paintbrush that created the PCX file. ZSoft has released updated revisions of the PCX format to keep up with the increasing functionality of its PC Paintbrush program and the burgeoning display adapter technology available for the PC. Each PCX file version has separate requirements for handling and displaying its image. Prior to version 2.5 of PC Paintbrush, the PCX image file format was considered proprietary information by ZSoft Corporation.

Possible values for Version are shown below:

Value	PC Paintbrush Version and Description
0	Version 2.5 with fixed EGA palette information
2	Version 2.8 with modifiable EGA palette information
3	Version 2.8 without palette information
4	PC Paintbrush for Windows
5	Version 3.0 of PC Paintbrush, PC Paintbrush Plus, PC Paintbrush Plus for Windows, Publisher's Paintbrush, and all 24-bit image files

Encoding indicates the type of encoding used on the image data. The only encoding algorithm currently supported by the PCX specification is a simple byte-wise run-length encoding (RLE) scheme indicated by a value of 1 in this byte. It would seem to follow that if a PCX file held unencoded image data this value would be 0. PCX files, however, always contain encoded image data, and currently the only valid value for the encoding field is 1.

BitsPerPixel is the number of bits per pixel per plane in the image data. The possible values are 1, 2, 4, and 8 for 2-, 4-, 16-, and 256-color images. The planar data in a scan line is often padded with extra data to align the scan line on an even byte boundary to prevent aliasing (the "jaggies"). PCX paint and conversion programs use this value to find where in a scan line pixel data stops and extra padding begins.

XStart, YStart, XEnd, and YEnd store the size of the image in pixels. These four values are the rectangular dimensions of the visible part of the PCX image (sometimes called the Picture Dimension Window) and its position relative to the physical display screen. Using these dimensions, the largest PCX image that can be stored is 65,535x65,535 pixels in size. The dimensions are the location of the upper-left and lower-right corners of the PCX image on the display screen. The upper-left corner of the screen is considered to be at location 0,0, and any PCX image with an XStart and YStart of 0 will start displaying at this location. If the XStart and YStart are values greater than zero, then a display program should start displaying the PCX image starting at those pixel coordinates. However, this is a feature rarely supported by PCX display programs.

Any PCX image may contain extra bytes of padding at the end of each scan line or extra scan lines added to the bottom of the image. To prevent this extra data from becoming visible, only the image data within the Picture Dimension Window coordinates is displayed.

HorzRes and VertRes are the horizontal and vertical size of the stored image in pixels per line or dots per inch (DPI). Scanned images have the DPI value of the device that created them. Typical DPI values for a scanned image may be 100x100 DPI or 300x300 DPI. An image produced by a FAX card can have a resolution of 100x200 DPI or 200x200 DPI. Images created by paint or screen dump programs will have pixel resolution values that reflect the resolution of the display mode under which they were created. For example, a typical VGA paint program saves images with a horizontal resolution of 320 pixels and a vertical resolution of 200 pixels. However, these values are not used when decoding image data.

Palette is a 48-byte array of 8-bit values that make up a 16-color EGA color palette. The earliest version of PC Paintbrush was not able to use a modifiable EGA palette and, therefore, used only the standard palette of the EGA. Subsequent versions have allowed the use of a modifiable palette enabling a PCX image file writer to choose which 16 (or fewer) of the 64 colors available to the EGA to use. Reserved1 is not currently used and should have a value of 00h. Older versions of PCX used this field for file identification or to hold the mode value of the display screen on which the PCX image was created. Several paint and graphics display programs will, in fact, claim that PCX file is invalid if this field is not set to 00h.

NumBitPlanes is the number of color planes that contains the image data. The number of planes is usually 1, 3, or 4 and is used in conjunction with the BitsPerPixel value to determine the proper video mode in which to display the image. PCX video display modes are shown below:

Color Planes	Bits per Pixel per Plane	Maximum Number of Colors	Video Mode
1	1	2	Monochrome
1	2	4	CGA
3	1	8	EGA
4	1	16	EGA and VGA
1	8	256	Extended VGA
3	8	16,777,216	Extended VGA and XGA

NumBitPlanes is also used to determine the maximum number of colors a PCX image may have. The number of bits per pixel per plane is multiplied by the number of color planes and shifted to the left by one:

```
MaxNumberOfColors = (1L << (BitsPerPixel * NumBitPlanes));
```

BytesPerLine is a 16-bit value indicating the size in bytes of a color plane in an unencoded scan line. This value may be multiplied by the NumBitPlanes value to find the total length of an unencoded scan line in bytes:

```
ScanLineLength = (BytesPerLine * NumBitPlanes);
```

PaletteType contains an indicator of information held in the color palette. A value of 1 indicates color or monochrome information, while a 2 indicates gray-scale information. This value is actually an indicator of whether the image should be displayed in color or gray-scale. (Only VGA is capable of displaying true gray-scale images.) PC Paintbrush and most other programs that use PCX files ignore this value.

HorzScreenSize and VertScreenSize were added to the PCX format starting with PC Paintbrush 4.0 and 4.0 Plus. These horizontal and vertical screen-size values represent the resolution of the screen on which the image was created. This allows graphical display programs to adjust their video mode to allow for proper display of the PCX image. Because these fields were added after the release of PC Paintbrush 3.0, there is no way to know if these fields contain valid information or are part of the Reserved2 field. Therefore, always check these values to be sure they are reasonable before you use them.

Reserved2 is the last field in the header and is a run of bytes with the value 00h. This filler field is used to pad the header out to a full 128 bytes and to save room for additional fields that might be added to the header in future revisions of the PCX format. The size of this field will be either 54 or 58 bytes in size, depending on whether or not the header contains the HorizScreenSize and VertScreenSize fields.

Palette

The color palette information within a PCX file varies depending upon the version of the PCX file.

16-Color EGA Palette

The first version of the PCX format did not support a modifiable color palette, so the values of the standard EGA color palette were always used. Later versions of PC Paintbrush could work with or without a modifiable palette, so two more versions of the PCX format appeared, one with palette information (modifiable palette) and one without palette information (standard EGA palette).

The EGA palette is a 48-byte array of sixteen RGB triples. Each color triple contains a red, green, and blue value, each with a range of 0 to 255. The palette will contain entries for 2, 4, 8, or 16 color triples with any remaining entries being set to 00h. No interpretation is necessary for display adapters using this format of color values. The EGA, however, has only four possible values for each RGB color (0 through 3), so each RGB value is shifted to the right by six to obtain the proper value. To extract the proper values to load into the EGA palette registers, the following code is used:

```
EgaColor0Red    = EgaPalette[0] >> 6;
EgaColor0Green  = EgaPalette[1] >> 6;
EgaColor0Blue   = EgaPalette[2] >> 6;
EgaColor1Red    = EgaPalette[3] >> 6;
EgaColor1Green  = EgaPalette[4] >> 6;
EgaColor1Blue   = EgaPalette[5] >> 6;
/* and so on . . .  */
```

4-Color CGA palette

The EGA color palette is also used for displaying CGA images. Two- or four-color images may be displayed on the CGA using one of eight possible color palettes, each consisting of three foreground colors and one background color.

The most significant four bits of the first byte of the EGA color palette contains the background color and is in the range of 0 to 15.

The most significant three bits of the fourth byte of the color palette contains the foreground color. The three bits of the foreground color correspond to the Color Burst Enable, Palette, and Intensity settings of the CGA, as shown below.

Color Burst Enable (Bit 7)	Palette (Bit 6)	Intensity (Bit 5)
0 (color)	0 (yellow)	0 (normal)
1 (monochrome)	1 (white)	1 (bright)

Code used to extract the CGA color-level data from the EGA color palette is shown below:

```
/* Get the CGA background color */
CgaBackgroundColor  = EgaPalette[0] >> 4;    /* 0 to 15 */

/* Get the CGA foreground palette */
CgaColorBurstEnable = (EgaPalette[3] & 0x80) >> 7;  /* 0 or 1 */
CgaPaletteValue     = (EgaPalette[3] & 0x40) >> 6;  /* 0 or 1 */
CgaIntensityValue   = (EgaPalette[3] & 0x20) >> 5;  /* 0 or 1 */
```

256-Color VGA palette

When PCX was conceived, the EGA was the premium display adapter available from IBM for the PC. The EGA could display only 16 colors from a palette of 64, so PCX was originally designed with a color palette large enough to hold only 16 colors.

The 16-color EGA technology of 1984, however, gave way to the 256-color VGA technology of 1987. PCX now fell short of VGA standard images that could contain up to 256 colors from a palette of 262,144, and a new color palette needed to be added to the PCX file format for VGA images. Because there was not enough room in the header for it, the designers of the PCX format appended it to the end of the PCX file itself.

This unconventional, if not inconvenient, location for the VGA palette presents a problem; because the size of the image data varies, the location of the VGA palette is different for every file. The position of the palette must be determined by its offset from the end of the file rather than from the beginning.

To see if a VGA palette is attached to a file, seek backwards 769 bytes from the end of the file. If the byte at this location is set to value C0h, then the 768 bytes following this value constitutes a VGA color palette. The PCX specification states that if the version number in the header (byte 1) is 5 (Version 3.0), then there might be a VGA color palette attached.

Normally, a PCX file must have a VGA color palette attached only if there are more than 16 colors in the image, otherwise the EGA palette can be used. However, many graphics programs create version 3.0 PCX image files without a VGA color palette, while other programs always attach a VGA color palette, even for 2-color images. To confuse things even more, 24-bit PCX images are always marked as version 3.0, yet never have an attached color palette.

A version 3.0 PCX image might not have a color palette; the value 768 bytes from the end of the file might be 0Ch by coincidence. In this rare case, a PCX reader would interpret the last 768 bytes of the encoded image data as a VGA palette, so a truly bizarre displayed image would result. One solution to this problem would be to first read all the image data and note whether the file pointer stopped 769 bytes from the end of the file. If so, then there is a VGA color palette present. Another method would be to check the three bytes following the 0Ch value. This is the first color of the color palette and is normally black, so the three bytes following the suspect VGA palette indicator value should all be zero.

When a VGA palette is present in the file, its information is always used to display the image data, rather than using any information that may be present in the EGA color palette. If the colors in an image do not display correctly, it may be necessary to disable the color palette so the display hardware may use its native color palette. Disabling the color palette is accomplished by changing the version number in the header (byte 1) from 5 to 3. The display software should recognize that this version of the format has no color palette and, therefore, should use its own default palette.

The VGA palette itself is an array of 768 bytes (256x3) containing the red, green, and blue values for each of the 256 possible colors in a VGA PCX image. Color values are organized into triples, as in the EGA palette. Bytes 0, 1, and 2 are the red, green, and blue values for the color 0; bytes 3, 4, and 5 are the red, green, and blues values for color 1; and so on. Each RGB value is in the range of 0 to 255.

In fact, the VGA palette is simply a much longer version of the EGA palette. VGA display devices, however, require that palette color values be in the range of 0 to 63, so all RGB values should be divided by four (shifted to the right twice). VGA images may have 2-, 4-, 8-, 16-, 32-, 64-, 128-, or 256-color entries in the palette.

Reading the PCX Header

The PCX specification does not specifically state that the PCX image file format must use the least-significant-byte ordering scheme used on Intel 80x86 processors, but we may safely assume that this is so because the PCX format was developed for use on Intel-based machines. If code that reads PCX-format files will only be executed on Intel machines, it is possible, although not portable, to use the fread() function to read the header on a little-endian machine:

```
PCXHEADER pcx;
if(fread(&pcx, sizeof(char), sizeof(PCXHEADER), fp) !=
        sizeof(PCXHEADER))
    fputs("Error reading PCX header.", stderr);
```

Compressing PCX Data

The data-encoding algorithm used in PCX files is a simple 1-byte/2-byte run-length encoding scheme. While this type of encoding is not the most effective in terms of reducing data size, it is very quick in its operation and quite easy to implement.

An image normally contains many series of pixel runs, that is, two or more contiguous pixels of the same value. Using the run-length data compression scheme, a run of pixels several bytes in length may be converted to a run code only two bytes in length.

The encoded data is read one byte at a time. If the two most significant bytes (MSB) of the first byte read are set to 1, then this byte is the first byte of a 2-byte run code. The first byte in a 2-byte run code always contains the run count in its lower six bits, which is the length of the pixel run. Therefore, a pixel run may be 1 to 63 pixels in length.

Using the two most significant bits to indicate a 2-byte code rather than just one, MSB is a hold-over from the early CGA days of Paintbrush. Use of only one MSB resulted in poor compression for CGA data, so two were used instead.

The second byte of a 2-byte run code is the value of the pixel run itself. This value may be in the range 0 to 255 and is written to the output a number of times equal to the run count.

If a run-count byte is read and the two MSBs are both 0, then this byte is a run-value byte and the run count is considered to be 1. This 1-byte run code is used to prevent a 1-pixel run from encoding into a 2-byte run code.

The PCX RLE encoding scheme is not perfect, however. A 1-byte run code can contain a run value only in the range 0 to 63. If the pixel run value is in the range 64 to 255, a 2-byte run code must be used instead. If an image contains many single pixel runs of color values greater than 63, an increase of image data size can occur after PCX encoding. Such an increase in data size typically occurs only in very noisy or grainy images.

Decoding a PCX Format File

To decode a file in PCX format, you must read the header of the file and calculate the following data:

- Width of image in pixels

- Length of image in scan lines

- Number of bytes needed to hold a decoded scan line

- Number of padding bytes at the end of each scan line

Calculate the image width and height from the image dimension values as follows:

```
ImageWidth  = XEnd - XStart + 1; /* Width of image in pixels */
ImageHeight = YEnd - YStart + 1; /* Length of image in scan lines */
```

The number of bytes required to hold a decoded scan line is necessary if the decoded image data is to be stored in a buffer. It is also necessary to determine if the image data has been encoded across scan lines. The number of color planes multiplied by the number of bytes per line per plane yields this value:

```
ScanLineLength = NumBitPlanes * BytesPerLine;
```

The length of padding at the end of a scan line may be determined by calculating the number of pixels in an unencoded scan line and comparing this value with the pixel width of the displayed image:

```
LinePaddingSize = ((BytesPerLine * NumBitPlanes) *
                  (8 / BitsPerPixel)) - ((XEnd - XStart) + 1);
```

The decoding steps are the following:

1. Read a byte.

2. If the two MSBs are set to 1, then mask off the run count.

3. Read next byte.

4. Write the byte a number of times equal to the run count.

5. Else, if the two MSBs are set to 0, then mask off the run value.

6. Write the byte once.

7. Repeat steps 1 through 6 until the buffer is full.

The code used to decode a scan line of information is as shown below:

```
/*
** Decode a PCX scan line.
**
** In this example the size of Buffer[] and the value of BufferSize
** is equal to the scan line length. Data is read from the FILE
** stream fpIn and written to Buffer[].
*/
do
{
  byte = GetByte(fpIn);                  /* Get next byte       */
  if ((byte & 0xC0) == 0xC0)             /* 2-byte code         */

    runcount = byte & 0x3F;              /* Get run count       */
    runvalue = GetByte(fpIn);            /* Get pixel value     */
    }
  else                                   /* 1-byte code         */
    {
    runcount = 1;                        /* Run count is one    */
    runvalue = byte;                     /* Pixel value         */
    }
  /* Write the pixel run to the buffer   */
  for (total += runcount;                  /* Update total        */
    runcount && index < BufferSize;        /* Don't read past buffer */
  runcount-, index++)                    /* Update counters            */
  Buffer[index] = runvalue;                /* Assign value to buffer   */
  } while (index < BufferSize);            /* Read to end of buffer    */
```

The PCX specification states that a decoding break should occur at the end of each scan line. This means that when a run of data is being encoded, and the end of the scan line is reached, the run should stop and not continue across to the next scan line, if it is possible to stop it.

Decoding can be complicated by PCX files that have been encoded ignoring this rule. Encoding across scan lines gains a few extra bytes of compression, but the process of decoding a single scan line is made much more difficult.

Encoding PCX Image Data

The scheme for encoding a scan line is fairly straightforward with only a few exceptions. Raw data is read one byte at a time. The only information needed is the number of bytes in a scan line. The following is the procedure for encoding image data using the PCX compression algorithm:

1. Read a byte of pixel data and store the value.

2. Set counter to 1.

3. Read the next byte and check if it is the same as the stored value.

4. If it is the same, increment the counter.

5. If it is not the same and the count is greater than one, or the count is 63, or if the end of scan line has been reached, then mask on the two MSBs and output the count value.

6. Output the data value.

7. Repeat steps 1 though 7 until all scan lines have been read.

PCX Image Data Format

Once a scan line has been decoded, the format of the data it contains depends upon the BitsPerPixel and the NumBitPlanes values found in the header. Knowing the data format of a scan line is necessary so you can parse the pixel data from a scan line for display of the image or conversion of the image file from one format to another. All scan lines in a PCX file always have the same format.

Scan-line pixel data is stored in one of two ways—either pixel-oriented or plane-oriented. Pixel-oriented data is stored with all the pixel data (either real data or indexes into a color palette) in a contiguous line. Plane-oriented data unrolls the pixel data into its red, green, and blue components and groups them by color across the scan line.

Single-plane data is stored pixel by pixel in one long plane that runs the length of the scan line. The data in the scan line is not the actual image data itself, but is instead a series of index values into either the EGA or VGA color palettes. The exception for single-plane data is the 1-bit monochrome image, where each bit in a scan-line maps directly as a pixel value.

How much of the scan-line data a single pixel occupies is determined from the BitsPerPixel value. For example, with one bit per pixel, every byte of scan-line data contains eight pixel values. With eight bits per pixel, every byte of scan-line data contains one pixel value. Monochrome, CGA, and 256-color VGA images usually contain only a single plane per scan line.

Scan lines with three planes are uncommon, but they do exist. 24-bit PCX images are stored using three bytes per pixel spread over three planes. The 24-bit data values are the actual color values for the image, and no color palette is used. Paintbrush for Windows 2.0 uses a 3-plane/1-bit data format to store 8-color images, where each pixel value is an index into the EGA color palette.

Images with four planes are usually 16-color EGA images. In addition to the red, green, and blue planes, there is a fourth intensity color plane that is specific to the EGA display card. Scan-line data in 4-plane images contains index values into the EGA palette.

Related File Formats

Several other formats are direct spin-offs of the PCX file format. And in most cases they are just specialized versions of PCX.

PCC image file format

Earlier versions of PC Paintbrush had the capability of clipping and copying an area of a PCX image and saving it to a file using the Copy To... command. The resulting file was saved as a PCX-format file with the extension .PCC, possibly to indicate that the image the file contained was a portion of another image. The current version of PC Paintbrush does not use the .PCC extension and uses the .PCX extension instead.

DCX image file format

The PCX file format is capable of storing only a single image per file. Applications that require two or more PCX image files to be identified as belonging to the same group often use a naming convention that will identify a collection of PCX files as being related to each other.

One such application is FAX software, where each facsimile page is stored as an individual image in a separate file. PCX became a popular format for PC-based FAX software, because facsimile pages saved in this format could be viewed using many popular paint and image display programs that supported PCX. However, storing each FAX page as a separate file can become quite cumbersome and also confusing, if each image has a cryptic filename.

In an effort to store PCX files in a manner more appropriate to facsimile applications, the DCX file format was created. The DCX format stores up to 1023 PCX images within a single DCX file. Each image in the DCX file is a complete PCX image file, including header and palette information. In applications,

DCX files may contain all of the pages of a facsimile transmission, a series of images of the same subject, or all of the illustrations within a document. The DCX header follows:

```
typedef struct _DcxHeader
{
    DWORD Id;                        /* DCX Id number */
    DWORD PageTable[1024];           /* Image offsets */
} DCXHEAD;
```

Id is a 4-byte word used to identify the file. The value of this word is 3ADE68B1h (987,654,321 decimal).

PageTable is a table of 1024 4-byte word values. The values in this table are the offsets of each PCX image contained within the DCX file. The offset of each PCX image is measured from the beginning of the file (byte 0). The last entry of the page list is the terminator value and is always set to zero.

Typically, a DCX file contains an entire 4096-byte page list (1023 4-byte offset values followed by a 4-byte terminator value), even if most of the values in the list are zero. Some DCX file writers may try to save space by writing only the values of the offsets, followed by a 0 terminating word, but not the remaining part of the list. It is, therefore, important never to expect the page list to be a full 4096 bytes in length. DCX file readers should always read one value at a time and stop when a word value of zero is read. If the first offset value in the page list is 1004h (4100 decimal), then an entire 4096-byte page list is contained within the DCX file.

The DCX format is quite convenient and very easy to use; however, this format suffers from one major drawback. When a series of PCX files is concatenated into a DCX file, all the information within the PCX files is preserved, but the actual names of the PCX files are lost. No provision in the DCX format (or in the PCX format for that matter) exists for storing the MS-DOS filename of the PCX image files. Therefore, if the original PCX filenames are important to your application, you will have to devise some sort of name list that is maintained outside of the DCX file. Future revisions of the DCX format might correct this oversight (perhaps by appending a name list onto the end of the DCX file itself).

For Further Information

For further information about the PCX format, see the specification included on the CD-ROM that accompanies this book.

The PCX format was created and is maintained by ZSoft Corporation. For additional information, contact ZSoft at:

ZSoft Corporation
Attn: Shannon Donovan
450 Franklin Road, Suite 100
Marietta, GA 30067
Voice: 404-428-0008
Fax: 404-427-1150
BBS: 404-427-1045
CompuServe: 76702,1207

ZSoft publishes the following technical reference manual describing the PCX format:

ZSoft Corporation, *Technical Reference Manual*, Revision 5, Marietta, GA, 1990.

PCX is a very popular format that has been described in many books and magazine articles. The following manual and magazine articles also document the format and use of PCX files:

Ashdown, Ian, "PCX Graphics," *C Users Journal*, Volume 9 Number 8, August 1991, pp. 89-96.

Azer, S., "Working with PCX Files," *Microcornucopia*, Number 42, July-August 1988, p. 42.

Luze, Marv, "Printing PCX Files," *C Gazette*, Volume 5, Number 2, Winter 1990-91, pp. 11-22.

Quirk, K., "Translating PCX Files," *Dr. Dobb's Journal*, Volume 14, Number 8, August 1989, pp. 30-36, 105-108.

NAME:	PDS
ALSO KNOWN AS:	Planetary Data System Format
TYPE:	General data format
COLORS:	Unlimited
COMPRESSION:	None
MAXIMUM IMAGE SIZE:	Unlimited
MULTIPLE IMAGES PER FILE:	Yes
NUMERICAL FORMAT:	NA
ORIGINATOR:	NASA
PLATFORM:	All
SUPPORTING APPLICATIONS:	Many
SPECIFICATION ON CD:	No (specification is too lengthy)
CODE ON CD:	Yes (in xv package)
IMAGES ON CD:	Yes
SEE ALSO:	FITS, VICAR2
USAGE:	PDS is used by NASA and other institutions to store planetary data.
COMMENTS:	PDS is an ODL-based format similar in form and use to FITS and VICAR2.

Overview

The PDS (Planetary Data System) file format is a standard format devised by the Planetary branch of the National Aeronautics and Space Administration (NASA) for storing solar, lunar, and planetary data collected on Earth and by interplanetary spacecraft.

PDS is actually a set of rules for the construction of labels to describe the structure of a variety of data files, including images. The basis for the labels is an Object Description Language (ODL), which describes each separate component of the data file as a distinct object. These labels have been designated for use by NASA's Planetary Data System.

A PDS image file could conceivably contain a number of different elements. The label might be a part of the data file, or it might be in a separate file. Each image row could have some leading and trailing information. There could be color palette or image histogram data before or after the image. There could even be multiple images in a single file. All of these possibilities can be handled with the PDS syntax.

This syntax has been used on the CD-ROMs of spacecraft data distributed by the PDS, such as the 12-disk "Voyagers To The Planets" set. A number of software packages also support PDS labels.

File Organization

A PDS data file consists of a header (called the label) and a set of data objects. The label and data objects may reside in the same file or in separate files.

A PDS label is usually a collection of ASCII text records. The label records can be fixed length or variable length, although fixed length is more portable. Records are usually delimited by a carriage return and a linefeed character to ensure readability on the widest possible variety of computers.

The label uses ODL to give information about the data objects. The ODL object description has the general form:

```
OBJECT = object_name
        Information about the object
END_OBJECT
```

Statements within an object description all have the form:

```
name = value
```

where *name* is a keyword, the name of a particular attribute associated with the object, and *value* is the value of the attribute. The attribute name can be up to 32 characters in length. The first character must be alphabetic, but the remaining characters can be alphabetic, numeric or the underscore character. The attribute values can be numeric (integer, real, or real with units), literal or enumerated values, strings, times, or object names. The values can also be arranged into arrays.

Direct access to data objects is possible by utilizing pointers to the objects in the label. A pointer is expressed with the notation:

```
^object_name = location
```

The *location* may be numeric, in which case it represents a starting record number for the object, or it may be a string giving the name of an external file.

The first record of a PDS label may be a Standard Format Data Unit (SFDU) ID in the format:

```
nnnnnnnnnnnnnnnnnnnn = SFDU_LABEL
```

The ID is assigned by a central control authority (Consultative Committee for Space Data Systems), but it can be safely skipped by application software.

Each PDS label must end with a statement of the form:

```
END
```

Comments may be embedded in the label, and a comment begins with the pair of characters /* (slash asterisk). The comment ends either at the end of the line or with the pair of characters */ (asterisk slash).

The PDS ODL is an evolving syntax, although downward compatibility is maintained. A number of new enhancements are supported under the second version of the syntax standard.

File Details

Here is a sample PDS version 1 label. The label is treated as a single byte stream of 203 bytes. Notice the (now obsolete) pointer syntax.

```
FILE_TYPE            = IMAGE
HEADER_RECORDS       = 1
HEADER_RECORD_BYTES  = 203
IMAGE_LINES          = 512
LINE_SAMPLES         = 512
SAMPLE_BITS          =   8
IMAGE_POINTER        = OLDIMAGE.IMG
END
```

Here is sample PDS version 2 label. The image data starts at the tenth record in the file (that is, byte 2550).

```
NJPL1I00PDS100055825 = SFDU_LABEL
RECORD_TYPE   = FIXED_LENGTH
RECORD_BYTES  = 255
FILE_RECORDS  = 223 /* 210 image records + 13 label */
LABEL_RECORDS = 13
/* This is a pointer to the file record where the image starts
^IMAGE = 10
OBJECT = IMAGE
       LINES  = 210
```

```
        LINE_SAMPLES  = 255
        SAMPLE_BITS   = 8

  END_OBJECT
  END
```

Here is another sample PDS version 2 label for an image with a detached label file:

```
CCSD3ZF0000100000001NJPL3IF0PDS200000001 = SFDU_LABEL
/*          File Format and Length                  */
RECORD_TYPE                 = FIXED_LENGTH
RECORD_BYTES                = 1024
FILE_RECORDS                = 512
/*          Record Pointers to Major Objects        */
^IMAGE                      = 'SAMPLE.IMG'
/*          Descriptions of Objects in File         */
OBJECT = IMAGE
  LINES = 512
  LINE_SAMPLES = 512
  SAMPLE_BITS  = 16
END_OBJECT    = IMAGE
END
```

For Further Information

Because the PDS specifications are so lengthy, and because they are freely available, we have decided not to include them on the CD-ROM that accompanies this book. For additional information about PDS, contact the JPL customer support facility:

> National Aeronautics and Space Administration (NASA)
> Planetary Branch
> Jet Propulsion Laboratory
> Mail Stop 525-3610
> 4800 Oak Grove Drive
> Pasadena, CA 91109
> Voice: 818-354-7587
> *PDS_Operator@jplpds.jpl.nasa.gov*

There is a set of several documents on PDS labels available from this facility:

> Jet Propulsion Laboratory, *Standards for the Preparation and Interchange of Data Sets*, JPL Document D-4683, NASA, Pasadena, CA, 1988.

Jet Propulsion Laboratory, *Data Preparation Workbook*, JPL Document D-7669, NASA, Pasadena, CA, 1990.

Jet Propulsion Laboratory, *Planetary Data System Standards Reference*, JPL Document D-4683, NASA, Pasadena, CA, 1990.

Jet Propulsion Laboratory, *Specification for the Object Description Language*, NASA, Pasadena, CA, 1990.

Pictor PC Paint

NAME:	Pictor PC Paint
ALSO KNOWN AS:	PC Paint, PIC, .PIC, .CLP
TYPE:	Bitmap
COLORS:	24-bit maximum
COMPRESSION:	RLE, uncompressed
MAXIMUM IMAGE SIZE:	64Kbx64Kb pixels
MULTIPLE IMAGES PER FILE:	No
NEMERICAL FORMAT:	Little-endian
ORIGINATOR:	Paul Mace Inc.
PLATFORM:	MS-DOS
SUPPORTING APPLICATIONS:	Too numerous to list
SPECIFICATION ON CD:	Yes
CODE ON CD:	No
IMAGES ON CD:	No
SEE ALSO:	PCX

USAGE: Paint programs.

COMMENTS: A device-specific format designed for PC (MS-DOS) hardware.

Overview

The Pictor PC Paint format is device-dependent and is specifically designed around the needs of the IBM family of display adapters (CGA, EGA, VGA, and so on). Because of this, the PIC format resembles PCX, another popular paint file format designed specifically for IBM hardware. This format uses the .PIC extension.

File Organization

The header structure for the Pictor PC Paint format is 17 bytes long and consists of the following fields:

```
typedef struct _PicHeader
{
WORD  Id;               /* Magic number (always 1234h)   */
WORD  Width;            /* Width of image in pixels   */
```

```
WORD    Height;              /* Height of image in pixels    */
WORD    XOffset;             /* X of lower left corner of image    */
WORD    YOffset;             /* Y of lower left corner of image    */
BYTE    PlaneInfo;           /* BPP and number color planes    */
BYTE    PaletteFlag;         /* Color palette/video flag    */
BYTE    VideoMode;           /* Video mode of image    */
WORD    PaletteType;         /* Type of color palette    */
WORD    PaletteSize;         /* Size of color palette    */

} PICHEAD;
```

File Details

Id is an identification value. This value is always 1234h.

Width and Height contain the size of the image in pixels.

XOffset and YOffset indicate the position of the image on the display screen. The default values of 0 and 0 indicate that the image starts at the origin point in the lower-left corner of the screen.

PlaneInfo contains two values. Bits 0 through 3 contain the number of bits per pixel per plane in the image. Bits 4 through 7 contain the number of additional color planes; there is always a minimum of one color plane. This value is 0 for one color plane, 2 for three color planes, and so on. These values may be used to determine the type of display hardware for which the image data is formatted. A value of 02h in this field indicates CGA data; a value of 31h indicates EGA data; and a value of 08h indicates VGA data.

The original version of the PC Paint format did not include any information on video modes or color palettes. Version 2.0 of the format adds the ability to store this additional information and increases the size of the header.

PaletteFlag contains the value FFh if the version of the PC Paint file is 2.0 or greater. In this case, data is present for the remaining three fields of the header. If the Marker field value is not FFh, then image data immediately follows the header.

VideoMode contains a single ASCII alphanumeric character indicating the screen mode used to create the image. This is useful only for setting the screen mode before displaying the image. The following mode values are used:

0	40 column text	F	EGA 640x350x4	
1	80 column text	G	EGA 640x350x16	
2	Monochrome text	H	EGA 720x348x2 (Hercules)	
3	EGA 43-line text	I	EGA 320x200x16 (Plantronics)	
4	VGA 50-line text	J	EGA 320x200x16	
A	CGA 320x200x4	K	EGA 640x400x2 (AT&T or Toshiba 3100)	
B	EGA 320x200x16	L	VGA 320x200x256	
C	CGA 640x200x2	M	VGA 640x480x16	
D	EGA 640x200x16	N	EGA 720x348x16 (Hercules InColor)	
E	EGA 640x350x2	O	VGA 640x480x2	

PaletteType indicates the type of color palette that is found after the header. A value of 0 indicates that no color palette is present (i.e., the image does not use a color palette, typical of monochrome image data). A value of 1 indicates a CGA color palette and border color. A value of 2 indicates a PC Jr. or non-ECD 16-color palette. A value of 3 indicates an EGA palette. A value of 4 indicates a VGA palette.

The CGA palette data is a single byte in size and the border data is also one byte in size. (See the PCX article for information on interpreting CGA palette data.) PC Jr. palette data, which may also be a generic 16-color palette, is stored as a 16-byte palette, one color value per byte. The VGA palette is stored as 256 3-byte triples, the same as in the PCX format.

PaletteSize stores the number of bytes of palette data that follow the header. For a CGA palette, this value is 2. For the PC Jr. and EGA palettes, this value is 16. For a VGA palette, this value is 768.

Image Data Encoding

The image data in a Pictor Paint image file may be stored in a compressed RLE format. Following the color palette data (if present) is a 16-bit data word that indicates how many run-length encoded blocks of data follow. If the image data in the Pictor file is not compressed, this value is 0.

Raw Pictor images never contain any color palette information, although the color palette information fields may be present in the header. The image data begins immediately after the header and is displayed starting at the bottom-left corner of the display screen. The image data always is stored by scan line and in consecutive color planes.

The RLE scheme used in the PC Paint format encodes runs of identical pixel values into blocks (also called packets). The number of data blocks in an image file is indicated by the 16-bit value found after the color palette information.

Each run-length encoded block begins with a 5-byte header. This header, which contains the information necessary to decode the image data stored in its data block, has the following format:

```
typedef struct _PicBlockHead
{
WORD  BlockSize;     /* Size of encoded block including header  */
WORD  RunLength;     /* Size of decoded pixel data   */
BYTE  RunMarker;     /* Start-of-run indicator   */

} PICBLKHEAD;
```

BlockSize is the size of the entire block of encoded image data including the block header. This value is useful for reading the entire data block into memory before decoding it.

RunLength contains the total number of pixels encoded in this block.

RunMarker contains a unique character marker that identifies the start of an encoded run in this block. Data blocks may contain multiple runs of pixels, and this marker delineates the start of each encoded run in the block.

Each encoded data block may contain one or more runs of pixel data. The runs may be eight bits in length (1 to 255 pixels), or 16 bits in length (1 to 65,535 pixels). For buffering reasons, a run typically does not exceed 8192 pixels (or bytes) in length. It is also possible to store a literal run of pixels in a data block that is not encoded at all.

The first five bytes of an encoded data block make up the block header. Following the header is normally a RunMarker character designating the start of an encoded run. The byte following a RunMarker is the RunLength. This is an 8-bit value that stores the length of the pixel run. If this value is not zero, then the byte that follows it, the RunValue, is the actual pixel value that is to be repeated RunLength times:

```
WORD  BlockSize     Size of encoded block including header
WORD  RunLength     Size of decoded pixel data
BYTE  RunMarker     Start-of-run indicator
BYTE  RunMarker     Start-of-run indicator
BYTE  RunLength     Length of the pixel run (8-bit run length)
BYTE  RunValue      The value of the pixel run
```

If the RunLength value is 0 then a 16-bit word value, the RunCount, follows the RunLength field. The byte following the RunCount is the actual pixel run that is to be repeated RunCount times:

```
WORD   BlockSize    Size of encoded block including header
WORD   RunLength    Size of decoded pixel data
BYTE   RunMarker    Start-of-run indicator
BYTE   RunMarker    Start-of-run indicator
BYTE   RunLength    Length of the pixel run (8-bit run length)
WORD   RunCount     Length of the pixel run (16-bit run length)
BYTE   RunValue     The value of the pixel run
```

If the RunMarker is missing from a data block, the byte read is assumed to be a literal pixel value and is written directly to the output:

```
WORD   BlockSize    Size of encoded block including header
WORD   RunLength    Size of decoded pixel data
BYTE   RunMarker    Start-of-run indicator
BYTE   PixelValue   No RunMarker, literal pixel value
```

The RunMarker character is an arbitrary value chosen to delineate the start of each encoded run in a data block. The RunMarker value should not be the same as any RunValue or PixelValue in the data block. Each data block uses a RunMarker value appropriate to the data in the data block. The following example is of a data block that uses a RunMarker value that is the same as a pixel RunLength value. This arrangement could confuse a Pictor RLE decoder:

```
WORD   BlockSize    Size of encoded block including header
WORD   RunLength    Size of decoded pixel data
BYTE   RunMarker    Start-of-run indicator
BYTE   RunMarker    Start-of-run indicator
BYTE   RunLength    Length of the pixel run (8-bit run length)
BYTE   RunValue     The value of the pixel run
```

Because there is no "end of data block" marker, a PC Paint decoder must keep track of the number of pixels decoded in each data block, and must compare this value to the value of the RunLength field of the block header. When these values are equal, the block is finished and the next block, if any, should be read.

The decoded format of the image data varies depending upon the type of graphics display adapter that was used to create the image. Monochrome images are stored eight pixels per byte. EGA images are stored two pixels per byte in four planes of 4-bit index values each, in a BGRI order. VGA image data is stored one pixel per byte, each byte being an index value into the color palette. When there is more than one color plane, the image data is stored by plane first, then by pixel (plane 0, plane 1, plane 2, and so on).

The following pseudocode details the decoding process of the Pictor RLE image data:

```
StartOfDataBlock:
    Read BlockSize value from data block header
    Read RunLength value from data block header
    Read RunMarker value from data block header
StartOfRun:
    If the next byte is a RunMarker
        If the byte following the RunMarker is not 0
            Read the next byte as the RunLength
            Read the next byte as the RunValue
            Write the RunValue 'RunLength' times.
        else
            If the byte following the RunMarker is 0
                Read the next word as the RunCount
                Read the next byte as the RunValue
                Write the RunValue 'RunCount' times.
    else
        If the byte following the header is not a RunMarker
            Write the byte as a literal PixelValue
        If the number of pixels written so far equals the RunLength
            Goto StartOfDataBlock:
    else
        If the number of pixels written so far does not equal the RunLength
            Goto StartOfRun:
```

Below are several examples of Pictor PC Paint run-length encoded data blocks. These examples show how one or more different types of runs may be encoded in the same data block.

The following encoded data block is 10 bytes in size and contains a single run 800 pixels in length. The start-of-run indicator is the value FFh. The Run-Length field is 0, so the RunCount field contains the number of pixels in the run. The RunValue is the actual pixel value in the run.

WORD	BlockSize	Size of encoded block including header
WORD	RunLength	Size of decoded pixel data (800)
BYTE	RunMarker	Start-of-run indicator
BYTE	RunMarker	Start-of-run indicator (run 1)
BYTE	RunLength	Length of the literal run
WORD	RunCount	Length of the encoded run
BYTE	RunValue	The value of the pixel run

The following encoded data block is 13 bytes in size and contains two runs. A total of 8256 pixels are encoded in this data block and the RunMarker is the value 80h. This first run is 64 pixels in length and has a value of 7. The second run is 8192 pixels in length and has a value of 1.

WORD	BlockSize	Size of data block including header
WORD	RunLength	Size of decoded pixel data (64 + 8192)
BYTE	RunMarker	Start-of-run indicator
BYTE	RunMarker	Start-of-run indicator (Run 1)
BYTE	RunLength	Length of the pixel run
BYTE	RunValue	Value of the pixel run
BYTE	RunMarker	Start-of-run indicator (Run 2)
BYTE	RunLength	Value is 0, get 16-bit RunCount
WORD	RunCount	Length of the pixel run
BYTE	RunValue	Value of the pixel run

The following encoded data block is 1039 bytes in size and contains two encoded runs and a literal run. The RunMarker in this block is the value 00h. The value FFh cannot be used because the block contains a run with this value. The first run is 1024 pixels in length, and each pixel has the value 01h. Following this run are three literal pixel values which are considered the second run in the block (literal pixel runs are not prefaced with a RunMarker). The third run contains 12 pixels each of the value FFh.

WORD	BlockSize	Size of data block including header
WORD	RunLength	Size of decoded pixel data (1024+1+1+1+12)
BYTE	RunMarker	Start-of-run indicator
BYTE	RunMarker	Start-of-run indicator (Run 1)
BYTE	RunLength	Value is 0, get 16-bit RunCount
WORD	RunCount	Length of the pixel run
BYTE	RunValue	Value of the pixel run
BYTE	PixelValue	No RunMarker, literal pixel value (Run 2)
BYTE	PixelValue	No RunMarker, literal pixel value
BYTE	PixelValue	No RunMarker, literal pixel value
BYTE	RunMarker	Start-of-run indicator (Run 3)

```
BYTE   RunLength   Length of the pixel run
BYTE   RunValue    Value of the pixel run
```

HiColor format

Four changes were made to Pictor PC Paint to support hicolor (65.536K colors) and truecolor (16,777,216 colors) video modes, and to correct past problems in compressing text-mode images.

First, the two 4-bit fields for the number of bit planes and number of bits per pixel (PlaneInfo) were combined into one field to support pixel depths greater than eight bits. The newly supported modes, and their hex values, are:

```
01    1 bit plane     1 bit per pixel 2 colors
02    1 bit plane     2 bits per pixel 4 colors
04    1 bit plane     4 bits per pixel 16 colors
11    2 bit planes    1 bit per pixel 4 colors
31    4 bit planes    1 bit per pixel 16 colors
08    1 bit plane     8 bits per pixel 256 colors
10    1 bit plane     16 bits per pixel 32,768 and 65,536 colors
18    1 bit plane     24 bits per pixel 16,777,216 colors
28    3 bit planes    8 bits per pixel 16,777,216 colors
```

Second, all text-mode images are now stored at 16 bits per pixel instead of eight bits per pixel, as in the past.

Third, the video mode may now be specified using two letters. The mark field, which always contained the value 0xFF in the past, is now the second letter. Valid values for the mark field are currently the ASCII characters 1, 2, and 3.

The hicolor extensions expanded the list of video modes supported by the .PIC format:

```
0    10   40x25 color text
1    10   80x25 color text
2    10   80x25 B&W text
3    10   EGA 80x43, VGA 80x50 color text
4    10   VESA 80x60 color text
5    10   VESA 132x25 color text
6    10   VESA 132x43 color text
7    10   VESA 132x50 color text
8    10   VESA 132x60 color text
A    02   CGA 4 color
B    04   PCjr/Tandy 16 color
C    01   CGA 640x200 2 color
D    31   EGA 640x200 16 color
```

E	01	EGA 640x350 2 color
F	11	EGA 640x350 4 color
G	31	EGA 640x350 16 color
H	01	Hercules 720x348 2 color
I	31	VGA 640x350 16 color
J	31	EGA 320x200 16 color
K	01	AT&T/Toshiba 640x400 2 color
L	08	VGA/MCGA 320x200 256 color
M	31	VGA 640x480 16 color
N	31	Hercules InColor 720x348 16 color
O	01	VGA/MCGA 640x480 2 color
P	01	EGA/VGA 800x600 2 color
Q	31	EGA/VGA 800x600 16 color
R	08	S-VGA 640x400 256 color
S	08	S-VGA 640x480 256 color
T	08	S-VGA 800x600 256 color
U	01	S-VGA 1024x768 2 color
V	31	S-VGA 1024x768 16 color
W	08	VGA 360x480 256 color
X	08	S-VGA 1024x768 256 color
Y	31	S-VGA 1280x1024 16 color
Z	08	S-VGA 1280x1024 256 color
L1	10	S-VGA 320x200 hicolor 15
s1	10	S-VGA 640x480 hicolor 15
t1	10	S-VGA 800x600 hicolor 15
x1	10	S-VGA 1024x768 hicolor 15
z1	10	S-VGA 1280x1024 hicolor 15
l2	10	S-VGA 320x200 hicolor 16
s2	10	S-VGA 640x480 hicolor 16
t2	10	S-VGA 800x600 hicolor 16
x2	10	S-VGA 1024x768 hicolor 16
z2	10	S-VGA 1280x1024 hicolor 16
l3	18	S-VGA 320x200 hicolor 24
S3	18	S-VGA 640x480 hicolor 24
T3	18	S-VGA 800x600 hicolor 24
X3	18	S-VGA 1024x768 hicolor 24
Z3	18	S-VGA 1280x1024 hicolor 24

The last change modified the compression algorithm to include 16- and 24-bit images. Each packed block has a similar format to the original byte-packed blocks of the previous compression method.

The first two bytes are 16-bit lengths of packed data, including the 4-byte header. The second two bytes are 16-bit lengths of unpacked data. What follows is a signed, 16-bit integer which, if negative, is a repeat count followed by a 16-bit repeat value (or 24-bit repeat value in 24-bit images). If the signed 16-bit integer is positive, then it is a run count of the number of 16-bit values (or 24-bit values) which follow. This repeats until the end of the packed block is reached.

BSAVE format

Pictor PC Paint 1.0 was developed for Mouse Systems in 1984 and supported only the BSAVE unpacked screen file format and stored only images using the 4-color CGA mode. PC Paint 1.5 supported a modified BSAVE format that allowed images larger than the screen to be stored and supported a rudimentary form of image compression. This revision 1.5 format was very short-lived, and very few image files of this format exist.

The header for the BSAVE format is as follows:

```
typedef struct _BsaveHeader
{
    BYTE Marker;            /* Marker value for packed data */
    WORD ScreenSegment;     /* PC screen memory segment */
    WORD ScreenOffset;      /* PC screen memory offset */
    WORD DataSize;          /* Size of screen data */

} BSAVEHEAD;
```

Marker is the byte value used to mark the start of an packed data run. This value is typically FDh or FEh if the image data is packed.

ScreenSegment is the segment address of the CGA video memory on the PC creating the BSAVE file. This value is typically B800h.

ScreenOffset is the offset address of the CGA video memory on the PC creating the BSAVE file. This value is typically 00h.

DataSize is the size of the screen image data stored in the file. This value is 16,384 for 4-color images, 32,768 for 16-color images, and 00h if the image data is packed. If DataSize is not 00h, then the image data immediately follows the header and is written literally to the PC's video memory. If the value is 00h, then two additional fields appear in the header:

```
WORD SizeOfData;        /* Total size of unpacked data in bytes */
WORD NumberOfBlocks;    /* Number of packed blocks */
```

SizeOfData is the total size of unpacked image data in bytes.

NumberOfBlocks is the number of packed data blocks stored in the file.

Following these fields is the image data in packed format.

At offset 8000 in each BSAVE file is the string "PCPAINT 1.0" or "PC Paint V1.5" indicating the format of the file. This ID string is followed by a byte indicating the current palette number and a second byte current border color number.

Clipping format

Early versions of Pictor PC Paint supported an image file format used to store image sections "clipped" from larger images. This clipping format uses the file extension .CLP and may store data in either a packed or unpacked form.

The header of the Pictor PC Paint clipping format is 11 or 13 bytes in length, depending upon how the image data is stored. The following 11 bytes appear in the header of every .CLP file:

```
typedef struct _ClpHeader
{
    WORD NumberOfBytes;        /* Size of the file, including header */
    WORD XSize;                /* Width of image in pixels */
    WORD YSize;                /* Length of image in pixels */
    WORD XOffset;              /* Left offset of image on display */
    WORD YOffset;              /* Top offset of image on display */
    BYTE BitsPerPixel;         /* Pixel depth */

} CLPHEAD;
```

NumberOfBytes is the total number of bytes in the clipped image.

XSize and YSize specify the size of the image in pixels.

XOffset and YOffset specify the location of the image on the display.

BitsPerPixel is the size of each pixel in bits. If this value is FFh, then the clipped image data is stored packed; otherwise, it is stored unpacked. If the BitsPerPixel value is not FFh, then the uncompressed image data follows the 11-byte header. If the BitsPerPixel value is FFh, then two additional fields appear in the header:

```
    BYTE RealBits;             /* Number of bits per pixel */
    BYTE Marker;               /* Marker byte value for packed data */
```

RealBits contains the number of bits per pixel (the value stored in BitsPerPixel if the data were not packed).

Marker is the value used to mark the beginning of a packed run.

The packed data then follows these fields. Packed data is stored as three bytes: the marker value, the run count, and the run value. A run value is repeated run count times. If a byte is read, and it does not contain the expected marker value, then the byte is written literally to the output.

Overlay format

Pictor PC Paint supports an image file format used to store collections of other images (usually .PIC and .CLP) in a single file. This Overlay format uses the file extension .OVR. It is also possible for .OVR files to contain other types of data besides image data. This is accomplished by appending a dummy 11-byte .PIC header to the data to fool PC Paint.

The header of an .OVR file is a list of each image file stored in the Overlay file. There is one entry in this list for each file stored in the .OVR file, plus an additional NULL entry to mark the end of the list. The format of this array is as follows:

```
typedef struct _PictureName
{
   WORD SizeOfList;              /* Size of the name list in bytes */
   struct _NameList              /* List of files in .OVR file */
   {
      LONG FileOffset;           /* Location of image in the .OVR file */
      CHAR Name[12];             /* Name of image file */
   } NameList[SizeOfList / sizeof(NameList)];

} PICTURENAME[];
```

SizeOfList is the total size of the name list in bytes, including the NULL entry at the end of the list.

NameList is an array of structures. There is one element per file stored, plus an additional NULL entry to mark the end of the list.

FileOffset is the location of this entry's file in the .OVR file. This offset is measured from the beginning of the .OVR file, and this value is 00h for the NULL list entry.

Name is the original filename of the file. This field is NULL padded for names shorter than 12 bytes and contains all NULLs for the NULL list entry.

The actual images stored in the .OVR file follows the NULL list entry.

As an example, let's say we have two files called IMAGE.PIC (2048 bytes in size) and IMAGE1.CLP (384 bytes in size) stored in an .OVR file. The internal format of the .OVR file would be as follows:

```
Field Name      Value
SizeOfList      48
FileOffset      50
Name            "IMAGE.PIC\0\0\0"
FileOffset      2097
Name            "IMAGE.CLP\0\0\0"
FileOffset      0
Name            "\0\0\0\0\0\0\0\0\0\0\0\0\0"
[ Image data for IMAGE.PIC starting at offset 50 ]
[ Image data for IMAGE.CLP starting at offset 2097 ]
```

For Further Information

For further information about the Pictor PC Paint format, see the specification included on the CD-ROM that accompanies this book.

The Pictor PC Paint image file format is supported by Paul Mace Software. Contact:

Paul Mace Software
Attn: Steven Belsky
400 Williamson Way
Ashland, OR 97520
Voice: 503-488-0224
Fax: 503-488-1549
BBS: 503-482-7435

Pixar RIB

NAME:	Pixar RIB
ALSO KNOWN AS:	RenderMan Interface Bytestream, RIB
TYPE:	Scene description
COLORS:	Up to 24-bit
COMPRESSION:	NA
MAXIMUM IMAGE SIZE:	NA
MULTIPLE IMAGES PER FILE:	NA
NUMERICAL FORMAT:	NA
ORIGINATOR:	Pixar
PLATFORM:	All
SUPPORTING APPLICATIONS:	RenderMan, modeling applications, others
SPECIFICATION ON CD:	Yes (summary description)
CODE ON CD:	No
IMAGES ON CD:	No
SEE ALSO:	DKB, MTV, POV, QRT

USAGE: Storage of image scene descriptions for Pixar's RenderMan product.

COMMENTS: Although RIB is proprietary, RenderMan is a capable product available on a number of platforms, so an energetic aftermarket has developed. Enough applications besides RenderMan now read and write RIB files, which has pushed the format into prominence as a de facto standard for high-end rendering.

Overview

Pixar RIB files implement the RenderMan Interface Bytestream (RIB) Protocol, which was developed at Pixar to provide a "standard interface between photorealistic modeling and rendering programs." Because in practice RIB files are supported by other applications mainly to provide output readable by Pixar's RenderMan application, this description would be considered disingenuous, were it not for the fact that RenderMan is so highly regarded.

RenderMan is available on a number of platforms and has a certain currency among sophisticated computer graphics artists and animators. As an application, it provides photorealistic rendering capability, through calls to a comprehensive library of functions. Thus the files resemble scripts, or a series of function calls in a programming language. Each statement implements what Pixar calls a rendering primitive. A list of rendering primitives establishes a description of how a picture is to appear, without specifying how the rendering application should construct it.

File Organization

RIB files are written one byte at a time, and thus Pixar has avoided potential portability problems caused by byte sex differences. The RIB protocol implements a command language, and the data contained in the files can be either 7-bit ASCII or in a compressed binary form. The RIB protocol thus defines an abstract rendering model. In this sense, a RIB file takes the place of a rendering application (usually RenderMan). The user later applies a rendering application to the RIB file to produce an actual image. RIB files are streams of free-form data compatible with the abstract RIB rendering application.

Keeping this in mind, then, RIB files maintain a graphics state, which contains the information necessary to render a graphics primitive, such as color and the various coordinate mapping transformations. In some other rendering applications, "graphics state" refers to the set of attributes associated with any objects being rendered, but Pixar extends the terminology slightly.

RIB defines a number of 2D and 3D geometric primitives, some of them quite sophisticated.

File Details

The RIB rendering application is assumed to be an interpreter scanning a bytestream. To support this model, RIB files are contructed from a sequence of tokens. Tokens are delimited by a set of special characters (", #, [, and]), and the data stream may contain white space, defined as in the C language. Comments are strings preceded by a #.

Both signed real numbers and integers are supported, as are strings, and both also follow conventions similar to their counterparts in the C language.

Names, arrays, and parameter lists round out the data types defined in the specification. Names are usually text strings (or their binary counterparts) associated with RenderMan Interface requests, otherwise known as RenderMan commands. Alongside arrays and parameter lists, they allow the full specification of function calls to the rendering application.

A section of a RIB file might appear as follows:

```
Projection "perspective" "fov" [30.0]
Translate 0 1 0
Rotate 90 0 1 0
WorldBegin
Surface "wood" "roughness" [.3] "Kd" 1
Color [.2 .3 .9]
Polygon "P" [010 011 001 000]
WorldEnd
```

This is not an excerpt from a file, only an example of the kind of commands to be found in one.

For Further Information

For further information about the Pixar RIB format, see the article on the CD-ROM that accompanies this book; this article was prepared by Pixar specifically for this book. For additional information, contact:

Pixar
Attn: Ray Davis
1001 West Cutting
Richmond, CA 94804
Voice: 510-236-4000
FAX: 510-236-0388
rdavis@pixar.com

See these references for additional information about Pixar RIB:

Pixar, *The RenderMan Interface Bytestream Protocol File Format*, Pixar, June 1990.

Pixar, *The Renderman Interface*, Version 3.1, Pixar, September 1989.

Upstill, Steve, *The RenderMan Companion: A Programmer's Guide to Realistic Computer Graphics*, Addison-Wesley, Reading, MA, 1989.

The latter two documents are needed for a full understanding of the RIB format. The binary version of RIB is discussed in the following:

Pixar, *The RenderMan Interface, Version 3.1*, Appendix C, Pixar.

Plot-10

NAME:	Plot-10
ALSO KNOWN AS:	Tek Plot-10
TYPE:	Vector
COLORS:	NA
COMPRESSION:	Uncompressed
MAXIMUM IMAGE SIZE:	NA
MULTIPLE IMAGES PER FILE:	No
NUMERICAL FORMAT:	NA
ORIGINATOR:	Tektronix
PLATFORM:	All
SUPPORTING APPLICATIONS:	NA
SPECIFICATION ON CD:	No
CODE ON CD:	Yes (one variant in pbmplus package)
IMAGES ON CD:	No
SEE ALSO:	None

USAGE: Tektronix terminal control, occasionally written to files instead of to the terminal.

COMMENTS: If you need this information, you really need it badly, and good luck. Plot-10 files are basically dumps of terminal commands, written on-the-fly to a file.

Overview

Plot-10 is associated with a series of graphics terminals manufactured by Tektronix, which were widely used for a certain period of time, primarily at scientific and laboratory sites, before cheap, high-resolution raster display terminals became widely available in the 1980s. Tektronix no longer supports these terminals except under contract. Many owners of Tektronix terminals, however, saw fit through the years to code applications that saved Tektronix terminal commands in local files. A typical application might acquire data from an experiment, for instance, and provide a real-time display of it on a Tektronix terminal. If this data was interesting in any way, it was saved. Unfortunately, because Tektronix provided no guidelines for this, the application developer was forced to make up his or her own format on the spot.

The result of this situation is that there are a lot of "Plot-10" formats in existence. Because most scientific programming has been in Fortran, you might consider that any data you find, on an old tape, for example, may be organized in accordance with the Fortran formatting conventions.

Tektronix technical support has access to the documents describing several terminal communication protocols from that era. These include IDL, STI, and TCS. Unfortunately, they appear to be in offsite backup storage, and we were unable to obtain them from Tektronix, because the company wanted to charge a hefty fee even to look for them. We hope that these documents might be made available to us in a future edition of this book.

For Further Information

For further information about Plot-10, you might try contacting:

Tektronix
Attn: Technical Support
26600 Southwest Parkway
Wilsonville OR 97070-1000
Voice: 503-685-2418

Ask for information that will allow you to decode Plot-10 terminal dump files. Mentioning the IDL, STI, and TCS documentation may be helpful. Be sure to ask if there is a fee.

The pbmplus utilities included on the CD-ROM include an application to convert one of the Plot-10 versions.

POV

NAME:	POV
ALSO KNOWN AS:	POV-Ray, Persistence of Vision
TYPE:	Vector
COLORS:	Unlimited
COMPRESSION:	None
MAXIMUM IMAGE SIZE:	Unlimited
MULTIPLE IMAGES PER FILE:	Yes
NUMERICAL FORMAT:	ASCII
ORIGINATOR:	POV-Team
PLATFORM:	MS-DOS, Macintosh, Amiga, UNIX
SUPPORTING APPLICATIONS:	POV-Ray
SPECIFICATION ON CD:	Yes
CODE ON CD:	No
IMAGES ON CD:	No
SEE ALSO:	TGA, GIF
USAGE:	POV is a scene-description language used to mathematically represent image data that is rendered by the POV-Ray ray tracing engine.
COMMENTS:	One of the few formats described in this book that is created entirely by the human hand.

Overview

The POV (Persistence of Vision) format is used to store the scene description language used by the POV-Ray (Persistence of Vision Raytracer) software package. This format is very similar to other vector-based animation and ray tracing formats.

POV-Ray is capable of creating photorealistic, three-dimensional images using a graphical rendering technique called ray tracing. Simple shapes, textures, lights, and properties are available to render images. POV-Ray also supports many advanced ray tracing features, such as Bezier patches, blobs, height-fields, and bump and material mapping.

Images are created by a POV-Ray user writing mathematical code in an editor and rendering the image using the ray-tracing engine. POV-Ray then writes out the rendered image to a file using either the TGA (24-bit) or GIF (8-bit) raster file formats.

Because the process of creating a POV-Ray image is similar to the way in which a programmer writes and compiles code (rather than the way in which an artist uses a paint program), POV scene-description files are more akin to source code files than to typical graphics format files.

The information stored in a POV language file is a set of descriptions of the scenes in the rendered image. The POV scene description language may therefore be thought of as a PostScript-like page description language for ray-traced images.

File Organization

POV scene files contain three types of elements: camera, object, and light source. A *camera* is the angle of the view into the image. Different perspectives of the scene may be rendered by changing the angle of the camera view and the position of the camera within the image. An *object* is a visible shape that can be seen in the rendering. A *light source* is an invisible object that illuminates the visible objects in the scene. Each scene may have multiple objects and lights, but only one camera.

Let's look at a minimal POV scene file and examine the elements:

```
//
// The canonical red ball on a green floor
//
camera {
        location <0 1 -2>
        look_at <0 1 2>
}
object {
        sphere { <0 1 2> 1 }
        texture { color red 1 phong 1 }
}
object {
        plane { <0 1 0> 0 }
        texture { color green 1 }
}
object {
        light_source { <3 3 -3> color red 1 green 1 blue 1 }
}
```

POV *(cont'd)*

In this example we see a camera and three objects: a sphere, a plane, and a light source. The camera object contains two statements. The first, *location*, indicates the position of the camera within the rendering. It is followed by a parameter list containing the values of the X, Y, and Z coordinates of the physical camera location with respect to the origin point at location 0 0 0. In the example, the values 0, 1, -2 indicate that the camera is centered horizontally (X = 0), one unit up (Y = 1), and two units back (Z = -2) from the origin.

The second statement, *look_at*, specifies the direction the camera is pointing and the point of its focus. These points are also described using 3-dimensional coordinate values. In the example, the values 0, 1, 2 indicate that the camera is looking forward (X = 0), one unit up (Y = 1), and focused at a point two units in front of it (Z = 2).

The first object in the scene is the sphere. Being a visible object, this object contains a shape description and a material description. The shape description is a *sphere* statement, indicating the position of the sphere in the scene and the size of the radius. In the example, the sphere is located at the coordinates 0, 1, 2 and has a radius of 1 unit. The material description is a description is a *texture* statement specifying that the sphere is red in color and has a phong highlighting intensity value of 1.

The next object is the plane. The *plane* statement defines a plane with its surface normal along the Y axis and offset 0 units from the Y axis. The *texture* statement indicates that the plane is green in color.

The last object is the light source object. The parameters of the *light_source* statement indicate the position of the (omnidirectional) light source and its color (white).

As you can see, objects and cameras are written using code similar to that used in many computer languages. Each statement begins with a keyword and is followed by a function body with zero or more values or statements enclosed in braces. For example:

```
sphere { <0 1 0> -4 }
box { <-2 -4 -3.5> <2.5 5.0 2.5> }
color_map { [0.0 0.2 color red 1] [0.2 0.4 color red .5] }
camera { location <0,0,0> look_at <0 1 2> }
```

In this example, the sphere object has a body containing two values, a vector coordinate parameter list and a floating point value. The body of the box object contains two parameter lists. The color map body contains a two-element array. The camera object contains two statements, each statement in turn containing a parameter list.

There are many objects supported by the POV scene-description language and they are fully detailed in the POV documentation.

File Details

POV files are normal ASCII text and do not contain a header or any binary information. Text information in a POV file is case-sensitive. Lowercase words are reserved language keywords. Uppercase words are used for naming data constructs. A single character in double quotes is a literal character.

Comments in POV files use with the Standard C comment tokens /* */ or the C++ comment token //. The Standard C tokens may be nested. Data may be inserted into a POV file using the #include declaration, as follows:

```
#include "filename.inc."
```

POV include files normally have the extension ".inc" and contain information that is shared between multiple POV renderings.

One nice feature of POV is the ability to pre-define a set of data that is used repeatedly, similar to the type definition (*typedef*) feature found in the C language.

Predefinition is accomplished using the *#declare* keyword. In this example, we declare a texture with color parameters values for white:

```
texture { color red 1 green 1 blue 1 }
```

We can predefine the color white for visual clarity in meaning and for later reuse in the file:

```
#declare WHITE = color red 1 green 1 blue 1
texture { color WHITE }
```

For Further Information

For further information about the POV format, see the specification included on the CD-ROM that accompanies this book. Information about the POV-Ray description language can be found in the POV-Ray package itself. Versions of POV-Ray for MS-DOS, UNIX, Apple Macintosh, Commodore Amiga, and other computers are available from CompuServe, America Online, the Internet, and many BBSs.

The Internet home FTP archive site for POV-Ray is: *alfred.ccs.carleton.ca (134.117.1.1)*

The Waite Group has published an excellent book on ray tracing on the PC using POV-Ray. This book comes with the POV-Ray tracing software for the PC with many scenes and objects and also contains a nice introduction to the art and concepts of ray tracing. See the following:

Wells, Drew and Young, Chris, *Ray Tracing Creations: Generate 3D Photo-Realistic Images on the PC*, Waite Group Press, Corte Madera, CA. 1993.

If you have questions about POV-Ray, you can contact:

Drew Wells
POV-Team Leader
73767.1244@compuserve.com

NAME:	Presentation Manager Metafile
ALSO KNOWN AS:	MET
TYPE:	Metafile
COLORS:	Unlimited
COMPRESSION:	RLE
MAXIMUM IMAGE SIZE:	NA
MULTIPLE IMAGES PER FILE:	Yes
NUMERICAL FORMAT:	Little-endian
ORIGINATOR:	Microsoft Corp., IBM
PLATFORM:	OS/2
SUPPORTING APPLICATIONS:	Various under OS/2 Presentation Manager
SPECIFICATION ON CD:	Yes
CODE ON CD:	No
IMAGES ON CD:	No
SEE ALSO:	Microsoft Windows Metafile, OS/2 Bitmap

USAGE: Storage and transport of graphics information associated with the OS/2 Presentation Manager GUI. Seldom found ouside the OS/2 environment.

COMMENTS: A complex format mainly consisting of aliased calls to Presentation Manager supporting libraries. Difficult to support outside of that environment.

Overview

Presentation Manager Metafile (MET) files are used to store vector- and bitmap-format image data in memory or in disk files, for later playback to an output device. Although the Presentation Manager Metafile format is specific to IBM's Presentation Manager for OS/2, many third-party applications support this format as a method for interchanging data between applications under OS/2. Because of the confusion in the market engendered by the IBM-Microsoft split, and the subsequent increase in the installed base of Microsoft Windows, Presentation Manager Metafile has found little support in the larger market, even though the OS/2 installed base is substantial.

File Organization

Presentation Manager Metafiles consist of a sequence of what IBM calls structured fields, which are followed by the actual data. Structured fields and the associated data are organized into one or more functional components, which are large blocks of data—documents, for instance, or complex graphics objects. These functional components are delimited by "begin-component" and "end-component" structured fields.

File Details

Structured fields start with the following header:

```
typedef struct _MetHeader
{
  CHAR Length[2];
  CHAR ID[3];
  BYTE Flags;
  CHAR SegSeqNum[3];

} MetHeader;
```

Length is the length of the field, in bytes.

ID is a field identifier.

Flags contains Boolean information related to the disposition of the field by the rendering application. Currently this is always 0.

SegSeqNum contains what IBM calls a segment sequence number. Again, this is currently always 0.

Following the header structure, which is common to all structured fields, is information that IBM calls positional information. This information extends the header; its exact nature depends on the actual structured field. Following these positional fields are what IBM calls triplets, which consist of a short header of the following form:

```
typedef struct _Triplet
{
  BYTE Length;
  BYTE ID;

} Triplet;
```

Length is the length in bytes of the triplet header and the following data.

ID contains a value identifying the triplet.

Following this header is the actual data associated with the triplet. The bulk of the data found in the metafile is located here.

Structured fields defined in the documentation are listed below.

Field Name	Field ID	Parameters	Triplets
Begin Document	D3A8A8	10 bytes	3
Begin Resource Group	D3A8C6	08 bytes	0
Begin Color Attribute	D3A877	08 bytes	0
Color Attribute Table	D3B077	03 bytes	(varies)
End Color Attribute Table	D3A977	08 bytes	0
Begin Image Object	D3A8FB	08 bytes	0
Begin Resource Group	D3A8C6	08 bytes	0
End Resource Group	D3A9C6	08 bytes	0
Begin Object Environment Group	D3A8C7	08 bytes	0
Map Color Attribute Table	D3AB77	02 bytes	2
Image Data Descriptor	D3A6FB	09 bytes	0
Image Picture Data	D3EEFB	(varies)	(varies)
End Image Object	D3A9FB	08 bytes	0
Begin Graphics Object	D3A8BB	08 bytes	0
Map Coded Font	D3AB8A	02 bytes	3
Map Data Resource	D3ABC3	02 bytes	2
End Object Environment Group	D3A9C7	08 bytes	0
End Graphics Object	D3A9BB	08 bytes	0
End Resource Group	D3A9C6	08 bytes	0
End Document	D3A9A8	08 bytes	0

Perhaps the most common structured field is the Graphics Data Descriptor, which contains the actual graphics data:

Graphics Data Descriptor   D3A6BB

Parameter information associated with the Graphics Data Descriptor provides an elaborate description of the following data, which takes the place of what might be encoded in another format as a long, complex header. Its length varies, but it may be several hundred bytes long. Please see the specification included on the CD-ROM for details and further information. (Note that the document appears to contain an incomplete list of the structured fields likely to be found in a Presentation Manager Metafile.)

For Further Information

For further information about the Presentation Manager Metafile format, see the specification included on the CD-ROM that accompanies this book.

Presentation Manager Metafile is also documented in the following IBM publication:

IBM Corporation, *OS/2 2.0 Technical Library Presentation Manager Programming Reference Volume III, Part Number 10G627.*

Relevant information is contained in Appendixes D, G, and F of the IBM publication. This document is available for purchase through your local IBM dealer or salesperson.

Support responsibility for OS/2 is now solely in the hands of IBM. For information, contact:

IBM Corporation
Attn: Independent Vendor League
150 Kettletown Road
Southbury, CT 06488
Voice: 203-266-2000

OS/2 and the Presentation Manager Metafile format originated at Microsoft, and some documentation is still available there. You may be able to get some information by contacting:

Microsoft Corporation
One Microsoft Way
Redmond, WA 98052-6399
Voice: 206-882-8080
Voice: 800-426-9400
FAX: 206-883-8101

NAME:	PRT
ALSO KNOWN AS:	Parallel Ray Trace
TYPE:	Scene description
COLORS:	NA
COMPRESSION:	Uncompressed
MAXIMUM IMAGE SIZE:	NA
MULTIPLE IMAGES PER FILE:	NA
NUMERICAL FORMAT:	NA
ORIGINATOR:	Kory Hamzeh
PLATFORM:	All
SUPPORTING APPLICATIONS:	PRT ray trace application, others
SPECIFICATION ON CD:	Yes
CODE ON CD:	Yes (in pbrupluc package)
IMAGES ON CD:	No
SEE ALSO:	NFF, POV, QRT, Radiance

USAGE: Description of 3D scenes for ray-tracing or other rendering applications.

COMMENTS: A simple ray tracing format, notable because it is one of the few formats designed to support parallel processing.

Overview

PRT (Parallel Ray Trace) is the format associated with the PRT ray-tracing application created by Kory Hamzeh. It is apparently based loosely on Eric Haines' Neutral File Format (NFF). Its main distinguishing characteristic is that the PRT application was designed to support parallel rendering, that is, rendering by a number of machines at once, over a network.

File Organization

Other than the fact that PRT files consist of a number of ASCII lines, there is little mandatory structure. Lines consist of keywords and parameters.

The following keywords may be found in a PRT file:

from
at
up
angle
resolution
light
background
surface
cone
sphere
hsphere
polygon
ring
quadric
instance
end_instance
instance_of

Each file must start with the following:

```
from %g %g %g
at %g %g %g
up %g %g %g
angle %g
resolution %d %d
```

The parameters are listed below:

from	Eye location in XYZ world coordinates
at	Center of the image, in XYZ world coordinates
up	Vector indicating which direction is up
angle	Angle of image in degrees
resolution	Resolution in pixels in both the x and y directions

File Details

The following information is extracted from the documentation supplied by Kory Hamzeh, the creator of PRT, and explains the keywords listed above:

Light Sources

A light source is defined as follows:

    light X Y Z

Format:

```
light %g %g %g
```

This keyword defines the position of the light sources. All light sources must be defined before any objects are defined.

Background Color

A background color is defined as follows:

    background R G B y

Format::

```
background %g %g %g y
```

The background color is in RGB. The last field is used for color cueing (not yet implemented) and must always be 'y'.

Surface Properties

A surface property is defined as follows:

    surface Rr Rg Rb Ks Fr Fg Fb T Ar Ag Ab Dr Dg Db Sr Sg Sb P Ior

Format:

```
surface %g %g %g %g %g %g %g %g %g %g %g %g %g %g %g %g
        %g %g %g
```

Parameters are:

Rr Rg Rb   The reflective color triplet. This value should always be 1 1 1 (unless you want this surface to reflect a different percentage per color component).

Ks   The specular component. This value is the percentage of light that is reflected from this object. A value of 0 means no reflection, and a value of 1 means a perfect reflector (mirror).

Fr Fg Fb   The refractive color triplet. This value should always be 1 1 1 (unless you want this surface to refract a different percentage per color component).

T   Transparency value. The amount of light that can go through this object; a value of 0 means a totally opaque object. A value of 1 means a totally transparent object.

Ar Ag Ab   The ambient color for this object; this means the color of an object if it were fully shadowed. All objects are assigned this color before any shading algorithm is started.

Dr Dg Db   The diffuse color component

Sr Sg Sb   This value is the color of the specular highlights. Usually, it should be 1 1 1.

P   The Phong cosine power for highlights. The higher the number (for example 100), the smaller the highlight.

Ior   Index of refraction

Cylinder or Cone

A cylinder or cone is defined as follows:

```
cone
base.x base.y base.z base_radius
apex.x apex.y apex.z apex_radius
```

Format:

```
cone
%g %g %g %g
%g %g %g %g
```

Sphere

A sphere is defined as follows:

```
sphere center.x center.y center.z radius
```

Format:

```
sphere %g %g %g %g
```

Hollow Sphere

A hollow sphere is defined as follows:

sphere center.x center.y center.z radius thickness

Format:

```
sphere %g %g %g %g %g
```

Polygon

A polygon is defined as follows:

polygon total_vertices
vert1.x vert1.y vert1.z
[etc. for total_vertices vertices]

A polygon is defined by a set of vertices. With these databases, a polygon is defined to have all points coplanar. A polygon has only one side, with the order of the vertices being counterclockwise as you face the polygon (right-handed coordinate system). The first two edges must form a non-zero convex angle, so that the normal and side visibility can be determined.

Format:

```
polygon %d
[ %g %g %g ] <— for total_vertices vertices
```

Ring

A ring is defined as follows:

ring center.x center.y center.z p1.x p1.y p1.z p2.x p2.y p2.z or ir

A ring is a flat coplaner round-shaped object. For a ring object, you must specify the following: center, two points on the surface of the ring, the inner radius, and the outer radius. If the inner radius is non-zero, then the ring has a hole in the middle with the given radius.

PRT (cont'd)

Format:

```
ring %g %g %g %g %g %g %g %g %g %g %g
```

Quadratic

A quadratic is defined as follows:

```
quadric center.x center.y center.Z
min.x min.y min.z max.x max.y max.z
a b c d e
f g h i j
```

You can ray trace any quadratic object by specifying the center, minimum, maximum, and coefficients. This is a very powerful object type. It can do ellipsoids, hyperbolas, and any other quadratic surface.

In the model shown above, the fields "a" through "j" are the coefficients.

Format:

```
quadric %g %g %g
%g %g %g %g %g %g
%g %g %g %g %g
%g %g %g %g %g
```

Object Instances

You may define a group of objects (and surface properties) to an instance and assign a name to that instance. When the instance is used, all the objects in that instance are placed relative to the given origin. Note that instances by themselves do not create any objects; the objects are created when the instance is referenced. Instances cannot be nested.

An instance is defined as follows:

```
instance nameofthisinstance
   [ objects and surface properties ]
end_instance
```

where *nameofthisinstance* is a user-assigned name such as, for example, `tile_pattern`.

An instance is referenced as follows:

    instance_of *nameofinstance* loc.x loc.y loc.z

where:

nameofinstance
is the name assigned to a previously defined object instance.
`loc.x, loc.y, loc.z` represent the location of this object group.

For Further Information

For further information about the PRT format, see the specification included on the CD-ROM that accompanies this book. You can also contact:

Kory Hamzeh
Avatar
6217 Melba Avenue
Woodland Hills, CA 91367
kory@avatar.com

QRT

NAME:	QRT
ALSO KNOWN AS:	Quick Ray Trace
TYPE:	Scene description
COLORS:	NA
COMPRESSION:	Uncompressed
MAXIMUM IMAGE SIZE:	NA
MULTIPLE IMAGES PER FILE:	NA
NUMERICAL FORMAT:	NA
ORIGINATOR:	Steve Koren
PLATFORM:	All
SUPPORTING APPLICATIONS:	QRT ray-tracing application, others
SPECIFICATION ON CD:	Yes
CODE ON CD:	Yes
IMAGES ON CD:	No
SEE ALSO:	NFF, POV, PRT, Radiance

USAGE: Description of 3D scenes for ray tracing or other rendering applications.

COMMENTS: A solid scene description format similar to other ray-tracing formats described in this book. It is not used much today.

Overview

QRT (Quick Ray Trace) is associated with the QRT ray-tracing application created by Steve Koren. As such, it implements the QRT scene-description language. Each QRT file consists of a number of ASCII lines, which define objects in the QRT system, and operations, which can be performed by QRT.

File Organization

QRT files consist of a number of ASCII lines consisting of keywords. Like most ray-trace formats, it was designed to be human-readable and to be composed and altered with standard text-editing tools. Keywords may appear in any order in the file. Parameters associated with each keyword may appear in any order, provided that there is no ambiguity.

File Details

The following is a list of QRT keywords. Some of these must be found in every file. The rest are optional. Each keyword may be followed by one or more parameters.

SKY	FIRST_SCAN
QUADRATIC	END_BBOX
GROUND	LAMP
PATTERN	BEGIN_INSTANCES
FOC_LENGTH	SPHERE
RECTANGLE	END_INSTANCES
LAST_SCAN	PARALLELOGRAM
CIRCLE	INSTANCE_OF
FILE_NAME	TRIANGLE
POLYGON	DEFAULT
OBSERVER	RING
BEGIN_BBOX	

For Further Information

Although the author, Steve Koren, says that QRT is obsolete and has been for some time, we find that the QRT distribution is still widely available via FTP from various sites. It is also downloaded with some regularity from the major PC BBSs.

For further information about the QRT file format, see the PRT specification included on the CD-ROM that accompanies this book, and the *QRT Language Reference* found in the QRT distribution. You can also contact:

Steve Koren
koren@hpfcogv.fc.hp.com

QuickTime

NAME:	QuickTime
ALSO KNOWN AS:	QTM, QuickTime Movie Resource Format
TYPE:	Audio/video data storage
COLORS:	Up to 24 bits
COMPRESSION:	RLE, JPEG, others
MAXIMUM IMAGE SIZE:	64Kx64K pixels
MULTIPLE IMAGES PER FILE:	Yes
NUMERICAL FORMAT:	Little-endian
ORIGINATOR:	Apple Computer
PLATFORM:	Apple Macintosh, Microsoft Windows
SUPPORTING APPLICATIONS:	QuickTime, QuickTime for Windows, others
SPECIFICATION ON CD:	Yes
CODE ON CD:	No
IMAGES ON CD:	No
SEE ALSO:	JPEG, MPEG, RIFF

USAGE: Storage and interchange of time-based information under the Macintosh and Microsoft Windows environments.

COMMENTS: Currently the most widely-used audio-video format, although it competes with Microsoft's RIFF/AVI on Intel machines under Microsoft Windows.

Overview

QuickTime (sometimes called QTM) is the native method of storing audio and motion video information on the Apple Macintosh platform. It is used to record and play back multimedia information and store the data on magnetic or optical media. In this sense, it is similar to multimedia data formats. Quick-Time, however, is not only a data-storage format. It is also a collection of tools (the Movie Toolbox) that allows QuickTime movies to be modified (edit, cut, copy, paste, and so on), just as a word processor is capable of modifying an ordinary text file.

A QuickTime movie may be stored as a disk file or may be encoded on a DAT or a CD-ROM. Playback of audio and video data is quick, and the audio and video output at least matches the quality of a VCR-taped program.

The QuickTime format allows the storage of multiple tracks of audio and video data. Multiple audio tracks may be used to store the narration for a movie in several different languages. Multiple video tracks may be used to change the video output based on the user responses to an interactive multimedia application. QuickTime movies may also contain a preview, which is a five-second sequence of audio and video data from the movie, and a poster, which is a single frame displayed from the movie data. Both previews and posters are used to quickly identify a movie and its contents.

QuickTime movies are normally structured for the Macintosh environment. However, it is possible to store QuickTime movies in an interchange format, which allows time-based information to be exchanged between the Macintosh and other platforms. This ability allows many multimedia applications that run under non-Macintosh environments, such as Microsoft Windows, the capability of recording and playing back QuickTime movies.

The Movie Toolbox defines six different compression methods that may be used in a QuickTime movie. All of the compression methods used, except for JPEG (Joint Photographic Experts Group, described in Chapter 9, *Data Compression*), are proprietary to Apple Computer and are mentioned only briefly below.

- The Photo Compressor uses the JPEG compression method to compress single-frame images. Continuous-tone images with a pixel depth of eight to 24 bits compressed are the optimal source images for the photo compressor.

- The Video Compressor is a lossy, motion-video compression method, which uses both spatial and temporal compression techniques and has a very fast decompression time. The video compressor is for use with 24-bit, continuous-tone video images.

- The Compact Video Compressor is a lossy, motion-video compression method which is for use with 16- and 24-bit continuous-tone video images. The Compact Video Compressor offers higher image quality, greater compression ratios, and a faster playback speed than is possible when using the Video Compressor, but it requires much more time to perform the initial compression of the video information.

- The Animation Compressor uses a motion-video compression method to compress computer-generated and animation sequences. This compressor uses a run-length algorithm which operates on images of any pixel depth and may be selected to perform lossy or lossless compression. The lossy option offers greater data compression ratios at the expense of image quality. This compressor produces high compression ratios at the expense of a slower decompression speed.

- The Graphics Compressor employs a compression algorithm that is used to encode 8-bit still images and image sequences. This compressor produces lower compression ratios, but is able to decompress the image data very quickly. This method is used to encode sequences that will be stored on slower devices, such as CD-ROMs.

- The Raw Compressor is simply a conversion program that increases (pads) or reduces (decimates) the number of bits in a pixel. A 32-bit image is reduced to a 24-bit image by stripping off the alpha channel bits. A 16-bit image is decimated to an 8-bit image by throwing away the eight least significant bits of each pixel. A 4-bit image is padded out to an 8-bit image by adding four bits to each pixel. The Raw Compressor is used most for pre-processing image data to an appropriate pixel depth before it is encoded by another compressor.

Audio data in QuickTime movie files is digitally encoded into 8-bit samples. A sample is an amplitude value represented by the signed integer range of -128 to 127, with 0 representing silence (two's-complement sound encoding), or an unsigned integer range of 0 to 255, with 128 representing silence (offset-binary sound encoding). Samples stored using the Audio Interchange File Format (AIFF) use the two's-complement encoding method, while samples stored directly in a movie's sound media resource are offset-binary encoded.

The following sections describe only the basic format of the QuickTime movie file. For a complete explanation of the QuickTime file architecture, refer to the *Inside Macintosh* series, specifically the sections which describe QuickTime and the Movie Toolbox, or the QuickTime Developer Kit reference manuals and CD-ROM.

File Organization

A QuickTime movie is called a movie resource. In the Macintosh environment it is not necessary to know the internal arrangement of a movie resource. All of the functions available in the Movie Toolbox handle the reading, writing, and interpretation of the movie data for the programmer. In non-Macintosh environments that do not have an emulation of the Macintosh Movie Toolbox, functions must be written to read the movie resources directory, and the internal arrangement of the resources must therefore be known. This is necessary so non-Macintosh platforms may create and play back QuickTime movies.

In the Macintosh environment, QuickTime movies are normally stored in both the resource fork and the data fork of a file. The resource fork contains information about the QuickTime movie data. The data fork contains either the actual movie data or a reference to where the data is located.

A second type of QuickTime movie file, called the single-fork movie file, stores all of the movie data in the data fork, and the resource fork is left empty. This interchange format is used when the movie file will be transported to a non-Macintosh system. When most Macintosh files are moved to a non-Macintosh system, such as MS-DOS or UNIX, the useful information is mostly found in the data fork, and the resource fork information is discarded. When non-Macintosh files are transported to the Macintosh, a resource fork is either created for the file or the resource fork is simply left empty.

In the Macintosh environment movie files have the file type 'moov'. In non-Macintosh environments, movie files usually have the extension .QTM.

File Details

The basic data structure in a move file is called an *atom*. Each atom is a specific collection of data similar to a "chunk" found in the IFF and Microsoft RIFF file formats. The basic format of the atom is shown here:

```
typedef struct _Atom
{
   DWORD Size;          /* Size of the atom in bytes */
   DWORD Type;          /* Atom type identifier */
   ATOM  Atom;          /* One or more atom structures */
   DATA  Data;          /* One or more pieces of data contained with
                           this atom */

} ATOM;
```

Size indicates the size of the atom in bytes, including the Size and Type fields.

Type specifies the type and format of data that is stored in the atom.

Atom identifiers are always 4-character ASCII values.

An atom is the actual movie structure. Two varieties of atoms are defined for use in QuickTime movies: the container atom and the leaf atom. Container atoms may contain other atoms, including other container atoms. A leaf atom contains only data and no other atoms.

Two atom types are found in every data fork of a movie file. The first is the movie data atom which has the type identifier mdat. This atom contains the actual movie data. The second is the movie resource atom, which has the type identifier moov. This atom always follows the movie data atom and contains the description of the movie file. Other atoms may follow the movie resource atom, but only the mdat and moov atoms are required to occur in every movie file.

The movie resource atom is actually a directory of all of the information found in the movie and is the closest thing to a header that you will find in a Quick-Time movie file. The resource atom contains the following:

- Movie header atom (mvhd)

- Clipping atom (clip)

- One or more track atoms (trak)

- User-defined data (udta)

The clipping and track atoms can, in turn, contain a number of different types of atoms.

Each data stream in a movie file is stored in a track atom. There is one track atom per data stream stored in the movie file. A movie which contains a single audio and video data stream therefore contains two track atoms. Each track atom contains a track header and a media atom, which describes the actual stream data.

Using a C syntax-like notation, you can see the nested structure of atoms within a QuickTime movie file:

```
struct _MovieDirectory
{
  struct _MovieHeaderAtom;
  struct _ClippingAtom
  {
    struct _ClippingRegionAtom;
  }
  struct _TrackDirectory
  {
    struct _TrackHeaderAtom;
    struct _ClippingAtom
```

```
    {
      struct _ClippingRegionAtom;
    }
    struct _EditsAtom
    {
      struct _EditListAtom;
    }
    struct _MediaDirectory
    {
      struct _MediaHeaderAtom;
      struct _MediaHandlerAtom;
      struct _MediaInfoAtom;
      {
        struct _VideoMediaInfoAtom
        {
        }
        struct _SoundMediaInfoAtom
         {
           struct _SoundMediaInfoHeaderAtom
           {
             struct _SoundMediaInfoHeaderAtom;
           }
           struct _HandlerAtom;
           struct _DataReferenceAtom;
           struct _SampleTableAtom;
         }
       }
     }
    struct _UserDataAtom;
  }
  struct _UserDataAtom
  {
    struct _MoviesUserData
    {
    }
  }
}
```

This schematic of a QuickTime movie file shows the atoms nested down only to five levels. There are several more levels and dozens of additional atoms not shown here. In this article, we discuss only the main atom types—the movie, track, and media atoms and their respective header atoms. For information on all other atoms, see the references listed in the section called "Movie Resource Atom."

As stated, the movie resource atom is really a directory containing all the information about the movie except for the movie data itself. The movie resource atom has the following structure:

```
typedef struct _MovieDirectory
{
   LONG              AtomSize;      /* Size of this atom in bytes */
   LONG              AtomType;      /* Type of atom ('moov') */
   MOVIEHEADERATOM   MovieHeader;   /* Movie header atom for this atom */
   CLIPPINGATOM      MovieClip;     /* Clipping atom for this atom */
   TRACKDIRECTORY    Track[];       /* One or more track atoms */
   USERDATAATOM      UserData;      /* User Definable Extensions */

} MOVIEDIRECTORY;
```

AtomSize is the size in bytes of the atom.

AtomType is the type of atom.

MovieHeader is an atom containing global information about the MovieDirectory atom, the data it contains, and how the data is to be played back.

MovieClip is an atom containing data pertaining to the visual appearance of the movie.

Track is an atom containing an array for each track contained in the movie. There is one track per data stream found in the movie file.

UserData is an atom containing information such as the movie's date of creation, the copyright notice, and the names of the movie's director, producer, writers, and so on.

MovieHeader Atom

The structure of the MovieHeader atom is the following:

```
typedef struct _MovieHeaderAtom
{
LONG  AtomSize;       /* Size of this atom in bytes */
LONG  AtomType;       /* Type of atom ('mvhd') */
LONG  Flags;          /* Atom version and flags */
LONG  CreationTime;   /* Time/date atom was created */
LONG  LastModifyTime; /* Time/date atom was last modified */
LONG  TimeScale;      /* Time scale used for this movie */
```

```
LONG   Duration;          /* Duration of this movie */
DWORD  DataRate;          /* Rate at which to play this movie */
SHORT  Volume;            /* Movie loudness */
SHORT  Reserved1;         /* Not used */
LONG   Reserved2;         /* Not used */
LONG   Reserved3;         /* Not used */
DWORD  Matrix[3][3];      /* Transform matrix used by this movie */
LONG   PreviewTime;       /* Time in track the preview begins */
LONG   PreviewDuration;   /* Duration of the movie preview */
LONG   PosterTime;        /* Time in track the the poster begins */
LONG   SelectionTime;     /* Time in track current selection begins */
LONG   SelectionDuration; /* Duration of the current selection */
LONG   CurrentTime;       /* Movie time the current selection begins */
LONG   NextTrackID;       /* Next value to use for an track ID */

} MOVIEHEADERATOM;
```

AtomSize is the size of the atom in bytes.

AtomType is the type of atom.

The first byte of the Flags field indicates the version number of the movie header atom. The remaining three bytes of the Flags field are not used and are reserved for future use.

CreationTime holds the time and date stamp when the header atom was created. LastModifyTime indicates the time and date this atom was last modified. On the Macintosh, these fields are a number representing the number of seconds that have occurred since midnight January 1, 1904 and the actual time/date represented by these fields.

TimeScale contains the number of units per second in the time coordinate system used by this movie. A TimeScale value of 100 indicates that a single unit of time is 1/100th of a second in length.

Duration is the length of the movie in TimeScale units.

DataRate is the rate of data throughput necessary to properly play back the movie.

Volume indicates the volume level at which to play the movie.

Reserved1, Reserved2, and Reserved3 are not used and are set to 0.

Matrix is a two-dimensional array of integers used to transform one visual coordinate system to another.

PreviewTime indicates where in the track the movie preview begins.

PreviewDuration indicates the length of the preview.

PosterTime indicates where the movie poster occurs in the track.

SelectionTime and SelectionDuration indicate the location and length of the currently selected segment of the movie.

CurrentTime indicates the time at which the current selection appears within the movie.

NextTrackID is the track ID of the next occurring track in the movie.

TrackDirectory Atom

Each type of data stream in the movie file is represented by a TrackDirectory atom. These 'trak' atoms are stored as an array in the moov atom and have the following structure:

```
typedef struct _TrackDirectory
{
    LONG              AtomSize;      /* Size of this atom in bytes */
    LONG              AtomType;      /* Type of atom ('trak') */
    TRACKHEADERATOM   TrackHeader;   /* Standard track information */
    CLIPPINGATOM      TrackClip;     /* Clipping atom for this track*/
    EDITSATOM         Edits;         /* Edit atom for this track*/
    MEDIADIRECTORY    Media;         /* Media atom for this track */
    USERDATAATOM      UserData;      /* Additional data about this track*/

} TRACKDIRECTORY;
```

AtomSize is the size of the atom in bytes.

AtomType is the type of atom.

TrackHeader contains information specific to this track atom only.

TrackClip is an atom containing data which specifies the spatial clipping region for the track.

Edits is an atom specifing how to map the media data stored in the track.

Media is an atom containing information describing the actual media data represented by this track.

UserData contains user-definable extension data.

TrackHeader Atom

The structure of the TrackHeader atom is the following:

```
struct _TrackHeaderAtom
{
    LONG  AtomSize;         /* Size of this atom in bytes */
    LONG  AtomType;         /* Type of atom ('tkhd') */
    LONG  Flags;            /* Atom version and flags */
    LONG  CreationTime;     /* Time/date atom was created */
    LONG  LastModifyTime;   /* Time/date atom was last modified */
    LONG  TrackID;          /* Track ID number */
    LONG  Reserved1;        /* Not used */
    LONG  Duration;         /* Length of track */
    LONG  Reserved2;        /* Not used */
    LONG  Reserved3;        /* Not used */
    SHORT Layer;            /* Priority for this track in movie */
    SHORT AlternateGroup;   /* Track group ID value */
    SHORT Volume;           /* Loudness of the track */
    SHORT Reserved4;        /* Not used */
    DWORD Matrix[3][3];     /* Transform matrix used by this track*/
    LONG  TrackWidth;       /* Track width */
    LONG  TrackHeight;      /* Track height */

} TRACKHEADERATOM;
```

AtomSize is the size of the atom in bytes.

AtomType is the type of atom.

The first byte of the Flags field indicates the version number of the track header atom. The remaining three bytes of the Flags field are not used and are reserved for future use.

CreationTime and LastModifyTime fields indicate when this atom was first created and last modified respectively.

TrackID contains a unique value used to identify the track within the movie.

Reserved1 is not used and is set to 0.

Duration indicates the playing time of the track data.

Reserved2 and Reserved3 are not used and are set to 0.

Layer contains the layer level of this track.

AlternateGroup is an identification value associating this track with a specific group of data found within the movie.

Volume is the loudness setting for the track media.

Reserved4 is not used and is set to 0.

Matrix is an array containing a set of data that defines how to map points from one coordinate space into a different coordinate space.

TrackWidth and TrackHeight are the width and height of the rectangle that encloses a visual media track.

Media Atom

The description of the actual media data for this track is contained within the Media atom (mdia). A media atom can contain other atoms, such as a media header (mdhd), a handler reference (hdlr), media information (minf), and user-defined data (udta). Only the media header atom is required.

The media atom has the following structure:

```
typedef struct _MediaDirectoryAtom
{
    LONG              AtomSize;       /* Size of this atom in bytes */
    LONG              AtomType;       /* Type of atom ('mdia') */
    MEDIAHEADERATOM   MediaHeader;    /* Media attributes */
    HANDLERATOM       MediaHandler;   /* Media handler atom */
    MEDIAINFO         MediaInfo;      /* Media information atom */

} MEDIADIRECTORYATOM;
```

AtomSize is the size of the atom in bytes.

AtomType is the type of atom.

MediaHeader is an atom specifying the attributes of the media data stream contained within this media atom.

MediaHandler is an atom specifying the type of software service (media handler) that is to interpret the media data.

MediaInfo is an atom that stores information that the media handler uses to interpret the actual media data. The format of this atom varies depending upon the type of media stored.

Media Header Atom

The structure of the MediaHeader atom is as follows:

```
struct _MediaHeaderAtom
{
    LONG  AtomSize;        /* Size of this atom in bytes */
    LONG  AtomType;        /* Type of atom ('mdhd') */
    LONG  Flags;           /* Atom version and flags */
    LONG  CreationTime;    /* Time/date atom was created */
    LONG  LastModifyTime;  /* Time/date atom was last modified */
    LONG  TimeScale;       /* Time scale used for this media */
    LONG  Duration;        /* Length of this media */
    SHORT Language;        /* Language code for this media */
    SHORT Quality;         /* Quality rating for this media */

} MEDIAHEADERATOM;
```

AtomSize is the size of the atom in bytes.

AtomType is the type of atom.

The first byte of the Flags field indicates the version number of the media header atom. The remaining three bytes of the Flags field are not used and are reserved for future use.

CreationTime and LastModifyTime indicate when this atom was first created and last modified respectively.

TimeScale and Duration specify the type of time scale used and the duration of the media stream in TimeScale units.

Language indicates the language code of this atom.

Quality holds a quantitative value indicating the relative quality of the data stored in the media atom.

For Further Information

For further information about QuickTime, see the documentation included on the CD-ROM that accompanies this book.

The developer guide and kit for QuickTime are available from Apple. Information on Apple Computer programming products, development tools, and technical references also may be obtained directly from:

Apple Computer, Inc.
Attn: APDA
20525 Mariani Avenue
Mail Stop 33-G
Cupertino, CA 95014-6299
Voice: 800-282-2732 (United States)
Voice: 800-637-0029 (Canada)
Voice: 800-562-3910 (all other countries)
FAX: 408-562-3971

Information about Apple developer support programs may be obtained from:

Apple Computer, Inc.
Attn: Macintosh Developer Technical Support
20525 Mariani Avenue
Mail Stop 75-3T
Cupertino, CA 95014-6299
Voice: 408-974-4897

Information about QuickTime can also be found in the following:

Apple Computer, *Inside Macintosh*, Imaging and QuickTime volumes, Addison-Wesley, Reading, MA.

NAME:	Radiance
ALSO KNOWN AS:	None
TYPE:	Scene description
COLORS:	NA
COMPRESSION:	Uncompressed
MAXIMUM IMAGE SIZE:	NA
MULTIPLE IMAGES PER FILE:	NA
NUMERICAL FORMAT:	NA
ORIGINATOR:	Greg Ward
PLATFORM:	All
SUPPORTING APPLICATIONS:	Radiance, others
SPECIFICATION ON CD:	Yes
CODE ON CD:	Yes
IMAGES ON CD:	No
SEE ALSO:	DKB, NFF, POV, PRT, QRT, Rayshade, RTrace
USAGE:	3D scene description for use by ray-tracing applications and other renderers.
COMMENTS:	A well-documented, well-thought-out format.

Overview

Radiance is a rendering application created by Greg Ward. It is well regarded and has been widely distributed through the Internet graphics community, although perhaps not as widely distributed as some of the other ray-tracing applications. There are actually two formats associated with the Radiance application: the input (or scene description) format and the output format. The input format is well-documented, carefully conceived, flexible, and extensive. The output is a simple bitmap format.

File Organization

The input format consists of a series of ASCII lines implementing the scene description language used by the Radiance application. The output format consists of an ASCII information header terminated by an empty line, followed by the bitmap data.

File Details

The input file consists of a list of surfaces and materials. Surface types include spheres, polygons, cones, and cylinders. Materials can be plastic, metal, glass, and others. Light sources known to the system are distant disks as well as local spheres, disks, and polygons.

This section is adapted from the Radiance documentation:

A scene description file represents a three-dimensional physical environment in Cartesian (rectilinear) world coordinates. It is stored as ASCII text, with the following basic format:

```
# comment
modifier PM identifier n S1 S2 S3 ... Sn
0
m R1 R2 R3 ... Rm
modifier (alias identifier reference)
! command
```

A comment line begins with a pound sign (#).

The scene description primitives all have the same general format and can be either surfaces or modifiers. Here are some definitions:

- A primitive has a modifier, a type, and an identifier.

- A modifier is either the identifier of a previously defined primitive, or "void" (no modifier).

- An identifier can be any string (i.e., a sequence of non-blank characters).

The arguments associated with a primitive can be strings or real numbers. The first integer following the identifier is the number of string arguments, and it is followed by the arguments themselves (separated by white space). The next integer is the number of integer arguments, followed by the integer arguments themselves. (There are currently no primitives that use them, however.) The next integer is the real argument count, and is followed by the real arguments.

An alias gets its type and arguments from a previously defined primitive. This is useful when the same material is used with a different modifier, or as a convenient naming mechanism. Surfaces cannot be aliased.

A line beginning with an exclamation point (!) is interpreted as a command. It is executed by the shell, and its output is read as input to the program. The command must not try to read from its standard input, or confusion will result. A command may be continued over multiple lines using a backslash (\) to escape the newline.

Blank space is generally ignored, except as a separator. The exception is the newline character after a command or a comment.

Commands, comments, and primitives may appear in any combination, as long as they are not intermingled.

The following example defines a sphere by specifying its center and radius:

```
mod sphere id
0
0
4 xcent ycent zcent radius
```

For other examples, see the CD-ROM that accompanies this book.

For Further Information

For further information about the Radiance format, particularly the Radiance parameters and their primitives, see the Radiance specification and other documents included on the CD-ROM that accompanies this book. On the CD-ROM you will also find source code for reading and writing Radiance format files. You can also contact the author:

Lawrence Berkeley Laboratory
Attn: Gregory J. Ward
Lighting Systems Research Group
Energy & Environment Division
University of California
Building 90-3111
1 Cyclotron Road
Berkeley, CA 94720
Voice: 510-486-4757
FAX: 510-486-4089
GJWard@lbl.gov

The source code for the Radiance application is maintained at

hobbes.lbl.gov

At that site there are several directories containing files associated with the application:

pub/models
pub/objects
pub/pics

NAME:	Rayshade
ALSO KNOWN AS:	None
TYPE:	Scene description
COLORS:	NA
COMPRESSION:	Uncompressed
MAXIMUM IMAGE SIZE:	NA
MULTIPLE IMAGES PER FILE:	NA
NUMERICAL FORMAT:	NA
ORIGINATOR:	Craig Kolb
PLATFORM:	All
SUPPORTING APPLICATIONS:	Rayshade, others
SPECIFICATION ON CD:	Yes
CODE ON CD:	No
IMAGES ON CD:	No
SEE ALSO:	DKB, MTV, NFF, POV PRT, QRT
USAGE:	Description of scenes meant to be rendered by programs such as Rayshade.
COMMENTS:	A well-constructed format that has influenced writers of more recent ray-tracing programs.

Overview

Rayshade is a ray-tracing application created by Craig Kolb. It is well-respected and has been widely distributed, particularly on the Internet and throughout the PC/MS-DOS world, but it has largely been superseded by more recent ray-trace programs.

The format implements a scene description language, which could be (and has been) used as a model for later rendering applications. It would be a good model to study if you are in the process of writing yet another ray trace or 3D scene-rendering application.

File Organization

Like many ray-trace formats, Rayshade files consist of a series of ASCII lines that implement a proprietary command language, this one associated with the Rayshade application.

File Details

The following summary information about the Rayshade format is extracted from the *Rayshade 4.0 Quick Reference* document by Craig Kolb, which is included on the CD-ROM that accompanies this book.

Reals and integers may be written in exponential notation, with or without a decimal point. Reals are truncated to integers when need be.

Numbers may also be written as expressions surrounded by a matched pair of parentheses. Sub-expressions may be parenthesized to control the order of evaluation.

Variables may be defined and used in parenthesized expressions.

Predefined variables include the following:

> time (current time)
> frame (current frame number, 0 - frames - 1)
> pi
> dtor (pi/180)
> rotd (180/pi)

Available operators include the following:

> + (addition)
> − (subtraction and negation)
> * (multiplication)
> / (division)
> % (remainder)
> ^ (exponentiation)

Functions include the following:

> sin
> cos
> tan
> asin
> acos

atan
sqrt
hypot

Strings are written as non-quoted strings that may include include uppercase and lowercase letters, non-leading digits, and the following special characters:

- / (slash)
- – (dash)
- _ (underscore)
- . (period)

The following command-line options are supported. These override options are set in the input file:

–A frame	First frame to render
–a	Toggle alpha channel
–C cutoff	Adaptive tree cutoff
–c	Continued rendering
–D depth	Maximum ray tree depth
–E eye_sep	Eye separation
–e	Exponential RLE output
–F freq	Report frequency
–f	Flip triangle normals
–G gamma	Gamma exponent
–g	Use Gaussian filter
–h	Help
–j	Toggle jittered sampling
–l	Render left eye view
–m	Produce sample map
–N frames	Total frames to render
–n	No shadows
–O outfile	Output filename
–o	Toggle opaque shadows
–P cpp-args	Arguments for cpp
–p	Preview-quality
–q	Run quietly
–R xres yres	Resolution
–r	Right eye view
–S samples	Use Samples^2 samples
–s	Toggle shadow caching

Rayshade (cont'd)

–T r g b	Contrast threshold
–u	Toggle use of cpp
–V filename	Verbose file output
–v	Verbose output
–W lx hx ly hy	Render subwindow
–X l r b t	Crop window

Here are the author's specifications for the construction of the input file:

```
File: /* Input file consists of . . .*/
   <Item> [<Item> ... ]

Item:
   <Viewing>
   <Light>
   <Atmosphere>
   <RenderOption>
   <ObjItem>
   <Definition>

ObjItem: /* Items used in object definition blocks */
   <SurfDef>
   <ApplySurf>
   <Instance>
   <ObjDef>

Viewing:
   eyep Xpos Ypos Zpos         /*  Eye position (0 -10 0)  */
   lookp Xpos Ypos Zpos        /*  Look position (0 0 0)  */
   up Xup Yup Zup              /*  "up" vector (0 0 1)  */
   fov Hfov [Vfov]            /*  Field of view in degrees
                                  (horiontal=45)  */
   aperture Width              /*  Aperture width (0)  */
   focaldist Distance          /*  Focal distance (|eyep - lookp|)  */
   shutter Speed               /*  Shutter speed (0 -> no blur)  */
   framelength Length          /*  Length of a single frame (1)  */
   screen Xsize Ysize          /*  Screen size  */
   window Xmin Xmax Ymin Ymax /*  Window (0 xsize-1 0 ysize-1)  */
   crop left right bot top     /*  Crop window (0 1 0 1)  */
   eyesep Separation           /*  Eye separation (0)  */

SurfDef: /*  Give a name to a set of surface attributes  */
   surface Name <SurfSpec> [<SurfSpec> ...]
```

```
Surface: /*  Surface specification  */
    <SurfSpec>                    /*  Use gven attributes  */
    Surfname [<SurfSpec> ...]
            /*  Use named surface w/ optional mods */
    cursurf  [<SurfSpec> ...]
            /*  Use cur. surface w/mods - see ApplySurf  */

SurfSpec: /* Surface attribute specification */
   ambient R G B              /*  Ambient contribution */
   diffuse R G B              /*  Diffuse color */
   specular R G B             /*  Specular color */
   specpow Exponent           /*  Phong exponent */
   body R G B                 /*  Body color */
   extinct Coef               /*  Extinction coefficient */
   transp Ktr                 /*  Transparency */
   reflect Kr                 /*  Reflectivity */
   index N                    /*  Index of refraction */
   translu Ktl R G B Stpow    /*  Translucency, transmit
                                  diffuse, spec exp */
   noshadow                   /*  No shadows cast
                                  on this surface */

Effect: /* Atmospheric Effects */
   mist   R G B Rtrans Gtrans Btrans Zero Scale
   fog    R G B Rtrans Gtrans Btrans

Atmosphere: /* Global atmosphere */
   atmosphere [Index] <Effect> [<Effect>...]
            /*  Global index, effects  */

ApplySurf:
   applysurf <Surface>
            /*  Apply surf to all following objs w/o surface  */

Instance:                       /* Instance of an object */
   <Object> [<Transforms>] [<Textures>]

Object:
   Primitive              /*  Primitive object  */
   Aggregate              /*  Named aggregate  */

ObjDef:                         /*  Define a named object  */
   name Objname <Instance>
```

```
Primitive:                        /*  Primitive object  */
  plane     [<Surface>] Xpos Ypos Zpos Xnorm Ynorm Znorm
  disc      [<Surface>] Radius Xpos Ypos Zpos Xnorm Ynorm Znorm
  sphere    [<Surface>] Radius Xpos Ypos Zpos
  triangle  [<Surface>] Xv1 Yv1 Zv1
                        Xv2 Yv2 Zv2  Xv3 Yv3 Zv3
              /* flat-shaded triangle  */
  triangle  [<Surface>] Xv1 Yv1 Zv1 Xn1 Yn1 Zn1
                        Xv2 Yv2 Zv2 Xn2 Yn2 Zn2
                        Xv3 Yv3 Zv3 Xn3 Yn3 Zn3
              /* Phong-shaded triangle  */
  polygon   [<Surface>] Xv1 Yv1 Zv1
                        Xv2 Yv2 Zv2  Xv3 Yv3 Zv3 [Xv3 Yv4 Zv4 ...]
  box       [<Surface>] Xlow Ylow Zlow
                        Xhi  Yhi  Zhi
  cylinder  [<Surface>] Radius Xbase Ybase Zbase Xapex Yapex Zapex
  cone      [<Surface>] Rbase Xbase Ybase Zbase  Rapex Xapex Yapex
Zapex
  torus     [<Surface>] Rswept Rtube Xpos Ypos Zpos Xnorm Ynorm
Znorm
  blob      [<Surface>] Thresh Stren Rad Xpos Ypos Zpos
                        [Stren Rad X Y Z ...]
  heightfield [<Surface>] Filename

Aggregate:
  Grid
  List
  Csg

Grid:
  grid X Y Z <ObjItem> [<ObjItem> ...]  end

List:
  list <ObjItem> [<ObjItem> ...] end

Csg:
  union      <Object> <Object> [<Object> ...] end
  intersect  <Object> <Object> [<Object> ...] end
  difference <Object> <Object> [<Object> ...] end
  /* CSG only works properly when applied to closed objects, e.g.:
   * sphere, box, torus, blob, closed Aggregate, other Csg object
   */
```

```
Transforms: /*  Transformations  */
   translate    Xtrans Ytrans Ztrans
   scale        Xscale Yscale Zscale
   rotate       Xaxis Yaxis Zaxis Degrees
   transform A   B   C
             D   E   F
             G   H   I
             [Xt  Yt  Zt]


Textures:
   texture     <TextType> [Transforms] [<Texture>
               [Transforms] ...]


Texture:
   checker     <Surface>
   blotch      Scale <Surface>
   bump        Bumpscale
   marbl       [Colormapname]
   fbm         Offset Scale H Lambda Octaves Thresh [Colormapname]
   fbmbump     'Offset Scale H Lambda Octaves
   wood
   gloss       Glossiness
   cloud       Scale H Lambda Octaves Cthresh Lthresh Transcale
   sky         Scale H Lambda Octaves Cthresh Lthresh
   stripe      <Surface> Width Bumpscale [<Mapping>]
   windy       Scale Wscale Cscale Bscale Octaves Tscale Hscale Offset
   image       Imagefile [<ImageTextOption>
               [<ImageTextOption> ...]]


ImageTextOption:
   component   <SufComp>
   range       Lo Hi
   smooth
   textsurf    <Surface>
   tile        U V
   <Mapping>


SurfComp:
   ambience
   diffuse
   reflect
   transp
```

```
      specular
      specpow

  Mapping:
    map uv
    map cylindrical    [Xorigin Yorigin Zorigin Xup Yup Zup Xu Yu Zu]
    map planar         [Xorigin Yorigin Zorigin Xv  Yv  Zv  Xu Yu Zu]
    map spherical      [Xorigin Yorigin Zorigin Xup Yup Zup Xu Yu Zu]

  Light:
    light R G B <LightType>     [noshadow]
    light Intensity <LightType> [noshadow]

  LightType:
    ambient
    point         Xpos Ypos Zpos
    directional   Xdir Ydir Zdir
    extended      Radius Xpos Ypos Zpos
    spot          Xpos Ypos Zpos Xat Yat Zat Coef Thetain Thetaout
    area          Xorigin Yorigin Zorigin Xu Yu Zu
                  Usamples Xv Yv Zv Vsamples

  RenderOption:
    samples      Nsamp [jitter | nojitter]
    /*  Use Nsamp^2 pixel samples (3^2 jittered) */
    background R G B    /* Background color (0 0 0) */
    outfile    Filename /* Output file name (written to stdout) */
    frames     Nframes  /* Number of frames to render (1) */
    starttime  Time     /* Time corresponding to start of frame 0 */
    contrast   R G B    /* Maximum contrast w/o supersampling */
    maxdepth   Depth    /* Maximum ray tree depth (5)  */
    cutoff     Factor   /* Minium spawned ray contribution (.001) */
    report [verbose] [quiet] [Freq] [Statfile]
                        /* Reporting mode (false false 10 stderr) */
    shadowtransp        /* Toggle object opacity affects shadows */

  Definition:          /* Variable definition */
    define Name Expr    /* Assign value for Name */
```

For Further Information

For further information about the Rayshade format, see *Rayshade 4.0 Quick Reference,* included on the CD-ROM that accompanies this book.

You can also contact the author:

Princeton University
Attn: Craig Kolb
Department of Computer Science
35 Olden Street
Princeton, NJ 08544
cek@princeton.edu

The Rayshade application package is available from various archive sites on the Internet and from many PC/MS-DOS BBSs. For further information, contact the author at the above address.

▌RIX

NAME:	RIX
ALSO KNOWN AS:	RIX Image File, ColoRIX VGA Paint
TYPE:	Bitmap
COLORS:	Up to 32 bits per pixel
COMPRESSION:	Undocumented
MAXIMUM IMAGE SIZE:	64Kx64K
MULTIPLE IMAGES PER FILE:	No
NUMERICAL FORMAT:	Little-endian
ORIGINATOR:	RIX SoftWorks
PLATFORM:	MS-DOS
SUPPORTING APPLICATIONS:	ColoRIX VGA Paint
SPECIFICATION ON CD:	Yes
CODE ON CD:	No
IMAGES ON CD:	No
SEE ALSO:	NA

USAGE: Storage of bitmap files with few colors under MS-DOS.

COMMENTS: RIX's programs have been bundled with several video cards for the PC running MS-DOS.

Overview

In most respects, the RIX format appears to be a nice format to support. Unfortunately, although the rest of the format, which we have included on the CD-ROM that accompanies this book, is reasonably well-documented, the compression algorithm used in the files is not. RIX SoftWorks says that the algorithm is not published because it is, "extremely complicated." The ColoRIX VGA Paint document goes on to explain that:

> Although some compression schemes are more efficient for some pictures, the RIX compression scheme performs extremely well with a broad range of picture types.

Expert opinion is mixed between skepticism and outright dismissal, so it is a shame that there is no way to verify this claim. Certainly, an advance in compression technology would bring RIX more than a modest portion of riches and fame. In any case, until RIX decides to publish its full format specification, you'll just have to wing it with the information provided here.

File Organization

The RIX format is a simple bitmap format, consisting of a fixed header, a palette, and bitmap data.

File Details

The RIX header is structured as follows:

```
typedef struct _RIX_HEAD
{
   CHAR ID[3];              /* Three-character ID field, "RIX" */
   WORD Width;              /* Image width in pixels */
   WORD Height;             /* Image height in lines */
   CHAR PaletteType;        /* Palette type code */
   CHAR StorageType;        /* Format of bitmap data */

} RIX_HEAD;
```

Width and Height represent the size of the image.

PaletteType identifies the type of display device and can have any of the values listed below. These are calculated using a scheme discussed in the specification document.

Value	Type of Display Device
CB	EGA
AB	Extended EGA
AF	VGA
E7	Targa 16
9F	IBM PGA
10	Targa 16
18	Targa 24
20	Targa 32

StorageType can have any of the the values listed below. Refer to the specification document for a discussion of the scheme used to calculate these values.

Value	Type of Data
80	Compressed
40	Extension block
20	Encrypted
00	Linear, one byte per pixel
01	Planar (0213), similar to EGA
02	Planar (0123), similar to EGA
03	Text

If the storage type value indicates an extension block value, it is followed by a byte containing an extension format value. Some typical format extension types are illustrated below.

Value	Type of Extension
00	ASCII text
01	Original image origin
02	Original image screen resolution
03	Encryptor's ID
04	Bitmap palette in use; length is either 2 or 32 bytes

After the extension format value is a byte containing the total number of bytes in the extension block. The actual extension block data follows immediately afterward.

RIX suggests that developers with special extension needs request an extension storage type value less than 128.

Following the header is a palette, which is either 48 or 768 bytes long. Palette entries are stored as RGB triples, one for each color. Following the palette is the image data. If the image data is not encrypted or compressed, the data format can be deduced from the storage type value.

For Further Information

For further information about the RIX format, see the specification included on the CD-ROM that accompanies this book. You can contact:

RIX SoftWorks, Inc.
Attn: Richard Brownback
18023 Sky Park Circle, Suite J

Irvine, CA 92714
Voice: 714-476-8266

You can also contact:

Paul Harker
Voice: 714-476-8486

The RIX file format is also documented in the *ColoRIX VGA Paint* manual, available by purchasing a copy of the program from RIX SoftWorks.

RTrace

NAME:	RTrace
ALSO KNOWN AS:	SFF, SCN
TYPE:	Scene description
COLORS:	NA
COMPRESSION:	Uncompressed
MAXIMUM IMAGE SIZE:	NA
MULTIPLE IMAGES PER FILE:	NA
NUMERICAL FORMAT:	NA
ORIGINATOR:	António Costa
PLATFORM:	All
SUPPORTING APPLICATIONS:	RTrace
SPECIFICATION ON CD:	Yes
CODE ON CD:	No
IMAGES ON CD:	No
SEE ALSO:	DKB, NFF, POV, PRT, QRT, Rayshade
USAGE:	3D scene description used for ray-trace and other rendering applications.
COMMENTS:	RTrace is a simple but well-designed format that could find general use for describing 3D scenes.

Overview

The RTrace format (called SFF by its author) was created by António Costa and is associated with his ray-trace application, RTrace. Work on both the application and the format date from 1988. The format itself was designed to support the description of 3D scenes. Although it was originally intended for ray-trace applications, it could just as well be used for other renderers. RTrace would be a good format to study if you are in the process of writing yet another ray trace or rendering application.

In his program documentation, António Costa mentions, as a motivation for producing a new format, limits embodied in Eric Haines' NFF format.

File Organization

Like many ray trace formats, RTrace implements the scene description language in its own application. The RTrace format consists of a series of ASCII text lines and is designed to be human-readable and easily edited.

File Details

The following information is based on António Costa's documentation, *The SFF Ray-Tracing Format, Version 8.*

An RTrace (SFF) file is divided into five sections (sometimes six, for compatibility reasons). In each, there are definitions, which may be of several types:

- Viewing
- Ambient/Background
- Lights
- Surfaces
- Objects, Textures, and Transformations

Viewing Section

The Viewing section is the first to appear. It has five lines consisting of:

Comments
Eye point
Look point
Up vector
Horizontal and vertical view angles

Each of these items must be on a separate line. Comments can follow up to the end of the line.

Example:

```
viewr
8 0 0- Eye <EOL>
0 0 0- Look <EOL>
0 1 0- Up <EOL>
20 20- View angles (horizontal and vertical) <EOL>
```

Ambient and Background Section

The Ambient and Background section follows the Viewing section. It contains three lines:

- Comments
- Background color
- Ambient color

Both background color and ambient color are defined in RGB format.

After each item there may be comments up to the end of the line.

Example:

```
colors<EOL>
0.1 0.5 0.7- Sky blue(red=0.1 green=0.5 blue=0.7) <EOL>
0.2 0.2 0.2- Dark gray(red=0.2 green=0.2 blue=0.2) <EOL>
```

Lights Section

The Lights section contains a series of lines:

- Comments
- One line for each light definition
- Empty line

There are three types of light definitions:

Point light

> To define a point light, specify the point code (1), a position, and RGB brightness.

Direction light.

> To define a direction light, specify the directional code (2), a position, RGB brightness, direction, angle, and attenuation factor. This kind of light radiates from a point in the specified direction inside the solid angle, and the transition may be sharp (factor ~= 1) or soft (factor >> 1). A truly directional light may be simulated by positioning it far away from the objects and defining its brightness to be negative. Normally, illumination decreases with distance; to make illumination distance-independent, make at least one component of the brightness negative (at least one component).

Extended light.

To define an extended light, specify the extended code (3), a position, RGB brightness, radius and samples. This kind of light is simulated by a sphere of specified radius, which is sampled to calculate the actual illumination (a low value for frequency of samples produces undesirable effects).

Example:

```
lights<EOL>
1  4 5 1  0.9 0.9 0.9- White point light <EOL>
2  0 10 0  0 0 1  0 -1 0  15 5- Blue spot light <EOL>
3  8 1 -3  0 1 0  0.3 8- Green extended light <EOL>
1  1000 1000 1000  -1 -1 -1- Directional light <EOL>
<EOL>
```

Surfaces Section

The Surfaces section defines all of the surfaces. It consists of a series of lines:

- Comments
- One line for each surface definition
- Empty line

There are two types of surface definitions:

Code 1 definition.

A code 1 surface definition defines a surface by body RGB color, diffuse RGB factor, specular RGB factor, specular exponent factor, metalness factor, and transmission RGB factor. The RGB's colors and factors must be in the [0,1] range. The diffuse RGB factor defines the quantity of light coming from all directions. The specular RGB factor defines the quantity of light coming from the ideal reflection direction. The exponent factor controls the shininess of the surface (the surface is very shiny with a factor bigger than 10; if the factor is near zero, the surface appears dull). The metalness factor makes the reflected light appear white if it is small (as in plastic) or metallic if it is near 1. The transmission RGB factor defines the transparency. The sum of diffuse, specular, and transparency RGB factors should be equal or approximately 1.

Code 2 definition.

A code 2 surface definition has a body RGB color, a smoothness RGB factor, a metalness RGB factor, and a transmission RGB factor. This method is an alternative for defining surfaces, but it is more intuitive. The smoothness RGB factor controls the shininess of the surface.

Example:

```
surfaces<EOL>
1  1 0 0  1 1 1  0 0 0  0 0  0 0 0    - Matte <EOL>
1  0 1 0  0.5 0.5 0.5  0.5 0.5 0.5  10 0.5   0 0 0 <EOL>
1  0 0 1  0.7 0.8 0.9  0.3 0.2 0.1  100 1    0 0 0  - Metallic <EOL>
1  1 1 1  0.1 0.1 0.1  0.1 0.1 0.1  200 0.8  0.8 0.8 0.8 <EOL>
2  1 1 0  0 0 0  0 0 0  0 0 0    - Matte <EOL>
2  1 0 1  1 1 1  1 1 1  0 0 0    - Mirror <EOL>
<EOL>
```

Objects, Textures, and Transformations Section

The Objects, Textures, and Transformations section defines the 3D objects, and, optionally, the textures and transformations. It consists of a series of lines, plus one line for each object definition.

All objects are defined by a code, a surface index (which specifies one of the previously defined surfaces, starting in 1), a refraction index, and then the data itself.

Example 1:

The object with code 1 is a sphere and has a center point and radius.

```
1  3  1.0  4 3 2  0.5- Sphere centered at (4,3,2) radius=0.5 <EOL>
*
```

Example 2:

The object with code 2 is a parallelipiped aligned with the XYZ axis. It requires a center point and three dimensions, for the X, Y, and Z directions.

```
2  2  1.0  1 0 0  10 1 3- Box at (1,0,0)
            with sizes (+-10,+-1,+-3) <EOL>
```

Example 3:

The object with code 3 is a bicubic patch or a group of bicubic patches. It is followed by a translation vector, three scale factors for X, Y, and Z, and a filename or -. If there is a filename, then the patch's geometry is read from that file; otherwise, it is read from the following lines in the SFF file, ending with an empty line:

```
3  1  1.0  0 0 0  1 1 1  example.pat
               - Read from file example.pat <EOL>
3  2  1.0  0 0 0  2 1 1
               - Read from the next lines <EOL>
```

A bicubic patch is defined by 12 points.

```
1 2 4 5 6 7 9 10 11 12 14 15- Patch 1<EOL>
2 3 5 6 7 8 10 11 12 13 15 16- Patch 2<EOL>
<EOL>
0 -0.5 -1- Vertex 1 <EOL>
0 0 -2- Vertex 2 <EOL>
0 -0.5 -3 <EOL>
1 0 0 <EOL>
1 0 -1 <EOL>
1 0.5 -2 <EOL>
1 0 -3 <EOL>
1 0 -4 <EOL>
2 0 0 <EOL>
2 0 -1 <EOL>
2 0.5 -2 <EOL>
2 0 -3 <EOL>
2 0 -4 <EOL>
0 -0.25 -1 <EOL>
0 0 -2 <EOL>
0 0 -3 <EOL>
<EOL>
```

Example 4:

The code 4 object is a cone or cylinder. It has an apex center point and radius, followed by a base center point and radius. The apex radius must be less than (in the case of a cone) or equal to (for a cylinder) the base radius. The cone/cylinder are opened objects (i.e., they do not have any circular surfaces in the apex or base).

```
4  1  1.0  0 1 0  0  0 0 0  1- Cone <EOL>
4  1  1.0  0 1 0  1  0 0 0  1- Cylinder <EOL>
```

Example 5:

The code 5 object is a polygon or a group of polygons, similar to patches. It is followed by a translation vector, three scale factors for X, Y, and Z, and by a filename or -. If there is a filename, then the polygon's geometry is read from that file; otherwise, it is read from the following lines in the RTrace file, ending with an empty line.

```
5  1  1.0  0 0 0  1 1 1  example.pol- Read from file example.pol <EOL>
5  2  1.0  0 0 0  1 1 1
                    - Read from the next lines <EOL>
```

A polygon is defined by its vertices in counterclockwise order. A file with polygons is composed of two parts. In the first part are the number of polygons and the polygon's definitions, using indices into the vertex list. In the second part (after an empty line) is the vertex list, is terminated by another empty line.

```
5   1 2 3 4 5- polygon 1 <EOL>
3   1 6 2- polygon 2 <EOL>
<EOL>
0 0 -2- vertex 1 <EOL>
1 0 0- vertex 2 <EOL>
2 0 -1- vertex 3 <EOL>
2 0 -3- vertex 4 <EOL>
1 0 -4- vertex 5 <EOL>
0.5 2 -1- vertex 6 <EOL>
<EOL>
```

Example 6:

The code 6 object is a triangle or a group of triangles, similar to a polygon but also specifying each vertex normal vector. (These triangles are also known as Phong triangles.) It is followed by a translation vector, three scale factors for X, Y, and Z, and a filename or –. If there is a filename, then the triangle's geometry is read from that file; otherwise, it is read from the following lines in the RTrace file, ending with an empty line.

```
6  1  1.0  0 0 0  1 1 1  example.tri- Read from file example.tri <EOL>
6  2  1.0  0 0 0  1 1 1- Read from the next lines <EOL>
   . . .
```

A triangle is defined by its vertices (data and normal) in counterclockwise order. A file with triangles is composed of the triangle's definitions: first data and normal vertices, followed by the second data and normal vertices, and finally the third data and normal vertices. It is terminated by another empty line.

```
0 0 0 0 1 0  1 0 0 0 1 0  1 0 -1 0 1 0- Triangle 1 <EOL>
0 0 0 1 1 0  0 1 0 1 0 0  0 1 -1 1 0 1- Triangle 2 <EOL>
```

Example 7:

The code 7 object is an extruded primitive derived from closed segments composed of lines and splines. This object is very well-suited to trace high-quality text, although it may be used for many other purposes. It is followed by a file-name or -. If there is a filename, then the character's geometry is read from that file; otherwise, it is read from the following lines in the RTrace file, ending with an empty line.

```
spacing      0.1<EOL>
orientation  0 0 -1  0 1 0  1 0 0 <EOL>
encoding     ascii.ppe <EOL>
font         roman.ppf <EOL>
scale        0.4 0.4 0.2 <EOL>
at           1 1 2  "RTrace /copyright/ António Costa 1993"<EOL>
font         times.ppf <EOL>
scale        0.5 0.6 0.3 <EOL>
at           0 3 0  "Etc" <EOL>
  . . .
```

The spacing keyword defines the separation between characters. Most of the supplied fonts have their characters enclosed in a one-unit square.

The orientation keyword defines how the text appears in the 3D space; the first vector defines the text direction, the second the up direction, and the third the extrusion direction. As these are independent, it is possible to slant the text or create more complex effects.

The encoding keyword specifies a file that contains translations from character names to character codes, which are used to access the character data.

The font keyword specifies a file that contains the character's data (number of closed segments—lines and splines—and other data for each character).

The scale keyword defines the scaling for the characters, using the directions specified by the orientation keyword.

The at keyword specifies the starting baseline position and which characters to trace. With the supplied font files, it is possible to use PostScript names for the characters in almost all languages; in this case, the character name must be enclosed in / /.

The next codes are not used to define primitive objects, but rather to associate, transform, or texture objects. The code 64 defines a texture to be applied to an object, usually the previous one. It is followed by a type, an object ID, a trans-formation matrix, and local data. The supported types are:

Type	Name	Parameters
0	Null	
1	Checker	surface
2	Blotch	scale surface [file(colormap)]
3	Bump	scale
4	Marble	[file(colormap)]
5	FBM	offset scale omega lambda threshold octaves
6	FBM Bump	offset scale lambda octaves
7	Wood	color(red) color(green) color(blue)
8	Round	scale
9	Bozo	turbulence [file(colormap)]
10	Ripples	frequency phase scale
11	Waves	frequency phase scale
12	Spotted	[file(colormap)]
13	Dents	scale
14	Agate	[file(colormap)]
15	Wrinkles	scale
16	Granite	[file(colormap)]
17	Gradient	turbulence direction(x) direction(y) direction(z) file(colormap)]
18	Imagemap	turbulence mode axis(horizontal) axis(vertical) file(image)
19	Gloss	scale
20	Bump	3D scale size

For Further Information

For further information about the RTrace format, see the specifications included on the CD-ROM that accompanies this book.

The RTrace application is available for downloading at many Internet archive sites and on PC/MS-DOS BBSs. For further information, contact:

> ISEP/INESC
> Instituto de Engenharia de Sistemas e Computadores
> Attn: António Costa
> Computer Graphics & CAD Group
> Largo Mompilher 22
> Apartado 4433

4100 Porto Codex Portugal
acc@asterix.inescn.pt

SGI Image File Format

NAME:	SGI Image File Format
ALSO KNOWN AS:	SGI, RLE, Haeberli
TYPE:	Bitmap
COLORS:	16 million
COMPRESSION:	RLE
MAXIMUM IMAGE SIZE:	64Kx64K pixels
MULTIPLE IMAGES PER FILE:	No
NUMERICAL FORMAT:	Big-endian
ORIGINATOR:	Silicon Graphics
PLATFORM:	UNIX
SUPPORTING APPLICATIONS:	SGI graphics software
SPECIFICATION ON CD:	Yes
CODE ON CD:	No
IMAGES ON CD:	No
SEE ALSO:	None

USAGE: The SGI image file format is a generic bitmap format used for storing black-and-white, gray-scale, and color images.

COMMENTS: SGI is one of the few formats to make use of a scan-line offset table to indicate the beginning of each scan line within compressed image data. SGI files may also contain only color maps or alpha channel data, and they may have a very large number of bit planes.

Overview

The SGI image file format is actually part of the SGI image library found on all Silicon Graphics machines. SGI image files may store black-and-white (.BW extension), color RGB (.RGB extension), or color RGB with alpha channel data (.RGBA extension) images. SGI image files may also have the generic extension .SGI as well.

The SGI image file format was developed by Paul Haeberli at Silicon Graphics.

File Organization

The SGI image file format header is 512 bytes in size and has the following structure:

```
typedef struct _SGIHeader
{
    SHORT Magic;          /* Identification number (474) */
    CHAR Storage;         /* Compression flag */
    CHAR Bpc;             /* Bytes per pixel */
    WORD Dimension;       /* Number of image dimensions */
    WORD XSize;           /* Width of image in pixels */
    WORD YSize;           /* Height of image in pixels */
    WORD ZSize;           /* Number of bit planes */
    LONG PixMin;          /* Smallest pixel value */
    LONG PixMax;          /* Largest pixel value */
    CHAR Dummy1[4];       /* Not used */
    CHAR ImageName[80];   /* Name of image */
    LONG ColorMap;        /* Format of pixel data */
    CHAR Dummy2[404];     /* Not used */

} SGIHEAD;
```

Magic is the SGI file identification value; it is always decimal 474.

Storage indicates whether the image data is compressed using an RLE algorithm (value of 01h) or is stored uncompressed (value of 00h).

Bpc is the number of bytes per pixel. This value may be 01h or 02h; most SGI images have a value of 01h, or one byte per pixel.

Dimension indicates how the image data is stored. A value of 01h indicates that a single-channel image is stored as one long scan line. A value of 02h indicates a single-channel bitmap whose dimensions are indicated by the XSize and YSize header field values. A value of 03h indicates a multi-channel bitmap with the number of channels shown by the value of the ZSize header field.

XSize and YSize are the width and height of a bitmap image in pixels.

ZSize is the number of channels in a bitmap image. Black-and-white images typically have a ZSize of 01h, RGB images a ZSize of 03h. RGB images with an alpha channel have a ZSize of 04h.

PixMin specifies the minimum pixel value in the image. This value is typically 00h.

PixMax specifies the maximum pixel value in the image. This value is typically FFh.

Dummy1 is a 4-byte NULL character field that is not used.

ImageName is an 80-byte character field used to store the name of the image. The name string may be up to 79 characters in length and must be terminated with a NULL.

ColorMap specifies how the pixel values are to be regarded. Values are shown below:

00h	Normal pixel values. Black-and-white images have one channel, color images have three channels, and color images with an alpha value have four channels.
01h	Dithered image with only one channel of data. Each dithered pixel value is one byte in size, with the red channel value stored in bits 0, 1, and 2; the green value in bits 3, 4, and 5; and the blue value in bits 6 and 7.
02h	Single-channel image. The image contains pixels that are index values into a color map stored in another SGI file.
03h	Stored image data is a color map to be used for other images and should not be displayed.

SGI files with ColorMap values of 01h and 02h are considered obsolete.

Dummy2 is a 404-byte NULL character field used to pad the header out to an even 512 bytes in size.

In SGI files containing uncompressed image data, the image data appears immediately after the header. In SGI files with compressed image data, a scan-line offset table follows the header, and the compressed image data follows the table.

File Details

The majority of SGI files store single-channel, 8-bits-per-pixel, black-and-white images. Such images typically have a Bpc of 01h, a Dimension of 01h, and a ColorMap of 01h. Color RGB images typically have a Bpc of 01h, a Dimension of 02h (or 03h if an alpha channel is present), a ZSize of 03h (or 04h if an alpha channel is present), and a ColorMap of 01h.

The origin (0,0) for all SGI images is the lower-left corner of the display with the first scan line starting at the bottom of the image.

SGI files are found in two basic flavors: run-length encoded and verbatim (uncompressed). Verbatim image data is written out by plane as scan lines. For example, a 3-channel image has all of the data for its first plane written first, followed by the data for the second plane, and finally by the data for the third. If Bpc is set to 01h, then each scan line contains an XSize number of BYTEs; if Bpc is set to 02h, then each scan line contains an XSize number of SHORTs.

In RLE image data, a scan-line offset table is used to keep track of the offset where each scan line begins within the compressed image data. The offset table appears immediately after the header and before the compressed image data. The table contains one entry per scan line, determined by multiplying the YSize and ZSize values together. Each entry is a LONG (4-byte) value.

The offset table is actually two tables written consecutively to the SGI file. The first table contains the starting offset values of each scan line; each offset is calculated from the beginning of the file. If the image data is stored as two or more bit planes (ZSize > 1), then all of the offset values for the first plane are stored first, followed by all of the offsets for the second plane, and so on. The second table stores the compressed length of each encoded scan line in BYTEs. And, once again, if the data is stored in more than one bit plane, the offset values are stored by plane.

Note that the scan-line table cannot be ignored during the reading of compressed data, even if you are decoding the image completely from beginning to end. There are several reasons for this:

1. The SGI specification dictates that scan lines need not be stored in consecutive order; only planes are required to be stored consecutively. It is therefore possible that a scan line might be stored in an interleaved fashion (0, 4, 8, 12, ... rather than 0, 1, 2, 3, ...).
2. Multiple entries in the scan-line table might point to the same scan line. An image with many identical scan lines (containing all white pixels, for example) might encode only one such scan line and have all identical entries in the offset table pointing to the same line. It is also possible that a gray scale image stored as three planes (RGB) would have each plane pointing towards the same scan line.

The RLE algorithm used to compress the SGI image data varies in format depending upon the value of the Bpc field in the header. If the Bpc is 01h, this indicates one byte per pixel. A simple 2-byte RLE encoding scheme is used, in which the lowest seven bits of the first byte is the run count. The high bit in this byte is the run-count flag. If this bit is set to 0, then the next byte (the run value) is repeated a number of times equal to the run count. If the run count flag is 1, then the run count indicates the number of BYTEs to copy literally from the input stream to the output stream.

If the Bpc value is 02h, then each pixel is stored in a 2-byte SHORT value. The RLE algorithm is basically the same, with each RLE packet being three BYTEs long, rather than two. Bits 0 through 6 of the low byte are the run count, and bit 7 is the run-count flag. The run value is the SHORT value following the run-count byte. If bit 7 is set to 0, this indicates a repeat run count of SHORT pixel values. If bit 7 is set to 1, this indicates a literal run count of SHORT pixel values. Using either pixel size, each decompressed scan line should be XSize pixels in length.

For Further Information

For further information about the SGI image format, see the specification included on the CD-ROM that accompanies this book. Information on all Silicon Graphics file formats may be obtained directly from SGI:

Silicon Graphics Inc.
Attn: Visual Magic Marketing
2011 North Shoreline Blvd.
Mountain View, CA 94039-7311
Voice: 800-800-4SGI

SGI also maintains an anonymous FTP site *sgi.com*, which contains information on several formats and many Silicon Graphics products.

If you are using a Silicon Graphics workstation, you may refer to the documentation on the *–limage* library by using the man command *man 4 rgb*.

NAME:	SGI Inventor
ALSO KNOWN AS:	IRIS, 3D Interchange File Format
TYPE:	3D scene description
COLORS:	Unlimited
COMPRESSION:	Uncompressed
MAXIMUM IMAGE SIZE:	Unlimited
MULTIPLE IMAGES PER FILE:	Yes
NUMERICAL FORMAT:	NA
ORIGINATOR:	Silicon Graphics
PLATFORM:	UNIX
SUPPORTING APPLICATIONS:	Many
SPECIFICATION ON CD:	Yes
CODE ON CD:	Yes
IMAGES ON CD:	No
SEE ALSO:	SGO

USAGE: Known primarily through SGI's IRIS Inventor system.

COMMENTS: SGI Inventor was designed for the exchange of 3D modeling information between software applications.

Overview

The SGI Inventor file format was first released in July 1992 by Silicon Graphics, and was specifically designed for the exchange of 3D modeling information between software applications. It has been used by CAD, chemistry, financial data, scientific visualization, art history, earth sciences, creative, presentation, architecture, animation, and other applications.

The SGI Inventor file format was created as part of the IRIS Inventor 3D Toolkit. The toolkit is an object-oriented 3D class library for the C and C++ languages that enables programmers to write interactive 3D graphics programs. IRIS Inventor's file format is used by a large assortment of 3D applications, such as SGI's Showcase, SGI's Explorer Scientific Visualization System, Industrial Light and Magic's animation system, SDRC, Parametric Technology, and many more.

The toolkit is based on an object-oriented database (OODB) to represent a 3D hierarchical scene. The scene database contains many types of objects, such as groups, transformations, labels, materials, drawing styles, cameras, lights, 18 different geometry types, and so on. And because SGI Inventor is object-oriented, the file format can be extended to support custom objects. The SGI Inventor file format therefore is an ASCII version of a scene database.

File Organization

The SGI Inventor file format may write either binary or ASCII data, depending on how the file is to be used. The data in both file types are machine-independent. The internal format of the Inventor binary format is proprietary and cannot be discussed in depth in this article.

SGI Inventor ASCII files contain only 7-bit, ASCII information and are parsed just as any other text file would be when read. Each line of information in an Inventor ASCII file is terminated by a linefeed (ASCII 0Ah) character. Lines beginning with the # are comments and are generally ignored.

Inventor ASCII files contain the following header signature:

```
#Inventor V1.0 ascii
```

while Inventor binary files contain the following header signature:

```
#Inventor V1.0 binary
```

Although these signatures may vary in design in future versions of the Inventor file formats, they will never be longer than 80 characters and will always begin with the # comment character.

File Details

Following the header signature is a series of data nodes that contain the actual rendering information. All information in an Inventor file is conceptualized as objects called nodes. Nodes may contain other nodes (called child nodes) and may also be grouped into collections of nodes called graphs. The syntax for a node is as shown below:

```
nodename {
    fieldname1 value1 value2
    fieldname2 value1 value2 value3
    fieldname3
    fieldnameN value
}
```

A node contains a node name followed by a series of data field names and data field values. The fields may appear in any order within a node and are not written out if their values are the default values for the field. The fields of a node are always enclosed in braces.

Nodes may also contain other nodes called child nodes:

```
nodename {
    fieldname1 value
    fieldname2 value
    fieldnameN value
    childnode1 {
        fieldname1 value
        fieldname2 value
        fieldnameN value
    }
    childnode2 {
        fieldname1 value
        fieldname2 value
        fieldnameN value
    }
}
```

The values in each field are defined for each node. A field may contain one or more values. Each value is separated by a white space character. A field containing multiple groups of values surrounds the entire grouping with brackets, and commas separate each group; for example:

```
nodename {
    fieldname1 value1 value2 value3
    fieldname2 [ value1a value1b value1c, value2a value2b value2c ]
}
```

The format used to write field values depends upon their data type, as shown below:

100	Integers
100.0	Floating point
1.0e2	Floating point
"name"	Strings
mnemonic	Enumerations and bit fields
~	Ignore this field

A field name which contains a tilde (˜) for a value is ignored by the SGI Inventor file reader. The following is a fragment of an SGI Inventor ASCII file:

```
Separator {
    Normal {
        vector  0 1 0
    }
    Material {
        ambientColor   0.2 0.2 0.2 ~
        diffuseColor   0.720949 0.714641 0.492981
        specularColor  0.2 0.2 0.2 ~
        emissiveColor  0 0 0 ~
        shininess      0 ~
        transparency   0 ~
    }
    Coordinate3 {
        point [  0.0   0.0  0.0,   # 0
                 1.0   0.0  0.0,   # 1
                 1.0   1.0  0.0,   # 2
                 2.0   0.0  0.0,   # 3
                 2.0   1.0  0.0,   # 4
                 2.0   1.0  0.0,   # 5
                 3.0   0.0  0.0,   # 6 ]
    }
    IndexedTriangleMesh {
        coordIndex    [ 0, 1, 2, 3, 4, 5, -1 ]
    }
}
```

Each node stored in an Inventor file represents a 3D shape, property, or grouping. All SGI Inventor nodes are divided into five classes:

- Shape

- Property

- Group

- Light

- Camera

Shapes include geometric objects. Properties are the qualitative aspects of the objects. Group indicates the type of organization applied to one or more nodes. Light and Camera information affect the appearance of the rendered image.

The following list contains the Inventor nodes grouped by class:

Shape:

Cone	IndexedNurbsCurve	PointSet
Cube	IndexedNurbsSurface	QuadMesh
Cylinder	IndexedTriangleMesh	Sphere
FaceSet	LineSet	Text2
IndexedFaceSet	NurbsCurve	Text3
IndexedLineSet	NurbsSurface	TriangleStripSet

Property:

BaseColor	MatrixTransform	Texture2
Complexity	Normal	Texture2Transform
Coordinate3	NormalBinding	TextureCoordinate2
Coordinate4	NurbsProfile	TextureCoordinateBinding
DrawStyle	PackedColor	TextureCoordinateCube
Environment	PickStyle	TextureCoordinateCylinder
Font	ProfileCoordinate2	TextureCoordinateEnvironment
Info	ProfileCoordinate3	TextureCoordinateFunction
Label	ResetTransform	TextureCoordinatePlane
LightModel	Rotation	TextureCoordinateSphere
LinearProfile	RotationXYZ	Transform
Material	Scale	Translation
MaterialBinding	ShapeHints	Units

Group:

Array	LayerGroup	Separator
CustomNode	MultipleCopy	Switch
File	PathSwitch	
Group	Selection	

Light:

DirectionalLight	PointLight	SpotLight

Camera:

OrthographicCamera	PerspectiveCamera

For Further Information

For further information about the SGI Inventor format, see the following documents included on the CD-ROM that accompanies this book.

Silicon Graphics, Inc., *How to Write an IRIS Inventor File Translator*, Release 1.0.

Silicon Graphics, Inc., *How to Write an Open Inventor File Translator*, Release 2.0.

Silicon Graphics, Inc., *IRIS Inventor Nodes Quick Reference Guide*, Release 1.0.

Silicon Graphics, Inc., *IRIS Inventor Nodes Quick Reference Guide*, Release 2.0.

Information on the SGI Inventor file format may also be found in the following document, available directly from Silicon Graphics:

SGI Inventor Programming Guide, Volume I: Using the Toolkit.

The following book contains a chapter describing the SGI Inventor file format for Release 2.0:

Wernecke, Josie, *The Inventor Mentor*, Addision-Wesley, Reading, MA, 1994.

For additional information, contact:

Silicon Graphics Inc
Attn: Visual Magic Marketing
2011 North Shoreline Blvd.
Mountain View, CA 94039-7311
Voice: 800-800-4SGI

You can also contact:

Gavin Bell
Silicon Graphics Inc.
FAX: 415-390-6056
gavin@sgi.com

SGI also maintains an anonymous FTP site, *sgi.com*, which contains information on Inventor in *sgi/inventor*, including a "Quick Reference Guide" that summarizes the file format of each object.

NAME:	SGI YAODL
ALSO KNOWN AS:	Yet Another Object Description Language, Power-Flip Format
TYPE:	3D scene description
COLORS:	Millions
COMPRESSION:	Uncompressed
MAXIMUM IMAGE SIZE:	Unlimited
MULTIPLE IMAGES PER FILE:	Yes
NUMERICAL FORMAT:	ASCII, big-endian
ORIGINATOR:	Silicon Graphics
PLATFORM:	SGI
SUPPORTING APPLICATIONS:	Powerflip
SPECIFICATION ON CD:	No
CODE ON CD:	No
IMAGES ON CD:	Yes
SEE ALSO:	SGI Inventor

USAGE: A simple format used for storing 3D vector data.

COMMENTS: YAODL is not widely used at Silicon Graphics and is constantly in danger of being rendered obsolete by more robust 3D imaging formats, such as SGI Inventor.

Overview

YAODL (Yet Another Object Description Language) is a description language used for storing 3D object data to disk files. YAODL is a rather obscure format that was created specifically for the Silicon Graphics Powerflip demo program, and it is not widely supported by SGI. However, it is a simple example of a basic vector-object description language.

YAODL supports a small collection of object types, including NURBS, polygons, and quad-meshes. Object properties such as normals (facet or vertex), colors (object, facet, and vertex), and texture coordinates are also supported.

Advanced features of YAODL include hierarchical models, coordinate transformations (rotations, scales, translations, and so forth), and instancing (using the same data more than once).

File Organization

A YAODL file begins with the comment header #YAODL, followed by one or more YAODL objects. Each object can be completely independent of all other objects in the YAODL file, or it can rely on previously defined object data within the same file.

Each object may be written to a YAODL file using either an ASCII or binary data format. Therefore, a YAODL file may contain entirely ASCII data, entirely binary data, or a mixture of the two.

The advantage of ASCII objects is that they are easy to modify using a simple text editor and are portable between different machine platforms. And while binary objects are less portable, they are smaller and faster to load than their ASCII equivalents.

Comments may be inserted into ASCII YAODL files either by enclosing the comment in the Standard C comment tokens /* and */, or by including the UNIX shell-style comment # at the beginning of each line. All comments and white space characters are ignored by YAODL file parsers.

File Details

An ASCII YAODL file contains one or more YAODL objects, delimited by commas. Each object may have one of the following syntaxes:

```
(object_type argument1, argument2, ... )
(object_type argument1, ... : property1, property2, ... )
integer integer integer ...
float float float ...
"some character String"
name = { one of the forms above }
name
```

Each YAODL object may contain zero or more arguments and have zero or more properties. For example, a colors object contains a minimum of three arguments:

```
(colors 0.0 1.0 0.0),
```

The three arguments here are RGB float values and define the color green. It is possible for many objects to have multiple groups of arguments. For example, a colors object may define more than one color, with each color represented by a set of three float values:

```
(colors 0.0 1.0 0.0   0.0 1.1 0.0   0.0 1.2 0.2),
```

An object may be used by other objects that take objects as their arguments or properties. For example, we may define a red polygon with four vertices in the following way:

```
(polygons
  (vertices -1. -1. 0.  1. -1. 0.  1. 1. 0.  -1. 1. 0.),
  : colors  0.0 1.0 0.0
),
```

Here we have a polygons object that takes one vertex's object as its argument and a color object as its properties. We can shorten this declaration by assigning a name to the colors object and using the new name in the properties list of the polygons object:

```
green = (colors    0.0 1.0 0.0),
(polygons
  (vertices -1. -1. 0.  1. -1. 0.  1. 1. 0.  -1. 1. 0.),  : green),
```

Note that the colors object, green, is a property of the polygons object, and object properties affect only the object to which they are assigned. The properties of each object must be explicitly specified or their default value(s) are assumed.

You probably have noticed that all the objects we've seen so far are described using their plural inflection, such as polygons rather than polygon. This is because it is possible to describe more than one rendered object within a YAODL object. For example, we could create three polygons, each red, green, and blue, using three polygon objects:

```
/* Three polygons */
red = (colors 1.0 0.0 0.0),
green = (colors    0.0 1.0 0.0),
blue = (colors 0.0 0.0 1.0),
(polygons
  (vertices -1. -1. 0.  1. -1.0.  1. 1. 0.  -1. 1. 0.),  : red),
(polygons
  (vertices 1. -1. 0.  1. 1.0.  -1. 1. 0.  -1. -1. 0.),  : green),
```

```
(polygons
   (vertices  1.  1. 0. -1.  1.0.  -1.-1. 0.   1. -1. 0.),   : blue),
```

Or we could nest all of these descriptions together to achieve exactly the same rendering using a single polygon object:

```
(polygons
   (vertices -1. -1. 0.   1. -1. 0.   1. 1. 0.   -1.  1. 0.),
   (vertices  1. -1. 0.   1.  1. 0.  -1. 1. 0.   -1. -1. 0.),
   (vertices  1.  1. 0.  -1.  1. 0.  -1. -1. 0.   1. -1. 0.),
   : colors 1.0 0.0 0.0  0.0 1.0 0.0  0.0 0.0 1.0,
),
```

It is important to realize that a YAODL reader does not perform any data type conversion, so be careful not to use an integer when a float is needed, and so on.

Normally, each name and object defined in an ASCII YAODL file has a global scope across the entire file starting at the point where it is defined. Braces { } may be used to create limited, block-scope variables within a YAODL file. Names defined within this local scope have precedence over identical names declared in the global scope and do not exist outside of their block.

```
blue = (colors 0.0 0.0 1.0), /* Define the color blue */
(polygons
   (vertices  1. 1. 0.   2. 2. 0.), : blue), /* Draw a blue line */

{
blue = (colors 0.0 0.15 1.0),
         /* Redefine the color blue for this block only */
(polygons
   (vertices  2. 2. 0.   2.5 2.5 0.), : blue), /* Draw a blue line */ }
# This line is drawn in the original blue.
(polygons
   (vertices  2.5 2.5 0.   3. 3. 0.), : blue), /* Draw a blue line */
```

In all cases, names must be defined before they are referenced.

Hierarchies may be created within YAODL objects using the group object. A group object may have any number of arguments, each of which is a YAODL object. A group object may also contain properties, but each property must have a definition for each object in the group. For example:

```
(group V =
 (vertices -0.175000 0.350000 0.020000),
N =
 (normals 0.000000 0.000000 1.000000),
I =
 (indices 0 1 2),
half = (indexpolygons V, I, : N), half,
(group half,
 : (rotates 180.000000 0.000000 0.000000 1.000000),
),
),
```

As previously mentioned, objects within a YAODL file may also be stored using a binary format. Binary YAODL objects start with an @ character followed by a NULL-terminated ASCII string identifying the name of an object. Valid object names are:

colors	regularMesh
contours	rotates
indexpolygons	scales
indices	texcoords
group	textures
normals	translates
nurbs	trimcurves
polygons	vertices

Following the object name string is an 8-byte integer specifying the number of bytes of binary data that follow. The format of the binary data depends on the type of data used by the object. Integer and floating-point data are stored normally, using the native byte order of the machine. Indices are stored using the following format:

The number_of_lists specified is an integer indicating how many arguments (groups of integers) the object has. The array length is a list of integers specifying the length of each group of integers. Following this array is the integer data for each list.

The following is an example of a small YAODL file that renders a cube:

```
#YAODL
v =
(vertices 0.250000 -0.250000 -0.250000 0.250000 0.250000 -0.250000
 -0.250000 0.250000 -0.250000 -0.250000 -0.250000 -0.250000
 0.250000 0.250000 0.250000 0.250000 -0.250000 0.250000
```

```
-0.250000 0.250000 0.250000 -0.250000 -0.250000 0.250000 ,),
i =
(indices
0 1 2 3 ,
0 1 4 5 ,
4 1 2 6 ,
7 6 2 3 ,
0 5 7 3 ,
7 6 4 5 ,
)
,
(indexpolygons v,
i,
: (colors 1.000000 1.000000 0.400000 0.700000 0.500000 0.200000
0.000000 0.000000 1.000000 0.300000 1.000000 1.000000
0.200000 1.000000 0.700000 1.000000 0.700000 0.700000 ,),
(normals 0.000000 0.000000 -1.000000 1.000000 0.000000 0.000000
0.000000 1.000000 0.000000 -1.000000 0.000000 0.000000
0.000000 -1.000000 0.000000 0.000000 0.000000   1.000000
,),
),
```

For Further Information

For further information about YAODL, see the YAODL(6D) manual page found on the Silicon Graphics system. For more information, contact:

Silicon Graphics Inc.
Attn: Visual Magic Marketing
2011 North Shoreline Blvd.
Mountain View, CA 94039-7311
Voice: 800-800-4SGI

NAME:	SGO
ALSO KNOWN AS:	Showcase, Silicon Graphics Object
TYPE:	3D vector
COLORS:	Unlimited
COMPRESSION:	None
MAXIMUM IMAGE SIZE:	Unlimited
MULTIPLE IMAGES PER FILE:	No
NUMERICAL FORMAT:	Big-endian
ORIGINATOR:	Silicon Graphics
PLATFORM:	UNIX
SUPPORTING APPLICATIONS:	SGI Showcase
SPECIFICATION ON CD:	Yes
CODE ON CD:	No
IMAGES ON CD:	No
SEE ALSO:	SGI Inventor

USAGE: Used primarily with Silicon Graphics Showcase.

COMMENTS: A useful format to examine if you are interested in interchange strategies.

Overview

SGO (Silicon Graphics Object) is a binary format used to store 3D image-rendering information. SGO was originally created for internal use at Silicon Graphics, but is now associated with the Silicon Graphics Showcase application. SGO is used primarily as a way to import 3D models into Showcase, although the SGI Inventor format is generally preferred over SGO as an interchange medium. (See the SGI Inventor article for information about this format.)

File Organization

The SGO file format does not have an actual header as most image file formats do. The first two bytes of every SGO file is a magic number value of 5424h. This value identifies the file as being an SGO data file.

Following the magic number is a series of data objects. Each object begins with a data token value indicating the type of data the object stores. Valid data token values are:

01h   Quadrilateral List
02h   Triangle List
03h   Triangle Mesh
04h   End Of Data

An SGO data file may contain any number of these objects in any order, except that there is only one End Of Data object per file, and it must appear as the last object stored in the data file. An End Of Data object contains only a token value and no data.

File Details

The SGO Quadrilateral List and SGO Triangle List data objects have the same structure, shown below:

```
typedef struct _QuadTriListObjects
{
  LONG ObjectToken;                /* Object token identifier */
  LONG DataSize;                   /* Size of the data in this
                                      object in  WORDs */

  struct _Vertex                   /* Object vertex structure(s) */
  {
    FLOAT XNormalVector;           /* X axis of the normal vector
                                      at the vertex */
    FLOAT YNormalVector;           /* Y axis of the normal vector
                                      at the vertex */
    FLOAT ZNormalVector;           /* Z axis of the normal vector
                                      at the vertex */
    FLOAT RedVertexComponent;      /* Red color component
                                      at the vertex */
    FLOAT GreenVertexComponent;    /* Green color component at the
                                      vertex */
    FLOAT BlueVertexComponent;     /* Blue color component at
                                      the vertex */
    FLOAT XVertex;                 /* X axis of the vertex */
    FLOAT YVertex;                 /* Y axis of the vertex */
    FLOAT ZVertex;                 /* Z axis of the vertex */
```

```
    } Vertices[DataSize / 9];

} SGOQUADLIST, SGOTRIANGLIST;
```

ObjectToken is the object token identification value. This value is 01h for Quadrilateral List objects and 02h for Triangle List objects.

DataSize is the size in WORDs of the data contained within this object. The size of the ObjectToken and DataSize fields are not included in this value.

Each vertex in the object is encoded as an array of one or more 18-byte structures. Each vertex structure contains nine fields of data defining a vertex in the object. The fields in each structure are defined as follows:

XNormalVector, YNormalVector, and ZNormalVector contain the position of the normal vector at this vertex.

RedVertexComponent, GreenVertexComponent, and BlueVertexComponent hold the RGB values for the color of this vertex.

XVertex, YVertex, and ZVertex contain the position of the vertex itself.

The structure of the SGO Triangle Mesh data object is similar to the List objects, but adds a few more fields of information:

```
    typedef struct _TriMeshObject
    {
      LONG ObjectToken;              /* Object token identifier */
      LONG DataSize;                 /* Size of the data in this object in
                                        WORDs */
      LONG VertexSize;               /* Size of the vertex data in WORDs */
      struct _Vertex                 /* Object vertex structure(s) */
      {
        FLOAT XNormalVector;              /* X axis of the normal vector
                                             at the vertex */
        FLOAT YNormalVector;              /* Y axis of the normal vector
                                             at the vertex */
        FLOAT ZNormalVector;              /* Z axis of the normal vector
                                             at the vertex */
        FLOAT RedVertexComponent;         /* Red color component
                                             at the vertex */
        FLOAT GreenVertexComponent;       /* Green color component
                                             at the vertex */
        FLOAT BlueVertexComponent;        /* Blue color component
                                             at the vertex */
        FLOAT XVertex;                    /* X axis of the vertex */
```

```
    FLOAT YVertex;                 /* Y axis of the vertex */
    FLOAT ZVertex;                 /* Z axis of the vertex */
    } Vertices[DataSize / 9];
struct _MeshControl                /* Mesh Control structure(s) */
{
    LONG MeshControlId;            /* Mesh Control identifier */
    LONG NumOfIndicies;            /* Number of indices stored in the
                                      control */
    LONG Indices[NumOfIndicies];   /* Index values */
    } Vertices[];

} SGOTRIANGMESH;
```

ObjectToken is the object token identification value. This value is 03h for Triangle Mesh objects.

DataSize is the size in bytes of the data contained within this object. The size of the ObjectToken and DataSize fields are not included in this value.

VertexSize is the number of WORDs required to store the vertex data in the object.

Each vertex in the object is encoded as an array of one or more 18-byte structures. Each vertex structure contains nine fields of data defining a vertex in the object. The fields in each vertex structure are defined as follows:

XNormalVector, YNormalVector, and ZNormalVector contain the position of the normal vector at this vertex.

RedVertexComponent, GreenVertexComponent, and BlueVertexComponent hold the RGB values for the color of this vertex.

XVertex, YVertex, and ZVertex contain the position of the vertex itself.

Following the vertices array is an array of mesh control structures. These structure hold data that specifies how the vertex data is to be linked together. The fields in each mesh control structure are defined as follows:

MeshControlId is the identifier for the type of mesh control. The valid values for this field are:

01h	Begin Triangle Mesh
02h	Swap Triangle Mesh
03h	End Begin Triangle Mesh
04h	End Triangle Mesh

NumOfIndicies indicates how many indices are stored in this mesh control. Indices is an array of the index values for this mesh control.

For Further Information

For further information about the SGO file format, see the specification included on the CD-ROM that accompanies this book. In addition, see the references in the SGI Inventor article and the following article, available from SGI:

> Silicon Graphics, *IRIS Showcase User's Guide,* Appendix C, "Graphics Library Programming Guide."

Contact:

> Silicon Graphics Inc.
> Attn: Visual Magic Marketing
> 2011 North Shoreline Blvd.
> Mountain View, CA 94039-7311
> Voice: 800-800-4SGI

SGI also maintains an anonymous FTP site, *sgi.com,* that contains information on many SGI applications and products.

Sun Icon

NAME:	Sun Icon
ALSO KNOWN AS:	ICO
TYPE:	Bitmap
COLORS:	Mono
COMPRESSION:	None
MAXIMUM IMAGE SIZE:	64x64 pixels
MULTIPLE IMAGES PER FILE:	No
NUMERICAL FORMAT:	Big-endian
ORIGINATOR:	Sun Microsystems
PLATFORM:	SunOS
SUPPORTING APPLICATIONS:	Many UNIX-based
SPECIFICATION ON CD:	No
CODE ON CD:	Yes (in pbmplus package)
IMAGES ON CD:	Yes
SEE ALSO:	Sun Raster
USAGE:	Used to store iconic images found in the Sun GUI environments.
COMMENTS:	Sun Icon is an ASCII representation of a bitmap image format.

Overview

The icons found in the Open Look and SunView Graphical User Interfaces available on the Sun Microsystems UNIX-based platforms are stored in a simple format known as the Sun Icon format.

File Organization

Sun Icon files are ASCII text files that may be created and modified using a simple text editor. Sun icons are typically 64x64 pixels in size and contain black-and-white image data. Files contain an ASCII header followed by a hexadecimal representation of the bitmapped image data.

The header is found in the first 78 bytes of the icon file. The header contains five fields of information composed of printable ASCII characters. Each field has a *keyword=value* syntax and is delineated by a comma and a space character.

The header begins and ends with the standard C comment tokens /* */. A linefeed character (ASCII 0Ah) is preset at offset 49h within the header.

File Details

When you use a text editor to examine a Sun Icon header, you can see the format shown below:

```
/* Format_version=1, Width=64, Height=64, Depth=1,
   Valid_bits_per_item=16
 */
```

Format_version is the version of the icon file format and is always 1.

Width and Height are the size of the icon in pixels; both are typically set to a value of 64.

Depth is the number of bits per pixel in the icon image data and is usually 1.

Valid_bits_per_item is the number of bits of image data contained in each item of hexadecimal bitmapped data. Typical values for this field are 16 and 32.

The image data that follows the header is a series of hexadecimal numbers called *items*. Each item represents a number of pixels equal to the Valid_bits_per_item value divided by the Depth value. For images with a Valid_bits_per_item value of 16 and a Depth of 1, each hexadecimal number represents 16 pixels and is two bytes in size.

Items are separated by commas, and every eighth item is delimited by a linefeed character. All hexadecimal numbers begin with the standard C hexadecimal notational prefix 0x. The following illustration is a complete Sun Icon image file. The <LF> symbols indicate the location of a linefeed character.

```
/*
Format_version=1,Width=64,Height=64,Depth=1,Valid_bits_per_item=16<LF>
*/<LF>
0x0000,0x0000,0x0000,0x0000,0x01E0,0x3C00,0x0000,0x0000,<LF>
0x1F5C,0xEB00,0x0000,0x0000,0x7AAB,0xB5C0,0x0000,0x0000,<LF>
0xD555,0x6B00,0x0000,0x0000,0xFAAA,0xDC00,0x0000,0xC600,<LF>
0x0FF7,0x0000,0x0001,0x2900,0x0000,0x0000,0x0000,0x1000,<LF>
0x0000,0x0000,0x8000,0x0000,0xE000,0x0000,0x8000,0x0000,<LF>
0x5804,0x0001,0xC318,0x0000,0xAE06,0x0001,0x44A4,0x018C,<LF>
0x5587,0x0001,0xC040,0x0252,0xAE05,0x0001,0x6000,0x0020,<LF>
0xF006,0x8082,0xA000,0x0000,0x0005,0x4083,0x6000,0x0000,<LF>
0x0002,0xC0C2,0xB020,0x0000,0x0003,0x6145,0x5060,0x0000,<LF>
0x0002,0xB1A6,0xB060,0x0000,0x0003,0x5165,0x50A0,0x00C0,<LF>
```

```
0x0001,0xB9B6,0xA9A0,0x0340,0x0001,0x575D,0x5940,0x0D80,<LF>
0x0041,0xAAAA,0xAAC0,0x7B00,0x0071,0xD77F,0xD541,0xD500,<LF>
0x803C,0xAF80,0x3EC6,0xAA00,0x602B,0xD815,0x035D,0x5400,<LF>
0x7815,0xE140,0x28EA,0xA800,0x2E1A,0x8400,0x0235,0x5800,<LF>
0x15CB,0x1000,0x009A,0xB000,0x0ABC,0x4000,0x0005,0x6000,<LF>
0x055D,0x0000,0x0022,0xC000,0x0550,0x0000,0x0009,0x4000,<LF>
0x02A4,0x7800,0x0000,0xFFF0,0x01A0,0x8400,0x0002,0xAAA0,<LF>
0x0150,0x8000,0x0000,0x5540,0xFF80,0x8000,0x0001,0x2A80,<LF>
0x55A0,0x80E7,0x3700,0x3500,0x2B00,0x7842,0x1880,0x9B00,<LF>
0x1540,0x0442,0x1080,0x1600,0x1E00,0x0442,0x1080,0x4C00,<LF>
0x0A80,0x8442,0x1080,0x0C00,0x0600,0x8442,0x1080,0x2B80,<LF>
0x0680,0x783C,0x38C0,0x0AF0,0x3C00,0x0000,0x0000,0x155F,<LF>
0xED00,0x0000,0x0000,0x06AC,0x5400,0x0000,0x0000,0x1550,<LF>
0x2D00,0x0000,0x0000,0x06A0,0xFFD5,0x5555,0x5555,0x5FFF,<LF>
0xFF88,0x8888,0x8888,0xB7FF,0xDDE2,0x2222,0x2222,0x5DDD,<LF>
0xBBD4,0x4444,0x4444,0xFBBB,0xFFFF,0xFFFF,0xFFFF,0xFFFF,<LF>
0x0000,0x0000,0x0000,0x0000,0x0000,0x0000,0x0000,0x0000,<LF>
0x0000,0x0000,0x0000,0x0000,0x0000,0x0000,0x0000,0x0000,<LF>
0x0000,0x0000,0x0000,0x0000,0x0000,0x0000,0x0000,0x0000,<LF>
0x0000,0x0000,0x0000,0x0000,0x0000,0x0000,0x0000,0x0000,<LF>
0x0000,0x0000,0x0000,0x0000,0x0000,0x0000,0x0000,0x0000,<LF>
0x0000,0x0000,0x0000,0x0000,0x0000,0x0000,0x0000,0x0000
```

For Further Information

For further information about the Sun Icon format, refer to the following files on SunOS systems:

/usr/include/suntool/icon.h
/usr/include/suntool/icon_load.h

These files contain the declaration for the Sun Icon format, as well as other information about the format.

You can also try getting information from Sun at:

Sun Microsystems Incorporated
2550 Garcia Avenue
Mountain View, CA 94043
Voice: 415-960-1300

There are also many available UNIX-based tools for reading, writing, and converting Sun Icon files. See the pbmplus package on the CD-ROM, described in Appendix A, *What's on the CD-ROM?*

NAME:	Sun Raster
ALSO KNOWN AS:	RAS
TYPE:	Bitmap
COLORS:	Variable
COMPRESSION:	RLE
MAXIMUM IMAGE SIZE:	Variable
MULTIPLE IMAGES PER FILE:	No
NUMERICAL FORMAT:	Big-endian
ORIGINATOR:	Sun Microsystems
PLATFORM:	SunOS
SUPPORTING APPLICATIONS:	Many UNIX-based
SPECIFICATION ON CD:	Yes (summary description)
CODE ON CD:	Yes (in FBM, ImageMagick, pbmplus, xli, xloadimage, and xv packages)
IMAGES ON CD:	No
SEE ALSO:	Sun Icon
USAGE:	Sun Raster is the native bitmap format of the Sun UNIX platforms.
COMMENTS:	A simple bitmap format with wide distribution, particularly in the UNIX world.

Overview

The Sun Raster image file format is the native bitmap format of the Sun Microsystems UNIX platforms using the SunOS operating system. This format is capable of storing black-and-white, gray-scale, and color bitmapped data of any pixel depth. The use of color maps and a simple Run-Length data compression are also supported. Typically, most images found on a SunOS system are Sun Raster images, and this format is supported by most UNIX imaging applications.

File Organization

The basic layout of a Sun Raster file is a header, followed by an optional color map, and then by the bitmapped image data.

File Details

The Sun Raster file header is 32 bytes in length and has the following format:

```
typedef struct _SunRaster
{
    DWORD MagicNumber;       /* Magic (identification) number */
    DWORD Width;             /* Width of image in pixels */
    DWORD Height;            /* Height of image in pixels */
    DWORD Depth;             /* Number of bits per pixel */
    DWORD Length;            /* Size of image data in bytes */
    DWORD Type;              /* Type of raster file */
    DWORD ColorMapType;      /* Type of color map */
    DWORD ColorMapLength;    /* Size of the color map in bytes */

} SUNRASTER;
```

MagicNumber is used to identify a file as a Sun Raster image and always contains the value 59a66a95h. This value is stored in big-endian byte order, as are the entire contents of every Sun Raster file. Reading this magic number using the little-endian byte order (as is possible on the Intel-based Sun 386i system) produces the value 956aa659h, a clue that you are not reading the raster file using the proper byte order.

Width and Height specify the size of the image in pixels. The width of a scan line is always a multiple of 16 bits, padded when necessary.

Depth is the number of bits per pixel of the image data. The typical values for this field are 1, 8, 24, and 32; a value of 32 indicates 24-bit values with a pad byte preceding the pixel values. Note that 24- and 32-bit pixel data (assuming no color map) is in BGR format, rather than RGB, unless the image type is RGB.

Length is the actual size of the bitmapped data in the bitmap file (that is, the file size minus the header and the color map length). Do not expect this value to always be accurate, however. In the original release of the Sun Raster format, this field indicated the type of encoding used on the bitmapped data and was always set to 00h (no encoding). In the second release, this field was renamed and was used to indicate the length of the bitmapped data.

Therefore, older raster files will appear to have a length of 00h. In this case, the Length must be calculated by multiplying together the values of the Height, Width, and Depth fields.

Type is the version (or flavor) of the bitmap file. The following values are typically found in the Type field:

0000h	Old
0001h	Standard
0002h	Byte-encoded
0003h	RGB format
0004h	TIFF format
0005h	IFF format
FFFFh	Experimental

Both Old and Standard formats are the same. They indicate that the image data within the file is not compressed, and most Sun Raster files you will encounter are stored in this manner.

The Byte-encoded type indicates that the image data is compressed using a Run-length encoding scheme (described later in this section).

The TIFF and IFF format types indicate that the raster file was originally converted from either of these file formats.

The Experimental type is implementation-specific and is generally an indication that the image file does not conform to the Sun Raster file format specification.

ColorMapType indicates the type of color map included in the raster file, or whether a color map is included at all. The following values are typically found in the ColorMapType field:

0000h	No color map
0001h	RGB color map
0002h	Raw color map

ColorMapLength contains the number of bytes stored in the color map.

If ColorMapType is 0000h (no color map), ColorMapLength is 0000h. If ColorMapType is 0001h (RGB color map) or 0002h (raw color map), ColorMapLength is the number of bytes in the color map. In the case of an RGB color map, the colors are separated into three planes, stored in RGB order, with each plane being one-third the size of the ColorMapLength value. For example, a 256-element color map for a 24-bit image consists of three 256-byte color planes and has a length of 768 bytes (Depth = 24, ColorMapType = 01h, ColorMapLength = 768). A raw color map is any other type of color map not defined by the Sun Raster file format and is stored as individual byte values.

Bitmap files with a Depth of 1 contain 2-color image data. Typically, 1-bit bitmap images do not have a color map. Each bit in the bitmap represents a pixel, with a value of 0 representing black and a value of 1 representing white (the bits are stored most significant bit first within each byte). If a color map is present in a 1-bit image file, it is a 2-color map, each color being 24 bits in length (Depth = 1, ColorMapType = 01h, ColorMapLength = 6). Each bit of image data is then an index pointing to one of these two colors in the map.

Raster files with a Depth of 8 may contain either color or gray-scale image data. Images with pixels eight or fewer bits in depth do not include a color map (Depth = 8, ColorMapType = 00h, ColorMapLength = 0). Each byte of image data contains the value of the color it stores. If a color map is present in an 8-bit raster file, the pixel values are index pointers into the color map. Such an image, although it may contain a 24-bit color map (Depth = 8, ColorMapType = 01h, ColorMapLength = 768), can contain only a maximum of 256 colors.

Raster files with a Depth of 24 (or 32) normally do not have color maps. Instead, the colors values are stored directly in the image data itself (truecolor bitmap). If a 24-bit image has a color map, it is either a raw color map, or an RGB color map that contains more than 256 elements.

The Run-length encoding (RLE) scheme optionally used in Sun Raster files (Type = 0002h) is used to encode bytes of image data separately. RLE encoding may be found in any Sun Raster file regardless of the type of image data it contains.

The RLE packets are typically three bytes in size:

- The first byte is a Flag Value indicating the type of RLE packet.
- The second byte is the Run Count.
- The third byte is the Run Value.

A Flag Value of 80h is followed by a Run Count in the range of 01h to FFh. The Run Value follows the Run count and is in the range of 00h to FFh. The pixel run is the Run Value repeated Run Count times.

There are two exceptions to this algorithm. First, if the Run Count following the Flag Value is 00h, this is an indication that the run is a single byte in length and has a value of 80h. And second, if the Flag Value is not 80h, then it is assumed that the data is unencoded pixel data and is written directly to the output stream.

For example, a run of 100 pixels with the value of 0Ah would encode as the values 80h 64h 0Ah. A single pixel value of 80h would encode as the values 80h 00h. The four unencoded bytes 12345678h would be stored in the RLE stream as 12h 34h 56h 78h.

Note also that the Sun Raster bitmap is read as if it is a single stream of data. Therefore, the encoding of pixel runs does not stop at the end of each scan line.

For Further Information

For further information about the Sun Raster format, see the summary description included on the CD-ROM that accompanies this book and the SunOS manual page entitled *rasterfile*. The man page entry describes only the basic layout of the Sun Raster format. Information about the order of bit planes or the RLE encoding used on the image data is not included. The following file contains the Sun Raster header declaration and field values:

> */usr/include/rasterfile.h*

You can also try getting information from Sun Microsystems at:

Sun Microsystems Incorporated
2550 Garcia Avenue
Mountain View, CA 94043
Voice: 415-960-1300

In addition, there are also many publicly available UNIX-based image file viewers and converters that support the Sun Raster format. See the FBM, ImageMagick, pbmplus, xli, xloadimage, and xv packages on the CD-ROM, described in Appendix A, *What's on the CD-ROM?*

▌TDDD

NAME:	TDDD
ALSO KNOWN AS:	Turbo Silver 3D Data Description, T3D
TYPE:	3D vector and animation
COLORS:	16 million
COMPRESSION:	Uncompressed
MAXIMUM IMAGE SIZE:	Unlimited
MULTIPLE IMAGES PER FILE:	Yes
NUMERICAL FORMAT:	Big-endian
ORIGINATOR:	Impulse
PLATFORM:	All
SUPPORTING APPLICATIONS:	Turbo Silver
SPECIFICATION ON CD:	Yes (summary description)
CODE ON CD:	No
IMAGES ON CD:	No
SEE ALSO:	Interchange File Format

USAGE: Interchange of 3D image information, primarily on the Amiga.

COMMENTS: A slightly modified version of IFF that is widely used.

Overview

The TDDD (Turbo Silver 3D Data Description) format is used to store object data created by the Turbo Silver 3.0 application from Impulse. The TDDD format is actually the Electronic Arts Interchange File Format (IFF) with modifications to two of its chunks. For this reason, please read the IFF article before you read this article about TDDD.

File Organization

Like IFF files, TDDD files consist of a series of sections called chunks. The FORM chunk of a TDDD file uses only two types of IFF chunks: INFO and OBJ.

The INFO chunk stores information describing observer data and appears in *cell* files. Each INFO chunk contains standard IFF sub-chunks. The INFO chunk is optional and might not appear at all in the FORM chunk.

The OBJ chunk contains data which describes an object hierarchy and appears in both cell and object files. One or more OBJ chunks are contained in the FORM chunk and each OBJ chunk contains one or more sub-chunks.

There are three types of OBJ sub-chunks:

1. EXTR describes an "external" object in a separate file.

2. DESC describes a single node of a hierarchy.

3. TOBJ marks the end of a hierarchy chain.

Each hierarchy node is described either by an EXTR chunk or by a DESC and TOBJ chunk pair.

The TOBJ sub-chunks contain no data and have a length of zero. The DESC and EXTR sub-chunks contain sub-chunks as defined by the IFF file format. Unrecognized sub-chunks are skipped over by TDDD readers, and the default values are assumed for any missing sub-chunks.

The object hierarchy contains a head object and one or more brothers. Each brother may have child objects; the children may have grandchildren; and so on. The brother nodes are stored in a doubly linked list, and each node has a pointer to a doubly linked "child" list. (If no child is present, then the pointer is NULL.) Child lists point to grandchildren lists and back to their parent, and so on.

Each of the "head" brothers is written in a separate OBJ chunk, along with all its descendants. Each child, grandchild, and so on in the descendant hierarchy begins a DESC chunk and ends with a TOBJ chunk. Objects stored in external files are described only with a single EXTR chunk. The children and grandchildren of this external object are also stored in the same external file.

File Details

Several data types are used to represent fields within several sub-chunks. RGB values are always represented by an array of three BYTE values and the values are stored in RGB order. Fractional (FRACT) and point values are stored as LONG values. A VECTOR is an array of three FRACT values and a MATRIX is an array of three VECTOR values. With this in mind, here are the structures for these data types:

```
typedef BYTE COLOR[3];    /* Red, Green, and Blue values */
typedef LONG FRACT;       /* Point */
typedef struct _Vectors
{
  FRACT X;
  FRACT Y;
  FRACT Z;

} VECTOR;
typedef struct _Matrices
{
  VECTOR I;
  VECTOR J;
  VECTOR K;

} MATRIX;
```

The following structure is used in generating animated cells from a single cell. It can be attached to an object or to the camera. It is also used for Turbo Silver's "extrude along a path" feature.

```
typedef struct _Story
{
  BYTE   Path[18];       /* Name of object */
  VECTOR Translate;      /* Translate vector */
  VECTOR Rotate;         /* Rotate vector */
  VECTOR Scale;          /* Scale vector */
  WORD   Info;           /* Coordinate flags */

} STORY;
```

Path is the name of a named object in the cell data.

Translate is not used.

Rotate specifies rotation angles about the X, Y, and Z axes of the vector.

Scale specifies X, Y, and Z factors of the scale vector.

Info contains a collection of bitfield flags with the following definitions:

0x0001	ABS_TRA	Translate in world coordinates (not used)
0x0002	ABS_ROT	Rotation in world coordinates
0x0004	ABS_SCL	Scaling in world coordinates
0x0010	LOC_TRA	Translate in local coordinates (not used)

0x0020	LOC_ROT	Rotation in local coordinates
0x0040	LOC_SCL	Scaling in local coordinates
0x0100	X_ALIGN	Not used
0x0200	Y_ALIGN	Align Y axis to path's direction
0x0400	Z_ALIGN	Not used
0x1000	FOLLOW_ME	Children follow parent on path

INFO Chunk

The following sub-chunk structures are found only in the INFO chunk. All of these INFO sub-chunks are optional, as is the INFO chunk itself. If a sub-chunk is not present, then its default value is assumed. The base default values for an INFO chunk are the following:

- No brushes, stencils, or textures defined

- No story for the camera

- Horizon and zenith and ambient light colors set to black

- Fade color set to (80, 80, 80)

- Unrotated, untracked camera at (-100, -100, 100)

- Global properties array set to [30, 0, 0, 0, 0, 100, 8, 0]

- Global properties array set to [30, 0, 0, 0, 0, 100, 8, 0]

The BRSH sub-chunk defines a brush. There may be up to eight brushes defined in an INFO chunk.

```
typedef struct _Brush
{
   WORD BrushNumber;      /* Brush number (0 to 7) */
   CHAR FileName[80];     /* IFF ILBM filename */

} BRSH;
```

BrushNumber is the identification number of the brush, and this value may be in the range of 0 to 7.

FileName is the name of the IFF file which stores the brush information.

The STNC sub-chunk defines a stencil. There may be up to eight stencils defined in an INFO chunk.

```
typedef struct _Stencil
{
  WORD StencilNumber;    /* Stencil number (0 to 7) */
  CHAR FileName[80];     /* IFF ILBM filename */

} STNC;
```

StencilNumber is the identification number of the stencil, and this value may be in the range of 0 to 7. FileName is the name of the IFF file which stores the stencil information.

The TXTR sub-chunk defines a text resource. There may be up to eight resources defined in an INFO chunk.

```
typedef struct _Text
{
  WORD TextNumber;       /* Text number (0 to 7) */
  CHAR FileName[80];     /* Code module name */

} TXTR;
```

TextNumber is the identification number of the resource, and this value may be in the range of 0 to 7.

FileName is the name of a code module that can be loaded using the Load-Seg() function found in Turbo Silver.

The OBSV sub-chunk specifies the location, position, and focal length of the camera observer. The rotation angles are in degrees and specify the degree of rotation around the X, Y, and Z axes.

```
typedef struct _Observer
{
  VECTOR Camera;    /* Camera position */
  VECTOR Rotate;    /* Camera rotation angles */
  FRACT  Focal;     /* Camera focal length */

} OBSV;
```

The OTRK sub-chunk specifies the name of an object; otherwise the camera always follows the tracked object.

```
typedef struct _ObjectTrack
{
  BYTE TrackName[18];    /* Name of tracked object */

} OTRK;
```

The OSTR sub-chunk contains the story information for the camera.

```
typedef struct _ObjectStory
{
   STORY CStory;              /* STORY structure for the camera */
} OSTR;
```

FADE contains the parameters for a fading operation.

```
typedef struct _Fade
{
   FRACT FadeAt;              /* Distance to start fade */
   FRACT FadeBy;              /* Distance of total fade */
   BYTE  Pad;                 /* Pad byte (always 0) */
   COLOR FadeTo;              /* RGB color to fade to */

} FADE;
```

The SKYC sub-chunk defines the color of a rendered sky.

```
typedef struct SkyColor
{
   BYTE     Pad1;             /* Pad byte (always 0) */
   COLOR    Horizon;          /* Horizon color */
   BYTE     Pad2;             /* Pad byte (always 0) */
   COLOR    Zenith;           /* Zenith color */
} SKYC;
```

The AMBI sub-chunk defines the ambient light color of the rendering.

```
typedef struct _AmbientLightColor
{
   BYTE     Pad;              /* Pad byte (always 0) */
   COLOR    Ambient;          /* Ambient light color */

} AMBI;
```

The GLB0 sub-chunk contains an array of eight global property values used by Turbo Silver.

```
typedef struct _GlobalProperties
{
   BYTE Props[8];             /* Eight global properties */

} GLB0;
```

The elements are defined as follows:

0	GLB_EDGING	Edge level value
1	GLB_PERTURB	Perturbance value
2	GLB_SKY_BLEND	Sky blending factor
3	GLB_LENS	Lens type
4	GLB_FADE	Sharp/fuzzy focus
5	GLB_SIZE	Apparent size
6	GLB_RESOLVE	Resolve depth
7	GLB_EXTRA	Genlock sky flag

GLB_EDGING and GLB_PERTURB correspond to the edging and perturbance values heuristics control in ray tracing.

GLB_SKY_BLEND is zero for no blending and 255 for full blending.

The GLB_LENS value corresponds to the boxes in the "camera" requester, and may be 0 (manual), 1 (wide angle), 2 (normal), 3 (telephoto), or 4 (custom).

GLB_FADE turns the "fade" feature ON (non-zero) and OFF (zero).

GLB_SIZE is 100 times the "custom size" parameter in the camera requester and is used to set the focal length for a custom lens. GLB_RESOLVE specifies the number of rays the ray tracer will shoot for a single pixel.

The GLB_EXTRA flag indicates if the sky is colored or is set to the "genlock" color (color 0 to black) in the final picture. If "genlock" is set in TurboSilver, a "zero color" is written into the bitplanes for genlock video to show through.

DESC Chunk

The following sub-chunk structures are only found in the DESC chunk. Many of these sub-chunks are optional (the SHAP sub-chunk is required to appear), and all have default values if they are not present. Note that if there is a FACE chunk, there must also be a CLST, an RLST, and a TLST sub-chunk as well, all with matching Count fields.

The default for the DESC chunk sub-chunks are: Colors set to (240,240,240); reflection and transmission coefficients set to zero; illegal shape; no story or special surface types; position at (0,0,0); axes aligned to the world axes; size fields all 32.0; intensity at 300; no name; no points/edges or faces; texture parameters set to zero; refraction type 0 with index 1.00; specular, hardness and roughness set to zero; blending at 255; glossy off; phong shading on; not a light source and not brightly lit.

The NAME sub-chunk contains the name of the object itself and is used by a number of operations, including camera tracking and specifying story paths.

```
typedef struct _ObjectName
{
   BYTE Name[18];            /* The name of the object */

} NAME;
```

The SHAP sub-chunk defines the visible appearance of an object.

```
typedef struct _ObjectShape
{
   WORD Shape;               /* Object type */
   WORD Lamp;                /* Lamp type */

} SHAP;
```

Shape values include:

0   Sphere
1   Stencil
2   Axis
3   Facets
4   Surface
5   Ground

Lamp values include:

0   No lamp
1   Light is sunlight
2   Light is from a lamp, and intensity falls off with distance

The POSI sub-chunk specifies the position of an object in a rendering.

```
typedef struct _ObjectPosition
{
   VECTOR  Position;     /* The object's position in space */

} POSI;
```

Legal coordinates are in the range -32768 to 32767 and 65535/65536.

The AXIS sub-chunk describes a direction (orthogonal unit) vector for the object coordinate system.

```
typedef struct _VectorAxis
{
   VECTOR  XAxis;                  /* X axis of vector */
```

```
        VECTOR   YAxis;              /* Y axis of vector */
        VECTOR   ZAxis;              /* Z axis of vector */

      } AXIS;
```

The SIZE sub-chunk is used by a variety of operations requiring a vector size value.

```
      typedef struct _Size
      {
        VECTOR Size;                 /* Object size */

      } SIZE;
```

The PNTS sub-chunk stores all the points defining a custom objects.

```
      typedef struct _Points
      {
        WORD    PCount;              /* Point count */
        VECTOR Points[PCount];       /* Points */

      } PNTS;
```

The EDGE sub-chunk contains the edge list for custom objects.

```
      typedef struct _EdgeList
      {
        WORD ECount;                 /* Edge count */
        WORD Edges[ECount][2];       /* Edges */

      } EDGE;
```

The FACE sub-chunk contains the triangle (face) list for custom objects.

```
      typedef struct _FaceList
      {
        WORD    TCount;              /* Face count */
        WORD    Connects[TCount][3]; /* Faces */

      } FACE;
```

The COLR sub-chunk contains the main object color coefficients.

```
typedef struct _Color
{
  BYTE  Pad;                    /* Pad byte (always 0) */
  COLOR Color;                  /* RGB color */

} COLR;
```

The REFL sub-chunk contains the main object reflection coefficients.

```
typedef struct _Reflection
{
  BYTE  Pad;                    /* Pad byte (always 0) */
  COLOR Color;                  /* RGB color */

} REFL;
```

The TRAN sub-chunk contains the main object transmission coefficients.

```
typedef struct _Transmission
{
  BYTE  Pad;                    /* Pad byte (always 0) */
  COLOR Color;                  /* RGB color */

} TRAN;
```

The CLST sub-chunk contains the main object color coefficients for each face in custom objects.

```
typedef struct _ColorList
{
  WORD Count;                   /* Count of colors */
  COLOR Colors[Count];          /* Colors */

} CLST;
```

The count should match the face count in the FACE chunk and the ordering corresponds to the face order.

The RLST sub-chunk contains the main object reflection coefficients for each face in custom objects.

```
typedef struct _ReflectionList
{
  WORD Count;                    /* Count of colors */
  COLOR Colors[Count];           /* Colors */

} RLST;
```

The count should match the face count in the FACE chunk and the ordering corresponds to the face order.

The TLST sub-chunk contains the main object transmission coefficients for each face in custom objects.

```
typedef struct _TransmissionList
{
  WORD Count;                    /* Count of colors */
  COLOR Colors[Count];           /* Colors */

} TLST;
```

The count should match the face count in the FACE chunk and the ordering corresponds to the face order.

The TPAR sub-chunk contains a list of parameters for texture modules when texture mapping is used.

```
typedef struct _TextureParameters
{
  FRACT Params[16];              /* Texture parameters */

} TPAR;
```

The SURF sub-chunk contains an array of five surface property specifications.

```
typedef struct _SurfaceProperties
{
  BYTE SProps[5];                /* Object properties */

} SURF;
```

The elements are defined as follows:

0	PRP_SURFACE	Surface type
1	PRP_BRUSH	Brush number
2	PRP_WRAP	IFF brush wrapping type

| 3 | PRP_STENCIL | Stencil number for stencil objects |
| 4 | PRP_TEXTURE | Texture number if texture mapped |

PRP_SURFACE is the type of surface. Values for this element include 0 (normal), 4 (genlock), and 5 (IFF brush).

PRP_BRUSH is the brush identification number if the brush is mapped to an IFF file.

PRP_WRAP is the IFF brush-wrapping type. Values for this element may be 0 (no wrapping), 1 (wrap X), 2 (wrap Z), or 3 (wrap X and Z).

PRP_STENCIL is the stencil number for stencil objects.

PRP_TEXTURE is the texture number if the object is texture-mapped.

The MTTR sub-chunk contains refraction data for transparent or glossy objects. Type may have a value of 0 for air (refraction index of 1.00), 1 for water (1.33), 2 for glass (1.67), 3 for crystal(2.00), or 4 for a custom index (1.00 to 3.55). Index contains the value of the custom refraction index.

```
typedef struct _RefractionData
{
    BYTE Type;     /* Refraction type (0-4) */
    BYTE Index;    /* Custom index of refraction */
} MTTR;
```

The SPEC sub-chunk contains specularity information.

```
typedef struct _SpecularInfo
{
BYTE Specularity;   /* Specular reflection (0 to 255) */
BYTE Hardness;      /* Specular exponent (0 to 31) */
} SPEC;
```

Specularity contains the amount of specular reflection in the range of 0 (none) to 255 (fully specular).

Hardness specifies the "tightness" of the specular spots. A value of zero gives broad specular spots and a value of 31 gives smaller spots.

The PRP0 sub-chunk contains an array of object properties that programs other than Turbo Silver might support.

```
typedef struct _MiscProperties
{
    BYTE Props[6];   /* Object properties */
} PRP0;
```

The elements are defined as follows:

0	PRP_BLEND	Blending factor
1	PRP_SMOOTH	Roughness factor
2	PRP_SHADE	Shading flag
3	PRP_PHONG	Phong shading flag
4	PRP_GLOSSY	Glossy flag
5	PRP_QUICK	Quickdraw flag

PRP_BLEND controls the amount of dithering used on the object in the range of 0 to 255 (255 being fully dithered).

PRP_SMOOTH specifies how rough the object should appear in the range of 0 (completely smooth) to 255 (maximal roughness).

PRP_SHADE indicates how the object is shaded. If the object is a light source and the flag is ON, then the object casts a shadow; otherwise it does not. If the object is a normal object and the flag is ON, the object is always considered fully lit and is not affected by other light sources.

PRP_PHONG indicates that phong shading is on by default. Any non-zero value turns it off.

PRP_GLOSSY indicates if an object is to be rendered as glossy or normal.

PRP_QUICK flag, when set, indicates that the image should not be drawn with all the points and edges, but instead should be drawn as a rectangular solid centered at the object position using sizes determined by the axis lengths.

The INTS sub-chunk is the intensity field for light source objects.

```
typedef struct _Intensity
{
   FRACT Intensity;        /* Light intensity */

} INTS;
```

An intensity of 255 for a sun-like light fully lights object surfaces which are perpendicular to the direction to the light source. For lamp-like light sources, the necessary intensity will depend on the distance to the light.

The STRY sub-chunk contains the story information for the description.

```
typedef struct _Story
{
   STORY CStory;

} STRY;
```

The EXTR chunk only contain sub-chunks which are required to appear.

EXTR Chunk

MTRX is used to represent a set of matrix coordinates.

```
typedef struct _Matrix
{
   VECTOR Translate;      /* Translation vector */
   VECTOR Scale;          /* X, Y, and Z scaling factors */
   MATRIX Rotate;         /* Rotation matrix */

} MTRX;
```

Translate is the translation vector in world coordinates.

Scale is the scaling factors with respect to local axes.

Rotate is the rotation matrix with respect to the world axes.

The LOAD sub-chunk contains the name of an external, FORM TDDD object file. which may contain any number of objects, possibly grouped into one or more hierarchies.

```
typedef struct _FileName
{
    BYTE FileName[80];       /* External object file name */
} LOAD;
```

For Further Information

For further information about TDDD, see the summary description included on the CD-ROM that accompanies this book. See also the article about TTDDD, an ASCII format based on TDDD, and the article on IFF, the format on which TDDD is based.

TGA

NAME:	TGA
ALSO KNOWN AS:	Targa Image File, VST, VDA, ICB, TPIC
TYPE:	Bitmap
COLORS:	8-bit, 16-bit, 24-bit, 32-bit
COMPRESSION:	RLE, uncompressed
MAXIMUM IMAGE SIZE:	None
MULTIPLE IMAGES PER FILE:	No
NUMERICAL FORMAT:	Little-endian
ORIGINATOR:	Truevision Inc.
PLATFORM:	MS-DOS, Windows, UNIX, Atari, Amiga, others
SUPPORTING APPLICATIONS:	Too numerous to list
SPECIFICATION ON CD:	Yes
CODE ON CD:	Yes
IMAGES ON CD:	Yes
SEE ALSO:	Lumena Paint, RIX

USAGE: Used for the storage and interchange of deep-pixel images, paint, and image manipulation programs.

COMMENTS: A well-defined, well-documented format in wide use, which is quick and easy to read and decompress. It lacks, however, a superior compression scheme.

Overview

The TGA (Targa Image File) format is used widely in paint, graphics, and imaging applications that require the storage of image data containing up to 32 bits per pixel. TGA is associated with the Truevision product line of Targa, Vista, and NuVista graphics adapters for the PC and Macintosh, all of which can capture NTSC and/or PAL video image signals and store them in a digital frame buffer. For this reason, TGA has also become popular in the world of still-video editing.

Early work on the the TGA file format was performed at the EPICenter division of AT&T. EPICenter (Electronic Photography and Imaging Center), established in 1984 to manufacture graphics boards, was purchased by EPICenter employees from AT&T in 1987 and renamed Truevision.

The first product produced by EPICenter was called the VDA (Video Display Adapter), which had a resolution of 256x200 and a 24-bit palette providing 16 milllion colors. At the time, it competed with the CGA from IBM. EPICenter's second product was the ICB (Image Capture Board), which launched both EPICenter and AT&T into the realm of video graphics (that is, video capture, manipulation, and output).

At this time, EPICenter purchased a paint package, written by Island Graphics, that later came to be known as TIPS (Truevision Image Paint System). TIPS gave VDA and ICB (and later Targa and TrueVista) users the ability to capture live video images, to create and overlay graphics, and to perform a variety of image-processing functions on bitmap data.

Although there was only one original TGA file format, applications using it created many different filename extensions—one for every graphics display board that EPICenter, and later Truevision, produced. Therefore, .VDA, .ICB, .TGA, and .VST image files created by Truevision applications all are actually in TGA format. Today, the only filename extensions supported are TGA and TPIC on the Macintosh and .TGA on the PC and other platforms.

In 1989, the TGA format was revised, and Truevision has chosen to designate the old and new formats as original TGA format and new TGA format. The original TGA format is very simple in design and quite easy to implement in code. This makes it an appealing format to work with for many developers. As the available hardware technology has become more complex, however, additional file format features, such as the storage of gamma and color correction information and pixel aspect ratio data, have become necessary. The new TGA format was created as a wrapper around the original TGA format to add functionality without sacrificing backwards compatibility with older applications.

Today the TGA format is used on many different platforms world-wide for a variety of image storage, processing, and analysis needs. The Truevision solutions source book lists more than 200 software applications that support the TGA format.

The TGA format became popular primarily because it was the first 24-bit, true-color bitmap format generally available to the PC community, even predating 24-bit support in TIFF.

TGA is device-dependent in that the structure of the format is designed to fit the requirements of certain display hardware manufactured by Truevision. In practice, this is not a severe limitation, with one minor caveat: TGA does not support the storage of image data as planes of color information.

TGA comes in several flavors, the most common of which are usually referred to as the Targa 16, Targa 24, and Targa 32 formats. These designations identify the type of Truevision hardware that created the file, and the numbers indicate the depth (number of bits per pixel) of the image data the files contain. Less commonly found variants include VDA, ICB, and Targa M8.

All of the Truevision adapters were originally designed to interface with the ISA bus found in the IBM PC platform. For this reason, all data in a TGA format file, including the image data, is stored in little-endian format. This includes TGA files created by the NuVista card residing in the otherwise big-endian Macintosh.

File Organization

The original TGA format (version 1.0) is structured as follows:

- Header containing information on the image data and palette

- Optional image identification field

- Optional color map

- Bitmap data

The new TGA format (version 2.0) contains all of the structures included in the original TGA format, and also appends several data structures onto the end of the original TGA format. The following structures may follow the bitmap data:

- Optional developer directory; which may contain a variable number of tags pointing to pieces of information stored in the TGA file

- Optional developer area

- Optional extension area, which contains information typically found in the header of a bitmap file

- Optional color-correction table

- Optional postage-stamp image

- Optional scan-line table

- Footer, which points to the developer and extension areas and identifies the TGA file as a new TGA format file

As you can see, both the new and original TGA format files are identical in structure from the header to the image data area. For this reason, applications that read only original TGA format image files should have no problem reading new TGA format images. All information occurring after the image data may be ignored.

The TGA format specification available from Truevision is detailed and well-written. It is, in fact, one of the best written format specifications that was reviewed for this book, and we heartily congratulate Truevision on their effort. The TGA format is complex, but the clarity of the description in Truevision's specification makes it easy to read and understand. Truevision also distributes on floppy disk the Truevision TGA Utilities which is a collection of utilities and C source code used to manipulate both TGA-format files and Targa video-graphics display adapters.

File Details

This section describes the various components of a TGA file in greater detail.

Header

The TGA header is eighteen bytes in length and is identical in both versions of the TGA file format. The structure of the TGA header is as follows:

```
typedef struct _TgaHeader
{
    BYTE IDLength;          /* 00h  Size of Image ID field      */
    BYTE ColorMapType;      /* 01h  Color map type              */
    BYTE ImageType;         /* 02h  Image type code             */
    WORD CMapStart;         /* 03h  Color map origin            */
    WORD CMapLength;        /* 05h  Color map length            */
    BYTE CMapDepth;         /* 07h  Depth of color map entries  */
    WORD XOffset;           /* 08h  X origin of image           */
    WORD YOffset;           /* 0Ah  Y origin of image           */
    WORD Width;             /* 0Ch  Width of image              */
    WORD Height;            /* 0Eh  Height of image             */
    BYTE PixelDepth;        /* 10h  Image pixel size            */
    BYTE ImageDescriptor;   /* 11h  Image descriptor byte       */

} TGAHEAD;
```

IDLength is the number of significant bytes in the image identification field starting at byte 12h (following the header), and may be in the range of 0 to 255. When the IDLength is set to 0, this is an indication that there is no image identification field in the TGA file.

ColorMapType indicates whether the TGA file includes a palette. A value of 1 indicates the presence of a palette, while a value of 0 indicates that no palette is included. If the value of this field is not 0 or 1, then it is probably a value specific to the program or developer that created the TGA file. Truevision reserves the ColorMapType values 0 to 127 for its own use and allots values 128 to 255 for use by developers.

ImageType indicates the type of image stored in the TGA file. There are currently seven TGA image types. Color-mapped images (pseudocolor) use a palette. Truecolor images do not use a palette and store their pixel data directly in the image data, although truecolor TGA image files may contain a palette that is used to store the color information from a paint program. Truevision reserves the ImageType values 0 to 127 for its own use and allots values 128 to 255 for use by developers.

Valid ImageType values are listed below:

Image Type	Image Data Type	Color Map	Encoding
0	No image data included in file	No	No
1	Color-mapped image data	Yes	No
2	Truecolor image data	No	No
3	Monochrome image data	No	No
9	Color-mapped image data	Yes	Yes
10	Truecolor image data	No	Yes
11	Monochrome image data	No	Yes

The next three fields are known collectively as the Color Map Specification; the information contained in these fields is used to manipulate the image palette. If the ColorMapType field value is zero, then all three of these fields have a value of zero.

CMapStart defines the offset of the first entry in the palette. Although all palette entries must be contiguous, the entries may start anywhere in the palette; for example, 16-color values may be stored in a 64-element palette starting at entry 31 rather than at entry 0.

CMapLength defines the number of elements in the color map. If an image contains only 57 colors, then it is possible to construct a 57-element palette using this field.

CMapDepth contains the number of bits in each palette entry. The value is typically 15, 16, 24, or 32 and need not be the same value as the image data pixel depth. Table TGA-1 shows valid entries for different types of TGA palettes.

TABLE TGA-1: *TGA Palette Entry Sizes*

Truevision Bits Per Display Adapter	Attribute Color Map Entry	Bits Per Pixel	Color Formats Supported
Targa M8	24	0	Pseudo
Targa 16	15	1	True
Targa 24	24	0	True
Targa 32	32	8	True
ICB	0	0	True
VDA	16	0	Pseudo
VDA/D	16	0	Pseudo
Vista	24 or 32	0 or 8	True, Pseudo, Direct

The next six fields in the header (the last 10 bytes) are referred to collectively as the image specification. The data in these fields is used to describe the image data found in the TGA file.

XOffset and YOffset describe the position of the image on the display screen. Normally, the coordinate 0,0 defaults to the lower-left corner of the screen, but any of the four corners may be designated the origin point by the ImageDescriptor field (the last field in the header).

Width and Height are the size of the image in pixels. The maximum size of a TGA image is 512 pixels wide by 482 pixels high.

PixelDepth is the number of bits per pixel, including attribute bits, if any. Typical PixelDepth values are 8, 16, 24, and 32, although other depth values may be specified, as shown in Table TGA-1.

ImageDescriptor contains two pieces of information. Bits 0 through 3 contain the number of attribute bits per pixel. Attribute bits are found only in pixels for the 16- and 32-bit flavors of the TGA format and are called alpha channel, overlay, or interrupt bits. Bits 4 and 5 contain the image origin location (coordinate 0,0) of the image. This position may be any of the four corners of the display screen. When both of these bits are set to zero, the image origin is the lower-left corner of the screen. Bits 6 and 7 of the ImageDescriptor field are unused and should be set to 0.

Image ID

The Image ID (image description) field is an optional field that may appear immediately after the TGA header. The Image ID field stores information that identifies the image in some way (filename, author name, serial number, and so on). This field is not required to be NULL-terminated, although it should be if it is used to store string data. The size of this field is indicated by the value of the IDLength field in the header. This value may be in the range 0-255. A value of 0 indicates that no Image ID field is present in the TGA file.

Color Map

The TGA format defines three methods of arranging image data: psuedo-color, direct-color, and truecolor.

Pseudocolor images store an index value into a palette in each pixel value of data. It is the palette which contains the actual pixel values that are displayed. Pseudocolor image palettes store each pixel value as a single element in the palette. The color channels of each pixel value are not accessible individually.

Direct-color images are similar to pseudocolor images, except that each color channel (red, green, and blue) is stored in separate elements and may be individually altered. Each pixel value of direct-color image data contains three index values, one for each color channel in the color map.

Truecolor images store the pixel color information directly in the image data and do not use a palette.

The presence of a palette and the format of the image data found in a TGA file is determined by the type of Truevision hardware that was used to create the image data (see Table TGA-1). TGA images created with a Targa 24 are only truecolor images and therefore never use a palette. TGA images created with a VDA/D card are only in the pseudocolor format and will therefore always use a palette. The Vista series of cards (ATVista and NuVista) may create and store TGA data in any of the three color formats. A palette is present in a TGA file if the ColorMapType field is set to 1. A value of 0 indicates that no palette is present in the TGA file.

It is important to realize that a palette may be present in a TGA image file even if it is not used by the image data. All TGA image files created by the TIPS paint program contain a palette which stores the 256 colors found in the TIPS color palette. This palette is not actually used to display the image data, but is instead used by TIPS. A TGA reader should therefore never assume that truecolor TGA files never contain a palette.

The TGA format supports variable-size palettes. Most other formats require a palette to have a fixed number of entries based on the pixel depth of the image data. Thus, an 8-bit image contains a 256-element color map even if only four colors are needed to reproduce the image. The TGA format, however, does not determine the number of color map elements based on the pixel depth, so an image with 57 colors may only have a 57-element palette. The number of elements in the palette is contained in the CMapLength field in the header.

The size of each palette element in bits is found in the CMapDepth field of the header. The depth of a pixel and the depth of a palette element are not always the same. A 24-bit image may contain a 256-element palette, with each element having a depth of 24 bits, but it may contain pixel data with only an 8-bit depth. This is because 8 bits is all that is required to index a 256-element palette. It is also possible for a TGA image to contain a 4096-element palette where each element is eight bits in depth. Each pixel value of the image data therefore needs to have a minimum depth of 12 bits for indexing into the palette, although 16-bit pixel values are easier to read and write. The depth of a palette element always includes alpha channel, overlay, or interrupt bit information, if any.

Image Data Encoding

Image data stored in a TGA file is normally raw (unencoded). For this reason, TGA files tend to be quite large, especially when the bitmap data is 24 or 32 bits deep. To address this problem, the TGA specification incorporates a simple, but effective, RLE compression scheme. For more detailed information on Run-length encoding, see Chapter 9, *Data Compression.*

The RLE encoding method used by the TGA format encodes runs of identical pixels rather than runs of identical bits or bytes. This achieves a higher compression ratio over a bit-wise or byte-wise RLE scheme, because TGA pixel data often occurs as multiple byte values rather than single byte values. Therefore, contiguous runs of identical bytes in TGA image data often occur only in very short lengths.

Data encoded using the TGA RLE scheme may contain two types of encoded data packets. The first type is a run-length packet which is used to encode multiple runs of the same pixel value into a single data packet. A run-length packet begins with a single byte used as the pixel count. The value for the lower seven bits of this byte is in the range of 0 to 127 and the count is always one plus this value (1 to 128). There can never be an encoded run-length of zero pixels.

The high bit of the pixel count value is always set to 1 to indicate that this is a run-length encoded packet. Following the pixel count is the pixel data value. This value is the number of bits equal to the Pixel Depth value in the Image Specification section of the header. Because the size of TGA pixels can range from one to four bytes in size, this value varies from between two to five bytes in length, depending upon the type of TGA image data encoded.

The second type of packet is the raw or non-run length encoded packet. When a run of pixel values is too short in length to justify using the run-length packet format, the run is encoded using the raw packet format. Raw packets start with a byte that is used as the pixel count. Just as with the encoded packet, the count value is in the range of 0 to 127, with the actual pixel count being one plus this value (1 to 128). A run length of zero pixels can never be encoded. Raw packets, however, have the high bit of the count byte always set to zero. This differentiates raw packets from encoded packets, in which the high byte is always one. Following the count byte is the number of pixels equal to the count. The number of bytes that follows the raw count is equal to the count value multiplied by the number of bytes per pixel.

The following TGA RLE pseudocode algorithm is used to encode a pixel run using an encoded packet:

    Set counter to zero
    Read a pixel of scan-line data
    Read a second pixel of scan-line data
    If the first pixel is the same as the second pixel
        increment the counter
    Else
        write the counter value (with high bit ON)
        write the pixel value

The following TGA RLE pseudocode algorithm is used to encode a pixel run using a raw packet:

    Set counter to zero
    Read a certain number of pixels of scan-line data
    Increment the counter for each pixel read
    Write the counter value (with high bit OFF)
    Write all pixel values read

Figure TGA-1 shows the RLE packet types for various pixel sizes.

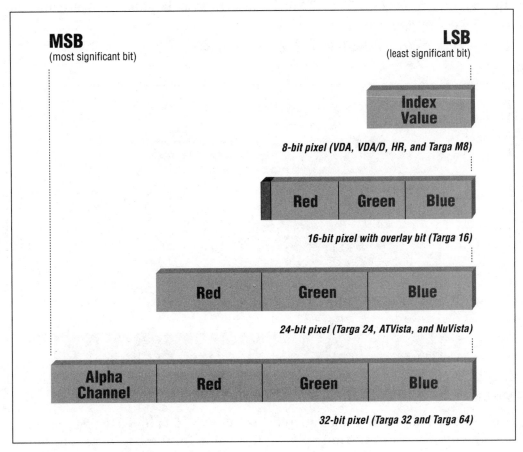

FIGURE TGA-1: *Run-length encoding packet types*

Image Data

Image data is usually found following the header, but may occur after a palette or Image ID field if these are present in the TGA file. For this reason, never read image data from a TGA file without first checking for the presence of palette and Image ID fields. If you do, you will quickly notice that the displayed image is skewed, because the image was read starting at the wrong offset. (See the section called "Color Map" above.)

The size of a TGA image is limited to 65,535 pixels high by 65,535 pixels wide. This is because a 16-bit field is used to store the size of the image in the header. Otherwise, the size of a TGA image would be unlimited. A typical size for Targa

16, 24, and 32 images is 512x482 pixels; the NuVista is 640x480 pixels; and the ATVista is 756x486 pixels.

Figure TGA-2 shows different pixel data formats.

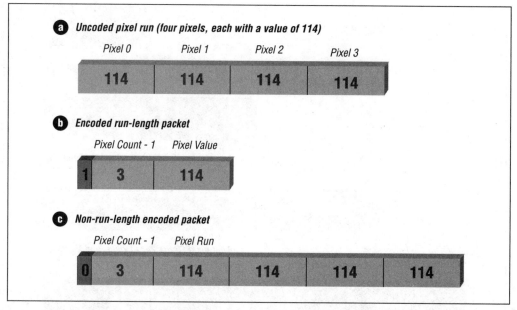

FIGURE TGA-2: *Pixel data formats*

Most of the Truevision display adapters store pixel data in 8-, 16-, 24-, or 32-bit increments. Reading or writing pixel information for these formats is as simple as reading and writing bytes of data. Targa 16-bit pixel data, however, is slightly more complicated, as described below.

When a value of 15 appears in the PixelDepth field of the Image Specification section of the header, there are five bits each of red, green, and blue pixel data and one bit of overlay data in each pixel (see the section below called "Pixel Attribute Bits"). This is the format the Targa 16 uses to store data. Because these 16 bits are stored in two bytes of data, a little shifting and masking is required to read and write these pixel data values.

In the following example, a scan line of unencoded pixel data is stored in the byte array pixeldata[]. The red, green, and blue values are five bits in size, and the overlay attribute is a single bit in size. Data from the first pixel (array elements 0 and 1) are read and stored in the variables defined:

```
/*
** Reading and writing 16-bit pixel data stored
** in an 8-bit BYTE array.  Note that the green
** value is split between two bytes.
*/
BYTE red, green, blue, overlay;
BYTE pixeldata[SCAN_LINE_LENGTH];
/* Read */
red    = (pixeldata[0] & 0xf8) >> 3;
green  = ((pixeldata[0] & 0x07) << 2) | ((pixeldata[1] & 0xfb)
>> 6);
blue   = (pixeldata[1] & 0x3e) >> 1;
overlay =  pixeldata[1] & 0x01;

/* Write */
pixeldata[0] = (red  << 3)            | (pixeldata[0] & 0x07);
pixeldata[0] = ((green & 0x1c) >> 2)  | (pixeldata[0] & 0xf8);
pixeldata[1] = ((green & 0x03) << 6)  | (pixeldata[1] & 0xf8);
pixeldata[1] = (blue << 1)            | (pixeldata[1] & 0xc1);
pixeldata[1] =  overlay               | (pixeldata[1] & 0xfe);

/*
** Reading and writing 16-bit pixel data stored
** in a 16-bit WORD array
*/
BYTE red, green, blue, overlay;
WORD pixeldata[SCAN_LINE_LENGTH];

/* Read */
red     = (pixeldata[0] & 0xfc00) >> 11;
green   = (pixeldata[0] & 0x07e0) >> 6;
blue    = (pixeldata[0] & 0x003f) >> 1;
overlay =  pixeldata[0] & 0x0001;

/* Write */
pixeldata[0] = (red   << 11) | (pixeldata[0] & 0x03ff);
pixeldata[0] = (green << 6)  | (pixeldata[0] & 0xfc1f);
pixeldata[0] = (blue  << 1)  | (pixeldata[0] & 0xffc1);
pixeldata[0] =  overlay      | (pixeldata[0] & 0xfffe);
```

Pixel Attribute Bits

The names of the Targa display adapters include a designation that indicates the number of bits per pixel that they are capable of storing. This seems logical for the Targa 16 and the Targa 24, but the Targa 32 and Targa 64? 32 and 64 bits per pixel? That's correct, but realize that color data is not the only information you can store in a pixel.

Referring back to Figure TGA-1, look at the column labelled "Attribute Bits Per Pixel." This value is the number of bits a pixel may contain that are not directly associated with the color value of the pixel. Bits 0 through 3 of the ImageDescriptor field of the header contains the number of attribute bits per pixel.

In the case of the Targa 16, only 15 of the 16 pixel bits are used for color information. The sixteenth bit, also called the overlay bit, is used to indicate whether the pixel is transparent (invisible) or opaque (visible) when displayed on a video monitor. The ICB board also uses 15 bits per pixel for color information and a single bit for overlay control. The VDA/D board is similar in that it uses five bits per primary color and uses the sixteenth bit for interrupt control. The Targa 32 and the TrueVista boards (ATVista and NuVista) each use 32 bits per pixel. Color information is stored in 24 bits, and the additional eight attribute bits in each pixel are used as an alpha channel value.

Alpha channel is a nondescript name that indicates the degree of transparency of a displayed pixel. Alpha channel and overlay values are used when one image is overlaid onto another image or onto a live video picture. A single overlay bit (as in the Targa 16) can only indicate that the pixel is visible or invisible. Eight bits of precision can vary the visibility of a pixel from completely transparent (0) to completely opaque (255).

The alpha channel value also describes the degree to which a pixel from an image is mixed with a live video source. An alpha value of 0 displays the pixel entirely from the graphical image stored in the frame buffer memory. An alpha value of 255 displays the pixel entirely from the live video source. An alpha value of 84 displays the pixel as 33 percent graphical image (85 of 256) and 67 percent live video (171 of 256). A pixel with an alpha value of 84 appears as a translucent graphical image overlaid on a field of live video.

The ability to control graphical and live video images using 256 alpha channel levels allows the superimposing of graphical text over video, fading into and out of an image, and cross-fading between graphical images and live video. All of these effects can be rendered using the Truevision Targa+ and NuVista+ graphical display boards.

When storing pixel data or pixel size, the attribute bits are always included in any reads, writes, or calculations. Attribute bits are also stored in color maps and lookup tables, although in these cases their values are usually set to zero and ignored.

The New TGA Format

Version 2 adds several features to the original TGA format, which increases the amount of information the TGA format can support. The original TGA format is fairly simple in design, which allows it to be quickly and easily implemented in software. However, it does not contain many features needed by developers—features that are found in several other image file formats. Therefore, extensions have been added to the TGA format to allow the storage of additional image information and to create a customizable area for the storage of developer-specific information.

The extensions added by the new TGA format are called the Developer Area, the Extension Area, and the TGA File Footer. These areas were appended to the original TGA format without making any changes to the TGA file header. Applications that read only original TGA image files should have no problems reading new TGA format files unless the Developer or Extension Areas contain information necessary to read or display the image data properly. For newer applications that support the new TGA format, it is important to correctly interpret as much of the Extension and Developer Area information as possible.

Footer
The footer is 26 bytes in length and is always the last piece of information found in a version 2.0 TGA format file. It contains a total of three fields that are represented in the following structure:

```
typedef struct _TgaFooter
{
  DWORD ExtensionOffset;        /* Extension Area Offse */
  DWORD DeveloperOffset;        /* Developer Directory Offset */
  CHAR Signature[18];           /* TGA Signature */

} TGAFOOT;
```

ExtensionOffset is a 4-byte offset value of the extension area of the TGA file. If this value is zero, then there is no extension area present in the TGA file.

DeveloperOffset is the number of bytes from the beginning of the file (byte 0) to the first byte of the developer directory. If this value is zero, then the TGA file does not contain a developer area.

Signature contains an identifying signature string. The TGA format does not contain a field in the header indicating the version of the format. Instead, version 2.0 includes a footer containing a 16-byte character string that identifies the version of the file.

To determine the version of a TGA file, read the file footer and check bytes 8 through 23 of the footer for the presence of the character string TRUEVISION-XFILE. If this signature string is present, the TGA file is version 2.0 and thus may contain a Developer and Extension area.

Following the signature is the ASCII value 2Eh (period) and the ASCII value 00h (NULL). All of these fields must contain the correct information for the file to be recognized as a version 2.0 TGA format file.

A version 1.0 TGA file may be converted to a version 2.0 TGA file simply by appending a footer with the appropriate signature string, a period, and NULL characters. In this case, you could set the ExtensionOffset and DeveloperOffset to 0. Be cautious about doing this, however. This conversion adds nothing to the functionality of the file unless an Extension or Developer Area is added. It will not, however, interfere with the ability of older, pre-version 2.0 TGA format software to read the file.

Developer Area

The Developer Area begins with a directory that resembles the structure of the Image File Directory found in the TIFF format. The first entry in the directory is the number of directory entries, or tags, that the directory contains. This field is two bytes in size. The offset value of this field is stored in the footer described in the previous section.

Following the number of directory entries is a series of 10-byte tags, one for each entry specified. The structure of a Developer Area tag is as follows:

```
typedef struct _TgaTag
{
    WORD   TagNumber;      /* ID Number of the tag */
    DWORD  DataOffset;     /* Offset location of the tag data */
```

```
    DWORD DataSize;          /* Size of the tag data in bytes */

} TGATAG;
```

TagNumber is the identification number of the tag. Tag number values from 0 to 32767 are reserved for developer use, while tag number values 32768 to 65535 are reserved for use by Truevision only. Tags may be registered with the Truevision Developer Services to assure permanent and exclusive use by your application.

DataOffset contains the offset location of the data in the TGA file. Note that offsets are always calculated from the beginning of the file.

DataSize is the size of the data in bytes.

The tags in the developer directory are always stored as a contiguous block, and the tags do not have to be sorted by tag number. Tags do not indicate the type of data pointed to by the tag (BYTE-, WORD-, or DWORD-oriented data), so an application that is reading tag data is required to have prior knowledge of the type of data the tag points to.

Extension Area

The Extension Area can be thought of as a second header that contains information not found in the original TGA format header. The offset of the Extension Area is stored in the TGA footer. The size of the Extension Area in version 2.0 is 495 bytes. The structure of the Extension Area is as follows:

```
typedef struct _TgaExtension
{
    WORD   Size;                    /* Extension Size              */
    CHAR   AuthorName[41];          /* Author Name                 */
    CHAR   AuthorComment[324];      /* Author Comment              */
    WORD   StampMonth;              /* Date/Time Stamp: Month      */
    WORD   StampDay;                /* Date/Time Stamp: Day        */
    WORD   StampYear;               /* Date/Time Stamp: Year       */
    WORD   StampHour;               /* Date/Time Stamp: Hour       */
    WORD   StampMinute;             /* Date/Time Stamp: Minute     */
    WORD   StampSecond;             /* Date/Time Stamp: Second     */
    CHAR   JobName[41];             /* Job Name/ID                 */
    WORD   JobHour;                 /* Job Time: Hours             */
    WORD   JobMinute;               /* Job Time: Minutes           */
    WORD   JobSecond;               /* Job Time: Seconds           */
    CHAR   SoftwareId[41];          /* Software ID                 */
    WORD   VersionNumber;           /* Software Version Number     */
```

```
    BYTE  VersionLetter;            /* Software Version Letter  */
    DWORD KeyColor;                 /* Key Color                */
    WORD  PixelNumerator;           /* Pixel Aspect Ratio       */
    WORD  PixelDenominator;         /* Pixel Aspect Ratio       */
    WORD  GammaNumerator;           /* Gamma Value              */
    WORD  GammaDenominator;         /* Gamma Value              */
    DWORD ColorOffset;              /* Color Correction Offset  */
    DWORD StampOffset;              /* Postage Stamp Offset     */
    DWORD ScanOffset;               /* Scan-Line Table Offset   */
    BYTE  AttributesType;           /* Attributes Types         */

} TGAEXTEN;
```

Size specifies the number of bytes in the extension area. This value is 495 for version 2.0 of the TGA format.

AuthorName allows the name of the TGA file creator to be stored using up to 40 characters. Unused characters are padded with spaces and the field is NULL-terminated.

AuthorComment is also a string field containing 324 bytes (four 80-character lines) in which to store information. This field is similar to the Image ID field that follows the header. This field is also padded with spaces and is NULL-terminated.

The six Stamp fields contain the time and date the image was created or last modified. These fields may have the following values:

StampMonth	1 to 12
StampDay	1 to 31
StampYear	0000 to 9999
StampHour	0 to 23
StampMinute	0 to 59
StampSecond	0 to 59

Unused fields are set to zero.

JobName is a 4-byte, NULL-terminated string identifying the production job with which the image is associated. JobHour, JobMinute, and JobSecond indicate the amount of time expended on the job.

SoftwareID field is a 40-character, NULL-terminated string that identifies the software application that created the file. The VersionNumber and VersionLetter fields contain the version of the software application.

KeyColor contains the background color of the image. This is the pixel color used to paint the areas of the display screen not covered by the image or the color used to clear the screen if the image is erased. The default value for this field is 0, which corresponds to black.

PixelNumerator and PixelDenominator store the aspect ratio of the pixels used in the image. If no aspect ratio is specified, then these fields are set to 0.

GammaNumerator and GammaDenominator are the gamma correction values to be used when displaying the image. If both fields are 0, then a gamma value is not used.

ColorOffset contains an offset value of the color correction table. If the file does not contain a color correction table, then value of this field is set to 0.

StampOffset field contains an offset value of the postage-stamp image included in the TGA file. If no postage-stamp image is present, the value of this field is 0.

ScanOffset contains the offset value of the scan-line offset table.

AttributesType describes the type of alpha channel data contained within the pixel data. A value of 00h indicates that the image data contains no alpha channel value. A value of 01h, 02, 04h, or 08h indicates the presence of alpha channel data (see the TGA specification for more information on this field).

Scan-line Table, Postage-stamp Image, and Color Correction Table
A new TGA format file may contain three additional data structures not found in the original TGA format. These structures are the scan line table, the postage-stamp image, and the color correction table. There may only be one of each of these data structures per TGA file, and offsets to these structures appear in the Extension Area.

The scan-line table is a method of accessing scan lines at any location within raw or compressed image data. The table is an array of DWORD values. Each value is the offset location from the beginning of the file to the beginning of the corresponding scan line in the image data. There is one entry in the scan-line table per scan line in the image. Entries are written to the table in the order in which the scan lines appear within the image.

The postage-stamp image is a smaller rendering of the primary image stored within the TGA file. The first byte of the postage-stamp data specifies the width of the stamp in pixels, and the second byte specifies the height, also in pixels.

Postage stamps should not be larger than 64x64 pixels, are typically stored in the same format as the primary image, and are never compressed.

The color correction table is an array 1000 bytes in length, which contains 256 entries used to store values used for color remapping. The entire table has the following format:

```
typedef struct _TGAColorCorrectionTable
{
   SHORT Alpha;
   SHORT Red;
   SHORT Green;
   SHORT Blue;

} TGACCT[256];
```

The fields Alpha, Red, Green, and Blue store the color values for each entry. The range of each value is 0 to 65535. Black is 0,0,0,0, and white is 65535,65535,65535,65535.

For Further Information

For further information about the TGA format, see the specification and code example included on the CD-ROM that accompanies this book.

The TGA format is maintained by Truevision Inc. Sometime prior to this writing Truevision was acquired by RasterOps, Inc., but for the time being Truevision remains an independent subsidiary. Copies of the latest TGA specification, including a sample code disk, may be obtained directly from Truevision:

Truevision Incorporated
7340 Shadeland Station
Indianapolis, IN 46256-3925
Voice: 317-841-0332
FAX: 317-576-7700
BBS: 317-577-8783

NAME:	TIFF
ALSO KNOWN AS:	Tag Image File Format
TYPE:	Bitmap
COLORS:	1- to 24-bit
COMPRESSION:	Uncompressed, RLE, LZW, CCITT Group 3 and Group 4, JPEG
MAXIMUM IMAGE SIZE:	$2^{32}-1$
MULTIPLE IMAGES PER FILE:	Yes
NUMERICAL FORMAT:	See article for discussion
ORIGINATOR:	Aldus
PLATFORMS:	MS-DOS, Macintosh, UNIX, others
SUPPORTING APPLICATIONS:	Most paint, imaging, and desktop-publishing programs
SPECIFICATION ON CD:	Yes
CODE ON CD:	Yes
IMAGES ON CD:	Yes
SEE ALSO:	Chapter 9, *Data Compression* (RLE, LZW, CCITT, and JPEG)

USAGE: Used for data storage and interchange. The general nature of TIFF allows it to be used in any operating environment, and it is found on most platforms requiring image data storage.

COMMENTS: The TIFF format is perhaps the most versatile and diverse bitmap format in existence. Its extensible nature and support for numerous data compression schemes allows developers to customize the TIFF format to fit any peculiar data storage needs.

Overview

The TIFF specification was originally released in 1986 by Aldus Corporation as a standard method of storing black-and-white images created by scanners and desktop publishing applications. This first public release of TIFF was the third major revision of the TIFF format, and although it was not assigned a specific version number, this release may be thought of as TIFF Revision 3.0. The first widely used revision of TIFF, 4.0, was released in April 1987. TIFF 4.0 added support for uncompressed RGB color images and was quickly followed by the release of TIFF Revision 5.0 in August 1988. TIFF 5.0 was the first revision to add the capability of storing palette color images and support for the LZW compression algorithm. TIFF 6.0 was released in June 1992 and added support for CMYK and YCbCr color images and the JPEG compression method. (See the section called "Color" in Chapter 2, *Computer Graphics Basics*, for a discussion of these color images. See Chapter 9, *Data Compression*, for a discussion of JPEG compression.)

Today, TIFF is a standard file format found in most paint, imaging, and desktop publishing programs and is a format native to the Microsoft Windows GUI. TIFF's extensible nature, allowing storage of multiple bitmap images of any pixel depth, makes it ideal for most image storage needs.

The majority of the description in this chapter covers the current TIFF revision 6.0. Because each successive TIFF revision is built upon the previous revision, most of the information present in this chapter also pertains to TIFF Revision 5.0 as well. And, although there are currently more images stored in the TIFF 5.0 format than any other revision of TIFF, there are still quite a few TIFF 4.0 image files in existence. For this reason, information is also included that details the differences between the TIFF 4.0, 5.0, and 6.0 revisions.

TIFF has garnered a reputation for power and flexibility, but it is considered complicated and mysterious as well. In its design, TIFF attempts to be very extensible and provide many features that a programmer might need in a file format. Because TIFF is so extensible and has many capabilities beyond all other image file formats, this format is probably the most confusing format to understand and use.

A common misconception about TIFF is that TIFF files are not very portable between software applications. This is amazing considering that TIFF is widely used as an image data interchange format. Complaints include, "I've downloaded a number of TIFF clip-art packages from some BBSs and my paint program or word processor is able to display only some of the TIFF image files, but not all of them," "When I try to display certain TIFF files using my favorite image display program, I get the error message 'Unknown Tag Type' or 'Unsupported Compression Type'," and "I have a TIFF file created by one application and a second application on the same machine cannot read or display the image, even though TIFF files created by the second application can be read and displayed by the first application."

These complaints are almost always immediately blamed on the TIFF image files themselves. The files are labeled as "bad," because they have been munged during a data-file transfer or were exported by software applications that did not know how to properly write a TIFF file. In reality, most TIFF files that do not import or display properly are not bad, and the fault usually lies, instead, with the program that is reading the TIFF file.

If an application only uses black-and-white images, it certainly does not need to support the reading and writing of color and gray-scale TIFF image files. In this case, the application should simply, and politely, refuse to read non-black-and-white TIFF image files and tell you the reason why. By doing this, the application would prevent the user from trying to read unusable image data and would also cut down on the amount of TIFF code the application programmers need to write.

Some applications that read TIFF image files—or any type of image files, for that matter—may just return an ambiguous error code indicating that the file could not be read and may leave the user with the impression that the TIFF file itself is bad (not that the application could not use the image data the TIFF file contained). Such an occurrence is the fault of the application designer in not providing a clearer message informing the user what has happened.

Sometimes, however, you may have an application that should be able to read a TIFF file, and it does not, even though the type of image data contained in the TIFF file is supported by the application. There are numerous reasons why a perfectly good TIFF file cannot be read by an application, and most of them have to do with the application programmer's lack of understanding of the TIFF format itself.

A major source of TIFF reader problems is the inability to read data regardless of byte-ordering scheme. The bytes in a 16-bit and 32-bit word of data are stored in a different order on little-endian architectures (such as the Intel iAPX86), than on big-endian machines (such as the Motorola MC68000A). Reading big-endian data using the little-endian format results in little more than garbage.

Another major source of problems is readers that do not support the encoding algorithm used to compress the image data. Most readers support both raw (uncompressed) and RLE-encoded data, but do not support CCITT T.4 and T.6 compression. It is also surprising how many TIFF readers support the reading of color TIFF files, which are either stored as raw or RLE-compressed data, but do not support the decompression of LZW-encoded data.

Most other TIFF reader problems are quite minor, but usually fatal. Such problems include failure to correctly interpret tag data, no support for colormapped images, or the inability to read a bitmap scan line that contains an odd number of bytes.

File Organization

TIFF files are organized into three sections: the Image File Header (IFH), the Image File Directory (IFD), and the bitmap data. Of these three sections, only the IFH and IFD are required. It is therefore quite possible to have a TIFF file which contains no bitmapped data at all, although such a file would be highly unusual. A TIFF file which contains multiple images has one IFD and one bitmap per image stored.

TIFF has a reputation for being a complicated format in part because the location of each Image File Directory and the data the IFD points to—including the bitmapped data—may vary. In fact, the only part of a TIFF file that has a fixed location is the Image File Header, which is always the first eight bytes of every TIFF file. All other data in a TIFF file is found by using information found in the IFD. Each IFD and its associated bitmap are known as a TIFF *subfile*. There is no limit to the number of subfiles a TIFF image file may contain.

Each IFD contains one or more data structures called *tags*. Each tag is a 12-byte record that contains a specific piece of information about the bitmapped data. A tag may contain any type of data, and the TIFF specification defines over 70 tags that are used to represent specific information. Tags are always found in contiguous groups within each IFD.

Tags that are defined by the TIFF specification are called *public tags* and may not be modified outside of the parameters given in the latest TIFF specification. User-definable tags, called *private tags*, are assigned for proprietary use by software developers through the Aldus Developer's Desk. See the TIFF 6.0 specification for more information on private tags.

Note that the TIFF 6.0 specification has replaced the term *tag* with the term *field*. Field now refers to the entire 12-byte data record, while the term tag has been redefined to refer only to a field's identifying number. Because so many programmers are familiar with the older definition of the term tag, the authors have choosen to continue using tag, rather than field, in this description of TIFF to avoid confusion.

Figure TIFF-1 shows three possible arrangements of the internal data structure of a TIFF file containing three images. In each example, the IFH appears first in the TIFF file. In the first example, each of the IFDs has been written to the file first and the bitmaps last. This arrangement is the most efficient for reading IFD data quickly. In the second example, each IFD is written, followed by its bitmapped data. This is perhaps the most common internal format of a multi-image TIFF file. In the last example, we see that the bitmapped data has been written first, followed by the IFDs. This seemingly unusual arrangement might occur if the bitmapped data is available to be written before the information that appears in the IFDs.

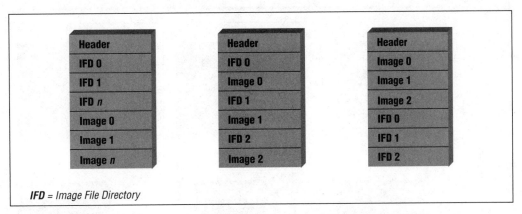

Each IFD is a road map of where all the data associated with a bitmap can be found within a TIFF file. The data is found by reading it directly from within the IFD data structure or by retrieving it from an offset location whose value is stored in the IFD. Because TIFF's internal components are linked together by offset values rather than by fixed positions, as with stream-oriented image file formats, programs that read and write TIFF files are often very complex, thus giving TIFF its reputation.

The offset values used in a TIFF file are found in three locations. The first offset value is found in the last four bytes of the header and indicates the position of the first IFD. The last four bytes of each IFD is an offset value to the next IFD. And the last four bytes of each tag may contain an offset value to the data it represents, or possibly the data itself.

NOTE

Offsets are always interpreted as a number of bytes from the beginning of the TIFF file.

Figure TIFF-2 shows the way data structures of a TIFF file are linked together.

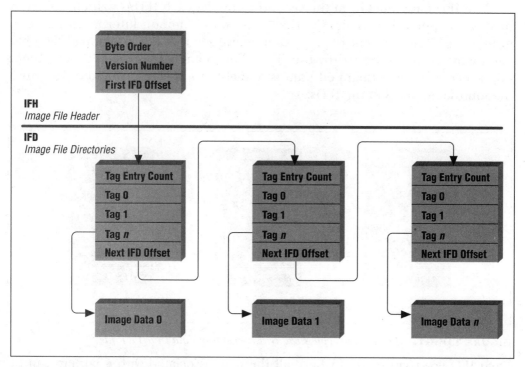

FIGURE TIFF-2: *Logical organization of a TIFF file*

File Details

This section describes the various components of a TIFF file.

Image File Header

TIFF, despite its complexity, has the simplest header of all of the formats described in this book. The TIFF Image File Header (IFH) contains three fields of information and is a total of only eight bytes in length:

```
typedef struct _TiffHeader
{
    WORD  Identifier;  /* Byte-order Identifier */
    WORD  Version;     /* TIFF version number (always 2Ah) */
    DWORD IFDOffset;   /* Offset of the first Image File Directory*/

} TIFHEAD;
```

Identifier contains either the value 4949h (II) or 4D4Dh (MM). These values indicate whether the data in the TIFF file is written in little-endian (Intel-format) or big-endian (Motorola-format) order, respectively. All data encountered past the first two bytes in the file obey the byte-ordering scheme indicated by this field. These two values were chosen because they would always be the same, regardless of the byte order of the file.

Version, according to the TIFF specification, contains the version number of the TIFF format. This version number is always 42, regardless of the TIFF revision, so it may be regarded more as an identification number, (or possibly the answer to life, the universe, etc.) than a version number.

A quick way to check whether a file is indeed a TIFF file is to read the first four bytes of the file. If they are:

```
49h 49h 2Ah 00h
```

or:

```
4Dh 4Dh 00h 2Ah
```

then it's a good bet that you have a TIFF file.

IFDOffset is a 32-bit value that is the offset position of the first Image File Directory in the TIFF file. This value may be passed as a parameter to a file seek function to find the start of the image file information. If the Image File Directory occurs immediately after the header, the value of the IFDOffset field is 08h.

Image File Directory

An Image File Directory (IFD) is a collection of information similar to a header, and it is used to describe the bitmapped data to which it is attached. Like a header, it contains information on the height, width, and depth of the image, the number of color planes, and the type of data compression used on the bitmapped data. Unlike a typical fixed header, however, an IFD is dynamic and may not only vary in size, but also may be found anywhere within the TIFF file. There may be more than one IFD contained within any file. The format of an Image File Directory is shown in Figure TIFF-3.

One of the misconceptions about TIFF is that the information stored in the Image File Directory tags is actually part of the TIFF header. In fact, this information is often referred to as the "TIFF Header Information." While it is true that other formats do store the type of information found in the IFD in the header, the TIFF header does not contain this information, although it is possible to think of the IFDs in a TIFF file as extensions of the TIFF file header.

A TIFF file may contain any number of images, from zero on up. Each image is considered to be a separate *subfile,* that is a bitmap, and has an IFD describing the bitmapped data. Each TIFF subfile can be written as a separate TIFF file or can be stored with other subfiles in a single TIFF file. Each subfile bitmap and IFD may reside anywhere in the TIFF file after the headers, and there may be only one IFD per image.

This may sound confusing, but it's not really. We have seen that the TIFF header contains an offset value that points to the location of the first IFD in the TIFF file. To find the first IFD, all we need do is seek to this offset and start reading the IFD information. The last field of every IFD contains an offset value to the next IFD, if any. If the offset value of any IFD is 00h, then there are no more images left to read in the TIFF file.

An IFD may vary in size, because it may contain a variable number of data records, called *tags.* Each tag contains a unique piece of information, just as fields do within a header. However, there is a difference. Tags may be added and deleted from an IFD much the same way that notebook paper may be added to or removed from a 3-ring binder. The fields of a conventional header, on the other hand, are fixed and unmovable, much like the pages of this book. Also, the number of tags found in an IFD may vary, while the number of fields in a type header is fixed.

The format of an Image File Directory is shown in the following structure:

```
typedef struct _TifIfd
{
    WORD    NumDirEntries;    /* Number of Tags in IFD  */
    TIFTAG  TagList[];        /* Array of Tags  */
    DWORD   NextIFDOffset;    /* Offset to next IFD  */

} TIFIFD;
```

NumDirEntries is a 2-byte value indicating the number of tags found in the IFD. Following this field is a series of tags; the number of tags corresponds to the value of the NumDirEntries field. Each tag structure is 12 bytes in size and in the sample code above is represented by an array of structures of the data type definition TIFTAG. (See the next section for more information on TIFF tags.) The number of tags per IFD is limited to 65,535.

NextIFDOffset contains the offset position of the beginning of the next IFD. If there are no more IFDs, then the value of this field is 00h.

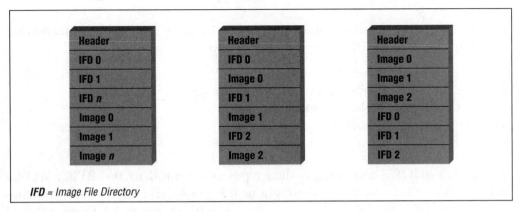

IFD = Image File Directory

FIGURE TIFF-3: *Format of an Image File Directory*

Tags

As mentioned in the previous section, a tag can be thought of as a data field in a file header. However, whereas a header data field may only contain data of a fixed size and is normally located only at a fixed position within a file header, a tag may contain, or point to, data that is any number of bytes in size and is located anywhere within an IFD.

The versatility of the TIFF tag pays a price in its size. A header field used to hold a byte of data need only be a byte in size. A tag containing one byte of information, however, must always be twelve bytes in size.

A TIFF tag has the following 12-byte structure:

```
typedef struct _TifTag
{
    WORD    TagId;        /* The tag identifier   */
    WORD    DataType;     /* The scalar type of the data items   */
    DWORD   DataCount;    /* The number of items in the tag data   */
    DWORD   DataOffset;   /* The byte offset to the data items   */

} TIFTAG;
```

TagId is a numerical value identifying the type of information the tag contains. More specifically, the TagId indicates what the tag information represents. Typical information found in every TIFF file includes the height and width of the image, the depth of each pixel, and the type of data encoding used to compress the bitmap. Tags are normally identified by their TagId value and should always be written to an IFD in ascending order of the values found in the TagId field.

DataType contains a value indicating the scalar data type of the information found in the tag. The following values are supported:

1	BYTE	8-bit unsigned integer
2	ASCII	8-bit, NULL-terminated string
3	SHORT	16-bit unsigned integer
4	LONG	32-bit unsigned integer
5	RATIONAL	Two 32-bit unsigned integers

The BYTE, SHORT, and LONG data types correspond to the BYTE, WORD and DWORD data types used throughout this book. The ASCII data type contains strings of 7-bit ASCII character data, which are always NULL-terminated and may be padded out to an even length if necessary. The RATIONAL data type is actually two LONG values and is used to store the two components of a fractional value. The first value stores the numerator, and the second value stores the denominator.

The TIFF 6.0 revision added the following new data types:

6	SBYTE	8-bit signed integer
7	UNDEFINE	8-bit byte
8	SSHORT	16-bit signed integer
9	SLONG	32-bit signed integer
10	SRATIONAL	Two 32-bit signed integers
11	FLOAT	4-byte single-precision IEEE floating-point value
12	DOUBLE	8-byte double-precision IEEE floating-point value

The SBYTE, SSHORT, SLONG, and SRATIONAL data types are used to store signed values. The FLOAT and DOUBLE data types are used specifically to store IEEE-format single- and double-precision values. The UNDEFINE data type is an 8-bit byte that may contain untyped or opaque data and is typically used in private tags. An example of the use of this data type is to store an entire data structure within a private tag specifying the DataType as UNDEFINE (value of 7) and a DataCount equal to the number of bytes in the structure.

With the exception of the SMinSampleValue and SMaxSampleValue tags (which may use any data type), none of these newer data types is used by any TIFF 6.0 tags. They are therefore found only in private tags.

DataCount indicates the number of items referenced by the tag and doesn't show the actual size of the data itself. Therefore, a DataCount of 08h does not necessarily indicate that eight bytes of data exist in the tag. This value indicates that eight items exist for the data type specified by this tag. For example, a DataCount value of 08h and a DataType of 03h indicate that the tag data is eight contiguous 16-bit unsigned integers, a total of 32 bytes in size. A DataCount of 28h and a DataType of 02h indicate an ASCII character string 40 bytes in length, including the NULL terminator character, but not any padding if present. And a DataCount of 01h and a DataType of 05h indicate a single RATIONAL value a total of eight bytes in size.

DataOffset is a 4-byte field that contains the offset location of the actual tag data within the TIFF file. If the tag data is four bytes or less in size, the data may be found in this field. If the tag data is greater than four bytes in size, then this field contains an offset to the position of the data in the TIFF file. Packing data within the DataOffset field is an optimization within the TIFF specification and is not required to be performed. Most data is typically stored outside the tag, occurring before or after the IFD (see Figure TIFF-3).

Table TIFF-1 lists all of the public tags included in the TIFF 4.0, 5.0, and 6.0 specifications. Note that some tags have become obsolete and are not found in the current revision of TIFF; however, we provide them because the TIFF 4.0 and TIFF 5.0 specs are still in some use. Also, note that several tags may support more than one data type.

In the table below, an asterisk (*) means that the tag is defined, a hyphen (-) means that the tag is not defined and an "x" means that the tag is obsolete.

TABLE TIFF-1: *TIFF Tag Types Arranged Alphabetically by Name*

Tag Name	Tag ID	Tag Type	4.0	5.0	6.0
Artist	315	ASCII	-	*	*
BadFaxLines	326	SHORT or LONG	-	-	-
BitsPerSample	258	SHORT	*	*	*
CellLength	265	SHORT	*	*	*
CellWidth	264	SHORT	*	*	*
CleanFaxData	327	SHORT	-	-	-
ConsecutiveBadFaxLines	328	LONG or SHORT	-	-	-
ColorMap	320	SHORT	-	*	*
ColorResponseCurve	301	SHORT	*	*	x
ColorResponseUnit	300	SHORT	*	x	x

Compression	259	SHORT	*	*	*
Uncompressed	1		*	*	*
CCITT 1D	2		*	*	*
CCITT Group 3	3		*	*	*
CCITT Group 4	4		*	*	*
LZW	5		-	*	*
JPEG	6		-	-	*
Uncompressed	32771		*	x	x
Packbits	32773		*	*	*
Copyright	33432	ASCII	-	-	*
DateTime	306	ASCII	-	*	*
DocumentName	269	ASCII	*	*	*
DotRange	336	BYTE or SHORT	-	-	*
ExtraSamples	338	BYTE	-	-	*
FillOrder	266	SHORT	*	*	*
FreeByteCounts	289	LONG	*	*	*
FreeOffsets	288	LONG	*	*	*
GrayResponseCurve	291	SHORT	*	*	*
GrayResponseUnit	290	SHORT	*	*	*
HalftoneHints	321	SHORT	-	-	*
HostComputer	316	ASCII	-	*	*
ImageDescription	270	ASCII	*	*	*
ImageHeight	257	SHORT or LONG	*	*	*
ImageWidth	256	SHORT or LONG	*	*	*
InkNames	333	ASCII	-	-	*
InkSet	332	SHORT	-	-	*
JPEGACTTables	521	LONG	-	-	*
JPEGDCTTables	520	LONG	-	-	*
JPEGInterchangeFormat	513	LONG	-	-	*
JPEGInterchangeFormatLength	514	LONG	-	-	*
JPEGLosslessPredictors	517	SHORT	-	-	*
JPEGPointTransforms	518	SHORT	-	-	*
JPEGProc	512	SHORT	-	-	*
JPEGRestartInterval	515	SHORT	-	-	*
JPEGQTables	519	LONG	-	-	*
Make	271	ASCII	*	*	*
MaxSampleValue	281	SHORT	*	*	*
MinSampleValue	280	SHORT	*	*	*
Model	272	ASCII	*	*	*
NewSubFileType	254	LONG	-	*	*
NumberOfInks	334	SHORT	-	-	*
Orientation	274	SHORT	*	*	*

PageName	285	ASCII	*	*	*
PageNumber	297	SHORT	*	*	*
PhotometricInterpretation	262	SHORT	*	*	*
WhiteIsZero	0		*	*	*
BlackIsZero	1		*	*	*
RGB	2		*	*	*
RGB Palette	3		-	*	*
Tranparency Mask	4		-	-	*
CMYK	5		-	-	*
YCbCr	6		-	-	*
CIELab	8		-	-	*
PlanarConfiguration	284	SHORT	*	*	*
Predictor	317	SHORT	-	*	*
PrimaryChromaticities	319	RATIONAL	-	*	*
ReferenceBlackWhite	532	LONG	-	-	*
ResolutionUnit	296	SHORT	*	*	*
RowsPerStrip	278	SHORT or LONG	*	*	*
SampleFormat	339	SHORT	-	-	*
SamplesPerPixel	277	SHORT	*	*	*
SMaxSampleValue	341	Any	-	-	*
SMinSampleValue	340	Any	-	-	*
Software	305	ASCII	-	*	*
StripByteCounts	279	LONG or SHORT	*	*	*
StripOffsets	273	SHORT or LONG	*	*	*
SubFileType	255	SHORT	*	x	x
T4Options	292	LONG	*	*	*
T6Options	293	LONG	*	*	*
TargetPrinter	337	ASCII	-	-	*
Thresholding	263	SHORT	*	*	*
TileByteCounts	325	SHORT or LONG	-	-	*
TileLength	323	SHORT or LONG	-	-	*
TileOffsets	324	LONG	-	-	*
TileWidth	322	SHORT or LONG	-	-	*
TransferFunction	301	SHORT	-	-	*
TransferRange	342	SHORT	-	-	*
XPosition	286	RATIONAL	*	*	*
XResolution	282	RATIONAL	*	*	*
YCbCrCoefficients	529	RATIONAL	-	-	*
YCbCrPositioning	531	SHORT	-	-	*
YCbCrSubSampling	530	SHORT	-	-	*
YPosition	287	RATIONAL	*	*	*
YResolution	283	RATIONAL	*	*	*

TIFF (cont'd)

| WhitePoint | 318 | RATIONAL | - | * | * |

Notes:

Tag 292 was renamed from Group3Options to T4Options in TIFF 6.0.

Tag 293 was renamed from Group3Options to T6Options by TIFF 6.0.

The name of tag 301 was renamed from ColorResponseCurve to TransferFunction by TIFF 6.0.

Tags BadFaxLines, CleanFaxData, and ConsecutiveBadFaxLines are part of TIFF Class F now maintained by Aldus and are not actually defined by the TIFF 6.0 specification.

Organization of TIFF Tag Data

To keep developers from having to guess which tags should be written to a TIFF file and what tags are important to read, the TIFF specification defines the concept of baseline TIFF images. These baselines are defined by the type of image data they store: bilevel, gray-scale, palette-color, and full-color. Each baseline has a minimum set of tags, which are required to appear in each type of TIFF file.

In the TIFF 5.0 specification, these baselines were referred to as TIFF classes. Each TIFF file consisted of a common baseline (Class X) and was modified by an additional class depending upon the type of image data stored. The classes were Class B (bilevel), Class G (gray-scale), Class P (palette-color), and Class R (full-color RGB).

The TIFF 6.0 specification redefines these classes into four separate baseline TIFF file configurations. Class X is combined with each of the other four classes to form the bilevel, gray-scale, color-palette, and full-color baselines. Although TIFF 6.0 largely does away with the concept of TIFF classes, it is likely that because more TIFF 5.0-format files exist than any other, TIFF files will be referred to by these class designations for many years to come.

It is worth mentioning that a de facto TIFF class, Class F, exists specifically for the storage of facsimile images using the TIFF format. This class of TIFF file, created by Cygnet Technologies, is used by Everex products to store facsimile data, and is also known as the Everex Fax File Format. Although Cygnet Technologies is no longer in business, TIFF Class F remains in use and is considered by some to be an excellent storage format for facsimile data.

Table TIFF-2 lists the minimum required tags that must appear in the IFD of each TIFF 6.0 baseline. Note that several of these tags have default values which are used if the tag does not actually appear in a TIFF file:

- Bilevel (formerly Class B) and gray-scale (formerly Class G) TIFF files must contain the thirteen tags listed. These tags must appear in all revision 5.0 and 6.0 TIFF files regardless of the type of image data stored.

- Palette-color (formerly Class P) TIFF files add a fourteenth required tag that describes the type of palette information found within the TIFF image file.

- RGB (formerly Class R) TIFF files contain the same tags as bilevel TIFF files and add a fourteenth required tag, which describes the format of the bitmapped data in the image.

- YCbCr TIFF files add four additional tags to the baseline.

- Class F TIFF files add three tags.

TABLE TIFF-2: *Minimum Required Tags for Each TIFF Class*

Class Name	Tag Type	Tag Name
Bilevel and	254	NewSubfileType
Gray-scale	256	ImageWidth
	257	ImageLength
	258	BitsPerSample
	259	Compression
	262	PhotometricInterpretation
	273	StripOffsets
	277	SamplesPerPixel
	278	RowsPerStrip
	279	StripByteCounts
	282	XResolution
	283	YResolution
	296	ResolutionUnit

The following classes contain the above 13 tags plus the following tags:

Palette-color	320	ColorMap
RGB	284	PlanarConfiguration
YCbCr	529	YCbCrCoefficients
	530	YCbCrSubSampling
	531	YCbCrPositioning
	532	ReferenceBlackWhite

Class F	326	BadFaxLines
	327	CleanFaxData
	328	ConsecutiveBadFaxLines

All other tags found in the TIFF specification are available to meet developer's needs. While a TIFF reader must be able to support the parsing and interpretation of all tags it considers necessary, it is certainly not necessary for a TIFF writer to include as many tags as possible in every TIFF file written.

Image Data

TIFF files contain only bitmap data, although adding a few tags to support vector or text-based images would not be a hard thing to do. As we have seen, the bitmapped data in a TIFF file does not always appear immediately after the image header, as with most other formats. Instead, it may appear almost anywhere within the TIFF file. And, because the majority of the work performed by a TIFF reader and writer is the creation and manipulation of the image data, a thorough understanding of how the image data is stored within a TIFF file is necessary, starting with the concept of *strips*.

NOTE

TIFF 6.0 images may contain tiles rather than strips.

Strips

It is always amusing to come across a TIFF reader or viewer whose author posts the caveat in the source code "This TIFF reader does not support striped images." A large proportion of TIFF readers that fail to read certain TIFF image files do so because the author of the reader did not quite understand the concept of how image data can be organized within a TIFF file. In this case, not only did the author of the reader fail to understand how to write code to read strips, he or she also failed to realize that every TIFF 5.0 (and earlier) image contains strips.

A strip is an individual collection of one or more contiguous rows of bitmapped image data. Dividing the image data into strips makes buffering, random access, and interleaving of the image data much easier. This concept exists in several other image file formats, and is given names such as *blocks*, *bands*, and *chunks*. TIFF strips differ from other such concepts in several important ways due to the structure of the TIFF format.

Three tags are necessary to define the strips of bitmapped data within a TIFF file. These three tags are RowsPerStrip, StripOffsets, and StripByteCounts.

The first required tag, RowsPerStrip, indicates the number of rows of compressed, bitmapped data found in each strip. The default value for RowsPerStrip is 2^32-1, which is the maximum possible size of a TIFF image. All of the strips in a TIFF subfile must use the same compression scheme and have the same bit sex, color sex, pixel depth, and so on. To find the number of strips in a non-YCbCr subfile image, we would use the RowsPerStrip tag, the Image-Length tag, and the following calculation:

```
StripsInImage =
    floor((ImageLength * (RowsPerStrip - 1)) / RowsPerStrip);
```

The second required tag, StripOffsets, is important because without it a TIFF reader has absolutely no hope of locating the image data within a TIFF file. This tag contains an array of offset values, one per strip, which indicate the position of the first byte of each strip within the TIFF file. The first value in the array is for the first strip, the second value for the second strip, and so on. If the image data is separated into planes (PlanarConfiguration = 2), StripOffsets contains a two-dimensional array of values which is SamplesPerPixel in width. All of the columns for color component (plane) 0 are stored first, followed by all the columns for color component (plane) 1, and so forth. The strips of planar image data may be written to the TIFF file in any order, but are typically by plane (RRRRGGGGBBBB) or by color component (RGBRGBRGBRGB). StripOffsets values are always interpreted from the beginning of the file.

The StripOffsets tag allows each strip in a TIFF file to have a completely independent location from all other strips in the same subfile. This means that strips may occur in any order and be found anywhere within the TIFF file. Many "quick and dirty" TIFF readers find the beginning of the first strip and then attempt to read in the image data as one large chunk without checking the StripOffset array for the position of each additional strip. This technique works if all the strips in the TIFF file are contiguously written to the TIFF file and are in the same consecutive order as the original rows in the bitmap. If the strips are stored out of sequence, perhaps in a planar or interlaced fashion, or are aligned on paragraph or page boundaries, the image data read will not be in its proper order, and the image will appear sliced up and rearranged on the display. If the strips are stored in a fairly random fashion, a large part of the data read might not be part of the image, or even the TIFF file itself. In this case, anything that is displayed would be mostly garbage.

The value of the RowsPerStrip tag and the size of each element in the array of the StripOffsets tag is usually a LONG (32-bit) value. TIFF 5.0 added the ability of this tag to use SHORT (16-bit) values instead. Very old TIFF readers may expect the values in this tag to always be LONG and will therefore read the offset values improperly if they are SHORT. This modification was made primarily for TIFF readers that read the StripOffsets values into an array in memory before using them. The TIFF 6.0 specification suggests that the offset values should not require such an array to be larger than 64K in size.

The third tag, StripByteCounts, maintains an array of values that indicates the size of each strip in bytes. And, like the StripOffsets tag, this tag is also an array of values, one per strip, one-dimensional for chunky format and two-dimensional for planar format, each of which is calculated from the number of bytes of compressed bitmapped data stored in each strip.

This tag is necessary because there are several cases in which the strips in an image may each contain a different number of bytes. The first case occurs when using compressed bitmapped image data. As we have said, the Strip-BytesCounts value is the size of the image data *after* it is compressed. Although there is a fixed number of bytes in an uncompressed row, the size of a compressed row varies depending upon the data it contains. Because we are always storing a fixed number of rows, not bytes, per strip, it is likely that most strips will be of different lengths because each compressed row will vary in size. Only when the bitmap data is not compressed will each strip be the same size.

Well, almost.... The last strip in an image is sometimes an exception. TIFF writers typically attempt to create strips so that each strip in a TIFF image has the same number of rows. For example, a bitmap with 2200 rows can be divided into 22 strips, each containing 100 rows of bitmapped data. However, it is not always possible to divide the number of rows equally among the desired number of strips. For example, if we needed to divide a bitmap containing 482 rows into strips containing five rows each, we would end up with a total of 97 strips, 96 strips containing five rows of data and the 97th strip containing the remaining two rows. The RowsPerStrip tag value of 5 would be correct for all strip lengths except for the last strip.

The truth is that a TIFF reader does not need to know the number of rows in each strip to read the image data, only the number of bytes. Otherwise, the TIFF specification would require that every "short" strip be padded with additional rows of dummy data, but it doesn't. Instead, we simply read the last StripByteCounts value to determine how many bytes to read for the last strip. What the TIFF specification doesn't make clear is that the RowsPerStrip value specifies the *maximum* value, and not the required value, of the number of rows per strip. Many TIFF files, in fact, store a single strip of data and specify an arbitrarily large RowsPerStrip value.

There are several advantages to organizing bitmap data in strips.

First, not all applications can read an entire file into memory. Many desktop machines still have only one megabyte or less of memory available to them. And even if a system has gobs of memory, there is no guarantee that a TIFF reader will be able to use it. Such a TIFF reader can allocate the largest buffer it can manage and then read in the bitmapped data one strip at a time until the buffer is filled. If the image is panned or scrolled, data in the buffer can be discarded and more strips read in. If the entire image can fit in memory, all the strips in the TIFF file would then be read.

Because compressed strips can vary in size, the StripByteCounts values cannot be accurately used by an application to dynamically allocate a buffer in memory (unless every value is read and the largest value is used to allocate the buffer). Therefore, it is recommended that each strip be limited to about 8K in size. If a TIFF reader can allocate a much larger buffer than 8K, then multiple strips may be read into the buffer. Although TIFF strips can be larger, perhaps to support an image where each compressed or uncompressed row is greater than 8K in size, the size of a strip should never exceed 64K. Allocating a buffer greater than 64K can be a bit tricky when using certain system architectures.

Second, having access to a table of strip offsets makes random access of the bitmapped data easier. If a TIFF reader needed to display the last 100 rows of a 480-row image, and the bitmaps were divided into 48 strips of 10 rows each, the reader would skip over the first 380 rows and read in the strips stored at the last 10 offsets in the StripOffsets tag array. If no strip offsets were present, the entire image would need to be read to find the starting position of the last 100 rows.

And while it is possible that the bitmap in a TIFF file may be written out as one long strip—and many TIFF files are written this way—it is not a good idea to do so. These so-called unstripped images often fail because an application must attempt to allocate enough memory to hold the entire image. For large images, or small systems, enough memory may not be available to do so. One can only hope that a TIFF file reader would exit from such a situation gracefully.

Tiles

Strips are not the only possible way to organize bitmapped data. TIFF 6.0 introduced the concept of *tiled*, rather than stripped, bitmapped data. A strip is a one-dimensional object that only has a length. A tile can be thought of as a two-dimensional strip that has both width and length, very similar to a bitmap. In fact, you can think of each tile in an image as a small bitmap containing a piece of a larger bitmap. All you need to do is fit the tiles together in their proper locations to get the image. (This concept only serves to remind me that I must replace the linoleum in my bathroom one day.)

Dividing an image into rectangular tiles rather than horizontal strips has the greatest benefit on very large high-resolution images. Many Electronic Document Imaging applications cannot manipulate images larger than E size (6848 pixels wide by 8800 pixels long) because of the large amount of memory required to buffer, decompress, and manipulate even a few hundred rows of image data. Even if you just wanted to display the upper-left corner of an image you would still be forced to decompress the entire strip and maintain it in memory. If the image data were tiled, however, you would only decompress the tiles that contained the image data for the part of the image you wanted to display.

Many compression algorithms, such as JPEG, compress data not as one-dimensional strips, but instead as two-dimensional tiles. Storing the compressed data as tiles optimizes the decompression of the data quite a bit. In fact, the support of two-dimensional compression algorithms is perhaps the primary reason why the capability of tiling image data was added to TIFF 6.0.

When tiles are used instead of strips, the three strip tags, RowsPerStrip, StripByteCounts, and StripOffsets, are replaced by the tags TileWidth, TileLength, TileOffsets, and TileByteCounts. As you might have guessed, the tile tags are used in much the same way that the strips tags are. And, like strips, tiles are either all uncompressed, or all compressed using the same scheme. Also, TIFF images are either striped or tiled, but never both.

TileWidth and TileLength describe the size of the tiles storing the image data. The values of TileWidth and TileLength must be a multiple of 16, and all tiles in a subfile are always the same size. These are important compatibility considerations for some applications, especially when using the tile-oriented JPEG compression scheme. The TIFF 6.0 specification recommends that tiles should contain 4K to 32K of image data before compression. Finally, tiles need not be square. Rectangular tiles compress just as well.

The TileWidth and TileLength tag values can be used to determine the number of tiles in non-YCbCr image subfiles:

```
TilesAcross = (ImageWidth + (TileWidth - 1)) / TileWidth;
TilesDown = (ImageLength + (TileLength - 1)) / TileLength;
TilesInImage = TilesAcross * TilesDown;
```

If the image is separated into planes (PlanarConfiguration = 2), the number of tiles is calculated like this:

```
TilesInImage = TilesAcross * TilesDown * SamplesPerPixel;
```

The TileOffsets tag contains an array of offsets to the first byte of each tile. Tiles are not necessarily stored in a contiguous sequence in a subfile. Each tile has a separate location offset value and is independent of all other tiles in the subfile. The offsets in this tag are ordered left-to-right and top-to-bottom. If the image data is separated into planes, all of the offsets for the first plane are stored first, followed by the offsets for the second plane, and so on. The number of offset values in this tag are equal to the number of tiles in the image (PlanarConfiguration = 1) or the number of tiles multiplied by the Samples-PerPixel tag value (PlanarConfiguration = 2). All offset values are interpreted from the beginning of the TIFF file.

The final tag, TileByteCounts, contains the number of bytes in each compressed tile. The number of values in this tag is also equal to the number of tags in the image, and the values are ordered the same way as the values in the TileOffsets tag.

Normally, a tile size is chosen that fits an image exactly. An image 6400 pixels wide by 4800 pixels long may be divided evenly into 150 tiles, each 640 pixels wide by 320 pixel long. However, not all image dimensions are divisible by 16. An image 2200 pixels wide by 2850 long cannot be evenly divided into tiles whose size must be multiples of 16. The solution is to choose a "best-fit" tile size and fill out the image data with padding.

To find a best-fit tile size, we must choose a tile size that minimally overlaps the size of the image. In this example, we want to use tiles that are 256 pixels wide by 320 pixels long, roughly the same aspect ratio as the image. Using tiles this size requires that 104 extra pixels of padding be added to each row and that 30 additional rows be added to the image length. The size of the image data plus padding is now 2304 pixels wide by 2880 pixels long and can be evenly divided among 81 of our 256 by 320 pixel tiles.

In this example, you may notice that the total amount of padding added to the image before tiling is 365,520 pixels. For a 1-bit image, this equals an extra

45,690 bytes of image data. No appreciable gain in compression results from tiling small images. Also, avoid using tiles that are excessively large and require excessive amount of padding.

Compression

TIFF supports perhaps more types of data compression than any other image file format. It is also quite possible to use an unsupported compression scheme just by adding the needed user-defined tags. TIFF 4.0 supported only Run-Length Encoding (RLE) and CCITT T.4 and T.6 compression. These compression schemes are typically only for use with 8-bit color, and gray-scale and 1-bit black-and-white images, respectively. TIFF 5.0 added the LZW compression scheme, typically for color images, and TIFF 6.0 added the JPEG compression method for use with continuous-tone color and gray-scale images. (All of these data compression schemes are discussed in Chapter 9, *Data Compression*, including a variety of RLE algorithms.)

TIFF uses the PackBits RLE compression scheme found in the Macintosh toolbox. PackBits is a simple and effective algorithm for compressing data and is easy to implement. The name "PackBits" would lead a programmer to believe that it is a bit-wise RLE, packing runs of bits. However, PackBits is a byte-wise RLE and is most efficient at encoding runs of bytes.

PackBits actually has three types of data packets that may be written to the encoded data stream. The first is a two-byte *encoded run packet*. The first byte (the run-count byte) indicates the number of bytes in the run, and the second byte stores the value of each byte in the run. The actual run count value stored is in the range 0 to 127 and represents the values 1 to 128 (run count + 1).

Another type of packet, the *literal run packet*, stores 12 to 128 bytes literally in the encoded data stream without compressing them. Literal run packets are used to store data with very few runs, as found in very complex or noisy images. The literal run packet's run count is in the range of -127 to -1, indicating that 2 to 128 run values (-(run count) + 1) follow the run count byte.

The last type of packet is the no-op packet. No-ops are one byte in length and have a value of -128. The no-op packet has no use in the PackBits compression scheme and is therefore never found in PackBits-encoded data.

Decompressing PackBits-encoded data is a simple matter of reading a packet of encoded data and converting it to the appropriate byte run. Once again, the run count byte value is stored one less than the actual number of bytes in the run. It is therefore necessary to add one to the run count value before using it.

Refer to the TIFF 6.0 specification for more information on PackBits compression and to Chapter 9, *Data Compression*, for more information on RLE algorithms.

Problems With TIFF 6.0 JPEG

Commentary by Dr. Tom Lane of the Independent JPEG Group, a member of the TIFF Advisory Committee

TIFF 6.0 added JPEG to the list of TIFF compression schemes. Unfortunately, the approach taken in the 6.0 specification is a very poor design. A new design is being worked on by the TIFF Advisory Committee. If you are considering implementing JPEG in TIFF, I strongly urge you to wait for the new design to be published.

The fundamental problem with TIFF 6.0's JPEG design is that JPEG's various tables and parameters are broken out as separate fields, which the TIFF control logic must manage. This is bad software engineering—that information should be private to the JPEG compressor/decompressor. Worse, the fields themselves are specified without thought for future extension and without regard to well-established TIFF conventions. Here are some of the more significant problems:

- The JPEG table tags use a highly nonstandard layout: rather than containing data directly in the tag structure, the tags hold pointers to information elsewhere in the file. This requires special-purpose code to be added to *every* TIFF-manipulating application. Even a trivial TIFF editor (for example, a program to add an ImageDescription field to a TIFF file) must be explicitly aware of the internal structure of the JPEG-related tables, or it will probably break the file. (Every other auxiliary tag in TIFF follows the normal rules and can be copied or relocated by common code.)

- The specification requires the TIFF control logic to know a great deal about JPEG details, for example, such arcana as how to compute the length of a Huffman code table—the length is not supplied in the tag structure and can be found only by inspecting the table contents.

- The design neglects the fact that baseline JPEG codecs may support only two sets of Huffman tables; they specify a separate table for each color component. This implies either wasting space (by storing duplicate Huffman tables) or violating the TIFF convention that prohibits duplicate pointers. Furthermore, decoders must test to see which tables are identical, a waste of time and code space.

• The JPEGInterchangeFormat tag again violates the proscription against duplicate pointers; it envisions having the normal strip/tile pointers pointing into the larger data area pointed to by JPEGInterchangeFormat. TIFF editing applications must be specifically aware of this relationship, because they must maintain it or, if they can't, must delete the JPEGInterchangeFormat tag.

• The JPEGQTables tag is fixed at a byte per table entry; there is no way to support 16-bit quantization values. This is a serious impediment to extending TIFF to use 12-bit JPEG.

• The design cannot support using different quantization tables in different strips/tiles of an image (so as to encode some areas at higher quality than others). Furthermore, because quantization tables are tied one-for-one to color components, the design cannot support table switching options that are likely to be added in JPEG 2.

In addition to these major design errors, the TIFF 6.0 JPEG specification is seriously ambiguous. In particular, several incompatible interpretations are possible for its handling of JPEG restart markers, and Section 22, "Data Sample Format," actually contradicts Section 15, "Document Storage and Retrieval," about the restrictions on tile sizes.

Finally, the 6.0 design creates problems for implementations that need to keep the JPEG codec separate from the TIFF control logic—consider using a JPEG chip that was not designed specifically for TIFF. JPEG codecs generally want to produce or consume a standard JPEG datastream, not just raw data. (If they do handle raw data, a separate out-of-band mechanism must be provided to load tables into the codec.) With such a codec, the TIFF control logic must be prepared to parse JPEG markers to create the TIFF table tags (when encoding) or to synthesize JPEG markers from the tags (when decoding). Of course, this means that the control logic must know a great deal more about JPEG than we would like. The parsing and reconstruction of the markers also represents a fair amount of unnecessary work.

Due to all these problems, the TIFF Advisory Committee is working on a replacement JPEG-in-TIFF scheme. The rough outline is as follows:

1. Each image segment (strip or tile) in a JPEG-compressed TIFF image contains a legal JPEG datastream, complete with all markers. This data forms an independent image of the proper dimensions for the strip or tile.

2. To avoid duplicate tables in a multi-segment file, segments may use the JPEG "abbreviated image data" datastream structure, in which DQT and DHT tables are omitted. The common tables are to be supplied in a JPEG "abbreviated table specification" datastream, which is contained in a newly defined "JPEGTables" TIFF field. Because the tables in question typically amount to 550 bytes or so. the savings is worthwhile.

3. All the field definitions in the existing Section 22, "Data Sample Format," are deleted. (In practice, those field tag values will remain reserved indefinitely, and this scheme will use a new Compression tag, probably Compression=7. Implementations that have 6.0-style files to contend with may continue to read them, using whatever interpretation of 6.0 they did before.)

If you are considering implementing JPEG in TIFF, please contact the Aldus Developer's Desk to find out the status of this replacement design. The 6.0 JPEG design has not been widely implemented and with any luck it will stay that way.

For Further Information

For further information about the TIFF format, see the specification included on the CD-ROM that accompanies this book.

The primary source of information about TIFF is the Aldus Developer's Association (ADA). The ADA distributes the official TIFF specification, and the latest news on TIFF can be found in the *Aldus Developer's Newsletter*. All inquiries about TIFF, including joining the Aldus Developer's Association or obtaining the TIFF Developer's Kit, should be directed to the Developer's Desk at Aldus Corporation:

TIFF *(cont'd)*

Aldus Corporation
Attn: Aldus Developer's Desk
411 First Avenue South
Seattle, WA 98104-2871
Voice: 206-628-6593
Voice: 800-331-2538
FAX: 206-343-4240
tiff-input@aldus.com

Aldus also distributes the TIFF Class F specification, and it is available in the Aldus forum on CompuServe. The ADA supports a FAXback service in which information may be requested automatically via a facsimile machine. This service may be reached at:

206-628-5737

Order document #9001 to receive the index of all information available via this service.

See the following references for more information about TIFF:

Murray, James. "TIFF File Format," *C Gazette*, Winter 1990-91, pp. 27-42.

Campbell, Joe. *The Spirit of TIFF Class F*, Cygnet Technologies, Berkeley, CA. April 1990.

Aldus Corporation. *TIFF Developer's Toolkit*, Revision 6.0, Seattle, WA. June 1992

Aldus Corporation. *TIFF Developer's Toolkit*, Revision 5.0. Seattle, WA. November 1988.

Hewlett-Packard Company. *HP TIFF Developer's Manual*, Greeley, CO. November 1988.

Aldus Corporation. *Aldus Developer News*, Seattle, WA.

NAME:	TTDDD
ALSO KNOWN AS:	Textual Three-Dimensional Data Description
TYPE:	Vector/animation
COLORS:	16 million
COMPRESSION:	None
MAXIMUM IMAGE SIZE:	Unlimited
MULTIPLE IMAGES PER FILE:	Yes
NUMERICAL FORMAT:	ASCII
ORIGINATOR:	Glenn Lewis
PLATFORM:	All
SUPPORTING APPLICATIONS:	T3DLIB
SPECIFICATION ON CD:	Yes (documentation by the author)
CODE ON CD:	Yes
IMAGES ON CD:	Yes
SEE ALSO:	Interchange File Format, TDDD

USAGE:	Used primarily as a method of editing and interchanging TDDD file format information.
COMMENTS:	For a complete understanding of TTDDD you need to read about the IFF and TDDD file formats as well.

Overview

The TTDDD (Textual Three-Dimensional Data Description format) is an ASCII data representation of the TDDD (T3D) file format used by Impulse for its Turbo Silver and Imagine rendering and animation software products. In fact, so much of the information in the TDDD specification is relevant to TTDDD that no official separate TTDDD file format specification has ever been written.

TTDDD was created as part of two, now obsolete, programs, ReadTDDD and WriteTDDD. These programs were capable of reading a TDDD file and writing out a TTDDD file and vice versa. They have now been replaced by the newer T3DLIB shareware library and utilities. (See "For Further Information" below for more details about T3DLIB.)

File Organization

All TTDDD files are simple ASCII files that may be read with any text editor. Each line contains a 4-letter case-insensitive keyword, followed by an optional parameter name and one or more values. Array subscripts need not be contained within double quotes. Comments may appear in TTDDD files in the form of the standard C comment tokens /* */ surrounding the comment, or the TeX token % appearing at the beginning of the comment. Here are some examples of valid keyword/parameter/value combinations:

```
NAME "Fred"                   % Keyword and value
NAME Fred                     % Same, but no double quotes
BRSH[0]="Brush 0"             % String assigned to array element 0
BRSH 0 =Brush 0               % Same, but no double quotes or
                              % brackets

OBSV Focal  2.82              % Keyword, parameter, and one value
OBSV Rotate Z=2.7 X=4.3       % Keyword, parameter, and two values
FADE FadeTo 23 99 254         % Keyword, parameter, and three values
OSTR Info ABS_TRA Z_ALIGN     % Keyword, parameter, and two flags
```

File Details

TTDDD files do not have a header, other than possibly a few comment lines identifying the file contents, author, and time and date of creation. The actual vector data is organized as a series of chunks, each enclosed by a BEGIN and END keyword pair. The INFO chunk usually appears first in older TTDDD files. Newer TTDDD files do not typically have an INFO chunk because the Imagine product does not use them.

An example of an INFO chunk is shown here:

```
INFO Begin
  NAME "Gizmo"
  BRSH[0]="This is the IFF ILBM filename of Brush 0"
  BRSH 1 ="Brush 1"               % Brackets are optional.
  STNC[0] "Stencil 0 filename"    % etc.
  TXTR[0] Texture                 % Quotes not necessary here.
  OBSV Camera X=5.0 Y=2.7 Z=5.3

                                  % Default: -100 -100 100
  OBSV Rotate Z=2.7 X=4.3         % In this case, Y=0.0
  OBSV Focal 2.82
  OTRK "Object for Camera Tracking"
```

```
                              % If parameters are too long,
                              % they are simply truncated.
OSTR Path "Path object name"
OSTR Translate X=2.8 Y=7.3 Z=2.1
                              % Defaults to zero.
OSTR Rotate Y=90              % Defaults to zero.
OSTR Scale 2.5
OSTR Info ABS_TRA Z_ALIGN     % Keep all flags on THIS LINE!
FADE FadeAt 50.0
FADE FadeBy 500
FADE FadeTo 23 99 254         % "R=23 G=99 B=254"
                              % Defaults to 80 80 80
                              % Defaults to zero.
SKYC Horizon R=12 B=30
SKYC Zenith R=2 B=50
AMBI 5 27 32                  % Also RGB
GLB0[0] 5                     % Edging
GLB0 1 2                      % Perturb
GLB0[2] 255                   % Sky_Blend
GLB0[3] 2                     % Lens
GLB0 4 1                      % Fade
GLB0[5]=9                     % Size
GLB0 6 =2                     % Resolve
GLB0[7] 0                     % Extra
End INFO
```

The order of data within each Begin/End block pair is completely arbitrary, except for variable-length arrays. These arrays must begin with the Count field, specifying the number of entries in the array, followed by the values for the array starting with the first element.

Following the INFO chunk will always be one OBJ chunk per object hierarchy stored in the TTDDD file. Each OBJ chunk contains one DESC sub-chunk or an EXTR sub-chunk. DESC sub-chunks describe object data stored internally within the TTDDD file. EXTR sub-chunks describe the same type of data stored in an external file. Newer TTDDD files typically do not have EXTR sub-chunks. External information is usually imported directly into the TTDDD file as a DESC sub-chunk.

Following is an example of a DESC and an EXTR sub-chunk:

```
OBJ Begin
/*
** DESC sub-chunk
*/
```

TTDDD *(cont'd)*

```
DESC Begin
  NAME "Gizmo"                        % Object name. Defaults to no name
  SHAP Shape 2                        % This must be supplied!
  SHAP Lamp 0                         % ditto
  POSI X=5.7 Y=200.9 Z=132.7          % Defaults to zero.
  AXIS XAxis X=1                      % Defaults to 1 0 0
  AXIS YAxis Y=1                      % Defaults to 0 1 0
  AXIS ZAxis Z=1                      % Defaults to 0 0 1
  SIZE X=1 Y=1 Z=1                    % Defaults to 32.0
  PNTS PCount 3
  PNTS Point[0] 12 27 52              % Brackets and "X= . . . " optional
  PNTS Point 1  21 72 25              % ditto
  PNTS Point[2] 72 25 21              % ditto
  EDGE ECount 3
  EDGE Edge[0] 0 1                    % Edge connection between two points
  EDGE Edge 1  1 2                    % Brackets optional
  EDGE Edge 2  2 0
  FACE TCount 1
  FACE Connect[0] 0 1 2               % List of 3 edges to make a triangle
  COLR 87 23 232                      % RGB. Defaults to 240 240 240
  REFL G=12 R=240 B=97                % RGB. Defaults to zero.
  TRAN 25 72 53                       % RGB. Defaults to zero.
  CLST Count 1                        % Must match TCount above.
  CLST Color[0] 240 12 57             % RGB. Defaults to 240 240 240
  RLST Count 1                        % Must match TCount above.
  RLST Color[0] 120 24 23             % RGB. Defaults to zero.
  TLST Count 1                        % Must match TCount above.
  TLST Color[0] 255 92 87             % RGB. Defaults to zero.
  TPAR[0] 42.73
  TPAR[12]=72.67                      % Defaults to zero.
  SURF[2]=0
  SURF[4] 1                           % Defaults to zero.
  MTTR Type 4                         % Defaults to zero.
  MTTR Index 2.972                    % Defaults to 1.0.
                                      % (1.00 <= Index <= 3.55)
  SPEC Specularity 28                 % Defaults to zero.
  SPEC Hardness 16                    % Defaults to zero.
  PRP0[0] 100                         % Blending factor. Defaults to 255.
  PRP0[1]=5                           % Roughness factor. Defaults to 0.
  PRP0 2 =1                           % Shading On/Off flag (1/0).
                                      % Defaults to 1.
  PRP0[3] 1                           % Phong shading flag. Defaults to 1
  PRP0[4]=0                           % Glossy flag. Defaults to 0
```

```
    PRPO 5  1                    % Quickdraw flag. Defaults to 1
    INTS 200                     % Defaults to 300
    STRY Path "Path object name"
    STRY Translate 2.8 7.3 2.1   % Defaults to zero.
    STRY Rotate Z=90   % Defaults to zero.
    STRY Scale 3.5
    STRY Info ABS_TRA X_ALIGN     % Keep all the flags on THIS LINE!
End DESC
% Possible child (including external) objects go here to
% build object hierarchy.
/*
** EXTR sub-chunk
*/
EXTR Begin
    MTRX Translate 34 72 56      % Defaults to zero.
    MTRX Scale 1 5 9             % Defaults to 1.
    MTRX Rotate 1 0 0 0 1 0 0 0 1
                                 % A Matrix MUST be in the proper
                                 % order!
    LOAD "External file name"
End EXTR
TOBJ   % Ends current object hierarchy.
End OBJ
```

For Further Information

For further information about TTDDD, see the documentation included on the CD-ROM that accompanies this book. TTDDD was created by Glenn M. Lewis for his shareware package T3DLIB. The current revision of T3DLIB contains many useful utilities and a platform-independent library for C programmers to use that allows easy manipulation of TDDD objects algorithmically.

You can obtain the T3DLIB package via FTP from *ftp.wustl.edu* or *ftp.luth.se* in the */pub/aminet/gfx/3d* directory. The T3DLIB files have R42 in their names.

You can also contact the author for information:

Glenn M. Lewis
8341 Olive Hill Court
Fair Oaks, CA 95628

Voice: 916-721-7196
glewis@pcocd2.intel.com
glewis@netcom.com

NAME:	uRay
ALSO KNOWN AS:	DBW_uRay, Microray
TYPE:	Scene description
COLORS:	NA
COMPRESSION:	Uncompressed
MAXIMUM IMAGE SIZE:	NA
MULTIPLE IMAGES PER FILE:	NA
NUMERICAL FORMAT:	NA
ORIGINATOR:	David B. Wecker
PLATFORM:	All
SUPPORTING APPLICATIONS:	uRay ray tracing application
SPECIFICATION ON CD:	Yes
CODE ON CD:	Yes
IMAGES ON CD:	No
SEE ALSO:	NFF, POV, PRT, QRT, Radiance

USAGE: Description of 3D scenes for ray tracing or other rendering applications.

COMMENTS: A simple scene description format useful for specifying 3D objects. This is a good format to look at if you are considering building your own ray-trace format or application.

Overview

uRay is the format created by David B. Wecker for use by the uRay (Microray) ray tracer. It provides a simple way of specifying a small number of 3D objects.

File Organization

Like those of many other ray-trace formats, uRay files consist of a number of ASCII lines implementing a proprietary command language, in this case the uRay scene description language.

File Details

Commands used in writing uRay files may consist of the following:

DEPTH   Recursion depth

COLS   Columns in an image

ROWS   Rows in an image

START   Row number at which to begin rendering operations

END   Row number at which to end rendering operations

BPP   Bits per pixel in output image (12 or 24)

AOV   View angle

ASPECT   Image aspect ratio

NEAR   Background color for "sky" near eye

FAR   Background color for "sky" far from eye

GROUND   Background color below horizon

BASE   Blackness of shadows

WAVES n   where n is the number of lines following the WAVES keyword. Each line consists of the following:

     x y z   Wave center

     amp   Starting amplitude of the wave

     phase   Starting phase shift

     length   Wave length

     damp   Damping between successive waves

ATTRIBUTES n

     where n is the number of lines following the ATTRIBUTES keyword. Each line consists of the following:

     r g b   Diffuse color

     Kd   Diffuse coloring

     Ks   Reflection

     Kt   Transmission

     Ir   Index of refraction

     Kl   Self lighting

     dist   Inverse square law distance

Kf	Fuzz	
Wave	Wave number	
tex	Texture; may be one of the following:	
	0	No texture
	1 r g b x y z	Checks in color (r g b) at scale (x y z)
	2 r g b	Random mottling
	3 r g b a b c	Blend in x direction
	4 r g b a b c	Blend in y direction
	5 r g b a b c	Blend in z direction

The following objects are predefined:

SPHERE	Sphere
QUAD	Rectangle
TRIANGLE	Triangle
RING	Ring

See the uRay documentation for detailed information about parameters.

For Further Information

For further information about the uRay format, see the uRay documentation included on the CD-ROM accompanying this book. You can also contact the author:

David B. Wecker
Digital Equipment Corporation
Cambridge Research Lab
One Kendall Square
Cambridge, MA 02139
Voice: 617-621-6699
FAX: 617-621-6650
wecker@crl.dec.com

Utah RLE

NAME:	Utah RLE
ALSO KNOWN AS:	RLE
TYPE:	Bitmap
COLORS:	256
COMPRESSION:	RLE
MAXIMUM IMAGE SIZE:	32Kx32K
MULTIPLE IMAGES PER FILE:	No
NUMERICAL FORMAT:	Little-endian
ORIGINATOR:	University of Utah
PLATFORM:	UNIX, others
SUPPORTING APPLICATIONS:	Utah Raster Toolkit, others
SPECIFICATION ON CD:	Yes
CODE ON CD:	Yes (in FBM, ImageMagick, JPEG, xli, and xloadimage packages)
IMAGES ON CD:	No
SEE ALSO:	Chapter 9, *Data Compression*
USAGE:	Primarily used in support of the Utah Raster Toolkit, though other applications, mainly on UNIX platforms, occasionally choose to support it.
COMMENTS:	A simple, well-defined and well-documented bitmap format. Too bad it's not in wider use. Consider using it in a pinch for interapplication exchange of 8-bit images if you have no alternative.

Overview

The Utah RLE format was developed by Spencer Thomas at the University of Utah Department of Computer Science. The first version appeared around 1983. The work was partially funded by the NSF, DARPA, the Army Research Office, and the Office of Naval Research. It was developed mainly to support the Utah Raster Toolkit (URT), which is widely distributed in source form on the Internet. Although superseded by more recent work, the Utah Raster Toolkit remains a source of ideas and bitmap manipulation code for many.

Utah RLE was intended to be device-independent. Documentation associated with the URT claims that Utah RLE format files often require about one-third of the available space necessary for most "image synthesis"-style images. If the image data does not compress well, the format accommodates storage as uncompressed pixel data with little extra overhead. Despite its age, slightly idiosyncratic terminology, and some missing information, the Utah RLE format specification is well-written and reasonably clear. Aspiring format creators, take note!

File Organization

The file consists of a header, followed by palette information, a comment area, and the bitmap data.

File Details

The header looks like this:

```
typedef struct _RLE_Header
{
  WORD  Magic;        /* Magic number */
  SHORT Xpos;         /* Lower left x of image */
  SHORT Ypos;         /* Lower left y of image */
  SHORT Xsize;        /* Image width */
  SHORT Ysize;        /* Image height */
  BYTE  Flags;        /* Misc flags */
  BYTE  Ncolors;      /* Number of colors */
  BYTE  Pixelbits;    /* Number of bits per pixel */
  BYTE  Ncmap;        /* Number of color channels in palette */
  BYTE  Cmaplen;      /* Color map length */
  BYTE  Redbg;        /* Red value of background color */
  BYTE  Greenbg;      /* Green value of background color */
  BYTE  Bluebg;       /* Blue value of background color */

} RLE_HEADER;
```

Magic is, naturally enough, a magic number identifying the file type. Unfortunately, the magic number is not documented in the specification.

Xpos and Ypos are the position of the lower-left corner of the image, in pixels.

Xsize and Ysize are the size of the image, in pixels.

Flags is an 8-bit field used by the format writer to store miscellaneous information.

Ncolors is the total number of colors in the image, limited to 256.

Pixelbits provides information on the number of bits per pixel in the image. This is currently limited to 8.

Ncmap denotes the number of colors channels in the palette.

Cmaplen provides the number of bits in the palette and limits ncolors (defined above), the total number of colors in the image. For example, a cmaplen value of 8 denotes a 256-color palette.

Redbg, Greenbg, and Bluebg together provide a 24-bit specification of the image background color.

A key concept used in the Utah RLE format specification is that of the color channel. Each color channel contains eight bits, and the format supports up to 255 of them. This makes for an extremely flexible color model, but one, perhaps, that has never been utilized fully. Gray-scale images, for example, normally use one color channel; 24-bit RGB images use three channels; and RGBA, where an alpha channel is included, uses four channels.

The comment area is a series of null-terminated ASCII strings, each of which is preceded by a 16-bit length value. Each comment is WORD-aligned and is padded if necessary. Comments have the form:

```
name=value
```

The bitmap data is in stream format and is amply documented in the specification and the sample code.

For Further Information

For further information about the Utah RLE format, see the following article included on the CD-ROM:

> Thomas, Spencer W., *Design of the Utah RLE Format*, University of Utah, Department of Computer Science.

See also the Utah Raster Toolkit for actual implemention details.

The URT package may be obtained via FTP from the sites listed below.

cs.utah.edu
weedeater.math.yale.edu
freebie.engin.umich.edu

You will find the package in the *urt-3.0.tar.Z* file, and sample images in *urt-img.tar.Z*.

URT is copyrighted, but is freely redistributable on a GNU-like basis. You can send questions about the URT or Utah RLE to either of the following:

toolkit-request@cs.utah.edu
urt-request@caen.engin.umich.edu

VICAR2

NAME:	VICAR2
ALSO KNOWN AS:	Planetary File Format
TYPE:	Bitmap
COLORS:	Unlimited
COMPRESSION:	Uncompressed
MAXIMUM IMAGE SIZE:	Unlimited
MULTIPLE IMAGES PER FILE:	No
NUMERICAL FORMAT:	Little-endian
ORIGINATOR:	NASA
PLATFORM:	VAX/VMS
SUPPORTING APPLICATIONS:	Many
SPECIFICATION ON CD:	Yes
CODE ON CD:	Yes (in ImageMagick, xloadimage,and xv packages)
IMAGES ON CD:	No
SEE ALSO:	FITS, PDS

USAGE: Storage of bitmap data.

COMMENTS: You are unlikely to see the VICAR2 format unless you deal with planetary data from NASA or JPL.

Overview

The VICAR2 image file format is used primarily for storing planetary image data collected by both interplanetary spacecraft and Earth-based stations. Many astronomical and astrophysical organizations use and support the VICAR2 format.

File Organization

VICAR2 is very similar in construction to the FITS and PDS image file formats. A VICAR2 image file is divided into an ASCII header (called a label) and a collection of binary image data.

File Details

This section contains information on the label and image data in a VICAR2 file.

Labels

A VICAR2 label contains system label items and may contain history label items as well. History label items are added to the label during software processing, and it is possible for history label items not to be present in a VICAR2 label at all. If history label items do exist, they always occur following the last system label item.

The history label section may also contain other, software-specific keywords called user labels. They are for informational purposes for any software application that knows how to interpret them. If a VICAR2 reader does not recognize them, then they are ignored and always preserved whenever the file is written or read.

The label is always located at the beginning of the file, starting on the first byte, and is always arranged in system-/history-/user-section order.

All label sections contain one or more fixed-length records in the form of ASCII character strings. Because all records in the label must be the same length, the last record must be padded out to the proper size with NULL (ASCII 00h) characters if it is too short.

All records in the label use the standard *keyword=value* format for storing information about the image. Keywords are written in uppercase and have a maximum of eight characters. The value may be one of four data types:

- INTEGER (fixed-point)
- REAL (floating-point)
- DOUBLE (double-precision REAL)
- STRING

STRING data is delimited by single quotation marks (') containing any printable ASCII characters and spaces except for single quotation mark characters. Strngs may be from 1 to 512 characters in length.

A *keyword=value* pair is always separated by an equals sign (=). There are never any spaces between the equal sign and the keyword/value data. Each *keyword=value* pair is separated from the next pair by one more spaces.

The following is a list of valid VICAR2 label keywords. Refer to the VICAR2 specification on the CD-ROM for an explanation of each keyword and the data format of its associated value:

BUFSIZE	N4
LBLSIZE	NB
DAT_TIM	NBB
DIM	NL
EOL	NLB
FORMAT	NS
HOST	ORG
INTFMT	REALFMT
N1	RECSIZE
N2	TASK
N3	USER

The first keyword of the system section of the label is always LBLSIZE, which specifies the total number of bytes in the label, including any NULL bytes used for padding out the last record. LBLSIZE is always a multiple of the file record size.

A system label may end with the keyword TASK, which marks the beginning of the history section of the label. If no history section exists, then the label ends with an ASCII NULL value, or simply after the number of characters specified by LBLSIZE.

If the EOL KEYWORD is present in the label and has a VALUE of 1, then an additional label record appears at the end of the file following the image data. Your guess is as good as ours as to the use of this End-Of-File trailing record.

Image Data

The image data begins on the next record boundary following the label. The image data contains one record per scan line in the image. The size of each record is a number of bytes equal to the number of bytes in one scan line.

The image data is represented by one of the following data types, indicated by the FORMAT keyword in the image label:

BYTE	8 bits
HALF	16 bits
FULL	32 bits

REAL	32 bits
DOUB	64 bits
COMPLEX	64 bits

The following is a typical VICAR2 label section, including history and user records. Note that in this example, carriage returns have been inserted for clarity; none actually exist in a real label.

```
LBLSIZE=1680 FORMAT='BYTE' TYPE='IMAGE' BUFSIZ=20480 DIM=3 EOL=0
RECSIZE=840 ORG='BSQ' NL=738 NS=840 NB=1 N1=840 N2=738 N3=1
N4=0 NBB=0 NLB=0 HOST='VAX-VMS' INTFMT='LOW' REALFMT='VAX'
TASK='LOGMOS' USER='HXS343' DAT_TIM='Fri Nov 2 17:41:32 1990'
SPECSAMP=493943 PROJSAMP=4096 PROJ_L ON=350.7789496599263
PRODTYPE='F-MIDR' PIXSIZ=75 SEAM='CORRECTED' MAP_PROJ='SINUSOIDAL'
SEAMLOC='NO' IMAGE='RADAR CROSS SECTION POWER' DN_UNITS='DECI BELS'
SPECLINE=38724 LAT_UR=27.5 LAT_UL=27.5 LAT_LR=22.4102769981245
LAT_LL =22.4102769981245 LON_UL=347.5 LON_UR=354.0578993198525
LON_LL=347.6328878639 307 LON_LR=353.9250114559218
M_SPDN_1='MISSING DATA' LOW_REP=-20.0 HI_REP=30 .0 LOW_DN=1
HI_DN=250 N_SPDN=1 SPDN_1=0 REV_STRT=460 REV_END=4 93
PRODUCT='F-MIDR.25N351;1' TASK='COPY' USER='DNJ345'
DAT_TIM='Sat Apr 20 12:29:24 1991' TASK='STRETCH' USER='DNJ345'
DAT_TIM='Sat Apr 20 12:29: 39 1991' PARMS=' LINEAR STRETCH:
71 TO     0 AND  155 TO   255'
```

For Further Information

For further information about VICAR2, see the documentation included on the CD-ROM that accompanies this book. You can also contact:

National Aeronautics and Space Administration (NASA)
Attn: Bob Deen
Image Processing Laboratory
Jet Propulsion Laboratory
4800 Oak Grove Drive
Pasadena, CA 91109
rgd059@mipl3.jpl.nasa.gov

You can also obtain VICAR2 images from the FTP archive site *ames.arc.nasa.gov*, in the directory *pub/SPACE/VICAR.*

NAME:	VIFF
ALSO KNOWN AS:	Khoros Visualization/Image File Format
TYPE:	Bitmap
COLORS:	Unlimited
COMPRESSION:	None, RLE
MAXIMUM IMAGE SIZE:	Unlimited
MULTIPLE IMAGES PER FILE:	Yes
NUMERICAL FORMAT:	Any
ORIGINATOR:	Khoral Research
PLATFORM:	UNIX (X Window)
SUPPORTING APPLICATIONS:	Khoros
SPECIFICATION ON CD:	Yes
CODE ON CD:	Yes (in ImageMagick package)
IMAGES ON CD:	Yes
SEE ALSO:	None

USAGE: Used by the Khoros System as its native format.

COMMENTS: The VIFF format is capable of storing any type of information generated by the Khoros System, making VIFF a very diverse and feature-rich format.

Overview

VIFF (Khoros Visualization/Image File Format) is the native file format of the Khoros System environment. Khoros is a visual programming and software development environment used to create image processing and visualization tools for commercial and scientific research. Khoros is implemented using UNIX and the X Window System.

Khoros contains a complete visual programming language, code generators, and a user interface editor. Khoros' capabilities include interactive image display; image, numerical, and signal processing and analysis functions; and two- and three-dimensional plotting.

Khoros is especially useful for conducting research in the areas of image and signal processing, pattern recognition, machine vision, remote sensing, and geographic information systems. Khoros is capable of converting many image file formats to and from VIFF, including TIFF, TGA, FITS, PBM, XBM, DEM, DLG, MATLAB, BIG, ELAS, Sun raster, ASCII, and raw binary. This capability makes the Khoros source code distribution a prime source of image file format information (see "For Further Information" below).

File Organization

All VIFF files contain a header, which is followed by either image data or one or more data (color) maps, or both. If both image and colormap data is present, the image data precedes the map data. VIFF image data need not use a colormap to be valid, and colormaps may be stored in VIFF files with only a header and no image data.

The VIFF specification uses the term "bands" to indicate color channels. An RGB image divided into its component color planes (R,G,B) is said to contain "three bands" of data. Also, multiband data is stored "by pixel" rather than "by plane." In other words, each pixel is stored as an RGB triplet, rather than three separate color planes.

Single-band VIFF images contain a single channel (or plane) of index values and a colormap. Many of the Khoros image-processing functions require that three-band images be converted into single-band pseudocolor images before they can be used.

File Details

This section describes the VIFF header, the data maps, and the location and image data in a VIFF file.

Header

The VIFF header is 1024 bytes in size and has the following format:

```
typedef struct _ViffHeader
{
  CHAR  FileId;          /* Khoros file ID value (always ABh)*/
  CHAR  FileType;        /* VIFF file ID value (always 01h) */
  CHAR  Release;         /* Release number */
  CHAR  Version;         /* Version number */
  CHAR  MachineDep;      /* Machine dependencies indicator */
  CHAR  Padding[3];      /* Structure alignment padding (always 00h)*/
  CHAR  Comment[512];    /* Image comment text */
  DWORD NumberOfRows;    /* Length of image rows in pixels */
```

```
    DWORD NumberOfColumns;     /* Length of image columns in pixels */
    DWORD LengthOfSubrow;      /* Size of any sub-rows in the image */
    LONG  StartX;              /* Left-most display starting position */
    LONG  StartY;              /* Upper-most display starting position */
    FLOAT XPixelSize;          /* Width of pixels in meters */
    FLOAT YPixelSize;          /* Height of pixels in meters */
    DWORD LocationType;        /* Type of pixel addressing used */
    DWORD LocationDim;         /* Number of location dimensions */
    DWORD NumberOfImages;      /* Number of images in the file */
    DWORD NumberOfBands;       /* Number of bands (color channels) */
    DWORD DataStorageType;     /* Pixel data type */
    DWORD DataEncodingScheme;  /* Type of data compression used */
    DWORD MapScheme;           /* How map is to be interpreted */
    DWORD MapStorageType;      /* Map element data type */
    DWORD MapRowSize;          /* Length of map rows in pixels */
    DWORD MapColumnSize;       /* Length of map columns in pixels */
    DWORD MapSubrowSize;       /* Size of any subrows in the map */
    DWORD MapEnable;           /* Map is optional or required */
    DWORD MapsPerCycle;        /* Number of different maps present */
    DWORD ColorSpaceModel;     /* Color model used to represent image */
    DWORD ISpare1;             /* User-defined field */
    DWORD ISpare2;             /* User-defined field */
    FLOAT FSpare1;             /* User-defined field */
    FLOAT FSpare2;             /* User-defined field */
    CHAR  Reserve[404];        /* Padding */
} VIFFHEADER;
```

FileId is a magic number indicating that this is a VIFF file. This value is always ABh.

FileType is a value indicating the type of Khoros file. This value is always 01h, indicating a VIFF file.

Release indicates the release number of the *viff.h* file in which the VIFF file information structure is defined. This value is currently 01h and does not necessarily match the Khoros system release number.

Version indicates the version number of the *viff.h* file in which the VIFF file information structure is defined. This value is currently 03h and does not necessarily match the Khoros system version number.

MachineDep contains a value indicating the format of the image data and how the image data was last processed. Values currently defined for this field are:

02h	IEEE and big-endian byte ordering
04h	Digital Equipment Corporation/VAX byte ordering
08h	NS32000 and little-endian byte ordering
0Ah	Cray byte size and ordering

Padding is a 3-byte field containing the values 00h 00h 00h. This field is used only to word-align the header structure.

Comment is a 512-byte field typically containing ASCII plain-text information documenting the contents of a VIFF image data. This field may also be used for other purposes, but such uses are strictly user-defined and are not supported by Khoros.

NumberOfRows and NumberOfColumns indicate the size of the image data in pixels (the number of data items). If these two values are set to 00h, then no image data is present in the file, but a colormap may still exist.

LengthOfSubrow is the length in pixels of any subrows that may exist in the image data.

StartX and StartY specify the location of a sub-image within a parent image. The home coordinate (0,0) is always the upper-left corner of the image. If these values are equal to 00h, then the image is not a sub-image.

XPixelSize and YPixelSize indicate the actual size of the pixels in meters. The ratio of these two values gives the aspect ratio of the pixels in the image data.

LocationType indicates whether the image data contains implicit (01h) or explicit (02h) locations.

LocationDim has a value of 00h if the locations are stored implicitly (Location-Type is 01h); in this case, there is no location data stored in the VIFF file. Location data is present in the image file if the locations are stored explicitly (LocationType is 02h); in this case, LocationDim indicates the number of dimensions represented by the location data (typically 00h, 01h, or 02h for 1-, 2-, and 3-dimensional data).

NumberOfImages contains a value equal to the number of images stored in the VIFF file.

NumberOfBands indicates the number of bands per image (or dimensions per vector). A three-band RGB image would have a value of 03h in this field.

DataStorageType specifies the data type used to store each pixel. Supported values include:

00h	Bit
01h	BYTE
02h	WORD
04h	DWORD
05h	Single-precision float
06h	Complex float
09h	Double-precision float
0Ah	Complex double

Note that when pixels are stored as bits, eight pixels are packed per BYTE, least-significant bit first, and are padded out to end on a BYTE boundary.

DataEncodingScheme indicates the type of encoding used to compress the image data. Defined values for this field include:

00h	No compression
01h	ALZ
02h	RLE
03h	Transform-based
04h	CCITT
05h	ADPCM
06h	User-defined

Only values 00h and 01h are currently supported by Khoros 1.0.

MapScheme indicates the type of mapping present in the VIFF file. Possible values are:

01h	Each image band uses its own map
02h	The image is displayed by cycling through two or more maps
03h	All bands share the same map
04h	All bands are grouped together to point into one map

The mapping scheme indicated by a MapScheme value of 04h is not supported by Khoros 1.0.

MapStorageType specifies the type of data in the map or the resulting pixel data type after the mapping has been performed. Valid values for this field are:

00h	No data type
01h	Unsigned CHAR
02h	Short INT

04h	INT
05h	Single-precision float
06h	Complex float
07h	Double-precision float

MapRowSize and MapColumnSize indicate the width and height of the map.

MapSubrowSize stores the number of sub-rows in the map, if any.

MapEnable indicates whether the image data is valid if it is not mapped. Possible values for this field are:

01h	Image data may be used without first mapping it
02h	Map data must be applied to the image data before it can be used.

MapsPerCycle is the number of maps used to cycle the image when it is displayed. The value of this field is valid only if MapScheme is equal to a value of 02h.

ColorSpaceModel specifies the color model used to interpret the image data. The recognized values for this field are:

00h	No color space model used
01h	NTSC RGB
02h	NTSC CMY
03h	NTSC YIQ
04h	HSV
05h	HLS
06h	IHS
07h	CIE RGB
08h	CIE CMY
09h	CIE YIQ
0Ah	CIE UCS UVW
0Bh	CIE UCS SOW
0Ch	CIE UCS Lab
0Dh	CIE UCS Luv
0Eh	User-defined
0Fh	User-defined RGB

ISpare1, ISpare2, FSpare1, and FSpare2 are spare fields included for use by a user application. These fields are typically used to store data while the header is stored in memory and may not contain any information when the format is stored to a disk file.

Reserve is a chunk of padding which fills out the VIFF header to 1024 bytes in length. The bytes in this field are normally set to 00h, but may contain user-defined data as well.

Maps

Following the header may be a collection of one or more data maps. A data map contains information that is used to transform the image data in a specified way. By far the most common example of a map is a simple colormap, where each pixel contains an index value that references a color value stored in the map. Although VIFF data maps may contain any type of data necessary to interpret the image data properly, the image data always contains index values if a data map is present in the file.

All maps are stored as 1-dimensional data, and all map values are referenced as elements in an array. The size of the map is indicated in the MapRowSize and MapColumnSize header fields. The size of each element of the map is specified by the MapStorageType field.

Although there may be only one physical map data structure per VIFF file, the map may be divided into two more logical maps, each containing specific data. For example, 3-band image data might use three separate maps (one for each band), or it might use a single map for all three bands. Multiple maps may also be stored that are continually read in sequence as the image is displayed. Such a technique is used to render the image as an animation rather than as a still image.

Maps may also be specified as optional or forced. An optional map need not be used in the interpretation of the image data. A forced map is data that is required in order for the image data is to have any real validity. Forced maps are more common and usually indicate that the map contains color data and that the image data contains map index values.

Location and Image Data

Following any map data in a VIFF file may be a block of data called the location data. This data, if present, stores the coordinate information for each pixel in the image. Location data is a 1-dimensional array of float values and may contain one or more bands (dimensions) of location data. Each location value corresponds to a pixel in the image data. But before we can talk of pixel locations, we must understand how VIFF expresses the pixel data itself.

Pixels may be addressed as if they reside either in a 1-dimensional or in a multi-dimensional space. These addressing types are called implied locations and explicit locations, respectively. The implied location of a pixel is a reference to a pixel stored in a 1-dimensional array, but using the canonical 2-dimensional XY coordinates. For example, if we have a 256x256 image stored in a 1-dimensional array and we need to reference the value of the pixel at location 100x135, we use its implicit coordinates:

```
WORD ImageWidth = 256;                  /* Number of pixel in X axis */
WORD ImageLength = 256;                 /* Number of pixel in Y axis */
BYTE PixelArray[ImageWidth * ImageLength];      /* 256x256 image */
BYTE PixelValue;

/* Get the value of the pixel at 100x135 */
PixelValue = PixelArray[ (100 * ImageWidth) + 135 ];
```

You can see that the formula array [(X * ImageWidth) + Y] yields the value we need. Note that this formula assumes that the pixels in the array are stored by row. If the pixel data is stored by column, then ImageLength value should be used in place of the ImageWidth.

Explicit pixel locations are used to reference pixel data stored in two or more dimensions. If explicit pixel locations are indicated, a block of location data appears in the VIFF file just prior to the image data. This location data stores the coordinates of each pixel in the rendered space. For example:

```
WORD   ImageWidth = 256;             /* Number of pixel in X axis */
WORD   ImageLength = 256;            /* Number of pixel in Y axis */
WORD   NumberOfDims = 2;             /* Dimensions of pixel locations */
BYTE   PixelArray[ImageWidth * ImageLength];      /* 256x256 image */
FLOAT  LocationArray[ImageWidth * ImageLength * NumberOfDims];
BYTE   PixelValue;
FLOAT  LocationX;
FLOAT  LocationY;

/* Get the value of the pixel at 100x135 */
PixelValue = PixelArray[ (100 * ImageWidth) + 135 ];

/* Get the location of the pixel at 100x135 */
LocationX = LocationArray[ (100 * ImageWidth) + 135 ];
LocationY = LocationArray[ (100 * ImageWidth) + 135
             + (ImageWidth * ImageLength)];
```

As you can see, the image data is referenced in the same way for explicit data as it is for implicit data. If a map is present, the pixel values serve as indices into that map. If no map is present, then the pixel values are the actual color or intensity values of the image data.

Location data is stored as bands, but in a planar fashion. In the case of 2-dimensional data, all of the X location values are stored first, followed by all of the Y location values. And although a VIFF image can support thousands of dimensions, 1-, 2-, and 3-dimensional pixel locations are the most common.

For Further Information

For further information about VIFF, see the documentation and sample code included on the CD-ROM that accompanies this book.

The Khoros System is owned and copyright by Khoral Research, Inc. and is maintained by the Khoros Consortium. To obtain further information on the Khoros package and its distribution, or to support further research and development of software environments for data processing and visualization, contact:

Khoral Research, Inc.
6001 Indian School Road NE
Suite 200
Albuquerque, NM 87110
Voice: 505-837-6500
Fax: 505-881-3842
khoros-request@chama.eece.unm.edu

You can also contact the Khoros User Group at:

khoros@chama.eece.unm.edu

You can join the Khoros mailing list by sending email to:

khoros-request@bullwinkle.eece.unm.edu.

Khoros information may also be found posted in the USENET newsgroup *comp.soft-sys.khoros*, which is the home of the Khoros FAQ, posted weekly to this group and to *news.answers*. This and other Khoros FAQs, in addition to the complete Khoros distribution, may also be found in the */release* directory of the Khoros System distribution at the following FTP sites:

ftp.eece.unm.edu:/pub/khoros
ftp.uu.net:/pub/window-sys/khoros
popeye.genie.uottawa.ca:/pub/khoros
ipifidpt.difi.unipi.it:/pub/khoros
ftp.waseda.ac.jp:/pub/khoros

Your best source of further VIFF information is the Khoros package itself. The Khoros System distribution is quite large (65 megabytes, not including executables), and it is not practical to download the entire package just to find VIFF information. Instead, you should obtain the files you need from an installed Khoros System or one of the distribution sites previously listed. Information specifically about the VIFF format can be found in the following directories:

src/file_formats/no_format
> Programs for converting VIFF files to and from raw binary and ASCII data

src/file_formats/remote_gis
> Programs for converting VIFF files to and from remote sensing and GIS file formats.

src/file_formats/standard
> Programs for converting VIFF files to and from many other file formats

include/viff.h
> VIFF format header file

data/images, data/kernels, data/lut
> Sample VIFF image files

The VIFF format is also described in Chapter 1 of *Volume II, Programmer's Manual*, of the Khoros Manual Set. Both Chapter 1 and the *viff.h* file are included on the CD-ROM.

VIS-5D

NAME:	VIS-5D
ALSO KNOWN AS:	Visualization-5D, McIDAS, Grid File Format
TYPE:	Vector
COLORS:	NA
COMPRESSION:	Uncompressed
MAXIMUM IMAGE SIZE:	Unlimited
MULTIPLE IMAGES PER FILE:	No
NUMERICAL FORMAT:	Big- and little-endian
ORIGINATOR:	University of Wisconsin - Madison
PLATFORM:	UNIX
SUPPORTING APPLICATIONS:	VIS-5D, McIDAS
SPECIFICATION ON CD:	Yes
CODE ON CD:	Yes
IMAGES ON CD:	No
SEE ALSO:	None

USAGE: Designed to support the VIS-5D application by providing for the storage of multi-dimensional data.

COMMENTS: Although VIS-5D was designed to support scientific applications, multi-dimensional data visualization is a growing area. This format may become more important outside of scientific circles in the future.

Overview

The VIS-5D (Visualization-5D) format is the native file format of the VIS-5D scientific visualization UNIX application. VIS-5D is used to store a three-dimensional rendering of numerical data. Such data is typically acquired from scientific sources such as weather data and topographical measurements. Because the numerical data often contains a time component, VIS-5D file data may be animated to show changes over time, such as the movements of cloud patterns.

The VIS-5D application is actually a stand-alone subsystem of the proprietary McIDAS (Man-computer Interactive Data Access System) system maintained by the Space Science and Engineering Center of the University of Wisconsin at

Madison. McIDAS also uses the VIS-5D format to store data, and users of both systems often refer to VIS-5D files as "McIDAS 5D grid files", or simply as "grid files."

Because the VIS-5D system is distributed under the GNU public license, it is freely available with full source code. This makes the VIS-5D distribution itself your best source of information for this file format.

File Organization

All VIS-5D files contain three sections of data:

- The 5D file header
- A sequence of 3D grid information headers
- An array of 3D grid data sequences

The file header contains information about the contents of the entire file. The grid information headers are a directory of the grid data sequences stored in the file. The data is a sequence of one or more 3D grids, each of which defines a coordinate point in the numerical data.

There is one 3D grid information header per grid stored in the file. The information header stores the size and location, time and date stamp, variable name, and unit description of a grid or grid point. Each grid point is constructed of five floating-point values referred to as a five-dimensional data set. The five values stored are the three coordinate locations of the grid point, a time step value, and the physical variable name of the grid point.

The three coordinate locations store the spatial dimensions of latitude, longitude, and altitude (rows, columns, and levels) of a point in the three-dimensional grid data set. The time step value indicates the moment in time that the point exists. The variable name is the label used to refer to the point.

Grid points are divided into logical groupings called grid sequences. A grid sequence is one or more grid points that all exist in the same moment in time. A grid sequence is and similar to a single still-image frame in an animation. Displaying the grid sequences in their orderly succession causes the numerical data to become animated.

The duration of time between each grid sequence is called a time step. The time step increments may be as short as one second or as long as years. All of the time steps in a grid data set are the same length of time, and the rate at which the data is displayed by an application may or may not depend on the size of these increments.

Time step values are derived from the time and date stamp data associated with each grid. Time stamps are constructed using the familiar HHMMSS (hours, minutes, seconds) format. For example, 183426 would be 6:34 p.m. and 26 seconds. Date stamps are constructed using the less familiar YYDDD format, where YY is the last two digits of the year and DDD is the number of the day of the year. For example, June 20th is the 171st day of the year 1994 and would be represented by the date format 94171.

In the following hypothetical example, we have a data set containing 20 grid points. Each point is identified by an integer starting with 1. The data set contains five grid sequences, each containing four grid points. There are five time steps, one per grid sequence, starting on April 7, 1994 at 11:00 p.m. and advancing in 30-minute increments. Each time step is composed of four grid points using the physical variable names A, B, C, and D. Each grid contains data in all three spatial dimensions:

Grid	Seq.	Date	Time	Var.	Latitude	Longitude	Altitude
1	1	94097	230000	A	34076.67	123543.90	4365.7
2	1	94097	230000	B	29086.56	135789.74	4405.6
3	1	94097	230000	C	32567.67	129086.56	4445.5
4	1	94097	230000	D	16095.34	116865.91	4495.4
5	2	94097	233000	A	34184.22	123543.90	4375.7
6	2	94097	233000	B	29006.56	135789.75	4415.6
7	2	94097	233000	C	32567.67	129186.56	4455.5
8	2	94097	233000	D	16567.34	115765.91	4505.4
9	3	94098	000000	A	34262.47	123543.90	4385.7
10	3	94098	000000	B	29008.22	135789.76	4425.6
11	3	94098	000000	C	32567.67	129286.56	4465.5
12	3	94098	000000	D	16456.34	114365.91	4515.4
13	4	94098	003000	A	34666.14	123543.90	4395.7
14	4	94098	003000	B	28055.46	135789.77	4435.6
15	4	94098	003000	C	32567.67	129386.56	4475.5
16	4	94098	003000	D	16234.34	112165.91	4525.4
17	5	94098	010000	A	34776.20	123543.90	4405.7
18	5	94098	010000	B	28006.01	135789.78	4445.6
19	5	94098	010000	C	32567.67	129486.56	4485.5
20	5	94098	010000	D	16123.34	120486.91	4535.4

As you can see, this data is animated by displaying each successive grid sequence as a frame in a movie. In this example, the four grid points are displayed in sequence and would appear to move as their position changes over time.

Although it is possible to construct a simple data set consisting of one dimension, no time dynamic, and only one variable, it is more likely that data stored using the VIS-5D format will use all five dimensions.

Grid files are typically named using file mask GR3Dnnnn, where nnnn is a zero-padded number in the range of 0001 to 9999. This number is referred to as the grid file number and is used to sequence and identify grid files associated with a project. Grid files typically do not use a file extension.

A single grid file may contain a maximum of 100,000,000 grid points, which is 400 megabytes of data. If this is not enough for your application, VIS-5D allows single data sets to span multiple disk files.

File Details

All VIS-5D files begin with a 256-byte header in the following format:

```
typedef struct _Vis5DHeader
{
    CHAR  Identifier[32];   /* File description field */
    LONG  ProjectNumber;    /* Project number */
    LONG  CreationDate;     /* Date file was created */
    LONG  MaximumSize;      /* No. of data points in largest 3D grid */
    LONG  NumberOfGrids;    /* No. of 3D grids in the data */
    LONG  FirstGrid;        /* Location of first grid */
    LONG  Padding[51];      /* Alignment padding */
} VIS5DHEADER;
```

Identifier is a 32-byte field used to store a NULL-terminated character string which is used to identify the file and its contents. This field, when blank, may be filled with all NULL (00h) or SPACE (20h) characters.

ProjectNumber is a user-defined value used to identify the project to which a VIS-5D file belongs. If a project number is not required, this value may then equal the grid file number used to construct the file name, or may be set to 00h.

CreationDate is the date the VIS-5D file was created in YYDDD format. A value of 01h indicates that no creation date was specified.

MaximumSize is the number of data points in the largest 3D grid. This value is the product of the number of rows, columns, and levels in the largest grid.

NumberOfGrids is the total number of 3D grids in the data. This value is the product of the number of time steps and parameters in the data.

FirstGrid is the offset location of the first grid in the data. This offset value is the number of 4-byte LONG values from the first grid to the beginning of the file. The first grid usually follows the last 3D grid information header in the file.

Padding is 204 bytes of filler used to pad the header out to a length of 256 bytes. This field is set to a value of 00h.

Following the header is a sequence of 3D grid information headers. Each header may be thought of as an entry in a directory of grid point data found in a grid file. There will be one information header per grid point stored in the file, and the number of grids is equal to the product of the number of time steps and physical parameters.

All 3D grid information headers are 256 bytes in length and have the following format:

```
typedef struct _3DGridInformationHeader
{
    LONG  Size;               /* Number of data points */
    LONG  NumberOfRows;       /* Number of rows */
    LONG  NumberOfColumns     /* Number of columns */
    LONG  NumberOfLevels;     /* Number of levels */
    LONG  DataLocation;       /* Location of grid data */
    LONG  Date;               /* Grid date stamp */
    LONG  Time;               /* Grid time stamp */
    LONG  Padding1;           /* Alignment padding */
    CHAR  ParamName[4];       /* 4-character variable or parameter name */
    CHAR  UnitsDesc[4];       /* 4-character units description */
    LONG  Padding2[11];       /* Alignment padding */
    LONG  IType;              /* Always 04h */
    LONG  NorthLatitude;      /* North latitude * 10000 */
    LONG  WestLongitude;      /* West longitude * 10000 */
    LONG  LatitudeIncrement;  /* Latitude increment * 10000 */
    LONG  LongitudeIncrement; /* Longitude increment * 10000 */
    LONG  Padding3[4];        /* Alignment padding */
    LONG  IhType;             /* Always 01h */
    LONG  TopAltitude;        /* Top altitude * 1000 */
    LONG  AltitudeIncrement;  /* Altitude increment * 1000 */
```

```
    LONG  Padding4[31];  /* Alignment padding */
} 3DGRIDINFOHEADER;
```

Size is equal to the number of 4-byte data points in the grid. This value is always equal to NumberOfRows * NumberOfColumns * NumberOfLevels.

NumberOfRows, NumberOfColumns, and NumberOfLevels are the number of rows, columns, and levels, respectively, in the grid data.

DataLocation is the location of the grid data in the file stored as the number of 4-byte LONG values from the beginning of the file.

Date is the date stamp of the grid data in YYDDD format.

Time is the time stamp of the grid in HHMMSS format.

Padding1 is four bytes of filler used to align the first seven fields of the header on a 32-byte boundary. This field is set to a value of 00h.

ParamName is a 4-character ASCII string which is the physical variable name used to represent the grid point. This field is not NULL-terminated and is padded with SPACE (20h) characters if needed.

UnitsDesc is a 4-character ASCII string which describes the unit of measure used by the grid point. This field is not NULL-terminated and is padded with SPACE (20h) characters if needed.

Padding2 is 44 bytes of filler used to align the previous ten fields. This field is set to a value of 00h.

IType is always set to the value 04h.

NorthLatitude is the Northern-most latitude in the grid data multiplied by 10000.

WestLongitude is the Western-most longitude in the grid data multiplied by 10000.

LatitudeIncrement is the latitude increment multiplied by 10000.

LongitudeIncrement is the longitude increment multiplied by 10000.

Padding3 is 16 bytes of filler used to align the previous 16 fields. This field is set to a value of 00h.

IhType is always set to the value 01h.

TopAltitude is the highest altitude multiplied by 1000.

AltitudeIncrement is the altitude increment multiplied by 1000.

Padding4 is 124 bytes of filler used to pad the information header out to a length of 256 bytes. This field is set to a value of 00h.

The actual grid data is a five-dimensional array of floating-point values:

```
FLOAT GridArray[TimeSteps][Parameters][Levels][Columns][Rows];
```

TimeSteps is the number of time steps in this grid data set.

Parameters is the number of physical parameters used by the grid data set.

Levels is the number of levels (altitude).

Columns is the number of columns (longitude).

Rows is the number of rows (latitude).

An array containing only one grid using one time step and one variable would be declared as:

```
FLOAT GridArray[1][1][1][1][1];
```

while an array containing 1644 grids using 12 parameters and 137 time steps in each sequence would be declared as:

```
FLOAT GridArray[137][12][1644][1644][1644];
```

The Northwest-bottom corner of the data set is:

```
GridArray[TimeSteps][Parameters][0][0][0];
```

The Southeast-top corner is:

```
GridArray[TimeSteps][Parameters][Levels - 1][Columns - 1][Rows - 1];
```

Empty or missing data in a grid element is indicated by a value of 1.0e35.

For Further Information

For further information about VIS-5D, see the documentation and sample code on the CD-ROM that accompanies this book. For additional information or to be added to the VIS-5D mailing list, contact:

Space Science and Engineering Center
Attn: Bill Hibbard or Brian Paul
University of Wisconsin - Madison
1225 West Dayton Street
Madison, WI 53706
Bill Hibbard: *whibbard@macc.wisc.edu*
Brian Paul: *brianp@ssec.wisc.edu*

The VIS-5D distribution is available via FTP at the following site:

iris.ssec.wisc.edu (in the *pub/vis5d directory*)

There is no official VIS-5D file format specification, but the files *README* and *util/sample.c* (included on the CD-ROM) should be of special interest.

Vivid and Bob

NAME:	Vivid, Bob
ALSO KNOWN AS:	None
TYPE:	Scene description
COLORS:	NA
COMPRESSION:	No
MAXIMUM IMAGE SIZE:	NA
MULTIPLE IMAGES PER FILE:	NA
NUMERICAL FORMAT:	NA
ORIGINATOR:	Stephen Coy
PLATFORM:	All
SUPPORTING APPLICATIONS:	Vivid and Bob ray tracers, other ray-trace applications
SPECIFICATION ON CD:	No
CODE ON CD:	No
IMAGES ON CD:	No
SEE ALSO:	DKB, NFF, P3D, POV, PRT, QRT, Radiance, Rayshade
USAGE:	Vivid has been widely distributed on the Internet.
COMMENTS:	You might want to look at these if you're thinking about writing a ray tracer, mainly because the code is available.

Overview

Vivid and Bob are two separate ray-trace applications originated and maintained by their author, Stephen Coy. They both use proprietary scene-input formats designed by the author. We are not able to include file format specifications for Vivid and Bob on the CD-ROM that accompanies this book, although we would like to, because these formats have had a substantial impact on other ray trace formats. About Vivid, Mr. Coy writes:

> Vivid's file format is constantly changing, so that anything I could give you would be out-of-date even before you could publish it. In the last year since version 2.0 came out, I've released 18 new test versions covering bug fixes and new features, with several hundred lines of notes and

changes to the documentation. Vivid 3.0 will be released within the next couple of months, but until that time there's no single document fully describing the file format as it currently is.

About Bob, he writes:

The Bob file formats are documented in the book *Photorealism and Ray Tracing in C,* which anyone who is legally using Bob already has.

File Organization and Details

We've pulled together what information we have been able to obtain about the Vivid and Bob formats here.

The Vivid input module is case-sensitive, and the system understands a right-hand coordinate system. Colors are expressed as RGB triplets, and each of R, G, and B falls into the range 0 to 1. Certain mathematical operations are available, and are designed for use with both vectors and numerical values. Vector operations include the following:

Addition
Subtraction
Scalar multiplication
Dot and cross products

Scalar operations include the following:

Addition
Subtraction
Multiplication
Division
Exponentiation

The system also supports the following functions:

Sine
Cosine
Tangent
Arcsine
Arccosin
Arctangent
Square roots

Operator precedence appears to be poorly developed, so liberal use of parentheses in complex expressions is recommended.

Comments are the same as in ANSI C, which means that both

```
/* a comment */
```

and

```
// a comment
```

are supported.

Normal files contain what the documentation refers to as a studio description, which consists of the image size, antialiasing state, and viewpoint. This description is followed by definitions of lights, surfaces, and objects. Lights and surface definitions persist until redefined. Objects, as in most systems of this type, are simply geometric descriptions.

The Vivid system is implemented partly through the use of a preprocessor. Some versions of Vivid leave a temporary file, *XYZZY.V* subsequent to invocation. This appears to be an error in the system, but it may have some utility in debugging. Macros are contained between normal parentheses, and multiline macros, as in the C preprocessor, must have each line terminated with the line continuation character (\).

For Further Information

For further information about the Vivid and Bob file formats, refer to the documentation that comes with the applications. In particular, for Bob, refer to the following book that comes with the system:

> *Photorealism and Ray Tracing in C*

For information about obtaining these applications, contact the author:

Stephen Coy
coy@plato.ds.boeing.com

NAME:	Wavefront OBJ
ALSO KNOWN AS:	Wavefront Object, OBJ
TYPE:	3D Vector
COLORS:	Unlimited
COMPRESSION:	Uncompressed
MAXIMUM IMAGE SIZE:	Unlimited
MULTIPLE IMAGES PER FILE:	Yes
NUMERICAL FORMAT:	NA
ORIGINATOR:	Wavefront
PLATFORM:	UNIX
SUPPORTING APPLICATIONS:	Advanced Visualizer
SPECIFICATION ON CD:	Yes
CODE ON CD:	No
IMAGES ON CD:	No
SEE ALSO:	Wavefront RLA

USAGE: Used to store and interchange 3D vector data.

COMMENTS: Because of the high-end market for Wavefront services, this format has not been widely distributed to date, but it is worth taking a look at.

Overview

Wavefront OBJ (Object) files are used by Wavefront's Advanced Visualizer application to store geometrical objects to disk and to interchange data with other software applications. The current release of the OBJ format is 3.0, which supersedes the previous 2.11 release.

Object files may be stored in ASCII format (using the .OBJ file extension) or in binary format (using the .MOD extension). The binary format is proprietary to Wavefront, and therefore only the ASCII format is described here.

In the 3.0 release, the OBJ file format supports both polygonal and free-form objects. Polygonal geometry uses points, lines, and faces to define objects, while free-form geometry uses curves and surfaces. Rational and non-rational forms of curve or surface types supported include Bezier, B-spline, Cardinal (Catmull-Rom splines), and Taylor.

File Organization

OBJ files do not have any sort of header. Each line in an OBJ file begins with a keyword and is followed by the data for that keyword. Keyword lines are read and their data processed until the 'end' keyword is reached.

Comments may appear anywhere in an OBJ file and are ignored by OBJ file readers. A comment is any line that begins with the '#' character; in a multi-line comment, each line must begin with a # character.

```
# This is a comment line
```

The following keywords may be included in an OBJ file. In this list, keywords are arranged by data type, and each is followed by a brief description.

Vertex data:

v	Geometric vertices
vt	Texture vertices
vn	Vertex normals
vp	Parameter space vertices

Free-form curve/surface attributes:

deg	Degree
bmat	Basis matrix
step	Step size
cstype	Curve or surface type

Elements:

p	Point
l	Line
f	Face
curv	Curve
curv2	2D curve
surf	Surface

Free-form curve/surface body statements:

parm	Parameter values
trim	Outer trimming loop

hole	Inner trimming loop
scrv	Special curve
sp	Special point
end	End statement

Connectivity between free-form surfaces:

con	Connect

Grouping:

g	Group name
s	Smoothing group
mg	Merging group
o	Object name

Display/render attributes:

bevel	Bevel interpolation
c_interp	Color interpolation
d_interp	Dissolve interpolation
lod	Level of detail
usemtl	Material name
mtllib	Material library
shadow_obj	Shadow casting
trace_obj	Ray tracing
ctech	Curve approximation technique
stech	Surface approximation technique

File Details

This section contains examples of OBJ files:

Bezier Patch

```
# 3.0 Bezier patch
v -5.000000 -5.000000 0.000000
v -5.000000 -1.666667 0.000000
v -5.000000 1.666667 0.000000
v -5.000000 5.000000 0.000000
v -1.666667 -5.000000 0.000000
```

```
v -1.666667 -1.666667 0.000000
v -1.666667 1.666667 0.000000
v -1.666667 5.000000 0.000000
v 1.666667 -5.000000 0.000000
v 1.666667 -1.666667 0.000000
v 1.666667 1.666667 0.000000
v 1.666667 5.000000 0.000000
v 5.000000 -5.000000 0.000000
v 5.000000 -1.666667 0.000000
v 5.000000 1.666667 0.000000
v 5.000000 5.000000 0.000000

# 16 vertices

cstype bezier
deg 3 3
surf 0.000000 1.000000 0.000000 1.000000 13 14 \
               15 16 9 10 11 12 5 6 7 8 1 2 3 4
parm u 0.000000 1.000000
parm v 0.000000 1.000000
end
# 1 element
```

Cardinal Curve

```
# 3.0 Cardinal curve

v 0.940000    1.340000 0.000000
v -0.670000 0.820000 0.000000
v -0.770000 -0.940000 0.000000
v 1.030000 -1.350000 0.000000
v 3.070000 -1.310000 0.000000
# 6 vertices

cstype cardinal
deg 3
curv 0.000000 3.000000 1 2 3 4 5 6
parm u 0.000000 1.000000 2.000000 3.000000 end
# 1 element
```

Texture-mapped Square

```
# A 2 x 2 square mapped with a 1 x 1 square
# texture stretched to fit the square exactly.

mtllib master.mtl

v  0.000000 2.000000 0.000000
v  0.000000 0.000000 0.000000
v  2.000000 0.000000 0.000000
v  2.000000 2.000000 0.000000
vt 0.000000 1.000000 0.000000
vt 0.000000 0.000000 0.000000
vt 1.000000 0.000000 0.000000
vt 1.000000 1.000000 0.000000
# 4 vertices

usemtl wood
f 1/1 2/2 3/3 4/4
# 1 element
```

Cube with Materials

```
# This cube has a different material
# applied to each of its faces.

    mtllib master.mtl

    v  0.000000    2.000000    2.000000
    v  0.000000    0.000000    2.000000
    v  2.000000    0.000000    2.000000
    v  2.000000    2.000000    2.000000
    v  0.000000    2.000000    0.000000
    v  0.000000    0.000000    0.000000
    v  2.000000    0.000000    0.000000
    v  2.000000    2.000000    0.000000
    # 8 vertices

    g front
    usemtl red
    f 1 2 3 4
    g back
    usemtl blue
    f 8 7 6 5
```

```
g right
usemtl green
f 4 3 7 8
g top
usemtl gold
f 5 1 4 8
g left
usemtl orange
f 5 6 2 1
g bottom
usemtl purple
f 2 6 7 3
# 6 elements
```

Cube Casting a Shadow

```
# In this example, the cube casts a shadow on the other objects
# when it is rendered with Image. The cube, which is stored in
# the file cube.obj, references itself as the shadow object.
```

```
mtllib master.mtl
shadow_obj cube.obj

v  0.000000    2.000000    2.000000
v  0.000000    0.000000    2.000000
v  2.000000    0.000000    2.000000
v  2.000000    2.000000    2.000000
v  0.000000    2.000000    0.000000
v  0.000000    0.000000    0.000000
v  2.000000    0.000000    0.000000
v  2.000000    2.000000    0.000000
# 8 vertices

g front
usemtl red
f 1 2 3 4
g back
usemtl blue
f 8 7 6 5
g right
usemtl green
f 4 3 7 8
g top
```

```
usemtl gold
f 5 1 4 8
g left
usemtl orange
f 5 6 2 1
g bottom
usemtl purple
f 2 6 7 3
# 6 elements
```

Cube Casting a Reflection

```
# This cube casts its reflection on any reflective objects when
# it is rendered with Image. The cube, which is stored in the
# file cube.obj, references itself as the trace object.

    mtllib master.mtl
    trace_obj cube.obj

    v  0.000000      2.000000      2.000000
    v  0.000000      0.000000      2.000000
    v  2.000000      0.000000      2.000000
    v  2.000000      2.000000      2.000000
    v  0.000000      2.000000      0.000000
    v  0.000000      0.000000      0.000000
    v  2.000000      0.000000      0.000000
    v  2.000000      2.000000      0.000000
    # 8 vertices

    g front
    usemtl red
    f 1 2 3 4
    g back
    usemtl blue
    f 8 7 6 5
    g right
    usemtl green
    f 4 3 7 8
    g top
    usemtl gold
    f 5 1 4 8
    g left
    usemtl orange
```

```
f 5 6 2 1
g bottom
usemtl purple
f 2 6 7 3
# 6 elements
```

For Further Information

For further information about the Wavefront OBJ format, see the specification included on the CD-ROM that accompanies this book.

You can also contact:

Wavefront Technologies
530 East Montecito Street
Santa Barbara, CA 93103
Voice: 805-962-8117

Wavefront also maintains a toll-free support number and a BBS for its customers. Many Wavefront users' groups exist to support customers.

NAME:	Wavefront RLA
ALSO KNOWN AS:	RLA, RLB, Run-length Encoded Version A, Run-length Encoded Version B
TYPE:	3D bitmap
COLORS:	16 million
COMPRESSION:	RLE
MAXIMUM IMAGE SIZE:	64Kx64K pixels
MULTIPLE IMAGES PER FILE:	Yes
NUMERICAL FORMAT:	Big-endian
ORIGINATOR:	Wavefront
PLATFORM:	UNIX
SUPPORTING APPLICATIONS:	Wavefront Advanced Visualizer
SPECIFICATION ON CD:	Yes
CODE ON CD:	No
IMAGES ON CD:	No
SEE ALSO:	None

USAGE: Storage of 3D output data.

COMMENTS: Proprietary, but associated with a well-known application, so likely to be important in the future.

Overview

The Wavefront RLA (Run-Length Encoded Version A) image file format is used to store three types of data:

- Graphics images
- Field-rendered images captured from live video
- Three-dimensionally rendered image data

RLA is used primarily by the Wavefront Advanced Visualizer animation package to store output data and to exchange graphical data with other software applications. There are actually three variations of the RLA image file format.

Prior to 1990, the original RLA format was in use. In this format, RLA was capable of storing only standard graphics images, such as those found in many other bitmap file formats.

In 1990, the capabilities of RLA expanded to include the storage of field-rendered images. Rather than revising RLA (and upsetting many customers in the process), Wavefront created the RLB (Run-Length Encoded Version B) image file format to incorporate these new features. RLB is essentially the original RLA format with a few extra fields added to the header.

Some time later, Wavefront released version 3.0 of the Advanced Visualizer animation package and updated the original RLA format to include all of the new fields found in the RLB format. Wavefront also added and expanded several fields in the header to include the capability of storing multichannel rendered image data—a feature not supported by the RLB format. Thus, the new RLA image file format was born.

Today, the new RLA image file format is the standard format for Wavefront software applications. Both RLB and the original RLA format are considered to be outdated, and future support of these two older formats by Wavefront is questionable.

File Organization

Both RLA formats and the RLB format are always stored using the big-endian byte order. Floating-point data is always stored as ASCII strings to avoid problems with machine-dependent representations of floating-point data. String data stored in the header is composed entirely of ASCII data and is always NULL-terminated. Blank character fields contain all NULL (ASCII 00h) values.

All three formats contain three major sections:

- Header
- Scan-line offset table
- Image data

File Details

This section contains information about each of the components in an RLA or RLB file.

Header

The RLA header is 740 bytes in length and has the following format:

```
typedef struct _WavefrontHeader
{
    SHORT WindowLeft;                /* Left side of the full image */
    SHORT WindowRight;               /* Right side of the full image */
    SHORT WindowBottom;              /* Bottom of the full image */
    SHORT WindowTop;                 /* Top of the full image */
    SHORT ActiveLeft;                /* Left side of the viewable image */
    SHORT ActiveRight;               /* Right side of viewable image */
    SHORT ActiveBottom;              /* Bottom of the viewable image */
    SHORT ActiveTop;                 /* Top of the viewable image */
    SHORT FrameNumber;               /* Frame sequence number */
    SHORT ColorChannelType;          /* Data format of the image
                                        channels */
    SHORT NumOfColorChannels;        /* Number of color channels in
                                        image */
    SHORT NumOfMatteChannels;        /* Number of matte channels in
                                        image */
    SHORT NumOfAuxChannels;          /* Number of auxiliary channels in
                                        image */
    SHORT Revision;                  /* File format revision number */
    CHAR  Gamma[16];                 /* Gamma setting of image */
    CHAR  RedChroma[24];             /* Red chromaticity */
    CHAR  GreenChroma[24];           /* Green chromaticity */
    CHAR  BlueChroma[24];            /* Blue chromaticity */
    CHAR  WhitePoint[24];            /* White point chromaticity*/
    LONG  JobNumber;                 /* Job number ID of the file */
    CHAR  FileName[128];             /* Image file name */
    CHAR  Description[128];          /* Description of the file contents */
    CHAR  ProgramName[64];           /* Name of the program that created
                                        the file */
    CHAR  MachineName[32];           /* Name of machine used to create
                                        the file */
    CHAR  UserName[32];              /* Name of user who created the file */
    CHAR  DateCreated[20];           /* Date the file was created */
    CHAR  Aspect[24];                /* Aspect format of the image */
    CHAR  AspectRatio[8];            /* Aspect ratio of the image */
    CHAR  ColorChannel[32];          /* Format of color channel data */
    SHORT Field;                     /* Image contains field-rendered data */
    CHAR  Time[12];                  /* Length of time used to create the
                                        image file */
```

```
        CHAR  Filter[32];              /* Name of post-processing filter */
        SHORT NumOfChannelBits;        /* Number of bits in each color
                                          channel pixel */
        SHORT MatteChannelType;        /* Data format of the matte channels */
        SHORT NumOfMatteBits;          /* Number of bits in each matte
                                          channel pixel */
        SHORT AuxChannelType;          /* Data format of the auxiliary
                                          channels */
        SHORT NumOfAuxBits;            /* Number of bits in each auxiliary
                                          channel pixel */
        CHAR  AuxData[32];             /* Auxiliary channel data description */
        CHAR  Reserved[36];            /* Unused */
        LONG  NextOffset;              /* Location of the next image header
                                          in the file */
    } WAVEFRONT;
```

WindowLeft, WindowRight, WindowBottom, and WindowTop specify the absolute size of the image in pixels. The home position of the window is normally the bottom-left corner of the display. An image displayed starting from this position has WindowLeft and WindowBottom values of 0.

ActiveLeft, ActiveRight, ActiveBottom, and ActiveTop define the part of the image that is actually stored in the file. Normally, these values are the same as the WindowLeft, WindowRight, WindowBottom, and WindowTop values. However, if the stored image is a clip from a larger image, these values indicate the position of the stored image on the original image. Only the clipped portion of the original image is stored in the file.

The size of the image may be determined using the following calculations:

```
    ImageHeight = (ActiveBottom - ActiveTop) + 1;
    ImageWidth = (ActiveRight - ActiveLeft) + 1;
```

FrameNumber is the image number if the image is one frame in a sequence. Values for this field start at 01h.

ColorChannelType indicates the format of the color-channel data. A value of 0 indicates that the data is stored as 8-bit BYTEs. A value of 1 indicates that the data is stored as 16-bit WORDs. A value of 2 indicates that the data is stored as 32-bit DWORDs. And a value of 3 indicates that 32-bit IEEE floats are used to store the data.

NumOfColorChannels specifies the number of color channels in the file. There are typically three color channels (red, green, and blue) in an image.

NumOfMatteChannels specifies the number of matte information channels in the file. There is typically only one matte channel, or possibly one matte channel per color channel.

NumOfAuxChannels specifies the number of auxiliary information channels in the file. There are normally no auxiliary channels (unless the file contains 3D image data), and this field is set to 00h.

Revision holds the current revision identifier for the image format. This value is always FFFEh. This field holds an auxiliary data-mask value in original RLA format images.

Gamma contains an ASCII floating-point number representing the gamma correction factor applied to the image before it was stored. A value of 2.2 is considered typical. A value of 0.0 indicates no gamma setting.

RedChroma, GreenChroma, BlueChroma, and WhitePoint specify the X and Y chromaticity values for the red, green, and blue primary colors and the white-point reference value. These values are written as ASCII floating-point numbers and have the standard NTSC chromaticity values as their default:

	X	Y
Red	0.670	0.330
Green	0.210	0.710
Blue	0.140	0.080
White	0.310	0.316

JobNumber is a user-defined number that identifies the project or task of which the image is part.

FileName is the name of the image file which stores the data. A maximum of 128 characters may be stored in this field.

Description is a string describing the contents of the image file. A maximum of 128 characters may be stored in this field.

ProgramName is the name of the software program that created the file. A maximum of 64 characters may be stored in this field.

MachineName is the name of the computer system that created the image file. A maximum of 32 characters may be stored in this field.

UserName is the name of the user or system account that created the image file. A maximum of 32 characters may be stored in this field.

DateCreated is the date that the image file was created. A maximum of 20 characters may be stored in this field. Wavefront images typically use the date format MMM DD hh:mm yyyy (e.g., SEP 17 16:30 1994).

Aspect is a user-defined string describing the aspect ratio of the image. This string is used to locate size and aspect ratio information stored in a table. A maximum of 24 characters may be stored in this field. Following is a list of aspect description strings defined by Wavefront:

Description	Width	Height	Aspect
1k_square	1024	1024	1.00
2k_square	2048	2048	1.00
3k_square	3072	3072	1.00
4k_square	4096	4096	1.00
5k_square	5120	5120	1.00
6k_square	6144	6144	1.00
7k_square	7168	7168	1.00
8k_square	8192	8192	1.00
Creator	640	484	1.33
ImageNode	512	486	1.33
Iris-8-10	3000	2400	1.25
Abekas	720	486	1.33
ccir_pal	720	576	1.33
full_1024	1024	768	1.33
full_1280	1280	1024	1.33
iris_1400	1022	768	1.33
iris_2400	1024	768	1.33
iris_ntsc	636	484	1.33
iris_pal	768	576	1.33
matrix_2k	2048	1366	1.50
matrix_2k_ntsc	1821	1366	1.33
matrix_4k	4096	2732	1.50
matrix_4k_ntsc	3642	2732	1.33
ntsc_4d	646	485	1.33
ntsc_512	512	484	1.33
ntsc_512_fld	512	242	1.33
ntsc_636	636	484	1.33
ntsc_636_fld	636	242	1.33
ntsc_640	640	486	1.33
ntsc_640_fld	640	243	1.33

pal_768	768	576	1.33
pal_780	780	576	1.33
pixar	1024	768	1.33
pixar_ntsc	640	486	1.33
pv_2k	2048	1638	1.25
pv_3k	3072	2457	1.25
pv_ntsc	646	486	1.33
pv_pal	768	576	1.33
qnt_pal	720	576	1.33
qtl_ntsc	720	486	1.33
screen	1280	1024	1.25
shiba_soku	1600	1045	1.33
sony_hdtv	1920	1035	1.855
tek_ntsc	720	486	1.33
tek_pal	720	576	1.33
texture_512	512	512	1.00
tga_486	512	486	1.33
tga_ntsc	512	482	1.33
vc_ntsc	640	486	1.33
vfr_comp	768	486	1.33
vfr_rgb	720	486	1.33
vst_hires	1024	768	1.33
vst_ntsc	756	486	1.33
vst_pal	738	576	1.33
vst_pal2	740	578	1.33
vst_targa	512	486	1.33
vtc_mvbhm	1440	1200	1.33
vte_720	720	576	1.33
window	1024	820	1.25

AspectRatio is an ASCII floating-point number used to determine the pixel aspect ratio of the image. This number is the display width divided by the display height.

ColorChannel is an ASCII string identifying the color space model used to represent the image data. Values for this field may be rgb, xyz, or sampled.

Field is set to 01h if the file contains a field-rendered image. Otherwise, the value of this field is 00h.

Time is a string storing the amount of CPU time in seconds that was required to create the image. A maximum of 12 characters may be stored in this field.

Filter is the name of the filter used to post-process the image data before storage. A maximum of 32 characters may be stored in this field.

NumOfChannelBits specifies the number of bits per pixel in each color channel. The value for this field may be in the range of 1 to 32.

MatteChannelType indicates the format of the matte channel data. A value of 0 indicates that the data is stored as 8-bit BYTEs. A value of 1 indicates that the data is stored as 16-bit WORDs. A value of 2 indicates that the data is stored as 32-bit DWORDs. And a value of 3 indicates that the data is stored as 32-bit IEEE floats.

NumOfMatteBits specifies the number of bits per pixel in each matte channel. The value for this field may be in the range of 1 to 32.

AuxChannelType indicates the format of the auxiliary channel data. A value of 0 indicates that the data is stored as 8-bit BYTEs. A value of 1 indicates that the data is stored as 16-bit WORDs. A value of 2 indicates that the data is stored as 32-bit DWORDs. And a value of 3 that indicates that the data is stored as 32-bit IEEE floats.

NumOfAuxBits specifies the number of bits per pixel in the auxiliary channel. The value for this field may be in the range 1 to 32.

AuxData indicates the format of the auxiliary channel data. Valid strings for this field are range and depth.

Reserved is unused space that is reserved for future header fields. All bytes in this field are always set to 00h.

NextOffset is the offset value to the header of the next image stored in the file. The value of this field is 00h if no other images appear in the file.

Scan-Line Offset Table

Immediately following the header is a scan-line offset table. This table is a one-dimensional array of 4-byte integers indicating the starting position of each scan line in the image data.

Each scan line in an RLA and RLB image file is run-length encoded. Because of the variable lengths of the RLE records and packets, it is impossible to detect easily where any scan line begins unless the image is decoded from the beginning.

To locate easily any scan line in the image data, store the offsets to the beginning of each encoded scan line in the scan-line offset table. Each entry in the offset table is four bytes in size, and there is one entry per scan line in the image. All offsets are calculated from the beginning of the image file, even if a file contains multiple images.

Image Data

The image data in RLA and RLB files is separated into one or more color channels (also called *color planes*) and one or more matte channels (also called *alpha channels*). An image using the RGB color model contains three color channels, one each for red, green, and blue color information.

Typically, there is only one matte channel per image, although one matte channel per color channel is possible. The matte channel contains information on the visual appearance of each pixel in the image and indicates the degree of transparency or opaqueness of each pixel when the image is displayed.

The channel information is organized into scan lines. Each scan line of image data therefore contains four (or more) channels of information in the order of red, green, blue, and matte. When a scan line is read, all of the red information is read first, followed by the green information, then blue, and so on.

Multiple images may be stored in a single disk file by simply appending them together. The NextOffset value in the header of one image should contain the offset value of the first byte of the header of the next image. The last image in a file will have a NextOffset value of 00h. This is common way to store a full-sized image and a postage-stamp image (called a *swatch* in Wavefront lingo) in the same file.

Field-Rendered Images

The RLB and the newer RLA format have the capability of storing field-rendered image data. Normally, an image bitmap contains both odd- and even-numbered scan lines. Interlaced video signals, such as those used by television, display frames of video data as alternating fields of odd- and even-numbered scan lines. There are always two fields per frame.

When an interlaced video field is captured and stored as an image, only half of the scan lines in the frame are present in the field. It is therefore possible to store a captured video frame as two separate fields by using two RLA or RLB image files. Odd-numbered scan lines are stored in one file, and even-numbered scan lines are stored in the other. Images stored in this way usually have file names with odd and even numbers to indicate frame and field designations.

Note that in field-rendered images, the header values ActiveBottom and Active-Top indicates the full size of the frame image. The actual number of scan lines stored in each field-image file is half the difference between these values. For example, a 640-line frame creates two 320-line field-image files.

3D Image Data

New RLA images normally contain four channels of information in the form of red, green, blue, and matte data. If a 3-dimensional scene has been rendered to an image, a fifth channel, known as the auxiliary channel, is present and contains information on the depth of each pixel relative to the camera's, or viewer's, location. Auxiliary channel information is stored as floating-point data in the range 0.00 to 1.00 inclusive.

Run-Length Encoding

Each channel of image data in RLA and RLB image files is always run-length encoded (RLE). Each channel within a scan line is encoded into a separate RLE record. Each record begins with a 2-byte value indicating the number of bytes of encoded data in the record. This count byte is followed by the encoded channel data itself. There may be a maximum of 65,535 bytes of encoded data in any record.

Image data with a pixel depth of one byte (one to eight bits) is encoded into packets containing a run-count byte and a run-value byte. If the run-count value is a positive value, then the run value is repeated "run count + 1" times. If the run-count value is negative, the following "run count" bytes are repeated literally. Only runs of three or more pixels are encoded into repeated runs.

Image data with a pixel depth of two bytes (nine to 16 bits) is encoded using a similar algorithm, but the actual bytes of pixel data are read in an interleaved fashion. Two separate passes are made over the pixel data in each channel. The first pass run-length encodes the least significant byte of each pixel in the channel; the second pass encodes the most significant byte of each pixel in the channel.

With image data that contains four bytes (17 to 32 bits) per pixel, a 4-pass process is used, encoding from the least to most significant byte in each pixel. The same algorithm is used for encoding each pass of 2- and 4-byte pixel data as is used for 1-byte pixel data.

For Further Information

For further information about the Wavefront RLA and RLB formats, see the specification included on the CD-ROM that accompanies this book.

The specification for the RLA and RLB file formats is also available in Appendix B of the *Wavefront Advanced Visualizer User Manuals* available from Wavefront:

Wavefront Technologies
530 East Montecito Street
Santa Barbara, CA 93103
Voice: 805-962-8117

Wavefront also maintains a toll-free support number and a BBS for its customers. Many Wavefront users' groups exist to support customers.

WordPerfect Graphics Metafile

NAME:	WordPerfect Graphics Metafile
ALSO KNOWN AS:	WPG
TYPE:	Metafile
COLORS:	256
COMPRESSION:	RLE
MAXIMUM IMAGE SIZE:	NA
MULTIPLE IMAGES PER FILE:	Yes
NUMERICAL FORMAT:	Big-endian
ORIGINATOR:	WordPerfect Corporation
PLATFORM:	MS-DOS, Microsoft Windows, Macintosh, UNIX
SUPPORTING APPLICATIONS:	WordPerfect, other word-processing programs
SPECIFICATION ON CD:	No
CODE ON CD:	No
IMAGES ON CD:	Yes
SEE ALSO:	None

USAGE: Used for storage of document and image data.

COMMENTS: WPG is supported by other applications mainly for compatibility, due to the widespread distribution of WordPerfect for MS-DOS, which is the number one word-processing application on that platform in terms of unit sales. Not used much as an interchange format.

Overview

The WordPerfect Graphics Metafile (WPG) file format is a creation of Word-Perfect Corporation (WPC) specifically for use with its line of software products. WPG image files are likely to be found in any environment that is supported by WPC products, including MS-DOS, UNIX, and the Apple Macintosh.

WPG files are capable of storing both bitmap and vector data, which may contain up to 256 individual colors chosen from a palette of more than one million total colors. It is also possible to store Encapsulated PostScript (EPS) code in a WPG file.

The particular version described in this article is the WordPerfect Graphic file format as created by the WPC products WordPerfect 5.x and DrawPerfect 1.x. For a complete description of the WPG format, refer to the WordPerfect Corporation Developer's Toolkit for IBM PC Products. Information on how to obtain this toolkit is provided in the "For Further Information" section later in this article.

A WPG-format file created using WordPerfect 5.0 can store either bitmap or vector image data, but not both at once. WPG files created under WordPerfect versions 5.1 and later can store both bitmap and vector image data in the same file. Unfortunately, there is no way to tell whether a WPG file contains both bitmap and vector data by reading the header. The actual record data from the body of the file must be read and interpreted.

File Organization

In WPC terminology, a WordPerfect Graphics Metafile contains a prefix area (the header) and a record area (the graphics data). All data in the metafile is written using the big-endian byte order.

File Details

This section contains information about the prefix and record areas of a WordPerfect Graphics Metafile.

Prefix

The prefix is 16 bytes in length and has the following format:

```
typedef struct _WordPerfectGraphic
{
  BYTE  FileId[4];     /* File Id Code (always FFh 57h 50h 43h) */
  DWORD DataOffset;    /* Stat of data in the WPG file (always 10h)*/
  BYTE  ProductType;   /* Product Code (always 1) */
  BYTE  FileType;      /* WPC File Code (always 16h) */
  BYTE  MajorVersion;  /* Major Version Code (always 1) */
  BYTE  MinorVersion;  /* Minor Version Code (always 0) */
  WORD  EncryptionKey; /* Password Checksum (0 = not encrypted) */
  WORD  Reserved;      /* Reserved field (always 0) */

} WPGHEAD;
```

FileId values are four contiguous bytes that contain the standard WPC File ID code. All WPC files starting with version 5.0 of WordPerfect begin with this code. The values for these fields, in order, are FFh, 57h, 50h, and 43h.

DataOffset contains an offset value pointing to the start of the record data in the WordPerfect Graphics Metafile. Because the record data always immediately follows the prefix, and the prefix is always 16 bytes in length, this value is always 10h.

ProductType identifies the WPC software product that created the WPG file. This field always contains the value 01h, indicating that the file was created by the WordPerfect word processor. This value is always the same, even if the WPG file was created by a third-party software application.

FileType identifies the type of data the file contains. For WPG files, the value of this field is always 16h.

MajorVersion and MinorVersion contain the internal version number of the product for which the WPG file was created (which may not match the published, external version number of the product). For all WPG files, the MajorVersion field always contains a value of 01h, and the MinorVersion field always contains a value of 00h.

EncryptionKey normally contains a value of 00h if the file is not encrypted. If the value of this field is non-zero, then the value is used as the checksum of the password and is used to decrypt the file. In the current version, WPG files are never encrypted and therefore the value of this field is always 00h.

Reserved is not currently used and always contains a value of 00h.

Record Area

Following the prefix in WordPerfect Graphics Metafile is the record area. This area contains a sequence of objects and their attributes; this information is used to render the image. Any color maps, bitmaps, and sections of PostScript code are also considered objects within the WPG file record area.

Each record begins with a record prefix (a header in almost any other format). The record prefix may be two, four, or six bytes in length depending on the type of record it precedes. Here are the three possible record prefix formats:

```
/* Two-byte prefix */
typedef struct _TwoByteRecPrefix
```

```
{
   BYTE   RecordType;    /* The Record Type identifier */
   BYTE   RecordLength;  /* The length of the record in bytes (0-FEh)*/

} RECPREFIX2BYTE;

/* Four-byte prefix */
typedef struct _FourByteRecPrefix
{
   BYTE   RecordType;     /* The Record Type identifier */
   BYTE   SizeIndicator;/* WORD or DWORD length follows (always FFh)*/
   WORD   RecordLength;   /* The length of the record in bytes */

} RECPREFIX4BYTE;

/* Six-byte prefix */
typedef struct _SixByteRecPrefix
{
   BYTE   RecordType;     /* The Record Type identifier */
   BYTE   SizeIndicator;/* WORD or DWORD length follows (always FFh)*/
   DWORD  RecordLength;   /* The length of the record in bytes */

} RECPREFIX6BYTE;
```

RecordType, the first field of each record, contains a value that identifies the type of data stored in the record as follows:

Record Type	Record Description
01h	Fill attributes
02h	Line attributes
03h	Marker attributes
04h	Polymarker
05h	Line
06h	Polyline
07h	Rectangle
08h	Polygon
09h	Ellipse
0Ah	Reserved
0Bh	Bitmap (Type 1)
0Ch	Graphics text (Type 1)
0Dh	Graphics text attributes
0Eh	Color map

0Fh	Start of WPG data (Type 1)
10h	End of WPG data
11h	PostScript data follows (Type 1)
12h	Output attributes
13h	Curved polyline
14h	Bitmap (Type 2)
15h	Start figure
16h	Start chart
17h	PlanPerfect data
18h	Graphics text (Type 2)
19h	Start of WPG data (Type 2)
1Ah	Graphics text (Type 3)
1Bh	PostScript data follows (Type 2)

RecordLength, the second field of each record, may be a BYTE, WORD, or
DWORD in size, depending upon the value stored in the first BYTE of this
field (SizeIndicator above). Because it is possible for the same RecordType to
have a different size each time it appears in the same WPG file, each record
cannot be be assigned a RecordType field of a fixed size. You must therefore
determine the size of the RecordLength field when you read the record prefix.

If the BYTE value read after the RecordType field is in the range of 00h to FEh,
the RecordLength field is a BYTE in size, and this value is used as the number
of bytes in the record. If the BYTE is the value FFh, then the RecordLength
field is either a WORD or a DWORD in size.

The next WORD of the prefix is then read. If the high bit of this WORD is 0,
then this value is the length of the record. If the high bit is 1, then this value is
the upper WORD value of a DWORD length value. The next WORD is read
and is used as the lower WORD value in the DWORD. This DWORD value is
then the length of the record. The following code should help to clarify this
logic:

```
BYTE  RecordType;
DWORD RecordLength;
FILE *fp;

RecordType = GetByte(fp);          /* Read the RecordType */
RecordLength = GetByte(fp);        /* Read the RecordLength */

if (RecordLength == 0xFF)           /* Not a BYTE value */
{
```

```
      RecordLength = GetWord(fp);        /* Read the next WORD value */
      if(RecordLength & 0x8000)      /* Not a WORD value */
      {
         RecordLength <<= 16;      /* Shift value into the high WORD */
         RecordLength += GetWord(fp);     /* Read the low WORD value */
         }
   }
```

Example Records

The following is a description of several of the records found in the WPG format. For a complete listing of all records and values, refer to the WordPerfect Developer's Toolkit.

The first record of a WPG file is always the Start WPG Data (0Fh) record. This record contains information on the size of the image and the version number of the WPG file and has the following format:

```
typedef struct _StartWpgRecord
{
   BYTE        Version;          /* WPG Version Flags (always 01h) */
   BYTE        WpgFlags;         /* Bit flags */
   WORD        Width;            /* Width of image in WP Units */
   WORD        Height;           /* Height of image in WP Units */

} STARTWPGREC;
```

Version indicates the WPG file version. This value is currently defined to be 01h.

The eight bits in the WpgFlags field are used as flag values. If Bit 0 is set to 0, then there is no PostScript code included in this WPG file. If Bit 0 is set to 1, then PostScipt code is included in this file. Bits 1 through 7 are reserved and always set to 0.

Width and Height contain the size of the image in WP Units (WPU), each of which is equal to 1/1200th of an inch.

A Color Map (0Eh) record normally follows the StartWpgRecord, unless the image is black and white. If no Color Map record is present, then the default color map is used instead. There is only one color-map record per WPG file, regardless of how many bitmap or vector objects the file contains. The current WPG format does not provide a way to assign separate color maps to specific vector objects and bitmaps.

All images stored in a WPG file, both bitmap and vector, use index values into the color map to define their colors. This record may define an entire color map unique to this image, or it may define only a smaller color map used to overlay a portion of the default color map. To avoid problems with WPC products, the first 16 colors in the color map should never be changed from their default values. The ColorMapRecord has the following format:

```
typedef struct _ColorMapRecord
{
   WORD  StartIndex;      /* The starting index of this color map */
   WORD  NumberOfEntries;/* The number of entries in this color map*/
   BYTE  *ColorMap[][3]; /* Color map triples */

} COLORMAPREC;
```

StartIndex indicates the starting color index number of this map.

NumberOfEntries indicates the number of contiguous entries in the color map from the starting index. If entries 178 though 244 in the default color map were being replaced by this color map, the value of StartIndex would be 178, and the value of NumberOfEntries would be 66. If the entire color map were being replaced, the values of these fields would be 0 and 256 respectively.

These two fields are followed by a sequence of three-byte triples, which hold the actual color map-data. The number of triples is equal to the value stored in the NumberOfEntries field. The number of bytes in this field is calculated by multiplying the value of the NumberOfEntries field by 3. The default colormap for WPG files is the same as the IBM VGA standard color table defined in the PS/2 Display Adapter manual.

The VGA color map structure is also shown in Chapter 2, in the section called "Examples of Palettes."

This color map contains 256 color entries, each with a 1-byte red, green, and blue color value for a total of 768 map elements. The first 16 colors are those of the IBM EGA color table. Colors 17 through 32 are 16 gray-scale shades. The remaining 224 colors are a palette of 24 individual colors, each with three different intensity and three different saturation levels. The WPG color map uses eight bits for red and six bits each for green and blue.

When displaying WPG images using a display adapter with fewer bits per primary color, such as the VGA, the color values are truncated starting with the least significant bits. For a VGA adapter that has only 6 bits for red, all 8-bit red values in the color table are shifted to the right twice before the value is used. The green and blue values are not changed.

As previously mentioned, a WPG file created with WordPerfect 5.0 can store either bitmap or vector image data, but not both. This is due to a limitation of the Bitmap (0Bh) record structure. This record is now considered obsolete and should not be used when you create new WPG files. The structure of this record is as follows:

```
typedef struct _BitmapType1
{
  WORD   Width;         /* Width of image in pixels */
  WORD   Height;        /* Height of image in pixels */
  WORD   Depth;         /* Number of bits per pixel */
  WORD   HorzRes;       /* Horizontal resolution of image */
  WORD   VertRes;       /* Vertical resolution of image */

} BITMAP1REC;
```

Width and Height describe the size of the bitmap in pixels.

Depth contains the number of bits per pixel. The possible values of this field are 1, 2, 4, or 8 for 2-, 4-, 16-, and 256-color images.

HorzRes and VertRes are the horizontal and vertical resolution of the original bitmap in pixels per inch. These values can also describe the minimum resolution of the screen required to display the image.

The bitmap data follows this record structure. The Bitmap (0Bh) record was superseded by the Bitmap Type 2 (14h) record introduced with WordPerfect 5.1. This new record added five fields not found in the Bitmap Type 1 record. These fields contain information on the position of the bitmap on the output device. If you use a Bitmap Type 2 record, it is also possible to store multiple bitmaps in a single WPG file.

The structure of the Bitmap Type 2 record is shown below:

```
typedef struct _BitmapType2
{
  WORD   RotAngle;      /* Rotation angle of bitmap (0-359) */
  WORD   LowerLeftX;    /* Lower-left X coordinate of image */
  WORD   LowerLeftY;    /* Lower-left Y coordinate of image */
  WORD   UpperRightX;   /* Upper-right X coordinate of image */
  WORD   UpperRightY;   /* Upper-right Y coordinate of image */
```

```
WORD  Width;       /* Width of image in pixels */
WORD  Height;      /* Height of image in pixels */
WORD  Depth;       /* Number of bits per pixel */
WORD  HorzRes;     /* Horizontal resolution of image */
WORD  VertRes;     /* Vertical resolution of image */
} BITMAP2REC;
```

RotAngle is the rotation angle of the bitmap in degrees. This value may be in the range of 0 to 359, with 0 indicating the image is not rotated.

LowerLeftX and LowerLeftY describe the location of the lower-left corner of the image in WPUs.

UpperRightX and UpperRightY describe the location of the upper-right corner of the image in WPUs. Note that the origin point (0,0) of all WPG images is the lower left-hand corner of the output device.

The remaining five fields, Width, Height, Depth, HorzRes, and VertRes, are identical to those in the Bitmap Type 1 record.

It is possible to store two or more images in a WPG file by using multiple Bitmap records. The coordinate information found in a Bitmap Type 2 record will allow the images to be positioned on the output device so they do not overlap. The size of a bitmap in bytes may be determined by multiplying the Height, Width, and Depth fields and then dividing the product by 8:

```
SizeInBytes = (Height * Width * Depth) / 8;
```

Bitmap data is always stored in a WPG file using a byte-wise run-length encoding (RLE) algorithm (see Chapter 9, *Data Compression*, for more information on run-length encoding algorithms.) Each scan line is encoded separately.

There are four possible types of RLE packets in the WPG algorithm:

- Encoded packet
- Literal packet
- All-bits-on packet
- Repeat scan-line packet

An encoded packet may encode a run of from 1 to 127 bytes in length. An encoded packet always has the most significant bit (MSB) as 1 and the seven least significant bits (LSB) are a non-zero value. The length of the run is the value of the seven LSBs. If the MSB of this byte is 1, but the seven LSBs are set to 0, then next byte is read as the run count and the byte value FFh is repeated "run count" times. If the MSB of the byte read is 0, and the seven LSBs are a non-zero value, then this is a literal run. The seven LSBs hold the run-count value and the next "run count" bytes are read literally from the encoded data stream. If the run count is 0, then the next byte is read as the run count and the previous scan line is repeated 'run count' times.

The pseudocode for the WPG RLE algorithm is shown below:

```
Read a BYTE
If the Most Significant Bit is ON
    If the 7 LSB are not 0
        The RunCount is the 7 least significant bits
        Read the next BYTE and repreat it RunCount times
    If the 7 LSB are 0
        Read the next BYTE as the RunCount
        Repeat the value FFh RunCount times
    If the Most Significant Bit is OFF
        If the 7 LSB are not 0
            The RunCount is the 7 least significant bits
            The next RunCount BYTEs are read literally
        If the 7 LSB are 0
            Read the next BYTE as the RunCount
            Repeat the previous scan line RunCount times
```

Encapsulated PostScript (EPS) data may be included in a WPG file by using the PostScript Data Type 1 (11h) record or the PostScript Data Type 2 (1Bh) record. The PostScript Data Type 1 record contains a set of output commands needed to print the EPS code included in the WPG file on a PostScript printer. The structure for the PostScript Data Type 1 record is as follows:

```
typedef struct _PsDataType1
{
  WORD   BbLowerLeftX;     /* Lower left X coordinate of image */
  WORD   BbLowerLeftY;     /* Lower left Y coordinate of image */
  WORD   BbUpperRightX;  /* Upper right X coordinate of image */
  WORD   BbUpperRightY;  /* Upper right Y coordinate of image */

} PSTYPE1REC;
```

The four fields in this record contain the bounding-box values of the PostScript image in points. These are the values found in the %%Bounding-Box field in the EPS header. The EPS data immediately follows this record. The PostScript Data Type 2 record is used to store one or more EPS images. If the EPS data also contains a TIFF, PICT, WMF, or EPSI image, as is found in a

Display PostScript file, this data is converted to a Bitmap Type 2 record that follows the PostScript Data Type 2 record.

The structure for the PostScript Data Type 2 record is shown below:

```
typedef struct _PsDataType2
{
    DWORD RecordLength;          /* Length of the following record */
    WORD  RotAngle;              /* Angle of roation of image */
    WORD  LowerLeftX;            /* Lower-left X coordinate of image */
    WORD  LowerLeftY;            /* Lower-left Y coordinate of image */
    WORD  UpperRightX;           /* Upper-right X coordinate of image */
    WORD  UpperRightY;           /* Upper-right Y coordinate of image */
    BYTE  FileName[40];          /* File name of original EPSF file */
    WORD  BbLowerLeftX;          /* Lower-left X coordinate of bounding
                                    box */
    WORD  BbLowerLeftY;          /* Lower-left Y coordinate of bounding
                                    box */
    WORD  BbUpperRightX;         /* Upper-right X coordinate of bounding
                                    box */
    WORD  BbUpperRightY;         /* Upper-right Y coordinate of bounding
                                    box */

} PSTYPE2REC;
```

RecordLength indicates the number of bytes occuring in the Bitmap Type 2 record following the EPS data. If the EPS data does not have an associated Bitmap Type 2 record, then the value of this field is 0.

The RotAngle, LowerLeftX, LowerLeftY, UpperRightX, and UpperRightY fields have the same meaning as in the Bitmap Type 2 (14h) record.

FileName contains the name of the original EPSF file from which this EPSF code was derived.

The BbLowerLeftX, BbLowerLeftY, BbUpperRightX, and BbUpperRightY fields are the same as in the PostScript Data Type 1 (11h) record.

The EPSF code immediately follows this record. The PostScript Data Type 2 record found in WordPerfect 5.1 and DrawPerfect supersedes the PostScript Data Type 1 record found only in WordPerfect 5.0 and DrawPerfect 1.0. You should always use the Type 2 record rather than the Type 1 when creating new WPG files.

The last record in every WPG file is the End of WPG Data (10h) record. This record has a NULL body; it merely marks the end of the WPG record stream.

For Further Information

The WordPerfect Graphics Metafile format was created and is maintained by WordPerfect Corporation. You can try to get information from:

WordPerfect Corporation
1555 North Technology Way
Orem, UT 84057
Voice: 801-222-4477
Voice: 800-526-5068
FAX: 801-222-5077
BBS: 801-225-4414

A complete description of the WPG format and other technical information associated with WordPerfect software applications may be found in the Word-Perfect Corporation Developer's Toolkit for PC Products. This toolkit is available directly from WordPerfect by calling:

WordPerfect Information Services
Voice: 801-225-5000

You can submit technical questions regarding the toolkit to:

WordPerfect Manufacturer/Developer Relations Department
Voice: 801-228-7700
FAX: 801-228-7777
CompuServe: 72567,3612

Please direct all FAX and CompuServe correspondence to "Developer's Toolkit."

XBM

NAME:	XBM
ALSO KNOWN AS:	X BitMap
TYPE:	Bitmap
COLORS:	Mono
COMPRESSION:	None
MAXIMUM IMAGE SIZE:	Unlimited
MULTIPLE IMAGES PER FILE:	Yes
NUMERICAL FORMAT:	ASCII
ORIGINATOR:	X Consortium
PLATFORM:	Any supporting X Window System
SUPPORTING APPLICATIONS:	BRL-CAD
SPECIFICATION ON CD:	No
CODE ON CD:	Yes
IMAGES ON CD:	Yes
SEE ALSO:	XPM
USAGE:	Primarily used for the storage of cursor and icon bitmaps for use in the X graphical user interface.
COMMENTS:	XBM is a monochrome bitmap format in which data is stored as a C language data array.

Overview

Normally, we think of images as data being stored as binary information in a file. In many cases, however, it is more convenient to represent smaller bitmapped images as collections of ASCII data rather than binary data. If such a small bitmapped image is being used by a software application, such as the cursors and icons found in all graphical user interfaces, the images may be stored as an array of ASCII characters, or even as an array of data values stored in the actual software source code.

Storing small amounts of image data directly as C language source code is the philosophy behind the XBM (X BitMap) format. Small images that will be compiled into a software program are stored as simple arrays of data values, with one array used per stored image. XBM files are therefore nothing more than C language source files that are read by a compiler, rather than by a graphical display program or bitmap editor, as are most other graphical files.

XBM bitmap data is mostly found in C source header files (with a .h file extension) and in separate XBM bitmap files (with no file extension). Multiple XBM image-data arrays may be stored in a single file, but none of the images may have the same name, or a naming conflict will result.

The XPM (X PixMap) format is similar to XBM. XPM is a cousin of XBM and is capable of storing color bitmap image data and a colormap. XPM is also an ASCII format and is described in the XPM article.

File Organization

XBM files have a height and width, and may define an optional hotspot within the image. The hotspot is used for bitmapped cursors and indicates the absolute position of the cursor on the screen. The hotspot on an arrow cursor is the tip of the arrow, which is usually located at position 0,0 in the bitmap.

In place of the usual image file format header, XBM files have two or four #define statements. The first two #defines specify the height and width of the bitmap in pixels. The second two specify the position of the hotspot within the bitmap, and are not present if no hotspot is defined in the image.

The labels of each #define contain the name of the image. Consider an image that is 8x8 pixels in size, named FOO, with a hotspot at pixel 0,7. This image contains the following #define statements:

```
#define FOO_width 8
#define FOO_height 8
#define FOO_x_hot 0
#define FOO_y_hot 7
```

The image data itself is a single line of pixel values stored in a static array. Data representing our FOO image appears as follows:

```
static unsigned char FOO_bits[] = {
    0x3E, 0x80, 0x00, 0x7C, 0x00, 0x82, 0x41, 0x00};
```

Because each pixel is only one bit in size, each byte in the array contains the information for eight pixels, with the first pixel in the bitmap (at position 0,0) represented by the high bit of the first byte in the array. If the image width is not a multiple of eight, the extra bits in the last byte of each row are not used and are ignored.

XBM files are found in two variations: the older X10 format and the newer (as of 1986) X11 format. The only difference between these formats is how the pixel data is packed. The X11 flavor stores pixel data as 8-bit BYTEs. The older X10 flavor stores pixel data as 16-bit WORDs. There are no markers separating the rows of image data in either of these formats, and the size of an XBM array is limited only by the compiler and machine using the bitmap.

The X10 XBM is considered obsolete. Make sure that any X software you write is able to read both the XBM X10 and X11 formats, but when you write data, use only the X11 XBM format.

File Details

Following is an example of a 16x16 XBM bitmap stored using both its X10 and X11 variations. Note that each array contains exactly the same data, but is stored using different data word types:

```
/* XBM X10 format */
#define xlogo16_width 16
#define xlogo16_height 16

static unsigned short xlogo16_bits[] = {
    0x0f80, 0x1e80, 0x3c40, 0x7820, 0x7810, 0xf008, 0xe009, 0xc005,
    0xc002, 0x4007, 0x200f, 0x201e, 0x101e, 0x083c, 0x0478,
    0x02f0};

/* XBM X11 format */
#define xlogo16_width 16
#define xlogo16_height 16

static unsigned char xlogo16_bits[] = {
    0x0f, 0x80, 0x1e, 0x80, 0x3c, 0x40, 0x78, 0x20, 0x78, 0x10,
    0xf0, 0x08, 0xe0, 0x09, 0xc0, 0x05, 0xc0, 0x02, 0x40, 0x07,
    0x20, 0x0f, 0x20, 0x1e, 0x10, 0x1e, 0x08, 0x3c, 0x04, 0x78,
    0x02, 0xf0};
```

For Further Information

For further information about the XBM format, see the code examples included on the CD-ROM that accompanies this book.

The XBM format is part of the X Window System created by the X Consortium. The X11 source code distribution contains many XBM files (in the

/bitmaps directory) and C language source code functions (such as XCreateBitmapFromData, XReadBitmapFile, and XWriteBitmapFile), which operate upon XBM data. The central FTP distribution site for X11 is *ftp.x.org*.

Other references containing information on XBM include the following:

Gettys, James, Robert W. Scheiffler, et al. *Xlib-C language X Interface*, X Consortium Standard, X Version 11, Release 5, First Revision, August 1991.

Nye, Adrian, *Xlib Programming Manual*, third edition, O'Reilly & Associates, Inc., Sebastopol, CA, 1992.

XPM

NAME:	XPM
ALSO KNOWN AS:	X PixMap
TYPE:	Bitmap
COLORS:	Unlimited
COMPRESSION:	Uncompressed
MAXIMUM IMAGE SIZE:	NA
MULTIPLE IMAGES PER FILE:	Yes
NUMERICAL FORMAT:	NA
ORIGINATOR:	Groupe Bull
PLATFORM:	X Window
SUPPORTING APPLICATIONS:	XPM Library
SPECIFICATION ON CD:	No
CODE ON CD:	Yes
IMAGES ON CD:	Yes
SEE ALSO:	XBM

USAGE: Used to store X Window pixmap information to a disk file.

COMMENTS: XPM is a de facto format only. There is no official standard file format for storing X multibit bitmap data.

Overview

The XPM (X PixMap) format is the current de facto standard for storing X Window pixmap data to a disk file. This format is supported by many image editors, graphics window managers, and image file converters. (See "For Further Information" later in this article.)

XPM is capable of storing black-and-white, gray-scale, or color image data. Hotspot information for cursor bitmaps may also be stored. Although small collections of data, such as icons, are typically associated with XPM files, there is no limit to the size of an image or the number of colors that may be stored in an XPM file.

File Organization

XPM stores image data in the form of ASCII text formatted as a Standard C character string array. This type of format allows XPM files to be edited easily with any text editor, to have comments inserted at any point within the file, to be included as data in C and C++ programs, and to be easily transmitted via electronic mail.

Also, because of its human-readable, plain-text format, XPM does not support any native form of data compression. External compression programs, such as the UNIX *compress* program, must be used to reduce the physical size of an XPM file.

File Details

The basic syntax of an XPM file is:

```
/* XPM */
static char * <pixmap_name>[] = {
<Values>
<Colors>
<Pixels>
<Extensions>
};
```

XPM files always start with the string XPM, delimited by Standard C comment tokens. This is an identifier indicating that the file contains an XPM data structure. Following this identification comment is a Standard C array containing the actual pixmap data in the form of character strings. The data in this array is arranged into four sections: Values, Colors, Pixels, and Extensions.

The <Values> section is similar to an image file format header. It contains values indicating the width and height of the pixmap, the number of colors in the image, the number of characters per pixel, the hotspot coordinates in the image, and a marker indicating whether the XPM file contains an optional extension section. The hotspot values and the extension marker are optional values and need not appear if there is no hotspot or extension section.

The expanded syntax of the <Values> section is shown below:

```
<width><height><numcolors><cpp> [ <x_hotspot><y_hotspot> ] [ XPMEXT ]
```

The <Colors> section defines the ASCII characters that represent the pixmap data in the <Pixels> section of this array. There is one string in this section per color in the pixmap. Each string in the <Colors> section may be defined using the following expanded syntax:

```
<character> { <key> <color> } { <key> <color> }
```

The <character> is the character(s) used to present a single pixel. The actual number of characters in this field equals the <cpp> value in the <Values> section. The <character> is followed by one or more groups of values. These groups define the type of color(s) each <character> represents.

The <key> indicates the type of color or data represented, and may have one of the following values:

m   Mono
s   Symbolic name
g4   Four-level gray scale
g   Gray scale (more than four levels)
c   Color

The <color> is any of the following:

- A color name
- A # followed by the RGB code in hexadecimal
- A % followed by the HSV code in hexadecimal
- A symbolic name
- The string None, indicating that the pixel is transparent and is part of a masking bitmap rather than a pixmap.

The <Pixels> section contains the actual bitmap data. There is <height> number of strings, each containing <width> number of characters. Each character in a pixel string is a character previously defined in the <Colors> section.

The <Extension> section lets additional string information be stored in the XPM file data. If the XPMEXT marker appears in the <Values> section, then an extension block is found after the <Pixels> section. If there is no marker, then the XPM file extension section does not appear and is said to be empty.

An <Extension> section is composed of one or more sub-sections. Each sub-section may have one of two possible formats. The first format is a single extension composed of only one string:

```
XPMEXT <extension_name> <extension_data_string>
```

The second format is a single extension sub-section composed of multiple strings:

```
XPMEXT <extension_name> <extension_data_string1>
        <extension_data_string2>
```

The <Extension> section always ends with the XPMENDEXT marker.

The following is an example of an XPM file containing a bitmap, a hotspot, four bitmap character colors, and an extension section with four sub-sections:

```
/* XPM */
static char * plaid[] =
{
/* plaid pixmap */
/* width height ncolors chars_per_pixel */
"22 22 4 2 0 0 XPMEXT",
/* colors */
"    c red       m white  s light_color",
"Y   c green     m black  s ines_in_mix",
"+   c yellow    m white  s lines_in_dark ",
"x               m black  s dark_color ",
/* pixels */
"x   x   x x x   x   x x x x x x + x x x x x ",
"  x   x   x   x   x   x x x x x x x x x x x ",
"x   x   x x x   x   x x x x x x + x x x x x ",
"  x   x   x   x   x   x x x x x x x x x x x ",
"x   x   x x x   x   x x x x x x + x x x x x ",
"Y Y Y Y Y x Y Y Y Y Y + x + x + x + x + x + ",
"x   x   x x x   x   x x x x x x + x x x x x ",
"  x   x   x   x   x   x x x x x x x x x x x ",
"x   x   x x x   x   x x x x x x + x x x x x ",
"  x   x   x   x   x   x x x x x x x x x x x ",
"x   x   x x x   x   x x x x x x + x x x x x ",
"          x               x x x Y x x x ",
"          x             x   x   Y   x   x   ",
"          x               x x x Y x x x ",
"          x             x   x   Y   x   x   ",
"          x               x x x Y x x x ",
"x x x x x x x x x x x x x x x x x x x x x x ",
"          x               x x x Y x x x ",
"          x             x   x   Y   x   x   ",
"          x               x x x Y x x x ",
```

```
"          x           x  x  Y  x  x   ",
"          x            x x x Y x x x ",
"XPMEXT ext1 data1",
"XPMEXT ext2",
"data2_1",
"data2_2",
"XPMEXT ext3",
"data3",
"XPMEXT",
"data4",
"XPMENDEXT"
};
```

For Further Information

For further information about the XPM format, see the code examples included on the CD that accompanies this book.

The XPM file format was created by Arnaud Le Hors and Colas Nahaboo of the KOALA Project at Groupe Bull Research. If you have questions or comments about XPM, you can contact:

> BULL Research
> c/o INRIA
> 2004 route des Lucoiles
> 06565 Valbonne Cedex
> FRANCE
> *lehors@sophia.inria.fr*

You can subscribe to the XPM mailing list by sending an email request to:

> *xpm-talk-request@sophia.inria.fr*

The XPM Library is a collection of Xlib-level functions for the X Window System that read, write, and manipulate XPM data in both files and in memory. The latest version of this library may be obtained by anonymous FTP from:

> *avahi.inria.fr* in the directory *contrib/xpm.tar.Z*
> or
> *export.lcs.mit.edu*

The current version of the XPM library is 3.2g (April 1993).

Other applications capable of generating XPM output include xsnap and pixt, both available via anonymous FTP from *avahi.inria.fr* or *ftp.x.org*. A number of software packages included on the CD-ROM also support the conversion of

XPM files; see the discussion of FBM, ImageMagick, pbmplus, xli, XLoadimage, and xv in Appendix C, *What's On The CD-ROM?*.

A collection of XPM icons also exists in *ftp.x.org* in the directory *contrib/AIcons*.

XWD

NAME:	XWD
ALSO KNOWN AS:	X Window Dump
TYPE:	Bitmap
COLORS:	Unlimited
COMPRESSION:	Uncompressed
MAXIMUM IMAGE SIZE:	64Kx64K
MULTIPLE IMAGES PER FILE:	No
NUMERICAL FORMAT:	Big- and little-endian
ORIGINATOR:	X Consortium
PLATFORM:	UNIX X Windows
SUPPORTING APPLICATIONS:	Many
SPECIFICATION ON CD:	Yes
CODE ON CD:	Yes (in FBM, ImageMagick, pbmplus, xli, xloadimage, and xv packages)
IMAGES ON CD:	No
SEE ALSO:	None

USAGE: XWD is used to store images of captured X window displays.

COMMENTS: Many image-processing and display applications and toolkits read and write XWD format image files.

Overview

The XWD (X Window Dump) format is used specifically to store screen dumps created by the X Window System. Under X11, screen dumps are created by the *xwd* client. Using *xwd*, the window or background is selected to dump and an XWD file is produced containing an image of the window. If you issue the following command:

```
% xwd -root > output.xwd
```

the entire contents of the current display are saved to the file *output.xwd*. The *id* of the window to dump may also be specified by using the *–id* command-line flag on versions of *xwd* prior to Release 5.

File Organization

The first version of the X Window System to support window dumps was X10. Only gray-scale and color-mapped dumps were supported, and the bitmapped data was never compressed. The X10 version of XWD contains the following header:

```
typedef struct _X10WindowDump
{
    LONG  HeaderSize;            /* Header size in bytes */
    LONG  FileVersion;          /* X10 XWD file version (always 06h) */
    LONG  DisplayType;          /* Display type */
    LONG  DisplayPlanes;        /* Number of display planes */
    LONG  PixmapFormat;         /* Pixmap format */
    LONG  PixmapWidth;          /* Pixmap width */
    LONG  PixmapHeight;         /* Pixmap height */
    SHORT WindowWidth;          /* Window width */
    SHORT WindowHeight;         /* Window height */
    SHORT WindowX;              /* Window upper left X coordinate */
    SHORT WindowY;              /* Window upper left Y coordinate */
    SHORT WindowBorderWidth;    /* Window border width */
    SHORT WindowNumColors;      /* Number of color entries in window */

} X10WINDOWDUMP;
```

HeaderSize is the size of the header in bytes. This value is always 40.

FileVersion contains the version number of the XWD file. This value is always 06h.

DisplayType is the type of the display from which the image was dumped.

DisplayPlanes is the number of color planes in the image data. This value is typically 01h or 03h.

PixmapFormat indicates the format of the bitmap. A value of 00h indicates a single-plane bitmap (XYFormat), and a value of 01h indicates a bitmap with two or more planes (ZFormat).

PixmapWidth and PixmapHeight represent the size of the image in pixels.

WindowWidth and WindowHeight represent the size of the window to display.

WindowX and WindowY represent the position of the window on the display.

WindowBorderWidth indicates the width of the window border in pixels.

WindowNumColors specifies the number of colors that can be displayed in the window.

If the image is a PseudoColor image, a color map immediately follows the header. The color map contains one entry per color in the image, and each entry has the following format:

```
typedef struct _X10ColorMap
{
  WORD EntryNumber;     /* Number of the color-map entry */
  WORD Red;             /* Red-channel value */
  WORD Green;           /* Green-channel value */
  WORD Blue;            /* Blue-channel value */
} X10COLORMAP[WindowNumColors];
```

EntryNumber is the number of the color-map entry. This value starts at 00h. Color maps typically do not exceed 256 entries in size.

Red, Green, and Blue are the RGB channel values for this entry. The range of each of these values is typically 0 to 65535; often, only the high byte of the value is set (i.e., the value is 0-255 shifted left eight bits.)

The XWD format was revised for Version 11 of the X Window System. The new format can store more types of image data and many fields have been added to the header and to the color map, reflecting the increased graphics capabilities of X11 over X10.

The Version 11 XWD file format contains the following header:

```
typedef struct _X11WindowDump
{
  DWORD HeaderSize;      /* Size of the header in bytes */
  DWORD FileVersion;     /* X11WD file version (always 07h) */
  DWORD PixmapFormat;    /* Pixmap format */
  DWORD PixmapDepth;     /* Pixmap depth in pixels */
  DWORD PixmapWidth;     /* Pixmap width in pixels */ /
  DWORD PixmapHeight;    /* Pixmap height in pixels */
  DWORD XOffset;         /* Bitmap X offset */
  DWORD ByteOrder;       /* Byte order of image data */
  DWORD BitmapUnit;      /* Bitmap base data size */
  DWORD BitmapBitOrder;  /* Bit-order of image data */
  DWORD BitmapPad;       /* Bitmap scanline pad*/
  DWORD BitsPerPixel;    /* Bits per pixel */
  DWORD BytesPerLine;    /* Bytes per scanline */
  DWORD VisualClass;     /* Class of the image */
```

```
        DWORD RedMask;           /* Red mask */
        DWORD GreenMask;         /* Green mask */
        DWORD BlueMask;          /* Blue mask */
        DWORD BitsPerRgb;        /* Size of each color mask in bits */
        DWORD NumberOfColors;           /* Number of colors in image */
        DWORD ColorMapEntries;          /* Number of entries in color map */
        DWORD WindowWidth;       /* Window width */
        DWORD WindowHeight;      /* Window height */
        LONG  WindowX;           /* Window upper left X coordinate */
        LONG  WindowY;           /* Window upper left Y coordinate */
        DWORD WindowBorderWidth;        /* Window border width */

    } X11WINDOWDUMP;
```

HeaderSize is the size of the header in bytes. This value is always 40.

FileVersion contains the version number of the XWD file. This value is always 07h.

PixmapFormat is the format of the image data. A value of 00h indicates a 1-bit (XYBitmap) format. A value of 01h indicates a single-plane bitmap (XYPixmap). A value of 02h indicates a bitmap with two or more planes (ZPixmap).

PixmapDepth is the depth of the bitmap in pixels. This value is 1 to 32.

PixmapWidth and PixmapHeight represent the size of the image in pixels.

XOffset specifies the number of pixels to ignore at the beginning of each scanline.

ByteOrder indicates the byte order of the image data. Values for this field are 00h for least significant byte first, and 0 for most significant byte first.

BitmapUnit is the size of each data unit in each scan line. This value may be 8, 16, or 32.

BitmapBitOrder indicates the order of the bits within each byte of image data. Values for this field are 00h for least significant byte first, and 0 for most significant byte first.

BitmapPad is the number of bits of padding added to each scan line. This value may be 8, 16, or 32.

BitsPerPixel contains the size of each pixel in bits. For StaticGray and GrayScale images, this value is 1. For StaticColor and PseudoColor images, this value is 2 to 15 (typically 8). For TrueColor and DirectColor images, this value is 16, 24, or 32.

BytesPerLine is the size of each scan line in bytes.

VisualClass indicates the format of the image data:

- Even-numbered values indicate fixed-image data that cannot be changed in memory.

- Odd-numbered values indicate dynamic image data that may be altered.

- The values 00h (StaticGray) and 01h (GrayScale) specify a gray-scale image.

- The values 02h (StaticColor) and 03h (PseudoColor) indicate a color mapped image.

- The values 04h (TrueColor) and 05h (DirectColor) indicate true-color image data.

RedMask, GreenMask, and BlueMask are the RGB mask values used by ZPixmaps.

BitsPerRgb is the size of each RedMask, GreenMask, and BlueMask in bits.

NumberOfColors specifies the number of colors in the image. This value also indicates the number of colors for colormapped images as well.

ColorMapEntries contains the number of entries in the color map. This value is 00h if there is no color map.

WindowWidth and WindowHeight are the size of the window to display.

WindowX and WindowY contain the position of the window on the display.

WindowBorderWidth is the width of the X Window border in pixels. If the border has not been captured in the dump, this value is 00h.

The color map immediately follows the header. Each entry in the color map is 12 bytes in size and has the following format:

```
typedef struct _X11ColorMap
{
    DWORD EntryNumber;    /* Number of the color map entry */
    WORD  Red;            /* Red-channel value */
    WORD  Green;          /* Green-channel value */
    WORD  Blue;           /* Blue-channel value */
    CHAR  Flags;          /* Flag for this entry */
    CHAR  Padding;        /* WORD-align padding */

} X11COLORMAP[ColorMapEntries];
```

EntryNumber is the number of the color map entry. This value starts at 00h. Color maps typically do not exceed 256 entries in size.

Red, Green, and Blue are the RGB channel values for this entry. The range of each of these values is typically 0 to 65535; often, only the high byte of the value is set (i.e., the value is 0-255 shifted left eight bits.)

Flags indicates which of the color channels in the color map are actually used. The value of this field is typically 07h, indicating that all three channels are used.

Padding is a byte set to a value of 00h and used to pad the color map entry out to an even WORD boundary in size.

For Further Information

For further information about the XWD format, see the documentation included on the CD-ROM that accompanies this book.

The XWD format is part of the X Window System created by the X Consortium. Information about the XWD format, and, indeed, all of the file formats associated with the X Window System, is scattered over a wide variety of header files (in */usr/include/X11*) and UNIX manual pages.

The central FTP distribution site for X11 is *ftp.x.org*.

Many image-processing and display applications and toolkits included on the CD-ROM read and write XWD-format image files, and documentation for those tools may contain additional information about XWD. See the discussion of FBM, ImageMagick, pbmplus, xli, xloadimage, and xv in Appendix A, *What's on the CD-ROM?*

## PART THREE

Appendices

What's On The CD-ROM?

This book includes a CD-ROM (Compact Disc-Read-Only Memory) containing a great deal of information that will help you understand, use, convert, manipulate, and otherwise make sense of the nearly 100 graphics file formats described in this book.

CD-ROMs provide a durable, cost-effective distribution medium that is becoming the standard way to distribute operating systems, third-party software, and other types of information. On this particular CD-ROM, we've collected a cornucopia of material that you'd otherwise have to beg from vendors, search for through FTP archives, and borrow from friends and colleagues. In many cases, we have been able to obtain the rights to include specifications and software that have never before been publicly available. Enjoy!

NOTE

In addition to reading this appendix, be sure to read the informational files on the CD-ROM for specific instructions for using the CD-ROM that accompanies this book. There are two types of informational files in the various directories on the CD-ROM: *readme.txt* files are provided by the vendor or author of the file format specification or software package; *read_gff.txt* files are written by us and describe file types, necessary file renamings, and cross-reference information.

Using the CD-ROM

If you are new to CD-ROMs, you will need to learn about some specific CD-ROM issues before you can use the information on the CD-ROM that accompanies this book.

The CD-ROM can be used in two different ways:

- It can be mounted just long enough for text files or software to be copied onto a local hard disk. In this respect, it is a distribution medium similar to magnetic tapes or floppy disks. For example, you might mount the CD-ROM, copy the particular file format specification (e.g., TIFF, FaceSaver, etc.) you want to view or print or the particular software package (e.g., pbmplus, Picture Man) you want to run.

- It can be mounted so that it is always present and available as a local read-only hard disk. It will appear as a drive or filesystem, and you can use familiar commands or menu options to peruse it.

The CD-ROM Format

Because graphics file formats are of interest to users of many different platforms—by their very nature, these formats are meant for interchange between platforms—we have chosen to develop a multi-platform CD-ROM for inclusion in this book. This CD-ROM conforms to the ISO standard 9660. Virtually all CD-ROM drives support this standard, although there are some differences in how the files are read and presented, as we'll describe below.

ISO 9660 is the standard approved by the International Standards Organization (ISO) in 1987. This standard is adapted slightly from the original standard proposed by CD-ROM application developers and computer vendors. That original standard was known as the High Sierra format. You will sometimes see the terms High Sierra and ISO 9660 used interchangeably, but they are actually slightly different. ISO 9660 is the standard that will be supported from now on, although ISO 9660-compliant CD-ROM drives will continue to be able to read disks created in the older High Sierra format.

The ISO 9660 standard has the major advantage that it is relatively consistent across platforms. It does, however, impose a few limitations on files and directories:

- Directories may not be more than eight levels deep.

- Directory names may contain up to eight characters with no extensions. The name may consist only of the characters A-Z (or a-z, but cases may not be mixed) and the digits 0-9.

- All file and directory names are monocase. Depending on the driver program associated with your particular CD-ROM drive, they will appear as either all uppercase or all lowercase. For example, the *ATARI.TXT* filename may be displayed as either *ATARI.TXT* or *atari.txt*.

- A filename may contain up to eight characters, with an extension of up to three characters. Filenames (both the name and the extension) may consist only of the characters A-Z (or a-z, but cases may not be mixed), the digits 0-9, and the underscore (_).

With some CD-ROM driver programs, you will notice that a period is appended to the filename (if the filename does not have an extension). You will also notice that a semicolon, followed by a version number, is appended. For example, the *ATARI.TXT* filename might be displayed as any of the following, depending on which system and CD-ROM driver you use:

ATARI.TXT
ATARI.TXT;1
atari.txt
atari.txt;1

For PC users, ISO 9660 will have familiar characteristics because it is basically an MS-DOS format (for example, the familiar 8-character filenames with 3-character extensions).

For UNIX users, ISO 9660 will look quite different. Lengthy UNIX filenames and multiple extensions have had to be changed to conform to the ISO 9660 standard.

For Macintosh users, ISO 9660 will also look quite different. If you are using a Macintosh, you will perhaps be more familiar with the native HFS format for CD-ROMs. On the Macintosh, ISO 9660 is supported by Macintosh CD-ROM drives, including Apple's, but it is considered to be a "foreign format." On the Macintosh, lengthy Macintosh names (and names containing spaces) have had to be changed to conform to the ISO 9660 standard. You will also need to perform an extra step to view files or run programs, as described in "Using the CD-ROM With the Macintosh."

The next few sections describe the structure of the directories and files on the CD-ROM and what to do if you don't have a CD-ROM drive. Next, separate sections describe the specifics of using the CD-ROM and its files on the main platforms we support: MS-DOS, Windows, OS/2, UNIX, and the Macintosh. The final sections summarize the software packages included on the CD-ROM and tell you what to do if you have problems.

Don't Have a CD-ROM Drive?

If you don't have a CD-ROM drive, we strongly suggest that you get one. And not just for this disc—CD-ROM is quickly becoming the distribution method of choice, and not just for software.

To get a CD-ROM drive, the first thing we recommend is to call your system vendor or supplier. Because CD-ROM formats are still in flux, you need to be sure that the drive you get is compatible with both your hardware and your operating system.

Another approach is to call CD-ROM manufacturers directly and ask them whether their drive will work on your platform. This would be helpful if you intend to use the same drive on several different systems, manufactured by different vendors.

On the low end, street prices for CD-ROM drives are now less than $200. On the high end . . . well, the sky's the limit. As the price of the drive goes up, so does its speed. If you want to use the same drive on several different machines, you need to spend more for an external drive.

Using FTP

If you don't have a CD-ROM and won't be getting one any time soon, you can still get a lot of the material provided on this CD-ROM—as long as you have Internet access and/or access to a commercial service such as CompuServe. When a specification or a piece of software is available from one of these sources, we'll tell you in the book. This appendix also describes specifically how you can get software from various sites, and how the filenames and formats correspond to what we've provided on the CD-ROM.

NOTE

All FTP site names and filenames shown in this appendix are subject to change. Because filenames at FTP sites so often include an indication of the program version (e.g., *winjp251.zip* indicates Version 2.51 of the software), the filenames we reference here may change as new versions of the software become available.

Even if you have a CD-ROM drive, you may want to check out these sites as time goes by, because much of the software, the FAQs (Frequently Asked Questions), and even some of the specifications included on the CD-ROM will be updated to new versions over time.

If you are not familiar with FTP and the Internet in general, we highly recommend that you take a look at Ed Krol's book, *The Whole Internet User's Guide and Catalog* (second edition, O'Reilly & Associates, 1994), which describes alternatives to FTP. See also the discussion in Appendix B, *Graphics and Imaging Resources*, for a summary of Internet and commercial resources beyond those described here.

The following shows a very brief example of an FTP session. Here, the user is obtaining the latest version of the PhotoLab software for Windows. (Bold shows what the user types.)

```
%ftp oak.oakland.edu
Connected to oak.oakland.edu.
220 oak.oakland.edu FTP server (Version wu-2.4(3)) Thu Apr 14 22:09:55
Name (oak.oakland.edu:debby): anonymous
331 Guest login OK, send your complete e-mail address as password.
Password:    (Type your user name and host here.)

(Welcome message displayed here.)

230 Guest login OK, access restrictions apply.
ftp> cd pub/msdos/windows3
250 CWD command successful.
ftp> binary         (Very important! You must specify binary
                     transfer for compressed files; you do not need to
                     specify it for ASCII files.)
200 Type set to I.
ftp> mget pholab18.zip
mget pholab18.zip? y
200 PORT command successful.
150 Opening BINARY mode data connection for pholab18.zip (118170 bytes).
226 Transfer complete.
local: pholab18.zip remote: pholab18.zip
118179 bytes received in 59 seconds (2 Kbytes/s)
ftp> quit
221 Goodbye.
%
```

The *pholab18.zip* file is deposited in your current directory. (See the description of PhotoLab later in this appendix for what to do next.)

Contents of the CD-ROM

The CD-ROM contains two top-level directories:

formats
software

These directories contain the various subdirectories described in this section. Figure A-1 shows the general structure of the directories. Tables A-1 and A-2 show the detailed contents.

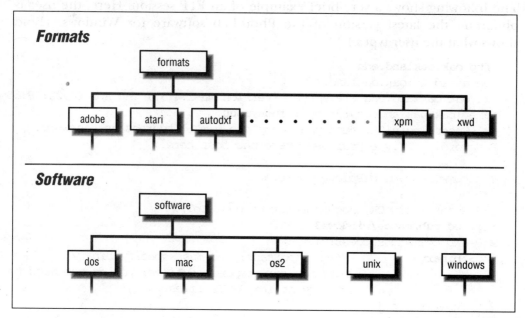

FIGURE A-1: *CD-ROM directory structure*

The formats Directory

The *formats* directory contains one subdirectory for each file format described in this book (except for those few formats for which we have not been able to obtain permission to include any electronic information). For example, there is a subdirectory called *gif* containing information about the GIF file format; there is another subdirectory called *tiff* containing information about the TIFF file format; and so on. (A full listing of the formats supported is included later in this appendix.)

Each file format subdirectory contains whatever resources we've been able to pull together for that format. We've tried to include information in three subdirectories: *spec, code,* and *image.* For example, for the GIF file format there is information in all of the following subdirectories:

formats/gif/spec
formats/gif/code
formats/gif/image

Other formats may contain only a *spec, code,* or *image* subdirectory. In future editions of this book and CD-ROM, we hope that vendors and readers may contribute additional files.

spec

In this subdirectory, we've included the official specification documents obtained from the vendor who owns or supports the file format. In some cases, there is a single document, sometimes quite lengthy. In other cases, the vendor distributes multiple documents, each describing one version or facet of the file format. In general, we have included these documents just as we've received them from the vendors.

However, we have also tried to make the specifications as useful as possible to as large an audience as possible. Although some vendors distribute their specifications in ASCII, many others distribute them in other forms: PostScript, Microsoft Word for Windows, WordPerfect, Macintosh binaries, FrameMaker, etc. When possible, we have converted these formats to ASCII so you will be more readily able to browse through them electronically. (We've usually included the original documents as well.) We've named these ASCII files consistently; for example, in the Microsoft RIFF format directory, the Microsoft Word file is named *ms_riff.doc*, and our ASCII conversion of it is named *ms_riff.txt*.

In some cases, because of copyright or licensing restrictions, we have not been able to convert the ASCII (usually because the vendor was concerned about the potential support problems that could arise because of inconsistent page numbering). In these cases, we have included only the original specification in its original format.

A word of warning about the file format specifications you will find on this CD-ROM: Most of these are internal documents—working specifications rather than polished user documentation. In many cases, we have not had permission to make any changes to these documents, even cosmetic ones. Therefore, you will find that the documents are of uneven quality. Some contain misspellings, missing sections or figures, notes about planned revisions, and other informalities. Nevertheless, these documents are likely to be invaluable to you as you do your work. We chose to be inclusive and not to exclude specifications that happened to be formatted unattractively or that may not be readily readable on your particular platform. You may find that you need to do some conversion on your local system or to read the file using a particular word processor.

On balance, we believe that we have managed to pull together a vast amount of file format information (however uneven in places) that you would have had a great deal of difficulty locating and acquiring on your own. We trust that you will understand that in some cases we have had to make tradeoffs in order to make this information available at all.

NOTE

All of the ASCII text files on the CD-ROM have PC line breaks (a carriage return/linefeed at the end of each line). If you are working on a UNIX or Macintosh system and would prefer more familiar line breaks, you can convert the files using the *crlf* script in the *software/unix/crlf* directory or the *crlf* program in the *software/dos/crlf* directory. Instructions for use are included in the two directories.

code

In this subdirectory, we've included sample code that we have developed, or that we have been able to obtain from the vendors. This code shows how you can read, write, and display files in different formats. We have not included complete standalone applications, but simply segments of code that will help you develop your own applications. This code is written in ANSI C and is platform-independent whenever possible.

A note about the code examples: Many of the software packages on the CD-ROM (in the *software* directory) include source code that demonstrates, far more completely than we can in these short examples, how to read, write, and otherwise manipulate many different file formats. All of the UNIX packages are distributed in source form; several of the other packages also include source. Refer to these packages for additional examples of code.

image

In this subdirectory, we've included sample images associated with the file format; these range from simple line drawings to elaborate images of lizards, planets, X-rays, and Corvettes. Sometimes, we have provided one or two images for a format to help you in testing whether you've implemented the format correctly. Sometimes, we have been able to acquire a large set of images. Not all formats have corresponding sample images; we simply couldn't find programs that made some types of images!

The software Directory

The *software* directory contains software that displays, manipulates, and converts graphics files. We have been fortunate enough to obtain permission to include some excellent software on this CD-ROM.

The *software* directory contains one subdirectory for each major platform: DOS, Windows, OS/2, UNIX, and the Macintosh. Within that subdirectory is a subdirectory for each software package we have elected to include. For example, the directory called *windows* contains the following subdirectories: *convasst*, *lview*, *paintpro*, *photolab*, *pictman*, *pixfolio*, and *winjpeg*.

Each program subdirectory contains whatever files the software author or vendor has provided us. In general, we have preserved the original format of the distribution, so that you can use the standard documentation for these packages.

In a few cases, we have had to change the filenames or compress or expand the files to conform to the ISO 9660 CD-ROM standard. Platform-specific sections included later in this appendix describe these changes. See also the *read_gff.txt* files on the CD-ROM for specific information about filename changes, etc.

All of the UNIX software is provided in the form of source code, just as the authors distribute it on the Internet. Because there are so many possible UNIX platforms, we chose not to try to provide binaries for all of them. You should be able to build the binaries for your own UNIX system without too much difficulty, using the documentation provided with the software.

In most cases, the PC and Macintosh software is provided in the form of executables for the specific platform supported by the author or vendor. These vendors do not typically provide source code.

We have included brief descriptions of the packages in this appendix. We have also included on the CD-ROM any readme and help files and any other online documentation included with the packages.

An important note about the software: We have chosen to include certain packages on the CD-ROM as an extra bonus to readers. To a large extent, this software is beyond the the scope of this book, whose focus is graphics file formats and the specifications that define them. We believed that this software would add to the overall value of the CD-ROM, and we have selected a handful of applications that seemed to be good ones from the many packages available from publicly available sources.

However (this is the important part!), we have not played any part in developing this software, nor can we vouch for it. We have tested the packages on certain platforms and systems, and we have tested for viruses, but we have not been able to do anything resembling a thorough quality assurance on this software.

This is a caveat emptor: We hope you enjoy this software and find it useful. There are many satisfied users. But, O'Reilly & Associates and the authors are not able to support the software ourselves. We don't own it and, in most cases, we don't even have access to the source code. We've provided information on how to contact the vendors and authors at the end of this appendix, and online files and welcome screens contain that information as well. If you have comments or questions, contact them directly, just as you would if you had obtained the packages from the Internet or from a commercial service or bulletin board.

Another important note: Most of the software on the CD-ROM is publicly available, sometimes with a few restrictions, but some of it is shareware. When you execute the programs, you will see a screen informing you of the terms of distribution. You may also find readme files or other documentation in the CD-ROM directories that describe the terms and conditions. In some cases, you will be asked to register and/or pay a fee to obtain more extensive versions of the software and its full documentation. O'Reilly & Associates in no way benefits from these fees, nor can we offer any additional releases or features.

Directory Listings

This section lists the contents of the two top-level directories on the CD-ROM: *formats* and *software*.

formats

As we've discussed above, within each of the formats subdirectories listed in Table A-1 there may be one or more of the following subdirectories: *spec*, *code*, and *image*.

A note about the *compress* subdirectory: It contains the FAQ (Frequently Asked Questions) document for the newsgroup *comp.compression*. This document contains a good deal of helpful information about data compression. Because the FAQ did readily not fall into any format, we've put it in its own directory under *formats*.

TABLE A-1: *formats Directories*

Directory	Format	Spec	Code	Image
adobe	Adobe Photoshop	x	–	–
atari	Atari ST Graphics Formats	x	x	–
autodesk	AutoCAD DXF	x	x	–
bdf	BDF	x	x	x
brl	BRL-CAD	x	–	–
bufr	BUFR	x	–	–
cals	CALS Raster	–	–	x
cgm	CGM	–	–	x
cmu	CMU Formats	x	x	–
compress	Compression FAQ	x	–	–
–	DKB	–	–	–
dore	Dore Raster File Format	x	–	–

Directory	Format	Spec	Code	Image
drhalo	Dr. Halo	x	—	x
eps	Encapsulated PostScript	x	x	x
face	FaceSaver	x	x	—
fax	FAX Formats	—	x	—
fits	FITS	x	x	x
fli	FLI	x	—	x
gemras	GEM Raster	—	x	x
—	GEM VDI	—	—	—
gif	GIF	x	x	x
grasp	GRASP	x	—	—
grib	GRIB	x	—	—
—	Harvard Graphics	—	—	—
hdf	Hierarchical Data Format	x	—	—
—	IGES	—	—	—
inspix	Inset PIX	x	—	x
intdvi	Intel DVI	x	—	—
iff	Interchange File Format	x	x	x
jpeg	JPEG File Interchange Format	x	x	x
—	Kodak Photo CD	—	—	—
kodycc	Kodak YCC	x	x	—
—	Lotus DIF	—	—	—
—	Lotus PIC	—	—	—
lumena	Lumena Paint	x	—	—
macpaint	Macintosh Paint	—	x	x
macpict	Macintosh PICT	x	x	x
mspaint	Microsoft Paint	—	—	x
msriff	Microsoft RIFF	x	—	—
msrtf	Microsoft RTF	x	—	
—	Microsoft SYLK	—	—	—
msbmp	Microsoft Windows Bitmap	x	x	x
msmeta	Microsoft Windows Metafi	x	—	—
miff	MIFF	x	x	x
mpeg	MPEG	x	x	x
mtv	MTV	x	x	—
naplps	NAPLPS	x	—	x
nff	NFF	x	—	—
off	OFF	x	x	—
os2bmp	OS/2 Bitmap	x	x	—
p3d	P3D	x	—	—
pbm	PBM, PGM, PNM, and PPM	x	x	—
pcx	PCX	x	x	—
pds	PDS	—	x	x
pictor	Pictor PC Paint	x	—	—

Directory	Format	Spec	Code	Image
pixrib	Pixar RIB	x	—	—
plot10	Plot-10	—	x	—
pov	POV	x	—	—
presman	Presentation Manager Metafile	x	—	—
prt	PRT	x	x	—
qrt	QRT	x	x	—
qt	QuickTime	x	—	—
radiance	Radiance	x	x	—
rayshade	Rayshade	x	—	—
rix	RIX	x	—	—
rtrace	RTrace	x	—	—
sgiimage	SGI Image File Format	x	—	—
sgiinv	SGI Inventor	x	x	—
sgiyaodl	SGI YAODL	—	—	x
sgo	SGO	x	—	—
sunico	Sun Icon	—	x	x
sunras	Sun Raster	x	x	—
tddd	TDDD	x	—	—
tga	TGA	x	x	x
tiff	TIFF	x	x	x
ttddd	TTDDD	x	x	x
uray	uRay	x	x	—
utahrle	Utah RLE	x	x	—
vicar	VICAR2	x	x	x
viff	VIFF	x	x	x
vis5d	VIS-5D	x	x	—
—	Vivid and Bob	—	—	—
waveobj	Wavefront OBJ	x	—	—
waverla	Wavefront RLA	x	—	—
wpg	WordPerfect Graphics Metafile	—	—	x
xbm	XBM	—	x	x
xpm	XPM	—	x	x
xwd	XWD	x	x	—

software

There are five subdirectories in the software subdirectory, one for each of the following platforms: MS-DOS, Windows, OS/2, UNIX, and the Macintosh. Table A-2 lists the main subdirectories; note that we have not listed those that contain only cross-references to other directories and files.

TABLE A-2: *software Directories*

Directory	Package
dos/	
crlf	PC/UNIX line break conversion programs
imdisp	IMDISP (Image Display)
mpeg	ISO MPEG-2 Codec (MPEG Encoder and Decoder)
pbmplus	pbmplus (Portable Bitmap Utilities)
vpic	VPIC
windows/	
convasst	Conversion Assistant for Windows
lview	LView
paintpro	Paint Shop Pro
photolab	Photo Lab
pictman	Picture Man
winjpeg	WinJPEG (Windows JPEG)
os2/	
gbm	GBM (Generalized Bitmap Module)
pmjpeg	PMJPEG (Presentation Manager JPEG)
unix/	
crlf	UNIX/PC line break conversion programs
fbm	FBM (Fuzzy Bitmap Manipulation)
immagick	ImageMagick
jpeg	IJG (Independent JPEG Group's Library)
libtiff	libtiff (TIFF Library)
mpeg	ISO MPEG-2 Codec (MPEG Encoder and Decoder)
pbmplus	pbmplus (Portable Bitmap Utilities)
sao	SAOimage (Smithsonian Astrophysical Observatory Image)
xli	xli
xloadimg	xloadimage
xv	xv (X Viewer)
mac/	
bbedit	BBEdit text editor for file display
gifconv	GIFConverter
grphconv	GraphicsConverter
jpegview	JPEGView
nihimage	NIH Image
sparkle	Sparkle (MPEG)

Note that in addition to including the source code for pbmplus in the *unix* directory, we have included a port of pbmplus for MS-DOS. The sources for several other packages (FBM, JPEG, libtiff) have been compiled for PC systems as well, although we have not been able to include them on this CD-ROM.

Using the CD-ROM With MS-DOS

This section describes what you need to know about using the CD-ROM with MS-DOS on the PC.

Accessing the CD-ROM Under MS-DOS

Under MS-DOS, the CD-ROM is simply another drive (a read-only one). Insert the CD-ROM, following the directions for your own system and CD-ROM drive. The CD-ROM will be available on the next available drive after your floppy and hard disk drives and partitions (often, this will be D:).

Accessing Specs, Code, and Images Under MS-DOS

You should have no trouble reading the contents of the *formats* directory under MS-DOS.

You can view any of the ASCII specification files (*.txt* files in the *spec* directories) using the type or edit commands or any MS-DOS editor.

As mentioned above, you'll also find PostScript, Word for Windows, Frame, and other types of files in the *spec* directories. You'll need the appropriate applications to read and/or print these files. Some files are specifically Macintosh-format files. We have tried, wherever possible, to include ASCII versions of such files (the *.txt* files in the directory).

The files in the *code* directories are text files as well, and they follow the same conventions as those described for the *spec* directories.

The images in the *image* directories are of various types (e.g., GIF, BMP, TIFF, TGA). You will need to view these files with programs specifically designed for that purpose. Many such programs are found on the CD-ROM.

Accessing Software Under MS-DOS

We have included a number of popular MS-DOS packages on the CD-ROM. Each MS-DOS package is stored in its own directory under *software/dos*. The MS-DOS programs are supplied only in binary form.

To run a program, you'll typically execute the *.exe* file in the directory and follow any directions provided. Be sure to read the readme files for the program, because some of the programs may require you to run a special setup or configuration program. In some cases, you will need to copy the files from the CD-ROM first because the program will need to write files in the current directory (and the CD-ROM is read-only). See the program documentation for details.

Removing the CD-ROM Under MS-DOS

When you are finished using the CD-ROM, you can remove it by simply pressing the eject button on your CD-ROM drive. No program commands are required. Note that on some systems you cannot remove the CD-ROM if you have files open on the device or if you are in a directory of the CD-ROM.

Using the CD-ROM With Windows

This section describes what you need to know about using the CD-ROM with Windows on the PC.

Accessing the CD-ROM Under Windows

Under Windows, the CD-ROM is simply another drive (a read-only one). Insert the CD-ROM, following the directions for your own system and CD-ROM drive. The CD-ROM will be available on the next available drive after your floppy and hard disk drives and partitions (often, this will be D:). Use the File Manager to select the CD-ROM drive. Use the files just as you would any other read-only files.

Accessing Specs, Code, and Images Under Windows

You should have no trouble reading the contents of the *formats* directory under Windows.

For any of the ASCII specification files (*.txt* files in the *spec* directories), you can simply click on the file to invoke the Windows Notepad application automatically; Notepad will read and display the file. You can also use Write, edit, or any Windows editor to view files.

As mentioned above, you'll also find PostScript, Word for Windows, Frame, and other types of files in the *spec* directories. You'll need the appropriate applications to read and/or print these files. Some files are specifically Macintosh-format files. We have tried, wherever possible, to include ASCII versions of such files (the *.txt* files in the directory).

The files in the *code* directories are simply text files as well, and they follow the same conventions as those described for the spec directories.

The images in the *image* directories are of various types (e.g., GIF, BMP, TIFF, TGA). You will need to view these files with programs specifically designed for that purpose. Many such programs are found on the CD-ROM.

Accessing Software Under Windows

We have included a number of popular Windows packages on the CD-ROM. Each Windows package is stored in its own directory under *software/windows*. The Windows programs are supplied only in binary form.

To run a program, you'll typically click on the *.exe* file in the directory and follow any directions provided. Be sure to read the readme files for the program, because some of the programs may require you to run a special setup or configuration program. In some cases, you will need to copy the files from the CD-ROM first because the program will need to write files in the current directory (and the CD-ROM is read-only). See the program documentation for details.

Removing the CD-ROM Under Windows

When you are finished using the CD-ROM, you can remove it by simply pressing the eject button. No program commands are required. Note that on some systems you cannot remove the CD-ROM if you have files open on the CD-ROM or if you are in a directory of the CD-ROM.

Using the CD-ROM With OS/2

This section describes what you need to know about using the CD-ROM with OS/2 on the PC.

Accessing the CD-ROM Under OS/2

Under OS/2, the CD-ROM is simply another drive (a read-only one). Insert the CD-ROM, following the directions for your own system and CD-ROM drive. The CD-ROM will be available on the next available drive after your floppy and hard disk drives and partitions (often, this will be D:). You can use either the MS-DOS-type command interface or the graphical interface. If you use the former, you will handle the CD-ROM files just as described for MS-DOS. If you use the latter, click on the Drives icon in the OS/2 System Folder to open the CD-ROM. Now, use the files just as you would any other read-only files.

Accessing Specs, Code, and Images Under OS/2

You should have no trouble reading the contents of the *formats* directory under OS/2.

For any of the ASCII specification files (.*txt* files in the *spec* directories), you can simply click on the file. OS/2 typically uses the default editor, the OS/2 System Editor. You can also use Notepad or edit if they are available on your system, or any OS/2 editor, to read and display the files.

As mentioned above, you'll also find PostScript, Word for Windows, Frame, and other types of files in the spec directories. You'll need the appropriate applications to read and/or print these files. Some files are specifically Macintosh-format files. We have tried, wherever possible, to include ASCII versions of such files (the .*txt* files in the directory).

The files in the *code* directories are simply text files as well, and they follow the same conventions as those described for the *spec* directories.

The images in the *image* directories are of various types (e.g., GIF, BMP, TIFF, TGA). You will need to view these files with programs specifically designed for that purpose. Many such programs are found on the CD-ROM.

Accessing Software Under OS/2

We have included several popular OS/2 packages on the CD-ROM. Each OS/2 package is stored in its own directory under *software/os2*. Some programs are supplied only in binary form; for GBM, both source and binary are included.

To run a program, you'll typically click on the .*exe* file in the directory or run the .*exe* file from an OS/2 command-line session, and follow the directions provided. Be sure to read the readme files for the program, because some of the programs may require you to run a special setup or configuration program. In some cases, you will need to copy the files from the CD-ROM first because the program will need to write files in the current directory (and the CD-ROM is read-only). See the program documentation for details.

Removing the CD-ROM Under OS/2

When you are finished using the CD-ROM you can remove it by simply pressing the eject button. No program commands are required. Note that on some systems you cannot remove the CD-ROM if you have files open on the CD-ROM or if you are in a directory of the CD-ROM.

Using the CD-ROM With UNIX

This section describes what you need to know about using the CD-ROM with UNIX.

Watching Out for Version Numbers

There is one thing you will need to be careful of if your CD-ROM driver program is one that appends a version number to the filename, as described earlier in this appendix. As we mentioned, some CD-ROM drivers automatically append the characters ;1 to each filename. For example, the file *rtf.txt* might be displayed as *rtf.txt;1*, and this becomes the actual filename. There is nothing we can do about this; it's done by your CD-ROM driver. However, depending on what UNIX platform you are using, your mount command may offer an option (noversion) that you can use to suppress these version numbers.

If you do end up with version numbers appended to your files, you need to be careful when specifying filenames in commands. When you access a filename—for example, to copy it to your system, you must be sure to include the version number in the name. If you are specifying that name in a UNIX shell, you will need to escape the semicolon character using a backslash or to single-quote the entire filename, as shown below.

```
% cp /cdrom/formats/gif/spec/gif_code.txt\;1 gif_code.txt
```

```
% cp '/cdrom/formats/gif/spec/gif_code.txt;1' gif_code.txt
```

If you don't quote or escape the semicolon, you'll get a message like this, because the UNIX shell interprets a semicolon as the delimiter between two commands:

```
% cp /cdrom/formats/gif/spec/gif_code.txt;1 gif_code.txt
Usage: cp [-ip] f1 f2; or: cp [-ipr] f1 ... fn d2
1: Command not found
```

Mounting the CD-ROM Under UNIX

Under UNIX, the CD-ROM is simply another filesystem (a read-only one).

To mount the CD-ROM physically, follow the directions for your own CD-ROM drive. To mount the CD-ROM logically, use the standard UNIX mount command. This command usually has the form:

```
% mount options device-name mount_point
```

The CD-ROM options and device name vary depending on the type of UNIX system. If you do not know the device name, consult the documentation that comes with your system. On some systems, the SCSI ID of the CD-ROM device can vary. The SCSI ID is part of the device name—for example, */dev/rz3c* is the CD-ROM at SCSI ID 3 on a DECstation.

The *mount point* is simply a directory that will become the parent directory of the CD-ROM when it is mounted.

Most systems do not provide a way for unprivileged users to mount the CD-ROM, so you probably need to become the superuser. If you do not have permission to su root, you need to have your system administrator mount the CD-ROM for you.

Because the CD-ROM is read-only, you may have to specify this fact to the mount program or it will generate an error if it tries to open the CD-ROM device for writing. Some systems also need to be told the type of filesystem being mounted if it is not the default (usually ufs or nfs). There may be options to the mount program that control whether all the ISO 9660 features (such as version numbers) are turned on.

For example, the CD-ROM can be mounted on a SunOS 4.1.1 system with the command:

```
# /etc/mount -r -t hsfs /dev/sr0  /cdrom
```

This command mounts the CD-ROM (/dev/sr0) on the mount point (/cdrom) on a High Sierra/ISO 9660-type filesystem (hsfs) in a read-only fashion (–r). If you omit the –r option, mount displays the following error:

```
mount_hsfs:  must be mounted readonly
mount:  giving up on:
    /cdrom
```

If you omit the filesystem type of hsfs, mount displays the following error:

```
mount:  /dev/sr0 on /cdrom:  Invalid argument
mount:  giving up on:
    /cdrom
```

The procedure for mounting a CD-ROM varies with each type of operating system. Here are some additional examples of mount commands for various UNIX systems:

Sun4 and Sun3 SunOS 4.1.1
```
# /etc/mount -r -t hsfs /dev/sr0 /cdrom
```

Solaris 2.0
```
# etc/mount - hsfs -r /dev/c0t6d0s0 /mnt
```

IBM RS/6000 AIX 3.2
```
# /etc/mount -r -v cdrfs /dev/cd0 /cdrom
```

DECstation Ultrix 4.x
```
# /etc/mount -t cdfs noversion  /dev/rz3c /cdrom
```

HP 700 HP-UX
```
# /etc/mount -r -s cdfs /dev/dsk/c201d2sr0 /cdrom
```

SCO UNIX
```
# /etc/mount -r -fHS,lower,intr,soft,novers   /dev/cd0 /cdrom
```

SGI IRIX 4.x
```
# /etc/mount -o ro,notranslate -t iso9660 /dev/scsi/sc0d510 /cdrom
```

You can also start up the cdromd process as follows:

```
# cdromd -o ro,notranslate -d /dev/scsi/sc0dd510 /cdrom
```

To mount, insert the CD-ROM in the drive. To unmount, use the eject command.

OSF/1 for Alpha AXP
```
# /etc/mount -t cdfs -o noversion /dev/rz3c /cdrom
```

Linux
```
# /etc/mount -r -t iso0660 /dev/sr0 /cdrom
```

or (depending on your distribution):

```
# /etc/mount -r -t iso0660 /dev/scd0 /cdrom
```

To get more information for your own system, consult the manual pages for the mount command and look for a mention of CD-ROM, ISO 9660, or High Sierra:

```
% man mount
```

Once the CD-ROM has been mounted, you can change directory to the mount point you specified (the CD-ROM directory name) and can use the files as you would any other read-only files.

For example:

```
% cd /cdrom
```

Accessing Specs, Code, and Images Under UNIX

You should have no trouble reading the contents of the *formats* directory under UNIX.

For any of the ASCII specification files (*.txt* files in the *spec* directories), you can view or print using standard UNIX commands.

As mentioned above, you'll also find PostScript, Word for Windows, Frame, and other types of files in the *spec* directories. You'll need the appropriate applications to read and/or print these files. Some files are specifically PC- or Macintosh-format files. We have tried, wherever possible, to include ASCII versions of such files (the *.txt* files in the directory).

The files in the *code* directories are simply text files as well, and they follow the same conventions as those described for the spec directories.

The images in the *image* directories are of various types (e.g., GIF, BMP, TIFF, TGA). You will need to view these files with programs specifically designed for that purpose. Many such programs are found on the CD-ROM.

Accessing Software Under UNIX

We have included a number of popular UNIX packages on the CD-ROM. Each UNIX package is stored in its own directory under *software/unix*. All of the software is provided in source form, written in C. Although most often these packages are designed for a UNIX environment, in fact they can be, and some have been, ported to other platforms as well. The pbmplus and ISO MPEG-2 Codec ports are included on the CD-ROM, and pointers are provided to several other ports. All of the packages are publicly available.

Because there are many possible types of UNIX systems, we have not provided binaries for the software described in this section. You will find instructions for installing, compiling, and building the software in the online documentation that comes with the packages.

The UNIX software is distributed in the form of uncompressed *tar* files. If you are simply copying the software from the CD-ROM to your own system (the way most users do it), this format is most efficient for you, because you will have to copy only one file. Then, on your UNIX system, you can untar the file to extract from it the many individual files and directories that comprise it.

We have chosen to distribute *tar* files rather than individual program files partly because of ISO 9660 CD-ROM format restrictions. The file-naming and directory structures of these packages conform, in most cases, to standard UNIX, and not to the more restrictive ISO 9660 requirements. Thus, filenames of individual program files are often much longer than the names allowed on the CD-ROM, and directories are, in some cases, deeper than the eight levels allowed.

If you are familiar with the way these UNIX packages are distributed on the Internet, you will note that on the net the files are compressed (e.g., *fbm.tar.Z*), whereas on the CD-ROM they are uncompressed (e.g., *fbm.tar*). Because ISO 9660 does not allow two extensions and because we had plenty of room on the CD-ROM, we chose to simply include the packages in uncompressed format.

To untar a UNIX *tar* file, type the following command (or an appropriate command for your own system):

```
% tar -xvf filename
```

This extracts the individual files from the *tar* file, displays a list of them as it extracts, and places them in your current directory. For example, if you type:

```
% tar -xvf xloadimg.tar
```

you will see this output:

```
xloadimage/
xloadimage/Imakefile
xloadimage/Makefile
xloadimage/Makefile.std
xloadimage/README
xloadimage/build-imake
xloadimage/extract
xloadimage/xloadimage.man
xloadimage/patchlevel
xloadimage/mcidas.h
xloadimage/pbm.h
xloadimage/pcx.h
xloadimage/rle.h
```

xloadimage/sunraster.h
xloadimage/xloadimage.h
xloadimage/xwd.h
xloadimage/cmuwmraster.h
xloadimage/copyright.h
xloadimage/fbm.h
xloadimage/g3.h
xloadimage/gif.h
xloadimage/image.h
xloadimage/img.h
xloadimage/imagetypes.h
xloadimage/jpeg.h
xloadimage/kljcpyrght.h
xloadimage/mac.h
xloadimage/mit.cpyrght
xloadimage/mrmcpyrght.h
xloadimage/options.h
xloadimage/tgncpyrght.h
xloadimage/bright.c
xloadimage/clip.c
xloadimage/cmuwmraster.c
xloadimage/compress.c
xloadimage/dither.c
xloadimage/faces.c
xloadimage/fbm.c
xloadimage/fill.c
xloadimage/g3.c
xloadimage/gif.c
xloadimage/halftone.c
xloadimage/imagetypes.c
xloadimage/img.c
xloadimage/jpeg.c
xloadimage/mac.c
xloadimage/mcidas.c
xloadimage/mc_tables.c
xloadimage/merge.c
xloadimage/misc.c
xloadimage/new.c
xloadimage/options.c
xloadimage/path.c
xloadimage/pbm.c
xloadimage/pcx.c
xloadimage/reduce.c
xloadimage/rle.c
xloadimage/rlelib.c

```
xloadimage/root.c
xloadimage/rotate.c
xloadimage/send.c
xloadimage/smooth.c
xloadimage/sunraster.c
xloadimage/value.c
xloadimage/window.c
xloadimage/xbitmap.c
xloadimage/xloadimage.c
xloadimage/xpixmap.c
xloadimage/xwd.c
xloadimage/zio.c
xloadimage/zoom.c
```

See your own system's UNIX documentation for more information about tar options.

Unmounting the CD-ROM Under UNIX

When you are finished with the CD-ROM, you can unmount it with the umount command, specifying only the mount point as the argument:

```
# /etc/umount   /cdrom
```

To eject the physical CD-ROM, follow the directions for your own CD-ROM drive.

Using the CD-ROM With the Macintosh

This section describes what you need to know about using the CD-ROM with the Macintosh.

NOTE

If you have an Apple CD-ROM drive, be sure that you have the Foreign File Access extension and the ISO 9660 File Access extension installed. These extensions are automatically installed for you when you install the CD-ROM hardware and software, but some users delete them. If you don't have them installed, your CD-ROM drive will not be able to read an ISO 9660 CD-ROM.

Accessing the CD-ROM on the Macintosh

On the Macintosh, the CD-ROM is simply another drive (a read-only one). Insert the CD-ROM, following the directions for your own system and CD-ROM drive. You will see an icon for the GFF_CD. Click on it to access the drive. You will now see the GFF_CD window.

Accessing Specs, Code, and Images on the Macintosh

Reading the CD-ROM files on the Macintosh is not as simple as on the other platforms, but we have tried to make the process as smooth as possible by providing tools that can help you.

Because we are committed to the notion of providing one set of files on a single multi-platform ISO 9660 standard CD-ROM, we have not been able to include the resource forks that the Macintosh uses in opening files while still preserving PC and UNIX compatibility. To read the ASCII files on the Macintosh, rather than clicking to open you'll need to use an editor. We describe a number of options in the sections below.

Using TeachText or SimpleText

When the Macintosh tries to open one of the ASCII files on the CD-ROM, it will ask you if you want to open it with the TeachText or SimpleText editor. When TeachText displays the file, it will show □ characters at the beginning of each line (representing the PC-style line break characters in the file), and it may also wrap lines that are longer than its default line length. (With Simple-Text, available on the newest Macintoshes, you can change the font to a monocase, such as Courier, which strips the □ characters and nicely aligns the text.) TeachText and SimpleText can read only relatively short text files (those that are less than 27K or so).

Using Other Editors and Word Processors

There are a variety of other text and programmer's editors (e.g., Think C's) and word processors that you can use to read text files on the Macintosh. Some are better than others at filtering line breaks, but with a small amount of effort you will be able to view the text files and edit them to improve their readability.

For example, if you use Microsoft Word you can:

1. Open the file with Microsoft Word. Word asks you to "Select a Converter." Select "Text" to indicate that you want the file displayed literally, without conversion. Word now displays the text file, which looks much the way it does with TeachText.

2. To eliminate the wrapping of lines you can:

   a. Enlarge the margins to 80 characters.

   b. Reduce the point size of characters so each line fits in the margins with no wrapping.

   c. Change the font to a monospace font such as Courier or Monaco.

3. To delete the □ characters on the left, you can hold down the option key while you drag the mouse to select the first column of the entire file display. Then, press the Delete key to delete the entire set of first columns in a single operation. The text file should now be quite readable.

4. To save the changes, save the file as another filename (on another drive, of course, because you cannot write to the CD-ROM).

Using BBEdit

As an excellent alternative to viewing text files with TeachText or your own editor or word processor, consider using BBEdit, a text editor written by Rich Siegel of Bare Bones Software that we've included on the CD-ROM. Bare Bones also sells a commercial version and distributes a publicly available version.

If you do not already have a copy of the package, you can use the copy we've included on the CD-ROM in the *software/mac/bbedit* folder. Bare Bones Software has allowed us to distribute a demo version of the commercial product:

Here is what you need to do to copy the software to your Macintosh:

1. Copy the *bbedit.hqx* file from the *software/mac/bbedit* folder to your own Macintosh system. This file contains a set of BBEdit executables and documentation that have been compressed and combined in a way that allows them to be included on an ISO 9660 CD-ROM.

2. You will need to run Stuffit Expander (version 3.07 or later) or an equivalent program that can expand the files in the *hqx* file. Drag the *bbedit.hqx* file to the Stuffit Expander icon.

3. Once you have run Stuffit Expander, you will see the files shown in Figure A-2 on your Macintosh.

4. Drag your text file to the BBEdit 2.5 Demo icon to view the file.

Getting BBEdit and StuffitExpander

Many Macintosh users already have a copy of BBEdit on their systems because a version of this text editor is free and widely available on the Internet and on various commercial services. On the Internet, you will find a number of different versions of this software available via FTP at the *sumex-aim.stanford.edu* site (in the *info-mac/TextProcessing* directory) and its mirrors and at the *mac.archive.umich.edu* site. On CompuServe, you will find it in the DTPFORUM (Desktop Publishing Forum). On America Online, you will find it in the Macintosh Software Center.

To order BBEdit directly from the vendor, contact:

Bare Bones Software
One Larkspur Way 34
Natick, MA 01760
Voice: 508-651-3561
Fax: 508-651-7584
Internet: *bbedit@world.std.com*
CompuServe: 73051,3255
AppleLink: BARE.BONES

Most Macintosh users already have a copy of the publicly available version of Stuffit Expander because this program is widely available on the Internet and on various commercial services and because it is so valuable in file interchange. If you don't already have Stuffit Expander version 3.0.7 or later, here's how you can get it.

On the Internet, you will find the software available via FTP at the *sumex-aim.stanford.edu* site (in the *info-mac/Compress-Translate* directory) and its mirrors. On CompuServe, you will find it in the DTPFORUM (Desktop Publishing Forum) and in MACAP and APPHYPER. On America Online, you will find it in the Macintosh Software Center.

To order Stuffit directly from the vendor, contact:

Aladdin Systems
165 Westridge Drive
Watsonville, CA 95076
Voice: 408-761-6200
Fax: 408-761-6206

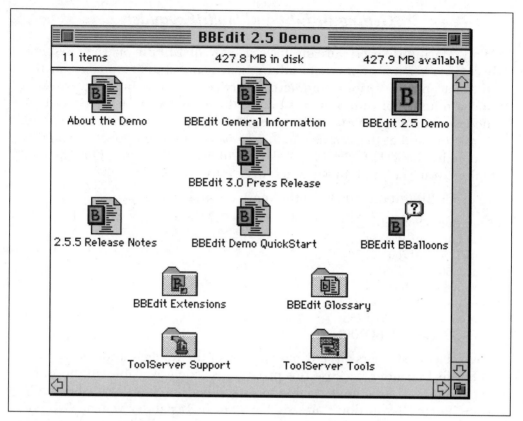

FIGURE A-2: *BBEdit files*

Accessing Software on the Macintosh

We have included a number of popular Macintosh packages on the CD-ROM. Each Macintosh package is stored in its own folder in the *software/mac* folder. One program, NIH Image, is included in both source and binary form; for the others, only binaries are included.

All of the software is provided in the form of *.hqx* files. As described for BBEdit in the preceding section, an *.hqx* file must be unBINHEXed and expanded into the full set of program files before you can execute the program. You expand the *.hqx* file (e.g., *jpegview.hqx*) by dragging it to the Stuffit Expander icon. Because the CD-ROM is read-only, you have to specify a desktop folder for the destination file.

For example, for JPEGView, you will see the files shown in Figure A-3.

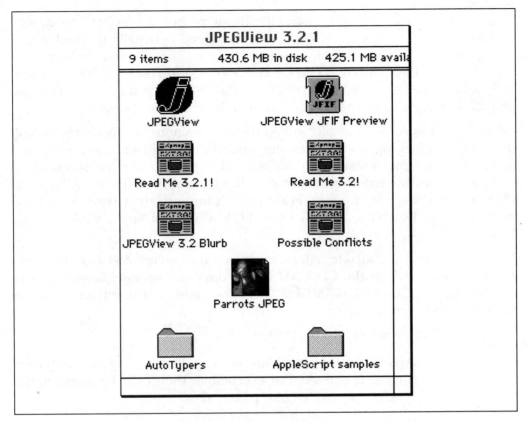

FIGURE A-3: *JPEGView files*

Removing the CD-ROM from the Macintosh

When you are finished using the CD-ROM, you can remove it by dragging the GFF_CD icon to the Trash.

Software Summaries

This section contains a brief description of each software package included on the CD-ROM.

MS-DOS Software

This software is contained in the *software/dos* directory.

IMDISP

IMDISP (Image Display) is an interactive image processing program written by Archie Warnock and Ron Baalke. It was designed originally to display and manipulate the Voyager and Magellan astronomical images that are stored on the Planetary Data System (PDS) CD-ROMs. (More than 30,000 of these images have been collected on CD-ROMs.) IMDISP can be used on a PC to display these images, as well as images stored on hard and floppy disks.

IMDISP performs such image manipulation functions as zooming, image-merging, brightening and darkening, smoothing, edge enhancement, and more. The program comes with built-in color palettes and performs color cycling and pseudo-coloring. For input, it supports the GIF, VICAR2, PDS, FITS, and raw raster file formats. For output, it supports the GIF, PDS, and raw raster formats. IMDISP runs with CGA, EGA, VGA, and Super VGA graphics boards.

IMDISP is publicly available software which runs under MS-DOS. The executable is included on the CD-ROM in the directory *software/dos/imdisp*. The version on the CD-ROM is IMDISP 7.9g, the most recent version available when we went to press.

On the CD-ROM, you will find these files:

imdis79g.exe   IMDISP distribution. This file is a self-extracting archive. When it runs, it extracts the executable, the documentation, and a number of pseudo-color palette files.

doc/   Documents describing IMDISP.

palettes/   Palettes that can be used by IMDISP.

There are also various help, display, and text files in the directory.

The documentation describes how to install and run IMDISP and the modifications you might want to make to your *AUTOEXEC.BAT* file. It also describes how to use IMDISP with a CD-ROM containing the PDS astronomical images, the various types of graphics boards, how to use the palette files, and how to perform various program functions.

If you have a problem with IMDISP that you cannot solve, you can contact the author:

Archibald Warnock
Archie.Warnock@hypatia.gsfc.nasa.gov

You can also request IMDISP source for non-commercial use.

ISO MPEG-2 Codec

The ISO MPEG Codec (MPEG-2 Encoder and Decoder) was written by Chad Fogg and Stefan Eckart to convert uncompressed video frames into MPEG-1 and MPEG-2 video-coded bitstream sequences, and vice versa. The program source, now being handled by the MPEG Software Simulation Group, will eventually become part of the MPEG-2 specification document, *ISO/IEC DIS 13818-2 (Part 5: Technical Report on the Software Simulation of Phase II)*. (For information about MPEG and references to additional sources of information, see the article about MPEG files in Part II of this book.)

MPEG-2 video is a generic method for compressed representation of video sequences using a common coding syntax (defined in an ISO standard). The MPEG-2 concept is similar to MPEG-1, but includes extensions to cover a wider range of applications. The most significant enhancement over MPEG-1 is the addition of syntax for efficient coding of interlaced video.

The ISO MPEG-2 Codec is publicly available and platform-independent. Although often used on UNIX systems, the source code has also been compiled for MS-DOS. The source code is included in the *software/unix/mpeg* directory on the CD-ROM. For a complete discussion, see the description in the

"UNIX Software" section below.

On the CD-ROM, we have included precompiled binaries for the ISO MPEG-2 Codec in the *software/dos/mpeg* directory. You will find these files:

mpeg2dec.exe   MPEG-2 decoder

mpeg2enc.exe   MPEG-2 encoder

emu387   387 emulator

You will also find readme files there.

The port to MS-DOS was accomplished using the djgpp development environment (a port of the Free Software Foundation's gcc/g++ compiler). In keeping with the requirements of the Free Software Foundation, we have included the source, as well as the binary, for djgpp (in the *software/dos/pbmplus/djgpp* directory).

Getting the ISO MPEG-2 Codec

If you do not have a CD-ROM drive, you can get a copy of the ISO MPEG-2 Codec from several sites on the Internet. The official version of the software is at the *ftp.uu.net* site (in the *graphics/mpeg* directory). Other sites may have copies of the software, but they are not guaranteed to be up-to-date. The *mpeg2v10.zip* file is a zip file containing the full MS-DOS distribution. You must run the unzip program to extract the individual files from the zip file.) Note that this filename may change as new versions become available. You will also find the source files and sample bitstreams in this directory, as described under "UNIX Software" below.

If you have a problem with the ISO MPEG-2 Codec that you cannot solve, you can contact:

MPEG@ftp.uu.net

or the authors:

Chad Fogg
cfogg@netcom.com

Stefan Eckart
stefan@lis.e-technik.tu-muenchen.de

Another good contact point for MPEG is the *comp.compression* newsgroup.

pbmplus

pbmplus (Portable Bitmap Utilities) is a toolkit used to convert various image formats. The toolkit was developed by Jef Poskanzer for UNIX and is described in "UNIX Software." The source has been ported to a number of other platforms. The binaries described here were built by Mike Castle and run under MS-DOS.

pbmplus uses several distinct internal formats and functions:

- PBM (Portable Bitmap) functions handle the conversion of black-and-white images (bitmaps, one bit per pixel.

- PGM (Portable Graymap) functions handle the conversion of gray-scale images.

- PPM (Portable Pixmap) functions handle the conversion of full-color images.

- PNM (Portable anymap) functions handle content-independent manipulations on all three of these internal formats; it also handles external formats that have multiple types.

pbmplus converts from one graphics file format to another by converting the source format into one of the portable formats and then converting the portable format into the destination format.

Each of the components is upward-compatible: PGM reads both PGM and PBM files and writes PGM; PPM reads all three file types and writes PPM; PNM reads all three file types and usually writes the same types that it reads (it notifies you of any exceptions).

pbmplus supports a very large number of formats, including CMU, Sun icon, GEM, Macintosh Paint, Atari, Bennett Yee "face," BBN BitGraph, Group 3 FAX, GIF, MTV, IFF, QRT, various X formats, Printronix, and many more. For a full list, see the documentation that comes with the package.

In addition to converting graphics file formats, pbmplus performs a number of image manipulation functions, including normalizing, performing bitwise arithmetic, cropping, applying gamma correction, scaling, smoothing, colorizing graymaps, creating fractal terrains, applying Conway's Rules of Life, and others.

The port to MS-DOS was accomplished using the djgpp development environment (a port of the Free Software Foundation's gcc/g++ compiler) and the 32-bit 80386 DOS extender it uses to operate. Both were written by D.J. Delorie. To run these, you need a 386 or better PC or PS/2 running MS-DOS.

The code for pbmplus, djgpp, and the DOS extender are provided on the CD-ROM in the *software/dos/pbmplus* directory. The version on the CD-ROM is based on the December 10, 1991 version of pbmplus, the most recent version available when we went to press.

The pbmplus distribution contains a number of directories, including:

bin/   Program binaries. The *pbmmerge.exe, pgmmerge.exe, pnmmerge.exe,* and *ppmmerge.exe* files are the main executables. The *go32.exe* file contains the DOS extender. The *emu387* file is an emulator for the 387.

man/   Reference pages.

src/ and *newsrc/*

Certain sources. Note that the entire pbmplus source is not included here; it is in *software/unix/pbmplus.*

patch/   Software patches.

You will also find some documentation and readme files in the directory.

In keeping with the requirements of the Free Software Foundation, we have also included the source, as well as the binary, for djgpp (in the *software/dos/pbmplus/djgpp* directory).

Getting pbmplus

If you do not have a CD-ROM on your system, you can get a copy of the MS-DOS pbmplus port from many sites on the Internet. The official version is at the *oak.oakland.edu* site (in the *pub/msdos/graphics* directory) and other Simtel-20 mirrors. Other sites may have copies of the software, but they are not guaranteed to be up-to-date. The distribution includes the DOS extender. The *pbmp191d.zip* file is a zip file containing the full pbmplus distribution. (You need to run the unzip program to extract the individual files from the zip file.) Note that this filename may change as new versions become available.

You can get the djgpp code from the *oak.oakland.edu* site (in the *pub/msdos/djgpp* directory) and other Simtel-20 mirrors.

If you have a problem with the MS-DOS port of pbmplus that you cannot solve, you can contact:

Mike Castle
mcastle@cs.umr.edu

D.J. Delorie
dj@ctron.com

VPIC

VPIC is a graphics file display and conversion program written by Bob Montgomery especially for GIF file viewing. It supports several different graphics file formats, including GIF, Windows BMP, PCX, Macintosh PICT, TGA, Dr. Halo, and TIFF. It supports most of the common EGA, MCGA, VGA, and Super VGA video cards and uses a plain text configuration file to tell VPIC which VGA chip your display card uses and which video modes it can use.

You can use VPIC to develop slide shows, animate pictures, develop composite pictures, resize, and perform other manipulations.

VPIC is shareware for MS-DOS. To run it, you need a 386 or better and an EGA, VGA, or Super VGA video card. The version on the CD-ROM is VPIC 6.1, the most recent version available when we went to press.

On the CD-ROM, you will find a number of files in the *software/dos/vpic* directory, including:

vpic.exe	Main VPIC executable.
whichvga.exe	Program that figures out what video card you are using.
config.exe	Contains the configuration program which allows you to use a menu to configure the system for your video card.
cfg files	Configuration files for many video cards.
gif files	Test image files.

There are also a number of documentation and readme files in the directory. See these files for detailed information about configuring VPIC.

Getting VPIC

If you do not have a CD-ROM drive on your system, you can get the VPIC software from CompuServe in the GRAPHSUPPORT forum. You may also be able to find the software on America Online. It is not currently available on the Internet.

If you have a problem with VPIC that you cannot solve, you can contact the author:

Bob Montgomery
Internet: *73357.3140@compuserve.com*
CompuServe: 73357,3140

Windows Software

This software is contained in the *software/windows* directory.

Conversion Assistant for Windows

Conversion Assistant for Windows is an image conversion program written by Mark Edmead of MTE Industries. With this product you can convert many different types of image file formats, including Windows BMP, TIFF, TGA, GIF, PCX, WPG, and JPEG. You can also export Macintosh PICT and can import encapsulated PostScript files. You can view images, change their contrast and brightness, rotate and resize them, and get detailed information about them.

Conversion Assistant for Windows is a drag-and-drop application. It lets you convert all of your files in a single step. You drag and drop the images, using the File Manager. If you drop an entire directory, Conversion Assistant for Windows selects only the image files for conversion.

Conversion Assistant for Windows is shareware for Windows 3.1 and above and Windows NT. The product is also available in a commercial version. The version on the CD-ROM is Conversion Assistant v1.4 Lite for Windows, a demo version of the commercial software and the most recent version available when we went to press.

Getting Conversion Assistant for Windows

If you do not have a CD-ROM drive on your system, you can get a copy of the shareware version of Conversion Assistant for Windows from CompuServe in the GRAPHSUPPORT forum library 4. At present, the software is not available on the Internet.

On the CD-ROM, the *capture.exe* and *convert.exe* files in the *software/windows/convasst* directory contain the Conversion Assistant for Windows executables. You will also find library, help, and text files there.

If you have a problem with Conversion Assistant for Windows that you cannot solve, you can contact the author:

Mark Edmead
Internet: *70323.1415@compuserve.com*
CompuServe: 70323,1415

LView

LView is an image file editor written by Leonardo Loureiro. It reads, writes, and edits files in a number of file formats, including JPEG, Windows BMP, OS/2 BMP, TGA, and GIF. You can use it to crop, copy and paste, rotate, flip, and perform a number of other manipulations.

LView is based in part on the work of the Independent JPEG Group. (See the discussion of the JPEG library in the "Software for UNIX" section.)

LView is publicly available software for Windows 3.1 and above. It also works under Windows NT and OS/2, although not as efficiently. You need a 386 or better, and a truecolor Super VGA video card is recommended, although the software will run with most other cards. The version on the CD-ROM is LView 3.1, the most recent version available when we went to press.

On the CD-ROM, the file *lview31.exe* in the *software/windows/lview* directory contains the main LView executable. You will also find additional library, help, and text files there.

Getting LView

If you do not have a CD-ROM drive on your system, you can get a copy of LView from many sites on the Internet. The official version is at the *oak.oakland.edu* site (in the *pub/msdos/windows3* directory). The file *lview31.zip* is a zip file containing the full LView distribution. (You must run the unzip program to extract the individual files from the zip file.) Note that this filename may change as new versions become available.

If you have a problem with LView that you cannot solve, you can contact the author:

Leonardo Loureiro
mmedia@world.std.com

Paint Shop Pro

Paint Shop Pro, developed by JASC, Inc., displays, converts, alters, scans, and prints images. It allows you to work with multiple images at a time. Paint Shop Pro converts between many common graphics file formats, including JPEG, Windows BMP, GIF, encapsulated PostScript, Interchange File Format (IFF) for the Amiga, Microsoft Paint, PCX, Macintosh PICT, TGA, TIFF, and WPG.

With Paint Shop Pro you can resize, crop, dither, adjust color, and apply filters. You can adjust an image's brightness, highlight and shadow, add a border, and use many different standard filters. Paint Shop Pro supports all TWAIN-compliant scanners. Palette manipulation functions let you change individual color values, save, and load palettes. You can use Paint Shop Pro to capture a full screen, a user-defined area, a window, or a Windows client area. Batch conversion allows many images to be converted at one time. Paint Shop Pro provides OLE server support to allow you to add image support to your other applications.

Paint Shop Pro is shareware for Windows 3.1 and above. You must have a 286 or higher, and a 256-color video driver is recommended. The version on the CD-ROM is Paint Shop Pro Shareware 2.01, the most recent version available when we went to press.

On the CD-ROM, you will find a number of files in the *software/windows/paintpro* directory. Note that you cannot simply copy the files to your hard disk, because the files are packed in a special way. The setup program (which you invoke by running *setup.exe*) unpacks these files and builds them on your working disk to install the program. *psp1.cmp* and *psp2.cmp* are compressed files containing the Paint Shop Pro executables.

The other files contain various types of documentation, including Windows Help. Note that more extensive documentation is available when you register the product.

Getting Paint Shop Pro

If you do not have a CD-ROM on your system, you can get a copy of Paint Shop Pro from the Internet. The official version is at the *ftp.winternet.com* site (in the *users/jasc* directory). Other sites may have copies of this software, but they are not guaranteed to be up-to-date. The *psp201.zip* file in that directory is a zip file containing the complete Paint Shop Pro distribution. You will also find a more limited version of the product in *ps30.zip*. (You must run the unzip program to extract the individual files from the zip files.) Note that filenames may change as new versions become available.

Paint Shop Pro is also available from CompuServe in the GRAPHSUP-PORT forum library 4. There is also a version available on America Online.

If you have a problem with Paint Shop Pro that you cannot solve, you can contact the vendor:

JASC, Inc.
612-930-9171
Internet: *72557.256@compuserve.com*
CompuServe: 72557,256

PhotoLab

PhotoLab is an image processing system written by Daniel Baker that allows you to view and modify scanned or digitized images on a PC. It processes GIF, TIFF, Windows BMP, and Windows DIB format files. Images can be cropped, rotated, mirrored, flipped, resized, resampled, dithered, brightened, darkened, and more. If you have an HP ScanJet IIc color scanner, you must be sure to load its device driver into your *CONFIG.SYS* file.

PhotoLab is publicly available software for Windows 3.1 and above systems with 256-color or better video capabilities. The program operates on 8-bit (256 colors), 16-bit (32,768 colors), and 24-bit (16.7 million colors) video systems. Although the program is freely available, you must register in order to obtain upgrades and fixes. (See the online documentation for details.) The version on the CD-ROM is PhotoLab 1.8, the most recent version available when we went to press.

On the CD-ROM, you will find that there are a number of files in the *software/windows/photolab* directory, including:

photolab.exe   PhotoLab executable.

photolab.hlp   Windows Help.

photolab.lft   Filter file.

Getting PhotoLab

If you do not have a CD-ROM drive on your system, you can get a copy of PhotoLab from many sites on the Internet. The official version of Photo-Lab is at the *oak.oakland.edu* site (in the *pub/msdos/windows3* directory). The *pholab18.zip* file in that directory is a zip file containing the complete PhotoLab distribution. (You need to run the unzip program to extract the individual files from the zip file.) Note that the filename may change as new versions become available.

If you have a problem with PhotoLab that you cannot solve, you can contact the author:

Daniel Baker
Internet: *71551.2300@compuserve.com*
CompuServe: 71551,2300

Picture Man

Picture Man is a truecolor processing tool developed by Igor Plotnikov and his colleagues, Michail Kuznetsov and Alexey Bobkov, at Potapov Works, Stoik Ltd. in Moscow. Picture Man is designed for truecolor image enhancement, retouching, painting, and the creation of special effects. The software allows you to not only process an image in a selected area, but also to retouch and paint with a variety of filters and transformations.

Picture Man supports truecolor and hicolor adapters. It offers true multitasking and virtual memory management. You can input images from any scanner, video capture board, or other input device that has a driver compatible with Picture Man.

Picture Man allows you to convert images in the Windows BMP, GIF, TIFF, JPEG, TGA, PCX, and encapsulated PostScript graphics file formats. It also contains an open interface to image file format filters, so you can use it to develop converters for other formats.

You can also use Picture Man to perform such functions as geometrical transforms, halftone/color correction, filtering, and filling with color, patterns, and gradients. You can retouch an image in various types of areas (e.g., rectangle, ellipsis, polygon, text, freehand) with shared or smooth edges.

Picture Man is shareware which runs under Windows 3.1 and above. The executable is included on the CD-ROM in the directory *software/windows/pictman*. The version on the CD-ROM is Picture Man 1.55, the most recent version available when we went to press.

On the CD-ROM, you will find a number of files, including:

pman.exe   Main Picture Man executable.

dll files   Libraries that read and write specific file formats; for example, *readgif.dll* reads files in the GIF format, and *writetif.dll* writes files in the TIFF format.

pman.wri   User manual.

There are also additional libraries, help files, and documentation.

Getting Picture Man

If you do not have a CD-ROM drive on your system, you can get a copy of Picture Man from many sites on the Internet. The official version of Picture Man is at the *oak.oakland.edu* FTP site (in the *pub/msdos/windows3* directory). Other sites may have copies of this software, but they are not guaranteed to be up-to-date. The *pman155.zip* file in that directory is a zip file containing the complete Picture Man distribution. (You must run the unzip program to extract the individual files from the zip file.) Note that this filename may change as new versions become available.

Picture Man is also available on Simtel-20 and CICA and the GRAPHSUP-PORT forum at CompuServe.

If you have a problem with Picture Man that you cannot solve, you can contact the author:

Dr. Igor Plotnikov
igor@corvette.insoft.com

WinJPEG

WinJPEG (Windows JPEG) is an image viewer developed by Ken Yee and Norman Yee of Pixel Vision Software. It displays and exports images in GIF, JPEG, TIFF, TGA, PCX, Windows BMP, OS/2 BMP, and PPM (pbmplus toolkit) format. Images can be displayed in monochrome, 16-color, 256-color, hicolor, or truecolor display modes, and with their full palettes.

You can also perform a variety of image manipulations, including rotating, flipping, resizing, cropping, cutting and pasting (using Clipboard), color balancing, and hue, saturation, and brightness adjustment. You can print an image with scaling or with best proportional fit on the page. You can develop slideshows by displaying selected files sequentially with a cycle option.

WinJPEG lets you capture a window, the client area of a window, or a portion or all of the desktop. It provides support for Windows 3.1 drag-and-drop and common dialog features.

WinJPEG is shareware for Windows 3.0 and above and Windows NT. There is a 386 version for 386s and better, and a 286 version for 286s or better. The shareware version is a fully functional 286 version. You can obtain the 386 version by registering WinJPEG as described in the documentation. There is also a special version for OS/2 called PMJPEG (provided in the *software/os2/pmjpeg* directory).

The executable is included on the CD-ROM in the directory *software/windows/winjpeg*. The version on the CD-ROM is WinJPEG 2.51, the most recent version available when we went to press. This version is the 286 version.

You will find a number of files on the CD-ROM, including:

winjpeg.exe   286 version of WinJPEG.

dll files   Program libraries

winjpeg.hlp   Windows Help.

You will also find a number of additional text files.

Getting WinJPEG

If you do not have a CD-ROM drive on your system, you can get a copy of WinJPEG from many sites on the Internet. The official version of WinJPEG is at the *ftp.cica.indiana.edu* site (in the *pub/pc/win3/desktop* directory) and its mirrors. You will also find it at *oak.oakland.edu* (in the *pub/msdos/windows3* directory). Other sites may have copies of the software, but they are not guaranteed to be up-to-date. The file *winjp251.zip* in that directory is a zip file containing the full distribution. (You will need to run the unzip program to extract the individual files from the zip file.) Note that this filename may change as new versions are made available.

You can also get a copy of WinJPEG from CompuServe in the Windows Utilities conference.

If you have a problem with WinJPEG that you cannot solve, you can contact the authors:

Ken Yee
kenyee@ksr.com

Norman Yee
nyee@osiris.ee.tufts.edu

OS/2 Software

This software is contained in the *software/os2* directory.

GBM

GBM (Generalized Bitmap Module) is an image-processing program written by Andy Key. It supports a variety of graphics file formats, including Windows BMP, GIF, PCX, TIFF, TGA, Interchange File Format (IFF) for the Amiga, XBM, Archimedes Sprite, IBM KIPS, and IBM Image Access Executive. You can use GBM to display, rotate, convert between palettes and bits per pixel, perform gamma correction, extract subrectangles of bitmaps, and more.

GBM is publicly available software for OS/2. It runs under OS/2 2.x, but the main part of GBM is highly portable 32-bit C code and has been compiled on AIX 3.2 and other systems as well. The version on the CD-ROM is GBM 1.0, the most recent version available when we went to press.

On the CD-ROM, you will find complete binary and source. In the *software/os2/gbm/bin* directory are several subdirectories containing executable files and associated documentation. There are several versions of GBM you might want to run:

gbmv.exe   Simple GBM bitmap viewer.

gbmv2.exe   A more sophisticated bitmap viewer with menus, dialogs, and full help.

gbmdlg.exe   Derived from WinFileDlg and designed to allow the user to specify the file for loading and saving.

gbm.txt   Documentation.

Some additional supporting files are also included in this directory.

All of the source code in the *software/os2/gbm/src* directory is written in the author's own Andy's Editor (AE), a source code editor which runs under MS-DOS, OS/2, or AIX. AE is generally available via the Internet. You might also be interested in RT, Mr. Key's ray tracer, which is available via FTP at many sites.

If you have a problem with GBM that you cannot solve, you can contact the author:

Andy Key
ak@vnet.ibm.com

PMJPEG

PMJPEG (Presentation Manager JPEG) is an image viewer developed by Ken Yee and Norman Yee of Pixel Vision Software. It is a port of the Windows package, WinJPEG, to OS/2 2.x. It is a native 32-bit Presentation Manager application.

Like WinJPEG, PMJPEG displays and exports images in GIF, JPEG, TIFF, TGA, PCX, Windows BMP, OS/2 BMP, and PPM (pbmplus toolkit) format. Images can be displayed in monochrome, 16-color, 256-color, hicolor, or truecolor display modes, and with their full palettes. See the discussion of WinJPEG in the "Windows Software" section for more complete information.

PMJPEG is shareware for OS/2 2.x. The executable is included on the CD-ROM in the directory *software/os2/pmjpeg*. The version on the CD-ROM is PMJPEG v.1.63, the most recent version available when we went to press.

On the CD-ROM, the *pmjpeg.exe* file contains the PMJPEG executable. You will also find several text and help files there.

If you have a problem with PMJPEG that you cannot solve, you can contact the authors:

Ken Yee
kenyee@ksr.com

Norman Yee
nyee@osiris.ee.tufts.edu

UNIX Software

This software is contained in the *software/unix* directory.

FBM

FBM (the Fuzzy Pixmap Manipulation library) was written by Michael Mauldin. It allows you to view and manipulate many types of color and black-and-white image formats. When you use FBM in conjunction with pbmplus, you'll have a complete package for manipulating and converting color and black-and-white images, including 24-bit RGB, 8-bit mapped color, 8-bit gray-scale, and 1-bit bitmapped images. Formats supported by the most recent version of FBM include GIF (87a and 89a), Sun raster, TIFF, Utah RLE, PCX, IFF, and the PBM format supported by the pbmplus software described later in this section. Several dozen programs (e.g., fbcat, fbesxt, fbnorm, idiff, and more) are included in FBM.

FBM is publicly available UNIX software. In addition to running under all varieties of UNIX systems, FBM has been ported to PCs and the Amiga. The source code is included on the CD-ROM in the directory *software/unix/fbm*. (Detailed instructions for obtaining, compiling, and building FBM are contained in the distribution.) The version on the CD-ROM is FBM 1.2, the most recent version available when we went to press.

The *fbm_1_2.tar* file on the CD-ROM in the *software/unix/fbm* directory contains the full FBM source. You can extract files from this *tar* file by following the directions included above in "Accessing Software under UNIX."

Getting FBM

If you do not have a CD-ROM drive, you can get a copy of FBM from many sites on the Internet. The official version of FBM is available at *nl.cs.cmu.edu* (in the */usr/mlm/ftp* directory). (Note that you must specify the whole path at once, because the intermediate directory is not publicly readable, and remember to specify the first / character.) Other sites may have copies of the software, but they are not guaranteed to be up-to-date. The *fbm.tar.Z* file in that directory is a compressed *tar* file containing the source code. (You need to uncompress the file and then run the tar program to extract the individual files. Note that this filename may change as new versions become available.

You will also find the PC implementation of FBM in this directory in the *fbmpc.tar.Z* file; please note that this version has not yet been fully tested. In addition, you will find some older versions of the software and some readme files.

If you have a problem with FBM that you cannot solve, you can contact the author:

Dr. Michael L. Mauldin
fuzzy@cmu.edu

ImageMagick

ImageMagick was written by John Cristy. It allows you to interactively display and manipulate images in the X Window System.

ImagMagick is publicly available software. Although it is usually used with UNIX, ImageMagick can be compiled on any machine that has a C compiler, virtual memory, and the X11 libraries. This includes all UNIX systems, Linux on the PC, and Digital Equipment Corporation's VMS.

ImageMagick consists of several programs that read and write many popular image formats, including Windows BMP, EPS, JPEG, TGA, TIFF, VIFF, encapsulated PostScript, various X formats, and the internal formats used by the pbmplus package described elsewhere in this appendix. ImageMagick uses as an intermediate format the Machine Independent File Format (MIFF) that is ImageMagick's native format. ImageMagick displays images on any workstation capable of running an X server and allows you to convert, annotate, and animate these images. It also allows you to transform images in various ways (scale, rotate, color reduce, etc.) and to create montages.

The source code is included on the CD-ROM in the directory *software/unix/immagick*. (Detailed instructions for obtaining, compiling, and building ImageMagick are contained in the distribution.) The version on the CD-ROM is ImageMagick 3.0, the most recent version available when we went to press.

You will find these files on the CD-ROM:

immag3_0.tar   ImageMagick source, including the display, import, animate, montage, mogrify, convert, combine, segment, and Xtp programs.

images.tar   Images.

animatn.tar   Animation examples.

You can extract files from these *tar* files by following the directions included above in "Accessing Software under UNIX."

ImageMagick requires the use of JPEG (the Independent JPEG Group's Library), as well as libtiff (the TIFF library).

Getting ImageMagick

If you do not have a CD-ROM drive, you can get a copy of ImageMagick from many sites on the Internet. The official version of ImageMagick is at the *ftp.x.org* site (in directory *contrib*). Note that files at *ftp.x.org* are usually placed first in the *R*contrib* release directory (e.g., *R5contrib* or *R6contrib*), so you may find the software there. Other sites may have copies of the software, but they are not guaranteed to be up-to-date. The *ImageMagick-3.0.tar.gz* is a GNU-zipped *tar* file containing the source code and all associated documentation. (You need to run the gunzip command to uncompress it and the tar program to extract the individual files.) Note that this filename may change as new versions are made available. You will also find in this directory a number of additional files containing sample images and animations.

If you have a problem with ImageMagick that you cannot solve, you can contact the author:

John Cristy
cristy@dupont.com

JPEG

JPEG (Independent JPEG Group's JPEG library) was written by Tom Lane, Philip Gladstone, Luis Ortiz, Lee Crocker, George Phillips, Gé Weijers, and others. This software converts between the JPEG (Joint Photographics Experts Group) JFIF format and various other formats, including GIF, TGA, Utah RLE, and the formats used by the pbmplus package. The JPEG code implements JPEG image compression and decompression. JPEG, described further in Chapter 9, *Data Compression* of this book, is a standardized compression method for full-color and gray-scale images. It is used particularly for the compression of "real world" scenes. This software implements JPEG baseline and extended sequential compression processes. It also includes additional software used for color quantization (e.g., to output to colormapped file formats or colormapped displays).

The JPEG software is intended to be used:

1. As canned software for JPEG compression and decompression.

2. As the basis for other JPEG programs. For example, you could incorporate the decompressor into a general image-viewing package by replacing the output module with write-to-screen functions. For a GUI-based system, you might want a different user interface—for example, for the Macintosh or the Amiga.

3. As a toolkit for experimentation with JPEG and JPEG-like algorithms.

JPEG is publicly available software. Although used frequently in the UNIX world, it is actually platform-independent. The JPEG code is very portable and has been implemented on a range of systems from PCs to Crays. The source code is included on the CD-ROM in the directory *software/unix/jpeg*. (Detailed instructions for obtaining, compiling, and building the Independent JPEG Library are contained in the distribution.) The version on the CD-ROM is JPEG 4a, the most recent version available when we went to press.

The *jpeg4a.tar* file on the CD-ROM contains the full JPEG source. You can extract files from this *tar* file by following the directions included above in "Accessing Software under UNIX."

Getting JPEG

If you do not have a CD-ROM drive, you can get a copy of the Independent JPEG Library from many sites on the Internet. The official version of JPEG is at *ftp.uu.net* (in the *graphics/jpeg* directory). Other sites may have copies of the software, but they are not guaranteed to be up-to-date. The file, *jpegsrc.4a.tar.Z* in that directory is a compressed *tar* file containing the source code. (You need to uncompress it and then run the tar program to extract the individual files. Note that this filename may change as new versions become available. In addition, you will find in this directory the JPEG Interchange File Format (JFIF) specification (which we have included in the *formats/jpeg*) directory, and additional readme and document files describing the software and how to obtain the full JPEG standard.

On CompuServe, you can obtain this software from the GRAPHSUPPORT forum (GO PICS), library 15; however, CompuServe is not guaranteed to have the very latest version.

To find out more about JPEG, read the description of JPEG compression in Chapter 9, as well as the JFIF article in Part II. You will also find the JPEG FAQ (Frequently Asked Questions) article to be a good source of information about JPEG. We have included on the CD-ROM (in the *formats/jpeg/spec/faq* file) the latest version available before we went to press. Every two weeks, this FAQ is posted to the Usenet newsgroups *comp.graphics*, *new.answers*, and other groups. For the latest version, look in the *news.answers* archive via FTP at *rtfm.mit.edu* in *pub/usenet/new.answers/jpeg-faq*. If you do not have FTP access, send email to *mail-server@rtfm.mit.edu* with the body of the message "send usenet/news/answers/jpeg-faq".

If you have a problem with JPEG that you cannot solve, you can contact:

jpeg-info@uu.net

or the author:

Dr. Tom Lane
Tom_Lane@g.gp.cs.cmu.edu

ISO MPEG-2 Codec

The ISO MPEG Codec (MPEG-2 Encoder and Decoder) was written by Chad Fogg and Stefan Eckart to convert uncompressed video frames into MPEG-1 and MPEG-2 video-coded bitstream sequences, and vice versa. The program source, now being handled by the MPEG Software Simulation Group, will eventually become part of the MPEG-2 specification document, *ISO/IEC DIS 13818-2 (Part 5: Technical Report on the Software Simulation of Phase II)*. (For information about MPEG and references to additional sources of information, see the article about MPEG files in Part II of this book.)

MPEG-2 video is a generic method for compressed representation of video sequences using a common coding syntax (defined in an ISO standard). The MPEG-2 concept is similar to MPEG-1, but includes extensions to cover a wider range of applications. The most significant enhancement over MPEG-1 is the addition of syntax for efficient coding of interlaced video.

The ISO MPEG-2 Codec is publicly available software. Although used frequently in the UNIX world, it is actually platform-independent. The programs have been compiled successfully on various UNIX and PC platforms. The source code is included on the CD-ROM in the directory *software/unix/mpeg*. (Detailed instructions for obtaining, compiling, and building the ISO MPEG-2 Codec are contained in the distribution.) The version on the CD-ROM is the ISO MPEG-2 Codec Version 1.1, the most recent version available when we went to press.

You will find the following files on the CD-ROM:

mpeg2_cd.tar   ISO MPEG-2 Codec source. Includes encoder and decoder source and documentation, including a Frequently Asked Questions list about MPEG.

mpeg2_vf.tar   Sample bitstreams and raw pictures.

samples/   Sample bitstream for MPEG.

You can extract files from the *tar* files by following the directions included above in "Accessing Software under UNIX."

Getting the ISO MPEG-2 Codec

If you do not have a CD-ROM drive, you can get a copy of the ISO MPEG-2 Codec from several sites on the Internet. The official version of the software is at *ftp.uu.net* (in the *graphics/mpeg* directory). Other sites may have copies of the software, but they are not guaranteed to be up-to-date. The *mpeg2codec_v1.0.tar.gz* file contains the source code and documentation. The *mpeg2codec_verify_v1.0.tar.gz* file contains sample bitstreams and raw pictures. The *mpeg2v10.zip* file contains MS-DOS executables. The *tar.gz* files are compressed *tar* files. (You need to run the gunzip program to uncompress them, and then run the tar program to extract the individual files.) Note that these filenames may change as new versions become available.

If you have a problem with the ISO MPEG-2 Codec that you cannot solve, you can contact:

MPEG@ftp.uu.net

or the authors:

Chad Fogg
cfogg@netcom.com

Stefan Eckart
stefan@lis.e-technik.tu-muenchen.de

Another good contact point for MPEG is the *comp.compression* newsgroup.

libtiff

libtiff (TIFF library) was written by Sam Leffler to read and write TIFF (Tag Image File Format) files. (For information about TIFF, see the article about TIFF files in Part II of this book.)

libtiff is publicly available software. Although used frequently in the UNIX world, it is actually platform-independent. The source code is included on the CD-ROM in the *software/unix/libtiff*. ((Detailed instructions for obtaining, compiling, and building libtiff are contained in the distribution.) The version on the CD-ROM is libtiff 3.3, the most recent version available when we went to press.

The *lbtif3_3.tar* file on the CD-ROM contains the full libtiff source. You can extract files from this *tar* file by following the directions included above in "Accessing Software under UNIX."

The libtiff code includes the following major pieces:

libtiff library   Used to read and write TIFF files that follow either the TIFF 5.0 or 6.0 specification. The libtiff library provides two separate interfaces, one for strip-based images and one for tile-based images.

Device-independent programs

These include more than a dozen programs that perform simple manipulations of TIFF images (e.g,. copying images, dithering, converting from one color palette or scale to another, etc.)

Device-dependent programs

The tiffgt program displays the contents of a TIFF file on a frame buffer. The tiffsv program saves all or part of a frame buffer in a TIFF file. Both programs were written for the Silicon Graphics Graphics Library (GL), but you can tailor them for other systems without too much difficulty.

sgi2tiff   This program converts SGI image files to TIFF and can be used only on SGI machines.

Contributed software

Scripts, viewers, and other programs provided by additional authors.

Documentation

Documentation about the programs and copies of various TIFF specifications, as well as various readme and howto files describing the libtiff contents and how to build and test the software.

Test images   Images for most formats supported by the library.

Getting libtiff

If you do not have a CD-ROM drive, you can get a copy of libtiff from many sites on the Internet. The official version of libtiff is at *sgi.com* (in the *graphics/tiff* directory). Other sites may have copies of the software, but they are not guaranteed to be up-to-date. The file, *V3.3.tar.Z*, in that directory is a compressed *tar* file containing the source code. (You need to uncompress it, and then run the tar program. Note that this filename may change as new versions become available. You will also find in this directory additional files containing test images, earlier versions of the software, and the TIFF file format specification. (We include this specification on the CD-ROM in the *formats/tiff/spec* directory.)

You can subscribe to the *libtiff* mailing list by sending a message (containing the line, "subscribe tiff" in the body of the message) to:

majordomo@whizzer.wpd.sgi.com

If you have a problem with libtiff that you cannot solve, you can contact:

tiff@sgi.com

or the author:

Sam Leffler
sam@asd.sgi.com

pbmplus

pbmplus (Portable Bitmap Utilities) is a toolkit written by Jef Poskanzer to convert various image formats to and from each other via a portable intermediate format. For information about pbmplus functions, see the discussion of the MS-DOS version earlier in the "MS-DOS Software" section.

pbmplus is publicly available software. The source code is included on the CD-ROM in the directory *software/unix/pbmplus*. (Detailed instructions for obtaining, compiling, and building pbmplus are contained in the distribution.) The version on the CD-ROM is the version dated December 10, 1991, the most recent version available when we went to press.

The *pbm_1291.tar* file on the CD-ROM contains the full pbmplus source. You can extract files from this *tar* file by following the directions included above in "Accessing Software under UNIX."

NOTE

If you have a copy of *UNIX Power Tools* (O'Reilly & Associates, 1993), you will find on the accompanying CD-ROM prebuilt binaries for pbmplus for a variety of UNIX systems.

Getting pbmplus

If you do not have a CD-ROM drive, you can get a copy of pbmplus from many sites on the Internet. The official version of pbmplus is at the ftp.x.org site (in the *contrib* directory, the file named *contrib/pbmplus10dec91.tar.Z*). Note that files at *ftp.x.org* are usually placed first in the *R*contrib* release directory (e.g., *R5contrib* or *R6contrib*), so you may find the software there. You will also find pbmplus at the *ftp.ee.lbl.gov* site (in the file *pbmplus10dec91.tar.Z*). Other sites may have copies of the software, but they are not guaranteed to be up-to-date. The *pbmplus10dec91.tar.Z* is a compressed *tar* file containing the source code and all associated documentation. (You need to uncompress the file and the run the tar program to extract the individual files. Note that this filename may change as new versions become available.

If you have a problem with pbmplus that you cannot solve, you can contact the author:

Jef Poskanzer
jef@well.sf.ca.us

SAOimage

SAOimage (Smithsonian Astrophysical Observatory Image) is a program written by Mike VanHilst of the Harvard Smithsonian Center for Astrophysics (and enhanced by various people from the Space Telescope Science Institute and the Harvard Smithsonian Center for Astrophysics. It is an interactive program based on the X Window System that displays color or halftone astronomical images. SAOimage is intended mainly for use with FITS (Flexible Image Transport System) images.

SAOimage also performs a number of image manipulation functions, including interactive contrast/brightness manipulation, image panning and zooming, scaling, and pseudo-color display of images. In standalone mode, you can use SAOimage to display FITS files directly. SAOimage can also be used as a display server for the IRAF (Image Reduction and Analysis Facility) package or any other client software using the IIS protocol for remote I/O.

SAOimage is publicly available UNIX software. The source code is included on the CD-ROM in the directory *software/unix/saoimage*. (Detailed instructions for obtaining, compiling, and building SAOimage are contained in the distribution.) SAOimage binaries have been built for the following systems: Sun (all models), DECStations running Ultrix, VAXStations running Ultrix or VMS, Silicon Graphics running IRIX, Hewlett Packard 9000 300, 400 and 700 models running HPUX, IBM RS6000 running AIX, MIPS computers, Alliant computers, Apollo computers, and VAX/VMS systems.

The source code is included on the CD-ROM in the directory *software/unix/saoimage*. (Detailed instructions for obtaining, compiling, and building SAOimage are included in the distribution.) The version on the CD-ROM is SAOimage 1.07, the most recent version available when we went to press.

The *sao1_01.tar* file on the CD-ROM contains the full SAOimage source. You can extract files from this *tar* file by following the directions included above in "Accessing Software under UNIX." You will also find several files on the CD-ROM containing extensive SAOimage documentation (user's manual, UNIX man pages, readme files), some in separate *.txt* files and some included in the *tar* file.

Getting SAOimage

If you do not have a CD-ROM drive, you can get a copy of SAOimage from many sites on the Internet. The official version of SAOimage is *iraf.noao.edu* (in directory *iraf.old*). Other sites may have copies of the software, but they are not guaranteed to be up-to-date. The file, *saoimage.tar.Z*, in that directory is a compressed *tar* file containing the source code. (You need to uncompress this file and then run the tar program to extract files from it. Note that this filename may change as new versions are made available. In addition, you will find files in this directory containing extensive documentation and versions for specific systems. You will find additional system-specific versions and binaries in the *contrib* directory at *iraf.noao.edu*. We have included all of those files on the CD-ROM.

The current version of SAOimage is being supported by the IRAF Project at the National Optical Astronomy Observatories (NOAO) in association with the Smithsonian Astrophysical Observatory (SAO).

If you have a problem with SAOimage that you cannot solve, you can contact:

iraf@noao.edu

or:

Michael Fitzpatrick
itz@noao.edu

An alternate contact for questions, especially those related to use with the PROS software, is:

rsdc@cfa.harvard.edu

xli

xli was written by Graeme Gill. It is based on the xloadimage package developed by Jim Frost and described elsewhere in this appendix; like xloadimage xli views images in a number of different types of file formats under the X Window System (X11) and loads images onto the X11 root window. xli can be used under UNIX and also under MS-DOS systems that run the DJGPP Version 1.09 compiler. Formats supported by the current version of the software include CMU, GEM, GIF (87a and 89a), JFIF, Macintosh Paint, PCX, Sun raster, TGA, Utah RLE, various X formats, and those used by the pbmplus and FBM software.

xli allows you to modify images in various ways before viewing; options include clipping, dithering, depth reduction, zooming, brightening, darkening, gamma correction, and image merging. In any cases these image options are performed automatically; for example, a color image that is being displayed on a monochrome screen is dithered automatically. The xlito utility allows these viewing options to be appended to the image files.

xli is publicly available UNIX software. The source code is included on the CD-ROM in the *software/unix/xli* directory. (Detailed instructions for obtaining, compiling, and building xli are contained in the distribution.) In addition to running under UNIX, xli has been ported successfully to MS-DOS. The version on the CD-ROM is xli 1.15, the most recent version available when we went to press.

The *xli_1_15.tar* file on the CD-ROM contains the full xli source. You can extract files from this *tar* file by following the directions included above in "Accessing Software under UNIX."

Getting xli

If you do not have a CD-ROM drive , you can get a copy of xli from many sites on the Internet. The official version of xli is at the *ftp.x.org* site (in the *contrib* directory). Note that files at *ftp.x.org* are usually placed first in the *R*contrib* release directory (e.g., *R5contrib* or *R6contrib*), so you may find the software there. Other sites may have copies of the software, but they are not guaranteed to be up-to-date. The file, *xli.1.15.tar.Z* in that directory is a compressed *tar* file containing the source code. (You need to uncompress it, and then run tar to extract the individual files. Note that this filename may change as new versions become available. In addition, you will find a readme file describing the software in this directory.

If you have a problem with xli that you cannot solve, you can contact the author:

Graeme W. Gill
graeme@labtam.oz.au

xloadimage

xloadimage is a utility written by Jim Frost to view images in a number of different types of file formats in the X Window System (X11). It also allows you to load images onto the X11 root window. Formats supported by the current version of the software include CMU, GEM, JFIF, JPEG, TIFF, Macintosh Paint, PCX, Sun raster, Utah RLE, various X formats, and those used by the pbmplus and FBM software.

xloadimage performs a number of image manipulation functions, such as scaling, cropping, clipping, zooming, brightening and darkening, merging images, and dithering. If an image is too large to fit within the display, xloadimage places it in a scrollable window. In many cases, these image options are performed automatically; for example, a color image that is being displayed on a monochrome screen is dithered automatically.

xloadimage is publicly available UNIX software. The source code is included on the CD-ROM in the directory *software/unix/xloadimg*. (Detailed instructions for obtaining, compiling, and building xloadimage are contained in the distribution.) The version on the CD-ROM is xloadimage 4.1, the most recent version available when we went to press.

The *xload4_1.tar* file on the CD-ROM contains the full xloadimage source. You can extract files from this *tar* file by following the directions included above in "Accessing Software under UNIX."

NOTE

If you have a copy of *UNIX Power Tools* (O'Reilly & Associates, 1993), you will find on the accompanying CD-ROM prebuilt binaries for xloadimage for a variety of UNIX systems.

Getting xloadimage

If you do not have a CD-ROM drive, you can get a copy of xloadimage from many sites on the Internet. The official version of xloadimage is at the *ftp.x.org* site (in the contrib directory). Other sites may have copies of the software, but they are not guaranteed to be up-to-date. Note that files at *ftp.x.org* are usually placed first in the *R*contrib* release directory (e.g., *R5contrib* or *R6contrib*), so you may find the software there. The file, *xloadimage.4.1.tar.gz* in that directory is a GNU-zipped *tar* file containing the source code. (You need to run the gunzip command to uncompress it and then run the tar program to extract the individual files.) Note that this filename may change as new versions become available. In addition, you will find files containing earlier and beta test versions of the software.

If you have a problem with xloadimage that you cannot solve, you can contact the author:

Jim Frost
jimf@centerline.com

xv

xv (X Viewer) is a program written by John Bradley to display and convert images in a number of different file formats under the X Window System. Formats supported by the current version of the software include GIF (87a and 89a), JPEG, TIFF, PDS, VICAR2, Sun raster, various X formats, and those used by the pbmplus and FBM software.

xv performs such image manipulation functions as cropping, scaling, rotating, magnifying, editing color maps, gamma correction, and more. xv displays one image at a time in an output window or on the root window. It allows you to click on the picture to determine pixel RGB values and XY coordinates. If you try to view an image that is larger than your display, xv automatically scales it to fit.

xv is shareware; instructions for use and payment are included in the readme file included in the distribution. The source code is included on the CD-ROM in the directory *software/unix/xv*. (Detailed instructions for obtaining, compiling, and building xv are contained in the distribution.) In addition to its use under UNIX, xy has been ported successfully to VMS. The version on the CD-ROM is xv 3.00a, the most recent version available when we went to press.

The *xv3a.tar* file on the CD-ROM contains the full xv source. You can extract files from this *tar* file by following the directions included above in "Accessing Software under UNIX." You will also find a *patches.txt* file on the CD-ROM; this file describes patches you should apply to the distribution.

Getting xv

If you do not have a CD-ROM drive, you can get a copy of xv from many sites on the Internet. The official version of xv is at *ftp.cis.upenn.edu* (in the *pub/xv* directory). Other sites may have copies of the software, but they are not guaranteed to be up-to-date. The file, *xv-3.00a.tar.Z* in that directory is a compressed *tar* file containing the source code. (You need to uncompress it and then run the tar program to extract the files.) Note that this filename may change as new versions become available. You will also find some earlier versions of the software in this directory.

If you have a problem with xv that you cannot solve, you can contact the author:

John Bradley
bradley@grip.cis.upenn.edu

Macintosh Software

This software is contained in the *software/mac* folder.

GIFConverter

GIFConverter was written by Kevin Mitchell for the Macintosh. It displays and converts GIF files, as well as files in a variety of other graphics file formats. The program can read the GIF, JPEG (JFIF), TIFF, Microsoft RIFF, MacPaint, Thunderscan, and Macintosh PICT formats; it can write any of these formats, plus black-and-white EPS files. GIFConverter prints on any Macintosh printer (halftones on the LaserWriter, color on the ImageWriter II or on any color PostScript printer, the LaserWriter 6.0, and many other color printers). The program allows you to adjust an image to a particular set of colors by dithering and producing halftones.

GIFConverter runs on any Macintosh with 128K ROMs or newer, including Macintosh Plus, II, LC, Quadra, Centris, Performa, and PowerBook. The

Power Macintosh is currently emulated, but a subsequent version will offer native features. The program uses 168K of RAM minimum. Four megabytes is recommended for larger images with full color.

GIFConverter is shareware for the Macintosh. The executable is included on the CD-ROM in the *software/mac/gifconv* folder. The version on the CD-ROM is GIFConverter 2.3.7, the most recent version available when we went to press.

On the CD-ROM, the *gifconv.hqx* file contains the full GIFConverter distribution. This file is a self-extracting archive. You can extract the complete set of Macintosh files needed to run GIFConverter by running the Stuffit Expander program on this *.hqx* file. (See the discussion of Stuffit Expander above in "Accessing Software on the Macintosh.")

Getting GIFConverter

If you do not have a CD-ROM drive on your system, you can get a copy of GIFConverter from many sites on the Internet. Two good sources are the *mac.archive.umich.edu* site (in the *mac/graphics/graphicsutil* directory), the *sumex-aim.stanford.edu* site (in the *info-mac/grf/util* directory), and mirrors of these sites, as well as sites on the *macgifts* mailing list. Other sites may have copies of the software, but they are not guaranteed to be up-to-date. In these directories, you will find the GIFConverter executable, *gifconverter-237.hqx*, as well as a number of earlier versions and updates. (You need to uncompress and extract files from this *.hqx* file. Note that this filename may change as new versions become available.

The software is also available from CompuServe in the GRAPHSUPPORT forum library 3, *GIFCNV.SEA*, and on America Online in the Macintosh Graphics and CD-ROM Forum (keyword MGR).

If you have a problem with GIFConverter that you cannot solve, you can contact the author:

Kevin Mitchell
Internet: *kam@mcs.com*
CompuServe: 74017,2573

Graphics Converter

GraphicsConverter was written by Thorsten Lemke for the Macintosh. It converts more than 40 different graphics file formats to and from MS/DOS, Windows, UNIX, Amiga, and Atari formats. You can use the program to do batch conversions of complete folders. It can also produce slide shows and perform a variety of image manipulations (e.g., dithering).

To run GraphicsConverter, you must have a Macintosh with ColorQuickDraw, at least a 68020 or Power Macintosh with System 7 or later, and two megabytes of free RAM.

GraphicsConverter is shareware for the Macintosh. The executable is included on the CD-ROM in the *software/mac/grphconv* folder. The version on the CD-ROM is GraphicsConverter 1.7.8, the most recent version available when we went to press.

On the CD-ROM, the *grphconv.hqx* file contains the full GraphicsConverter distribution. This file is a BINHEXed, stuffed file. You can extract the complete set of Macintosh files needed to run GraphicsConverter by running the Stuffit Expander program on this *.hqx* file. (See the discussion of Stuffit Expander above in "Accessing Software on the Macintosh.") You will also find readme files in the folder.

Getting GraphicsConverter

If you do not have a CD-ROM drive on your system, you can get a copy of GraphicsConverter from many sites on the Internet. The official version is at the *sumex-aim.stanford.edu* (in the *info-mac/grf/util* directory) or its mirrors. Other sites may have copies of the software, but they are not guaranteed to be up-to-date. The GraphicsConverter executable is in the file *graphics-converter-178.hqx*. (You need to uncompress and extract files from this *.hqx* file. Note that this filename may change as new versions become available.

You can also get this software from CompuServe in the GRAPHSUPPORT and MACAP forums.

If you have a problem with GraphicsConverter that you cannot solve, you can contact the author:

Thorsten Lemke
Internet: *thorsten-lemke@pe.maus.de*
CompuServe: 100102,1304

JPEGView

JPEGView is an image viewer written by Aaron Giles for the Macintosh. It allows you to view files in the JPEG, TIFF, Windows BMP, GIF, Macintosh PICT, and Startup Screen formats.

JPEG runs on Macintosh and Power Macintosh systems and uses QuickTime. It is considered to be shareware, but is actually readily available at low or no cost. The author requires you only to send a postcard to him. If you want a printed copy of the new help, there is a fee, described in the readme file.

JPEGView is included on the CD-ROM in the *software/mac/jpegview* folder. The version on the CD-ROM is JPEGView 3.2.1, the most recent version available when we went to press.

The *jpeg321.hqx* file on the CD-ROM contains the full JPEGView distribution (sometimes known as the "fat binary") that runs at full speed on any type of Macintosh (classic or Power Macintosh). This file is a BINHEXed, stuffed file. You can extract the complete set of Macintosh files needed to run JPEGView by running the Stuffit Expander program on the *.hqx* file. (See the discussion of Stuffit Expander above in "Accessing Software on the Macintosh.")

Getting JPEGView

If you do not have a CD-ROM drive on your system, you can get a copy of JPEGView from many sites on the Internet. The official version of JPEGView is at the *guru.med.cornell.edu* site (in the *pub/jpegview* directory). Other sites may have copies of the software, but they are not guaranteed to be up-to-date.

The *jpegview321.sit.hqx* file contains the so-called "fat binary" version of JPEGView. At some sites, you may find system-specific versions of JPEGView. *jpegview321.68k.sit.hqx* contains the "classic" Macintosh (not Power Macintosh) version. *jpegview321.ppc.sit.hqx* contains the Power Macintosh version. (You need to uncompress and extract files from these *.hqx* files.) Note that these filenames may change as new versions become available. You will also find some utility and readme files in the directory.

For the official America Online version, look for keyword "JPEGView" in the JPEGView software libary.

If you have a problem with JPEGView that you cannot solve, you can contact the author:

Aaron Giles
giles@med.cornell.edu

NIH Image

NIH Image is an image-processing and analysis program for the Macintosh written by Wayne Rasband at the National Institutes of Health. It can acquire, display, edit, enhance, analyze, print, and animate images. It reads and writes TIFF, Macintosh PICT and PICS, and MacPaint files. It also supports Data Translation and Scion frame-grabber cards for capturing images or movie sequences using a TV camera. You can then correct the shading and do frame averaging on the acquired gray-scale images.

You can use NIH Image to perform a variety of image-manipulation functions, including contrast enhancement, density profiling, smoothing, sharpening, edge detection, median filtering, and spatial convolution. You can also use NIH Image to measure area, average ray value, center, and angle of orientation of a user-defined region of interest. The software provides MacPaint-like editing of color and gray-scale images, including the ability to draw lines, rectangles, ovals, and text. It supports multiple windows and eight levels of magnification.

NIH Image incorporates a Pascal-like macro programming language that provides the ability to automate complex and frequently repetitive processing tasks.

NIH Image is publicly available Macintosh software. The code is included on the CD-ROM in the *software/mac/nihimage* folder. Both source (written in Think Pascal from Symantec) and executables are provided. The version on the CD-ROM is NIH Image 1.54, the most recent version available when we went to press.

You will find several *.hqx* files in the *software/mac/nihimage* folder. All of the *.hqx* files are in BINHEXed, stuffed format. You can extract the complete set of Macintosh files needed to run NIH Image by running the Stuffit Expander program on these *.hqx* files. (See the discussion of Stuffit Expander above in "Accessing Software on the Macintosh.")

nih_fpu.hqx	NIH Image executable for floating-point systems.
nih_nfpu.hqx	Executable for non-floating-point systems.
nih_beta.hqx	Source files.
nih_docs.hqx	Documentation in Microsoft Word.

You will also find a number of readme files containing readme information.

Getting NIH Image

If you do not have a CD-ROM drive on your system, you can get a copy of NIH Image from many sites on the Internet. The official version of NIH Image is at the *zippy.nimh.nih.gov* site (in the *pub/nih-image* directory). Other sites may have copies of the software, but they are not all guaranteed to be up-to-date.

There are several versions of the NIH Image software available via FTP. Those currently available are are listed below. (You need to uncompress and extract files from these *.hqx* files. Note that these filenames may change as new version of the software become available.

nih-image154.fpu.hqx
> Version used in floating-point systems

nih-image154.nonfpu.hqx
> Version used in non-floating-point systems

nih-image155beta62.hqx
> Beta version of a newer release

nih-image154.source.hqx
> Complete source code

nih-image154.docs.hqx
> Complete documentation, mainly in Microsoft Word format

You will also find assorted images, contributed programs, and readme files in the directory.

You can subscribe to the NIH Image mailing list by sending a message (containing the line, "subscribe NIH Image" in the body of the message) to:

nih-image@soils.umn.edu

If you have a problem with NIH Image that you cannot solve, you can contact the author:

Wayne Rasband
wayne@helix.nih.gov

Sparkle

Sparkle is an MPEG player for the Macintosh written by Maynard Handley. Sparkle plays images (movies) in the MPEG (Motion Picture Experts Group) format. (See the MPEG article in Part II of this book.) It can open multiple files at one time and uses the QuickTime movie controller to control MPEG viewing.

Sparkle runs on Macintoshes with a 68020 or greater, System 7 or greater, and QuickTime 1.6 or greater. It also runs on Power PCs under emulation, but does not yet run in native mode on those machines.

Sparkle is publicly available Macintosh software. The executable is included on the CD-ROM in the *software/mac/sparkle* folder. The version on the CD-ROM is Sparkle 2.02, the most recent version available when we went to press.

The *spark202.hqx* file on the CD-ROM contains the full Sparkle distribution. This is a BINHEXed, stuffed file. You can extract the complete set of Macintosh files needed to run Sparkle by running the Stuffit Expander program on this *.hqx* file. (See the discussion of Stuffit Expander above in "Accessing Software on the Macintosh.") You will also find readme files in the folder.

The distribution includes documentation containing a list of frequently asked questions about MPEG images and viewing, sources of MPEG images, the conversion of QuickTime movies to MPEG files, and more.

Getting Sparkle

If you do not have a CD-ROM drive on your system, you can get a copy of Sparkle from many sites on the Internet. The official version of Sparkle is at the *sumex-aim.stanford.edu* site (in the *info-mac/grf/util* directory) and all mirror sites; for example, at *mrcnext.cso.uiuc.edu* it is in *pub/info-mac/grf/util*. Other sites may have copies of the software, but they are not all guaranteed to be up-to-date. In these directories you will find the Sparkle executable, *sparkle-202.hqx*. (You need to uncompress and extract files from this *.hqx* file. Note that this filename may change as new versions become available.

If you have a problem with Sparkle that you cannot solve, you can contact the author:

Maynard Handley
maynard@elwing.otago.ac.nz

You can also contact him if you want to request a copy of the source.

What To Do If You Have Problems?

For problems with any of the programs included on the CD-ROM, contact the vendors or authors. See the list at the end of this appendix.

For problems with the CD-ROM itself that you and your colleagues are not able to solve, you can call O'Reilly & Associates. We will try to help you if we can, and, if we can't, we'll refer you to other organizations.

Graphics and Imaging Resources

Our thanks to Shari L.S. Worthington for her contribution to this summary. Many of the Internet resources listed here were included in her article, "Imaging on the Internet: Scientific/Industrial Resources" which appeared in *Advanced Imaging*, February 1994.

There are many excellent resources for electronic access to information on graphics and imaging. The emphasis in this summary is on Internet resources. Historically, graphics and imaging information available via the Internet has tended to be more academic than commercial; as Internet usage spreads, this situation is beginning to change, and more and more commercial information is becoming available. The main advantages of the Internet, when contrasted with commercial sources such as CompuServe, are the ready accessibility of information on the Internet and the fact that redistribution of materials found on archive sites is generally not a problem.

Commercial Resources

The amount of information from the commercial sector available and archived on CompuServe (and to a lesser extent on BIX, GENIE, the other commercial services) is extraordinarily high compared to the Internet, and the breadth of information available is much wider. In addition to CompuServe, BIX, GENIE, and the other large commercial services, a network of private PC/Macintosh/Amiga (and other) BBSs (as many as 20,000 by some estimates) covers the U.S. and parts of the rest of the world. By far the largest amount of traffic is in files, but the FIDONET, RIME, and ILINK networks provide conference services akin to the Internet newsgroups described in this summary. Some of the graphics files and programs eventually make their way to the Internet program file archive sites, but little of the message traffic does. Worldwide, traffic through CompuServe and the private BBSs has been estimated to be as much as 30 times the volume of traffic through the entire Internet. The number of files on these commercial and private services is perhaps 100 times greater than on the Internet.

Despite the plethora of valuable information on the commerical services, it is unfortunately often difficult to find what you want; CompuServe, for example, hosts more than 1,000 forums. Another disadvantage of CompuServe is that it's not possible to redistribute materials provided by vendors for their own customers' use. On the other hand, most major companies provide support through CompuServe, so if you know what graphics information you want, CompuServe is the first place to look. In particular, it's the place to go for system-specific programming information in the PC and Macintosh worlds.

The GRAPHSUPPORT forum on CompuServe is one important source of graphics information. It is the central distribution point of GIF-related materials (recall that GIF was designed, and continues to be maintained, by CompuServe engineers). Because of the widespread popularity of GIF, the GRAPHSUPPORT forum has become an attractive place to post more general graphics-related information and queries and to upload files, including images and program-related materials.

The following list of libraries (called file directories on CompuServe) will give you an idea what can be found in GRAPHSUPPORT. Aside from the GIF-specific information, there are approximately 200 other forums with similar topical material on CompuServe.

Graphics Support Forum Libraries Menu

1 'Go Graphics' Help
2 Online Viewing
3 Graphic Viewers
4 Format Conversion
5 Paint/Draw Programs
6 Digitizing Hardware
7 Video Adapters
8 Printing Graphics
9 Publishing Projects
10 GIF Tools
11 Animation Players
12 Graphics Demos
13 Developers' Den
14 Misc. Util & Code
15 Non-GIF Software
16 Standards and Specs
17 Copyright & More!

CompuServe also offers a Graphics File Finder (GO GRAPHFF), which helps you find the images you are looking for, and the 'Go Graphics' News service (GO GRAPHNEWS), which tells you what's new in the graphics forums and with graphics in general.

In future editions of this book, we hope to expand our coverage to describe CompuServe and other commercial resources that contain especially valuable graphics and imaging information. If you use particular resources heavily, we hope you'll let us know what they are.

Internet Access Methods

This section summarizes various access methods you can use to get at the major Internet resources described in subsequent sections. These include resources in areas of general imaging; chemical and biomedical imaging; metereological, oceanographic, and geophysical imaging; and astronomy and space. We hope you'll let us know if a particular resource you use is not included in this summary.

USENET Newsgroups and FAQs

A prime source of information on the Internet is USENET, a messaging and conferencing system distributed across the entire Internet. USENET contains a networked base of more than 7,000 separate conference discussions called newsgroups. Although the number of newsgroups on any given Internet host will vary greatly, anyone with USENET access can read and contribute to newsgroups.

When exploring a newsgroup, always first look for the FAQ (Frequently Asked Questions). Many newsgroups have FAQ files that will answer most of your general questions about a newsgroup subject. Always read the FAQ for a newsgroup before posting any questions you might have (except for perhaps "Does this newsgroup have a FAQ?"). Not all newsgroups have FAQs; in fact, most do not.

FAQs are typically updated and distributed once a month on most newsgroups and may contain the word "FAQ" or "Frequently Asked Questions" in their subject heading. If you cannot find a FAQ sheet posted in a newsgroup, then check the newsgroup news.answers (where all FAQ lists are posted), or on the FTP site *rtfm.mit.edu* in the directory */pub/usenet/news.answers* (where all FAQ lists are archived). FAQs are also archived in subdirectories of each newsgroup's name under the */pub/usenet* directory (the FAQ for *comp.graphics* may be found in */pub/usenet/comp.graphics*). You can request that a FAQ be emailed to you by sending an email message to *mail-server@rtfm.mit.edu* with the name and path of the FAQ in the body of the message. A few to try are:

```
send pub/usenet/news.answers/jpeg-faq
send pub/usenet/news.answers/image-processing/Macintosh
send pub/usenet/sci.answers/sci-data-formats
send index
```

Send a message with the word "help" in the body for detailed instructions on using the *rtfm.mit.edu* mail server.

Mailing Lists

Mailing lists are a less visible, and often less costly, alternative to USENET newsgroups. Mailing lists are also distributed across the Internet, but via email rather than through a mechanism such as USENET. This access method is less costly in that only basic email service is required to join a mailing list, so users of information services such as CompuServe may join any Internet mailing list. Having access to USENET is not required.

A mailing list is similar to a newsgroup in that it is a discussion composed of contributions made by the mailing list members. Members of the list receive other members' contributions to the list as email and may contribute their own. You can save the email listings you receive and review them later. Most mailing list sites also archive their users' contributions, so you can join a list, request (or FTP) the last few weeks worth of listings, and catch up on what you've missed.

To subscribe to a mailing list you normally append "-request" to the name of the list in the Internet address name. For example, to subscribe to the mailing list *cogneuro@ptolemy.arc.nasa.gov*, send an email message to *cogneuro-request@ptolemy.arc.nasa.gov*. In the body of the message put the word "subscribe" followed by the name of the list, such as "subscribe cogneuro" (or "unsubscribe cogneuro" to remove yourself from the mailing list). You may contribute to the list by sending email to the *cogneuro@ptolemy.arc.nasa.gov* address. Whenever any other subscriber contributes to the list, you will receive email of that subscriber's listing.

FTP

FTP (File Transfer Protocol) is the communications protocol used to transfer files between computers on the Internet. Using FTP, you can connect to a remote FTP server and transfer files between your local client machine and the remote server. Some FTP sites do not even require a login name and password to connect, but most do.

FTP is often referred to as anonymous FTP because you can log in with the name anonymous. Sometimes you can specify anonymous as your password as well, although it is now becoming more politic to give your Internet address name as your password, and some FTP servers even insist upon it. Most, however, will only scold you if you give a password that is not in the familiar *name@host* format.

Telnet

Telnet is the protocol used for actually logging into a remote computer. To provide services beyond simple file transfers, a Telnet archive allows users to login to the remote server, typically with a known login name and no password, and to access system services, usually through a menu.

Gopher

Gopher is a much easier alternative to Telnet and FTP for browsing through an on-line library, database, or file archive. Using only FTP, you must dig through a hierarchy of files and directories looking for the information you need, usually with only index and readme files to guide you along the way. Telnet archives can confuse you with a variety of user interfaces that are all different. Gopher servers present you with a consistent, easy-to-use menuing interface that allows easy browsing of documents and databases, quick navigation through archives, and convenient access to FTP for file transfers.

General Imaging Resources

The prime source of graphics information on USENET is the FAQ for the *comp.graphics* newsgroup. Information on file formats, image processing and analysis, books and journal articles, and graphics and imaging software packages is updated monthly in this FAQ.

The image-processing FAQ found in the *sci.image.processing* newsgroup gives Macintosh image-processing information available via FTP, gopher, USENET, email, telephone, and the postal service.

The Pilot European Image Processing Archive (PEIPA) is a repository and distribution service for software, digests, and newsgroup archives concerned with image processing, analysis, manipulation, generation, and the display of graphics. The PEIPA FTP site (*peipa.essex.ac.uk*) contains the British Machine Vision Association (BMVA) and Society for Pattern Recognition newsletter (directory *ipa/digest/bmva*), the International Association for Pattern Recognition newsletter (directory *ipa/digest/IAPR*), and the archives for the pixel (*ipa/digests/pixel*) and Vision-List (directory *ipa/digests/vision-list*) mailing lists.

Newsgroups

alt.3d	Three-dimensional imaging
alt.graphics	An alternative to *comp.graphics*
alt.graphics.pixutils	
	Discussion of image manipulation software
comp.ai.vision	Technical discussion about computer-based vision
comp.compression	
	Data compression algorithms and theory
comp.compression.research	
	Discussions about data compression research
comp.graphics	Computer graphics, art, animation, image processing
comp.graphics.animation	
	Technical aspects of computer animation
comp.graphics.research	
	Technical discussion on latest graphics research
comp.graphics.visualization	
	Information on scientific visualization
comp.multimedia	
	Interactive multimedia technologies
comp.sys.mac.scitech	
	Macintosh scientific and engineering applications
comp.sys.sgi.graphics	
	Graphics software and issues on SGI systems
sci.data.formats	Modeling, storage, and retrieval of scientific data
sci.image.processing	
	Scientific image processing and analysis

Mailing Lists

agocg-ip@mailbase.ac.ak

Discussion of all aspects of image processing

To subscribe: send an email message to *mailbase@mailbase.ac.uk* with the body: "join agocg-ip *yourfirstname yourlastname*"

arachnet@uottowa

Association of electronic lists and journals on electronic publishing

To subscribe: send email to *dkovacs@kentvm.kent.edu*

ingrafx@psuvm Interdisciplinary discussion of information graphics; for cartographers, graphic designers, psychologists, and scientific visualization researchers

To subscribe: send email to *listserv@psuvm.psu.edu*

listserv@mom.spie.org

International Society for Optical Engineering

To subscribe to the INFO-EI mailing list: send email to *info-optolink-request@mom.spie.org* with "info-ei" in the body of the message

nih-image@soils.umn.edu

Discussion of the NIH Image software package for the Macintosh

To subscribe: send email to *listserv@soils.umn.edu* with the body "subscribe nih-image *yourfirstname yourlastname*"

pixel@essex.ac.uk

British Machine Vision Association newsletter for all image processing, machine vision, pattern recognition, remote sensing, and related topics

To subscribe: send email to *pixel-request@essex.ac.uk*

vision-list@ads.com

Computer vision discussion of algorithms and techniques

To subscribe: send email to *vision-list-request@ads.com* with the body "subscribe vision-list" *ximage@expo.lcs.mit.edu*

Image processing using the X Window System

To subscribe: send email to *ximage-request@expo.lcs.mit.edu* with "subscribe ximage"in the body of the message

FTP Archives

avalon.chinalake.navy.mil

3-D object repository; archive of graphics file format specifications

Directory: */pub/format_specs*

ftp.cica.indiana.edu

Clearinghouse for Microsoft Windows applications, tips, utilities, drivers, and bitmaps

ftp.ncsa.uiuc.edu

National Center for Supercomputing Applications. Publicly available software for image processing, data analysis, and visualization for the Macintosh, PC, and UNIX platforms. Archive of graphics file specifications.

Directory: */misc/file.formats/graphics.formats*

ftp.sdsc.edu   San Diego Supercomputer Center (SDSC). Image Tools, ImageTyper, and Interactive Color Tutorial. Sound and image file archive.

ftp.uu.net   UUNET archive. Large collection of graphics and imaging software including the *comp.graphics* archive

Directory: */graphics*

mom.spie.org   International Society for Optical Engineering. Proceedings, programs, and information on Technical Working Groups, including electronic imaging.

peipa.essex.ac.uk

Pilot European Image Processing Archive. Contains many images and software packages, including the Khoros GUI development environment. Also contains a modest collection of graphics file formats specifications.

Directory: */ipa/file-formats* Directory: */ipa/khoros*

ra.nrl.navy.mil   Naval Research Laboratory Research Computation Division Visualization Laboratory. Mostly Macintosh programs for chemistry, biology, math, imaging, AI, data acquisition, etc.

photo1.si.edu   Smithsonian Institution photoimage archives.

Directory: */images*

sumex-aim.stanford.edu
Large repository of Macintosh software

Directory: */info-mac*

sunsite.unc.edu   University of North Carolina. Information on multimedia images, video, and sound. Graphical image collection.

Directory: */pub/multimedia*

telva.ccu.uniovi.es
Archive of graphics file format specifications.

Directory: */pub/graphics/file.formats*

wuarchive.wustl.edu
Mirror site for most major FTP archive sites. Also contains a large archive of graphics and images for math and life science educators.

Directory: */graphics/graphics/packages*

zamenhof.cs.rice.edu
Large archive of graphics software and graphics file format specifications and information

Directory: */pub/graphics.formats*

zippy.nimh.nih.gov
National Institutes of Health archive for the Macintosh NIH Image and related publicly available programs.

Directory: */pub/nih-image*

Gopher

skyking.oce.orst.edu
sci.image.processing newsgroup archive

Chemical and Biomedical Imaging Resources

The following resources contain information on the sciences of chemistry, biology, biomedicine, and nuclear medicine. The Biomedical Computer Laboratory (BCL) is supported by the National Institute of Health's (NIH) National Center for Research Resources (NCRR). The BCL promotes the application of advances in computer science and engineering, mathematics, and the physical sciences to research problems in the biological and medical fields by supporting the development of advanced research technologies. Emphasis is on quantitative imaging, including PET image reconstruction, computational optical-sectioning microscopy, shape modeling and segmentation, electron-microscopic autoradiography (EMA), image acquisition and quantitative analysis of DNA electrophoretic gels and autoradiograms, and parallel processing.

Mailing Lists

cogneuro@ptolemy.arc.nasa.gov

> Cognitive science and neuroscience discussion

> To subscribe: send email to *cogneuro-request@ptolemy.arc.nasa.gov* with the body "subscribe cogneuro"

medimage@polygraf

> Medical imaging discussion.

> To subscribe: send email to *listserv%polygraf.bitnet@mitvma.-mit.edu* with the body "subscribe medimage"

nucmed@uwovax.uwo.ca

> A discussion of nuclear medicine and related issues, including the format of digital images.

> To subscribe: send email to *nucmed-request@uwovax.uwo.ca* with the body "subscribe nucmed"

radsig@uwavm.u.washington.edu

> Radiology Special Interest Group

> To subscribe: send email to *listserv@uwavm.bitnet* with the body "subscribe radsig"

vetcai-l@cvdls.ucdavis.edu

> Veterinary medicine computer assisted instruction.

> Topics include imaging, expert systems, and LIMs.

To subscribe: send email to *listserv@cvdls.ucdavis.edu* with body
"subscribe vetcai-l"

FTP Archives

ftp.sdsc.edu   Computational chemistry and biology information.

Directory: */pub/sdsc*

ftp.sura.net   List of health and medical related Internet sources

Directory: */pub/nic/medical.resources*

omicron.cs.unc.edu

Archive of MRI and CT scan data and images of human anatomy and electron density maps of RNA. Exploratory Visualization Software.

Directory: */pub/softlab/CHVRTD* Directory: */pub/VIEW*

sunsite.unc.edu University of North Carolina. Information on astronomy, biology, chemistry, molecular modeling, geology, and GIS.

Directory: */pub/academic*

wubcl.wustl.edu Biomedical Computer Laboratory. Quantitative imaging data.

zaphod.ncsa.uiuc.edu

Chemical Visualization project for high school education

Directory: */Education/ChemViz*

Telnet Archives

130.199.112.132

Nuclear Data Center

Login: nndc

Gopher

bdt.ftpt.br   Bioline publications, text, graphics, and references to other biological sciences gophers.

gopher.hs.jhu.edu

Johns Hopkins University History of Science and Medicine. Included is an image library of architectural photographs.

huh.harvard.edu
> Biodiversity and biological collections, including images

Meteorological, Oceanographic, and Geophysical Imaging Resources

The latest weather data sources are located in the FAQ for the newsgroup *sci.geo.meteorology*. The FAQ contains current information on weather satellite data and images, and on meteorological, oceanographic, and geophysical research data. Information on Geographical Information Systems (GIS) may be found in the GIS-L mailing list, the newsgroup *comp.infosystems.gis*, or on the FTP site *csn.org*.

Newsgroups

comp.infosystems.gis
> Information on all aspects of Geographical Information Systems (GIS)

sci.geo.meteorology
> Discussion of meteorology

Mailing Lists

GIS-L@ubvmcc.buffalo.edu
> Forum for the discussion of Geographical Information Systems
>
> To subscribe: send email to *listserv@ubvmcc.buffalo.edu* with the body "subscribe GIS-L"

FTP Archives

csn.org
> Geologic, GIS, mapping, earth science software and resources for the PC and Macintosh
>
> Directory: */COGS*

ics.uci.edu
> Synthetic stereo satellite images of Earth
>
> Directory: */honig*

liasun3.epfl.ch
> Weather map of England, Europe, and the Earth in GIF format
>
> Directory: */pub/weather*

vmd.cso.uiuc.edu
Weather satellite images of North America and Surface Analysis weather maps in GIF format

Directory: */wx*

Telnet Archives

128.175.24.1   Ocean Information Center. Data sets related to oceanography.

Login: info

Gopher

info.er.usgs.gov   US Geological Survey. Information on geology, hydrology, cartography, and GIS.

wx.atmos.uiuc.edu
University of Illinois Weather Machine. Current weather conditions, National Weather Service forecasts, and satellite images.

Astronomy and Space Exploration Imaging Resources

The Internet abounds with information on astronomy, astrophysics, and space exploration. Archives contain thousands of images collected from telescopic, satellite, and spacecraft data.

The Space Telescope Electronic Information System (*stsci.edu*) is a very comprehensive resource for all astronomical information. It includes many space craft and Hubble Space Telescope images.

The NASA archive *toybox.gsfc.nasa.gov* contains not only a huge collection of images, but also references to other resources, such as UUNET, the Washington University archives, and the Lawrence Berkeley Labs.

Newsgroups

alt.sci.astro   An astronomy discussion

alt.sci.astro.figaro
Figaro data-reduction package discussion

alt.sci.astro.aips
Discussions on the Astronomical Image Processing System (AIPS)

sci.astro	An astronomy discussion
sci.astro.fits	Issues related to the Flexible Image Transport System (FITS)
sci.astro.hubble	Hubble Space Telescope data

sci.astro.planetarium
> A planetarium-oriented discussion

Electronic Journal

COSMIC UPDATE
> Information on new NASA software for astronomy and space exploration
>
> To subscribe: send email to *service@cossack.cosmic.uga.edu.*

FTP Archives

ames.arc.nasa.gov
> NASA/Ames Archives. Data files, GIF images, and NASA press releases and indexes.
>
> Directory: */pub/SPACE*

suncub.bbso.caltech.edu
> Big Bear Solar Observatory. Solar full-disk and high- resolution images.

toybox.gsfc.nasa.gov
> NASA images in GIF, JPEG, PostScript, Sun Raster, and X Bitmap format. Links to LBL, Washington University, and UUNET.
>
> Directory: */pub/images*

wuarchive.wustl.edu
> Planetary Data System (PDS) Geosciences Node and Magellan spacecraft images
>
> Directory: */graphics/magellan*

Telnet Archives

envnet.gsfc.nasa.gov
> EnviroNET (Space Environment Information Service). Space data from NASA and the European Space Agency.
>
> Username: envnet Password: henniker

lpi.jsc.nasa.gov   Lunar and Planetary Institute. Lunar and planetary mission information and images. Image Retrieval and Processing System (IRPS).

> login: lpi

nssdc.gsfc.nasa.gov
> *nssdca.gsfc.nasa.gov"* National Space Sciences Data Center. Archive for space and Earth science researchers.
>
> login: nodis

Gopher

stsci.edu   Space Telescope Electronic Information System. Information for Hubble Space Telescope proposers and observers. Many links to astronomy Internet resources.

4-bit color

    Refers to a way of representing bitmap or other data that can handle up to 16 (2^4) colors.

8-bit color

    Refers to a way of representing bitmap or other data that can handle up to 256 (2^8) colors.

15-bit color

    Refers to a way of representing bitmap or other data that can handle up to 32,768 (2^{15}) colors.

16-bit color

    Refers to a way of representing bitmap or other data that can handle up to 65,536 (2^{16}) colors.

24-bit color

    Refers to a way of representing bitmap or other data that can handle up to 16,777,216 (2^{24}) colors.

active information device

    An electronic device with which the user must constantly interact in order to obtain information. Video arcade games and most multimedia applications are active information devices. Contrast with *passive information device.*

adaptive encoding

An algorithm that has no certain prior knowledge about the format of the data it is encoding. It must adapt to the format of the data as it encodes it. LZW is an adaptive encoding algorithm.

additive system

A color system in which colors are created by adding colors to black. The more color that is added, the more the resulting color tends towards white.

alpha channel

An additional channel of bitmap data used to store transparency data for an image, which can be on a per-pixel, per-block, or per-image basis. The degree of pixel transparency for an 8-bit alpha value ranges from 0 (the pixel is completely invisible or transparent) to 255 (the pixel is completely visible or opaque). See also *overlay bit.*

animation

A sequence of two or more images displayed in a rapid sequence so as to provide the illusion of continuous motion. Animations are typically played back at a rate of 12 to 15 frames per second.

array of pixels

An ordered set of colored display elements on an output device. This term is used loosely to refer to an array of numerical values used by an application program to specify colored elements on an output device.

artifact

A detectable change in an image produced by a rendering application, such as a filter, or an editing tool, such as a paint program. Such changes are said to be introduced by human intervention and are therefore artifactual influences upon natural, ecofactual data.

aspect ratio

The ratio of the width to the height of an image. A widely used aspect ratio for video is 4:3.

band

See *strip.*

BBS

Bulletin Board System. A telecommunications program running on a computer that allows other computers with modems to dial in and access files. BBSs are a prime source of image files and file format information. Older names for BBSs include Computer Bulletin Board System (CBBS) and Electronic Bulletin Board Systems (EBBS).

big-endian

Refers to systems or machines that store the most-significant byte (MSB) at the lowest address in a word, usually referred to as byte 0. Contrast with *little-endian*.

bit depth

The size of a value used to represent a pixel in bitmap graphics data. This is usually stated as the number of bits comprising the individual data value, or sometimes the number of bytes. The number 2 raised to the power *bit depth* specifies the maximum number of values the pixel can assume. Same as *pixel depth*.

bitmap

A set of numerical values specifying the colors of pixels on an output device. In older usage, the term referred to data intended for display on an output device capable of displaying only two levels. It is used in this book as a synonym for *raster*.

bitmap data

The portion of a bitmap file containing information associated with the actual image.

bitmap image

A representation of a graphics work on a raster device or in a bitmap file. Redundant in our terminology.

bit order

The order of the bits within a byte. The first bit in a byte may be either the most-significant or the least-significant bit. See also *LSB* and *MSB*.

bit plane

A two-dimensional array of bits one bit deep. A bitmap containing pixels with a depth of eight bits may be said to contain eight bit planes. A monochrome image (one bit per pixel) is usually stored as a single bit plane.

bit sex

The state of a bit (0 or 1).

bits per pixel

See *bit depth.*

block

See *chunk.*

bpp

Same as bits per pixel.

byte order

The order of bytes within a word of data. The first byte in a word may be either the most-significant or least-significant byte. See also *big-endian, little-endian, LSB,* and *MSB.*

CAD

See *Computer Aided Design.*

CD

See *Compact Disc.*

CD-DA

Compact Disc-Digital Audio. The standard used for encoding audio data onto a compact disc.

CD-I

Compact Disc-Interactive. The standard used for encoding audio and video information onto compact discs for use in interactive multimedia systems.

CD-R

Compact Disc-Recordable. The standard for creating write-once compact discs that may be mastered on a standard PC.

CD-ROM

Compact Disc-Read-Only Memory. A compact disc containing data encoded using the CD-XA standard. See also *CD-XA* and *ISO-9660.*

CD-XA

Compact Disc-Extended Architecture. The standard used for encoding data onto what we know as a CD-ROM. See also *ISO-9660*.

chroma

Term used when referring to color. Same as *chrominance*.

chrominance

The color portion of an image. It is the mixture of hue and saturation, or the combination of three primary colors, such as red, green, and blue.

chunk

A collection of data with a known format within a graphics file. Chunks are also called blocks in some graphics file format specifications. See also *packet*.

CLUT

Color Look-Up Table. See *look-up table*.

CMY

Acronym for Cyan/Magenta/Yellow. A subtractive color system based on the primary colors cyan, magenta, and yellow.

CMYK

Acronym for Cyan/Magenta/Yellow/Key. A subtractive color system based on the primary colors cyan, magenta, and yellow. Key color is the color black, which is not reproducable using the CMY model alone.

color channel

One of the numerical elements used to specify a color in a particular color model when that color is specified using an ordered n-tuple. Green is one channel in the RGB color model, which is specified using the ordered triplet (R,G,B).

color definition scheme

A system by which colors are specified, usually by numerical values or ordered sets of numbers.

color gamut

The range of colors which can be displayed using a particular color model or output device.

color map

See *look-up table.*

color model

The way colors are broken down and specified in a particular application or system.

color space

When a particular color scheme uses an ordered n-tuple to specify color, all the possible values corresponding to colors can be plotted on an n-dimensional graph. All the points plotted, which correspond to colors in the color model, constitute the color space.

color table

See *look-up table.*

color values

Same as *pixel values.*

Compact Disc

A circular plastic disc used for the storage of audio, video, textual, and other data that can be represented in a digital form, and from which data can be retrieved using an optical process. Although there are various formats, the one in most common use is 4.75 inches (12 centimeters) in diameter. See also *CD-ROM.*

component video

Color video information transmitted using three separate signal channels. RGB, YIQ, and YUV are examples of component video signals.

composite color

A color specified in a color model where that color is specified using an ordered n-tuple. A system where more than one color channel value exists, and where more than one channel value is needed to specify the color.

composite video

Color video information transmitted using a single signal channel. NTSC, PAL, and SECAM are examples of composite video signals.

Computer Aided Design

The use of applications, usually vector-based, for the design and rendering of graphical data of architectural and mechanical drawings, electronic schematics, and three-dimensional models. Commonly referred to as *CAD*.

convenience revision

A file format version created by an application vendor to accommodate a bug or quirk in a program. This is sometimes caused by ignorance or honest error, but in many cases is intentional. There is ample evidence that at least one vendor, the custodian (but not the originator) of a file format specification, knowingly released format revisions so as to avoid shipping delays caused by bugs introduced by junior programmers.

convolution

The process of transforming the value of a pixel, or a field of pixels, based on a mathematical formula. Convolution is used to alter the color of an image (filtering), or to re-encode the data (compression).

data compression

The process of converting data from one format to another format that is physically smaller in size. The same logical information is stored using less physical infomation.

data element

Typically the smallest units of readable data with a collection of data. Bits, bytes, WORDs, and DWORDs are all data elements.

data encoding

A generic term for the process of converting data from one format to another. Data compression and data encryption are both forms of data encoding.

data encryption

The process of converting data from an intelligible format to an unintelligible, but decryptable, format.

digitizing

The process of converting an analog signal to a digital signal. See *sampling*.

digitizing device

A device that creates a version of a physical graphical representation by creating a digital version. Common digitizing devices are scanners, image capture boards that work with video cameras, and digital cameras.

display surface

The portion of an output device where an image appears. The screen of a monitor, or printed paper.

EDIP

See *Electronic Document Image Processing*

Electronic Document Image Processing

A subfield of image processing specializing in the creation, storage, and manipulation of black-and-white images derived from printed documents. At least 75 percent of the image-processing market today is based on EDIP systems and applications.

FAX Files

Graphics files produced by a program that manages FAX-modem hardware. These are generally bitmap files and may be compressed. They are often in a proprietary format, although versions of TIFF and PCX are popular.

field

A fixed-size data structure in a file.

file element

The smallest unit of logical information within a file. Examples include fields within graphics file headers and color triples used to store RGB pixel data.

file identifier value

A specific value, or set of values, used to positively identify a file as being of a particular file format. File ID values may be an integer, such as 59A66A95h, or a string of ASCII characters, such as BITMAP, and they usually appear in the first field of a file header. Also called *magic number*.

fixed

Refers to an element in a file that has a known position, usually identified by an offset from a landmark in a file.

format creator

The person or organization responsible for the definition of the physical structure of, and conventions associated with, a file format. Often this person is a programmer called on to produce a file format in association with an application. In some cases, the format creator is a standards committee.

frame

A single image. Multiple frames of slightly differing images displayed in rapid sequence are used to create animations.

FTP

File Transfer Protocol. A low-level protocol used to transfer files between computers over computer networks. FTP is the primary means by which binary files are transferred between machines on the Internet.

fullcolor display

A term sometimes used to imply that a device is capable of displaying 2^{15} (32,768) or 2^{16} (65,536) colors; however, this actually describes *hicolor*, and *fullcolor* tends to be a marketing term, rather than a technical one.

full-motion video

Video image frames displayed at a rate of 30 frames per second for NTSC and 25 frames per second for PAL.

graphic work

The end result of effort by a graphic artist. A drawing or other artifact.

graphics data

Data which may or may not have a physical representation, intended for display on an output device.

graphics file

A file containing graphics data.

graphics file format

The definition of, and conventions associated with, a file structure used for the storage of graphics data.

graymap

In older terminology, raster data composed of values with more than two levels, intended for an output device capable of displaying only shades of gray.

gray-scale

A term used when referring to an image. A gray shade is any color whose three primary colors are the same value. Gray shades only have intensity (luminance) and no color (chrominance).

HBL

Acronym for Hue/Brightness/Luminosity. See *HSI*.

hicolor display

A term used to imply that a device is capable of displaying 2^{15} (32,768) or 2^{16} (65,536) colors.

HLS

Acronym for Hue/Lightness/Saturation. See *HSI*.

HSB

Acronym for Hue/Saturation/Brightness. See *HSI*.

HSI

Acronym for Hue/Saturation/Intensity. An additive color system based on the attributes of color (hue), percentage of white (saturation), and brightness (intensity). Similar or identical color systems include HBL, HLS, HSB, HSL, and HSV.

HSL

Acronym for Hue/Saturation/Luminosity. See *HSI*.

HSV

Acronym for Hue/Saturation/Value. See *HSI*.

hue

Any color, such as red, violet, orange, and so on.

hybrid text

The storage and display of bitmap and textual data using a single graphics file format. GIF89A is an example of a format with a hybrid text capability.

hybrid database

The ability to store complex and highly organized database information in conjunction with graphical data. See also *hybrid text*.

hypertext

A collection of graphical and textual data organized in such a way as to facilitate easy access to all of the information it contains. Hypertext may be thought of as a precursor to multimedia, or simply as an extension of it. Certain extensions of hypertext are becoming known as *hypermedia*.

image

A visual representation of graphics data displayed on the display surface of an output device. Output of a rendering application. One end of the graphics production pipeline. A single frame from an animation or video sequence.

image bitmap

See *bitmap image*.

image data

A term used loosely to refer to bitmap data, or the portion of a bitmap file containing bitmap data.

index map

See *look-up table*.

index values

Pairs of numbers arranged in a table so that an application can match numbers it knows about to numbers representing colors that an output device knows about.

indirect color

The specification of colors through the use of a palette or look-up table.

input

Generic term in computer technology referring to any data which is processed or transformed.

interframe encoding

The creation of encoded data from two or more image frames. MPEG encoding is an interframe encoding method.

interpolation

The process of reconstructing lines and outlines from key points. This usually consists of the application of an algorithm that specifies which points to color between or related to the key points.

intraframe encoding

The creation of encoded data from a single image frame. JPEG encoding is an intraframe encoding method.

ISO-9660

A file system standard developed for CD-ROMs using the CD-XA encoding standard. An ISO-9660 file system is readable by many operating systems, including MS-DOS, Apple Macintosh, and UNIX.

key points

Points necessary for the reconstruction of a graphics object from vector data. These are usually the minimum needed to specify the object. Two points at the corners of a rectangle are the key points.

landmark

Refers to an element in a file from which other positions and offsets are calculated. The canonical landmarks are the beginning, end, and current position. Other features, such as prominent data structures, may at times act as landmarks.

little-endian

Refers to systems or machines which store the least-significant byte (LSB) at the lowest address in a word, usually referred to as byte 0. Contrast with *big-endian.*

logical pixels

Idealized pixels having perfectly-defined characteristics and occupying no physical extent. The graphics equivalent of a mathematical point. Contrast with *physical pixels.*

look-up table

A series of pairs of numerical values whereby a program can match a meaningful value to one which specifies a color on an output device.

lossless encoding

A data compression or encoding algorithm that does not lose or discard any input data during the encoding process.

lossy encoding

A data compression or encoding algorithm that loses, or purposely throws away, input data during the encoding process to gain a better compression ratio. JPEG is an example of a lossy encoding method.

luminance

The brightness or intensity of a color. The pixels in a monochrome image have a luminance of either 100 percent or 0 percent.

LSB

Depending on context, either the least-significant byte (of more than one juxtaposed bytes) or the least-significant bit (of the bits in a byte or word of data). Contrast with *MSB*.

LUT

See *look-up table*.

magic number

See *file identifier value*.

magic values

Arbitrary numbers or text strings, often picked "out of the air" by a format creator for the purpose of identifying the format.

metadata

Metadata is comprised of attributes, parameters, notebooks, and other types of miscellaneous complex data aggregates associated with primary scientific data.

metafile

A file format capable of storing two or more types of image data, usualy vector and bitmap, in the same file.

MIDI

Acronym for Musical Instrument Digital Interface. A standard for digital signals used to control electronic musical instruments. MIDI information may be stored as a data file and is found in many multimedia file formats.

monochrome

An image composed of a single color and black. Most monochrome images are black and white, although any color might be substituted for white. Also called 1-bit images. Although the term monochrome, of course, means single-colored, in computer graphics it is used to denote a system where two colors can be specified: the foreground color and the background.

MSB

Depending on context, either the most-significant byte (of more than one juxtaposed bytes) or the most-significant bit (of the bits in a byte or word of data). Contrast with *LSB*.

multi-channel palette

A palette with two or more individual color values per color element. Contrast with *single-color palette*.

multimedia

The concept of creating, storing, and playing back two or more forms of electronic information simultaneously. Such information includes still-images, motion-video, animations, digitized sound, and control information such as MIDI codes.

NTSC

Acronym for National Television Standards Committee. The standards committee responsible for, among other things, the creation of the color television signal used in the United States (NTSC video).

output

Generic term in computer technology meaning the result of any process or transformation of data.

output device

Physical mechanism used to create a display.

output device language

A computer language or set of commands created by a vendor to communicate with a particular output device, such as a printer. Hewlett Packard's PCL is one well-known output device language and is understood by Hewlett Packard printers and HP-compatible printers. It may or may not be easily human-readable. See *page description language*.

overlay bit

An additional bit found in a pixel or pixel plane that indicates whether the pixel is displayed as visible (opaque) or transparent (overlayed). See *alpha channel*.

packet
> A block of data with a known structure, usually used to denote elements of a stream.

page description language
> A computer language created by a vendor to communicate with output devices. It may be a fully functional language and is always human-readable. It is generally more sophisticated than an output device language and is not tailored to any particular output device. The most popular page description language in use today is Adobe's PostScript.

page table
> An array of offset values used to index the location of multiple bitmaps within a single graphics file. Each offset value indicates the starting position of each bitmap.

PAL
> Acronym for Phase Alternation Line. PAL is a standard of color television and video signals developed in West Germany and used throughout Europe (PAL video).

palette
> The gamut of colors which a device can display; a software data structure used to match numbers that are meaningful to a software program to numbers that cause colors to appear on an output device.

passive information device
> An electronic device with which the user need not interact in order to obtain data. Television and newspapers are examples of passive information devices. Contrast with *active information device.*

pel
> See *pixel.*

persistence
> A term often used in object-oriented technology to describe data that is stored in a static medium, such as a disk file or database. The data is said to "persist" even after the application that created it is no longer in memory. Spreadsheet, word processing, and graphics files are examples of persistent data.

physical pixels

The actual pixels which appear on the display surface of a raster output device. Contrast with *logical pixels*.

picture element

See *pixel*.

pixel

In traditional usage, short for "picture elements." These are irreducible elements of color created by an output device on its display surface. The term is sometimes used loosely to refer to the values of bitmap data elements used by an application to order the display of color elements on an output device.

pixel depth

See *bit depth*.

pixelmap

In older terminology, bitmap data composed of values with more than two levels, intended for an output device capable of displaying color.

pixel values

Numerical data items in a graphics file indicating the color or other information associated with an individual pixel.

pixmap

See *pixelmap*.

planar files

Graphics files with image data stored as bit planes or color planes rather than as pixels.

predictive encoding

An algorithm that has certain prior knowledge about the format of the data it is encoding. Huffman is a predictive encoding algorithm.

primary colors

Colors in a particular color model from which other colors can be constructed. In the RGB color model, red, green, and blue are the primary colors because other colors can be produced by mixing them.

production pipeline

The series of operations involved in defining, creating, and displaying an image, from conception to its realization or recording on an output device.

pseudocolor

A color specified through the use of a palette or look-up table.

quantization

The process of reducing the number of colors defined in the source data to match the number available on an output device.

quantization artifacts

Generally refers to features introduced in an image when the data used to render that image is converted to a data format capable of displaying fewer colors than the original. Banding and false color are two examples of possible quantization artifacts. Usually considered undesirable.

raster

Refers to graphics data represented by color values at points, which taken together describe the display on an output device. *Bitmap* is used in preference to *raster* in this book.

realization

The representation of an image on an output device. Sometimes meant to signify the current rendered version of some particular graphics data.

render

To produce a visual representation of graphics data on an output device.

rendering

The actual representation of an image on an output device.

representation

The actual artifact produced as the end result of the computer graphics production process, which may be an image on a monitor or on paper.

resolution

The measure of detail within an image. The resolution of an image is its physical size (number of pixels wide by number of scan lines long). The resolution of a display is the number of scan lines it may display (800x600 is a higher resolution than 320x200).

RGB

Acronym for Red/Green/Blue. An additive color system based on the primary colors red, green, and blue. The RGB model is loosely patterned after human eyes, which have a peak sensitivity to the colors red, green, and blue light.

sample rate

The number of digital samples recorded per second. The sample rate increases with the number of samples recorded per second. Same as *sample resolution*.

sample resolution

See *sample rate*.

sampling

The process of reading an analog signal at specific increments in time (sample rate) and storing the data as digital values. Sampling is the basic process used to create digital audio and video.

saturation

The percentage of white in a color. Zero percent saturation is full white (no color). 100 percent saturation is no white (pure color).

scan line

A row of pixels. The term comes from the scanning action of raster CRT output devices, which produces successive lines of output on the display surface.

scan-line table

An array of offset values used to index the location of each scan line or tile within a collection of bitmap data, which may or may not be compressed. Each offset value indicates the starting position of each scan line or tile.

scene description language

A computer language used to describe the position and attributes of objects within a two- or three-dimensional image. A file produced by such a language is called a scene format or scene description file.

SECAM

Acronym for Sequential Coleur Avec Memoire (sequential color with memory). SECAM is a standard of color television and video signals used in France and several other European countries (SECAM video).

single-channel palette

A palette with one color value per element. Contrast with *multi-channel palette*.

stream

Data with no fixed position in a file, composed of sub-elements with a known structure.

strip

A collection of one or more contiguous scan lines in a bitmap. Scan lines are often grouped in strips to buffer them in memory more efficiently. Also called *bands* in some file format specifications.

subtractive system

A color system in which colors are created by subtracting colors from white. The more color that is added, the more the resulting color tends towards black.

tag

A data structure in a file which can vary in both size and position.

tile

A two-dimensional sub-section of a bitmap. For example, a bitmap 100x100 pixels in size may be divided into four 25x25 pixel tiles. Pixels are often grouped as tiles rather than scan lines to achieve a more efficient use of memory.

transform

See *convolution*.

transparency

The degree of visibility of a pixel against a fixed background. A totally transparent pixel is invisible. See also *alpha channel*.

trichromatic colorimetric

Color models that use three color channels to specify a color. The RGB color model is a trichromatic colorimetric system.

truecolor display

A term used to imply that a device is capable of displaying $2^{\wedge}24$ (16,777,216) colors or more (said to match or exceed the color-resolving power of the human eye). *Truecolor* formerly referred to any device capable of displaying $2^{\wedge}15$ (32,768) colors or more, but *hicolor* more accurately describes the display of $2^{\wedge}15$ (32,768) or $2^{\wedge}16$ (65,536) colors.

vector

Refers to graphics data composed mainly of representations of lines and outlines of objects, which can be compactly represented by specifying sets of key points. A program displaying vector data must know how to draw lines by interpolating points between the key points.

virtual output

Data or an image that is produced, but that can't be seen—in other words, for which no physical representation yet exists. Data in a file.

voxel

A three-dimensional pixel. Voxels contain all of the components of a pixel (such as color values) and include an extra component that specifies the distance of the voxel from the point of observation.

YIQ

The color model used by NTSC video signals. See NTSC.

YUV

Acronym for Y-signal, U-signal, and V-signal, which is based on early color television terminology. A luminance/chrominance-base color model (Y specifies gray-scale or luminance, U and V chrominance) used by many video compression algorithms, such as MPEG.

INDEX

About the Authors

James D. Murray started his computer career in 1981 on a Version 6 UNIX system running on a PDP-11/45 and programming in C. Over the years he has specialized in serial communications, image processing and analysis, and UNIX systems programming. Currently he works for a telecommunications company developing object-oriented workstation software using C++ in the Microsoft Windows and X Windows System operating environments. James lives in Southern California, has a degree in cultural anthropology, has studied computer science and both Western and non-Western music, and practices the Japanese martial arts of Aikido and Iaido (Japanese swordsmanship).

William vanRyper has been writing state-of-the-art graphics software since 1982. He was chief scientist at Flamingo Graphics, a company providing truecolor, object-oriented drawing, and antialiasing technology to a host of OEM's on all the major platforms. He has designed visualization systems, animation, and drawing packages for many major corporate clients. He is the president of uvr, a private consulting firm in Cambridge, MA, and is currently researching, writing, and speaking about the frontiers of consciousness, science, and technology.

Colophon

The cover was designed and produced by Edie Freedman in QuarkXpress 3.3. The cover image is from the Dover Pictorial Archive. Inside layouts were designed by Jennifer Niederst. The cover and the contents of the book were formatted using Copperplate and New Baskerville fonts from Adobe.

Text was prepared in SGML using the DocBook 2.1 DTD. The print version of this book was created by translating the SGML source into a set of gtroff macros using a filter developed at ORA by Norman Walsh. Steve Talbott designed and wrote the underlying macro set on the basis of the GNU gtroff -gs macros; Lenny Muellner adapted them to SGML and implemented the book design. The GNU groff text formatter version 1.08 was used to generate PostScript output.

The figures were created by Chris Reilley in Aldus Freehand 4.0, and imported into the final page layouts.

USING

UNIX AND X

Books from O'Reilly & Associates, Inc.

FALL/WINTER 1994-95

–Basics–

Our UNIX in a Nutshell *guides are the most comprehensive quick reference on the market—a must for every* UNIX *user. No matter what system you use, we've got a version to cover your needs.*

UNIX in a Nutshell: System V Edition

By Daniel Gilly & the staff of O'Reilly & Associates
2nd Edition June 1992
444 pages, ISBN 1-56592-001-5

You may have seen UNIX quick-reference guides, but you've never seen anything like *UNIX in a Nutshell*. Not a scaled-down quick reference of common commands, *UNIX in a Nutshell* is a complete reference containing all commands and options, along with generous descriptions and examples that put the commands in context. For all but the thorniest UNIX problems, this one reference should be all the documentation you need. Covers System V, Releases 3 and 4, and Solaris 2.0.

"This book is the perfect desktop reference.... The authors have presented a clear and concisely written book which would make an excellent addition to any UNIX user's library."
—*SysAdmin*

"Whether you are setting up your first UNIX system or adding your fiftieth user, these books can ease you through learning the fundamentals of the UNIX system."
—Michael J. O'Brien, Hardware Editor,
  ABA/Unix/group Newsletter

SCO UNIX in a Nutshell

By Ellie Cutler & the staff of O'Reilly & Associates
1st Edition February 1994
590 pages, ISBN 1-56592-037-6

The desktop reference to SCO UNIX and Open Desktop®, this version of *UNIX in a Nutshell* shows you what's under the hood of your SCO system. It isn't a scaled-down quick reference of common commands, but a complete reference containing all user, programming, administration, and networking commands.

Contents include:
- All commands and options
- Shell syntax for the Bourne, Korn, C, and SCO shells
- Pattern matching, with *vi, ex, sed,* and *aw*k commands
- Compiler and debugging commands for software development
- Networking with email, TCP/IP, NFS, and UUCP
- System administration commands and the SCO sysadmsh shell

This edition of *UNIX in a Nutshell* is the most comprehensive SCO quick reference on the market, a must for any SCO user. You'll want to keep *SCO UNIX in a Nutshell* close by as you use your computer: it'll become a handy, indispensible reference for working with your SCO system.

Learning the UNIX Operating System

By Grace Todino, John Strang & Jerry Peek
3rd Edition August 1993
108 pages, ISBN 1-56592-060-0

If you are new to UNIX, this concise introduction will tell you just what you need to get started and no more. Why wade through a 600-page book when you can begin working productively in a matter of minutes? It's an ideal primer for Mac and PC users of the Internet who need to know a little bit about UNIX on the systems they visit.

Topics covered include:

- Logging in and logging out
- Window systems (especially X/Motif)
- Managing UNIX files and directories
- Sending and receiving mail
- Redirecting input/output
- Pipes and filters
- Background processing
- Basic network commands

This book is the most effective introduction to UNIX in print. The third edition has been updated and expanded to provide increased coverage of window systems and networking. It's a handy book for someone just starting with UNIX, as well as someone who encounters a UNIX system as a visitor via remote login over the Internet.

"Once you've established a connection with the network, there's often a secondary obstacle to surmount.... *Learning the UNIX Operating System* helps you figure out what to do next by presenting in a nutshell the basics of how to deal with the 'U-word.' Obviously a 92-page book isn't going to make you an instant UNIX guru, but it does an excellent job of introducing basic operations in a concise nontechnical way, including how to navigate through the file system, send and receive E-mail and—most importantly—get to the online help...."
—Michael L. Porter, Associate Editor, *Personal Engineering & Instrumentation News*

"Whether you are setting up your first UNIX system or adding your fiftieth user, [this book] can ease you through learning the fundamentals of the UNIX system."
—Michael J. O'Brien, *ABA/Unix/group Newsletter*

Learning the vi Editor

By Linda Lamb
5th Edition October 1990
192 pages, ISBN 0-937175-67-6

A complete guide to text editing with *vi*, the editor available on nearly every UNIX system. Early chapters cover the basics; later chapters explain more advanced editing tools, such as *ex* commands and global search and replacement.

"For those who are looking for an introductory book to give to new staff members who have no acquaintance with either screen editing or with UNIX screen editing, this is it: a book on *vi* that is neither designed for the UNIX in-crowd, nor so imbecilic that one is ashamed to use it."
—*;login*

Learning the Korn Shell

By Bill Rosenblatt
1st Edition June 1993
363 pages, ISBN 1-56592-054-6

A thorough introduction to the Korn shell, both as a user interface and as a programming language. This book provides a clear explanation of the Korn shell's features, including *ksh* string operations, co-processes, signals and signal handling, and command-line interpretation. *Learning the Korn Shell* also includes real-life programming examples and a Korn shell debugger (*kshdb*).

"Readers still bending back the pages of Korn-shell manuals will find relief in...*Learning the Korn Shell*...a gentle introduction to the shell. Rather than focusing on syntax issues, the book quickly takes on the task of solving day-to-day problems with Korn-shell scripts. Application scripts are also shown and explained in detail. In fact, the book even presents a script debugger written for *ksh*. This is a good book for improving your knowledge of the shell."
—*Unix Review*

MH & xmh: E-mail for Users & Programmers

By Jerry Peek
2nd Edition September 1992
728 pages, ISBN 1-56592-027-9

Customizing your email environment can save time and make communicating more enjoyable. *MH & xmh: E-Mail for Users & Programmers* explains how to use, customize, and program with the MH electronic mail commands available on virtually any UNIX system. The handbook also covers *xmh*, an X Window System client that runs MH programs.

The second edition added a chapter on *mhook*, sections explaining under-appreciated small commands and features, and more examples showing how to use MH to handle common situations.

"The MH bible is irrefutably Jerry Peek's *MH & xmh: E-mail for Users & Programmers*. This book covers just about everything that is known about MH and *xmh* (the X Windows front end to MH), presented in a clear and easy-to-read format. I strongly recommend that anybody serious about MH get a copy."
—James Hamilton, *UnixWorld*

The USENET Handbook

By Mark Harrison
1st Edition Winter 1994-95 (est.)
250 pages (est.), ISBN 1-56592-101-1

The USENET Handbook describes how to get the most out of the USENET news network, a worldwide network of cooperating computer sites that exchange public user messages known as "articles" or "postings." These postings are an electric mix of questions, commentary, hints, and ideas of all kinds, expressing the views of the thousands of participants at these sites.

Tutorials show you how to read news using the most popular newsreaders—*tin* and Trumpet for Windows and *nn*, *emacs* and *gnus* for UNIX. It also explains how to post articles to the Net.

The book discusses things you can do to increase your productivity by using the resources mentioned on USENET, such as anonymous FTP (file transfer protocol), mail servers, FAQs, and mailing lists. It covers network etiquette, processing encoded and compressed files (i.e., software, pictures, etc.), and lots of historical information.

Learning the GNU Emacs

By Debra Cameron & Bill Rosenblatt
1st Edition October 1991
442 pages, ISBN 0-937175-84-6

An introduction to the GNU Emacs editor, one of the most widely used and powerful editors available under UNIX. Provides a solid introduction to basic editing, a look at several important editing modes (special Emacs features for editing specific types of documents), and a brief introduction to customization and Emacs LISP programming. The book is aimed at new Emacs users, whether or not they are programmers.

"Authors Debra Cameron and Bill Rosenblatt do a particularly admirable job presenting the extensive functionality of GNU Emacs in well-organized, easily digested chapters.... Despite its title, *Learning GNU Emacs* could easily serve as a reference for the experienced Emacs user."
—Linda Branagan, Convex Computer Corporation

Using UUCP and Usenet

By Grace Todino & Dale Dougherty
1st Edition February 1986 (latest update October 1991)
210 pages, ISBN 0-937175-10-2

Shows users how to communicate with both UNIX and non-UNIX systems using UUCP and *cu* or *tip* and how to read news and post articles. This handbook assumes that UUCP is already running at your site.

"Are you having trouble with UUCP? Have you torn out your hair trying to set the Dialers file? *Managing UUCP and Usenet* and *Using UUCP and Usenet* will give you the information you need to become an accomplished net user. The companion book is *!%@:: A Directory of Electronic Mail Addressing & Networks*, a compendium of world networks and how to address and read them. All of these books are well written, and I urge you to take a look at them."
—*Root Journal*

X User Tools

By Linda Mui & Valerie Quercia
1st Edition October 1994 (est.)
750 pages (est.) (CD-ROM included)
ISBN 1-56592-019-8

 *X User Tools* provides for X users what *UNIX Power Tools* provides for UNIX users: hundreds of tips, tricks, scripts, techniques, and programs—plus a CD-ROM—to make the X Windowing System more enjoyable, more powerful, and easier to use.

This browser's book emphasizes useful programs, culled from the network and contributed by X programmers worldwide. Programs range from fun (games, screensavers, and a variety of online clocks) to business tools (calendar, memo, and mailer programs) to graphics (programs for drawing, displaying, and converting images). You'll also find a number of tips and techniques for configuring both individual and systemwide environments, as well as a glossary of common X and UNIX terms.

The browser style of organization—pioneered by *UNIX Power Tools*—encourages readers to leaf through the book at will, focusing on what appeals at the time. Each article stands on its own, many containing cross-references to related articles. Before you know it, you'll have covered the entire book, simply by scanning what's of interest and following cross-references to more detailed information.

The enclosed CD-ROM contains source files for all and binary files for some of the programs—for a number of platforms, including Sun 4, Solaris, HP 700, Alpha/OSF, and AIX. Note that the CD-ROM contains software for both *emacs* and *tcl/tk*.

Volume 3: X Window System User's Guide

Standard Edition
By Valerie Quercia & Tim O'Reilly
4th Edition May 1993
836 pages, ISBN 1-56592-014-7

 *The X Window System User's Guide* orients the new user to window system concepts and provides detailed tutorials for many client programs, including the *xterm* terminal emulator and window managers. Building on this basic knowledge, later chapters explain how to customize the X environment and provide sample configurations. The *Standard Edition* uses the *twm* manager in most examples and illustrations. Revised for X11 Release 5. This popular manual is available in two editions, one for users of the MIT software, and one for users of Motif. (see below).

"For the novice, this is the best introduction to X available. It will also be a convenient reference for experienced users and X applications developers."
—*Computing Reviews*

Volume 3M: X Window System User's Guide

Motif Edition
By Valerie Quercia & Tim O'Reilly
2nd Edition January 1993
956 pages, ISBN 1-56592-015-5

This alternative edition of the *User's Guide* highlights the Motif window manager for users of the Motif graphical user interface. Revised for Motif 1.2 and X11 Release 5.

Material covered in this second edition includes:

- Overview of the X Color Management System (Xcms)
- Creating your own Xcms color database
- Tutorials for two "color editors": *xcoloredit* and *xtici*
- Using the X font server
- Tutorial for *editres*, a resource editor
- Extensive coverage of the new implementations of *bitmap* and *xmag*
- Overview of internationalization features
- Features common to Motif 1.2 applications: tear-off menus and drag-and-drop

UNIX Power Tools

By Jerry Peek, Mike Loukides, Tim O'Reilly, et al.
1st Edition March 1993
1162 pages (includes CD-ROM)
Random House ISBN 0-679-79073-X

Ideal for UNIX users who hunger for technical—yet accessible—information, *UNIX Power Tools* consists of tips, tricks, concepts, and freeware (CD-ROM included). It also covers add-on utilities and how to take advantage of clever features in the most popular UNIX utilities.

This is a browser's book... like a magazine that you don't read from start to finish, but leaf through repeatedly until you realize that you've read it all. You'll find articles abstracted from O'Reilly Nutshell Handbooks®, new information that highlights program "tricks" and "gotchas," tips posted to the net over the years, and other accumulated wisdom. The goal of *UNIX Power Tools* is to help you think creatively about UNIX and get you to the point where you can analyze your own problems. Your own solutions won't be far behind.

The CD-ROM includes all of the scripts and aliases from the book, plus *perl*, GNU *emacs*, *pbmplus* (manipulation utilities), *ispell*, *screen*, the *sc* spreadsheet, and about 60 other freeware programs. In addition to the source code, all the software is precompiled for Sun3, Sun4, DECstation, IBM RS/6000, HP 9000 (700 series), SCO Xenix, and SCO UNIX. (SCO UNIX binaries will likely also run on other Intel UNIX platforms, including Univel's new UNIXware.)

"Chockful of ideas on how to get the most from UNIX, this book is aimed at those who want to improve their proficiency with this versatile operating system. Best of all, you don't have to be a computer scientist to understand it. If you use UNIX, this book belongs on your desk."
—Book Reviews, *Compuserve Magazine*

"*Unix Power Tools* is an encyclopedic work that belongs next to every serious UNIX user's terminal. If you're already a UNIX wizard, keep this book tucked under your desk for late-night reference when solving those difficult problems."
—Raymond GA Côté, *Byte*

Making TEX Work

By Norman Walsh
1st Edition April 1994
522 pages, ISBN 1-56592-051-1

TeX is a powerful tool for creating professional-quality typeset text and is unsurpassed at typesetting mathematical equations, scientific text, and multiple languages. Many books describe how you use TeX to construct sentences, paragraphs, and chapters. Until now, no book has described all the software that actually lets you build, run, and use TeX to best advantage on your platform. Because creating a TeX document requires the use of many tools, this lack of information is a serious problem for TeX users.

Making TEX Work guides you through the maze of tools available in the TeX system. Beyond the core TeX program there are myriad drivers, macro packages, previewers, printing programs, online documentation facilities, graphics programs, and much more. This book describes them all.

The Frame Handbook

By Linda Branagan & Mike Sierra
1st Edition October 1994 (est.)
500 pages (est.), ISBN 1-56592-009-0

A thorough, single-volume guide to using the UNIX version of FrameMaker 4.0, a sophisticated document production system. This book is for everyone who creates technical manuals and reports, from technical writers and editors who will become power users to administrative assistants and engineers. The book contains a thorough introduction to Frame and covers creating document templates, assembling books, and Frame tips and tricks. It begins by discussing the basic features of any text-formatting system: how it handles text and text-based tools (like spell-checking). It quickly gets into areas that benefit from a sophisticated tool like Frame: cross-references and footnotes; styles, master pages, and templates; tables and graphics; tables of contents and indexes; and, for those interested in online access, hypertext. Once you've finished this book, you'll be able to use Frame to create and produce a book or even a series of books.

Exploring Expect

By Don Libes
1st Edition Winter 1994-95 (est.)
500 pages (est.), ISBN 1-56592-090-2

Written by the author of Expect, this is the first book to explain how this new part of the UNIX toolbox can be used to automate *telnet, ftp, passwd, rlogin,* and hundreds of other interactive applications. Based on *Tcl* (Tool Control Language), Expect lets you automate interactive applications that have previously been extremely difficult to handle with any scripting language.

The book briefly describes *Tcl* and how Expect relates to it. It then describes the *Tcl* language, using a combination of reference material and specific, useful examples of its features. It shows how to use Expect in background, in multiple processes, and with standard languages and tools like C, C++, and *Tk,* the X-based extension to *Tcl.* The strength in the book is in its scripts, conveniently listed in a separate index.

"Expect was the first widely used *Tcl* application, and it is still one of the most popular. This is a must-know tool for system administrators and many others."
—John Ousterhout, John.Ousterhout@Eng.Sun.COM

sed & awk

By Dale Dougherty
1st Edition November 1990
414 pages, ISBN 0-937175-59-5

For people who create and modify text files, *sed* and *awk* are power tools for editing. Most of the things that you can do with these programs can be done interactively with a text editor; however, using *sed* and *awk* can save many hours of repetitive work in achieving the same result.

"*sed & awk* is a must for UNIX system programmers and administrators, and even general UNIX readers will benefit. I have over a hundred UNIX and C books in my personal library at home, but only a dozen are duplicated on the shelf where I work. This one just became number twelve."
—*Root Journal*

Learning Perl

By Randal L. Schwartz, Foreword by Larry Wall
1st Edition November 1993
274 pages, ISBN 1-56592-042-2

Learning Perl is ideal for system administrators, programmers, and anyone else wanting a down-to-earth introduction to this useful language. Written by a Perl trainer, its aim is to make a competent, hands-on Perl programmer out of the reader as quickly as possible. The book takes a tutorial approach and includes hundreds of short code examples, along with some lengthy ones. The relatively inexperienced programmer will find *Learning Perl* easily accessible. Each chapter of the book includes practical programming exercises. Solutions are presented for all exercises.

For a comprehensive and detailed guide to advanced programming with Perl, read O'Reilly's companion book, *Programming perl.*

"All-in-all, *Learning Perl* is a fine introductory text that can dramatically ease moving into the world of *perl*. It fills a niche previously filled only by tutorials taught by a small number of *perl* experts.... The UNIX community too often lacks the kind of tutorial that this book offers."
—Rob Kolstad, *;login*

Programming perl

By Larry Wall & Randal L. Schwartz
1st Edition January 1991
482 pages, ISBN 0-937175-64-1

This is the authoritative guide to the hottest new UNIX utility in years, coauthored by its creator, Larry Wall. Perl is a language for easily manipulating text, files, and processes. Perl provides a more concise and readable way to do many jobs that were formerly accomplished (with difficulty) by programming in the C language or one of the shells.

Programming perl covers Perl syntax, functions, debugging, efficiency, the Perl library, and more, including real-world Perl programs dealing with such issues as system administration and text manipulation. Also includes a pull-out quick-reference card (designed and created by Johan Vromans).

O'Reilly & Associates—
GLOBAL NETWORK NAVIGATOR

The Global Network Navigator (GNN)™ is a unique kind of information service that makes the Internet easy and enjoyable to use. We organize access to the vast information resources of the Internet so that you can find what you want. We also help you understand the Internet and the many ways you can explore it.

In GNN you'll find:

Navigating the Net with GNN

 The *Whole Internet Catalog* contains a descriptive listing of the most useful Net resources and services with live links to those resources.

 The *GNN Business Pages* are where you'll learn about companies who have established a presence on the Internet and use its worldwide reach to help educate consumers.

 The *Internet Help Desk* helps folks who are new to the Net orient themselves and gets them started on the road to Internet exploration.

News

 NetNews is a weekly publication that reports on the news of the Internet, with weekly feature articles that focus on Internet trends and special events. The Sports, Weather, and Comix Pages round out the news.

Special Interest Publications

 Whether you're planning a trip or are just interested in reading about the journeys of others, you'll find that the *Travelers' Center* contains a rich collection of feature articles and ongoing columns about travel. In the *Travelers' Center*, you can link to many helpful and informative travel-related Internet resources.

The *Personal Finance Center* is the place to go for information about money management and investment on the Internet. Whether you're an old pro at playing the market or are thinking about investing for the first time, you'll read articles and discover Internet resources that will help you to think of the Internet as a personal finance information tool.

All in all, GNN helps you get more value for the time you spend on the Internet.

 The Best of the Web

GNN received "Honorable Mention" for **"Best Overall Site," "Best Entertainment Service,"** and **"Most Important Service Concept."**

The *GNN NetNews* received "Honorable Mention" for **"Best Document Design."**

Subscribe Today

GNN is available over the Internet as a subscription service. To get complete information about subscribing to GNN, send email to **info@gnn.com**. If you have access to a World Wide Web browser such as Mosaic or Lynx, you can use the following URL to register online: `http://gnn.com/`

If you use a browser that does not support online forms, you can retrieve an email version of the registration form automatically by sending email to **form@gnn.com**. Fill this form out and send it back to us by email, and we will confirm your registration.

O'Reilly on the Net—
ONLINE PROGRAM GUIDE

O'Reilly & Associates offers extensive information through our online resources. If you've got Internet access, we invite you to come and explore our little neck-of-the-woods.

Online Resource Center

Most comprehensive among our online offerings is the O'Reilly Resource Center. Here, you'll find detailed information and descriptions on all O'Reilly products: titles, prices, tables of contents, indexes, author bios, CD-ROM directory listings, reviews... you can even view images of the products themselves. We also supply helpful ordering information: how to contact us, how to order online, distributors and bookstores around the world, discounts, upgrades, etc. In addition, we provide informative literature in the field, featuring articles, interviews, bibliographies, and columns that help you stay informed and abreast.

 The Best of the Web

The *O'Reilly Resource Center* was voted "**Best Commercial Site**" by users participating in "Best of the Web '94."

To access ORA's Online Resource Center:

Point your Web browser (e.g., `mosaic` or `lynx`) to:

`http://gnn.com/ora/`

For the plaintext version, `telnet` or `gopher` to:

`gopher.ora.com`

(telnetters login: `gopher`)

FTP

The example files and programs in many of our books are available electronically via FTP.

To obtain example files and programs from O'Reilly texts:

`ftp` to:

`ftp.uu.net`

`cd published/oreilly`

or

`ftp.ora.com`

Ora-news

An easy way to stay informed of the latest projects and products from O'Reilly & Associates is to subscribe to "ora-news," our electronic news service. Subscribers receive email as soon as the information breaks.

To subscribe to "ora-news":

Send email to:
listproc@online.ora.com

and put the following information on the first line of your message (not in "Subject"):
subscribe ora-news "your name" **of** "your company"

For example:
subscribe ora-news Jim Dandy of Mighty Fine Enterprises

Email

Many other helpful customer services are provided via email. Here's a few of the most popular and useful.

Useful email addresses

nuts@ora.com
For general questions and information.

bookquestions@ora.com
For technical questions, or corrections, concerning book contents.

order@ora.com
To order books online and for ordering questions.

catalog@ora.com
To receive a free copy of our magazine/catalog, "ora.com" (please include a snailmail address).

Snailmail and phones

O'Reilly & Associates, Inc.
103A Morris Street, Sebastopol, CA 95472
Inquiries: **707-829-0515, 800-998-9938**
Credit card orders: **800-889-8969**
FAX: **707-829-0104**

O'Reilly & Associates—
LISTING OF TITLES

INTERNET

!%@:: A Directory of Electronic Mail
    Addressing & Networks
Connecting to the Internet: An O'Reilly Buyer's Guide
Internet In A Box
MH & xmh: E-mail for Users & Programmers
The Mosaic Handbook for Microsoft Windows
The Mosaic Handbook for the Macintosh
The Mosaic Handbook for the X Window System
Smileys
The Whole Internet User's Guide & Catalog

SYSTEM ADMINISTRATION

Computer Security Basics
DNS and BIND
Essential System Administration
Linux Network Administrator's Guide (Fall 94 est.)
Managing Internet Information Services (Fall 94 est.)
Managing NFS and NIS
Managing UUCP and Usenet
sendmail
Practical UNIX Security
PGP: Pretty Good Privacy (Winter 94/95 est.)
System Performance Tuning
TCP/IP Network Administration
termcap & terminfo
X Window System Administrator's Guide: Volume 8
X Window System ,R6, Companion CD (Fall 94 est.)

USING UNIX AND X

BASICS

Learning GNU Emacs
Learning the Korn Shell
Learning the UNIX Operating System
Learning the vi Editor
SCO UNIX in a Nutshell
The USENET Handbook (Winter 94/95 est.)
Using UUCP and Usenet
UNIX in a Nutshell: System V Edition
The X Window System in a Nutshell
X Window System User's Guide: Volume 3
X Window System User's Guide, Motif Ed.: Vol. 3M
X User Tools (with CD-ROM) (10/94 est.)

ADVANCED

Exploring Expect (Winter 94/95 est.)
The Frame Handbook (10/94 est.)
Making TeX Work
Learning Perl
Programming perl
sed & awk
UNIX Power Tools (with CD-ROM)

PROGRAMMING UNIX, C, AND MULTI-PLATFORM

FORTRAN/SCIENTIFIC COMPUTING

High Performance Computing
Migrating to Fortran 90
UNIX for FORTRAN Programmers

C PROGRAMMING LIBRARIES

Practical C Programming
POSIX Programmer's Guide
POSIX.4: Programming for the Real World
    (Fall 94 est.)
Programming with curses
Understanding and Using COFF
Using C on the UNIX System

C PROGRAMMING TOOLS

Checking C Programs with lint
lex & yacc
Managing Projects with make
Power Programming with RPC
Software Portability with imake

MULTI-PLATFORM PROGRAMMING

Encyclopedia of Graphics File Formats
Distributing Applications Across DCE and
    Windows NT
Guide to Writing DCE Applications
Multi-Platform Code Management
Understanding DCE
Understanding Japanese Information Processing
ORACLE Performance Tuning

BERKELEY 4.4 SOFTWARE DISTRIBUTION

4.4BSD System Manager's Manual
4.4BSD User's Reference Manual
4.4BSD User's Supplementary Documents
4.4BSD Programmer's Reference Manual
4.4BSD Programmer's Supplementary Documents
4.4BSD-Lite CD Companion
4.4BSD-Lite CD Companion: International Version

X PROGRAMMING

Motif Programming Manual: Volume 6A
Motif Reference Manual: Volume 6B
Motif Tools
PEXlib Programming Manual
PEXlib Reference Manual
PHIGS Programming Manual (soft or hard cover)
PHIGS Reference Manual
Programmer's Supplement for R6 (Winter 94/95 est.)
Xlib Programming Manual: Volume 1
Xlib Reference Manual: Volume 2
X Protocol Reference Manual, R5: Volume 0
X Protocol Reference Manual, R6: Volume 0 (11/94 est.)
X Toolkit Intrinsics Programming Manual: Vol. 4
X Toolkit Intrinsics Programming Manual,
    Motif Edition: Volume 4M
X Toolkit Intrinsics Reference Manual: Volume 5
XView Programming Manual: Volume 7A
XView Reference Manual: Volume 7B

THE X RESOURCE

A QUARTERLY WORKING JOURNAL FOR X PROGRAMMERS

The X Resource: Issues 0 through 12
    (Issue 12 available 10/94)

BUSINESS/CAREER

Building a Successful Software Business
Love Your Job!

TRAVEL

Travelers' Tales Thailand
Travelers' Tales Mexico
Travelers' Tales India (Winter 94/95 est.)

AUDIOTAPES

INTERNET TALK RADIO'S "GEEK OF THE WEEK" INTERVIEWS

The Future of the Internet Protocol, 4 hours
Global Network Operations, 2 hours
Mobile IP Networking, 1 hour
Networked Information and
    Online Libraries, 1 hour
Security and Networks, 1 hour
European Networking, 1 hour

NOTABLE SPEECHES OF THE INFORMATION AGE

John Perry Barlow, 1.5 hours

O'Reilly & Associates—
INTERNATIONAL DISTRIBUTORS

Customers outside North America can now order O'Reilly & Associates books through the following distributors. They offer our international customers faster order processing, more bookstores, increased representation at tradeshows worldwide, and the high quality, responsive service our customers have come to expect.

EUROPE, MIDDLE EAST, AND AFRICA

(except Germany, Switzerland, and Austria)

INQUIRIES
International Thomson Publishing Europe
Berkshire House
168-173 High Holborn
London WC1V 7AA
United Kingdom
Telephone: 44-71-497-1422
Fax: 44-71-497-1426
Email: danni.dolbear@itpuk.co.uk

ORDERS
International Thomson Publishing Services, Ltd.
Cheriton House, North Way
Andover, Hampshire SP10 5BE
United Kingdom
Telephone: 44-264-342-832 (UK orders)
Telephone: 44-264-342-806 (outside UK)
Fax: 44-264-364418 (UK orders)
Fax: 44-264-342761 (outside UK)

GERMANY, SWITZERLAND, AND AUSTRIA

International Thomson Publishing GmbH
O'Reilly-International Thomson Verlag
Attn: Mr. G. Miske
Königswinterer Strasse 418
53227 Bonn
Germany
Telephone: 49-228-970240
Fax: 49-228-441342
Email: gerd@orade.ora.com

THE AMERICAS, JAPAN, AND OCEANIA

O'Reilly & Associates, Inc.
103A Morris Street
Sebastopol, CA 95472 U.S.A.
Telephone: 707-829-0515
Telephone: 800-998-9938 (U.S. & Canada)
Fax: 707-829-0104
Email: order@ora.com

ASIA

(except Japan)

INQUIRIES
International Thomson Publishing Asia
221 Henderson Road
#05 10 Henderson Building
Singapore 0315
Telephone: 65-272-6496
Fax: 65-272-6498

ORDERS
Telephone: 65-268-7867
Fax: 65-268-6727

AUSTRALIA

WoodsLane Pty. Ltd.
Unit 8, 101 Darley Street (P.O. Box 935)
Mona Vale NSW 2103
Australia
Telephone: 61-2-979-5944
Fax: 61-2-997-3348
Email: woods@tmx.mhs.oz.au

NEW ZEALAND

WoodsLane New Zealand Ltd.
21 Cooks Street (P.O. Box 575)
Wanganui, New Zealand
Telephone: 64-6-347-6543
Fax: 64-6-345-4840
Email: woods@tmx.mhs.oz.au

TO ORDER: **800-889-8969** *(CREDIT CARD ORDERS ONLY);* **ORDER@ORA.COM**

A GRAPHICS INFORMATION RESOURCE

The enclosed CD-ROM is truly an information resource. It contains a great deal of information about graphics file formats that has never before been pulled together in one place—nearly 2000 files for five different platforms. The CD-ROM contains a collection of specification documents gathered from many vendors, as well as code examples, test images, and a sampling of contributed software.

The software packages included on this CD-ROM will help you read, write, convert, and otherwise make sense of the nearly 100 file formats described in this book. Collected from publicly available sources, this software gives you the tools you need to view, convert, and manipulate graphics files in many different formats. For example, you'll find:

- For MS-DOS: IMDISP, VPIC, port of pbmplus (Portable Bitmap Utilities), etc.

- For Windows: Conversion Assistant for Windows, Paint Shop Pro, PhotoLab, Picture Man, WinJPEG, etc.

- For OS/2: GBM (Generalized Bitmap Module), PMJPEG, etc.

- For UNIX: sources for pbmplus, libtiff (TIFF library), Independent JPEG Group's JPEG Library, ISO MPEG-2 Codec, etc.

- For the Macintosh: GIFConverter, JPEGView, Sparkle (MPEG Motion Picture Player), etc.

The CD-ROM is in the multi-platform ISO 9660 format. To use it, you need a CD-ROM drive that reads this format on your system. (Virtually all modern drives do.) If you use a Macintosh, you also must have a copy of the publicly available Stuffit Expander program. (If you don't, we'll tell you how you can obtain it.)

O'REILLY BOOK/CD-ROM COMPANIONS

By bundling online files and programs with documentation, you get everything you need in one convenient package. CD-ROMs provide a durable, cost-effective distribution medium that is becoming the standard way to distribute operating systems and third-party software.